Editorial Board

Encyclopedia of
Children and Childhood
In History and Society

Paula S. Fass, Editor in Chief

Volume 2
F-R

**MACMILLAN
REFERENCE
USA™**

New York • Detroit • San Diego • San Francisco • Cleveland • New Haven, Conn. • Waterville, Maine • London • Munich

THOMSON

GALE

Encyclopedia of Children and Childhood: In History and Society
Paula S. Fass, Editor in Chief

For permission to use material from this
product, submit your request via Web at
http://www.gale-edit.com/permissions, or you
may download our Permissions Request form
and submit your request by fax or mail to:

Permissions Department
The Gale Group, Inc.
27500 Drake Road
Farmington Hills, MI 48331-3535
Permissions Hotline:
248-699-8006 or 800-877-4253, ext. 8006
Fax: 248-699-8074 or 800-762-4058

While every effort has been made to
ensure the reliability of the information presented in this publication, The Gale Group,
Inc. does not guarantee the accuracy of the
data contained herein. The Gale Group, Inc.
accepts no payment for listing; and inclusion
in the publication of any organization,
agency, institution, publication, service, or
individual does not imply endorsement of the
editors or publisher.

Errors brought to the attention of the
publisher and verified to the satisfaction of
the publisher will be corrected in future editions.

LIBRARY OF CONGRESS CATALOGING-IN-PUBLICATION DATA

Encyclopedia of children and childhood : in history and society / edited
by Paula S. Fass.
      p. cm.
   Includes bibliographical references and index.
      ISBN 0-02-865714-4 (set hardcover : alk. paper) — ISBN 0-02-865715-2
(Volume 1) — ISBN 0-02-865716-0 (Volume 2) — ISBN 0-02-865717-9
(Volume 3)
      1. Children—Encyclopedias. I. Fass, Paula S.

HQ767.84.E53 2003
305.23'03—dc21   2003006666

This title is also available as an e-book.
ISBN 0-02-865915-5

Contact your Gale sales representative for ordering information.

Printed in the United States of America
10 9 8 7 6 5 4 3

F

Fairy Tales and Fables

Fables provided instructional reading for European children from the Middle Ages well into the nineteenth century. Fairy tales for children, on the other hand, were relative latecomers for child readers, appearing in the early eighteenth century but becoming popular only from the later eighteenth century onward.

Fables

In the western world, brief animal fables with an appended moral are generally identified as *Aesop's fables*. Although attributed to Aesop, reputedly a freed Greek slave living in the sixth century B.C.E., the body of work took shape over centuries, absorbing tales from disparate sources, such as the Hellenistic *Recensio Augustana*, whose animal protagonists typically had predictable characteristics: a cunning fox, a strong lion, a proud eagle.

Aesopic fables have dramatic plots, clear construction, and striking dialogue leading to a general moral that can easily be summarized in proverbial form. Fables are above all a didactic genre. Many Romans—Ennius, Lucilius, Horace, Livy—used Aesopic fables as exempla (short stories that illustrate a particular moral or argument), but Phaedrus strengthened their didactic elements in order to produce a guide for moral instruction.

Medieval Aesopica flowered in the eleventh century and grew larger in the twelfth century, as Johannes of Capua's edition absorbed fables from the Indian *Panchatantra*. The *Panchatantra* (Five Books or Five Teachings)—a story cycle consisting of fables about animals whose actions demonstrate the wise conduct of life and the knowledge of ruling—had emerged sometime before 250 C.E. Translated into Persian as *Kalila and Dimna* in the sixth century, these Eastern fables spread in multitudinous reworked forms in Arabic translation from the Middle East to northern Africa and Moorish Spain. Once Aesopic fables with their *Panchatan-*

tra / Kalila and Dimna admixture were incorporated into the Latin exempla collection for use in church sermons in the thirteenth through the fifteenth centuries, the way had been prepared for their use in schools throughout Christian Europe. From the High Middle Ages through Galland's early eighteenth-century translation, fables powerfully influenced European storytelling.

The sudden flourishing of published animal fables for children in late seventeenth-century England reveals the presence of a reading appetite no longer satisfied by a rigorous diet of gory Protestant martyrdoms, fervid child deaths, and earnest religious directives. Much of England's Christian practice had softened, as evidenced by the runaway success of the popular religious writer John Bunyan's allegorical narratives. Many of hymn-writer Isaac Watts's *Moral Songs*, though religious in category, nonetheless taught children about living harmoniously within a close family circle. Fables went one step further and provided moralized worldly narratives about how to live on earth. Isolated editions appeared in the sixteenth and seventeenth centuries, but the sudden publishing success of Aesopica between the 1690s and the 1740s demonstrates that parental child-rearing imperatives had moved far away from purely religious injunction in those years. The narrative-cum-moral form, so warmly recommended by English philosopher JOHN LOCKE, enabled Enlightenment educationists to incorporate interpretations that expressed rational values.

Internationally, Jean de La Fontaine's book of 245 fables (in three parts 1668, 1678–1679, 1693) prepared the way for an enormous efflorescence of fables in England, Germany, Italy, and France in the eighteenth century. In England, fables' success can be measured by their remarkable publishing history. Caxton printed an English translation of Aesop's fables in 1484; Roger l'Estrange's 1692 collection, *Fables of Aesop and other eminent mythologists (Barlandus-Anianus-Abstemius-Poggius) with morals and reflexions*, was republished with remarkable frequency throughout the late seventeenth and early eighteenth century. The success of L'Estrange's fables encouraged imitators and competitors, and so Reverend Samuel Croxall produced his *Fables of Aesop and Others* in 1722. It, too, enjoyed an enormous success (being reprinted five times between 1722 and 1747), as did John Gay's Aesopic fables (1727, 1738).

Fables passed early into school use. The London publisher S. Harding marketed *Amusing and Instructive Fables in French and English* in 1732. La Fontaine's *Fables and Tales . . . in French and English* (1734) and Daniel Bellamy's translation of Phaedrus's *Fifty Instructive and Entertaining Fables* (1734, 1753), both intended for youth in schools, immediately joined them, as did FRANÇOIS FÉNELON's *Tales and Fables* (1736) and Gabriel Faerno's *Fables in English and French Verse* (1741). The latter also appeared in Latin and French (1743, 1744). Benjamin Cole put his name on a collection, *Select Tales and Fables* (1746). In 1747 *The Instructive and Entertaining Fables of Bidpai* (tales derived from the *Panchatantra*) appeared in English for the first time. The pace of newly introduced fable books attests to market success for this genre, as each printing evidently sold out quickly enough to warrant new printings and new versions. As always England's chapbook (small, inexpensive paper booklets) publishers picked up whatever sold well, and in this case the Dicey printing house put out John Bickham's *Fables and Other Short Poems* as early as 1737.

John Newbery included several fables in *Little Pretty Pocket-Book* (1744) and *Goody Two-Shoes* (1766), and in 1757 Newbery himself produced *Fables in Verse. For the Improvement of the Young and the Old*. Attributed jokily to Abraham Aesop, Esq., Newbery's book was reprinted on ten separate occasions. Other fable books appeared, such as the simply entitled 1759 *Fables* and Robert Dodsley's *Select Fables of Aesop and Other Fabulists* (1761). Children read these and other fable books long after their original dates of publication, as attested by the multigenerational ownership inscribed onto many of these books' flyleaves.

When fables had to share the market with fairy tales from the end of the eighteenth century onward, they diminished in significance. Nonetheless, fables have continued to form a staple of children's literature and children's reading in a broad variety of (principally illustrated) editions to the present day. The classic historian of children's literature, Harvey Darton, wrote that fables "had been regimented for schools and decked out for fashion. It had been Everyman's and now was Everychild's" (p. 23).

Animal stories of the late eighteenth, nineteenth, and twentieth centuries may also be understood as a natural outgrowth of eighteenth-century Aesopic fables. An outstanding change from 1800 onward was a shift in animal attributes towards positive personal characteristics of courage, patience, loyalty, and endurance that remains evident in twentieth-century stories such as *Lassie* and *Black Beauty*.

Fairy Tales

Fairy tales, as they exist today, took shape in sixteenth-century Italy as literature for adults in a handful of tales in *Pleasant Nights* (1551, 1553) by Giovan Francesco Straparola. These made their way to France, as did the *Pentamerone* (1634–1636) of Giambattista Basile, where both underlay French fairy tales published from 1697 onward by Marie Catherine Jumel de Barneville, Baroness d'Aulnoy (c. 1650–1705), Charles Perrault (1628–1703), and other French retellers of the genre. In England, fairy tales were not a presence during the seventeenth century. At that time it was chapbook romances, whose heroes bravely encountered and courageously vanquished magical or gigantic opponents, that fired boys' imaginations. If girls read chapbook romances recreationally in the same period, women's memoirs do not mention it, generally reporting only devotional reading.

England's fairies and elves, which offered little in the way of narrative adventure, were chiefly anecdotal and explanatory rather than narrative figures. Only with the introduction of French fairy narratives can extended tales about fairies and fairy tales be said to have begun an English existence. Despite decades of assertions about the oral transmission of fairy tales from nursemaids to children in times past, no evidence exists to support the belief. Tom Thumb, whose adventures included a fairy patroness, was created in the early seventeenth century by Richard Johnson; Jack, the killer of giants, came to life a century later. Both supplied English imaginations with thumping good magic for centuries, but both are, strictly speaking, folk, not fairy, tales.

In the eighteenth century two bodies of fairy literature reached English shores. From 1699 to 1750 Mme d'Aulnoy's tales were translated and published for adult women readers, first for the upper class, and later for ever lower social classes. Robert Samber's 1729 translation of Charles Perrault's tales for child readers did not sell well as leisure reading; in consequence, its publishers attempted to recast the book as a French-English schoolbook. With many other dual-language texts available for school use, however, Perrault's tales foundered, perhaps because of their inclusion of "The Discreet Princess" with its questionable morality.

It was Mme Le Prince de Beaumont who made fairy tales socially acceptable for middle and upper-middle class girls in her *Magasin des Enfants* (starting in 1756), when she alternated highly moralized versions of existing fairy tales with equally moralized Bible stories, interleaving both with lessons in history and geography. Of all Mme Le Prince's fairy tales, only her "Beauty and the Beast" has survived.

Selected tales from the *Arabian Nights* began to appear in English chapbooks from about 1715 onward; the tales of Perrault and Mme d'Aulnoy, on the other hand, spread via chapbooks to English readers only after the 1750s. Perhaps they picked up fairy tales' potential for popular consumption from John Newbery's 1743 inclusion of "Red Riding Hood" and "Cinderilla" [*sic*] in his *Pretty Book for Boys and Girls*. Ever cautious, Newbery gradually introduced fairy tales into his publications by including some of Fenelon's highly moralized fairy tales in his *Short Histories for the Improvement of the Mind* (1760); putting "Fortunatus" and a version of Perrault's "Diamonds and Toads" into a later edition of the *Pretty Book*, and introducing "Puss in Boots" into *The Fairing* in 1767. Later firms, however, published all of Perrault's tales, minus "The Discreet Princess," and propelled those tales, along with Mme d'Aulnoy's "Yellow Dwarf" and "White Cat," into their nineteenth-century popularity.

Despite the disapproval of sober educators such as Sarah Trimmer, Robert Bloomfield, and Mary Martha Sherwood, England's nineteenth-century fairy tales were joined by Edward Taylor's translation of the Grimms' tales (vol. 1 in 1823, vol. 2 in 1826); Hans Christian Andersen's tales in 1846; Basile's bowdlerized *Pentamerone* in 1848; *The Fairy Tales of All Nations* in 1849; and Scandinavian myths, folk tales, and fairy tales in the 1850s. All of these tales were recirculated through late nineteenth-century editions, a practice that continued in the twentieth century. However, fairies and fairy tales enjoyed far more currency in England than in the United States in the nineteenth century.

The relationship of fairy tales to the lives of children is much debated. In the United States and England in the wake of World War II, a distrust of the Grimms' tales developed (the ferocious gore in some of their tales was thought to have encouraged genocide), a distrust that Bruno Bettelheim countered in *The Uses of Enchantment* (1976). Bettelheim implied that fairy tales arose from children's own subconscious as he sought to demonstrate that fairy tales accurately projected children's psychological needs and neatly described their psychosexual development. However, his neo-Freudian approach to textual analysis was often flawed by lapses in logic and by the substitution of assertion for proof. In contrast, Kristin Wardetzky's research in the 1980s, based on a sample of 1,500 schoolchildren, rested on an awareness that children's early and continuing exposure to books of fairy tales suffused their consciousness with fairy-tale characters, norms, and motifs. Wardetzky's analysis of fairy tales written by children themselves demonstrated that their narratives used standard fairy-tale motifs to bring evil under control and to (re)establish domestic harmony.

See also: **ABC Books; Children's Literature.**

BIBLIOGRAPHY

Bettelheim, Bruno. 1976. *The Uses of Enchantment*. New York: Knopf.

Bottigheimer, Ruth. 2002. "Misperceived Perceptions: Perrault's Fairy Tales and English Children's Literature." *Children's Literature* 30.

Darton, Harvey. 1982. *Children's Books in England: Five Centuries of Social Life*. Revised by Brian Alderson. Cambridge, UK: Cambridge University Press.

Opie, Iona, and Peter Opie. 1980 [1974]. *The Classic Fairy Tales*. New York: Oxford University Press.

Wardetzky, Kristin. 1992. *Märchen—Lesarten von Kindern: Eine empirische Studie*. Frankfurt, Germany: Lang.

Wheatley, Edward. 2000. *Mastering Aesop: Medieval Education, Chaucer, and His Followers*. Gainesville: University Press of Florida.

RUTH B. BOTTIGHEIMER

Family Patterns

Throughout history, family composition has affected children's lives in important ways. The size and structure of the family and its capacity to sustain itself has played a critical role in how children are raised, their level of formal education, and whether or not they participate in the labor force. The principal household structures are nuclear, extended, and blended. The nuclear household contains two generations, parents and children. Extended families are multigenerational and include a wide circle of kin and servants. In blended households—the result of divorce or the death of a spouse followed by remarriage and a new generation of children—mothers and fathers can be both biological parents and STEPPARENTS simultaneously.

Patterns of Family Structure through the Modern Era

Household structure took a variety of forms throughout Europe and North America during the fifteenth to eighteenth centuries. Research during the late twentieth century on European family systems situated these forms within sharp geographical boundaries over time. Those models, however, have since been adjusted, with consensus that geographical areas held more than one family pattern contemporaneously. Moreover, household systems sometimes changed over historical cycles. Finally, households were not necessarily autonomous but part of a wider network of relations with the community. The nuclear family, with late marriage preceded by a term of service in another household, was one common form in northwest Europe and North America, while multigenerational households were common to southern and eastern Europe. In Albania, Bulgaria, and European Russia as well as some parts of Italy, Greece, Spain, and Portugal, new households were formed when large ones divided or small ones combined. Marriage was not restricted to one son or daughter, there were few servants save for the rich, and households were home to multiple married couples. Children thus were supervised by co-resident adult kin. Elsewhere, in parts of central and southern France, Italy, Austria, and Germany, nuclear households combined with the fission and fusion processes of the East and South. Others contained two residential married couples consisting of parents and a married son. This usually occurred when there was not enough land to start a separate household.

Age at marriage and life expectancy were two important variables influencing household structure. Early marriage permitted a longer cycle of fertility than marrying late. Late marriage for women, from the mid to late twenties, was a means of restricting the number of births per household. Late marriage for men may or may not have affected the household's fertility cycle. It did, however, impinge upon the number of years fathers would be available to their children. The same was true for mothers. In fact one or both parents could be expected to die during the child's lifetime during the early modern period, creating the potential for economic hardship. There was a large percentage of ORPHANS, many of whom were farmed out to other families as servants, laborers, or apprentices. They lived with their employers rather than in their natal households. In other cases, the death of a parent brought remarriage, new stepsiblings, and the constitution of a blended family. This was common, for example, in New England and the Chesapeake area of North America during the colonial era. Children too died young. INFANT MORTALITY rates were very high during the early modern period, making it highly uncertain whether parents could expect their children to reach an age when they could help support the family household or sustain them in their elderly years.

INHERITANCE practices also affected household structure. Primogeniture in the nuclear family insured that the patrimony remained intact, under the authority of the eldest son upon his father's death. That son was expected to marry and carry on the family's future over time. In a stem family, common in Austria, brothers might work for the eldest sibling but would not be allowed to marry or to inherit. Sisters might marry or take vows, yet only the eldest son would inherit the family estate. Partible inheritance, on the other hand, allowed for the formation of separate households among all children. Extended families, whose size was generally limited by high mortality and low fertility, practiced joint inheritance, that is, shared ownership of their patrimony.

During the early modern period another important variable influencing household structure was the family's proximity to a means of production and its ability to sustain itself. Climate, geography, the productivity of the land, and the strength of the labor market all shaped household composition, and consequently childhood experience, in important ways. They helped determine whether or not people married and at what age, whether to try and restrict fertility, whether children worked and/or went to school, and whether or not they would be able to live at home under the supervision of their parents. Affluent households might have had less incentive to restrict fertility since they did not depend on offspring to contribute to the family economy. They did quite frequently, however, restrict marriage in order to keep the family patrimony intact. Modest households, however, presented another case, for there children were an economic liability. Children could remain under the family hearth only if there was a viable means of sustaining them. Otherwise

they were sent to work as domestic servants, laborers, or apprentices, living in employers' houses. Frequently in northwest Europe and North America, marriage took place only when the couple could afford to set up an independent household. Life-cycle servitude followed by late marriage was common because it was only at that stage that couples had accumulated the resources needed to set up the customary separate household. In extended families, on the other hand, where married children were joining a preestablished household, age at marriage was normally younger. The main consideration in deciding whether to marry was whether the new couple had the means to sustain a new family. Ten to 15 percent of the population never achieved the means to marry.

Until the end of the nineteenth century, land was perhaps the most important financial resource for the majority of the population. Its availability and how it was managed affected household composition. Firm assurance of land tenure, even in conditions where land was scarce, could encourage the establishment of more complex households, while adequate landed resources lent itself to the establishment of small, independent households. Peasant families required an adequate but not excess number of children to work the land. The nuclear household ideally contained several children spaced widely so that the oldest had left the household by the time the youngest came along, thus avoiding surplus mouths to feed. This was achieved by postponing marriage to the late twenties for men and early twenties for women, a practice that shortened their years of fertility. In addition, parents often sent their children to live and serve other households in need.

Yet not all peasants were able to avail themselves of land. Population growth and land shortage, characteristic of eighteenth-century North America, for example, forced sons to leave the family hearth. Landless villagers who sought employment where they could find it may not have formally married but procreated. This often resulted in pools of abandoned women and children. On the other hand, some peasant economies were replaced by more commercialized systems in which rural households were centers of production associated with the textile industry. Free markets created a greater demand for labor, drawing families into the production process. Children could remain at home rather than be farmed out to service if there was work allowing them to contribute to the sustenance of the household. This was also true when the center of production moved outside the home, a phenomenon characteristic of the nineteenth century. Fathers and children rather than mothers went to work in factories to support the family. In short, household composition and children's ability to remain living with their parents depended heavily on the availability of economic resources and employment.

The household as a center of production affected childhood experience. To age seven, even among slaveholders in

North America, children were generally exempt from work. But from then on they were gradually brought into the labor force. On farms young children collected firewood and worms on the vines, herded livestock, weeded, and helped around the house. After age ten boys might be trained outside in fields and stables to learn to be farmers or herders, while girls were tracked into domestic work. By the eighteenth century children were helping with sewing, spinning, lace making, and nail making. Slave children in North America had a similar experience, with light chores to age six and domestic or farm labor after age ten. In midwest and western North America, where the labor market was small, gender roles were less rigid than normal. Girls worked in the tobacco fields and did herding, harvesting, and hunting while boys took on domestic duties as well as working outside. On the frontier, children assumed duties earlier than in other regions. The young panned gold as well as performing a variety of domestic chores.

When the household did not offer a means of production it affected children in dramatic ways. In the nineteenth century they left school at the minimum required by the state and were put to work in factories, much to the horror of social reformers, and they were not normally under parental supervision. Cotton mills and coal mines, industries with steam power and machinery, drew children into the adult labor market. In the cities poor children took to street selling. All the while, domestic service was one of the largest employers of child labor. At the beginning of the nineteenth century children were 10 percent of the labor force in the American Northeast; by 1832 they constituted 40 percent.

Childhood experience during the early modern period was thus affected in numerous ways by family structure. First, their primary caretakers differed according to the configuration of the household. In nuclear families, parents normally assumed responsibility for raising their children, while in extended and blended families other adults besides the parents might be involved in the lives of the children. That might include uncles, aunts, and GRANDPARENTS in multigenerational extended families, while in a blended family, where one parent has remarried and constituted a new family, children might be raised by both a stepparent and a parent. In a nuclear household, children had economic and emotional relationships with their parents alone, while in extended and blended families the network of ties was potentially much larger. Domestic production in the home facilitated both parents assuming responsibility for child rearing. In the nineteenth century, when production moved outside the domestic hearth, mothers assumed more authority over children while fathers worked outside.

Another way household structure affected childhood was that the quality of a child's experience was directly affected by whether he or she was expected to contribute to the financial well-being of the household and whether he or she would inherit land. The latter determined whether or not marriage would be possible. Broader trends affected ability to marry as well. In periods of demographic rise and land shortage, marriage was delayed and restricted, while the opposite conditions encouraged early marriage. Although parents assumed responsibility for children's religious instruction, until the early twentieth century imparting vocational skills that would serve the means of production constituted the primary responsibility in child rearing.

The Twentieth Century

The parameters of household structure and childhood experience described above dramatically changed for the middle class during the first half of the twentieth century. The steady decline of the birthrate in Europe and North America from the nineteenth century was an important underpinning of this transformation. During the twentieth century highly reliable BIRTH CONTROL methods and legalized abortion made the one- or two-child family the norm. During the 1990s, for example, the average number of births per household in Italy was only 1.2, and in Muslim communities of Europe such as Albania they averaged no more than 2.5. With fewer children, parents devoted more time to their proper care and upbringing. Other developments that contributed to the transformations in household structure and childhood experience included state intervention in child labor, rising real wages, COMPULSORY SCHOOL ATTENDANCE, and new ideals of childhood and family life. Extended families also declined. In the nineteenth century, a grandparent often lived with an adult child and her children, and rates of co-residence in Europe actually increased. But in the 1920s older people began more consistently to live separately, a sign of quiet change in family structure.

Increasing prosperity had the effect of extending childhood beyond the minimum that had been experienced by working-class families. For the more fortunate, life shifted from the farm, domestic manufacture, factory, or streets to the home where parents nurtured and emotionally protected youngsters and socialized them for the wider world. While poorer children continued to receive minimum schooling so that they could help support their families, middle-class children increasingly withdrew from the labor force, enrolled in schools, and became the focus of parental investment both emotionally and financially. The age at which children became wage earners for their families was thus delayed to the late teens or beyond, and the period in which children remained living in the parental household was prolonged. Ethnicity and social class produced variation. Immigrants to North America, for example, brought their own customs. If they were poor, they depended more on their children to be wage earners rather than students. Socially mobile immigrants placed greater emphasis on schooling and higher education.

The transition from wage earner to schoolchild did not occur in a linear fashion. World War II, for example, disrupted all aspects of family life and the family economy due to separation, death, and financial hardship. Women entered the workforce while men were at war, and children were forced to mature more precipitously. However, from the 1950s, childhood in Europe and America became a defined stage of the life cycle which preceded formal schooling and vocational training and was clearly separate from the adult world of work. Age at marriage dropped, birthrates were exceptionally high compared to preceding periods, and divorce rates were low. There was a sharp gendered division of child-rearing responsibilities, with mothers at home, ideally giving affection and emotional support, and fathers out in the work force supporting their families. There was a marked preference for residential independence. In North America families moved to suburbs where, with economic prosperity, they could endow their children with material goods and better education. Middle-class children had more leisure time and money than ever before, but not without some cost: by the 1990s the majority of parents worked outside the home to maintain consumption standards, leaving children in care facilities.

The late twentieth century, especially in North America, produced quantitative leaps in the structure of the modern family. Divorce was relatively rare until the twentieth century. However, from 1900 onward it spread in both Europe and North America, becoming available to all social groups by the end of the century. By the 1980s birthrates had fallen dramatically and divorce rates had doubled or tripled. Women obtained greater property rights as well as the possibility of alimony and child support, making divorce a realistic option. Moreover, women could more effectively choose whether or not to marry. The result was a rise in single-parent households and households headed by women. Financial independence, coupled with desires for self-fulfillment and gender equality, caused more women than ever to enter the labor force. These developments reduced the amount of time mothers could spend with their children. Fathers took greater responsibility in nurturing their children as mothers contributed to the family economy, but in cases where both parents worked, parents in the United States struggled to find child care arrangements while parents in Europe usually placed children in day care facilities.

The late twentieth century ushered in new household structures, with unwed parents, gay parents, and remarried parents who brought with them a series of step-relations. Divorce, premarital pregnancy, and single parenthood lost some social stigma. Children in divorced families generally experienced independence at an earlier age. Some developed close relationships with more than one adult, and they developed new relationships with each parent. However, their sense of stability could not help but be disrupted by the breakup of the nuclear family unit, parents dating other people, and in some instances one or two new families being formed as a result of their parents' new relationships.

Blended families require considerable emotional if not financial adjustment. Children with SAME-SEX PARENTS also face complex social and emotional issues, including building perspective on gender roles as well as dealing with the community's reception of their nontraditional family structure. For the most part, in the early twenty-first century gay marriage has not been legally recognized in the United States and has been only marginally recognized in Europe. Children face larger challenges from society when their parents' relationship does not fit more familiar role models and is not supported by the institutional structures that uphold heterosexual marriage. On balance, same-sex parents are exceptionally committed to caring for and nurturing their children. The twenty-first century thus witnesses greater social complexities in household structure and family patterns that inevitably impact childhood, itself a structure continually in transition.

See also: **Apprenticeship; Child Labor in the West; Divorce and Custody; Economics and Children in Western Societies; European Industrialization; Fertility Rates; Siblings.**

BIBLIOGRAPHY

Cunningham, Hugh. 1995. *Children and Childhood in Western Society since 1500.* London and New York: Longman.

Demos, John. 1970. *A Little Commonwealth: Family Life in Plymouth Colony.* New York: Oxford University Press.

Gillis, John R., Lousie A. Tilly, and David Levine, eds. 1992. *The European Experience of Declining Fertility, 1850–1970: The Quiet Revolution.* Cambridge, MA: Blackwell.

Goody, Jack. 2000. *The European Family. An Historico-Anthropological Essay.* London: Blackwell.

Hajnal, John. 1965. "European Marriage Patterns in Perspective." In *Population in History: Essays in Historical Demography,* ed. D. V. Glass and D. E. C. Eversley. London: E. Arnold.

Heywood, Colin. 2001. *A History of Childhood: Children and Childhood in the West from Medieval to Modern Times.* Cambridge, UK: Polity Press.

Levine, David. 1977. *Family Formation in an Age of Nascent Capitalism.* New York: Academic Press.

Medick, Hans. 1976. "The Proto-Industrial Family Economy: The Structural Function of Household and Family during the Transition from Peasant Society to Industrial Capitalism." *Social History* 3: 291–315.

Mintz, Steven, and Susan Kellogg. 1988. *Domestic Revolutions: A Social History of American Family Life.* New York: Free Press; London: Collier Macmillan.

Popenoe, David. 1988. *Disturbing the Nest: Family Change and Decline in Modern Societies.* New York: A. de Gruter.

Quale, G. Robina. 1992. *Families in Context. A World History of Population.* New York: Greenwood.

JOANNE M. FERRARO

Fascist Youth

Fascism is a right-wing political movement rooted in nineteenth-century elitist nationalism and cultural romanticism.

A still from Leni Riefenstahl's Nazi propaganda film *Triumph of the Will* (1936), depicting the Nuremberg rallies of 1934. At these rallies thousands of Hitler Youth, along with members of other Nazi Party organizations, had the opportunity to see and hear their leader in person. The Kobal Collection.

It advocates authoritarian, single-party rule as the only solution for the socioeconomic problems of modern society. Fascism became a political force after World War I, when right-wing parties throughout Europe promised to restore health, moral order and a sense of purpose to their respective national communities. In 1921, the first self-proclaimed fascist party was founded by Benito Mussolini in Italy. Mussolini took the term *fascist* from an ancient Roman word meaning a bundle of sticks used as a disciplinary tool. As the term suggests, the National Fascist Party brought together various socioeconomic groups, particularly those who felt disenfranchised by World War I and/or the GREAT DEPRESSION—veterans, the lower middle class and youth.

Fascism's Appeal to Youth

Fascism recognizes youth as a vulnerable and politically significant population. In the 1920s and 1930s, fascist parties promised young people not only jobs and educational opportunities, but also a divine mission—to be the leaders of a revolutionary movement that would purify the nation. The fascists promoted a cult of the youthful, featuring young heroes in their music, film and literature, rejecting the ruling elite as cynical and complacent, and emphasizing the relative youthfulness of their own leaders. Fascism celebrated duty, loyalty and physical vitality, and challenged the young to use their natural energy, idealism and competitiveness for the good of the national community.

Fascist youth associations attracted large majorities of young people in Italy under Mussolini's rule and in Germany under the Nazi dictatorship. In these state-sponsored movements, young people found a variety of subsidized leisure opportunities, a strong national identity, and clearly defined gender roles. Because leaders encouraged members to put youth group duties above all other responsibilities, many youth joined in order to undermine the traditional authority of parents, school, or church. This practice reinforced core fascist beliefs that individuals owed primary allegiance to the state and that youth—not their elders—would shape the future.

National Variants: Italy and Germany

Benito Mussolini ruled Italy as a dictator from 1922 to 1945. His National Fascist Party offered a comprehensive array of clubs and service organizations for youth ages six to twenty-one, thereby challenging the traditional role of Catholic associations and sports clubs. The Fascists worked hard to attract older youth, particularly university students, but were most successful in mobilizing eight to fourteen-year-old boys into their *Balilla* organization, which promoted physical fitness and paramilitary training. Parallel groups for girls, such as the *Piccole Italiane*, promoted ideals of domesticity and motherhood.

In Germany, the NSDAP (Nazi Party), led by Adolf Hitler, won power in 1933 and immediately assumed dictatorial control of the country. The party's youth wing quickly evolved into a state-sponsored movement intended to simultaneously inspire, educate, and compel young Germans to serve the Nazi state. Like the Italian Fascists, the Nazis prescribed obedience, loyalty, and gender-specific roles. German youth were taught that racial purity would help Germany regain its proper dominant role among European nations. In their view, Jews, Gypsies, and other minorities had contaminated Germanic culture and weakened the nation. Through new national youth organizations, the Nazis recruited young Germans to help "cleanse" society of these racial impurities. In addition to ideological indoctrination and obedience, the boys' HITLER YOUTH emphasized preparation for future service in the German army or navy. The parallel League of German Maidens promoted physical health, service and motherhood, encouraging older members to volunteer for a year or more of domestic service.

Smaller fascist youth movements (such as the French *Jeunesses Patriotes*) existed throughout Europe prior to World War II. The Hitler Youth, however, was by far the most successful. Through the Hitler Youth, the Nazi state controlled virtually all educational, vocational and recreational opportunities, and effectively coordinated propaganda, peer pressure and intimidation techniques to claim, at its peak, more than 95 percent of German youth as members.

Post-1945 Fascist Youth

After World War II, the Nazis' militant authoritarianism and nationalism were blamed for corrupting and exploiting an entire generation of young Germans, and fascist youth groups were banned in many countries. Isolated groups persisted, often in secret association with racist political association. The skinhead movement, originally a working-class youth subculture that emerged in the 1970s and 1980s, was initially associated with fascism. However, although both European and American skinheads typically embrace Nazi symbols (the swastika), aggressive behavior, and nationalism, they lack a clear political organization. Consequently, most observers describe the skinheads as a rebellious subculture rather than a fascist youth movement.

In contrast, true neofascist youth groups are usually associated with ultraconservative political organizations, and while promoting nationalism, also foster international contacts and cooperation. The European Confederation of National Youth, for example, draws support from far-right parties including the French Front National and the German *Republikaner*, while the British-based International Third Position (ITP) promotes ties between European neofascists and American white-supremacist groups. These contemporary organizations attract youth (mostly males) hard-hit by economic decline, particularly in Germany and Eastern Europe, but also throughout Western Europe, the United States, and elsewhere. Like their historical predecessors, contemporary neofascists advocate racist, paramilitary, and authoritarian programs. Since 1989, neofascist youth groups have attracted public attention—and new members—with aggressive anti-immigrant rhetoric and demonstrations.

Debates

Scholarly debates about fascist youth highlight questions of motivation and program content. First, does membership imply acceptance of fascist ideology? In Nazi Germany, the Hitler Youth oversaw virtually all educational and extracurricular activities, so that membership became almost compulsory, and former participants sometimes argued that they simply endured (or ignored) ideological messages in order to participate in other activities. Later neofascist youth groups, on the other hand, had no such monopoly, leaving ideology and rhetoric as their primary recruiting tools. Second, what, other than ideology, distinguishes fascist youth from other youth organizations? Both the Italian and German variants borrowed program content, methods and rhetoric from pre-existing groups such as the Scouting movement; the fascist youth organizations simply imbued activities, songs and traditions with more extremist political and social significance. In this context, later neofascist youth groups again stand out because, unlike mainstream youth organizations, which promote cooperation and tolerance, neofascists cultivate absolute obedience, racial elitism, and paramilitarism.

See also: **Communist Youth.**

BIBLIOGRAPHY

Eatwell, Roger. 1996. *Fascism: A History.* New York: Penguin.

Laqueur, Walter. 1996. *Fascism: Past, Present, Future.* New York: Oxford University Press.

Leeden, Michael A. 1969. "Italian Fascism and Youth." *Journal of Contemporary History* 4, no. 3: 137–154.

Payne, Stanley. 1995. *A History of Fascism 1914–1945.* Madison: University of Madison Press.

KIMBERLY A. REDDING

Fashion

Historically, children have been clothed to mirror the adult society responsible for producing and assembling their wardrobes. The protective wrapping of infants and children not old enough to physically clothe themselves has alternately served as fantasy in miniature or as a burdensome necessity for doting or struggling parents or guardians. As manifest through images and surviving textile artifacts, the study of children's clothing predominantly serves to testify to social class or ethnicity. Only within the recent epoch, beginning with the Age of ENLIGHTENMENT, has the physical design of children's dress evolved to acknowledge and facilitate their developmental stages.

Children's Dress as an Extension of the Adult

Other than religious representations of the infant Jesus, early Western images of infants and children are within the context of larger, adult-dominated pictorial scenes. When not portrayed in the nude, infants are almost universally shown constrained by SWADDLING bands. Depending on the period or locale, these were widths of linen or cotton looped around clothing or strips of material, intended to immobilize the baby and prevent injury resulting from its uninhibited flailings. Older children, portrayed within the context of crowd scenes, are shown wearing scaled-down versions of adult attire, comprising tunics, coats, and cloaks of amorphous shape with only head or armholes, and held at the waist by belts or girdles. This clothing was functionally plain, fabricated by hand from hand-spun linen or wool. As fashion became more complex it evolved to differentiate between and accentuate the features of the female and male anatomy. Children's garments emulate this aesthetic, with only minor simplifications. During and following the Renaissance, those at the pinnacle of society reinforced their rank by wearing conspicuous and sumptuous clothing. Contemporary portraiture vividly illustrates an opulent vocabulary of silk velvets, metallic brocades encrusted with pearls, embroidery, stiffened lace and linen collars, and jewelry in both adult clothing and that of their progeny. This miniaturization extends to the wearing of form-modifying undergarments, including tightly laced boned stays, horsehair-stiffened underskirts and hoops, and varying shapes. A rigidly constructed combination conspires to make any playful or spontaneous childish motion impossible.

Concurrently, depictions of children of the working classes show functional garments that have been cobbled and reconfigured from larger, previously worn clothing. As textiles are an inherently costly commodity, while hand sewing is self-provided and abundant, fabrics initially acquired for adult purposes are almost indefinitely reused to the point of rags. The practical necessity of recycling endures throughout the nineteenth and twentieth century, with successive siblings, relatives, and neighbors receiving still-useful cast-offs. Only the contemporary advent of inexpensive yard goods and lavish supplies of ready-to-wear clothing has served to diminish the financial hardship of purchasing new clothing.

Blue Boy (c. 1770), Thomas Gainsborough. Although Gainsborough's portrait was painted in the late eighteenth century, his preadolescent subject wears the fashions of a hundred years earlier. By the end of the eighteenth century, simpler clothing designed for children was being introduced, yet children continued to wear "fancy dress" for special occasions, including sitting for portraits. © Francis G. Mayer/CORBIS.

Ethnicity and Children's Clothing

In broad terms, children's dress and body adornment reinforce, and are derivative of, cultural ethnicity. In pursuit of an adult aesthetic, children have been subjected to an unmodified array of social customs, in some cases almost from birth. Head flattening, whereby an infant's skull is distorted through pressure applied by boards, pads, bindings, and massage, created a mark of high status among tribal peoples in North and South America through the nineteenth century. The practice of foot binding in China, which requires the irrevocable manipulation of pliant bones to produce the culturally desirable lily-shaped foot, subjected girls between the ages of five and six to a first, painful step toward their initiation into womanhood well into the twentieth century. The universal vogue for ear piercing is clearly apparent in Eighteenth Dynasty Egyptian depictions of royal children adorned with large, decorative glass earplugs. More elaborate and ornate body altering techniques, such as TATTOOS

In *The Richard K. Haight Family* (c. 1849), attributed to Nicolino Calyo, both the adolescent girl on the left and her toddler sister wear bodices that reveal their shoulders, a style also popular with adult women, while their brothers are dressed in skeleton suits, a clothing style that was uniquely for boys. (Gouache on paper. Museum of the City of New York. Bequest of Elizabeth Cushing Iselin).

and scarification, are reserved for adolescents as a rite of passage into adult societal status. Practiced by cultures of central Africa and by the Maoris of New Zealand and Dayak groups of Central Borneo respectively these remain as tools for reinforcing ethnic identities.

Specialized Clothing for Special Needs

The first customized children's accessories appeared in the seventeenth century to address the specific needs of toddlers, who were in particular peril of injury or death due to their inquisitive, sometimes unsupervised, adventures. The innovations of the pudding (a leather and textile padded cap) and leading strings (separate tethers or reigns cut as part of a dress bodice) were first introduced in Europe but remained in use through the colonial period in America. Other early attempts at protecting children included the ubiquitous presence of baby caps, as well as a superstitious and talismanic use of coral for jewelry and rattle handles as a safeguard against evil.

By the late eighteenth century, philosophical departures celebrating the inquisitive nature of childhood set the tone for innovations in the attire of children. Influenced by the writings of JEAN-JACQUES ROUSSEAU in *Émile* (1762), and reflecting his pursuit of nature in child-rearing practices, a dramatic revision in the formula of dress began by banishing corsets and SWADDLING clothes in western Europe. A new empathetic and rational approach expounded the wearing of high-waisted, loose-fitting muslin chemise gowns over long pantalets for small children of both sexes. A plentiful supply of cotton and linen goods brought on by the increased output of the Industrial Revolution underscored the appeal of this soft, picturesque fashion for women as well. The skeleton suit, a period novelty, was recommended as garb for slightly older boys. A more formal look, its tailored design facilitated ease of motion by providing trousers that buttoned into the suit's bodice. Short simple hairstyles were worn with soft, flat-soled slippers to compliment this neoclassical look for children and adults alike.

After a mid-nineteenth century return to miniaturized adult dress, the influence of both the aesthetic and dress reform movements at the century's end can be seen in the stylistic direction of children's styles. Popularized in the 1890s in the West and in Western-influenced societies a penchant for pastel-tinted natural dyes and soft smocked shapes supplanted the garish, synthetic palette and Parisian-derived silhouette fashionable in the mid-nineteenth century to join the permanent vocabulary of children's custom and ready-to-wear clothing for the next century.

Special Occasion Dressing

The prospect of dressing for a unique occasion furnishes children and their guardians with a varied menu of socially prescribed garments. RITES OF PASSAGE are enduring and momentous events that traditionally require clothing of formulaic and memorable design. Frequently worn only one time, attire for occasions such as christening, FIRST COMMUNION, BAR AND BAT MITZVAHS, quinceañera (a girl's fifteenth birthday celebration in Latino cultures), CONFIRMATION, and social debuts is envisioned as a timeless garment of fantasy. As if in theatrical costume, the fledgling wearer assumes an unfamiliar identity and acts out a culturally defined role. Accordingly, many of these garments reflect an ethnic aesthetic, and sometimes provide a single opportunity to resurrect a long-silent family history. Surviving images of children taken at these thresholds of life serve to document the transition and its accomplishment through the interaction between garment and wearer.

Children's Clothing and Gender

The inherent naïveté of infants and small children has traditionally precluded the relevance of gender-specific dressing. Even christening gowns failed to betray a baby's sexual identity until the advent of color-coded ribbon trim in the twentieth century. Following their release from the bondage of swaddling, toddlers of both sexes were androgynously garbed in skirted, feminine styles. During the seventeenth century, these were interpreted in the same heavy, stiffened silk or wool worn by older children and adults. By the beginning of the eighteenth century androgynous baby and toddler dresses of bleached linen or cotton were embellished with an inexhaustible range of intricate embroidery and openwork. The strengthening affect of the handwork, coupled with the presence of rows of growth tucks, simultaneously served to preserve and extend the life of the dresses. Frequently they passed from one sibling to another, many times being worn by children of opposite sexes.

For small boys, the sartorial rite of passage marking the transition from dressing in skirts to short trousers occurred somewhere between the ages of three and five, generally corresponding with a first haircut. Into the twentieth century, the age of BREECHING remained subjective, and was ultimately determined by sentimentality and the readiness of family members to release their baby on the path toward manhood. A preoccupation with gender-mandated roles characterized children's dress for most of the nineteenth century. Parroting the vocational demeanor and somber tones of men's attire, boys were costumed in sailor and Scottish suits, military uniforms, and a variety of tailored clothes. The somewhat effeminate tone of the theatrically derived Little Lord Fauntleroy suit made it the ideal transitional garment for recently breeched children.

The homemaking woman of the same period was advised by a newfound proliferation of ladies' companion and fashion publications. The increased accessibility of home-sewing patterns, augmented by the proximity of merchandise in department store displays, exposed all classes to the allure of fashion trends. Affluent young ladies were dressed in store-bought cage crinolines and bustles, while homemade interpretations sufficed for most. Distinct, sexually prescribed parameters continued to govern the fashionable look for children and adolescents throughout most of the twentieth century, before they were superceded by the overwhelmingly popular trend toward transgender dressing that became prevalent by the mid-1980s. The carefree, practical appeal of intermixing ready-to-wear components came to dominate the contemporary fashion scene for all ages.

Increased exposure to fashion trends through pop culture and marketing devices has progressively lowered the age of children's personal involvement in the selection of their own wardrobes. Clamoring for looks endorsed by media icons, contemporary children demand a historically unprecedented voice in the way they look. The modern emphasis on named or designer apparel has also strongly affected the youth and even infant market as trademarks designate the status and fashion savvy of the young and their parents. In the late twentieth and twenty-first centuries shoes have become part of this trend as choices for this formerly utilitarian and expensive item have been influenced by peer pressure.

See also: **Child Development, History of the Concept of; Consumer Culture.**

BIBLIOGRAPHY

Brooke, Iris. 1930. *English Children's Costume since 1775.* London: A. and C. Black.

Cunnington, Phillis, and Anne Buck. 1965. *Children's Costume in England.* New York: Barnes and Noble.

Ewing, Elizabeth. 1977. *History of Children's Costume.* New York: Scribner.

Felger, Donna H. 1984. *Boy's Fashion 1885–1905.* Cumberland, MD: Hobby Horse Press.

Macquoid, Percy. 1923. *Four Hundred Years of Children's Costume from the Great Master: 1400–1800.* London: Medici Society.

Moore, Doris. 1953. *The Child in Fashion.* London: Batsford.

Olian, JoAnne. 1994. *Children's Fashions, 1860–1912: 1,065 Costume Designs from "La Mode Illustree."* New York: Dover Publications.

Paoletti, Jo B. 1983. "Clothes Make the Boy, 1860–1910." *Dress: The Annual Journal of the Costume Society of America* 9:16–20.

Rose, Claire. 1989. *Children's Clothes since 1750.* London: Batsford.

Schorsch, Anita. 1979. *Images of Childhood: An Illustrated Social History.* New York: Mayflower Books.

Sichel, Marion. 1983. *History of Children's Costume.* London: Batsford.

Villa, Nora. 1989. *Children in Their Party Dress.* Trans. Donna R. Miller. Modena, Italy: Zanfi.

Worrell, Estelle Ansley. 1980. *Children's Costume in America: 1607–1910.* New York: Scribner.

Phyllis Magidson

Fathering and Fatherhood

According to conventional wisdom patriarchal fathers of old were stern authoritarians, fatherly solicitude for one's children is a recent phenomenon, and industrialization removed men from the home and weakened their role. Historical study has added complexity to our understanding of their roles in the past, noted their involvement in their children's lives, exposed the various impacts of the Industrial Revolution, and complicated a linear view of the history of fathering and fatherhood. Historians ask about the extent of fathers' legal and domestic authority, the division of responsibility with their wives, their role in rearing their children, and the differences in the PARENTING of girls and boys in the past.

Patria Potestas

The Roman concept of *familia* described the people in a household subject to the authority of the master of the household, the paterfamilias. Members of a household shared a common subjection to the father first and blood or other ties second. Fathers, as *patresfamilias*, had complete power over the household. This included sexual rights to the slaves and freedmen or women who comprised his household. The ultimate power, in fact, lay in a Roman father's hands: *patria potestas*, the power of life and death. At the birth of a child fathers both acknowledged paternity and decided the child's future by picking up the newborn son laid at their feet or refusing to do so. Daughters they ordered nursed, or not. No law required fathers to support their biological offspring. ABANDONMENT, common among Romans of all social classes, protected the patrimony or INHERITANCE and was a means of family limitation. While rejection could mean death, abandoned children were often raised as foster children or slaves in a nonrelated household. They could later be reclaimed by their birth fathers, so long as the father reimbursed the foster family for the child's upbringing. Roman fatherhood was volitional, legal, and social, rather than biological, and ADOPTION was common. Adoption also solved problems of inheritance and could be enacted posthumously in a deceased father's will.

The power of fathers in ancient Rome reverberated beyond the family to affect Roman public life in myriad ways. The father-son relationship was a model for political relationships between men of different rank. Fathers represented their entire household politically, including their sons. Members of the Roman senate addressed one another as *patres conscripti* ("assembled fathers"), indicating that they served as leaders of households and ruled as fathers of Rome. Sons received citizenship through their fathers, albeit a second-class one. Responsible for raising and educating their sons as future full citizens, fathers went about the city and their political duties accompanied by their sons.

Young men were expected to become fathers when they came of age but they only became fully independent upon their own father's death. Citizenship, military service, and fatherhood were men's responsibilities to Rome. Men divorced and remarried if a wife was barren and quickly remarried should their wives die in childbirth. Leaving behind many children was a civic duty, a necessary rite of citizenship.

Under Roman law paternal authority was complete. The law permitted fathers to disinherit sons and theoretically, it also permitted them to kill their sons, although in the few cases where fathers exercised this right it was for high crimes such as treason. Widowed pregnant women were monitored carefully, even sequestered, by their husband's family, for according to statute her child belonged to her husband solely. Fathers retained authority over married daughters, including the right to punish them for adultery or to remove them from one marriage in favor of another more beneficial family alliance.

To escape this paternal control, if only partially, adult sons of the aristocracy left their father's households upon marriage, indicating an appetite for independence that could be satisfied because of wealth. Sons received the means to live independently but ownership of property remained with the father. Stress on the paternal line meant that grandchildren were likely to be raised by paternal GRANDPARENTS or in the paternal grandparents' home should their families be disrupted by DIVORCE, death, or additional marriages. Marriage was a means of facilitating alliances among men, and first wives might find themselves sent back to their fathers when their husbands arranged a new match. Perhaps because of the long-term responsibilities ascribed to fathers with regard to their adult daughters, Romans placed a high value on the father-daughter relationship. Cicero said, "What has nature wanted to be more pleasurable to us, what has nature wanted to be more dear to us than our daughters" (quoted in Hallett, p. 63).

Roman writers urged against the free expression of anger in the home. While corporal punishment was the right of the father, Seneca distinguished the exercise of this right from any need for anger. This advice likely arose out of the dangers posed by the all-encompassing authority over the household invested in fathers by law.

Christianity introduced a challenge to paternal authority. Individuals became answerable to an authority outside the

Eugène Manet and Daughter at Bougival (1881), Berthe Morisot. Although the image of the Victorian patriarch looms large in the modern imagination, nineteenth-century fathers were much more domestic than fathers in previous centuries. In the nineteenth century fatherhood and the emotional life of the family were seen as a respite from the demands of the increasingly industrialized outside world. © Giraudon/Art Resource, NY. Private collection, Paris, France.

head of household when they became Christians, an earthly one in the form of Church and priest and a heavenly one as well.

The Middle Ages

In the period of late antiquity and the Early Middle Ages, German *hausvaters* could corporally punish, reject, sell, and kill their offspring by law. Village social customs that assigned responsibility for rejected, illegitimate, or abandoned children to the maternal family—such as maternal uncles serving as guardians to the children of their sisters, an example often found in literature—modulated the starkness of the law.

The conjugal family was the basic family unit quite early in European family history—most certainly by 1000. While this truncated family did not much alter a father's authority in law, it would seem to improve his wife's place in the home

slightly, now that marriage was seen as a lifelong bond, and it meant that fathers would expect to see their sons leave their household upon marriage. Hence, authority over the adults of the next generation declined. Population growth in the feudal household gave rise to affective changes in family life: greater parental concern with child rearing and education. Fathers took charge of sons' upbringing as they grew less dependent on their mothers for full-time care, a pattern that would persist in later centuries. Inheritance practices tended to heighten the emotional and economic dynamics of fathers' relationships with their oldest son.

Inheritance and thus fatherhood underwent a revolution in the eleventh century that resulted in a stronger patriarch. Partible inheritance (that is, inheritance that could be split among heirs), bilateral kinship (a system wherein lineage was traced on both maternal and paternal lines), and women's control over property declined sharply. The nobility pioneered the system of primogeniture wherein property passed from the father to the oldest son in its entirety. Fathers designated a single male heir and passed on not only an impartible inheritance, but also a surname that followed the male line. Control of family resources shifted almost entirely to males. Women lost all but the most fleeting control over property as dower became only a lifetime grant and a husband's consent was required to sell any land a wife had inherited prior to her marriage. The emerging system that gave rise to this revolution, feudalism, also made the heads of noble families the founders of dynasties who exercised not only household authority, but because they were responsible for the defense of their lands, in effect ruled in the territory around them.

Yet, medieval Christianity moderated paternal power and altered the view of fatherly responsibility. Children were no longer seen as the property of the fathers; instead they were a responsibility entrusted to their fathers' safekeeping by God. Fathers were now expected to support and protect their offspring, even their illegitimate children.

Ideally, men, as fathers and husbands, ruled with love while children honored their parents. Intergenerational conflict between fathers and sons occurred, however, because a father's longevity could keep a son from inheriting the land needed in order to have the economic wherewithal to marry and set out on their own. Fathers controlled the patrimony, but the Church claimed that the next generation should be launched regardless. Late medieval household size in the fifteenth century indicates that family practice reflected these ideals and multigenerational households were the exception rather than the rule. Significant intergenerational tension erupted over marital choice as fathers sought to make suitable economic arrangements and alliances through their children's marriages. Daughters of the nobility in conflict with their fathers over marital choice had an option—a life in the service of God—although their fathers might go to great lengths to prevent or persuade them from exercising it.

The late medieval cult of St. Joseph reveals prescriptions for fatherly deportment. Writers and iconographers celebrated St. Joseph for his ability to support and care for the Holy Family, pointing out that he was both affectionate and a hard worker. The famine and plague of the late medieval period made concerns over the survival of families and lineages, and the protective and loving role of fathers in securing this, paramount.

One duty of the wealthy medieval father was in hiring a wet nurse for his children and proceeding to check up on the care she provided. It was also the father's decision when the child was to be weaned and returned to the natal household. Fathers were responsible for the education of sons, once they reached the age of seven, and focused on guiding them into a suitable occupation. Among the aristocracy, fathers might decide upon the education of their sons, but would not carry out this education themselves. Instead boys were trained for knighthood in another noble house, perhaps that of a maternal or paternal uncle. Urban fathers of means apprenticed their sons, placing them under the authority of another father. Peasant fathers were those fathers most likely in medieval times to rear their children through ADOLESCENCE in their own households. By the medieval period, all the components of modern fatherhood were present: breadwinner, educator, and at least in imagery, playmate. However the weight and meaning assigned to these roles shifted over time.

Reformation- and Enlightenment-Era Fathers

Close scholarly focus on the emotional quality and affective ties of fatherhood begins with the PROTESTANT REFORMATION, largely because Protestantism encouraged self-scrutiny and produced the written records that enable a close study. Protestantism also demanded a new role of men in the home: that of religious educator. The Reformation has been described as the "heyday" of the patriarchal nuclear family. The Protestant Reformation and ensuing Counter-Reformation in the Catholic Church resulted in a reform of family life, often in ways that cemented fathers' authority. For example, the laws of marriage were changed across Europe, outlawing the secret marriages of children that the Catholic Church had validated. Statutes now required a public ceremony along with parental consent and parents were expected to take into consideration their children's well being. The goals of reformers may not have been so much to enhance the control of children by their parents as they were to shore up the institution of marriage and clarify the means by which it was entered. In Catholic France and Italy, young people who disagreed with parents over marital alliances could turn to the state (in France) or the Church (in Italy) to find an ally, while in England, canon law allowed elopement to continue unrestrained until reforms were enacted in 1753.

German advice books for fathers indicate that fatherly solicitude began while their offspring were still in the womb. The books prescribed foods and herbs for the health of the fetus and pregnant woman and deputized the father to summon the midwife as the time of the birth neared and to serve as aide during labor. Diary evidence from Protestant fathers records their presence and attentiveness at the births of their children.

Reformation-era Europeans placed great stock in the abilities of parents to shape their children's future nature. Parents, fathers as well as mothers, were responsible for their offspring's physical and, most importantly, moral health. Europeans of this era sang the praises of the well-behaved and pious child, but, if anything, advice literature from the time would indicate that in practice parents were too lax rather than too firm in the application of DISCIPLINE.

Social order and eternal salvation were the primary rationales behind a strict upbringing. Ideas about the inherent nature of the sexes delegated to fathers the task of physically disciplining the children; mothers were thought too gentle for such a task. Echoing Roman prescriptions regarding corporal punishments, Lutheran advisers preferred that cool heads prevail and children not be spanked in anger. As in medieval times, fathers reared male children after age six. Both fathers and sons expected that fathers would guide the education and career choice of the next generation, but would take into consideration a child's inclinations, talents, and happiness.

Sixteenth-century child mortality rates and Protestant concern over original sin appear not to have shaped a particularly callous style of fathering. The death of a child brought men intense personal grief, despite religious beliefs and sermons (sometimes written by grieving fathers) that exhorted men to show little outward sign of mourning, but rather to rejoice that their children were relieved of earthly suffering. To fathers, Protestantism ascribed the duty of catechizing their children, even though first-generation Protestants themselves had thrown over the faith of their fathers. The texts they taught their children emphasized an individualism likely to produce self-confidence. According to historian Steven Ozment, the challenge of fathering the next generation of Protestants, then, was to inculcate a firm sense of responsibility to society to balance that incipient individualism.

ENLIGHTENMENT thinkers both affirmed the propriety of the rule of fathers over their households and set limits on its expression. The notion of the contract permeated their family philosophy. The marriage compact was a consensual one, and the task of parenthood shared, according to JOHN LOCKE. Locke saw in fatherhood an obligation to care for children. Any cessation of care obviated children's need to obey. JEAN-JACQUES ROUSSEAU saw any father-child bond once children ceased to require the father's aid in order to survive as voluntary.

Fathers in Colonial America

Patriarchy received a boost when English colonists constructed communities in the New World. English colonists expanded on the English laws and practices of family government, creating fathers who were among the most powerful household heads in the Western world, largely because of their control of the labor of subordinate household members, children, servants, and slaves. According to Carole Shammas, no English fathers, or any in Western Europe, had the ability that fathers in the New World had to force marriage, sell servants, or the authority to take a life. Chattel SLAVERY and indentured servitude granted household heads control of their labor force and concentrated tremendous patriarchal power in the hands of wealthy men. In colonial America, 80 percent of the population was legally dependent

on a male household head. Colonial fathers assumed power over the lives of adult and juvenile laborers through their servitude, while fulfilling the function of poor relief and correctional systems for their local communities. Control over the lives of dependents, family religious authority in Puritan communities, and distance from obligations to the Crown enhanced fathers' authority even if laws limiting the spectrum of physical correction might have tempered it slightly.

With the full development of plantation slavery, patriarchal power of white male household heads reached its apex in the antebellum slave South. For enslaved African-American men, slavery meant a fatherhood quite different from that of white men. Enslaved children followed the condition of the mother and white masters held authority over the African-American slave family. Sale separated slave parents and children in the internal slave trade from the Atlantic seaboard to the Southwest and residential patterns of the enslaved often meant that fathers lived on separate, although not necessarily distant, plantations from their children. Emancipation during and after the Civil War marked the first time that most African-American men assumed the paternal right to control family labor and the ability to protect their families without automatically risking their lives.

The Victorian Era

The Victorian patriarch, the mythically autocratic and stern father largely removed from the affairs of the household, is more a construction of the present than the past. While it may not have absented fathers from the home completely, the Industrial Revolution changed the days and duties of men and families dramatically, affecting the location and meaning of work, leisure, and parenting.

In preindustrial households, children owed their labor to their fathers for as long as they lived in the same house. The same assumptions governed the master/apprentice relationship and applied to nonrelated young people within the home. Industrialization transformed the family economy from one where household members pooled labor to a family wage economy where they pooled money gained from productive labor outside the home. In working-class homes, young people began to earn wages and the dependence of working-class families on their wages diminished the power of fathers. In middle-class households, industrialization had a different impact, transforming fathers into breadwinners and mothers into primary caretakers within the home. When the location of work shifted to the public sphere, middle-class fathers ceded control of the direct education and guidance of their children. On the one hand, this increased maternal autonomy at fathers' expense, while on the other fathers maintained a continued connection to the resources of power outside the home. Middle-class fathers may not have been true patriarchs in their own home, but they still held the reins of family political, social, and economic capital.

The Victorian father was, contrary to popular belief, quite domestic, and according to historian John Tosh, in England, Victorian fathers were more domestic than fathers either before or since. Home was a place where men ruled, but also a place that ministered to men's emotional needs. The family in the home was to make up for the dramatic social and economic changes of industrialization that threatened to turn men into mere drones. Home life and fatherhood was expected to rejuvenate men and provide meaning in an increasingly "heartless" world. In addition, domestic life was expected to replace the more homosocial leisure distractions outside the home of the English male middle class. In the United States men were similarly urged to eschew the club for the pleasures of the domestic hearth. Yet within the home, fathers had duties as well as respite. As in eras past, male parenting was focused particularly on sons and a successful masculine son was a public symbol of a successful manly father. According to Stephen Frank, in America, this pattern produced more formal relationships between fathers and sons, who were encouraged to be independent and manly; in contrast, fathers developed greater intimacy with daughters, even bestowing expensive educations on them as evidence of their economic success.

Fathers' legal powers were winnowed quite significantly in the Victorian era. In the United States coverture, the common-law system in which males represented the household to the public, diminished with the passage of married women's property acts, laws that gave women control of their earnings, and those that provided custody to mothers in the case of divorce. In addition, public education systems took over the education of youth in nearly every state by 1880. Many of the nineteenth-century reform movements, including temperance and abolition, at heart, dealt with the problem of the corrupt or out-of-control patriarch.

The Twentieth-Century "Decline in Patriarchy"
Assumptions of complete authoritarian patriarchal control in families of the past do not often hold up to scrutiny. Affection, piety, practicality, and allies both within and outside the household often mediated fathers' powers. Nonetheless, historians find a new fatherhood evolving with the democratic or companionate family. The exact timing of this new father's emergence is debated.

Fatherly play took firm root in the nineteenth-century American middle-class family. In the home, fathers refreshed themselves in the joyful company of their brood. PLAY both carved a specific place for fathers in family life and marginalized their importance. By the turn of the century paternal play became a marker of middle-class identity and a means by which experts imagined the domestic sphere could be injected with masculinity.

During the 1930s when the global economic crisis prevented many men from performing as family breadwinners and as the psychological community embraced the theories of SIGMUND FREUD, advisors elaborated a new role for fathers beyond that of playful companions. Father was a role model for the proper sex role development of both sons and daughters. This attention reflected anxieties about masculinity in the home as massive unemployment reduced the power of fathers to provide for their families. Men and women saw male authority as derived from their breadwinning role. Work relief programs targeted men with the aim of getting breadwinners back to work. If the GREAT DEPRESSION brought concerns about too many economically emasculated dads hanging around the nation's families, World War II raised concerns over the impact of their complete absence. The stage was set for the re-embrace of the "pater-unfamiliar" as Americans experienced a resurgence of domesticity at the war's end.

Father as Equal Participant
Fatherhood's function as a male restorative and as sex-role modeling for the family was achieved largely through companionship and play. Both could spawn intimacy but often did not. Neither required reorganizing gendered child-rearing responsibilities greatly. By the mid-twentieth century, American fathers emerged as pals as well as providers. As defined by experts, the role of father involved childcare, but men performed such labor to "spell" mother or to foster relationships with children, not because the work had to be done. These notions reified the gender division of labor even as they assigned men a place in the home. Parenting was fatherplay and motherwork.

Three twentieth-century developments challenged this division of labor which has proven, not surprisingly, quite resistant to change. The postwar BABY BOOM (1946–1964) ushered the ideal of fatherly participation further into the mainstream. Experts, mothers, and fathers themselves insisted, "Fathers are parents, too!" Women brought expert advice into the home to back up their need for help as they coped with raising the baby boomers. As the baby boom family cycle progressed, men, torn between the demands of home and work, opted for the more familiar rewards of breadwinning, but they, their wives, and their children became increasingly aware that the emotional penalty paid when men failed to engage in the daily care or play of their children was high. Resignation and regret characterized the reflections of empty-nest mothers and fathers in the 1980s and unleashed a spate of literature by male boomers scarred by absent fathers.

The postwar years brought another change to American families and those in Western Europe as well: the increased participation of married women in the labor force. With fathers as primary breadwinners, the occasional child-care chore was all that most families demanded of men, but as women increasingly shared the breadwinning role while shouldering the lions' share of the child-care and household work, their demands and persuasive power escalated. Contemporary studies attest to the ongoing negotiation of gender responsibilities with regard to household work and child care in American homes. Finally, the feminist movement of the 1960s, 1970s, and 1980s offered a critique of patriarchy, promoted the idea that gender roles were social constructs rather than immutable biological inheritances, and proposed that equality in the public sphere for women would be impossible without lessening the inequality in the private sphere.

Linked to feminism in the popular mind, but enabled by both women's labor force participation and a welfare state, women have increasingly been able to remove themselves and their children—either through divorce or the choice not to marry—from fathers they deem abusive or unsatisfactory. This has led to an increase in the number of children living in poverty and calls on both sides of the Atlantic to require popularly dubbed "deadbeat dads" to support their children. These changes provoked cultural anxieties about the decline of male authority and "disappearance" or weakness of the fathers at the end of the twentieth century. The issue reveals the continued economic inequality between men and women and the volitional quality of participatory fatherhood in the new millennium as well as the strong association of fatherhood with power. Breadwinning remains father's principle responsibility and the workplace remains family unfriendly, while more and more, mothers must balance their commitments to work and family. Fathers are no longer patriarchs, but they strive to be more than breadwinners and pals. The twenty-first-century father looks for self-identity, meaning, and satisfaction in his relationships with his children.

See also: **Mothering and Motherhood.**

BIBLIOGRAPHY

Ago, Renata. 1997. "Young Nobles in the Age of Absolutism: Paternal Authority and Freedom of Choice in Seventeenth-Century Italy." In *A History of Young People, Ancient and Medieval Rites of Passage*, vol. 1, ed. Giovanni Levi and Jean-Claude Schmitt, pp. 283–322. Cambridge, MA: Belknap Press of Harvard University Press.

Boswell, John. 1988. *The Kindness of Strangers: The Abandonment of Children in Western Europe from Late Antiquity to the Renaissance.* New York: Pantheon Books.

Burguiere, Andre, et al. 1996. *A History of the Family. Volume I: Distant Worlds, Ancient Worlds.* Cambridge, MA: Belknap Press of Harvard University Press.

Demos, John. 1982. "The Changing Faces of Fatherhood: A New Exploration in Family History." In *Father and Child: Developmental and Clinical Perspectives*, ed. Alan Gurwitt Stanley and John M. Ross. Boston: Little, Brown.

Fossier, Robert. 1996. "The Feudal Era (Eleventh–Thirteenth Century)." In *A History of the Family. Volume I: Distant Worlds, Ancient Worlds*, ed. Andre Burguiere. Cambridge, MA: Belknap Press of Harvard University Press.

Frank, Stephen. 1998. *Life with Father: Parenthood and Masculinity in the Nineteenth-Century American North.* Baltimore, MD: Johns Hopkins University Press.

Gies, Frances, and Joseph Gies. 1987. *Marriage and the Family in the Middle Ages.* New York: Harper and Row.

Gottlieb, Beatrice. 1993. *The Family in the Western World from the Black Death to the Industrial Age.* New York: Oxford University Press.

Griswold, Robert. 1993. *Fatherhood in America: A History.* New York: Basic Books.

Griswold, Robert, ed. 1999. "Special Issue: The History of Fatherhood." *Journal of Family History* 24: 3.

Guichard, Pierre and Jean-Pierre Cuvillier. 1996. "Barbarian Europe." In *A History of The Family, Volume I: Distant Worlds, Ancient Worlds*, ed. Andre Burguiere. Cambridge, MA: Belknap Press of Harvard University Press.

Hallett, Judith P. 1984. *Father and Daughters in Roman Society: Women and the Elite Family.* Princeton, NJ: Princeton University Press.

Herlihy, David. 1985. *Medieval Households.* Cambridge, MA: Harvard University Press.

Johansen, Shawn. 2001. *Family Men: Middle-Class Fatherhood in Early Industrializing America.* New York: Routledge.

La Rossa, Ralph. 1997. *The Modernization of Fatherhood: A Social and Political History.* Chicago: University of Chicago Press.

Ozment, Stephen. 1983. *When Fathers Ruled: Family Life in Reformation Europe.* Cambridge, MA: Harvard University Press.

Rouselles, Aline. 1996. "The Family under the Roman Empire: Signs and Gestures." In *A History of The Family, Volume I: Distant Worlds, Ancient Worlds*, ed. Andre Burguiere. Cambridge, MA: Belknap Press of Harvard University Press.

Ryan, Mary. 1981. *Cradle of the Middle Class: The Family in Oneida County, New York, 1790–1865.* Cambridge, UK: Cambridge University Press.

Shahar, Shulamith. 1992. *Childhood in the Middle Ages.* London: Routledge.

Shammas, Carole. 2002. *A History of Household Government in America.* Charlottesville: University of Virginia Press.

Thomas, Jan. 1996. "Fathers as Citizens of Rome, Rome as a City of Fathers (Second Century BC–Second Century AD)." In *A History of The Family, Volume I: Distant Worlds, Ancient Worlds*, ed. Andre Burguiere. Cambridge, MA: Belknap Press of Harvard University Press.

Tosh, John. 1999. *A Man's Place: Masculinity and the Middle-Class Home in Victorian England.* New Haven, CT: Yale University Press.

Weiss, Jessica. 2000. *To Have and To Hold: Marriage, the Baby Boom and Social Change.* Chicago: University of Chicago Press.

Zoja, Luigi. 2001. *The Father: Historical, Psychological and Cultural Perspectives.* Philadelphia: Taylor and Francis.

JESSICA WEISS

Fear

Changes in the occurrence and handling of children's fears in the West fit into the pattern in which the history of childhood has been discussed in the late twentieth and early twenty-first centuries. Notions of the "discovery" of the child in early modern times and of the absence of emotional relations between parents and children seem less convincing now than they did in the 1970s, when enthusiasm for the idea that personal relations could change in a short period of time was fresh. But without any doubt, ideas about how children should be raised show considerable shifts, and the debate about education has intensified since the eighteenth century. The social position of children changed in a long process in which childhood came to take several decades instead of (for most social classes) one.

Fear as a Pedagogical Tool

Everyday life in traditional society seems to have been determined by fear, since ignorance of natural phenomena, long periods of disease, and social strife made daily existence insecure. Religion was for a long time supportive in this world full of fear, but from the sixteenth century on became divided and destabilized. With religious disputes dominating public life, basic fears were reported to have been experienced in the religious domain as well.

In his autobiography, *Grace Abounding*, John Bunyan, who was born in 1628, tells his readers about the "fearful dreams" and "dreadful visions" which afflicted him while sleeping, and which were caused by "Devils and wicked spirits" but were ultimately sent by God to punish him for his sins. His greatest fear was the Day of Judgment, on which he might be ordered to spend his time "amongst Devils and Hellish Feinds."

By the eighteenth century, however, an enhanced confidence in knowledge and rationality made fear an undesirable relict, which was soon labeled as childish. In traditional society, fear had been used extensively in the raising of small children. In circumstances where it was difficult to keep an eye on the little ones who crept around and were in danger of getting lost, drowned, or burned, the bogeyman was a powerful tool to prevent children's dangerous inquisitiveness. As children got older they could prove their fitness for adult society by discarding their fears of a whole range of monsters, batmen, toe-shearers, werewolves, and child-eating roosters that had been said to be after children all over Europe. Before 1800 only few autobiographers wrote about their childhood fears, but those who did usually mentioned frightening stories told by adults. Isabelle de Moerloose, born in Flanders around 1661, confessed that she was afraid of a man wearing a long cape, who roamed the land to kill babies by putting a ball in their mouths.

Autobiographical writings confirm that parents widely used the bogeyman as a pedagogical tool. Even an educated person such as the Dutch statesman and poet Constantijn Huygens, born in 1596, threatened his little daughter with a creepy doll in a black cape. Such dolls were made especially to serve this purpose. Nineteenth-century autobiographers still frequently complained about parents who frightened them. Willem van den Hull, for instance, wrote that to keep him away from the canals, his mother had taught him that death lived underwater and was lingering to grab his feet and pull him down under if he dared come too close.

Since the seventeenth century, a growing number of pedagogues warned against such methods. According to the Dutch writer Jacob Cats, bogeymen had such an impact on the "tender senses" of children that they would never lose their early fears. JOHN LOCKE, in his influential *Some Thoughts Concerning Education*, advised parents to keep children away from frights of all kinds and he warned against "telling them of Raw-Head and Bloody Bones." In the eighteenth century the practice was even more widely condemned. Betje Wolff, the first female Dutch pedagogue, protested the practice avidly, the more so because she was herself being scared by the "black man" in her youth. She called fear and fright "the poison of a child's heart."

To protect children from real dangers, bogeymen remained an acceptable practice, but writers on education warned that they should never be used for fun. Rational use of bogeymen, however, was embedded in a culture in which childhood and fear were still interwoven with deep-rooted beliefs and customs. Marina Warner, for instance, cites a particularly bad-tempered Italian lullaby: "Go to sleep, may you die in your sleep, that the priest come to take you to keep! Ninna . . . oh, Ninna! To whom shall I give this little girl? . . . To the bogeyman I'll give her, for a whole day he will keep her. . . . " Peasants who threatened children with the terrible corn mother to make them stay out of the fields may themselves have had a vague belief in ghosts and spirits.

Conquering Fear

In the new literature on childhood that began appearing in great supply in the second half of the eighteenth century, the conquest of fear became an important educational goal. As Peter Stearns and Timothy Haggarty have noted, the enthusiasm for actively encouraging children to master their fears prevailed in the nineteenth century, in advice literature as well as in stories and books for children. But the age at which is was considered fit to help children overcome their fear was lowered. It also became customary to think that adults (and especially mothers) were the source of children's fears because they transmitted their own fears to their children.

In feudal society, the show of fear had been functional in relations between the social classes, especially in the behavior of inferiors toward their superiors; only the aristocracy had been supposed to show defiance. Fearlessness had been admired intensely, as numerous FAIRY TALES testify, but most people could not afford it. During the eighteenth century, the ideal that men were free and equal left no room for people to consider fearfulness an acceptable attitude. As children in general lack the self-control needed to suppress expressions of fear, this changed attitude toward fear was one of the phenomena that enhanced the distance between children and adults. Children were banned from polite society as long as they were supposed to be unable to control themselves.

As the psychological costs of this suppression of fear became clear to psychiatrists, and possibly even more to artists and writers, toward the end of nineteenth century, the emphasis of advice-givers on the handling of children's fear shifted to avoiding fearful situations as much as possible. Actively instilling fear into children as an educational tool, which had already been discouraged during the nineteenth century, became an abhorrent type of miseducation in the twentieth century. As parents had more opportunities to supervise their children, or to have them supervised, instilling fear in children made little sense anymore. Thus the conditions for a modern attitude toward fear were first realized in the upper and middle classes. As most advice literature was meant for these groups, who were living in comfortable circumstances where children could be prevented from endangering themselves, bourgeois parents began to worry about the contact their children had with representatives of the lower classes. This is notable in the extensive warnings against the possibility of housemaids scaring the children in their care. In books on education, children's fears were taken much more seriously after the second half of the nineteenth century; parents were encouraged to pay attention to any sign of distress. Where fear had been seen as a moral defect, in the course of the twentieth century new psychological insights considered it a natural phenomenon, something children could never be blamed for.

The Experience of Fear

Advice manuals and children's books provide the material with which to write the history of emotional standards, but childhood memories bring us closer to the actual experience of how fear shaped the identities of children in the past. In the absence of systematic studies of childhood memories, some preliminary conclusions from a study-in-progress of 500 AUTOBIOGRAPHIES from the Netherlands and Flanders, covering the period from 1750 to 1970, show that one out of five of these autobiographies mentions fear, which makes it clear that it was a focal point. The social bias in the available authors commands caution, however: upper-class witnesses dominate the early period (up to 1850), whereas a solid majority from the middle class, with emphasis on white-collar professions, is evident throughout the nineteenth and twentieth centuries.

The earliest statements show a remarkable agreement with the normative sources: aristocratic boys remembered with pride that they had been put to the test of their fear of darkness, being asked to get a Bible out of a distant, unlit church or being ordered to fetch a bottle of gin from an inn on a night when there were rumors of burglars in the neighborhood. In particular they remembered the praise they received after fulfilling these commissions. They even remembered their mothers' protests against their being put to the test. Having to fight the dark outside the house has almost completely disappeared from twentieth-century childhood memories. Actively forcing children to overcome this fear by sending them out in the dark is only mentioned by a few lower-class boys; middle-class parents seem to have taken

the hints of educational reformers who opposed the practice. But autobiographies contradict the advice books too: the horror stories told by servants are duly reported, but for every child who was scared by them, at least one remembers them with delight—a fondly remembered exercise in the control of fear.

What were children afraid of? In search of their first memories, almost one in three of the autobiographers comes up with sudden frights. Being lost in a crowd, the parents being out of sight, or a fire can easily be understood as impressive moments that can trigger a first memory. But many more mysterious moments are remembered only as anxious distress whose immediate cause has been lost. Some autobiographers simply state they were afraid of everything when very young.

The dark has inspired by far the most memories of childhood fears. Though it would seem feasible that night was less horrifying when children slept in the same bed or at least in the same room with others, some witnesses claim that the presence of sleeping family members enhanced their fright. If the others were not snoring, was it a sign they had suddenly departed? Were the monsters only after the children who did not sleep? But most memories of terrible fears in the night have been delivered by middle-class children who slept in their own bedrooms, with noises coming from all sides while they were on their own to cope with them. Whether night lights were a help is questionable. Enough witnesses remember the disturbing shadows and the spluttering sound adding to their misery. But many children asked for a light and remember the struggles they had to wage to be allowed one. Mentions of this fear declined in later years, with the most recent mention by an autobiographer born in 1918, which supports the idea that electrical light made a big difference, especially since many children have lamps by their beds that they can operate themselves and few people now feel they have to be economical with electricity.

Thunder and lightning could be overwhelming experiences, especially when others who were present could not master their fear. Quite a few autobiographers remember older brothers and sisters in distress: it was a moment of triumph for the smaller children. When the person who was afraid was an adult, the distinction between children and adults was lifted for a moment as children saw to their amazement that they were more in control of themselves than the trembling aunt or maid. Fathers visibly affected by the tempest, however, were a too severe breach of security: they left their children feeling that the world itself could perish.

The ubiquity of death in traditional society was an emotional burden to children and adults alike. In modern times the mystery of death became a more explicit moment of fear as children remembered clearly the day they realized their mortality for the first time. Many record it as a nauseating panic against which parents were almost helpless. Generalizations are dubious here, however: some autobiographers tell about childhood confrontations with sudden deaths—bodies encountered, skeletons found—that seemed only comical and made an impression only because other people were scared.

Generalized fear of the future seems to be a relatively recent phenomenon, not mentioned in memories of youth before 1880. Children have coveted adulthood as an escape from humiliating childhood. They remember their desire, but at the same time considered the future a frightening place where one had to be able to do all kinds of things that seemed very difficult. By the time childhood came to be valued as a special period in life, in the later nineteenth century, autobiographers wrote more specifically about their reluctance to grow up. How could they master all the skills in time to hold their own? The proliferation of vague fears about the future is a symptom of the disappearance of childhood in the last decades of the twentieth century. Rumors of war tend to result in frantic war games among the boys, but also in stifling anxiety. The horrors of mass warfare during two world wars, with carpet bombing, gas attacks, genocide, and nuclear destruction, had a great impact on children, but it is difficult to say to what extent this impact differed from that of warfare in previous centuries.

Finally, since the eighteenth century, all forms of fear appear in children's books, and since the twentieth century in MOVIES and on TELEVISION, continuing a much older tradition of telling children folktales and ghost stories. Children's fears are today exploited by writers and film directors, because in a paradoxical way fears have a great attraction. Often, but not always, the causes of fear are presented in a sensible way and the level of anxiety is coupled to the age of the intended audience. Nevertheless, books and films that are read or watched by children younger than their intended audiences have in the last decades been a new source of fears.

See also: **Child-Rearing Advice Literature; Emotional Life.**

BIBLIOGRAPHY

Bakker, Nelleke. 2000. "The Meaning of Fear. Emotional Standards for Children in the Netherlands, 1850–1950: Was There a Western Transformation?" *Journal of Social History* 34: 369–391.

Dekker, Rudolf. 1999. *Childhood, Memory, and Autobiography in Holland from the Golden Age to Romanticism.* London: Macmillan.

Stearns, Peter N., and Timothy Haggerty. 1991. "The Role of Fear: Transistions in American Emotional Standards for Children, 1850–1950." *American Historical Review* 96: 63–94.

Warner, Marina. 1998. *No Go the Bogeyman: Scaring, Lulling, and Making Mock.* London: Chatto and Windus.

RUDOLF M. DEKKER
HUGO RÖLING

Female Genital Mutilation

The mutilation of the female genitals known as *female circumcision* takes place today primarily in AFRICA. The practice is prevalent in areas where ISLAM is dominant, but female circumcision is far older. Pharaonic circumcision, the name given to the most mutilating form, goes back to ancient Egypt. It is not found in North Africa, Saudi Arabia, or many Asian countries where Muslims are numerous. But the Christian Copts of Egypt and the Jewish Falacha of Ethiopia know of the practice. The Kikuyu of Kenya perform it while their neighbors, the Luo, do not. Similar practices can also be found in eastern Mexico, in Peru, and in western Brazil, where they were imported at the time of the slave trade. Female circumcision was also performed in the West during the nineteenth century to treat feminine "hysteria."

The least traumatizing of these practices are called *sunna,* meaning "tradition" in Arabic. The most benign form consists of removing the foreskin from the clitoris, although the whole clitoris is often removed. The procedure also entails the removal of the smaller labia, called *tahara* (purification). Young Gishri girls in Hausa country, barely pubescent, are sold at a very high price once they have been made ready for penetration by this procedure, which involves cutting their vaginas.

Infibulation eliminates a major portion of the inner labia. What is left is sewn together with a silk thread in Sudan and Ethiopia, and with acacia needles in Somalia. This practice can sometimes also be found in western Africa (northern Nigeria, Al Pular of Senegal). Cauterization is accelerated by a concoction called *mai-mai,* a mixture of gum and sugar, herbal compresses, and even ash and goat dung. The operation closes the vulva almost entirely, except for a narrow orifice kept open by the insertion of a stick or a straw. This orifice is intended to permit the later evacuation of urine and menstrual flow. The procedure is performed before or sometimes after the first marriage in order to ensure the young girl's virginity. It is the husband who, using a razor blade or something similar, must open it up again to allow penetration. The goal of this practice is to give the husband strict control of his wife's SEXUALITY.

These operations are performed on girls of various ages, anytime from birth to PUBERTY. Sometimes the opposite is done: the lengthening of the clitoris is a practice of some communities in Benin and among the Khoisan of South Africa. The elongation of the smaller lips is done by MASTURBATION in lake villages, and the Shona people perform enlargements of the vagina with the use of a stick. These operations are women's business, never spoken of to the husbands. Social pressure to perform female circumcision is very strong, and the older women are especially attached to the practice. Except in educated urban areas, young women who have not gone through female circumcision are deemed unmarriageable. It is also an event that girls await impatiently because it is a cause for celebration, rejoicing, and gift giving. Without it they would be ostracized.

The World Health Organization (WHO) estimates that about 40 percent of African women are subjected to such operations in more than thirty-six states. The negative short- and long-term consequences of these operations are many. Most practitioners are women who are unfamiliar with modern aseptic techniques. The most common side effects are hemorrhages, septicemia, and tetanus, not to mention painful psychological trauma. One report estimates that a third of young Sudanese girls do not survive the operation. Its consequences continue to affect women throughout their lives: repeated infections and sterility (and therefore, repudiation by their husbands) may result.

Mandatory prohibition of female genital mutilation has yielded little result. Even emigrants to western Europe from areas where female circumcision is prevalent have been known to sometimes continue the practice. Great Britain banned female circumcision in Sudan and Kenya in 1946. The practice has retreated the most in Egypt and Eritrea, thanks to the social and educational advances made during President Nasser's time. The clumsiness of Western feminists for a long time alienated African women's movements, but they nevertheless took up the fight in Khartoum in 1979, and in response, in 1982 the World Health Organization condemned female circumcision. Today the taboo is finally lifted and the subject is being openly discussed, but progress remains slow.

See also: **Circumcision.**

BIBLIOGRAPHY

Coquery-Vidrovitch, Catherine. 1997. *African Women: A Modern History.* Boulder, CO: Westview Press.

Rahman, Anika and Nahid Toubia. 2000. *Female Genital Mutilation: A Guide to Laws and Policies Worldwide.* London: Zed Books.

Shell-Duncan, Bettina, and Ylva Hernlund. 2000. *Female "Circumcision" in Africa: Culture, Controversy, and Change.* Boulder CO: Lynne Rienner Publishers.

World Health Organization, UNICEF, and United Nations Population Fund. 1997. *Female Genital Mutilation: A Joint WHO/ UNICEF/UNFPA Statement.* Geneva: World Health Organization.

CATHERINE COQUERY-VIDROVITCH

Fénelon, François (1651–1715)

French archbishop, theologian, writer, and royal tutor François de Salignac de La Mothe Fénelon played many diverse intellectual roles; among these, posterity has celebrated him as a philosopher with extraordinary views of education.

Fénelon was born in 1651 into an established noble family that had long served the French Church and Crown. After completing his theological studies, he was ordained a priest in 1676; in 1678 he was appointed director of the Nouvelles Catholiques, a college that converted young women from French Protestantism. Here he wrote his first important work, *Traité de l'éducation des filles* (1687; Treatise on the education of girls). The same year, he published his *Réfutation de Malebranche.*

In 1689 his noble birth, combined with his remarkable pedagogical skills, landed Fénelon the influential job of tutor to Louis, the duke of Bourgogne and grandson and heir to Louis XIV. Several honors resulted from this privileged position at court, including Fénelon's election to the French Academy in 1693. His greatest success, however, was his *Les Aventures de Télémaque, fils d'Ulysse* (1699; Telemachus, son of Ulysses), a poetic rewriting of *Ulysses* composed for the political education of the prince.

At the same time, however, Fénelon's support of Madame Guyou, the leader of the quietist movement in France, had given rise to the so-called Quarrel of Quietism (the Christian doctrine in which human passivity is supposed to generate divine activity). Actually, by arguing for the "disinterested" and "pure" love of God in his *Explication des maximes des saints sur la vie intérieure* (1697; Explanation of the sayings of the saints on the interior life), Fénelon generated much consternation within the authoritarian Church. His selection as archbishop of Cambrai the year before had been a disappointment for a man whose accomplishments and reputation legitimately could have been expected to earn him the bishopric of Paris. His disgrace became official in 1699, when first Louis XIV, and later Rome, banned Fénelon's *Explication.*

Exiled to his diocese, Fénelon remained a vigilant observer of political matters, although he did despair upon the death of his pupil the duke of Bourgogne in 1712. Three years later, he himself died in Cambrai.

In a century with few childhood and educational theorists Fénelon was indeed an exception—as his countrymen Michel Montaigne and François Rabelais had been in the previous century. Fénelon's first pedagogical work explored the neglected field of girls' education. Although France had several nuns' schools, and the Saint-Cyr girls' school had been founded in 1686 near Versailles, Fénelon pointed to the necessity of educating, from a global moral perspective, all French girls for their roles as future mothers and housewives. The pedagogical counsel and rules given in Fénelon's *Treatise,* however, included not only girls' instruction, but also education in general; he encouraged recognition of the child *as a child.* The schoolmaster was to follow the child's nature, preparing her for education even before she could speak, never forcing her to study when not absolutely necessary, and eliminating her FEAR and submission by teaching using PLAY, joy, and amusing stories.

Because of this educational philosophy, Fénelon did not write scholarly treatises or discourses, as the other royal tutors had done before him. Instead, he invented pleasant dialogues, fables, and a less predictable format: the didactic novel *Telemachus*, originally conceived as an insertion into *Ulysses*.

Telemachus, in search of his father, is guided by the wise Mentor, alias Minerva, on his perilous travels through various civilizations throughout the Mediterranean. By telling such an adventurous story, Fénelon not only initiated his royal pupil into Greek mythology, but he also awakened the prince's interest in politics, religion, and virtue. Furthermore, by helping his pupil to identify with the future king of Ithaca, Fénelon hoped to teach him the art of good government. When Telemachus considers the countries he visits— comparing their laws, manners, and customs— he is actually preaching humanity and peace in contrast to the violence and despotism characteristic of Louis XIV's reign. Nevertheless, *Telemachus* is basically a pedagogical work for the use of young people and their teachers. Fénelon's genius was to incorporate traditional topics into a new dynamic process of teaching and learning.

Entirely organized around the fundamental coupling of the master and the disciple, *Telemachus* is in fact as much a didactic method as an edifying narrative. If *mentor* (meaning a good master) has become an ordinary word, it is because Fénelon's creation, in accordance with the Jesuits' pedagogical ideal, transforms the act of instruction into a relationship—one full of love. The master must help the child acquire her own experiences, kindly and step-by-step, "arranging" pedagogical situations, and sometimes even leaving the child alone when necessary.

Advocating for an entirely experimental education, Fénelon's writings had enormous influence on the ENLIGHTENMENT, directly affecting two of the era's leading philosophers, JOHN LOCKE and JEAN-JACQUES ROUSSEAU. From the eighteenth until the mid-twentieth century, *Telemachus* was required reading in French schools, mainly as a means of imparting knowledge of Greek culture to the pupils.

See also: **Education, Europe; Girls' Schools.**

BIBLIOGRAPHY

Carcassonne, Elie. 1946. *Fénelon, l'homme et l'oeuvre.* Paris, Boivin.

Chérel, Albert. 1970. *Fénelon au XVIIIe siècle en France, son prestige, son influence.* Geneva: Slatkine.

Dédéyan, Charles. 1991. *Télémaque ou la Liberté de l'Esprit.* Paris: Librairie Nizet.

Goré, Jeanne-Lydie. 1968. "Introduction." In *Les aventures de Télémaque,* by François Fénelon. Paris: Garnier-Flammarion.

Granderoute, Robert. 1985. *Le roman pédagogique de Fénelon à Rousseau.* Geneva and Paris: Editions Slatkine.

ANNE ELISABETH SEJTEN

Fertility Drugs

Fertility drugs are prescription medications that stimulate the ovaries to produce eggs. They are also known as ovulation induction medications. Typically in the course of a female monthly cycle, one egg is produced in response to hormonal signals from the brain. This ovulatory function can be disturbed in a variety of medical conditions or with the increasing age of a woman. When ovulation does not proceed normally, female infertility can result and fertility drugs are often used to restore ovulation.

There are two major types of fertility drugs. The first is a drug called clomiphene citrate, which comes in pill form. It was first synthesized in 1956, and approved for clinical use in 1967. The second type is derived from the urine of menopausal women, and is therefore called human menopausal gonadotropins (hMG). It was first clinically used in 1969, and is only available in an injectable form. Although both types of drugs can cause multiple eggs to be produced at one time, this is more common with the hMG drugs, so they are thought of as more potent ovulation inducers and are prescribed only by specialists in infertility treatment.

Clomiphene is generally used to induce ovulation when conception will occur through heterosexual intercourse, or when sperm will be inseminated into a woman's vagina or uterus. The cumulative six-month conception rate with clomiphene approaches 60–75 percent. HMGs can also be used for conception through intercourse or insemination, and cumulative six-cycle conception rates approach 90 percent. HMGs are more commonly used in IN VITRO FERTILIZATION (IVF), where it is important for a woman to produce as many eggs as possible.

Multiple gestation—twin, triplet, or higher order pregnancies—are an important consequence of treatment with fertility drugs. The multiple pregnancy rate with clomiphene is approximately 10 percent, nearly all twins. Multifetal gestation rates are approximately 20–25 percent with hMG use and intercourse or insemination. With IVF, twin rates approach 35 percent, and triplet or higher order pregnancies occur in 6–7 percent of cases. Overall this represents a twentyfold increase in twins and a fifty to one-hundredfold increase in higher order multiples compared to rates of multiples in natural conceptions.

Ovarian hyperstimulation syndrome (OHSS) is another potential complication of fertility drugs. In OHSS women experience massive ovarian enlargement, large shifts in fluid and chemical balance in the body, and occasionally blood clots in major veins. Severe OHSS occurs in 1–2 percent of women undergoing fertility drug treatment, and can require hospitalization. In rare cases OHSS can lead to death.

Questions have been raised about the possible association of fertility drugs with later development of ovarian cancer.

Several retrospective studies concerning this association offer contradictory conclusions. As a result, the American Society for Reproductive Medicine—the major organization of infertility physicians in the United States—recommends that physicians caution patients that these medications may increase their lifetime risk of developing ovarian cancer.

Data from the National Survey of Family Growth (NSFG), the only source for up-to-date nationally representative infertility data, indicates that approximately 1.8 million U.S. women used ovulation-inducing medications in 1995, the last year for which data is available. Several social trends have influenced the use of fertility medications. First, there has been a recent increase in infertility rates, according to NSFG data. In 1995, 10 percent of women reported some form of fertility impairment, compared to 8 percent in 1988. This rate increase occurred across almost all age, marital status, income, and racial subgroups. This is the first year that the NSFG showed an increase in infertility rates since the survey began in 1973. It is unknown if this increase represents a "real" increase in infertility status or a change in recognition and reporting of fertility problems.

Second, there was a dramatic increase in absolute numbers of women with impaired fertility, out of proportion to the infertility rate change. The number of women with impaired fertility rose from 4.6 million to 6.2 million between 1988 and 1995. It is thought that the dramatic increase in numbers is due to delayed marriage and delayed childbearing trends among the baby boom cohort, who reached their less fertile reproductive years in the 1990s. Third, because older women attempting reproduction have fewer years in which to accomplish childbearing, baby boomers have pursued infertility therapies in great numbers. In 1995, 2.7 million women in the United States sought infertility services, compared to 1.8 million in 1982. Women who sought infertility services tended to be older, married, wealthier, and white.

See also: **Conception and Birth; Multiple Births.**

BIBLIOGRAPHY

Chandra, Anjani, and Elizabeth Stephen. 1998. "Impaired Fecundity in the United States: 1982–1995." *Family Planning Perspectives* 30, no. 1: 34–42.

Speroff, Leon, Robert Glass, and Nathan Kase. 1999. *Clinical Gynecologic Endocrinology and Infertility*, 6th ed. Philadelphia: Lipincott Williams and Wilkins.

INTERNET RESOURCES

American Society for Reproductive Medicine. 2002. Available from <www.asrm.org>.

National Survey of Family Growth. 2002. Available from <www.cdc.gov/nchs/nsfg.htm>.

LISA H. HARRIS

Fertility Rates

Almost all societies limit birth rates to some extent. BIRTH-CONTROL patterns change over time. Hunting and gathering societies often limited births through prolonged lactation; in contrast, agricultural societies combined two strategies: on the one hand, making sure enough children were available for work and to inherit family land and possessions, and on the other hand limiting birth rates to protect resources.

Differences in the ways societies limit family size affect children. Some societies focus on controlling how closely children are spaced, with implications for SIBLING relationships, while others limit the number of girls as a method of population control; this in turn affects relationships between boys and girls as well as unbalancing the sex ratio among adults, which makes marriage almost universal among the surviving girls but not among the overrepresented males. Furthermore, birth rate limitations often reflect socioeconomic status, as the very wealthy in preindustrial conditions usually had more children than poorer groups because the rich had more resources to support larger families.

Demography is the study of changes in population composition and in vital rates that combine to identify pivotal transformations in social life. In addressing the question of fertility, the issue that deserves to be considered first is how people without access to modern contraceptive technology restrict their numbers. Almost all anthropological investigations reveal a welter of cultural adaptations to the basic biological fact that human fertility is never close to its physiological maximum. According to Henri Leridon, "First, the biological maximum for women who remain fecund and exposed to risk from their fifteenth to their forty-fifth birthdays, and who do not breast-feed their children, would be 17 to 18 children" (p. 147). In point of fact, Leridon is somewhat ungenerous in his assessment of what earlier generations would have called prolific power. For example, in Quebec a tiny minority of women had more than twenty live births from the seventeenth century until the quiet revolution of social change in Quebec in the 1960s. And in any population some women would be sterile. The historical question that comes into focus concerns the difference between Leridon's "biological maximum" and observed total fertility rates. How low were these premodern fertility rates?

Fertility Control through Late Marriage

Daniel Scott Smith has summarized the findings of thirty-eight family reconstitution studies (twenty-seven of which described French villages from the late seventeenth and eighteenth centuries) as follows: "A woman who married at age 20 exactly, and survived to age 45 with her husband would bear nine children" (p. 22). Thus the potential maximum fertility was only about half of Leridon's biological maximum. And what is more, Smith's potential maximum fertility is an overstatement for two reasons: first, the average

age at first marriage for northwestern European women was not twenty and second about one-third of all marriages were broken by the death of one partner before age forty-five, which Smith is using as a shorthand measurement for the onset of menopause. In Smith's sample of thirty-eight villages, for example, the average age at first marriage for women was 25.7 years old; their husbands were 28.0 years old.

Basing his conclusions on fifty-four published studies describing age-specific marital fertility rates for women in early modern northwestern Europe, Michael Flinn agrees with Smith, describing an average age at first marriage for women that fluctuated around twenty-five. Flinn does not provide us with measurements to assess the spread of the distribution around this midpoint, but other studies have determined the standard deviation to be about six years, meaning that about two-thirds of all northwestern European women married for the first time between twenty-two and twenty-eight. A few teenaged brides were counterbalanced, as it were, by a similar number of women who married in their thirties. Perhaps one woman in ten never married. In the demographer's jargon, that tenth woman was permanently celibate.

So in answering our question concerning the relative lowness of high birth rates, the first point we have to keep in view is that, uniquely, northwestern Europeans married late. Or, to be more precise, the link between PUBERTY and marriage was dramatically more attenuated in early modern northwestern Europe than elsewhere. Modern demographic studies have shown that in eastern and southern Europe this puberty-marriage gap was about half as long, while in most African and Asian countries puberty and marriage roughly coincided as a girl entered womanhood (and adult status) with the onset of menstruation. Arranged marriages followed almost immediately thereafter.

The identification of this austere Malthusian regime has been the greatest achievement of early modern historical demography. These statistics provide us with a single measure that distinguishes the creation of new families in northwestern Europe from other societies. This unique marriage strategy was vitally important for two reasons: first, it provided a safety valve, or margin for error, in the ongoing adjustment between population and resources that characterized the reproduction of generations and social formations; and second it meant that the role of women was less dependent and vulnerable insofar as they were marrying as young adults, not older children. Arranged marriages were normal among the propertied Europeans, as they were in almost every other part of the world; most of these marriages were arranged while the girl was still a child and they were formalized after puberty.

What about the second point raised from a consideration of Smith's statistics, mortality during marriage? Before considering the impact of adult mortality on the fecundity of marital couples, we need to discount his estimate of potential maximum fertility (nine live births) in order to take into account the impact of permanent celibacy, which was the destiny of perhaps 10 percent of all adult women. In Smith's thirty-eight villages, the "maximum spinsterhood percentage" was 13.3, whereas the "minimum spinsterhood percentage" was 8.6. Averaging these figures out provides an agreement with our rough approximation of 10 percent never marrying. This yields a revised potential maximum fertility per woman of eight births.

Now we can return to the impact of adult mortality on fertility rates. How many of these eight potential births would not have been realized because the marriage was broken by the death of one of the partners? The demographic parameters of early modern society were heavily influenced by the omnipresence of death. However, the truly gloomy statistics about life expectation at birth—averaging in the thirty- to forty-year range—are not a sure guide to adult mortality, since the heavy concentration of deaths in the first years of life was not so much an indicator of general levels of health as a reflection of the fragility of life in a period when both public health and individualized medical care were essentially nonexistent. Overall, an average of two babies in ten died in the first year of life, and a similar number died in the next few years of early childhood; however, a person who reached the age of five had an even chance of living until he or she was fifty.

Women were uniquely susceptible to deaths relating to childbirth, which was both dangerous and traumatic, so that there was female excess mortality during the childbearing years. Perhaps 1 percent of all women died as a result of complications from childbirth; and, of course, the average woman had several births, which heightened her exposure to this risk; the cumulative impact of adult mortality was, therefore, substantial. Only about two partnerships in three were likely to survive intact from marriage to menopause (i.e., from age twenty-five to forty-five). The cumulative impact of this mortality regime on fertility levels was likewise substantial—we might estimate that almost one-third of all of the revised potential maximum fertility would have been lost as a result of marriages that broke up because of parental death. The reality of the early modern demographic regime was that the average number of births per woman was likely to have been somewhat over five—not the eight suggested by the first revision (which took into account permanent celibacy) and surely not Smith's nine.

Fertility Control through Infanticide

The northwestern European system of delaying marriage and concentrating fertility into only some of the years of a woman's reproductive years is just one example of the strategies that populations practiced throughout history. In China and Japan a rather different system was deployed. There the key ingredient was systematic infanticide, frequently the result of a strong gender-preference for boys. Marriage of women in premodern Asia took place at a much earlier age than in northwestern Europe, but the ultimate level of reproduction was essentially similar, although it was achieved through quite different means.

The Historical Methods Break Down

Before 1800, in both east Asia and northwestern Europe, levels of fertility were kept in line with mortality rates to create low rates of population growth. After 1800, the Malthusian system of prudential marriage was somewhat less effective among the newly emerging proletariat, and that led to rising levels of population growth in (and considerable out-migration from) northwestern Europe. In China, too, the older system of fertility regulation was strained in the nineteenth century and population growth rates in the poorest regions increased substantially. However, it is crucial to maintain some perspective on this point, since the older systems of restraint bent but they did not break. Both northwestern European and east Asian populations grew more slowly in the nineteenth century than did Third World populations in the twentieth century.

When populations grow it is usually reflected in a change in the age pyramid, which gets larger at its base as there are more births than deaths. Malthus postulated that growing populations would be subjected to "preventative checks" that would cause death rates to rise, but the evidence for this assertion is skimpy. More significantly, when populations grow they become younger and children represent a larger percentage of the total. The various systems of prudential restraint—delayed marriage in northwestern Europe and infanticide in east Asia—had the effect of keeping the proportion of children in the population at a lower level than is the case in the poorer parts of the world today. The reason for this widening gap is that many Third World populations have benefited from public health measures that dramatically lessen mortality but have not yet made compensatory adjustments in fertility.

So far, the argument has considered only global averages. To make sense of these averages additional factors have to be taken into consideration. The difference between Leridon's biological maximum and Smith's potential maximum—as well as between Smith's potential maximum and the reality of the early modern demographic system—is not explicable solely in terms of biological or physiological factors. Indeed, the largest part of this difference can only be accounted for by also referring to cultural—and historical—factors. As is described above, the role of prudential marriage in northwesern Europe or infanticide in East Asia reflected cultural choices.

Accounting for Low Premodern Fertility Rates

Why, then, were high birth rates in the past so low? To answer this question one has to consider not only such factors as the age and incidence of nuptiality but also coital frequen-

cy, which affected the likelihood of impregnation; abortions; and starvation-induced amenorrhea, which cut off conceptions before they could result in live births; and breast-feeding practices and ritual taboos that created a safe period after childbirth when a woman was either unlikely to conceive or was not permitted to engage in sexual intercourse. Fertility, therefore, was more the result of such cultural norms than of biological forces. Biological forces were never allowed to work themselves out in a "natural" fashion, so it is misleading to speak of "natural fertility" when all societies brought children into the world as a result of the way that each one worked out its own cultural economy of fertility.

Another range of factors reducing premodern fertility rates relates to rates of INFANT MORTALITY. When a baby died there was a shorter interval between its birth and the next one than the average interval that would have occurred if that first child had lived. So the relationship between fertility rates and mortality rates was interactive; crudely put, populations with extremely high rates of infant mortality also had extremely high rates of fertility, and vice versa. Furthermore, while a large number of marriages were likely to have been broken by adult mortality, from the demographic point of view it was only female mortality that mattered. This brings us to consider rates of widowhood, remarriage, separation or desertion, and so forth. Some societies practiced stringent refusal against remarriage for women, which effectively meant that a husband's death was, in demographic terms, the same as her own; she could keep living but could no longer engage in a sexual relationship or bear children. These cultural rules were incredibly flexible, ranging from the extreme example of some parts of India, where widows were burned on their dead husband's funeral pyres, to the situation that prevailed in parts of northwestern Europe, where a few women (like Chaucer's wife of Bath) outlived several husbands.

Fertility rates can only be understood by placing them in sociocultural context and by finding nondemographic explanations for them. By reconstituting demographic statistics from their biological and cultural elements, we can comprehend how children were brought into a world patterned by social relationships. The transformation of premodern reproductive patterns was part of a massive shift in the nature of social relations; social change in the cultural economy of fertility was the result of changing norms of family life and in particular the value of children. Parents were thinking people who reflected on this relationship and changed their behavior with regard to it.

Below-Replacement Fertility Rates and Immigration

The fertility transition—from five or six births per woman to the controlled rates of fertility that result in below-replacement fertility in some late-modern societies—has been neatly summarized by J. C. Caldwell, who argues that we can understand this process by focusing on the role of children within the family. In high-fertility regimes wealth flows upwards from children to parents, whereas in low-fertility regimes the child-centered family means that there is a concentration of time, money, and emotion on each individual child as resources flow downwards from parents to children. Caldwell calls this a compass swing, a metaphor that may be too dramatic for this change since there were already restraints on fertility in premodern societies.

To date, the Caldwellian compass has swung most dramatically in Europe, North America, Japan, and Australia. For example, in Quebec in the early twentieth century, about one child in two was born into a family of ten or more children, but in the early twenty-first century the so-called *pur laine* Quebecois (those descended from the original French settlers) have below-replacement fertility. In France, northern Italy, Japan, and most other regions of the developed world, the native-born population has below-replacement fertility whereas immigrant groups account for a disproportionate share of the children. In Toronto, for example, the reproduction rates of recent immigrants outstrip those of the native-born two-to-one; in some schools in Toronto (or Los Angeles or London or Paris, for that matter) immigrant children outnumber native-born children. In immigrant-receiving cities like Toronto, more than half of all children entering the public school system do not speak the dominant language of the civil society at home. Such children come from larger families, stay in school for a shorter period of time, and are much more likely to work after school and on weekends in order to contribute to their family's income even if they do stay in school. These children are also disproportionately poorer than the majority population. When the writer George Orwell visited the poor families of Wigan in the Depression of the 1930s, he asked rhetorically if these families were poor because they were large or large because they were poor. Either way, the migration flows of the twentieth century and early twenty-first century have kept large numbers of children in poverty in the midst of plenty. In other parts of the world, children dot the landscape in mushrooming numbers.

World Population Growth

How do we account for this massive acceleration in both fertility and child survival, which has led to the quadrupling of the world's population in less than a century when the previous doubling had taken two hundred years (from 1700 to 1900) and when before that it took several millennia? Perhaps the best way to visualize this process is by comparing it to the action of a pair of scissors. For most of the past few millennia, the two arms of the scissors were kept close together as population growth rates moved in tandem with mortality levels; in the twentieth century, however, public health measures dramatically improved the life expectation of both children and adults while fertility rates were slow to respond to this massive increase in survivorship. The opening of the demographic scissors has had two dramatic effects:

first, the rate of population growth, which hovered at about 0.5 percent in the nineteenth century, has grown four- and fivefold (and in some places, like Egypt, as much as sixfold) so that the time it now takes for a population to double has dropped from about two hundred years to about forty years; and second, as population growth rates have shot up, the percentage of the total population at the bottom of the age pyramid has increased. Children have become more numerous as the surviving generations are significantly larger than the preceding ones.

This modern demographic explosion has been like the problem facing the sorcerer's apprentice in that once the demographic scissors open it is extremely difficult to close it again, and once a new equilibrium is attained the global organization of population will be radically different from what existed several hundred years ago. In 1700, almost two humans in five were Chinese; now the comparable figure is just over one in five; in 1700 the proportion of Europeans was perhaps one in five, whereas it is now about one in ten. In contrast, the relative proportion of South Americans, Africans, and Asians has increased incrementally as the world population balance has swung in a new direction. Moreover, not only are most of the additional people in these areas children but because of the dynamics of uncontrolled fertility among the poorest peoples most of them grow up in large families. In BRAZIL, for example, the white, urban, and middle classes have families of two or three children whereas the black, rural, and landless classes have families of six or more children. A similar dynamic is at work in Egypt, India, Indonesia, Mexico, Nigeria, and a host of other countries with small economies and large populations to feed. It will take a full-fledged sorcerer to get the modern explosion of population back into a condition of equilibrium; without such a magic act, the new demographic dynamic of the twenty-first century means that an ever-larger proportion of the world's population will be composed of children from underprivileged backgrounds living in poor countries.

See also: **Family Patterns.**

BIBLIOGRAPHY

Bongaarts, John. 1975. "Why High Birth Rates Are So Low." *Population and Development Review* 1: 289–296.

Caldwell, J. C. 1978. "Theory of Fertility: From High Plateau to Destabilization." *Population and Development Review* 4: 553–577.

Daly, H. E. 1971. "A Marxian-Malthusian View of Poverty and Development." *Population Studies* 25: 25–38.

Daly, H. E. 1985. "Marx and Malthus in North-East Brazil: A Note of the World's Largest Class Difference in Fertility and Its Recent Trends." *Population Studies* 39: 329–338.

Flinn, Michael. 1981. *The European Demographic System.* Baltimore: Johns Hopkins University Press.

Henry, Louis. 1961. "Some Data on Natural Fertility." *Eugenics Quarterly* 8: 81–91.

Lee, James, and Wang Feng. 1999. *One Quarter of Humanity: Malthusian Mythology and Chinese Realities, 1700–2000.* Cambridge, MA: Harvard University Press.

Leridon, Henri. 1977. *Human Fertility*. Chicago: University of Chicago Press.

Orwell, George. 1937. *The Road to Wigan Pier*. London: Gollancz.

Smith, Daniel Scott. 1977. "A Homeostatic Demographic Regime: Patterns in West European Family Reconstitution Studies." In *Population Patterns in the Past*, ed. R. D. Lee. New York: Academic Press.

Smith, T. C. 1977. *Nakahara: Family Farming and Population in a Japanese Village, 1717–1830*. Stanford, CA: Stanford University Press.

DAVID LEVINE

Fetal Imaging. *See* Sonography.

Film. *See* Movies.

Flappers

Flappers were modern adolescent girls and young women whose FASHION and lifestyle personified the changing attitudes and mores of America and its youths in the 1920s. Magazines, books, and MOVIES depicted the flapper with short, bobbed hair, powdered face, and painted puckered lips, and they dressed her in rolled stockings and scanty, low-waist dresses that emphasized a boyish figure. The flapper drank and smoked like men, and played and worked with men. She exuded an overt SEXUALITY not only with her provocative clothing, but also in her actions: dancing to jazz, flirting with men, and attending petting parties unchaperoned.

The flapper was the subject of a great deal of controversy in public discussion. Many critics found her departure from the fashions and manners of the corseted women who came before her representative of a lapse in morality among the young and of an emerging generation gap. Indeed, the open sexuality and the sexual practices of the flapper generation were divergent from earlier generations: women coming of age in the 1920s were twice as likely to have had premarital sex as their predecessors. At a time when DATING, the use of BIRTH CONTROL, and frank discussion about sex was on the rise, the flapper became the symbol for the new sexual liberation of women. Portrayed as predominantly urban, independent, career-oriented, and sexually expressive, the flapper was hailed as an example of the New Woman.

Despite these stereotyped images, the flapper was not a revolutionary figure; rather she was an updated version of the traditional model of womanhood. Although she was freer in her sexuality and public conduct among men than her mother, the flapper had no intention of challenging the role of women in society or abandoning the path towards marriage and motherhood. On the contrary, like the rest of the middle-class younger generation that she exemplified, the flapper was conservative in her ultimate values and behavior. As contemporary suffragists and feminists complained, the flapper took up the superficial accoutrements of the emancipated woman, but she did not take up the ballot or the political pursuit for equal rights under the law.

In fact, the flapper and her lifestyle were reflective of mainstream American values and the emerging cult of youth that began to characterize popular culture in the 1920s. She represented the new vitality of a modern era. Advertisers used her image, combining youth and sex, to sell an array of goods, including automobiles, cigarettes, and mouthwash. In addition, although flapper fashion flourished to its fullest extent among the privileged and bohemian few, new innovations in the mass production of clothing made it possible for the fashion to have a wider influence in all of women's dress. Young teenagers could afford to follow fashion and made the style into a trademark among their peers. Even older women exposed to certain elements of flapper style in Sears Roebuck catalogs sported some of that look. While movie actresses like Clara Bow and personalities like Zelda Fitzgerald epitomized the flapper persona and philosophy, the flapper fad prevailed among middle-class youth, infusing its style and manner into mainstream American culture.

See also: **Adolescence and Youth; Bobby Soxers; Manners; Teenagers; Youth Culture.**

BIBLIOGRAPHY

Chafe, William H. 1991. *The Paradox of Change: American Women in the 20th Century*. New York: Oxford University Press.

Fass, Paula S. 1977. *The Damned and the Beautiful: American Youth in the 1920s*. New York: Oxford University Press.

Yellis, Kenneth A. 1969. "Prosperity's Child: Some Thoughts on the Flapper." *American Quarterly* 21: 44–64.

LAURA MIHAILOFF

Formula. *See* Infant Feeding.

Foster Care

Foster care refers to the informal and formal custodial care of children outside of their own biological family home when their parents are unable, unwilling, or prohibited from caring for them. Historically, foster care provided homes to poor and parentless children and served to maintain order in a changing society. The origins of contemporary American foster care date back to the colonial-era practice of indentureship or "binding out." Following English tradition, families frequently placed their child with a master who taught the child a trade and provided basic sustenance in exchange for the child's labor. Poor children were often involuntarily bound out through public auction when a family was unable to provide for their care; exploitation was quite common in these circumstances. Indentureship declined in the late eighteenth and nineteenth centuries as reformers promoted institutional living and believed that its structured and contained life of the institution offered the solution to poverty and its accompanying social ills, including the plight of dependent and orphaned children.

The Formalization of Foster Care

The practice of foster care grew more formalized with the development of an anti-cruelty movement and the establishment of SOCIETIES FOR THE PREVENTION OF CRUELTY TO CHILDREN (SPCC) in the late nineteenth century. These agencies provided a feeder most commonly to institutions and to a lesser degree to family-based foster care. As a result the number of ORPHANAGES tripled between 1865 and 1890. Voluntary SPCC agents were often granted police power and removed children from their biological homes due to physical abuse or, more commonly, poverty-related neglect. Yet some nineteenth-century reformers questioned institutional practices. Most famously, CHARLES LORING BRACE established the NEW YORK CHILDREN'S AID SOCIETY that sent urban orphaned, half-orphaned, and other poor children to reside with farm families. Espousing romanticized notions of countryside living and a belief that it was best to remove neglected and abused children from their families of origin, Brace's work constituted a response to the increased immigration, crime, and disease that characterized urban society. Brace, however, was not without his critics, particularly those who believed that the farm families exploited the children's labor and Catholic reformers who accused Brace of placing Catholic children in Protestant homes.

The Progressive Era witnessed a deepening concern with the plight of poor and orphaned children. The period's CHILD-SAVING movement portrayed children as vulnerable beings in need of family protection, nurture, and affection and argued that a child was best cared for by its own biological parents. The child savers focused on a variety of child welfare initiatives, such as mothers' pensions, day nurseries, and public health reforms that they hoped would reduce the need for out-of-home care. Yet reformers such as Holmer Folks also recognized the continued need for custodial care and strongly advocated family-based foster care, which they viewed as far superior to institutional arrangements. Even Progressive-era child-caring institutions were refurbished to provide more of a family-like setting through "cottage" style housing although the majority of dependent children continued to be cared for in institutional settings in this period. These voluntary and largely sectarian foster care agencies often engaged in discriminatory practices. Historians of both the anti-cruelty and child-saving movements highlight the class and ethnic biases of middle-class Anglo Saxon reform-

ers who intervened in the family life of poor immigrant families and often equated foreign cultural practices and poverty-ridden conditions with neglect. Moreover, the child welfare agencies typically denied AFRICAN-AMERICAN CHILDREN foster care services or provided only a small number of homes on a segregated basis. As a result, early-twentieth-century African-American reformers established their own organizations, although these agencies often suffered from a lack of adequate funding. Members of the African-American community also fostered children on an informal basis, taking in children of friends, neighbors and relatives when assistance was needed. Informal fostering practices were also common in many immigrant communities.

Modern Foster Care

Concern with child welfare and foster care declined in the conservative 1920s and even the welfare state architects of the New Deal era paid little attention to foster care as they believed that larger anti-poverty efforts would reduce and ultimately eliminate the out-of-home placement of children. But the New Deal reformers were far from correct in their assessment. The years following World War II actually saw the development of the contemporary child welfare bureaucracy. The federal government provided an increasing amount of funds for the establishment and expansion of public child welfare agencies that, unlike the voluntary sectarian agencies, had to serve all children, regardless of race, ethnicity, or faith. The postwar period also witnessed the "rediscovery" of CHILD ABUSE. Mid-century radiologists uncovered the phenomenon of multiple, repeat fractures in children resulting from parental abuse and in 1962 the *Journal of the American Medical Association* published a now famous paper entitled "The Battered Child Syndrome" by physician C. Henry Kempe and his associates. The article drew massive amounts of public attention and captured the imagination of a reform-minded America. Between 1963 and 1967 every state passed legislation mandating professionals to report suspected instances of child abuse and in 1972 Congress enacted the Child Abuse Prevention and Treatment Act that provided funds for a national center on child abuse and neglect. Not surprisingly, this legislation resulted in a huge increase in child abuse reports and ultimately a dramatic rise in the foster care population.

Disturbed by the growth in foster care, child welfare advocates of the 1970s uncovered the phenomenon of "foster care drift" in which children experienced multiple foster home placements. This phenomenon flew in the face of popular social scientific wisdom that stressed the importance of attachment and permanency for children's positive developmental outcomes. In response to this mounting critique, Congress passed the Child Welfare Act of 1980. The act attempted to reduce the foster care population by emphasizing family preservation and reunification programs and required state agencies to make "reasonable efforts" before removing a child from its home. It also institutionalized the previously informal practice of "kinship care" in which relatives serve as foster parents. While the act contributed to a temporary decline in the foster care population, from 1987 to 1992 the number of children in foster care grew from 280,000 to 460,000. While some suggest that the act suffered from inadequate funding, others partially attribute the rise in foster care to the development of an epidemic of drug use that ravaged low-income, inner-city America during the 1980s. At the same time, family preservation efforts came under fire as some research showed that intensive social work programs did little to prevent child removal and a series of highly publicized child abuse cases described how children were allowed to remain or return to the homes of their biological parents where they ultimately met their deaths. Other critics were especially concerned about the growing overrepresentation of African-American children in the foster care population, which some attributed to institutionalized racism within the child welfare system.

The backlash against family preservation along with ongoing concern regarding the number of children in foster care culminated in the passage of the federal Adoption and Safe Families Act (ASFA) of 1997. ASFA sought to reduce the foster care population and promotes permanency for children by stressing ADOPTION over family preservation efforts, although some money was set aside for family preservation. The act sped up the time line toward termination of parental rights, allowed for "concurrent planning" in which child welfare workers simultaneously prepare for family reunification and adoption, and provided states with financial incentives for adoption. Adoption advocates argue that with increased assistance safe and loving adoptive homes can increasingly be found for foster children who were previously considered "hard to place"—such as those experiencing physical or psychiatric disabilities or children of color who historically have experienced low adoption rates.

Ongoing Critiques

Critics of the contemporary child welfare system argue that it is not foster care in and of itself that produces poor outcomes for children but rather a dysfunctional, underfunded child welfare bureaucracy run by poorly trained and overwhelmed staff. The Child Welfare League of America observed that by 2002 caseworkers in some states had up to 55 children on their caseloads, while the League recommended a caseload of no more than 15 children. Others maintain that the inadequacy of the child welfare system stems from its inability to address the primary issue contributing to child neglect, abuse, and removal: poverty. Indeed, the overwhelming majority of children in foster care are born into poverty and some studies show that the primary predictor of child removal is not the severity of abuse but the level of the family's income. Critics noted that in the early twenty-first century the United States had the highest rate of child poverty of any industrialized Western nation and argued the income and social supports more typical of Western European nations,

such as family allowances, government-supported day care, family leave policies, more generous benefits for single mothers and their children, would reduce the number of American children in foster care.

See also: **Placing Out; Social Welfare.**

BIBLIOGRAPHY

Ashby, LeRoy. 1997. *Endangered Children: Dependency, Neglect, and Abuse in American History.* New York: Twayne.

Billingsley, Andrew and Jeanne Giovannoni. 1972. *Children of the Storm: Black Children and American Child Welfare.* New York: Harcourt Brace Jovanovich.

Duncan, Lindsey. 1994. *The Welfare of Children.* New York: Oxford University Press.

Gordon, Linda 1988. *Heroes of Their Own Lives: The Politics and History of Family Violence, Boston, 1880–1960.* New York: Viking.

Mason, Mary Ann. 1994. *From Father's Property to Children's Rights: The History of Child Custody in the United States.* New York: Columbia University Press.

Nelson, Barbara. 1984. *Making an Issue of Child Abuse: Political Agenda Setting for Social Problems.* Chicago: The University of Chicago Press.

Platt, Anthony. 1969. *The Child Savers: The Invention of Delinquency.* Chicago: University of Chicago Press.

Roberts, Dorothy. 2002. *Shattered Bonds: The Color of Child Welfare.* New York: BasicBooks.

Tiffin, Susan 1982. *In Whose Best Interest? Child Welfare Reform in the Progressive Era.* Westport, CT: Greenwood Press.

LAURA CURRAN

Foundlings

From as far back as Hellenistic antiquity and up through the first decades of the twentieth century, the large-scale ABANDONMENT of newborn babies features prominently in the history of Western Europe. Although sometimes confounded with infanticide, abandonment frequently occurred with the hope that someone would find and rear the child. In many cases, these abandoned infants, or foundlings, were left with tokens to aid in reclamation or to ensure that they would be well treated. By the thirteenth century, salt was left with foundlings as an indicator of their baptismal status. These tokens suggest some expectation, or at least hope, that the child would be found alive.

Until the later Middle Ages, infants were frequently left outside of public buildings or in open places where they might be easily seen. As Christianity spread, foundlings were increasingly deposited at churches. However, beginning in the twelfth century, the process of abandonment became more institutionalized. Aimed at preventing loss of life—especially when it occurred prior to BAPTISM—a system of foundling homes emerged in Italy and then spread throughout much of Europe. By the nineteenth century, over one hundred thousand foundlings were being abandoned annually to these institutions. The officially sanctioned system usually allowed for the abandonment to remain anonymous. In many parts of Europe, it was possible to abandon the infant via a device known as the wheel—a wooden turntable placed within the wall of the foundling home building, often containing a cradle of sorts. A person standing outside the foundling home could place an infant inside the wheel, and, in many instances, there would be a bell above the wheel to ring and alert someone inside, who could then turn the wheel and procure the foundling without seeing the person who left the child. Ideally, these institutions would place the foundling with paid foster parents, preferably in the countryside, who would then raise the child. Foundling homes differed in the age at which they stopped paying foster parents, but in most cases, female foundlings remained the wards of the home until marriage, while male foundlings were cut off from all support once payments to their foster families ceased.

Although abandoned children were not uncommon, especially in urban areas, the first foundling home in the United States was not established until 1856, in Baltimore, Maryland. In the years that followed, many more were established so that by the early twentieth century most large cities had at least one foundling home. However, in many other places separate homes were never established and foundlings were received by ORPHANAGES, county almshouses, or poorhouses. The fragmentation of the U.S. system makes it difficult to estimate the numbers of foundlings at any one time or to generalize about methods of care they employed. Indeed, there is evidence that some foundling homes opposed fostering while others actively pursued rapid foster placements. One sad generalization about institutionalization can be made, however. In both Europe and the United States, competition from middle-class families created a shortage of wet nurses who could foster children or who wanted to work, often feeding more than one child, in the cramped conditions of the foundling homes. As a consequence, prior to the safe pasteurization of milk in the late nineteenth century, many children died in foundling hospitals, both from disease and malnutrition, in their first months of life.

See also: **Adoption in the United States; Baby Farming; Bastardy; Foster Care; Orphans; Wet Nursing.**

BIBLIOGRAPHY

Boswell, John. 1988. *Kindness of Strangers: The Abandonment of Children in Western Europe from Late Antiquity to the Renaissance.* New York: Vintage Books.

English, P. C. 1984. "Pediatrics and the Unwanted Child in History: Foundling Homes, Disease, and the Origins of Foster Care in New York City, 1860–1920." *Pediatrics* 73: 699–711.

Lynch, Katherine A. 2000. "Infant Mortality, Child Neglect, and Child Abandonment in European History: A Comparative Analysis." In *Population and Economy: From Hunger to Modern Economic Growth*, ed. Tommy Bengtsson and Osamu Saito. Oxford, UK: Oxford University Press.

Tilly, Louise A., Rachel G. Fuchs, David I. Kertzer, and David L. Ransel. 1992. "Child Abandonment in European History: A Symposium." *Journal of Family History* 17: 1–23.

WENDY SIGLE-RUSHTON

Francke, Aug. Hermann (1663–1727)

August Hermann Francke grew up in Gotha in Prussia amid the ecclesiastical, pedagogical, and social reforms of Ernst the Pious, Duke of Sachsen-Gotha. After a conversion experience in 1687, Francke founded a circle of "awakened" students in Leipzig, where he was studying theology. In 1691, he was appointed pastor of Glaucha near Halle; the same year, he was named a professor at the University of Halle in Prussia. His close relationships with members of the Prussian royal dynasty, particularly Frederick William I, helped promote Francke's great educational experiment: the Hallesches Waisenhaus. Francke founded the Hallesches Waisenhaus (Halle Orphanage) at the university in 1695. In addition to various economic enterprises, the facility contained an ORPHANAGE, elementary schools for boys and girls, the LATIN SCHOOL, and the Pädagogium Regium.

Francke's significance for the history of childhood lies in his ground-breaking methods of school organization, teacher training, and the promotion of gifted children; these innovations developed under his direction in the various institutions of the Hallesches Waisenhaus. Beyond Francke's pedagogical writings, the educational techniques in the Hallesches Waisenhaus contributed a great deal to the modern understanding of education. On the threshold of the ENLIGHTENMENT, Lutheran Pietism found in Francke an ideal spokesperson. He sought to realize in his pedagogy the Pietist aspiration to devote all of life to Christian objectives. In doing so, Francke helped to establish a different view of children and to enhance the status of childhood as a stage of life.

The decisive characteristic of Francke's approach was the submission of educational activity to specific methods. His philosophy contributed to the development of one of the most effective pedagogical prescriptions of the modern age: exerting methodical influence on the child's emotional life with the aim of shaping him from within. By extending its scope of application to include all children, regardless of social status or sex, Francke elaborated this objective and its realization in the form of pedagogical ordering concepts designed to promote discipline. His most important writings in this field include *Kurzer und Einfältiger Unterricht . . .* (*Brief and simple instruction . . .*, 1702) and the preface to the German translation of FRANÇOIS FÉNÉLON'S *Über die Mädchenerziehung* (On the education of girls, 1705). In his writings, Francke developed a unified notion of the child independent of her social status; similarly, the pedagogical practice of the schools of the Hallesches Waisenhaus reflected a unified educational concept which was applied to all its students. The Waisenhaus soon gained the reputation of a model institution. It achieved a heightened control of affect and individualization of education through the external organization of schools; instruction and internal influence in the form of catechism, self-observation and the examination of conscience; and by the extraordinary alertness of its teachers to the intellectual and spiritual development of their pupils. Francke's influence on the Prussian state and its educational system is undisputed, but his philosophy extended far beyond the borders of Prussia, as evidenced by his international contacts and the broad geographical origins of the children who lived and studied in the Franckesche Stiftungen (Francke Institutes). Francke's life and work are splendidly documented in the archives of the Franckesche Stiftungen in Halle a.d. Saale.

Francke's influence on the development of a modern understanding of childhood continued in the writings and teachings of Nikolaus Graf von Zinzendorf (1700–1760), the founder of the Moravian Church; his pedagogy also left a profound mark on F. Schleiermacher's (1768–1832) Romantic notion of childhood. Francke thus occupies a prominent position in the development of childhood education. His followers, along with those of Jansenism in France and Pietism in Germany, not only led pedagogy to autonomous modes of thought but also had a decisive impact on cultural images of the child at the beginning of the Enlightenment and Romanticism.

See also: **Education, Europe; Rousseau, Jean-Jacques.**

BIBLIOGRAPHY

Francke, August Hermann. 1964. "Pädagogische Schriften." In *Schöninghs Sammlung pädagogischer Schriften*, 2nd edition, ed. Hermann Lorenzen. Paderborn, Germany: Schöningh.

Jacobi, Juliane, and Thomas Müller-Bahlke, eds. 1998. "Man hatte von ihm gute Hoffnung." *Das erste Waisenalbum der Franckeschen Stiftungen 1695–1749.* Tübingen, Germany: Verlag der Franckeschen Stiftungen Halle.

Menck, P. 2001. *Die Erziehung der Jugend zur Ehre Gottes und zum Nutzen des Nächsten. Die Pädagogik A. H. Franckes.* Tübingen, Germany: Verlag der Franckeschen Stiftungen Halle.

INTERNET RESOURCE

Francke Foundation. Available from <www.franckesche-stiftungen.uni-halle.de/francke.htm/forschung/index.html>.

JULIANE JACOBI

Frank, Anne (1929–1945)

Anneliese Marie (Anne) Frank was born on June 12, 1929, in Frankfurt am Main, Germany. She fled from her country of birth to the Netherlands in 1934, following her father, mother, and sister. Their hope to be freed from the German persecution of Jews disappeared when Germany invaded the Netherlands in 1940. From then on, anti-Jewish measures isolated the Frank family more and more. Anne was forced to go to a school established for Jewish children, the Joods Lyceum. Finally, in July 1942, the family went into hiding in the *achterhuis* (annex) of her father's office and warehouse. A month before that, Anne had started writing a diary, which now became an account of two years of living in isolation with the constant fear of discovery and betrayal. The diary also became an analysis of the tensions among eight people living closely together in hiding. Finally it is the personal story of a girl growing up during her thirteenth through fifteenth years.

In March 1944 Anne heard a radio announcement by the Dutch government in exile that after the war diaries would be collected to document the German occupation. From then on she rewrote her diary in a more polished form. This came to an end in August 1944, when Anne and the others were betrayed, arrested, and deported. Anne died in Bergen-Belsen in February or early March 1945. Her father Otto Frank survived. After his return one of the people who had provided food during the family's period of hiding, had saved Anne's diary and gave it back to her father. He made a typescript of the diary, which was published in 1947 under the title *Het achterhuis*. German, French, and English translations followed. A play based on the diary, written in 1955 by Frances Goodrich and Albert Hackett, became a success on Broadway, and in 1958 was made into a movie by Hollywood director George Stevens. Anne Frank posthumously became famous worldwide. Otto Frank was convinced that his daughter's diary would be a warning against racism for young readers, and to this end he corresponded with readers all over the world. Meanwhile, however, the image of Anne Frank developed from a young victim of the HOLOCAUST into that of some sort of humanist saint. In Amsterdam, the annex became a museum. In 1986 a thorough scholarly edition of the Dutch text was published (followed by an English translation in 1989), in which questions about the authenticity of the diary from neo-Nazis were countered by an extensive technical examination of the manuscript. All three versions of the diary are included in this edition: Anne's first version, her own rewritten version, and the 1947 edition as edited by Otto Frank.

Anne Frank's diary has now been translated into dozens of languages and has sold millions of copies, yet the first biography of the author was published only a few years ago. The diary has traditionally been given to young people to read from a pedagogical motivation; nevertheless, there are several other ways to read the text. Today more attention is given to Anne Frank's Jewish background, which previously was kept in the background, especially in the play and movie. However, it is clear from the diary that for Anne herself her Jewishness was not a very essential part of her identity. Another aspect now more clearly realized is that Anne Frank was only one of many young victims, and the context of the Holocaust therefore now receives more attention. Recently a history of her school, the Joods Lyceum, was published, partly based on interviews with surviving schoolchildren. Anne Frank is now also seriously studied as a woman writer. Writing a diary was in itself an activity typical of girls, and a diary written by another pupil of the Joods Lyceum, Ellen Schwarzschild, was published in 1999. Anne's diary must also be seen in a long tradition of autobiographical writing. During World War II in Holland, as in other periods of crisis, many people started writing diaries, and hundreds have survived, of which several are published. Anne saw her diary, at least the second version, as a literary achievement. The diary itself reveals which novels were an influence on her writing, especially those by the popular Dutch novelist Cissy van Marxveldt. Anne's ability as a writer, her creativity and orginality, are receiving more recognition than before. Finally, having arrived in Holland only in 1934, Anne's mastery of the Dutch language is remarkable. Scholarly research has intensified in recent years, and it has taken different roads, but reading Anne Frank's diary itself is still a starting point.

See also: **Autobiographies.**

BIBLIOGRAPHY

Dacosta, Denise. 1998. *Anne Frank and Etty Hillesum: Inscribing Spirituality and Sexuality.* New Brunswick, NJ: Rutgers University Press.

Enzer, Hyman Aaron, and Sandra Solotaroff-Enzer, eds. 2000. *Anne Frank: Reflections on Her Life and Legacy.* Urbana: University of Illinois Press.

Frank, Anne. 1989. *The Diary of Anne Frank: The Critical Edition,* ed. David Barnouw and Gerrold van der Stroom. Trans. Arnold J. Pomerans and B. M. Mooyaart. Prepared by the Netherlands State Institute for War Documentation. New York: Doubleday.

Graver, Lawrence. 1995. *An Obsession with Anne Frank: Meyer Levin and the Diary.* Berkeley and Los Angeles: University of California Press.

Hondius, Dienke. 2001. *Absent. Herinneringen aan het Joods Lyceum Amsterdam 1941–1943.* Amsterdam: Vassallucci.

Lee, Carol Ann. 1999. *Roses from the Earth: The Biography of Anne Frank.* London: Viking.

Melnick, Ralph. 1997. *The Stolen Legacy of Anne Frank: Lillian Hellman and the Staging of the Diary.* New Haven, CT: Yale University Press.

Rittner, Carol. 1998. *Anne Frank and the World: Essays and Reflections.* Armonk, NY: Sharpe.

Schwarzschild, Ellen. 1999. *Tagebuch. Niet lesen als 't U belieft. Nicht lesen Bitte. Onuitwisbare herinneringen 1933–1943.* Amstelveen, the Netherlands: privately published.

INTERNET RESOURCES

Anne Frank Center USA. Available from <www.annefrank.com/>.

Anne Frank House. Available from <www.annefrank.nl/>.

Anne Frank Trust UK. Available from <www.afet.org.uk/>.

"One Voice: From the Pen of Anne Frank." Available from <www.exploris.org/learn/exhibits/frank/>.

RUDOLF M. DEKKER

Freinet, Célestin (1896–1966)

Célestin Freinet was born in 1896 at Gars, a small town of Alpes-Maritimes, a then fairly poor region of southern France. He spent his childhood working in the fields and as a shepherd. He participated in World War I and was seriously wounded, an injury from which he never quite recovered. He returned to the region of his childhood as a teacher and after serious conflicts with local school authorities he founded his own school, establishing a free platform for his educational work. He developed a school program, laid the groundwork for a national movement of school reform, published several books on schooling and education, and wrote a great number of articles in professional and political journals like *Clarté.* He organized the production and sale of learning materials, organized several national and international conferences on progressive education, and edited the journal *L'Éducateur* (The educator). During the interwar years he participated in N.E.F., the federation of progressive educationalists. He died in 1966.

The hardships of everyday life in his native region and his injured health, not the heritage of educational theory, formed the basis of Freinet's ardent social, educational, and political critique of capitalistic and urbanized societies. His focus was on the process of learning. As a practitioner he brought innovations in the fields of reading, writing, spelling, and arithmetic based on what he called "techniques of living." He believed children should work in workshops or outdoors and learn as a process of experimental trial and error. He is best known for his printing press (now usually replaced by a computer) for learning spelling and developing free text.

Freinet held that education was a way to change humanity. The school of tomorrow should center on the full development of children as members of the community. He regarded learning as a serious labor in which children should find their own course. He was also inspired by the multidisciplinary teaching practiced by progressive Germans, by Belgian educational pioneer Ovide Décroly's approach to learning, and by GEORG KERSCHENSTEINER's approach to the process of labor.

Freinet's books and workbooks have been translated into several languages and his ideas, methods, and teaching aids have become known throughout the world. There are Freinet teacher groups in several countries, and he is especially popular in developing countries because of the simplicity of his methods and because his ideas are attractive to those fighting for freedom and self-determination.

See also: **Age and Development; Child Development, History of the Concept of; Education, Europe; Progressive Education.**

BIBLIOGRAPHY

Freinet, Célestin. 1990. *Cooperative Learning for Social Change: Selected Writings of Célestin Freinet*, ed. David Clanfield and John Sivell. Toronto, ONT: Our Schools/Our Selves Education Foundation.

Freinet, Célestin. 1990. *The Wisdom of Matthew: An Essay in Contemporary French Educational Theory.* Lewiston, NY: Edward Mellon.

Freinet, Célestin. 1993. *Education through Work: A Model for Child-Centered Learning.* Lewiston, NY: Edward Mellen.

Jörg, Hans. 1995. "Freinet's Educational Methodology and Its International Sphere of Influence." In *Progressive Education across the Continents: A Handbook*, ed. Hermann Röhrs and Volker Lenhart. New York: P. Lang.

Legrand, Louis. 1993. "Célestin Freinet." In *Thinkers on Education*, vol. 1, ed. Zaghloul Morsy. Paris: UNESCO.

ELLEN NØRGAARD

Freud, Anna (1895–1982)

Anna Freud, the youngest child of Austrian psychoanalyst SIGMUND FREUD, was born and raised in Vienna, Austria, where she trained as an elementary school teacher and psychoanalyst. After being psychoanalyzed by her father, she became a member of the Vienna Psychoanalytic Society in 1922. Freud never married; she lived with a lifelong companion: the American Dorothy Tiffany Burlingham, whose children she psychoanalyzed. She worked as her father's scientific and administrative guardian, and she also made significant contributions to the technique of child analysis, theories of child development, and ego psychology.

Anna Freud published the first book on child psychoanalysis in 1926. *Introduction to the Technique of Child Analysis* combined her pedagogical experience with psychoanalytical insight and described an approach aimed at strengthening the child's ego. The book also criticized the techniques of British child analyst MELANIE KLEIN. Freud saw Klein's methods as a dangerous probing of the child's unconscious fantasy life; this criticism led to a 1927 debate between Freud and Klein about child analysis. Freud's *The Ego and the Mechanisms of Defense* appeared in 1936. This classic work systematically explained her father's concept of the ego and forged her reputation as a pioneer of ego psychology, a theory which dominated American psychoanalysis throughout the second half of the twentieth century.

Through the late 1920s and the 1930s, Freud served as Secretary of the International Psychoanalytical Association and Chair of the Vienna Psychoanalytic Society. When Germany invaded Austria in 1938, the Freud family emigrated to London and Anna Freud became a member of the British Psychoanalytical Society. There she participated in a second debate with Klein and her followers about whether Klein's ideas were truly Freudian. These controversial discussions ended with the organization of separate Freudian and Kleinian training programs within the society.

Freud set up the Hampstead War Nurseries in 1940, where she conducted observational research on orphaned children described in her 1944 book *Infants Without Families: The Case For and Against Residential Nurseries.* The nurseries closed in 1945 but later were reincarnated as the renowned Hampstead Child Therapy Clinic, posthumously renamed The Anna Freud Center for the Psychoanalytic Study and Treatment of Children. Over the next few decades Freud analyzed many young patients, trained future child analysts, and focused her research on developing ways to assess the relative normality or pathology of children at different ages, which she published in her 1965 work *Normality and Pathology in Childhood.*

Freud's later work also involved the practical application of psychoanalysis to problems in education and child welfare, and she lectured to public audiences on diverse topics ranging from child-rearing to family law. In 1961 she joined the faculty of Yale Law School as Senior Fellow and Visiting Lecturer. She collaborated with Yale colleagues Joseph Goldstein and Albert Solnit on the influential 1973 book BEYOND THE BEST INTERESTS OF THE CHILD. Followed by two similar volumes, this book helped establish social and legal rights for children in America.

Anna Freud continued to research and lecture until she died from the effects of a stroke in 1982. Her papers were placed with the Freud Archives in the Library of Congress, in Washington, D.C.

See also: **Age and Development; Child Development, History of the Concept of; Child Psychology.**

BIBLIOGRAPHY

King, Pearl, and Ricardo Steiner, eds. 1991. *The Freud-Klein Controversies 1941–1945.* London: Routledge.

Sandler, Joseph, and Anna Freud. 1980. *The Technique of Child Psychoanalysis: Discussions with Anna Freud.* Cambridge, MA: Harvard University Press.

Sandler, Joseph, and Anna Freud. 1985. *The Analysis of Defense: The Ego and the Mechanisms of Defense Revisited.* New York: International Universities Press.

Young-Bruehl, Elizabeth. 1988. *Anna Freud: A Biography.* New York: Simon and Schuster.

GAIL DONALDSON

Freud, Sigmund (1856–1939)

A century before Sigmund Freud, the father of psychoanalysis, formulated his psychoanalytic developmental theory, the English poet William Wordsworth wrote about nature and nurture, "The Child is father of the Man." It is commonsense knowledge that from birth on the child undergoes physical maturation (e.g., sexual maturation) and the development of body, mind, and character (e.g., psychological growth, social interaction, and adaptation). Freud's develop-

Sigmund Freud's theories on childhood have not been without controversy, yet his work remains a strong influence on the field of child psychology. © Hulton-Deutsch Collection/CORBIS.

mental psychology grew out of his method of psychoanalytic investigation of adult emotional disorders and his readings in the medical sexology that preceded him.

The Early Process of Discovery

Freud first discovered that adult neurotic disorders, specifically hysteria, were caused by psychic shock, or trauma, which he saw as a three-part process: one, a traumatizing event, an actual assault or injury, happened, which, two, the victim experienced and perceived as traumatic or stressful, and to which, three, the person reacted to with psychological defense, such as dynamic (active) forgetting or repression. The repressed memory and the accompanying emotions would then result in the various manifest symptoms of an emotional disorder. The traumas were of both a nonsexual and sexual kind and the emotional component was the paramount factor. As he delved into the history of sexual traumas, Freud became "drawn further and further back into the past; one hoped at last to be able to stop at puberty . . . but the tracks led still further back into childhood and into its earlier years" (Freud 1953 [1914], p. 17). As far as childhood goes, Freud's predominant interest was in sexual traumas and emotions; he postulated the sexual emotions as the primary ones. His next step was the discovery of the

> posthumous operation of a sexual trauma in childhood. If the sexual experience occurs during the peri-

od of sexual immaturity and the memory of it is aroused during or after maturity, then the memory will have a far stronger excitatory effect than the experience did at the time it happened; and this is because in the meantime puberty has immensely increased the capacity of the sexual apparatus for reaction. *The traumas of childhood operate in a deferred fashion as though they were fresh experiences; but they do so unconsciously.* (Freud 1962 [1896], pp. 166–167; italics in original)

Freud's term for deferred action was *Nachträglichkeit*, literally, *afterwardness*. As the traumas were a result of sexual acts of seduction or overwhelming by family members, servants, or others, they came to be known as the *seduction theory*, though nowhere did Freud himself employ the term.

At a certain point Freud wavered regarding the validity of this theory when he realized that some "hysterical subjects [traced] back their symptoms to traumas that were fictitious; [but] the new fact [that emerged was] precisely that they create such scenes in *phantasy*, and this psychical reality requires to be taken into account alongside practical reality. . . . From behind the phantasies, the whole range of a child's sexual life came to light" (Freud 1957 [1914], pp. 17–18). He discovered INFANTILE SEXUALITY. Eventually Freud reaffirmed the importance of seduction (trauma) and widened the theoretical scope by underscoring the complementarity of reality and fantasy.

In addition to external trauma, Freud also recognized the importance of internal trauma, the stimulation from within, by such forces as hunger, sexual drives, and other drives or needs. It should be noted, however, that Freud did not generally view the parents as traumatizers, in sharp contrast to his prominent student Sandor Ferenczi, with whom Freud fought tooth and nail. In contrast to Freud, Ferenczi insisted that parents can actually abuse their children, and this insight has been borne out by recent discoveries about CHILD ABUSE.

Freud's canonical text on infantile sexuality is the *Three Essays on the Theory of Sexuality*, where he formulated the developmental stages of childhood psychosexuality: At each stage, he wrote, humans engage in a fusion of bodily and mental pleasure-seeking and displeasure-avoidant behavior, and he named these stages the oral, anal, and phallic (or genital) phases, or stages, of early childhood; these are followed by the changes of PUBERTY and adulthood. The sensuous bodily experiences were correlated with interactions, conflicts, and fantasies related to parents and other significant persons in the child's environment.

The Oedipus Complex

Freud also advanced the psychoanalytic theory of the Oedipus complex, that is, the oedipal or phallic phase. He saw the oedipal phase as a developmental milestone, a time to face the traumas pertaining to the triangular situation between the child and the parents, when he or she is drawn to each of the parents as objects of desire, fantasy, and identification, while at the same time facing the threat of castration (or for girls, genital mutilation), and rivalry and competition in the wake of the birth of siblings. A good resolution of this constellation is a universal developmental task and is achieved by means of a consolidated sense of conscience (superego) and self-identity. These formulations would later be confirmed by anthropological and social sciences.

It needs to be emphasized that although the original, literal, nonmythological, name was the INCEST complex, Freud was not concerned with cases of actual incest but with incestuous fantasies. Again, more recent histories of child abuse have included the trauma of actual incest as well, including the problems of true versus false memories of past traumas.

This oedipal milestone led to a further differentiation between oedipal and preoedipal organization, in which the infant and young child of either gender relates primarily to the mother; however, here it was found that aggression, both in the parent and child, was a much more important issue than sexual attraction or fantasies. Another developmental line ran from autoerotism (deriving pleasure and satisfaction from one's own body), to narcissism (self-love), and to the full mature LOVE of others. Freud did not define a developmental line for aggression or a drive for power.

Integrated developmental psychology eventually led to a genetic psychological explanation of a wide spectrum of adult behavior: the psychology of love relations, mental disorders (neurosis and psychosis), criminal behavior, character formation, and the behavior of groups and masses.

Freudianism after Freud

When women joined the psychoanalytic movement, a fuller picture of developmental theory emerged, with an emphasis on the nonsexual aspects of development. Freud's followers elaborated seminal ideas that Freud had already discussed. ANNA FREUD elaborated the role of the defense mechanisms (dynamisms). MELANIE KLEIN, Anna Freud's great rival, emphasized the defenses called the paranoid and the depressive position in the first month of life. JOHN BOWLBY stressed attachment and loss. ERIK ERIKSON elaborated what he called the epigenetic stages in the development of identity.

While Freud focused on the organismic, or monadic (self-contained), aspects of development, later investigators were more receptive to the dyadic, or interpersonal, conception of development in health and disease first introduced by the great American psychiatrist Harry Stack Sullivan. This approach was importantly confirmed by family studies. The interpersonal-dyadic approach is the way of the future. The guiding principle should thus be not an exclusionary either/or but an inclusionary, this-as-well-as-that approach, integrating Freud's important monadic observations and insights with the interpersonal psychological reality as ob-

served in everyday life and depicted in imaginative literature, film, and television. In literature, a well-known example of applying the Oedipus complex is the interpretation of Shakespeare's *Hamlet*. In religion, psychoanalytic ideas can be applied to the biblical sacrifice of Isaac and the crucifixion of Jesus Christ.

Freud's THEORIES OF CHILDHOOD were subjected to both criticism and elaboration. Critics claimed that Freud's childhood theories were too exclusively fixated on SEXUALITY and were merely far-fetched extrapolations from observations of analyzed adult neurotics, thus lacking the empirical warrant of direct infant and child observation. This gap was first closed by the work of early women psychoanalytic pioneers who practiced child analysis, Hermine von Hug-Hellmeth and Sabina Spielrein. Further evolution of adult and child analysis significantly extended ideas that were only insufficiently developed in Freud, such as nonerotic attachment love, dependence (Freud's anaclitic type), and the role of aggression and envy. Here belongs the work of Melanie Klein and John Bowlby. These elaborations did not, however, amount to a refutation but rather to a more balanced view of issues in development. Further important work in the field came from infant and child research and focused on the role of interpersonal factors in development, such as the work of Margaret Mahler on separation-individuation or of Daniel Stern and Berry Brazelton on early good and failed communications between mother and child, among others.

See also: **Age and Development; Child Development, History of the Concept of; Child Psychology.**

BIBLIOGRAPHY

Fenichel, O. 1945. *The Psychoanalytic Theory of Neuroses.* New York: Norton.

Ferenczi, Sandor. 1955. "Confusion of Tongues between Adults and the Child." In *Final Contributions to the Problems and Methods of Psychoanalysis,* by Sandor Ferenczi. New York: Basic Books.

Freud, Sigmund. 1953 [1905]. "Three Essays on the Theory of Sexuality." In *Standard Edition,* vol. 7. London: Hogarth Press and the Institute of Psycho-Analysis.

Freud, Sigmund. 1957 [1914]. "On the History of the Psycho-Analytic Movement." In *Standard Edition,* vol. 14. London: Hogarth Press and the Institute of Psycho-Analysis.

Freud, Sigmund. 1962 [1896]. "Further Remarks on the Neuro-Psychoses of Defense." In *Standard Edition,* vol. 3. London: Hogarth Press and the Institute of Psycho-Analysis.

Lothane, Zvi. 1987. "Love, Seduction, and Trauma." *Psychoanalytic Review* 74: 83–105.

Lothane, Zvi. 1997. "Freud and the Interpersonal." *International Forum of Psychoanalysis* 6: 175–184.

Lothane, Zvi. 2001. "Freud's Alleged Repudiation of the Seduction Theory Revisited: Facts and Fallacies." *Psychoanalytic Review* 88: 673–723.

ZVI LOTHANE

Friendship

Discussions of the experience and the value of friendship, construed primarily in male terms, pervade Western cultural and literary tradition. The late-twentieth-century feminist reassessment of the uniqueness and significance of female friendship stimulated a variety of empirical investigations of the characteristics and function of friendship in contemporary society as well as several social historical examinations of the nature of past friendships. The latter work yielded two major new insights: the recognition that friendship is a socially constructed, historical phenomenon, mediated by the dominant emotional culture and various social and structural factors in a particular period—gender socialization, for example—and the recognition that friends have played a variety of important, and sometimes central, roles in the lives of both women and men.

Recent social scientific studies indicate that friendship also plays a significant role in children's lives from birth to ADOLESCENCE. While social relations within the family constitute a major component of the social environments of children, peer relations, including friendships, represent another important context for socialization. Psychologists have observed friendships between infants as young as eight or ten months. By the age of three, the development of social skills creates a wide range of friendship possibilities, and by the age of five, children can pretend and PLAY creatively. Between the ages of seven and twelve, friends still function as playmates, but they also provide mutual respect and affirmation. In adolescence, as in adulthood, female friendship involves a major component of trust and personal disclosure.

As children's social groups expand to include more than one "best" friend or a small, informal circle of close friends, their friends may be drawn from organized peer groups such as school classes, athletic teams, special interest clubs, scout troops, or gangs. Such groups also comprised significant social environments for nineteenth- and twentieth-century children. Factors such as access to schooling, period of compulsory schooling, length of school day, school size, diversity versus homogeneity of student body, and urban or suburban setting shaped children's social worlds and thus influenced their friendship patterns in the past. The modern history of friendship must deal with the growing importance of schooling as a bastion of friendship and a need for friends. Increasingly precise age-grading within schools has had a strong effect on the range of children's friendships. However, data concerning children's actual interactions with one another are not readily available for the historian who seeks to trace change and continuity in those patterns.

Some historians argue that the high proportion of childhood deaths in the premodern Western world conditioned children not to invest emotionally in their playmates, but we know very little about childhood friendship prior to the

eighteenth century. The presence of large numbers of SIB-LINGS also affected friendships outside the family. As with the history of childhood more generally, accessible sources of information about children's friendships from the eighteenth century on primarily reflect the point of view of middle-class adults. For example, child-rearing manuals, children's books, travelers' accounts, and the diaries and correspondence of parents document middle-class standards and cultural prescriptions and expectations for children's friendships. Yet these sources reveal little regarding either children's actual friendship practices and experiences in small, face-to-face groups or their feelings about their friends. Direct information concerning the dynamics of young children's friendships is particularly difficult to find, but sources such as autograph books, photographs, diaries, journals, and letters can offer insight into the experiences and feelings of older children and adolescents. Autobiographic recollections can also provide data about individuals' childhood friendships, albeit through the filter of memory. Despite the limitations of the available sources and the absence of a fully developed historical perspective on friendship in general, the outlines of a history of this aspect of childhood experience are beginning to emerge.

Girls and Friendship

Late-eighteenth- and early-nineteenth-century Western culture promoted the development of strong female friendships. Didactic and prescriptive middle-class literature emphasized affiliation as opposed to achievement as the appropriate focus for women's lives and assigned them a subordinate place in the social hierarchy. Shared religious, educational, biological, and domestic experiences created powerful bonds between women and constructed a world of intimacy and support that distanced them from their male relatives. Victorian emotional standards, which began to take shape in the 1820s, also fostered close friendships, particularly through an emphasis on intense family love that extended into friendship. Middle-class, nineteenth-century families often discouraged daughters from playing with boys, although some preadolescent girls chose boys as companions. Nevertheless, most young girls, surrounded by models of intimate adult female friendship and exposed to periodical literature that romanticized such relationships, typically replicated them in their own lives, sometimes choosing cousins or sisters as their closest friends.

The rise of educational institutions for girls provided an important setting for the development of close friendships. From the middle of the eighteenth century, middle-class young women interacted with each other in boarding schools, female ACADEMIES, and seminaries where they formed intimate, often lifelong relationships. Affectionate language and suggestions of physical intimacy pervade the correspondence of nineteenth-century school friends and highlight the central role of friendship in their lives. In the early twentieth century, the enrollment of growing numbers of girls in JUNIOR HIGH and HIGH SCHOOLS provided additional opportunities for peer interaction and friendship.

Like their predecessors, adolescent girls in the first two decades of the twentieth century expressed affection for friends, shared confidences, and relied on one another for emotional support. However, this period marks the beginning of a transition to different expectations and priorities with less emphasis on female intimacy. A new emotional culture stressed emotional restraint, and an explicit cultural preference for heterosexual relations stigmatized same-sex intimacy. These influences discouraged emotional intensity and closeness between female friends. Preadolescent girls were encouraged to go to parties and dances and to talk to boys. By the 1950s, ten year olds were worrying about being popular with boys. This distinctly new heterosexual imperative also dominated high school relationships, as the content of female friendships increasingly focused on boys and DATING, and young women's friendship choices often explicitly reflected their efforts to be perceived as members of the right group of girls to insure popularity with the opposite sex.

Although late-twentieth-century feminism re-emphasized the value and importance of female friendship, the impact of this ideology on young girls and adolescents is not clear. Several current studies describe a culture of aggression, backstabbing, and exclusive cliques among junior and senior high school girls, suggesting that friendship is fraught with problems for young women in contemporary society. While these descriptions of mean, calculating, and devious young women may be unrepresentative or exaggerated, they invite further study in the context of the history of children's friendships.

Boys and Friendship

Prior to the nineteenth century, boys spent more time in the company of adults than with their peers. As soon as they were old enough, they helped their fathers with farm work or served as apprentices or servants in other families. Certainly they had opportunities to play, but the structure of their lives offered limited occasions for independent activities out of the presence of adults, and hence for building friendships. This situation changed as urbanization and longer periods spent in school exposed them to larger groups of peers on a regular basis. In this context, boys developed a distinctive peer culture in which friendship played an important role.

Unlike those of girls, the friendships of young boys were unstable and superficial. Boys played outdoors, roaming more freely than their sisters were permitted to do. They chose their friends, often cousins and neighbors, pragmatically, more by availability than by any feelings of special affinity. Their relationships emphasized loyalty and good companionship rather than intimate confidences. Boys made friends easily, but conflict and rivalry were integral to their culture. Hence, their friendships shifted regularly, and fights

between gangs from different neighborhoods, villages, or social classes were common. Frequently friends, as well as rivals, engaged in physical combat, such as boxing matches. Numerous informal clubs that met in attics and basements brought boys together for athletic and other activities. Because these groups typically excluded certain individuals from membership, they actually promoted division as well as unity and companionship among boys.

Nineteenth-century boyhood ended in the mid- or late teens when young men typically left home to find a job or pursue further education. In this period of transition, often referred to by historians as youth, friendships became stronger. Individuals relied on peers for reassurance as they entered a new stage of life. Formal, self-created youth organizations first appeared in the late eighteenth century as descendants of earlier apprentice societies, and they proliferated. These groups—literary and debate clubs, religious societies, secret societies, fraternities, and lodges—provided a setting in which young men often found one or more close friends. In contrast to boyhood relationships, these new friendships displayed qualities similar to those of adolescent young women's friendships—intimacy, sharing of thoughts and emotions, expressions of affection, and physical closeness. However, while many nineteenth-century women maintained such friendships throughout their lives, intense male attachments ended as young men reached manhood and took on the responsibilities of marriage and careers.

As in the case of young women's relationships, the stigmatization of HOMOSEXUALITY in late-nineteenth- and early-twentieth-century society and the post-Victorian emphasis on emotional restraint discouraged intimacy in young men's friendships. Affectionate male relationships disappeared as a new pattern of interpersonal distance between young men emerged in response to the fear of being labeled homosexual. Despite social criticism of this pattern in the context of concerns about the personal isolation experienced by late-twentieth-century boys and young men, and some efforts toward male bonding among adults, homophobic social pressures continue to influence the nature of male friendship from childhood through adulthood.

See also: **Boyhood; Emotional Life; Girlhood; Love.**

BIBLIOGRAPHY

Cahane, Emily, Jay Mechling, Brian Sutton-Smith, et al. 1993. "The Elusive Historical Child: Ways of Knowing the Child of History and Psychology." In *Children in Time and Place: Developmental and Historical Insights*, ed. Glen H. Elder Jr., John Modell, and Ross D. Parke. New York: Cambridge University Press.

MacLeod, Anne Scott. 2000. "American Girlhood in the Nineteenth Century." In *Childhood in America*, ed. Paula S. Fass and Mary Ann Mason. New York: New York University Press.

Rosenzweig, Linda W. 1999. *Another Self: Middle-Class American Women and Their Friends in the Twentieth Century*. New York: New York University Press.

Rotundo, Anthony E. 1989. "Romantic Friendship: Male Intimacy and Middle Class Youth in the Northern United States, 1800–1900." *Journal of Social History* 23: 1–26.

Rotundo, Anthony E. 1993. *American Manhood: Transformations in Masculinity from the Revolution to the Modern Era.* New York: Basic Books.

Simmons, Rachel. 2002. *Odd Girl Out: The Hidden Culture of Aggression in Girls.* New York: Harcourt.

Smith-Rosenberg, Carroll. 1985. "The Female World of Love and Ritual: Relations Between Women in Nineteenth-Century America." In *Disorderly Conduct: Visions of Gender in Victorian America*, ed. Carroll Smith Rosenberg. New York: Alfred A. Knopf.

Thompson, Michael, and Grace O'Neill, with Lawrence J. Cohen. 2001. *Best Friends, Worst Enemies: Understanding the Social World of Children.* New York: Ballantine Books.

Wiseman, Rosalind. 2002. *Queen Bees and Wannabes: Helping Your Daughter Survive Cliques, Gossip, Boyfriends, and Other Realities of Adolescence.* New York: Crown.

Yacovone, Donald. 1998. "'Surpassing the Love of Women': Victorian Manhood and the Language of Fraternal Love." In *A Shared Experience: Men, Women, and the History of Gender*, ed. Laura McCall and Donald Yacovone. New York: New York University Press.

LINDA W. ROSENZWEIG

Froebel, Friedrich Wilhelm August (1782–1852)

Childhood education pioneer Friedrich Wilhelm August Froebel was born at Oberweissbach in the Thuringia region of Germany. (Froebel is the English form of the German surname Fröbel.) Just as his last name was translated from his native language, his ideas and educational practices were adapted to a variety of international settings. Froebel's greatest contribution to the care and education of young children, however, was his invention called the KINDERGARTEN.

The principal accounts of Froebel's life were written either by himself or by his supporters. Most of these biographies draw extensively upon his correspondence, contain religious language, and present Froebel in an uncritical, sometimes hagiographical, manner. The accounts highlight Froebel's unhappy early childhood experiences, describing them as influencing his thoughts and actions as an adult. The most lasting of Froebel's contributions to early childhood education is his insistence that its curriculum be based on play. Although Froebel was not the first to recognize that PLAY could be instructive, he did synthesize existing educational theories with innovative ideas of his own. He was not a very clear thinker, however; his writing is sometimes difficult to follow unless the reader interprets it in the context of German Romanticism, Idealist philosophy, and Naturphilosophie, or Nature Philosophy. These intellectual concepts heavily influenced Froebel. He read works by the German poet Novalis (1772–1801) and the German philosophers Johann Gottlieb Fichte (1762–1814), Karl Krause (1781–1832), and Friedrich Schelling (1775–1854).

Froebel applied his so-called spherical philosophy to education and it, rather than empirical observation, guided his work. Because of his strong religious beliefs, some educators have argued that his approach is more accurately described as mystical rather than philosophical. His method was to counterpose opposites that would then be resolved through the mediation of a third element. For example, Froebel held that mind and matter, although opposites, are both subject to the same laws of nature in which God, the third element, is immanent. Another triad he used in relation to the child was unity, diversity, and individuality. Each child would spontaneously represent these elements, a process he referred to as all-sided, self-activity. This is the context of his statement that "play is the self-active representation of the inner from inner necessity."

Like the seventeenth-century Moravian bishop and educator JOHANN AMOS COMENIUS, Froebel thought that all personal development came from within. Therefore, he asserted that the task of the teacher was to provide the conditions for growth without intervening too much in the learning process. Froebel presented these ideas in his 1826 book *The Education of Man.* In this philosophical work, Froebel explains the aims and principles of his first school at Keilhau and describes the characteristics of the stages of BOYHOOD (never GIRLHOOD). Like the revolutionary Swiss-born French philosopher, JEAN-JACQUES ROUSSEAU (1712–1778), Froebel believed that education should be adapted to the needs and requirements of each stage. Also, like Rousseau, he advocated that teaching should follow nature, avoiding arbitrary interference in the life of the young child. Contrary to many religious beliefs at the time, this naturalist approach asserted that every child is born good.

After childhood the youngster begins school, and Froebel devoted a chapter to describing the subjects he thought appropriate for this stage. This discussion owes much to the theories of Swiss educator, JOHANN PESTALOZZI (1746–1827), whose work Froebel observed when he visited Pestalozzi's Yverdon Institute between 1808 and 1810. In the final part of his book, Froebel talks of the necessity of unity between the school and the family, thereby emphasizing the notion that education is most effective when the school and family complement each other.

Near the end of his life, Froebel turned his attention to the family and the education of young children through play. He invented his famous educational TOYS, which he called *gifts*, a graded series of wooden blocks together with a sphere and a cylinder. Later, he added learning activities, which he called *occupations*, such as paper-folding and -cutting, weaving, and clay modeling. At Blankenburg in 1837, Froebel gave the name *kindergarten* to his system of education for young children.

In 1843, Froebel published a book entitled *Mother's Songs, Games and Stories.* This was his most popular book; as the title suggests, it described action songs and finger plays (together with their musical notation) woodcut illustrations, and guidance on how to present the songs as well as the meanings that could be derived from them. The book's content was based in part on Froebel's observations of mothers singing to their children. Froebel wanted to help women educate their infants more effectively as a prerequisite for a better society. Many middle-class women in Germany and elsewhere, including the United States, opened kindergartens and used Froebel's methods to educate their children.

Educators have long debated the nature of the relationship between Froebel's philosophy and his pedagogy. While the gifts and occupations and games may not have been logically entailed by his philosophy, without it many teachers resorted to formalism and mechanical imitation. For the most part, his attempts to persuade public schools to adopt the kindergarten saw only limited success during his lifetime. After his death, however, his ideas and practices spread rapidly; other educators came to agree with Froebel's belief in the importance of early childhood education.

See also: **Child Development, History of the Concept of; Education, Europe; Education, United States; Progressive Education; Theories of Play.**

BIBLIOGRAPHY

Bowen, H. C. 1893. *Froebel and Education by Self-Activity.* London: William Heinemann.

Brehony, Kevin J., ed. 2001. *The Origins of Nursery Education: Friedrich Froebel and the English System.* 6 vols. London: Routledge.

Shapiro, M. S. 1983. *Child's Garden: The Kindergarten Movement from Froebel to Dewey.* University Park: Pennsylvania State University Press.

Wollons, R. L., ed. 2000. *Kindergartens and Cultures: The Global Diffusion of an Idea.* New Haven, CT: Yale University Press.

KEVIN J. BREHONY

Furniture

Furniture made especially for children is not a modern phenomenon but has existed independent of the ways in which adult views of children have changed. At the same time, its form reflects or rises from changing pedagogical views of childhood. Children's furniture has historically been defined not just by scale but also by pedagogical purpose.

The design of children's furniture is influenced by period, material, form, function, pedagogical views, and children's games and status. It reflects the grown-up world's imagining of children's needs and also its ideals of order, DISCIPLINE, HYGIENE, PLAY, and even stimulation. Children's furniture often tries to anticipate children's behavior—mostly proscribed behavior.

One can distinguish between children's furniture in private homes and children's furniture in institutions such as nurseries and KINDERGARTENS. The distinction reflects the identity of each sphere. Children's furniture in the home often reflects the contemporary attitude to interior design and material. Institutional furniture tends to reflect the contemporary attitude toward pedagogy and hygiene.

High and Low Chairs

Of the children's furniture that has survived from earlier periods, chairs tend to show the most variety. (A great deal of children's furniture has been lost, but the oldest preserved chairs originate from the late 1500s and the early 1600s.) A Greek vase painting dated 400 B.C.E. shows a child in a high chair facing a woman sitting on a stool. The earliest known example of a low child's chair originates from the Viking age. The remnants of the chair were found during excavations in Sweden in 1981. The low chair has been known throughout most of Europe. Before the Viking chair was found, the oldest existing example of a low child's chair was in a family portrait in a 1601 Swiss tapestry.

These examples indicate that special furniture for children was made at a very early stage in the history of furniture, and that equally early two basic models of children's chairs existed: the high and the low model. Scale is what most distinguishes children's furniture from that of grown-ups. The sitting height of children's furniture is mostly either above or beneath the average grown-up sitting height. When children's chairs are built for pedagogical purposes, they tend to follow the low strategy to make children self-sufficient. The high strategy, on the other hand, puts the child at the level of the grown-ups at a table and enables the child to learn how to behave there.

Furniture and Status

Children's furniture stresses the social position of the child in relation to both the environment and to adults. To have an individual piece of furniture indicates status and the right to a status in the home or institution. The very existence of children's furniture promotes the child's status in the home and institution, because the furniture is the property of the child and because the furniture physically occupies space—a choice that excludes other furniture and reflects a priority, stressing the child's social importance. If a child has a piece of furniture of his or her own, this acknowledges the status and rank of the child. The special form of children's furniture signals that childhood is considered an important period.

School Furniture

The production of children's furniture for schools was an important innovation. School classes in the old village schools had long, narrow benches on which the children sat close together. Not until the second half of the nineteenth century was the first pedagogical school furniture designed: school desks with room enough between seat and table for children to barely stand. Classrooms were small, and the new desks minimized the space between rows.

In the late 1800s and the early 1900s many desk designs were considered. So-called school hygiene supporters made detailed descriptions of the correct way for a student to sit when writing, reading, or doing arithmetic or needlework. From these, they calculated designs, relating the height of the desk and the distance between the desk and the seat to the size of the child. There were different views on about whether to bolt the desk to the floor or allow it to be pulled aside when the room was cleaned, and about designing desks in differing heights adapted to differing ages and sizes. The choice between single desks or twin desks, however, was very often made on the basis of economics.

With the development of nurseries and kindergartens in the beginning of the twentieth century, children's public space became a focus of experiments with small, movable furniture. Between World Wars I and II, a group of creative and progressive schools used individual chairs and tables, allowing new pedagogical opportunities in the classroom. The traditional organization—a master's desk facing rows of pupils' desks—continued, however, into the 1950s in Europe but had largely disappeared in the United States by then.

Light, air, and a clean environment were the 1930s ideals of European pedagogical architecture. They were meant to produce healthy, clean, sound children. The first nurseries and kindergartens were models of clinical hygiene and sanitation, derived from hospital clinics. Their furniture was designed for easy cleaning in order to minimize the risk of infection. Not only hygienic precautions, but also the practical organization of the nurseries and kindergartens were intended to form the children. Furniture built to a child's scale was meant to make children active and resourceful. Children were to learn how to organize their own playthings on child-sized shelves and bookcases. Moreover, they were to learn how to wash themselves at washbasins built to their height.

Furniture and Play

The purpose of playing has been perceived differently through the ages. It may be considered, for example, to have social value or to help in motor development or to be of value in its own right. Research on children and the design of children's playthings and furniture between 1930 and 1960 shows that they were intended to prepare the child for the grown-up world and the working sphere. Therefore constructive playthings and junction furniture were popular and supported by the dominant psychologists and pedagogues.

Scandinavian furniture designers between 1930 and 1960 followed the lead of NURSERY SCHOOLS, socially engaged designers, and experts in child rearing regarding the child's need to play. It was generally accepted that children liked to use furniture in their PLAY. The first educated furniture designers in Scandinavia began to make children's furniture when they had children themselves and they began to attach importance to the idea that children should be able to use their furniture for more than just sitting in (e.g., to stimulate their imagination or to use as play equipment). Previously, children's furniture for nurseries and kindergartens had been made by constructing architects and consequently was designed from a technical point of view, resulting in adult furniture scaled down to a child's size.

The youth revolution in 1968 and the changing views of authority changed pedagogy and the dominant perception of the child's world, moving both in an anti-authoritarian direction. These changing values were reflected in children's furniture, which now was designed for play and relaxed behavior.

Conclusion

Although children's furniture in the private home has a long history, children's furniture in the public sphere is a more recent phenomenon. On the other hand, all furniture originally made for the private home was made for the upper classes. It was not until the twentieth century that mass production allowed children's furniture—like TOYS—to be made for the middle classes. At the same time children and childhood came to be taken more seriously than they had been previously, creating a greater focus on and demand for children's furniture and toys.

Today the difference between the public and private sphere has been minimized since most children attend nurseries and kindergartens, encountering the same kinds of furniture there as they do at home. Contemporary furniture designers do not care whether children's furniture is used in nurseries, kindergartens, or private homes. It is primarily the spirit of the time that determines the understanding of the form, function, and creation of children's furniture.

See also: **Children's Spaces; School Buildings and Architecture.**

BIBLIOGRAPHY

Bollivant, Lucy, ed. 1997. *Kid Size: The Material World of Childhood.* Milan, Italy: Skira, Vitra Design Museum.

Calvert, Karin. 1992. *Children in the House: The Material Culture of Early Childhood, 1600–1900.* Boston: Northeastern University Press.

Gelles, Edward. 1982. *Nursery Furniture: Antique Children's Miniature and Doll's House Furniture.* London: Constable.

Kevill-Davies, Sally. 1991. *Yesterday's Children: The Antiques and History of Childcare.* Woodbridge, UK: Antique Collector's Club.

KIRSTEN HEGNER

G

Geddes, Anne

Anne Geddes has been called the most celebrated baby photographer in the world. Her style is instantly recognizable, and Geddes's images enjoy great popularity and unparalleled brand name status. Photographs by Geddes appear on posters, postcards, stationary, personal checks, bookmarks, jigsaw puzzles, and stickers. Geddes's greatest fame, however, has come from calendars and coffee-table books of her work. In 1997 Geddes's *A Collection of Images* was the number-one selling calendar in the United States. There are estimated to be more than 7.5 million Anne Geddes calendars and date books in print. Her book of photographs *Down in the Garden* (1996) sold more than 1.5 million copies, and reached number three on the *New York Times* best-seller list. As of 2002 over 15 million Anne Geddes titles had been sold worldwide.

Geddes's photographs are highly crafted and carefully staged. Most are taken indoors, in a studio setting, employing elaborate costumes and props. The images rely on jokes and puns, which are created by putting children in strange or anomalous situations. Geddes's most famous images blur the boundaries between the child modeling for the shot and the natural world around it. For instance, in *Sweet Peas* (1995), several newborn babies lie sleeping, each dressed in an individual cloth pea pod. Her work creates the illusion that children are adorable, passive objects, protected from real-world concerns, who exist solely for the delectation of adult viewers. Geddes often works with newborns less than four weeks old, or with premature babies, to ensure that the child will lay still for the duration of the shot. The sheer difficulty of photographing such young children is part of what makes Geddes's photographs so attention-grabbing.

Geddes's popularity is also due in large part to the fact that, in her calendars and books, she presents children as simultaneously innocent and sensual. One of her most famous photographs shows two children emerging from giant cabbages, a coy reference to the myth that babies come from the cabbage patch. Geddes's own favorite photograph, entitled *Cheesecake*, is of a nude baby, its genitals covered, lying on a bed of roses, grinning. The image makes a joke of the idea of children as sexual, while at the same time indulging the representation of baby flesh. Recently, Geddes's work has begun to change. She is focusing less on props and has begun to include more black and white photographs in her calendars and books.

Geddes was born and raised in Queensland, Australia, and is a self-trained photographer. She now lives and works in Auckland, Australia.

See also: **Images of Childhood; Photographs of Children.**

BIBLIOGRAPHY

Isaacs, Nora. 1996. "Monitor: Genesis; Geddes Gardening Tips." *American Photo* 7: 32.

Swazeny, Sue. 1996. "Interview with Anne Geddes." *Family Photo*: 28–31, 72.

INTERNET RESOURCE

The Official Anne Geddes Website. 2002. Available from <www.annegeddes.com>.

A. Cassandra Albinson

Gendering

"It's a Boy!" "It's a Girl!" Birth announcements with these headlines commonly appear in North American newspapers. Birth and adoption announcements sent through the mail to family and friends frequently signal the sex of the child by their use of the traditional colors—pink for a girl and blue for a boy—so that recipients know the sex even before they read the baby's name. Indeed, most of us would find it unsettling if the announcing parents did not inform us of the newborn or newly adopted child's sex. The importance we place

Jean Renoir Sewing (c. 1899), Pierre-Auguste Renoir (French 1841–1919). Twenty-first-century viewers might find it hard to identify the long-haired, beribboned child depicted here sewing as a boy, yet long hair and petticoats were common for young children of both sexes until the early twentieth century. (Oil on canvas, 55.9 x 46.6 cm, Mr. and Mrs. Martin Ryerson Collection, Art Institute of Chicago).

on the sex assigned to a newborn baby indicates just how significant this differentiating category remains in our culture. Many would argue that gender is the most fundamental of the multitude of categories employed in all cultures in all historical periods to divide individuals into distinct groups. To a greater or lesser degree our sex assignment at birth shapes our prospects in life and determines how we and others see ourselves.

Even today, most people in North America and around the world accept the validity and the stability of gender difference without questioning it, simply seeing it as "natural." Indeed most parents and others who participate in shaping a child's identity do not consciously reflect on their contribution to what sociologists and psychologists call socialization. "Boys will be boys," or "girls will be girls," people say, when boys hoot and holler and shoot at each other with toy guns, or when girls sit quietly playing with dolls. On the other hand, as researchers have pointed out, when girls engage in rough, noisy activities or boys play quietly with stuffed animals, the same people will either not notice such violations of gender stereotypes, or explain them away as exceptions to a general rule.

However, while its impact even in North America has been limited, there has been a revolutionary change in scholarly thinking about the differences between men and women, and about the role that child-rearing practices play in producing those differences. This profound change came about because of the rise of feminism in the nineteenth and twentieth centuries. During the "second wave" of the women's movement in the 1960s, feminism, especially in North America, emerged as a strong political force and, for the first time, had a significant influence on scholarly investigation in history and the social and biological sciences. The decade of the 1970s represents a high point, as the creative energy of feminist scholarship called into sharp question complacent notions about the immutability as well as the utility of our culture's gender roles. These new scholars, along with feminist and gay and lesbian political activists, articulated the insight that masculinity and femininity (like race or class or ethnic identity) are shaped primarily by culture, rather than biology.

With these new directions, new concepts emerged. The use of the word *gender* as a category of analysis was a key development. The term is now used in scholarly literature to point to the contrast between biological sex and learned behavior. "Gendering," the title of this entry, asks us to notice that newborns identified as female or male do not on their own develop into feminine and masculine adults: gendering is a major task of socialization which begins at the moment of birth. Parents, extended family, and caregivers all contribute to providing the cues that encourage the baby to adopt feminine or masculine patterns, and so also does the wider culture, which includes television, motion pictures, children's stories, toys, and clothing, and institutions like government, religion, and schooling.

Definitions of appropriate masculine and feminine behavior vary cross-culturally and over time. However, most cultures, to a greater or lesser degree, have favored males, who have throughout much of human history had more power and prestige than women. Historically, male power and dominance has affected the treatment of children. In ancient Greece, notably in Athens, unwanted infants were often left to die, and a large majority of such exposed infants were female. A Victorian Englishman could write explicitly and without guilt about his deep disappointment that his first child was not a boy. In rural China in the 1980s, a grandfather would refer to the birth of a boy as a "big happiness," whereas the birth of a girl was only a "small happiness." In cultures past and present, when there is a shortage of food, girls and women get less to eat than boys and men.

In all cultures, children adapt to or attempt to resist the gender roles appropriate to their culture by learning through example. Through explicit as well as unspoken messages, girls are encouraged to model themselves on their mothers and other women they know or encounter in stories, schoolbooks, and television programs. Boys are encouraged to model themselves on their fathers and other male figures. In cultures where dominant beliefs unequivocally define women as wives and mothers and restrict them to nurturing roles and narrowly defined definitions of appropriate work, the lessons a child learns will be explicit. Middle- and upper-class Victorian girls, for example, were given dolls and encouraged to mother them, and moreover they were taught to sew dolls' clothing, thus learning to "use their needle," a skill then thought to be essential to womanliness. They were, however, rarely allowed to study Latin or Greek, subjects that marked the educated man. In many Muslim cultures today, children are taught traditional gender roles in family and in school. In all settings, including those parts of the twenty-first century world where ideologies about gender are changing and gender roles themselves are more flexible, it is still the case that women nurture more and men less, and men are more visible in public roles and exercise more public power. Boys and girls alike do not fail to notice these differences.

Many people, including some who do scholarly work on gender, maintain that such inequality is justified because males are "naturally" smarter, more assertive, more creative, and physically stronger than women, whereas women are "naturally" more gentle, submissive, and nurturing. As two generations of gender historians have demonstrated, the supposed naturalness of gender difference has been used as a justification for continuing male privilege and male dominance throughout human history. For much of this history, religious beliefs have served as the primary justification for gender inequality, whereas legal codes have served as the primary enforcer.

Science, however defined, has also played a role. In the ancient world, men like the philosopher Aristotle or the physician Galen articulated theories about male superiority and female inferiority based on their understanding of human biology. Galen for example believed that women were less perfect than men because they were colder. In the twentieth and twenty-first centuries in many parts of the world, religion and law have continued to buttress gender inequality. However, especially in Europe and North America, serious discourse about sex and gender has come to be associated with science. On the one side are researchers like behavioral psychologist Doreen Kimura, whose *Sex and Cognition* sets out to prove that there are significant differences in cognition between men and women, and that these differences are based in biology. On the other side are researchers like geneticist Richard Lewontin, whose work emphasizes biological and genetic diversity. Lewontin points out the one-dimensional thinking of those on the "nature" side of the debate who fail to take account of the complex relationship between biology and nurture when they assert that gender, race, and class differences rest fundamentally on biology.

The contemporary "nurture versus nature" debate is about politics as well as science, with those on the nurture side tending, like Lewontin, to support social policies designed to rectify inequalities, whereas researchers like Kimura tend to be politically conservative. Researchers who look for biological differences in temperament between the sexes do find some evidence of them, though any differences that have been found are small, and even diehard supporters of "nature" accept that "nurture" or culture can have a significant influence.

For this reason, we can assert that biology, while it may play a role, is not destiny. If it were, we would not see the great variation in the way in which seemingly universal gender norms manifest themselves. For example, many cultures believe that sexual appetites differ in males and females, but the definition of such difference varies. In medieval and early modern Europe women were thought to be more highly sexed than men but by the late nineteenth century people assumed that men had ungovernable passions and that women were passionless. In sixteenth-century England, men with money dressed to show off their bodies, wearing as much lace and embroidery as they could afford and sporting hose that displayed the shape of their legs. By the nineteenth century, ornamented or revealing dress for men was considered to be unmanly. A particularly telling example of varying patterns of gendering in childhood has to do with dress and appearance. Today, few North American parents, even those who support flexibility in gender roles, would dress a boy in a frilly pinafore or give a girl a boy's haircut. Yet in Europe and North America right up until the twentieth century babies and small children were dressed alike: both were put in petticoats and both had long hair. It was only when a boy reached the age of six or seven that he was put into britches (breeched), the ritual signifying that he was from then on to assume masculine gender roles.

Comparative work done on twentieth-century Japan and the United States reveals contrasting points of view about certain traits that are independent of gender and reinforces the importance of socialization, rather than biology, in shaping masculine and feminine behavior. In Japan, cooperation and acceptance of dependence on others (a trait that many North Americans would associate with femininity) is valued in both males and females, and the Japanese socialize their children accordingly, even though Japanese culture remains more committed to traditional gender differences than American culture and remains more male dominated. In contrast, in the United States since the founding of the Republic, individualism and autonomy have been valued and these traits have been fostered in both sexes, although more explicitly and extensively in boys.

In conclusion then, a culture's ideology about gender and its assignment of authority, responsibility, and privilege to men or women determines the way in which babies and children learn about gender. Cultures that remain unequivocally patriarchal foster sharp gender divisions, whereas more egalitarian cultures offer greater role flexibility for both males and females. Those who support genuine equality of opportunity should not however be complacent about what has been achieved in more "advanced" secular cultures. Even in early twenty-first century North America and Europe, where feminism has brought about meaningful changes for the better in women's legal status, it is still the case that most child care and early childhood socialization remains the responsibility of women, be they mothers, caregivers, or teachers. On the other hand, most powerful leaders in government or the work world are men. Some people believe that only when parents nurture equally will we achieve gender equality. Only then will assertiveness in girls and gentleness in boys be valued in our culture, and only then will men and women share power and authority equally in public and in personal life.

In addition to offering comparative work on the definitions of gender, and on changes in these concepts, historians have undertaken research on categories of children who are less clearly gendered or are deliberately cross-gendered. Sometimes these arrangements are designed to provide certain kinds of workers in an otherwise gendered labor system. Finally, historians work on changes in the importance of gendering in childhood socialization. While twentieth-century emphasis on gender remains stronger than many adults realize, it seems less sweeping than was true in the nineteenth century. Less emphasis is placed on separate educational tracks or on separate emotional arsenals. Shifts in the level of significance of gendering is a vital, and not simply contemporary, facet of the history of childhood.

See also: **Boyhood; Breeching; Girlhood.**

BIBLIOGRAPHY

Ariès, Philippe. 1962. *Centuries of Childhood: A Social History of Family Life.* Trans. Robert Baldick. New York: Knopf.

Belotti, Elena Gianini. 1975. *Little Girls: Social Conditioning and Its Effects on the Stereotyped Role of Women During Infancy.* London: Writers and Readers Publishing Cooperative.

Brooks-Gunn, Jeanne, and Wendy Schempp Matthews. 1979. *He and She: How Children Develop Their Sex-Role Identity.* Englewood Cliffs, NJ: Prentice-Hall.

Dinnerstein, Dorothy. 1996. *The Mermaid and the Minotaur: Sexual Arrangements and Human Malaise.* New York: Harper and Row.

Ferdows, Adele K. 1995. "Gender Roles in Iranian Public School Textbooks." In *Children in the Muslim Middle East,* ed. Elizabeth Warnock Fernea. Austin: University of Texas Press.

Frieze, Irene H; Jacquelynne E. Parsons; Paula B. Johnson; et al. 1978. *Women and Sex Roles: A Social Psychological Perspective.* New York: Norton.

Gorham, Deborah. 1982. *The Victorian Girl and the Feminine Ideal.* Bloomington: Indiana University Press.

Gould, Stephen Jay. 1996 *The Mismeasure of Man.* New York: Norton.

Kimura, Doreen. 1999. *Sex and Cognition.* Cambridge, MA: MIT Press.

Lewontin, Richard. 1995. *Human Diversity.* New York: Scientific American Library.

Lewontin, Richard; Steven Rose; and Leon J. Kamin. 1984. *Not in Our Genes: Biology, Ideology, and Human Nature.* New York: Pantheon Books.

Miedzian, Myriam. 1991. *Boys Will Be Boys: Breaking the Link between Masculinity and Violence.* New York: Doubleday.

Shwalb, David W., and Barbara J. Shwalb, eds. 1996. *Japanese Childrearing: Two Generations of Scholarship.* New York: Guilford Press.

Rotundo, E. Anthony. 1993. *American Manhood: Transformations in Masculinity from the Revolution to the Modern Era.* New York: Basic Books.

Tosh, John. 1999. *A Man's Place: Masculinity and the Middle-Class Home in Victorian England.* New Haven, CT: Yale University Press.

DEBORAH GORHAM

Gesell, Arnold (1880–1961)

Arnold Gesell broke new ground in his use of careful observation of children's behavior as a method of studying the orderly sequence of neuromotor development. Profoundly influenced by early embryologists who mapped the ontogeny of organ systems during fetal development, Gesell proposed that psychological development followed a similar orderly sequence governed by "lawful growth processes" (Gesell and Amatruda, p. 4). In his detailed studies of a small group of infants and young children, Gesell set out to define the stages of these orderly sequences and the laws governing their progression—what children are like at what point in their lives and how they respond to specific stimuli and test situations at different age levels.

Gesell's work was part of an emerging interest in defining normative patterns of physical and mental development that began in the mid-1800s with several so-called baby biographers who had chronicled events in their own children's lives. These personal histories of children's lives were a rudimentary beginning of a scientific approach to understanding normative patterns in children's psychological development. At Clark University, G. STANLEY HALL began to establish a database on the normal behavior and development of children as gathered through compilations of parent reports. His student, Arnold Gesell, took the field many steps further by defining observational methods for the quantitative study of human behavioral development from birth through adolescence. He pioneered the use of motion picture cameras and one-way screens to study the details of children's behavioral responses to specific situations and test materials, and his observations on the growth of behavioral organization provide maps of the stages of neuromotor maturation which researchers and clinicians studying infancy have relied upon ever since.

Gesell was born in 1880. He was among the first generation of American-born children born to German immigrants who had settled in Alma, Wisconsin. After receiving his bachelor's degree in 1906 from the University of Wisconsin, he obtained his Ph.D. in psychology from Clark University. Gesell accepted an assistant professorship at Yale in 1911. In his first years at Yale, he also worked toward his M.D., which he earned in 1915. Soon after his arrival at Yale, Gesell set up a "psycho-clinic" at the New Haven Dispensary, later known as the Clinic of Child Development, which he directed as Professor of Child Hygiene at Yale from 1930 to 1948. Gesell's clinic was the forerunner of the Child Study Center at the Yale School of Medicine.

Gesell's initial work focused on developmentally disabled children, but he believed that it was necessary to understand normal infant and child development in order to understand abnormality. He began his normative studies with infants and preschool children and later extended his work to children of five to ten and ten to sixteen. Gesell was one of the first to describe expectable maturational sequences in various domains of neuromotor development from early infancy through school age. He believed that, just as the body developed in genetically encoded, sequenced patterns, so behavioral patterns emerged in sequences reflective of differentiation in the central nervous system. In his own words:

> A behavior pattern is simply a defined response of the neuro-motor systems to a specific situation. . . . A young baby follows a dangled object with his eyes; eye following is a behavior pattern. . . . Behavior patterns are not whimsical or accidental by-products. They are the authentic end-products of a total developmental process which works with orderly sequence. . . . These patterns are symptoms. They are indicators of the maturity of the nervous system. (Gesell and Amatruda, p. 4)

He gave primacy to maturational processes and to endowment, a primary emphasis that has generated criticism from contemporary developmentalists. But he also believed that experience and environment played a major role in determining the rate of maturational change, and he (and all psychologists since) defined experience, the developmental environment, as beginning at conception.

Through his accumulated observations of the maturational sequences of various behaviors (detailed in *An Atlas of Infant Behavior* and *The Embryology of Behavior*), he created the Gesell Development Schedules, which are applicable for children between four weeks and six years of age. The instrument measures responses to test materials and situations both qualitatively and quantitatively. Areas assessed include motor and language development, adaptive behavior, and personal-social behavior; the child's performance is expressed as developmental age, which is then converted into a developmental quotient, representing the proportion of normative abilities for that individual child at his or her age. Gesell's work made it possible to apply standards for many

aspects of development against which children may be compared to indicate how normally they are growing.

In the 1940s and 1950s, Gesell was regarded as a leading authority on child rearing and development, and his developmental schedules were widely used as a standard method for assessing children's developmental progress. He and his colleague, Francis L. Ilg, coauthored several books that are widely read by parents, including *Infant and Child in the Culture of Today* (1943), *The Child from Five to Ten* (1946), and *Youth: The Years from Ten to Sixteen* (1956), in which he applied his basic research and gave norms for behavior at successive stages of development. Although his original data were derived from what has been criticized as a small, unrepresentative sample, his efforts were nonetheless the first to base descriptions of children's normative development on systematically gathered, direct observations. Gesell's description of the invariant sequences of development, the growth principles, and the variability of rates of development are milestones in the history of developmental psychology.

See also: **Child Development, History of the Concept of; Child Psychology; Child-Rearing Advice Literature.**

BIBLIOGRAPHY

Gesell, Arnold, and Catherine S. Amatruda. 1941. *Developmental Diagnosis: Normal and Abnormal Child Development, Clinical Methods and Pediatric Applications.* New York: Hoeber.

LINDA C. MAYES

Girlhood

During the early modern period in Europe and the colonial period in America it was believed that children did not acquire sexual traits before the age of six; hence, young boys and girls were dressed almost identically, and little attention was paid to differences between them. Girlhood—as a distinctive or privileged experience—was not as important as the larger notion of childhood that encompassed it. After the age of six, girls were trained in women's household occupations and their daily life began to revolve around their mothers and sisters (while boys spent more time with their fathers). In this manner the end of childhood and the beginning of womanhood happened early and fairly seamlessly in colonial society. Filial obedience was perhaps the dominant ideal for both girls and boys in America during this period: moral and religious training, basic education, and social life were organized around the Judeo-Christian Fifth Commandment, "Obey thy father and thy mother: that thy days may be long upon the land."

In the late colonial and antebellum agrarian South in the United States, expectations for girls differed based on race and class. Daughters of the plantation elite were schooled in the ornamental feminine arts—needlepoint, drawing, danc-

Joshua Reynolds portrays his young upper-class subject as the model of well-behaved, innocent girlhood in his portrait, *Penelope Boothby* (1788). © Ashmolean Museum, Oxford.

ing, and French. Because girls were largely considered to be ladies-in-training, a certain delicacy of manner was encouraged. Enslaved girls, meanwhile, were not ascribed any of the attributes of their white mistresses. Expected to work in the fields alongside adult men and women, they were accorded no special privileges until they became pregnant, at which point their owners had a vested interest in protecting their health. In fact, when black girls claimed for themselves aspects of femininity that applied to white girls—particularly sexual innocence or ill health during their menstrual cycle—they were accused of "playing the lady." Similarly, in the industrializing Northeast as well as in urban centers in the South, native white and immigrant working-class girls toiled in factories in the late nineteenth and early twentieth centuries. Over 18 percent of all children between the ages of ten and fifteen were employed in factory work in 1890. Hence, many girls had to assume adult responsibilities and work alongside boys. Girls of the middle and upper classes, by contrast, led lives full of social experiences with other girls and older women—classmates, female teachers, their mothers, and other female relatives. Some went to all-female boarding schools, and they often formed extremely close bonds of FRIENDSHIP that lasted through adulthood.

It was among middle- and upper-class girls in cities along the Atlantic seaboard during the mid-nineteenth century

that the idea and experience of girlhood emerged in its modern form. As small-scale manufacturing declined, and as Irish immigration in particular brought more women and girls to the United States looking for household positions, many middle-class girls no longer needed to work within their own households at all. Consequently, the notion that girlhood was a period of "domestic apprenticeship" all but disappeared. Girls continued to "help" their mothers, but increasingly they were paid an allowance for such work; otherwise, they went to school, socialized among their peers, and spent their leisure time any way they wished. Freedom was especially granted to girls younger than the age of twelve. "A wholesome delight in rushing about at full speed, playing at active games, climbing trees, rowing boats, making dirt-pies and the like" was recommended for young girls, and the celebrated figure of the "tomboy" emerged at this time. Because of high rates of LITERACY, older girls often spent their leisure time reading novels or serialized fiction—both adventure and romance—and many kept diaries as well. In their journals they recorded their attempts to achieve that most vaunted of Victorian goals for girls: to be "good." Being good meant controlling one's emotions, especially anger, following a disciplined routine, and remaining sexually chaste. Boys were not expected to be as "good" as girls—especially when it came to considering others' welfare before their own or maintaining a subdued countenance in public.

Due in large part to the efforts of Progressive reformers at the turn of the century, CHILD LABOR among the working classes declined and school attendance more than doubled between 1870 and 1910. Settlement workers built playgrounds and founded CHILD GUIDANCE clinics in cities across the United States, and educators advocated more opportunities for "personal growth" within the school curriculum. Largely because of rising rates of education, girls began spending more time with their peers. Among working-class girls, the growth of commercial amusements—dance halls, movie theaters and amusement parks—created new opportunities for girls to participate in a subculture that was independent of their parents. As a result, a heterosocial YOUTH CULTURE became a defining aspect of the Americanization process, and it contributed to an increasing generation gap between immigrant parents and their American daughters. The growth of this culture did the most to establish the prevailing sensibility about girlhood that exists to this day: that levity, playfulness, and consumerism are the stuff of girlhood through the teenage years. As "young ladies" evolved into "girls," the designation *girl* was extended to any female who was not married. Young women who worked in the new department stores were called "shop girls," those who were unmarried were often referred to as "bachelor girls," and young women who went on dates with men were known as "charity girls." Calling unattached young adult women in a range of situations "girls" reflected the growth and celebration of the notion of girlhood itself, a time when life was organized

The Boit Children (1882–1883), John Singer Sargent. Sargent's painting hints at something mysterious about girlhood, especially as girls grow into young women—only the youngest children are shown clearly, while their older sisters stand in the shadows. © Francis G. Mayer/CORBIS.

around the search for individual style, dancing, and flirtation—in short, the pursuit of fun.

Over the course of the 1920s, the FLAPPER—a term that applied equally to fashionable college-aged and adolescent girls—emerged as a figure of cultural fascination in the United States. Flappers were girls who cultivated a worldly, tough, and somewhat androgynous exterior in an attempt to

rebel against Victorian assumptions about feminine delicacy and "goodness." Older ideas about girlish innocence remained, however, in such characters as SHIRLEY TEMPLE and Little Orphan Annie. Both were poor but sweet little girls who charmed the rich through their street smarts, winning ways, and heart-melting vulnerability, moving their patrons to intercede on behalf of the lower social classes. Thus, when older girls began dismantling traditional ideas about girls' selflessness and purity, society began to look to young (or "little") girls to embody the traditional notions of female purity and virtue.

Girls have been called the first TEENAGERS because, when the term was popularized in the mid-1940s, the kind of consumerism associated with the teen years—malted milkshakes, record collecting, and quirky fashions—were embraced by girls first. With the introduction of *Seventeen* magazine in 1944, a monthly devoted solely to girls' fads and fashions, the perception of girlhood as a time of self-centered fun was fully enshrined in American culture. As teenage girls began to have more money in the 1950s —mostly through baby-sitting and increased allowances— they became an important consumer market segment, catered to as never before by advertisers, film makers, and fashion designers. It has been argued that girls' new purchasing power enhanced their influence in the culture overall; that they became "consumer citizens" of a sort. Others have pointed out, however, that girls themselves were not in control of the images of them that proliferated, and that much of what was sold to teenage girls actually reinforced ideas about their dependence on their fathers for money and the frivolity of their desires.

After World War II, girls were increasingly allowed to date boys without the supervision of parents or chaperones. But girls did not necessarily become alienated from their parents as a result of their newfound sexual and consumer autonomy, as is commonly believed. Indeed, there is ample evidence that relationships between girls and their parents actually took on heightened social meaning and renewed cultural emphasis in the 1950s and 1960s. During the postwar period, psychologists and sociologists began to study how parents acted as "sex role models" for their daughters, and how adult femininity developed out of childhood Oedipal experiences. The discovery of the psychological depth and developmental importance of girls' relationships with their parents contributed to new forms of familial intimacy and parent-child bonding.

As the SEXUALITY of teenage girls gained a certain amount of acceptance, social commentators and child experts began to worry more about younger girls. The age of the arrival of MENARCHE (the first menstrual period) had been declining since the mid-nineteenth century, with the average age dropping from just over the age of fifteen in 1850 to the age of thirteen by the early twentieth century. The seeming precocity of girls, and thus the potential erotic appeal of young girls to adult men, became a cultural preoccupation in the 1950s with the publication of Russian-born American author Vladimir Nabokov's famous novel LOLITA (1956) and American author Grace Metalious' blockbuster best-seller about the sexual escapades of youth, *Peyton Place* (1957).

The feminist movement of the late 1960s and 1970s shifted attention from the consumerism and sexuality of girls to

their inner lives, personal struggles, and educational needs. When Congress passed TITLE IX of the Higher Education Act in 1972, girls could compete in a range of SPORTS formerly reserved for boys. The Ms. Foundation's national "Take Our Daughters to Work Day," also established in 1972, focused public attention on girls' professional aspirations. Furthermore, the feminist scholar Carol Gilligan, in her groundbreaking book *In a Different Voice* (1982), provoked unprecedented debate about whether girls develop moral values and emotional strengths differently from boys.

Nonetheless, the problem of sexuality continues to dominate contemporary thinking about girls—of all races and classes—at the turn of the twenty-first century. Scholars, social commentators, and fiction writers have focused such topics as: sexual desire during adolescence; girls' sexual vulnerability; the threat of teen pregnancy; speculation about whether girls lie about sexual abuse; the ways in which girls are socially defined by their peers as "sluts" or "bad girls"; the suggestiveness of current teen and pre-teen fashions; and the extent to which girls are developing at earlier ages. The unrelenting cultural focus on girls' sexuality, though some of it may be well intended, has contributed to a perception that girls are defined above all by their sexual identities. Moreover, it is worth pondering whether the scale of fascination with girls in the recent past, particularly on the part of advertisers and the media, has been entirely to their benefit. It is indisputable, however, that over the course of the twentieth century, girlhood has become one of the most studied, privileged, and treasured—if not always genuinely protected— cultural experiences.

See also: **Baby-Sitters; Bobby Soxers; Boyhood; Dating; Gendering; Victory Girls.**

BIBLIOGRAPHY

Ariès, Philippe. 1962. *Centuries of Childhood.* Trans. Robert Baldick. New York: Alfred A. Knopf.

Demos, John. 1970. *A Little Commonwealth: Family Life in Plymouth Colony.* New York: Oxford University Press.

Devlin, Rachel. 1998. "Female Juvenile Delinquency and the Problem of Paternal Authority, 1941–1965." In *Delinquents and Debutantes: Twentieth Century Girls' Culture,* ed. Sheri Inness. New York: New York University Press.

Douglas, Susan J. 1994. *Where the Girls Are: Growing Up Female with the Mass Media.* New York: Three Rivers Press.

Fass, Paula S. 1977. *The Damned and the Beautiful: American Youth in the 1920s.* New York: Oxford University Press.

Fox-Genovese, Elizabeth. 1988. *Within The Plantation Household: Black and White Women in the Old South.* Chapel Hill: University of North Carolina Press.

Gilligan, Carol. 1982. *In A Different Voice: Psychological Theory and Women's Development.* Cambridge, MA: Harvard University Press.

Jones, Jacqueline. 1985. *Labor of Love, Labor of Sorrow: Black Women, Work and the Family, From Slavery to the Present.* New York: Basic Books.

Hunter, Jane. 2002. *How Young Ladies Became Girls: The Victorian Origins of American Girlhood.* New Haven, CT: Yale University Press.

Lamb, Sharon. 2002. *The Secret Lives of Girls: What Good Girls Really Do—Sex Play, Aggression and Their Guilt.* New York: Free Press.

Muncy, Robyn. 1991. *Creating a Female Dominion in American Reform, 1890–1935.* New York: Oxford University Press.

Peiss, Kathy. 1986. *Cheap Amusements: Working Women and Leisure in Turn-of-the-Century New York.* Philadelphia, PA: Temple University Press.

Pollock, Linda A. 1983. *Forgotten Children: Parent-Child Relations from 1500 to 1900.* London: Cambridge University Press.

Smith-Rosenberg, Caroll. 1975. "The Female World of Love and Ritual: Relations Between Women in Nineteenth-Century America." *Signs: Journal of Women in Culture and Society* 1: 1–30.

Sommerville, C. John. 1992. *The Discovery of Childhood in Puritan England.* Athens: University of Georgia Press.

Tanenbaum, Leora. 2000. *Slut! Growing up Female with a Bad Reputation.* New York: Perennial.

Walkerdine, Valerie. 1997. *Daddy's Girl: Young Girls and Popular Culture.* Cambridge, MA: Harvard University Press.

RACHEL DEVLIN

Girl Scouts

Girl Scouts of the USA, the largest voluntary organization for girls in America, is the only major group largely run by women ever since its inception. In 2003, there were 3.8 million Girl Scouts; more than fifty million women and girls have belonged to the organization since its founding on March 12, 1912. Furthermore, the World Association of Girl Guides and Girl Scouts (WAGGS), formed in 1921, comprises an international sisterhood of more than 8.5 million members in 144 countries.

Juliette Gordon Low brought Girl Scouting to her hometown of Savannah, Georgia, with a troop of just eighteen girls. She envisioned, however, that Girl Scouting would eventually be "for all the girls of America." Although Low was completely untrained in girls' work and in organizing a national movement, her wide social network helped the group grow steadily. Initially called Girl Guides as their counterparts were in England (a similar group started by Lord ROBERT BADEN-POWELL and his sister, Agnes Baden-Powell), by 1913 they changed their name to Girl Scouts. The new name was to be analogous to BOY SCOUTS, which had began in America in 1908.

From the outset, Girl Scouts offered a program that combined traditional domestic roles with practical feminism that enlarged girls' worlds and heralded a new day for women. For instance, while the Girl Scouts awarded badges for domestic activities such as cooking, laundering, and child care, they also taught girls a wide array of nontraditional skills, such as flying, semaphoring, and camping.

Although the Girl Scouts saw themselves and the Boy Scouts as allies, there were sometimes disagreements. For example, one of the Boy Scouts' executive directors, James West, abhorred the name Girl Scouts. Believing it detracted from his boys' masculinity, West fought for years to have the Girl Scouts merge with the Camp Fire Girls (a name he believed to be far more feminine) to become a unified organization called Camp Fire Girl Guides. His rationale was that a "girl is to guide and a boy is to scout." While the Girl Scouts opened new gender roles for girls, the Boy Scouts reinforced traditional male roles. Furthermore, the Boy Scouts remain more socially conservative, as evidenced by their leadership's continuing reluctance to extend membership to homosexuals, in contrast to the Girl Scouts' philosophy of "welcoming diversity."

As the founder of the Girl Scouts, Low correctly intuited what activities girls would enjoy. She envisioned an organization that would combine play, work, and healthy values to shape girls into active, modern women. The group participated in outdoor activities, camping, and sports, attracting girls and women with leadership qualities. Training offered by the Girl Scouts involved adult women from the beginning and was held in communities as well as on college campuses. Many women were drawn to the organization because it opened up opportunities for both volunteer and paid work. By the 1970s, the Girl Scouts was the largest employer of women in management positions in America.

As the organization grew, it employed paid professional staff. By 1920, the Girl Scouts began a publication department, printing program materials such as *The Leader*, a magazine for adult leaders, and *The Rally*, which quickly became *The American Girl*, for many years the largest magazine for teenage girls in America. Over time, the Girl Scout Handbooks and program changed, responding to world events and contemporary ideas about girl development.

The Girl Scout Promise and Law stayed constant, however; these statements formed the basis for the organization's moral training, urging girls to try their best to be helpful to all, to revere God, and to become active citizens and leaders. The philosophy "A Girl Scout is a Sister to every other Scout" often helped girls stretch their normal boundaries. The sisterhood promoted participation by girls with disabilities, which began as early as 1913. Some Girl Scout troops challenged racial divisions in their communities, although troops throughout the South were segregated until the 1960s.

During World War I, Girl Scouts witnessed its first growth surge, with girls responding patriotically to the war effort. Raising money by selling war bonds and rolling bandages led these girls into public work they had never done before. Some Girl Scout troops began selling home-baked cookies to raise money for the war. By the 1920s Girl Scout cookie sales had become a successful trademark fundraiser, with girls selling boxes of commercially baked cookies to defer their costs.

In response to the Depression during the 1930s and the subsequent need for opportunities for youth, Girl Scouts expanded its programs to include girls beyond the middle class. Outreach to Dust Bowl migrants, Native Americans on reservations, and inner-city girls marked the decade and accounted for some membership growth. During World War II, thousands of girls joined Scouting, again responding to the war effort. By 1945, membership stood at over one million girls.

Throughout the 1950s the organization continued to grow, but it focused more on traditional domestic skills than it had previously. Even so, Girl Scouting provided one of the few outlets for girls who wanted to participate in outdoor experiences and nontraditional activities. The organization also greatly expanded its outreach to its sister Girl Guides in countries overseas. This internationalism, inherent in Girl Scouting since its inception, inspired the Veterans of Foreign Wars to accuse the U.S. Girl Scouts of promoting communist sympathies. This patently absurd accusation led many Americans to question the virulent anticommunism of the period.

Like other youth organizations during the 1960s, the Girl Scouts began to lose members and see its relevance questioned. Racial issues, the countercultural youth movement, the Vietnam War, and the new feminist movement all challenged the organization to change and become more "modern." Although the organization moved to adapt its program and be more inclusive, African-American Girl Scouts called for fundamental changes and reform, which the organization struggled to accomplish with mixed success.

In the early 1970s, seeking to reverse the universal membership decline in youth organizations, the Camp Fire Girls, by now much smaller than the Girl Scouts, decided to add boys and rename itself Camp Fire. Boy Scouts voted to include girls in their high-school-aged Explorer Scouts. The Girl Scouts, however, declared themselves a "feminist organization," endorsed the Equal Rights Amendment in its first political stand ever, and voted to remain single-sex. By the 1980s, the Girl Scouts' membership resumed its growth.

In the twenty-first century, the Girl Scouts persists as a strong organization. Still run primarily by women, it continues to be innovative and responsive to national issues. For example, the "troops in prisons" program was initiated so that incarcerated mothers can participate with their daughters weekly in Scouting activities. Although it has evolved from the organization Low founded, the Girl Scouts remains imbedded in the fundamentals she espoused: teaching girls to play, work, and live by moral values.

See also: **Girlhood; Organized Recreation and Youth Groups.**

BIBLIOGRAPHY

Brown, Fern G. 1996. *Daisy and the Girl Scouts: The Story of Juliette Low.* Morton Grove, IL: Whitman.

Choate, Ann Hyde and Helen Ferris, eds. 1928. *Juliette Low and the Girl Scouts: The Story of an American Woman.* Garden City, NY: Doubleday.

Girl Scouts of the U.S.A. 1986. *Seventy-Five Years of Girl Scouting.* New York: Girl Scouts of the U.S.A.

Girl Scouts of the U.S.A. 1997. *Highlights in Girl Scouting, 1912–1996.* New York: Girl Scouts of the U.S.A.

Inness, Sherrie A. 1993. "Girl Scouts, Campfire Girls and Woodcraft Girls: The Ideology of Girls." In *Continuities in Popular Culture: The Present in the Past and the Past in the Present and Future,* ed. Ray B. Browne and Ronald Ambrosetti. Bowling Green, OH: Bowling Green State University Popular Press.

Jeal, Tim. 1990. *The Boy-Man: The Life of Lord Baden-Powell.* New York: Pantheon.

Rosenthal, Michael. 1984. *The Character Factory: Baden-Powell and the Origins of the Boy Scout Movement.* New York: Pantheon.

Shultz, Gladys Denny, and Daisy Gordon Lawrence. 1958. *Lady from Savannah: The Life of Juliette Gordon Low.* Philadelphia, PA: Lippincott.

Tedesco, Lauren. 1998. "Making a Girl Into a Scout: Americanizing Scouting for Girls." In *Delinquents and Debutantes: Twentieth Century American Girls' Cultures,* ed. Sherrie Inness. New York: New York University Press.

INTERNET RESOURCES

Boy Scouts of America. Available from <www.scouting.org>.

Camp Fire USA. Available from <www.campfire.org/start.asp>.

Girls Scouts of the USA. Available from <www.girlscouts.org>.

MARY LOGAN ROTHSCHILD

Girls' Schools

Although girls' schools existed well before the early modern period, in Europe and North America their development and diversification date back to the late eighteenth century. This development was in large part inspired by ENLIGHTENMENT debates about the importance of reason and education, which concerned both men and women. From the outset, girls' schools were almost always strictly divided along social lines—a feature that continued well into the twentieth century; working-class and peasant girls attended primary schools, where they received lessons in the rudiments, while middle-class and aristocratic girls received what was considered secondary education in the company of their peers. In both sorts of schools, lessons tended to emphasize women's distinct role in society, thereby contributing to maintaining them in positions of inferiority.

The expansion of girls' schooling over the past two hundred years, however, has brought a number of changes: first, the growth of primary schools for girls stimulated female LITERACY and opened professional opportunities for women as teachers. Thus·the feminization of teaching and the spread of girls' schools went hand in hand. Second, girls' secondary schools, often under the impetus of a feminist movement, gradually aligned themselves with male standards of excellence, preparing girls for the same exams and offering opportunities to pursue higher education. By the 1980s, the distinction between girls' and boys' schools had mostly disappeared, as coeducation had become the norm throughout the Western world. The virtual disappearance of girls' schools (except in the Catholic school system) has not eliminated the impact of gendered differences in education; instead these differences have become part of what is often referred to as a hidden curriculum, where teachers unconsciously encourage the gendered patterns of behavior and learning which were openly encouraged in the girls' schools of previous centuries.

The Spread of Girls' Schools (1750–1850)

A number of intellectuals strongly supported the expansion of girls' education in the late eighteenth century. In France, for example, the revolutionary philosopher the Marquis de Condorcet insisted in 1791 that "Instruction should be the same for women and men" while in Germany the philosopher Theodore von Hippel defended similar ideas. More commonly, the champions of girls' education in this period envisioned the development of separate girls' schools, and most writers focused on middle-class girls and women. In the United States, the republican essayist Judith Sargeant Murray and the physician and politician Benjamin Rush helped forge the concept of Republican Motherhood as they defended more rigorous education for women in order for them to assume their responsibilities in the new nation. In Europe figures such as Hannah More, the English pedagogue, heralded the emergence of a new domesticity within the middle classes, where women, as mothers and wives, were expected to rejuvenate private life but also to moralize public life through the lessons they provided their sons. A wide range of girls' boarding schools and ACADEMIES emerged in the early nineteenth century in order to help women assume these tasks more effectively within the private sphere.

In Europe most middle-class institutions for girls were relatively small, privately run structures where, for a fee, girls were given lessons in a relatively wide range of subjects: literature, history, geography, some natural sciences, foreign languages (but generally not Latin and Greek), and religion, as well as the indispensable female accomplishments (sewing, embroidery, painting, music, etc.). Prior to state involvement, these institutions were run by individual proprietors; by religious orders, particularly in Catholic countries; by trustees; and even at times by parents (which was the case for the Dottreskolen academy for girls in Copenhagen). Their longevity depended a great deal on individual ingenuity and economic resources.

Scholars have long ignored these institutions, considering them evanescent features of the urban social fabric or mere finishing schools; recent historical research, however, emphasizes the diversity of these schools and the ways they contributed to building a network of girls' institutions. Indeed, a few institutions in both Europe and North America achieved long-lasting fame and recognition and served as models for other schools throughout the Western world. As early as 1686 Madame de Maintenon created a school for noble girls at Saint Cyr, France, while in Saint Petersburg, Russia, beginning in 1764, the Smolny Institute for Noble Girls offered an example of enlightened education for the elite. The Napoleonic creations, the Legion of Honor schools for the daughters of his military officers, were among the most renowned girls' schools in Europe, inspiring similar creations in Germany, Russia, and Italy. Placed under the headship of the well-known educator and pedagogue Jeanne Campan, the first institution at Ecouen introduced a rigorous curriculum for girls that went far beyond the modest academic ambitions of many private finishing schools of the period. In northern Europe influential women educators, such as the Dutch headmistress Anna Barbera Van Meerten-Schilperoort or the German Betty Gleim, opened schools and published books defending girls' education. In the United States, educators such as Emma Hart Willard and Catharine Beecher contributed significantly to improving the quality of girls' education thanks to the examples offered by their renowned institutions: Willard's Troy Female Seminary flourished between 1821 and 1872, while Beecher's Hartford Female Seminary acquired national fame thanks to her indefatigable energy in promoting women's role in teaching and education.

While separation of the sexes almost universally characterized secondary schools, elementary education was often mixed, notably in Protestant countries. In Catholic countries, however, efforts were made to separate the sexes, which often meant that girls' schools simply did not exist. This was not the case in Catholic Belgium or France, however, where separate elementary girls' schools grew apace over the course of the century, less as a result of state involvement than of religious initiatives. The 1850 French Falloux Law required communes with a population of 800 to open a separate school for girls, but even in the public sector religious teachers far outnumbered lay ones: in 1863, 70 percent of the teachers in public elementary schools were nuns. In England, the voluntary system of education led to the emergence of a variety of institutions attended by working-class girls: dame schools, SUNDAY SCHOOLS, Church of England National Schools, and schools founded by Unitarians. While these institutions were not systematically separated by sex, they certainly reinforced gender differences through their focus on religion and sewing for girls. Similarly, in North America the development of an URBAN SCHOOL SYSTEM generally integrated girls and boys in the same schools except in private schools that were oriented to the elite.

Catholic teaching orders and Catholic churches provided an important impetus for the spread of girls' primary schools throughout the Western world. This began as early as the

Catholic Counter-Reformation in the seventeenth century, when the Ursulines in particular devoted themselves to the education of girls. In Canada in the 1660s, Mère de l'Incarnation ran a boarding school for both French and "savage" girls. Often combining both teaching and nursing services, congregations such as the Daughters of Charity opened schools throughout cities and in rural areas, offering poor girls an education in the basics—reading, writing and arithmetic—in addition to religion. The spread of schools for lower-class girls was not motivated by any concern for promoting greater equality between the sexes. Instead, Sunday schools, day schools, and charity schools were all concerned with offering girls the lessons that would best suit them for their future responsibilities. Thus, the schools promoted minimal literacy while emphasizing religious lessons, since mothers were expected to transmit the first elements of religious faith to their infant children.

Diversification and Professionalization (1850–1900)

By the second half of the nineteenth century the numbers of girls' schools in Europe and North America had considerably expanded. More significantly, however, the rise of a self-consciously feminist women's movement placed girls' education at the forefront of its demands for change. These demands included better teacher training and more rigorous exams for girls and women as part of a concern with improving the professional character of girls' education as well as expanding the range of career opportunities such an education would offer. By the mid-nineteenth century, girls' schools no longer focused so exclusively on forming girls into good wives and mothers. They also envisioned more directly women's participation in the public sphere as workers and "lady" professionals.

A number of remarkable women around mid-century contributed not only to improving private schools for girls but also to the emergence of higher, or secondary, girls' schools. In Great Britain women such as Frances Buss, Dorothea Beale, and Emily Davies, and the Irishwoman Isabelle Tod all campaigned to improve the quality of girls' secondary education, and a number of reformed girls' institutions appeared to answer a broader social demand for a more rigorous education for girls: North London Collegiate School, Cheltenham Ladies' College, and the Ladies Institute of Belfast, as well as a number of "public" schools for girls (Roedean, St Leonards, etc.) modeled on the lines of male PUBLIC SCHOOLS, which were, in fact, private schools. Davies in particular fought to have women gain access to the Cambridge Local Examination on the same basis as boys; these prestigious exams testified to the quality of a pupil's secondary examination and opened doors for a professional future. In 1866, the Frenchwoman Julie-Victoire Daubié published an analysis, which was widely commented upon, *La Femme Pauvre*, emphasizing the need to improve girls' education at all levels. In Germany in 1890, the moderate feminist Helene Lange founded a Women's Teachers' Association and helped establish a *Realkurse* for women. This was a two-year program in mathematics, science, economics, history, modern languages, and Latin. The concern here was to give girls the knowledge necessary for further studies. All these endeavors were largely for upper and middle-class girls.

Trans-Atlantic and intercontinental European travel during this period encouraged the emergence of a common set of goals in the promotion of girls' education, even if the nature of the schools that developed took very different forms. The development of coeducational high schools in the United States as well as the early emergence of WOMEN'S COLLEGES (Vassar opened in 1865, Wellesley and Smith in 1875) attracted considerable attention among foreign pedagogues, even if neither model provoked many European imitations in the period prior to 1900; indeed, in Europe very few university-level female institutions ever developed. Instead the most remarkable changes involved the progressive development of secondary schools for girls, particularly within the public sector. In 1880, when the French state finally established public secondary education for girls in *collèges* and LYCÉES, the promoter of the law, Camille Sée, could offer a panoramic sweep of the Western world, noting the presence of serious secondary schools for girls in Russia (the first girls' *gymnasia* appeared in 1858), in Belgium (Isabelle Gatti de Gamond founded a model secondary school in 1864), in Austria (*Mädchenlyzeen* were created after 1870); even in Greece a private institution known as the *Arsakion* offered secondary education as well as teacher training. James Albisetti has argued that the German model of secular secondary girls' schools, which were already widespread in the 1860s, provided the impetus for many of these national developments; immediately after the French law, Italian reformers introduced the first state-run *istituti femminile*. In the United States and Canada, higher girls' schools did not vanish with the spread of coeducation, as Catholic families continued to prefer the single-sex environment of female academies or seminaries, such as those run by the Ladies of the Sacred Heart or the Sisters of Saint Joseph.

The appearance of more academically ambitious institutions for girls also encouraged developments in teacher training and certification throughout Europe and North America, which contributed to the improvement of elementary education for girls. The creation of normal schools (teachers' colleges) for girls accelerated notably in the second half of the nineteenth century, often thanks to the dynamism of religious organizations: in England the first normal school for women was founded by the Anglican National Society in the early 1840s (Whitelands Training College); a Catholic teaching order founded the first French normal school in 1838. Increasingly, however, the state also intervened, providing teacher training for girls throughout Europe: in 1858 in Piedmont, in 1860 in Florence, in 1866 in Belgium and Portugal, in 1869 in the Austro-Hungarian empire, in 1879 in France. The growth in normal schools for women both encouraged and accompanied a tendency throughout the Western world—the feminization of the elementary teaching profession. By 1851 in Quebec, 50 percent of government schoolteachers were women, and the proportion was higher in the United States. This tendency strongly accelerated in the twentieth century.

Transformations in the Twentieth Century

By the end of the nineteenth century, northern European women had largely overcome their educational disadvantage with respect to literacy. (In the United States, male and female literacy rates were nearly equal by 1850 among white men and women). This reflected the emergence of national systems of public education and an increasing recognition that girls as well as boys needed to be literate in an industrializing society. In Mediterranean countries, however, girls' schools were notably few and far between, contributing to high female illiteracy rates in Catholic Italy (54 percent of Italian women were illiterate in 1901); female illiteracy rates were also high in Ireland and Russia.

In 1900 social class continued to determine whether girls pursued only elementary schooling or went on to secondary education, but increasingly intermediate levels of education emerged, some of which catered to girls. In France, higher primary schools for girls multiplied, offering more vocationally oriented education. The emergence of scientific approaches to domestic economy or social work, which were seen as feminine subjects, spurred the creation of either special classes for girls or such institutions as the Dutch School for Social Work in Amsterdam in 1898 and Alice Salomon's German equivalent. KINDERGARTEN teaching, in particular, generated the creation of vocational training institutions, generally influenced by the ideas of FRIEDRICH FROEBEL. Nineteenth-century institutions such as the German, *Hoschschule für das weibliche Geschlect* or the French *Ecole Pape Carpentier*, spawned numerous imitations in the twentieth century. American workers' organizations also developed a range of innovative educational programs, such as the Bryn Mawr Summer School for Women Workers, which was supported by trade unions and was aimed at providing working women with training in economics, labor history, and public speaking, along with classes on literature, art, music, and women's health issues.

While girls' schools initially developed to provide girls with the lessons they needed to fill their role as wives and mothers adequately, the impulse toward maintaining separate institutions began to fade as women's work opportunities expanded. The exception to this trend was where strong religious or moral considerations prevailed, most notably in Catholic countries: in Ireland in the early 1980s, over half of all secondary schools in the public and private sectors combined were single-sex. Indeed, by the 1980s in most Western countries girls not only attended schools at the same rate as boys, they often performed far better academically. Nonetheless, women's access to the same educational opportunities as available to men has not redressed persistent inequalities in the professions, stimulating in part the current debates in many countries—especially in Germany, the United States, and Ireland, and France—about the need to return to single-sex schooling in order to give girls confidence in areas such as the sciences, where men continue to dominate.

See also: **Coeducation and Same-Sex Schooling; Parochial Schools; Private and Independent Schools.**

BIBLIOGRAPHY

Albisetti, James. 1993. "The Feminization of Teaching in the Nineteenth Century: A Comparative Perspective." *History of Education* 22: 253–263.

Albisetti, James. 1988. *Schooling German Girls and Women: Secondary and Higher Education in the Nineteenth Century.* Princeton, NJ: Princeton University Press.

Cullen, Mary, ed. 1987. *Girls Don't Do Honours: Irish Women in Education in the Nineteenth and Twentieth Centuries.* Dublin: Argus.

Eisenmann, Linda, ed. 1998. *Historical Dictionary of Women's Education in the United States.* Westport, CT: Greenwood Press.

Fahmy-Eid, Nadia, Micheline Dumont, and Francine Barry, eds. 1983. *Maîtresses de maison, maîtresses d'école: femmes, famille et éducation dans l'histoire du Québec.* Montréal: Boréal Express.

Gold, Carol. 1996. *Educating Middle Class Daughters. Private Girls Schools in Copenhagen, 1790–1820.* Copenhagen: Royal Library / Museum Tusculanum Press.

Hunt, Felicity, ed. 1987. *Lessons for Life. The Schooling of Girls and Women 1850–1950.* Oxford, UK: B. Blackwell.

Kerber, Linda. 1980. *Women of the Republic: Intellect and Ideology in Revolutionary America.* Chapel Hill: University of North Carolina Press.

Kleinau, Elke, and Claudia Opitz, eds. 1996. *Geschichte der Mädchen- und Frauenbildung*, 2 vols. New York: Campus Verlag.

Mayeur, Françoise. 1979. *L'éducation des filles en France au XIXe siècle.* Paris: Hachette.

Prentice, Alison, and Margert Theobald, eds. 1991. *Women who Taught: Perspectives on the History of Women and Teaching.* Toronto: University of Toronto Press.

Purvis, June. 1991. *A History of Women's Education in England.* Milton Keynes, UK: Open University Press.

Rogers, Rebecca. 1995. "Boarding Schools, Women Teachers, and Domesticity: Reforming Girls' Education in the First Half of the Nineteenth Century." *French Historical Studies* 19: 153–181.

Van Essen, Mineke. 1993. "'New' Girls and Traditional Womanhood: Girlhood and Education in the Netherlands in the Nineteenth and Twentieth Century." *Paedagogica Historica* 29: 125–151.

Woody, Thomas. 1929. *A History of Women's Education in the United States*, 2 vols. New York: Science Press.

REBECCA ROGERS

Girls' Sports. *See* Title IX and Girls' Sports.

Globalization

Globalization refers to the growing interconnectedness in economic, cultural, and political life. The use of the term has increased since the 1980s to reflect the greater ease with which people, products, information, and images move across space and, consequently, the ability of events in one part of the world to more easily affect circumstances in others. Globalization is also linked to the remarkable ascendancy of free-market philosophy and practice worldwide. The nature and extent of these changes is the subject of extensive debate. Central questions surrounding globalization are whether the nation-state can maintain its position as the principal institution of economic and political governance in the face of rapid transnational flows, and the degree to which cultures can remain relatively autonomous.

The Expansion of Global Markets

In uneven but persistent ways, technological developments have tended to reduce the "friction of space" and to link markets in labor, finance, and commodities more closely. Children, as consumers of commodity goods, health-care, and education, and in some cases as producers of commodities, have been acutely affected by what some people term the "shrinking" of the globe.

It is important to note that deepening economic and social integration, captured by the term globalization, is not unprecedented. Mercantilism and the Atlantic slave trade from the sixteenth to the eighteenth century and European colonialism, peaking at the end of the nineteenth, connected vast numbers of people across the globe; by the end of the nineteenth century, for instance, Britain's territory had been enlarged by a factor of forty through colonial plunder. From the mid-1970s, however, there occurred what David Harvey, in *The Condition of Postmodernity*, describes as a new round of "time–space compression." Intense economic restructuring signaled the collapse of the post–World War II development model consisting of Keynesian state-intervention and mass-production work methods. Responding to economic crisis, Prime Minister Margaret Thatcher in the United Kingdom in 1979 and President Ronald Reagan in the United States in 1980 began reforms aimed at freeing the power of the market to restore prosperity. Policies emphasized were privatization, cuts to government expenditures, and tax breaks to businesses. At the same time, new forms of communication, especially the personal computer and the Internet, made contact everywhere faster.

In the 1980s some regions in the Third World, under pressure through structural adjustment policies to earn foreign exchange to pay heavy debt, moved from exporting primary commodities, a pattern set by colonialism, towards manufacturing labor-intensive industrial goods for a global production system. Multinationals were central to this process. They became closely linked to globalization not only through aggressive advertising—promoting global icons such as Nike or Coke—but by relocating labor-intensive industries into the Third World to reduce costs. The other important international institution driving these changes was the World Trade Organization (WTO), which succeeded, with a larger scope, the General Agreement in Trade and Tariffs (GATT) in 1995. The WTO encouraged international trade by promoting reductions in trade tariffs.

The seemingly inexorable expansion of the market, reinforced by the collapse of communism at the end of the 1980s, made alternatives to capitalism appear increasingly unfeasible. Nevertheless, the perceived negative social effects of deregulation elicited a wave of criticism against globalization at the turn of the century. The 1997 East Asian financial crisis, fueled by massive currency speculation, suggested that markets could create not simply prosperity but great vulnerabilities. Moreover, antiglobalization protests at the 1999 Seattle summit of the World Trade Organization and subsequent international meetings focused further attention on the detrimental social effects of globalization.

Child Labor

The growing volume of industrial production in the Third World gave the issue of child labor a high profile from the 1980s. In contrast to similar concerns in the nineteenth and early twentieth century, however, child labor was framed primarily as a global and not simply a national problem. Despite the attention given to children working in export industries such as garments and rugs, the International Labour Organization (ILO) reports that most child labor in fact takes place in agriculture, domestic service, and the informal sector. Child workers in export industries probably amount to no more than 5 percent of total child labor, although the trend has been toward an increase in this figure. Another, less reported, link between globalization and child labor is through structural adjustment, which often results in cuts to social expenditure and reductions in formal work opportunities. In these circumstances, children's earnings can be used to supplement household incomes, particularly when education becomes unaffordable because of increased fees that result from cuts in education budgets.

These broad trends, however, need to be differentiated regionally and by the type of work that children undertake. Massive debt crisis and political instability largely excluded sub-Saharan Africa from investment in industrial production. China, although exporting large quantities of labor-intensive goods, does not have a significant reported history of child labor. In fact, at least half of all child laborers work in southern Asia and Southeast Asia, with a large amount of bonded labor (labor to pay off debts) reported in India, Pakistan, Nepal, and Thailand. Child labor can also encompass child soldiers as well as the survival activities of street children. The term *street children* refers to children whose usual home is the street even if they may still have relatives. According to Human Rights Watch, they are frequently subjected to physical abuse by police or criminally charged with offenses such as loitering, vagrancy, or petty theft. In some countries, participation in wars can offer children respect and material benefits. An estimated 300,000 children under the age of eighteen are involved in conflicts worldwide.

A related set of literature suggests that children's bodies have themselves increasingly become global commodities. According to Michelle Kuo, approximately 60 percent of Thailand's tourists visit solely to engage in sexual activities, including those with children. To keep the Thai sex trade "respectable" for international participants, those prostitutes found to be HIV positive are evicted to lower-class brothels, and younger children are recruited from Burma and China to replace them: the younger they are, the less likely they are thought to be infected with HIV. Similarly, Nancy Scheper-Hughes links economic globalism to an expanding trade in body organs, including those from children. Desperately poor individuals in BRAZIL, CHINA, INDIA, and other countries are forced to sell body parts in order to survive. Like sexual services, these organs follow a path from poor to rich, often from the Third World to the First World.

Global Child Standards

Clearly globalization, despite suggesting a process of homogenization, produces highly uneven patterns of development. A countervailing force against growing divergences is the institutionalization of global human rights standards for children. This is evidenced by the 1989 UN CONVENTION ON THE RIGHTS OF THE CHILD (ratified by all but two countries: Somalia and the United States), and the ILO's 1999 Convention 182 that seeks to end the "worst forms" of child labor, such as debt bondage, the trafficking or sale of children, CHILD PROSTITUTION, or work harmful to the health of children. Efforts to promote CHILDREN'S RIGHTS are also assisted by campaigns that stretch across nations. In 1996, for instance, trade unions and nongovernmental organizations (NGOs) launched the "foul-ball" campaign that successfully forced the Federation of International Football Associations (FIFA) to refuse to endorse soccer balls sewn by children. Particularly in the wake of antiglobalization protests in Seattle, transnational NGOs such as Amnesty International and Human Rights Watch have become key sources of information on issues such as child labor and child soldiers. They have been among the quickest organizations to embrace the Internet which, through listservs (forums for quickly exchanging information by e-mail among a large group of people), is used to coordinate global campaigning strategies regardless of the physical location of members. At the touch of a button, global activists can now be in almost continuous contact.

Global Identities

Whereas classic anthropology represented culture as being static and bounded, the framework of cultural globalization stresses how culture is produced through widening and deepening interconnections. Between 1980 and 1991, the global trade in goods with cultural content—such as printed matter, literature, music, visual arts, cinema, and photography—almost tripled. Worldwide, parents face intense pressure from their children to buy goods with global brand names. Although global icons are, in fact, typically produced in the United States, new global styles such as world music also celebrate cultures from outside of the dominant regions. With dramatic telecommunication advances, images are projected almost instantly around the world, expanding the geography through which childhood is constructed and experienced. In recognizing that identity is formed through more widely stretched interconnections, work on youth has moved away from long-established frameworks of subculture or deviance to show how the local, national, and global are intermeshed to produce children's identities. Icons such as Madonna, Britney Spears, and the Spice Girls, and technologies such as the Internet are the most potent symbols of these processes. Concerned about this globalization of consumption, however, the United Nations Educational, Scientific and Cultural Organization (UNESCO) and the United Nations Environment Programme (UNEP) are among groups actively engaged in research and interventions that promote more sustainable consumption behavior among youth.

See also: **Child Labor in Developing Countries; Consumer Culture; International Organizations; Juvenile Justice: International; Soldier Children: Global Human Rights Issues.**

BIBLIOGRAPHY

Gereffi, Gary. 1995. "Global Production Systems and Third World Development." In *Global Change, Regional Response: The New International Context of Development,* ed. Barbara Stallings. Cambridge, UK: Cambridge University Press.

Griffin, Christine. 2001. "Imagining New Narratives of Youth: Youth Research, the 'New Europe' and Global Culture." *Childhood* 8, no. 2: 147–166.

Harvey, David. 1989. *The Condition of Postmodernity.* Oxford: Basil Blackwell.

Hecht, Tobias. 1998. *At Home in the Street: Street Children of Northeast Brazil.* Cambridge: Cambridge University Press.

Held, David, Anthony Mcgrew, David Goldblatt, et al. 1999. *Global Transformations: Politics, Economics, and Culture.* Oxford: Blackwell.

Hirst, Paul, and Grahame Thompson. 1996. *Globalization in Question: The International Economy and the Possibilities of Governance.* Oxford: Blackwell.

Kuo, Michelle. 2000. "Asia's Dirty Secret." *Harvard International Review* 22, no. 2: 42–45.

Myers, William E. 1999. "Considering Child Labour: Changing Terms, Issues, and Actors at the International Level." *Childhood* 6, no. 1: 13–26.

Ohmae, Kenichi. 1990. *The Borderless World: Power and Strategy in the Interlinked Economy.* London: Collins.

Polanyi, Karl. 2001 [1944]. *The Great Transformation.* Boston: Beacon Press.

Scheper-Hughes, Nancy. 2000. "The Global Traffic in Human Organs." *Current Anthropology* 41, no. 2: 191–224.

Scheper-Hughes, Nancy, and Carolyn Sargent. 1998. *Small Wars: The Cultural Politics of Childhood*. Berkeley: University of California Press.

Seabrook, Jeremy. 1998. "Children of the Market: Effect of Globalization on Lives of Children." *Race and Class* 39, no. 4: 37–49.

Skelton, Tracey, and Gill Valentine. 1998. *Cool Places: Geographies of Youth Culture*. London: Routledge.

United National Development Program. 1999. *Human Development Report*. Oxford: Oxford University Press.

Weissman, Robert. 1997. "Stolen Youth: Brutalized Children, Globalization, and the Campaign to End Child Labor." *Multinational Monitor* 18, nos. 1–2: 10–17.

INTERNET RESOURCES

Global March. 2002. Available from <www.globalmarch.org>.

Human Rights Watch. 2001. Available from <www.hrw.org/children/street.htm>.

International Labour Organization. 2002. Available from <www.ilo.org/public/english/standards/ipec/index.htm>.

UNICEF. 2003. Available from <www.unicef.org>.

MARK HUNTER

Godparents

In the early Christian church, BAPTISM was only intended for adults. Their "godparents" were witnesses and vouched for the person's commitment, as expressed by the Latin legal term *sponsor*. As early as the end of the second century, baptism for infants appeared in Christian communities; the practice was believed to chase away the evil spirits present in every newborn baby. At the end of the fourth century, Saint Augustine enforced the rule of child baptism. At the time, parents were their own children's godparents. Between the sixth and eighth centuries, as child baptism became more widespread in Europe, the idea spread that for a child to have a spiritual rebirth, it needed to have new parents. Godparenting by parents was abandoned and even forbidden by the Mayence Council of 819, a law that endures to this day. A spiritual relationship, quite distinct from a blood relationship, is therefore created. The Church gives a it very specific religious goal: to ensure the Christian education of the child.

The metaphor of baptism as a second birth was expressed concretely in the beliefs and customary practices that made up the godparenting ceremony. Godfathers and godmothers were supposed to re-create the child and pass along some of their own personal qualities. Spiritual heredity was passed on in the NAMING of the godchild, in observance of prescribed customs or prohibitions, and through the giving of ritual gifts. These might include coins, medals, or crosses, cups, or silverware, first shoes, and first underwear for boys or earrings for girls. It was the duty of the godparents to help their godchildren become accomplished men and women until the child's marriage, which marked the end and the crowning of their ritual role. This relationship was considered sacred and was exhibited in the respect the godchild showed the godparents. The godchild's obligations reflected those of the godparents, and they were considered to be linked into the afterlife. Through baptism, the godparent opened eternal life to the godchild, and in return the godchild found favor and approbation for the godparent's soul in heaven.

The sharing of a child's double-birth created ties of co-parenthood between parents and godparents, the Christian form of ritual fraternities. This friendship was considered sacred, "to the life, to the death," with obligations of solidarity. Parents and godparents called each other "co-mother" and "co-father," addressed each other formally with mutual respect, and were forbidden to have sexual contact with one another, at the risk of committing INCEST. Such sexual prohibitions transformed the relationship into a spiritual parenting, considered superior to biological parenting. A sexual prohibition concerning a godfather and his goddaughter was enacted by Justinian in 530, and did not disappear in the West until 1983. In 692, the Council of Byzantium extended this restriction to the goddaughter's mother, and this lasted until 1917.

In medieval Europe, godparenting relations therefore created a network of friends, whether the godparent was chosen from the same social circle or among more prominent people (clergymen, nobles, or bourgeois) whose reputations were measured by the number of godchildren they had. In this case, their relationships were similar to those of patronage. Among Joan of Arc's eight godmothers, one was the wife of the mayor of Domremy, another the wife of the court clerk, and one of her four godfathers was town prosecutor with her father. Co-parents among Florentine merchants during the fifteenth century were useful politically, and mostly appeared in groups of two or three. But the record is held by a child who was given twenty-two godfathers and three godmothers in 1445. The Council of Trent (1545–1563) limited the number of spiritual parents to two godfathers and one godmother for boys, and two godmothers and one godfather for girls. It also limited the sexual prohibitions that had proliferated throughout the Middle Ages.

Though the close relationship between godparents and parents endured in southern Europe and South America, where ethnologists have studied it exhaustively, it slowly disappeared in western Europe during the Renaissance. First among the aristocracy, and then in the other social groups, only one godfather and godmother were chosen from the immediate family, one belonging to the father's family and the other to the mother's. In France the custom was that the eldest child should have his or her paternal grandfather as a godfather, and his or her maternal grandmother as a godmother. For the second born it would be the opposite (maternal grandfather, paternal grandmother). For later children, or if one of the grandparents had already died, the parents' brothers and brothers-in-law, then their sisters and sisters-in-law would be chosen, keeping a balance between maternal and paternal lines. The youngest children's godparents were often their own older siblings. This tying of parental spirituality to biological parenting—characteristic of western Europe—is related, among other things, to an imperative shared by many societies: that of having one's offspring named after their ancestors. Homonymy between godfathers and godsons first appeared in western Europe, in contrast with the Balkans, where godfathers were most often chosen outside the family. There a godfather would not name his godson after himself: the family would choose a first name for the child.

Today, even though practicing Christians are a minority in Europe, close to two-thirds of Christian children are christened in France before the age of two, and the proportions are higher in Spain and Italy. Often without going as far as baptizing the child, parents will designate a godfather and a godmother. A majority of children are thus still given godfathers and godmothers who are expected to stand in for the parents should they die. This commitment, which became widespread in the second half of the nineteenth century, was then and remains now largely unfulfilled, although starting in the eighteenth century, the law stipulated that orphans would be placed with a family member designated by the family. The tradition continues to favor choosing godfathers and godmothers from among close relatives or close friends, always considering the balance between maternal and paternal lines. The choice of a godparent generally creates emotion and gratitude in proportion to the importance ascribed to this symbolic gift of a child. It allows a family to transform a close friend into a relative, and relatives into friends. Often, privileged ties of complicity and affection develop between godparents and their godchildren. In the framework of the varying contemporary family configurations typical of Western societies, godparenting appears as a privileged, choice-based relationship created for the protection of the child. It could not enjoy such vitality in modern secular societies if it did not continue to convey values embedded in more than fifteen centuries of history.

See also: **Catholicism; Parenting.**

BIBLIOGRAPHY

Fine, Agnès. 1994. *Parrains, marraines. La parenté spirituelle en Europe.* Paris: Fayard.

Fine, Agnès. 1997. "Parrainage et marrainage dans la société française contemporaine." *Lien Social et Politiques—RIAC* 37: 157–170.

Gudeman, Stephen. 1971. "The Compadrazgo as a Reflection of the Natural and Spiritual Person." *Proceedings of the Royal Anthropological Institute* 45–71.

Héritier-Augé, Françoise, and Elisabeth Copet-Rougier, eds. 1995. *La parenté spirituelle. Textes rassemblés et présentés par Françoise Héritier-Augé et Elisabeth Copet-Rougier.* Paris: Archives contemporaines.

Jussen, Bernhard. 1992. "Le parrainage à la fin du Moyen-Age: savoir public, attentes théologiques et usages sociaux." *Annales ESC* 2: 467–502.

Klapisch-Zuber, Christiane. 1985. "'Kin, Friends and Neighbors': The Urban Territory of a Merchant Family in 1400." In *Women, Family and Ritual in Renaissance Italy* by Christian Klapisch-Zuber, p. 68–93. Chicago: University of Chicago Press.

Klapisch-Zuber, Christiane. 1990. *La maison et le nom.* Paris: Ed. de l'EHESS.

Klapisch-Zuber, Christiane. 1992. "Au péril des commères. L'alliance spirituelle par les femmes à Florence." *Femmes, Mariages, lignages. XIIè–XIVè siècles. Mélanges offerts à Georges Duby.* Brussels: De Boeck-Wesmaël.

Lynch, Joseph. 1986. *Godparents and Kinship in Early Medieval Europe.* Princeton, NJ: Princeton University Press.

Mintz, Sydney, and Eric Wolf. 1950. "An Analysis of Ritual Coparenthood." *Southwestern Journal of Anthropology* 6: 341–368.

AGNÈS FINE

Grammar School

Grammar schools have their roots in the medieval monastic and cathedral Latin grammar schools of western and central Europe. In preparation for the priesthood, pupils in such schools acquired a facility with the Latin syllables, words, and rules of grammar necessary to lead religious worship. Over time, particularly in Elizabethan England, these schools developed into institutions that educated future leaders of church and state. The curriculum was narrowly classical and humanistic, emphasizing the reading, writing, and speaking of Latin and providing an elementary knowledge of Greek and occasionally Hebrew. This course of study prepared pupils for higher education and stood in contrast to that of petty schools, which provided rudimentary instruction in reading and writing in the vernacular.

Grammar schools were formally introduced in the North American colonies with the founding of the Boston Latin School in 1635. This school accepted pupils, generally beginning at seven or eight years of age, who had previously received instruction in English. Pedagogy consisted of disciplined memorization and recitation and the curriculum was again comprised of Latin and the classics, becoming more precisely defined over the next several decades by the entrance requirements to Harvard College. Graduates usually completed their studies in seven years.

As in England, colonial grammar schools were heavily reliant upon tuition, resulting in a student population drawn primarily from the upper classes. In 1647, however, the General Court of Massachusetts, motivated by the Protestant conviction that all individuals should be able to read the Scriptures, passed the Old Deluder Satan Act, legally requiring towns of one hundred families or more to establish grammar schools. Over the next ten years, all eight towns of this size complied with the Act.

During the second half of the seventeenth century, the number of colonial grammar schools increased in response to similar laws throughout New England. As they did so, however, the character of these schools also changed, typically at the insistence of the communities that supported them. Grammar schools were compelled to expand curricula to remain competitive with newly developing ACADEMIES, which were more utilitarian and offered a vocational program for children of the growing middle class. By 1750, many grammar schools offered courses in arithmetic, geography, history, and even bookkeeping.

During the 1800s, in spite of this broadening curriculum the increasing availability of common or public schooling further limited the appeal of the grammar school. Its name, however, synonymous with elite, college preparatory education, was adopted by public schools as they began a system of age grading, separating younger students from older ones. Primary schools were established for children approximately five to nine years of age, corresponding with grades one through four. Intermediate or grammar schools were developed for students ten to fourteen years of age, corresponding with grades five through eight. By 1900, these two programs were united into a single, eight-year elementary school, also referred to as grammar school, which became the most prevalent type of school in the United States.

See also: **Aristocratic Education in Europe; High School; Gymnasium Schooling; Latin School; Lycée.**

BIBLIOGRAPHY

Butts, R. Freeman. 1947. *A Cultural History of Education: Reassessing Our Educational Traditions.* Ed. H. Benjamin. New York: McGraw-Hill.

Cremin, Lawrence. 1970. *American Education: The Colonial Experience, 1607–1783.* New York: Harper and Row.

Cremin, Lawrence. 1980. *American Education: The National Experience, 1783–1876.* New York: Harper and Row.

Middlekauff, Robert. 1963. *Ancients and Axioms: Secondary Education in Eighteenth-Century New England.* New Haven, CT: Yale University Press.

Noble, Stuart G. 1961. *A History of American Education,* 2nd ed. New York: Holt, Rinehart and Winston.

CHARLES DORN

Grandparents

The historical experience of grandparenthood reflects the influence of a wide range of social and cultural factors. Grandparent-grandchild relationships develop within multiple intersecting contexts. These include demographic variables, social structures and norms, cultural images of the family, gender, class; race, ethnicity, and location. Prior to the middle of the twentieth century, social scientists and historians rarely focused on grandparenthood as a distinct topic, but since the late twentieth century a growing body of empirical research has examined various aspects of the relationship between grandparents and grandchildren. This work has documented both direct and indirect ways in which grandparents can influence grandchildren positively (e.g., as advocates, advisors, motivators, mentors, and transmitters of ethnic and religious traditions) and negatively (e.g., as purveyors of unsolicited child-rearing advice that may foster intergenerational family conflict). Reciprocal influences from grandchildren to grandparents have also been identified. While most of the research has focused on grandmothers, some work has also concentrated on grandfathers.

No comprehensive historical analysis of the role of grandparents in individual children's lives has been attempted, but research on the history of aging has addressed aspects of grandparenthood in the past. Several studies suggest that grandparenthood in North America changed significantly from the colonial period to the end of the twentieth century. Although they differ with regard to the chronology of the transition, these studies argue that changes in the dominant cultural images and in the material circumstances of aging adults reduced the elderly from a traditional position of authority and esteem to one of obsolescence and dependence, and eventually brought them independence and autonomy. Furthermore, this transformation also altered the emotional condition of the aged, moving the balance between respect and affection in intergenerational relationships toward a new emphasis on LOVE and companionship between parents and children, and thus between grandparents and grandchildren. However, other work has challenged both the idea of a drastic change in attitudes toward old age and the notion that longevity automatically conferred honor and power on the elderly in early America. These conflicting views highlight the complexity of the historical study of old age and of the effort to locate grandparent-grandchild relationships in historical perspective.

Early American Grandparents

Although religious and cultural prescriptions stressed respect for the elderly and emphasized intergenerational familial obligations during the colonial and post-Revolutionary periods, grandparents, particularly grandfathers, exercised economic and social control primarily through their ownership of land in an agricultural society. Even when offspring married and established their own households, as long as they remained dependent on their parents' assets the latter maintained authority in the family. This situation changed if children migrated to another area or became financially independent. Only a small minority of the elderly lived with children and grandchildren; co-residence usually reflected necessity—illness, helplessness, and in the case of women, widowhood—rather than personal preference.

The characteristic Western demographic pattern of high mortality, high fertility, and late age of marriage determined that, unlike their twentieth-century counterparts, few adults in earlier American society experienced grandparenthood as a stage of life separate from active parenthood. Short life expectancies meant that grandparenthood was a rare experience altogether in seventeenth-century Chesapeake society, although grandparents played an increasingly important role in eighteenth-century Southern families. In contrast, in early New England settlers survived to old age in larger numbers than elsewhere in the colonies. Longer life expectancies and the tendency for women to marry at a younger age than men meant that few survived to experience the maturity and marriage of all their offspring, and it was not unusual for the birth of late children and early grandchildren to occur simultaneously. Demographic records from New England indicate that first- or second-born children were likely to know all of their grandparents in early childhood, and perhaps to have two or three surviving grandparents in adolescence, while their younger siblings experienced fewer opportunities to interact with grandparents. Evidence from wills, probate court records, and other contemporary documents suggests that despite the high mortality and fertility rates of the period, frequent contact and affectionate ties between grandparents and grandchildren in early American families were not unusual. Grandparents regularly left property and money to their grandchildren and often cared for them in childhood. In turn, older grandchildren provided care and assistance to frail grandmothers and grandfathers. Occasional references to grandparental overindulgence in child-rearing literature also suggest relationships characterized by love as well as respect and obligation.

Grandparents, 1830–1920

As a larger proportion of people lived into old age and people married younger and bore children earlier, the possibility that three generations of family members would be alive simultaneously increased, and co-residence became progressively more likely. Thus by 1900 the percentage of trigenerational households had reached its peak in American history. Aging widows comprised the majority of those who resided with children and grandchildren. While the possibility of co-residence grew, concerns about its negative effects also multiplied. Middle-class commentators at the turn of the century and beyond lamented the disruptive consequences of living with aging parents, especially the frequency of intergenerational conflict over grandparental interference in child rearing. At the same time, dislocated parents complained about ungracious treatment and the constraints of living with children and grandchildren. While co-residence undoubtedly created difficulties for some families, such domestic arrangements remained the exception. Even in 1900, 70 percent of Americans who were sixty or older lived either as head of the household or spouse of the head, suggesting that most grandparent-grandchild interactions were not shaped by intergenerational domestic friction. Nevertheless, emerging images of the elderly as nonproductive and superfluous in an increasingly industrially and technically sophisticated society, along with medical interpretations of aging

as a disease, fostered the perception of aging parents and grandparents as a burden to society and to the family.

Despite the proliferation of negative cultural representations of aging individuals during this period, nineteenth-century letters, diaries, and autobiographic recollections document frequent contacts and close, affectionate relationships between grandparents and grandchildren, often, but not exclusively, defined by gender. For example, grandmothers frequently cared for young children in times of stress or illness, and in turn, adult granddaughters provided companionship and help for frail grandmothers. Many nineteenth-century women who recorded their life histories stressed the influence of grandmothers as models. Grandparents of both genders expressed joy at the birth of grandchildren and followed their progress eagerly. Grandfathers as well as grandmothers corresponded frequently with grandchildren of all ages. Letters from young women express love and concern for grandparents, but letters from young men, for example during the Civil War, illustrate closeness between young men and their grandparents as well. As in earlier America, nineteenth-century references to indulgent grandparents are not unusual. Artistic representations of grandmothers, emphasizing their benign qualities, suggest more positive public images as well.

Post–1920 Grandparents

In response to negative representations of the aging and warnings from family experts regarding the threats posed by co-residency, growing numbers of Americans espoused the ideal of autonomous households. While the catastrophic economic impact of the Depression temporarily disrupted the process of achieving this goal, the decline of co-residence represents a major development in the decades after 1920. By the middle of the century, Social Security benefits, private pensions, and growing prosperity among older people made it possible for most grandparents to live independently, a major change in the structure of many households that met widespread implicit approval. This trend was reflected in revised cultural images. No longer portrayed as burdens, the elderly were now depicted as active, busy, autonomous individuals who could and should control their own lives. Prescriptive literature addressed to grandparents explicitly defined their roles as providers of love and companionship. In the context of this new image, indulging and spoiling grandchildren no longer represented inappropriate behavior.

A range of evidence reflects congruence between the revised image of grandparenthood and grandparent-grandchild interactions in the second half of the twentieth century. Empirical studies as well as correspondence by and about grandmothers, grandfathers, and grandchildren illustrate strong intergenerational bonds. Grandparents reported that a sense of emotional distance had characterized their relationships with their own grandparents, while they enjoyed warm bonds, shared interests, and a sense of relative equality with their grandchildren. They sent loving letters and whimsical drawings to younger children and generous gifts to adolescents and young adults, and they expressed their pleasure in grandparenthood to friends and relatives. Grandchildren wrote grateful thank-you notes, worried about grandparental health, described their own activities, and sometimes testified explicitly to the importance of grandmothers and grandfathers in their lives. Although many contemporary studies emphasize the positive nature of companionate grandparenthood in the second half of the twentieth century, some scholars suggest that the grandparent-grandchild relationships may have lost a valuable component when the balance between sentiment and more instrumental ties changed.

Diversity and Grandparents

Despite evidence of common experiences in the history of grandparent-grandchild relationships, it is important to acknowledge the danger of overgeneralizing. Diversity and heterogeneity have characterized grandparenthood in all historical periods. Although factors like gender, class, race, ethnicity, and location have not been fully analyzed as variables in this context, some examples of their impact can be cited. For instance, shared gender roles fostered special closeness between nineteenth-century grandmothers and granddaughters, while twentieth-century grandmothers developed warmer, more communicative relationships with grandchildren than their male counterparts did. At the turn of the century, co-residence with grandparents was experienced primarily by middle-class children whose families had the resources to support elderly relatives. African-American grandparents, especially grandmothers, have played prominent roles in the lives of their grandchildren from slavery to the present. In contrast to their white counterparts, they have remained deeply involved in the rearing of grandchildren, though not necessarily by choice. While providing a loving companionship, they have consistently assumed more functional responsibilities and more authority in response to the range of problems African-American families have faced over the centuries. Hence, substantial participation in grandchildren's lives became an integral part of African-American intergenerational family culture, and contemporary African-American grandmothers continue to reflect a distinctive, hands-on style in their interactions with grandchildren. Many immigrant families, Italian-Americans in particular, venerated the older generation, especially grandmothers who helped in the home. At the same time, language and cultural barriers could impede the development of close relationships between grandparents and grandchildren. Finally, strong bonds linked the generations in rural families, but this often changed when young people migrated to the city.

Conclusion

The links between changes in the social and cultural context of grandparenthood and in the actual experience of intergenerational relationships within families are complex. As with any aspect of family history, direct one-to-one correlations cannot be assumed. The research to date suggests that grandparenthood has changed structurally and emotionally from the preindustrial period to the present. In earlier periods, grandparents were in short supply. Grandparenthood occurred simultaneously with parenthood. Co-residency created family conflict. By the end of the twentieth century, older people enjoyed more leisure time, financial security, and independence than previously. Increased life expectancy meant that many older people lived long enough to experience grandparenthood as a separate stage of life over a lengthy period. Moreover they looked forward to grandparenthood as a goal. Now grandchildren, rather than grandparents, were in short supply as FERTILITY RATES declined. Although geographic distance often separated family members, ease of travel and communication allowed them to keep in touch. It is important to consider how these changes altered the nature of relationships between grandparents and grandchildren. Nevertheless, evidence of explicitly loving and affectionate relationships in earlier periods as well as in the twentieth century cautions against overstating the extent to which grandparent-grandchild interactions have changed over time. Further historical study of individual relationships as recorded in personal documents and other primary sources will be necessary to develop a fuller understanding of the balance between change and continuity in grandparenthood.

See also: **Godparents; Parenting; Siblings.**

BIBLIOGRAPHY

Achenbaum, W. Andrew. 1978. *Old Age in the New Land.* Baltimore, MD: Johns Hopkins University Press.

Brady, Patricia, ed. 1991. *George Washington's Beautiful Nelly: The Letters of Eleanor Parke Custis to Elizabeth Bordley Gibson 1794–1851.* Columbia: University of South Carolina Press.

Cherlin, Andrew J., and Frank F. Furstenberg Jr. 1986. *The New American Grandparent: A Place in the Family, A Life Apart.* New York: Basic Books.

deButts, Mary Sutis Lee, ed. 1984. *The Journal of Agnes Lee.* Chapel Hill: University of North Carolina Press.

Demos, John. 1983. "Old Age in Early New England." In *The American Family in Social-Historical Perspective,* 3rd edition, ed. Michael Gordon. New York: St. Martin's Press.

Fischer, David Hackett. 1977. *Growing Old in America.* New York: Oxford University Press.

Gratton, Brian, and Carole Haber. 1996. "Three Phases in the History of American Grandparents: Authority, Burden, Companion." *Generations* 20: 7–12.

Haber, Carole. 1983. *Beyond Sixty-Five: The Dilemmas of Old Age in America's Past.* New York: Cambridge University Press.

Haber, Carole, and Brian Gratton. 1994. *Old Age and the Search for Security: An American Social History.* Bloomington: Indiana University Press.

Kornhaber, Arthur, and Kenneth L. Woodward. 1985. *Grandparents/Grandchildren: The Vital Connection.* New Brunswick, NJ: Transaction.

Premo, Terri L. 1990. *Winter Friends: Women Growing Old in the New Republic, 1785–1835.* Urbana: University of Illinois Press.

Uhlenberg, Peter, and James B. Kirby. 1998. "Grandparenthood over Time: Historical and Demographic Trends." In *Handbook on Grandparenthood*, ed. Maximiliane E. Szinovacz. Westport, CT: Greenwood Press.

Linda W. Rosenzweig

Great Depression and New Deal

For millions of American children and teens the Great Depression brought years of hardship and heartache. At a time of economic distress and double digit unemployment, when, as President Franklin D. Roosevelt put it in his second inaugural address, "one-third" of the nation was "ill-housed, ill-clad, ill-nourished," the young bore a disproportionate burden of poverty. The Relief Census of 1933 found that although youths under sixteen years of age represented only 31 percent of the U.S. population they constituted 42 percent of all of the poverty-stricken Americans who became relief recipients.

The human toll that lay beneath these statistics can be gleaned from the thousands of letters that low income youths sent to First Lady Eleanor Roosevelt during the Depression. The letters came from despondent children and teens, many of whom wrote to Mrs. Roosevelt asking her for the shoes, clothing, books, and transportation they so badly needed to attend school. This correspondence underscores the fact that initially the economic crisis of the Great Depression was an educational crisis as well. Diminishing tax revenues closed some 20,000 schools in rural America in 1934 and shortened school terms. The letters also tell of inadequate access to medical and dental care, constricted opportunities for recreation, and the psychological burdens the young experienced in homes where adults had been thrown out of work and into poverty. In such homes, as the studies of social scientists Mirra Komarovsky and Glenn H. Elder Jr. confirm, paternal authority often declined as fathers proved unable to play the traditional role of breadwinner, and children, denied elements of a protected childhood, assumed more adult-like roles in family management and support. These conditions led Americans to speak of the "youth crisis" of the 1930s in which material deprivation and limited educational and employment opportunities threatened the future of the younger generation —a crisis symbolized by the falling marriage and birth rates and the soaring youth unemployment rates during the early Depression years.

New Deal liberals, concerned intellectuals, and student activists did much to call public attention to this youth crisis. The New Deal's Farm Security Administration funded such compassionate photographers as Dorothea Lange and Walker Evans whose memorable images documented the plight of impoverished children. Eleanor Roosevelt used her daily newspaper columns and weekly radio addresses to highlight youth issues and urged an expanded federal role in

Dorothea Lange's 1936 photograph of a destitute migrant worker and her children in California has become one of the most enduring images of the Great Depression. According to Lange, at the time this picture was taken, this woman, her husband, and their seven children had been living for days on frozen vegetables and some birds that the children had killed. The Library of Congress.

assisting the Depression's youngest victims. The left-wing student and youth protest movements of the 1930s founded national organizations, such as the American Youth Congress and the American Student Union, championing federal aid to needy students and to education and led the first national youth marches on Washington.

New Deal liberals did far more than talk about the youth crisis; they acted to ameliorate it through a historic expansion of federal aid to youth and education. From 1933 to 1939 New Deal funds assisted 70 percent of all new school construction and prevented thousands of school closings by coming up with emergency funds to pay teachers. In Arkansas, for example, such aid stopped the closing of some 4,000 schools. The Works Progress Administration (WPA) made nursery school accessible to workers for the first time, establishing almost 3,000 free nursery schools in 1933 and 1934. By the end of the Depression the WPA had provided more than a billion free school lunches to needy students. Work study jobs provided by the National Youth Administration (NYA) enabled more than two million low income students to continue their education and funded 2.6 million jobs for out-of-school youths, while the Civilian Conservation Corps also provided temporary work relief and training for male teens. Even adult-centered relief agencies indirectly aided youth, as parents funded by the Federal Emergency Relief Administration and the Works Progress Administration— though still poor—were better able to provide their children with the basic necessities of life.

This New Deal funding helped the United States to bounce back from the educational crisis of the early Depression years. Thanks in part to federal aid to students, high school enrollments rose from 4,399,422 at the opening of the Depression to 6,545,991 by the end of the 1930s. At the college level, NYA funds helped low income students stay in school by providing 12 percent of the college population with work-study jobs. Thus after a decline in enrollments from 1932 through 1934, college enrollment increased during the second half of the 1930s, so that in 1939 enrollment stood at 1.3 million, exceeding the pre-Depression peak of 1.1 million.

Beyond these emergency measures the New Deal enacted youth welfare legislation whose impact would endure far beyond the 1930s. The New Deal launched the AID TO DEPENDENT CHILDREN (ADC) program as part of the Social Security Act of 1935, which would become the central vehicle by which the welfare state provided aid to needy children. Title V of the Social Security Act established federal aid to the states to expand programs for neglected and abused children. With its passage of the Fair Labor Standards Act of 1938 the New Deal realized another long-term goal of Progressives, the outlawing of many forms of CHILD LABOR.

While historic in their expansion of the federal role in promoting child welfare, the ADC and the child labor ban had problems in both design and implementation which delayed and in some cases blocked their assistance to children. Traditions of localism and states' rights combined with budgetary constraints to delay the participation of southern states in the ADC, so that states such as Mississippi and Kentucky did not join in this child aid program until the 1940s. And southern states tended to apply standards in a racially discriminatory manner, denying aid to mothers of dependent children (especially in black families) when they deemed them "morally deficient." The child labor ban did not apply to some of the most exploitative fields where the young worked, including agriculture and the street trades.

The liberal reformist ethos of the 1930s affected child rearing and educational discourse. In *Babies Are Human Beings: An Interpretation* (1938), a popular child-rearing book by C. Andrews Aldrich and Mary M. Aldrich, parents were urged to heed the emotional needs of their children, to display affection towards them and provide them with security in a changing world. This was a warmer and more child-centered approach than the behaviorist parenting guides that had proven so influential in the 1920s. Child-centered pedagogy also made some headway, as is evidenced by the fact that the Progressive Education Association (PEA)—the leading national organization devoted to promoting JOHN DEWEY's educational vision— reached its zenith in terms of both membership and influence during the 1930s. With capitalism faltering, some educators leaned left, following George S. Counts and the "Social Frontiers" thinkers, advocating social reconstructionism: that the educational system should be used to help build a new social system, freed of the inequities that had afflicted the capitalist system.

It seems clear, however, that the progressivism of PEA and the radicalism of the Social Frontiers group had more impact on educational theory than practice. School systems, confronting tight budgets under the leadership of conservative superintendents, tended to cling to traditional modes of teacher-centered pedagogy. The largest study of classroom practice in the 1930s, for example, the Regents Inquiry, which focused on New York, found that most school instruction centered on drill, factual recitation, and textbook memorization, as it had for decades— this despite the fact that New York was the home of John Dewey and the center of progressive education, Teachers College. Historical studies of progressive education by David Tyack and Arthur Zilversmit suggest that it was mostly the affluent districts and schools that experimented with student-centered pedagogy during the Depression decade.

Much like Progressive education, New Deal liberalism promised more than it could deliver to the children of Depression America. The NYA, though assisting millions of needy youths, missed many more than it could help because of budget constraints, often operating programs on a racially segregated basis, and did not outlive the Roosevelt administration (though Lyndon Johnson, an NYA official in the 1930s, would revive the NYA-style federal aid in the Great Society youth programs during his presidency in the 1960s). New Deal dollars assisted impoverished students, but failed to reform the localistic school financing system which allowed for vast inequities between rich and poor school districts. Even the New Deal programs that endured beyond the 1930s, the ADC and child labor ban, though historic steps towards a more humane society, were too limited in scope and funding to protect all American children from the ravages of poverty and child labor. The ambiguity of this record on youth is reflected in the letters that low income children and teens sent to Mrs. Roosevelt in the 1930s, since they show that the New Deal's war on poverty evoked love and loyalty from these needy youths, but also disappointment that the new federal programs failed to meet their personal material needs or to advance their educational opportunities.

Reflecting its emergence in a time of crisis, Depression America's YOUTH CULTURE was more divided than youth culture had been in relatively placid eras. On the one hand, the values of CONSUMER CULTURE and the marketplace, which tended to set the tone of youth culture in more prosperous decades, were still visible in the 1930s. It could be seen among the elitist segment of college youth who argued that only the affluent should attend college. It was even visible in some of the letters that poor children wrote to Mrs. Roosevelt, which were sent to her because of the ways that ADVERTISING and the superior possessions of their friends left them sounding like acquisitive individualists who longed for the material goods enjoyed by the middle class—and so requested consumer goods in a youthful brand of "keeping up with the Joneses." On the other hand, the more cooperative ethos of labor, the Left, and the New Deal itself spread and made possible a challenge to the hold that the competitiveness of the consumer culture had over youth. This egalitarianism was evidenced in the rising degree of youth participation in the labor movement and the creation of the first mass student movement in American history, movements which championed an egalitarian social and political agenda. Prominent on that agenda and in the letters that poor children and teens wrote to Mrs. Roosevelt was accessible education and the left-liberal conviction that a just society was one that afforded all—not just the affluent—access to secondary and even higher education. It was no accident, then, that the generation of politicians who presided over postwar America's age of expanding educational opportunities and the Great Society's federal youth aid programs—from Head Start to the Job Corps—came of age politically in Depression America.

See also: **Social Welfare; Youth Activism; Youth Agencies of the New Deal.**

BIBLIOGRAPHY

Ashby, Leroy. 1985. "Partial Promises and Semi-Visible Youths: The Depression and World War II." In *American Childhood: A Research Guide*, ed. Joseph M. Hawes and N. Ray Hiner. Westport, CT: Greenwood Press.

Cohen, Robert, ed. 2002. *Dear Mrs. Roosevelt: Letters From Children of the Great Depression.* Chapel Hill: University of North Carolina Press.

Cohen, Robert. 1993. *When the Old Left Was Young: Student Radicals and America's First Mass Student Movement, 1929–1941.* New York: Oxford University Press.

Elder, Glenn H., Jr. 1999. *Children of the Great Depression: Social Change in Life Experience.* Boulder, CO: Westview.

Fass, Paula. 2000. "Children and the New Deal." In *Childhood in America*, ed. Paula Fass and Mary Ann Mason. New York: New York University Press.

Hawes, Joseph M. 1991. *The Children's Rights Movement: A History of Advocacy and Protection.* Boston: Twayne.

Lindenmeyer, Kriste. 1997. *"A Right to Childhood": The U.S. Children's Bureau and Child Welfare, 1912–1946.* Urbana: University of Illinois Press.

Komarovsky, Mirra. 1949. *The Unemployed Man and His Family: The Effect of Unemployment upon the Status of the Man in Fifty-Nine Families.* New York: Dryden.

Modell, John. 1989. *Into One's Own: From Youth to Adulthood in the United States, 1920–1975.* Berkeley: University of California Press.

Reiman, Richard. 1993. *The New Deal and American Youth: Ideas and Ideals in a Depression Decade.* Athens: University of Georgia Press.

Thompson, Kathleen, and Hilary MacAustin. 2001. *Children of the Depression.* Bloomington: Indiana University Press.

Tyack, David, Robert Lowe, and Elisabeth Hansot. 1984. *Public Schools in Hard Times: The Great Depression.* Cambridge, MA: Harvard University Press.

ROBERT COHEN

Greenaway, Kate (1846–1901)

Catherine (Kate) Greenaway was an English artist and children's book illustrator. She is best known for her distinctive images of children in simple clothes set in pastoral and garden landscapes. She was born in London, the second daughter of the engraver John Greenaway and Elizabeth Greenaway. When she was five her family moved to Islington, where her mother opened a successful shop selling children's clothing and trimmings. During the summers, Greenaway and her siblings lived with relatives in the country village of Rolleston in Nottinghamshire. A keen observer, she would draw on remembered details from her childhood in her art.

Greenaway began her artistic training at twelve, when she enrolled in the Finsbury School of Art, which trained its students for careers in commercial art. At nineteen, she began further design training at the Female School of Art in South Kensington and some years later she took life classes at the Slade School. In the late 1860s she began receiving commissions for magazine and book illustrations and designing greeting cards.

Greenaway's career reached a turning point in 1877 when her father introduced her to the printer Edmund Evans, who produced high-quality color wood engravings. Evans was already successfully engraving and printing books by Walter Crane and Randolph Caldecott, two well-known children's book illustrators, and he printed Greenaway's first book, *Under the Window*, with the publisher George Routledge in 1879. The book combined Greenaway's illustrations of children with her own simple verse. It was a huge success and sold out almost immediately. Her subsequent books in the same vein continued to be successful, and several publishers produced books imitative of her style.

During these prolific years, Greenaway began to correspond with the art critic John Ruskin, who admired her images of children. She finally met him in the early 1880s. Ruskin, twenty-eight years Greenaway's senior and already experiencing bouts of mental illness, would have a lasting influence on the rest of Greenaway's life. She fell in love with him, although she was only one among several women with whom he had a flirtatious relationship. The two conducted a lengthy, complicated correspondence, and they visited each other sporadically. He offered artistic advice and en-

From *Under the Window: Pictures and Rhymes for Children* (1878). Kate Greenaway's drawings of children in pastoral settings were a great success in late Victorian Britain. The distinctive images of children dressed in early-nineteenth-century fashions spoke to adults' nostalgia both for a simpler era before industrialization and for the innocence of their own childhood.

couraged her to pursue nature studies and watercolor painting. Although he championed her work in a lecture and essay entitled "In Fairy Land," Greenaway's career suffered when she diverted her attention away from illustration. By the mid-1880s, Greenaway's books began to diminish in popularity. Focusing more on exhibiting and selling watercolor painting in the last decade of her life, she struggled to support herself. Countless products appeared with her designs (or were modelled after them), but most were produced without her permission. Greenaway died of breast cancer in 1901.

Greenaway's art nostalgically linked a pastoral landscape and the simplicity of eighteenth- and early nineteenth-century styles of clothing with an ideal of childhood sheltered from adult experience. At the same time, her work's simple, clean lines, decorative details, and her choice of colors corresponded to the progressive tastes of the Aesthetic movement of the later nineteenth century. This visual formula easily transferred to other media. Greenaway's style was successful in an expanding market for images of children that continued well into the twentieth century. Her images of children appeared on greeting cards, advertisements, porcelain figures, tiles, wallpaper, and fabrics, while the distinctive style of dress she pictured in her work influenced children's fashions in England and elsewhere. The well-known store Liberty of London, for example, carried its "Greena-

way dress" into the early twentieth century. Although she herself did not benefit financially beyond the sales of her books and illustrations, Greenaway was one of the first women artists to achieve success in the growing childhood-related markets of the nineteenth and twentieth centuries.

See also: **Children's Literature; Images of Childhood; Victorian Art.**

BIBLIOGRAPHY

Chester, Tessa Rose, and Joyce Irene Whalley. 1988. *A History of Children's Book Illustration.* London: John Murray/Victoria and Albert Museum.

Engen, Rodney. 1981. *Kate Greenaway: A Biography.* London: Macdonald Future Publishers.

Lundin, Anne H. 2001. *Victorian Horizons: The Reception of the Picture Books of Walter Crane, Randolph Caldecott, and Kate Greenaway.* Lanham, MD: Children's Literature Association/Scarecrow Press.

Schuster, Thomas E., and Rodney Engen. 1986. *Printed Kate Greenaway: A Catalogue Raisonné.* London: T. E. Schuster.

Spielman, M. H., and G. S. Layard. 1905. *The Life and Work of Kate Greenaway.* London: Adam Charles Black. Reprint, 1986, London: Bracken.

Taylor, Ina. 1991. *The Art of Kate Greenaway: A Nostalgic Portrait of Childhood.* Gretna, LA: Pelican.

DIANE WAGGONER

Funerary portrait (c. 1909–1930), Juan de Dios Machain. *Angelito* photographs taken of children in their caskets were common in late-nineteenth- and early-twentieth-century Mexico, a sad commentary on child mortality rates before the mid-twentieth century. Research Library, The Getty Research Institute, Los Angeles (95.R.17).

Grief, Death, Funerals

Death is clearly part of human experience, and yet children's experience of death depends heavily on their cultures' social customs and discourses surrounding death and funeral practices, beliefs regarding the afterlife, and norms of grieving. Any understanding of children's experiences with death must begin with the degree to which children are exposed to, or protected from, death and dying.

Exposure to Death

In many traditional societies, children were exposed to death on a regular basis, as mortality rates were often quite high. During the seventeenth and eighteenth centuries, death rates among children in Europe and America were quite high: a third or more of those born died by the age of two. In contexts of such high child mortality rates, few people would reach early adulthood without having multiple siblings die. With about 10 percent of all women dying in childbirth, a noticeable minority of children also directly experienced the death of their mothers. Children in rural environments were also frequently exposed to the deaths of animals. Large-scale war, with its massive carnage among young men, contributed to the awareness of death as well, again for children and adults alike.

In contrast, where mortality rates are lower, children are less likely to routinely experience death. By the early twentieth century, the incidence of death in Western cultures began to shift dramatically, in ways that affected children particularly. Throughout the United States and most of Western Europe, the decades from 1880 to 1920 saw a rapid reduction in INFANT MORTALITY, from over 20 percent within the first two years of life to under 5 percent; deaths in childbirth also declined. However, mortality rates varied considerably across different groups in Western cultures, and continue to be high in many developing countries, meaning that many children still live in contexts of routine and frequent death.

The physical management of death also affects children's exposure to death. In traditional societies, death typically occurred in the home, as did preparation of the corpse for funeral rites, meaning that children would be routinely exposed to the process of dying as well as to the presence of dead bodies. The increasing professionalization of death management meant that death and its accompanying rituals increasingly occurred outside the home, in hospitals and funeral homes. Up until the late nineteenth century in the United States, most funerals and the preparation of the dead (e.g., embalming) occurred in the deceased's home, but by the 1920s death had largely moved from the home to the hospital and the funeral home. The timing of this shift was not uniform across countries, however; in Newfoundland, for example, people continued to prepare bodies at home, with little access to professional funeral services, until the late 1960s.

Apart from the physical exposure to death, the willingness of adults to discuss death with children and the ways in which death is discursively managed in interactions with children have changed over time in Western cultures. Until the early twentieth century, it was considered perfectly appropriate for children to hear about death from adults. In Puritan New England, adults routinely discussed death with children as part of a larger message of sin and the necessity of salvation to avoid eternal damnation. Children were advised not only of the inevitability of death for all persons but of the imminent likelihood of their own death, a message accurately reflecting the high child mortality rates but almost certainly instilling fear of death. In the Victorian era, death was openly discussed with children, but in a more benign context. Stories for children routinely included death scenes and references to death, often with an emphasis on the joys of heaven and the inevitable reunion with loved ones there. In the United States, the most popular reading primers, such as McGuffey's, carried these themes on into the 1860s. A "poetical lesson," from the 1866 *Fourth Eclectic Reader* included a poem entitled "What Is Death?" addressing both the physical and metaphysical aspects of a baby's death. While these messages were less frightening than the Puritans', they still served to remind children of death's inevitability and the need to live a blameless life because it could be so easily and unexpectedly snatched away. Consider the simple Christian prayer, designed particularly for children: "Now I lay me down to sleep. . . . . If I die before I wake, I pray dear God my soul to take."

By the 1920s, however, questions arose as to the appropriateness of exposing children to knowledge of death. Expert advice began to warn of the dangers of children's fears, including those of death, and parents were urged to use caution in their discussions of death with children. Using SLEEP as a metaphor for death was deemed problematic, for example, as it could cause children to be afraid at bedtime. Euphemisms began to replace direct references to death, and some purists even urged sidestepping confrontations with the death of PETS. Even the idea of heavenly reunions seemed too explicit to some, who were eager to banish all thoughts of death from the experience of childhood. It was best to encourage children to think of death as a remote result of old age; there was some hope that providing scientific facts would reduce fears of death for older children.

By the 1950s, a general silence had emerged on the topic of death in the United States, with some authors calling it a taboo topic, particularly in reference to children. David Sudnow's 1960s ethnographic work in two U.S. hospitals found that hospital workers made a significant effort to shield children from knowledge of death, both of other children and their own. Hospital staff avoided references to the future when speaking with dying children and adolescents, for example. Children's deaths were more upsetting to the staff than adults', reflecting the general attitude shared by both parents and doctors that death and children did not mix, a consensus that had emerged in the late nineteenth and early twentieth centuries.

Children's participation in funeral practices and death rituals also reflected this shift. Funeral practices themselves changed considerably over time and across social groups, but children were included in funerals up to the early twentieth century. No respectable funeral procession in the late Middle Ages was complete without a delegation of children from ORPHANAGES or FOUNDLING homes. In the Victorian era, wearing somber clothes or other signs of mourning became widespread, and children were included in the practice. Although funerals moved from the home to park-like cemeteries, which were often at a considerable distance, children were still in attendance. By the 1870s, death kits were available for dolls, complete with coffins and mourning clothes, as a means of helping to train girls for participating in, even guiding, death rituals and their attendant grief. In the case of newsboys, children even organized and contributed toward the funeral rites of deceased newsboys in the late nineteenth and early twentieth century, to honor their lives and avoid the looming threat of a pauper's burial, as well as to express group solidarity.

The early twentieth century, however, saw a decline in these elaborate mourning rituals, and the remaining rituals often excluded children. It was believed that children should be kept away from funerals, just as they were usually barred from hospital sick rooms (even those of close relatives or parents). This stemmed in part from an increasing concern with children's vulnerability to emotional stress. It was believed that funeral rituals and contexts of great emotional intensity were too difficult for children to endure. Some countercurrents began in the mid-twentieth century, however, such as the hospice movement, which stressed the importance of a family context for the terminally ill. In addition, some subgroups in American society continued to involve children in highly emotional funerals. Certainly the death taboo with children in the twentieth century was not absolute, as children continued to confront death (both human and animal), but death was less explicitly and frequently discussed with children, and when death was presented, it tended to be in a less emotional and immediate fashion.

Emotional Responses to Death

Historians have debated the emotional response to death in the premodern period. Some once argued that adults, at least, became inured to death, so that it did not occasion significant grief. The standard adult "good death" (most frequently from lingering respiratory infection) did allow family members to pay respects to the dying individual, permitting any outstanding scores to be settled, and this may indeed have blunted the emotional impact for other family members, including children. Even where children were concerned, certain adult practices, such as reusing the names of children who had died and, in some places, not naming children at all for a year or two, suggest the impact of frequent deaths on adult behavior. Attachment patterns can serve to minimize grief: Nancy Scheper-Hughes found that Brazilian women facing a high child mortality rate distanced themselves emotionally from young infants, particularly those who seemed sickly, as a way of minimizing their anticipated grief at the infants' death.

But newer interpretations of premodern Europe, often based on diaries and letters, emphasize how deeply adults were affected by the deaths of young children, however common their occurrence. Expressions of lingering grief, often remembered into later life, and a practice of using children's deaths as the key markers in family calendars, suggest powerful emotional reactions, in part because children, dying of causes such as diarrhea, and inarticulate in any event, could not have the kinds of good deaths available to older adults.

Children's emotional responses to death involve more than just grief, particularly in those cultures that use the fear of death as a disciplinary and religious tool. Fear of death was actively employed in Catholic Europe as a means of keeping children in line and also of illustrating the dire consequences of original sin (the same theme emerged in Puritan society, as noted previously). Holy days like All Saints' Day, which commemorated the dead but which were also often associated with stories of ghosts returning and misfortune, could play a lively part in children's imagination. (Even in modern Mexico and Central America, children may be kept home from school on All Saints Day because of the risk of disaster.) These messages were clearly influential, as children were indeed often terrified by the prospect of death and damnation.

The gradual secularization of culture in countries like France reduced these death fears by the eighteenth century. By the early nineteenth century death became romanticized for the middle class in some Western countries as part of the new, sentimental current in literature. Many novels portrayed tragic death scenes, designed to elicit tears and compassion for innocent (often young, often female) victims, and some of these were available for children as readers. Children may have been comforted, as well, by the growing belief that families would be lovingly reunited in heaven, a theme in popular religious and romantic fiction and poetry, as well as in nineteenth-century popular songs.

As attitudes toward death changed, ceremonies became more elaborate and expressive, and children and adults were encouraged to embrace the emotion of grief, which was seen as a strong, family-uniting emotional bond in a time of loss.

Many children, particularly girls, grew up knowing that sorrow and sentimentality over loss were an expected part of emotional life, a counterpart to love. Certainly the open intensity of grief upon the death of a child increased among adults. Diary entries portray a blinding sorrow, combining a sense of loss and a new feeling of guilt, indicating a belief that a child's death should somehow be preventable. Funeral markers for children became increasingly elaborate, in marked contrast to the bare mentions in family plots in the seventeenth and eighteenth centuries. However cushioned it was by the hope of heavenly reunion, adult anxiety about children's death inevitably spilled over into children's experiences as well.

Acceptance of grief declined in the early twentieth century, in part through a growing commitment to consumerism, which made both grief and death less popular than orientations more conducive to pleasure. Grief was increasingly reproved where adults were concerned, with excessive emotion seen a sign of psychological weakness and indicative of a need for therapy. Children's grief came under even stronger attack, stemming from beliefs that grief was particularly hazardous to children's psychological well-being. Parents were urged to sympathize with crying children but to keep signs of their own grief in check in order to minimize childish grief. Fictional representations also reflected this avoidance of grief; in contrast to nineteenth-century children's fiction, contemporary children's media presented death as graphic and gory but emotionless, with no pause for grief.

By the 1960s some reconsideration of the new antipathy toward death had emerged. A variety of experts urged that children were being harmed by having insufficient outlet for their real feelings of grief, and that they should be reintegrated with the rituals of death. Schools moved increasingly to provide therapy to students when a classmate died—another move to bridge the gap between children and death. But the dominant contemporary reaction remained cautious in associating children with death, as evidenced by the relatively small purview of death-accepting hospices compared to standard death-fighting hospitals. Children encountered death in abundance in media representations, which has been a source of ongoing concern to some adults starting in the days of comic books and radio and continuing on to contemporary Internet games. But real death was more removed from most childhood experience than ever before in human history, with the result that many children had very little idea of what death was about. What happens to children who do experience the death of someone close, and the grief that accompanies it, without much experience or ritual support, remains a significant question in twenty-first-century childhood.

See also: **Child-Rearing Advice Literature; Emotional Life; Rites of Passage.**

BIBLIOGRAPHY

Ariès, Philippe. 1981. *The Hour of our Death.* Trans. Helen Weaver. New York: Knopf.

Coffin, Margaret M. 1976. *Death in Early America: The History and Folklore of Customs and Superstitions of Early Medicine, Funerals, Burials, and Mourning.* New York: Thomas Nelson.

Delumeau, Jean. 1990. *Sin and Fear: The Emergence of a Western Guilt Culture, 13th–18th Centuries.* Trans. Eric Nicholson. New York: St. Martin's Press.

DiGirolamo, V. 2002. "Newsboy Funerals: Tales of Sorrow and Solidarity in Urban America." *Journal of Social History* 36, no. 1 (fall): 5–30.

Emke, I. 2002. "Why the Sad Face? Secularization and the Changing Function of Funerals in Newfoundland." *Mortality* 7: 269–284.

Pine, Vanderlyn R. 1975. *Caretakers of the Dead: The American Funeral Director.* New York: Irvington.

Rosenblatt, Paul C. 1983. *Bitter, Bitter Tears: Nineteenth-Century Diarists and Twentieth-Century Grief Theories.* Minneapolis: University of Minnesota Press.

Scheper-Hughes, Nancy. 1985. "Culture, Scarcity, and Maternal Thinking: Maternal Detachment and Infant Survival in a Brazilian Shantytown." *Ethos* 13: 291–317.

Stannard, David E., ed. 1975. *Death in America.* Philadelphia: University of Pennsylvania Press.

Stearns, Peter N. 1994. *American Cool: Constructing a Twentieth-Century Emotional Style.* New York: New York University Press.

Sudnow, David. 1967. *Passing On: The Social Organization of Dying.* Englewood Cliffs, NJ: Prentice-Hall.

DEBORAH C. STEARNS

Guilt and Shame

Guilt and shame have been classified as emotions that reflect self-consciousness and enforce morality, and that function as a way of constraining behavior to societal norms. As such, instilling feelings of guilt and shame are a central component of childhood socialization. Precise definitions of guilt and shame have varied; some have argued that the critical component of shame is public exposure of one's wrongdoing or inadequacies, while others identify shame as self degradation and feelings of worthlessness. In both cases, shame involves the desire to hide from others. Guilt, on the other hand, is associated with a desire to apologize, make reparations, and be forgiven. In distinguishing guilt from shame, some define guilt as stemming from a focus on one's bad behavior, in contrast with shame's focus on the global self; others see guilt as private, a matter of one's conscience, and shame as public, a matter of one's reputation.

While guilt and shame are, most likely, inevitable aspects of childhood, children's experience of these emotions is influenced by social factors, including cultural beliefs and practices. Anthropologists have often distinguished cultures on the basis on which of these two forms of socialization is emphasized. Historians have often described certain religious beliefs as resulting in an unusual degree of guilt in children, such as those emphasizing an uncertain relationship with God or the unworthiness of followers. Indeed, ERIK ERIKSON's analysis of the life of Martin Luther suggests that guilt was a key element of his childhood, which he then transferred to his emphasis on original sin in his version of Christianity. Children's experiences of guilt and shame are particularly influenced by patterns of DISCIPLINE and peer group activities.

Patterns of Discipline: Shifting from Shame to Guilt

To the extent that shame is related to the experience of public exposure, societies that rely heavily on public discipline will incur greater shame in children than those that emphasize more private discipline. Japanese children, for example, are exposed to relatively high degrees of shaming, in that wrongdoing is identified and corrected publicly, both at home and in school. For example, James Stigler and Michelle Perry describe a Japanese elementary school math class in which a child who was unable to draw a cube correctly was repeatedly sent to the blackboard to try again, each attempt being critiqued by his fellow students until he was able to do it correctly. The child's sense of right and self-worth is thereby made contingent on overt group approval. This pattern of discipline stems in part from broader ideals that emphasize the needs of the group and encourage group conformity. Guilt and shame are self-conscious emotions, and as such, are tied to culturally variable notions of self. Hazel Markus and Shinobu Kitayama have argued that a number of non-Western cultures emphasize an interdependent self, one which is tied to group membership and would be more shame prone, while modern Western cultures tend to emphasize an independent self, separate from group membership and more prone to feelings of guilt.

Public shaming was also characteristic of early Western societies, however. Historians have been especially interested in the transition from shame to guilt in childhood discipline between the eighteenth and nineteenth centuries, and particularly in those areas that became the United States. Shame was widely used in colonial America, sometimes bolstered by physical punishments. Children who misbehaved were routinely subjected to public ridicule by siblings or, still more commonly, other community members. Scolding was deliberately conducted in front of an audience, as were spankings or whippings. Children also participated actively in the shaming of others, not only other children but also miscreant adults, such as those put on public display in order to be reviled in the stocks, or those hanged in public. The experience of childhood, therefore, was influenced both by eagerly shaming others and the possibility of being shamed (although we can only speculate as to the impact of these experiences). This shaming tradition was long carried on, in schoolrooms, by the practice of forcing a misbehaving or poorly performing child to sit in a special corner, viewed by his classmates, sometimes wearing an identifying dunce cap or some other marker in addition.

In family discipline, however, a major change occurred between the late eighteenth and early nineteenth centuries. Discipline now became largely private. A characteristic ploy, widely reported in diaries and prescriptive literature alike, involved isolating an offending child, sending him (or, more rarely, her) to a solitary room, sometimes for days, to subsist on a meager diet. The goal was to induce introspection about the offending act and, through this, provoke an ultimate admission of guilt—upon which point the child could be readmitted to the loving family circle. Shame was not fully removed from this approach, for other members of the family would be aware of the proceedings, but the real goal was guilt, and the capacity to experience or anticipate guilt for future offenses as well. Guilt measures were particularly applied to childish offenses seen as dangerous or as carrying the potential for bad character in adulthood. Thus signs of sexual interest, including MASTURBATION, came in for special doses of guilt. The capacity for guilt was increasingly equated with maturity and was seen as critical to shaping good character. Not surprisingly, the excesses of guilt figured heavily in the treatment of disturbed children by the end of the nineteenth century, especially in Freudian therapy.

Although adults are an important part of children's lives, we cannot assume that children's actual experiences of shame and guilt directly inscribed adult guidelines. Shame came under increasing criticism, but it was still a part of children's lives. In part, this resulted from parents, and particularly teachers, who continued to use shaming in the face of expert advice to the contrary. However, children's peer experiences were also important contributors to their EMOTIONAL LIFE, and children continued to shame each other. In the nineteenth century, groups of boys induced conformity through peer pressure and the threat of group shame (e.g., the practice of publicly "daring" a timid boy to display courage).

The spread of consumerism among children from the late nineteenth century onward intensified yet another instigator of shame. By the 1890s, many observers noted that children who could not keep up with the latest styles in clothing or toys often felt shame. Children's efforts to conform to peer standards in consumerism throughout the twentieth century was powerfully motivated by a desire to avoid being shamed by peers. Even when adults did try to reduce shame, children might not conform. By the later twentieth century in the United States, legislation banned the shame-inducing practice of posting school grades in public—a clear sign of the ongoing power of the adult concern regarding children's shame. Many children, however, blithely reported grades to each other, maintaining this impetus for shame.

Guilt Comes Under Suspicion

The cultural emphasis on instilling guilt in children began to be questioned in the 1920s and 1930s in the United States, and by the 1950s in Europe. Experts began to argue that guilt was too heavy a burden to impose on children, and potentially distorted their development. Parents were urged to develop approaches that would avoid loading children with guilt, as prescriptive literature explicitly turned against what was now seen as the excessive repression of the nineteenth-century approach to socialization. Guilt was both too unpleasant and too intense, impeding the necessary development of a sense of self-esteem—rather than motivating children to behave appropriately, it was seen as incapacitating. Psychologists increasingly viewed children as vulnerable and unable to bear the character-building practices of the prior century. The new emphasis on consumerism may also have contributed to the shift away from guilt. Without abandoning standards, it was important to allow children, in childhood and as preparation for their adult consumer role, to feel comfortable with considerable self-indulgence, including buying things and entertainments—many advertisements explicitly urged their audience to cast aside any sense of guilt in the pursuit of the good life.

To replace guilt, three alternative approaches to childhood socialization were identified. First, adults were advised to help children avoid situations that might result in misbehavior, and thus eliminate the need for reprimands. This process was facilitated by greater tolerance for certain childish behavior (e.g., signs of sexual interest). Second, parents and teachers were encouraged to offer rewards for good behavior, as opposed to punishments for misdeeds. In schools, this resulted in the introduction of self-esteem programs and reevaluating the use of bad grades as sanctions. The behaviorist school in psychology was particularly influential in developing incentive strategies to modify children's behavior and in discouraging the use of guilt-inducing punishments, which they saw as largely harmful to CHILD DEVELOPMENT. A fearful child, for example, could be guided by bribes that would reward more confident behavior in entering a dark room or encountering a pet, rather than being stunned by blame, which would only exacerbate the emotional weakness. Third, when all else failed and some discipline became essential, experts and parents alike searched for emotionally neutral sanctions to substitute for the guilt-laden technique of isolating children from the family used in the Victorian era. It was always hoped that children would respond to rational discussion, without guilty overtones. But if this broke down, two characteristic approaches were urged from the 1920s onward in the United States. First, children might be fined—thus punished—but without the emotional tirade. Second, and still more commonly, they might be "grounded"—deprived of normal entertainments (such as radio or television) or the company of their peers, for a set period of time. Again, the goal was to provide corrective deprivation without resorting explicitly to guilt.

The new approach called for considerable parental investment in both time and self control. The injunctions to arrange children's lives to avoid the need for discipline could be burdensome to parents. Moreover, parents were increasingly urged to control their own emotions in dealing with children, because of the guilt potential involved in expressions of anger. Needless to say, actual parents varied in their responses to the new advice, some noting that determined misbehavers did not respond as well as others to a guilt-free environment. But the expert injunctions were widely discussed and some disciplinary changes resulted, including widespread use of grounding as a disciplinary technique.

The overall impact of these changes on children's experiences is difficult to evaluate. While there may have been a reduction in childhood guilt, it is clear that children continued to feel guilty even in families that worked hard to reduce the guilt experience. Of course, many families, ignoring expert advice, did not even try. Indeed, other social changes offered new opportunities for guilt, including higher parental expectations for school performance and the rising divorce rate (from the later nineteenth century onward), which may have led children to feel at fault for family failure. However, the growing suspicion of guilt did result in children becoming increasingly adept at identifying their own feelings of guilt and expressing dislike for the experience. The aversion to guilt could also be used to manipulate adult behavior. By the second half of the twentieth century, middle-class children felt authorized to inform a parent that she or he was "making me feel guilty," with the goal of reducing parental criticism in the face of potentially damaging feelings of guilt. While guilt and shame certainly remain a part of children's experience, their meanings and uses have shifted considerably as part of larger changes in family, school, and peer contexts. As powerful means to develop adult behavior, these forms of emotion have become part of how we historically examine childhood experience in a culture in which a fundamental form of analysis is the examination of the self.

See also: **Anger and Aggression; Consumer Culture; Fear.**

BIBLIOGRAPHY

Demos, John. 1988. "Shame and Guilt in Early New England." In *Emotion and Social Change: Toward a New Psychohistory*, ed. Carol Z. Stearns and Peter N. Stearns. New York: Holmes and Meier.

Erikson, Erik H. 1958. *Young Man Luther: A Study in Psychoanalysis and History*. New York: Norton.

Gay, Peter. 1985. *Freud for Historians*. New York: Oxford University Press.

Markus, Hazel Rose, and Shinobu Kitayama. 1991. "Culture and the Self: Implications for Cognition, Emotion, and Motivation." *Psychological Review* 98: 224–253.

Matt, Susan J. 2002. "Children's Envy and the Emergence of the Modern Consumer Ethic, 1890–1930." *Journal of Social History* 36, no. 2: 283–302.

Stearns, Peter N. 2003. *Anxious Parents: A History of Modern American Parenting*. New York: New York University Press.

Stigler, James W., and Michelle Perry. 1990. "Mathematics Learning in Japanese, Chinese, and American Classrooms." In *Cultural Psychology: Essays on Comparative Human Development*, ed. James W. Stigler, Richard A. Shweder, and Gilbert Herdt. New York: Cambridge University Press.

Tangney, June Price, and Kurt W. Fischer, eds. 1995. *Self-Conscious Emotions: The Psychology of Shame, Guilt, Embarrassment, and Pride*. New York: Guilford Press.

DEBORAH C. STEARNS

Gulick, Luther (1865–1918)

Luther Halsey Gulick was a leader in the promotion of the social and health benefits of play and physical education during the late nineteenth and early twentieth centuries. Born in Hawaii to missionaries Luther Halsey Gulick and Louisa Lewis Gulick, Gulick spent much of his youth in mission fields in Europe and Asia. He attended Oberlin College and New York University's medical school, where he graduated with an M.D. in 1889. He married Charlotte Vetter in 1887, and they were the parents of six children.

Until 1900, Gulick worked for the International Young Men's Christian Association College, then known as the School for Christian Workers, in Springfield, Massachusetts. After receiving his medical degree, he became head of its Gymnasium Department; he was also secretary for the Physical Education Department of the International Committee of the YMCA.

Gulick's combined interest in evangelical Christianity and recreation led him to promote "muscular Christianity," a concept that aligned physical and spiritual strength. He remained associated with the YMCA even as he moved to other institutions, returning in 1918 to assist with war work. One of Gulick's students at the YMCA Training School, James Naismith, invented BASKETBALL in 1891 in response to an assignment by Gulick to develop a team sport; Gulick worked with Naismith to develop the game's rules further.

Some of Gulick's work was done through traditional education institutions. He worked for a time as a teacher and as principal of Pratt High School in Brooklyn from 1900 to 1903 and served as Director of Physical Education for the New York City schools from 1903 to 1907. In 1903, he helped develop the Public School Athletic League, independent from the Board of Education, to give proper supervision to youth athletics. The Girls' Branch of the League focused particularly on folk dancing. In 1916, Gulick was instrumental in founding the American Folk Dance Society. In 1906, he helped to organize the Playground Association of America and served as its first president until 1910. The Russell Sage Foundation also initiated its work in the field of recreation by hiring him to chair its Playground Extension Committee, a position he held until 1913.

Gulick also helped to found the Boy Scouts of America in 1910. In 1911, Gulick and his wife joined with others to organize the Camp Fire Girls, a female counterpart to the BOY SCOUTS intended to prepare girls for future feminine roles. (Gulick had worked with his wife before: Charlotte Gulick's interest in child-study prompted him to lead the Springfield, Massachusetts Mothers' Club from 1898 to 1900.) Gulick became Camp Fire's president when it was incorporated in 1914, serving until shortly before his death in 1918.

Gulick headed the Russell Sage Foundation's Department of Child Hygiene and helped to promote school medical inspections. He was a founding member of the American School Hygiene Association in 1906. Throughout his career, Gulick wrote extensively, publishing numerous articles (some later gathered into books) to publicize his views on recreation and hygiene.

See also: **Sports; Youth Ministries; YWCA and YMCA.**

BIBLIOGRAPHY

Dorgan, Ethel Josephine. 1934. *Luther Halsey Gulick, 1865–1918.* New York: Teachers College.

Cavallo, Dominick. 1981. *Muscles and Morals: Organized Playgrounds and Urban Reform, 1880–1920.* Philadelphia: University of Pennsylvania Press.

ELLEN L. BERG

Guns

Although the subject of children and guns is a troubling contemporary issue, it created little controversy before the twentieth century. Smooth-bored, muzzle-loading muskets were common in the colonies and the early republic. The weapons were imported from Europe, since there were few gunsmiths in America. Some guns were old or broken, but many more were in working order and accessible to children. The popular image of the crack-shot American boy given a gun in his cradle is overstated, however. Before the improvement of rifles and pistols in the mid-nineteenth century there were few guns accurate enough to support sharpshooting. Yet the wide distribution of guns among private citizens meant that American children were more familiar with them than were children in Europe (where gun ownership was closely regulated by the state). Anecdotes to that effect can be found in the narratives of European visitors.

While there was little generalized anxiety concerning children and guns during the early American era, the same tragic mishaps occurred that filled newspapers in the late twentieth century. The Reverend David Osgood preached a funeral sermon in 1797 for a nine-year-old boy killed when a gun held by a friend accidentally discharged and struck him in the bowels. But Osgood took a very different lesson from the accident than would today's moralists, drawing attention to the uncertainty of life and warning his audience to receive grace before they too were taken. He acknowledged but did not decry the gun's lack of a guard, and made nothing of children using a gun.

The author of one of the earliest documents to look critically at children and guns worried less about the children's safety than about their cheapening of what had been an elite sport. In his 1814 *Instructions to Young Sportsmen*, Peter Hawker tried to acculturate working-class youth to the finer rituals of shooting. Fred Mather, a renowned nineteenth-century fisherman and hunter, worried about children and guns for the sake of the small creatures that crossed their paths. In his memoir, *Men I Have Fished With*, he fondly recalled boyhood adventures using a very old musket he co-owned with a friend to shoot birds, muskrats, and deer. But his recollections are tainted with regret at his immoderacy. He implores fathers not to give guns to their sons because boys are savage and bloodthirsty, and will kill everything they can.

In the second half of the nineteenth century, toy guns appeared on the market. The cap gun was invented in 1859, pop guns in the 1870s, and the Daisy Air Rifle (or BB gun) in 1888. These toy weapons were initially quite dangerous, which restricted their appeal, but their increasing safety prompted escalating sales in the twentieth century. In the 1930s, advertisers shifted from selling toy guns for target-practice games to accentuating their use in fantasy role-playing. Boys could become G-men, cowboys, or even gangsters. For some adults, these games were too evocative of the terrorizing "gunplay" in which real Depression-era gangsters were engaging. In 1934 and 1935, Rose Simone, an activist, led Chicago schoolchildren to throw their toy guns into bonfires to protest the toys' fostering of youth violence.

However, there is little evidence that youth, even those who belonged to bootlegging gangs, used guns in their fights. Knives were more common. Only in the 1960s did guns begin to play a prominent role in teen gang behavior; still they were predominately used to make an impression rather than to cause injury. Meanwhile, pacifist sentiment aroused by the anti–Vietnam War movement had sparked a new campaign against toy guns, leading Sears to eliminate toy guns from its catalogs and Dr. Benjamin Spock to recommended against allowing children to engage in "pistol play." That antipathy to toy guns, however, shrinks in significance compared to the impact made on children's games by the invention of a new technology. The video game secured the role of guns—whether represented graphically or as a hand-held plastic facsimile pointed at the screen—in children's games. Some contemporary social critics argue that video games desensitize children to violence and condition them to take actual lives; others disagree.

The danger posed to children by the mass influx of guns into the illegal market in crack cocaine that developed during the 1980s is beyond the realm of speculation. The low price of crack, and its sale in small quantities, caused the absolute number of drug sales to increase exponentially, necessitating a parallel increase in the number of salesmen. Thou-

Boys playing with guns, c. 1950s. Toy guns were first manufactured in the mid-nineteenth century, but as early as the 1930s critics claimed that the toys encouraged children to be violent. © Horace Bristol/CORBIS.

sands of urban youths became crack dealers. The fluidity of the market encouraged violent competition among the sellers of crack, and more and more young dealers began carrying guns for protection. Between 1984 and 1991 homicide rates by adolescents tripled, an increase directly attributable to rising rates of youth gun-ownership.

Government and the not-for-profits have responded to the crisis with a flurry of well-intentioned campaigns. The U.S. Congress held hearings on the subject of children and

guns in 1989 (as part of the "Save the Kids" campaign) and 1992. There have been proposals for special legislation (some of which has passed, such as the Gun-Free Schools Act of 1994) to curb the problem. The Carter Center, the Violence and Policy Center, CHILDREN'S DEFENSE FUND, and the American Youth Center have published reports since 1989 on the subject of children and guns. All argue for better gun control. A rash of well-publicized school shootings during the 1990s, most of which occurred in white rural and suburban communities, forced many Americans to recognize that the crisis is not restricted to inner-city African-American youth. In 1999, 4,205 children were killed by gunfire. Most were older teenagers, but 629 were under fifteen years old.

Nonetheless, strong sentiment remains favoring children's gunplay. The National Rifle Association (NRA) publishes a special magazine, *InSights*, for its junior members, which features glossy photographs of children holding guns and encourages its readers to target-shoot and hunt. Memoirs of childhood shooting with dad, or granddad, likewise are a popular feature of *American Rifleman*, the NRA's primary publication. It remains to be seen whether either the gun-safety education programs that the NRA promotes, or the gun-control measures advocated by the NRA's opponents, will stop the gun accidents and gun violence that threaten American children.

See also: **Delinquency; Drugs; Law, Children and the; Police, Children and the; School Shootings and School Violence; Street Games; Toys; Youth Gangs.**

BIBLIOGRAPHY

Cook, Philip J., ed. 1996. "Kids, Guns, and Public Policy." *Law and Contemporary Problems* 59, no. 1.

Cross, Gary. 1997. *Kids' Stuff: Toys and the Changing World of American Childhood.* Cambridge, MA: Harvard University Press.

Grossman, Dave. 1995. *On Killing: The Psychological Cost of Learning to Kill in War and Society.* Boston: Little, Brown.

Ward, Jill M. 1999. *Children and Guns.* Washington, DC: Children's Defense Fund.

RACHEL HOPE CLEVES

Gutmann, Bessie Pease (1876–1960)

Bessie Pease Gutmann's work was part of the explosion of images of children which flooded the American commercial art market at the beginning of the twentieth century. Gutmann's drawings appeared in illustrated books, on magazine covers, and in advertisements.

Bessie Pease was born on April 8, 1876 in Philadelphia, Pennsylvania. She showed an early interest in art and after high school, she attended the Philadelphia School of Design for Women and the New York School of Art. After training at the Art Student's League of New York from 1896 to 1898, she was invited to join the firm of Gutmann and Gutmann, which specialized in fine art prints and advertisements. She later married Hellmuth Gutmann, one of the owners of the firm. Gutmann often used the couple's three children, Alice, Lucille, and John, as models for her drawings.

Between 1906 and 1922 Gutmann designed twenty-two magazine covers, for publications such as *Women's Home Companion* and *McCalls*. She also illustrated many popular children's books, including *A Child's Garden of Verse* (1905) and *Alice in Wonderland* (1907). About seventy Gutmann images are known to have been published as postcards. Gutmann's best-known work was her print *A Little Bit of Heaven*, published by the Balliol Corporation in 1916. *A Little Bit of Heaven* presents a close-up view of Gutmann's daughter Lucille that allows the viewer to admire the sleeping child's plump cheeks and chubby fingers in intimate detail. In 1926 Gutmann published a similar image of an African-American child, titled *My Honey*. She also produced a series of images of cherubs, and one of mothers and children together. Eschewing the nostalgic costumes and backgrounds that characterized the work of her closest competitor, JESSIE WILLCOX SMITH, Gutmann focused on rendering the tangible, physical presence of her adorable subjects.

See also: **Greenaway, Kate; Images of Childhood.**

BIBLIOGRAPHY

Choppa, Karen. 1998. *Bessie Pease Gutmann: Over Fifty Years of Published Art.* Lancaster, PA: Schiffer Publishing.

Christie, Victor J. W. 1990. *Bessie Pease Gutmann: Her Life and Works.* Radnor, PA: Wallace-Homestead.

Higonnet, Anne. 1998. *Pictures of Innocence: The History and Crisis of Ideal Childhood.* London: Thames and Hudson.

A. CASSANDRA ALBINSON

GutsMuths, J. C. F. (1759–1839)

Johann Christoph Friedrich GutsMuths was born in 1759 in Quedlinburg, Germany, the son of an ordinary lower-middle-class family. GutsMuths's father died when he was twelve years old and in order to contribute financially to the family he worked as a private teacher for the two sons of the Ritter family while he attended high school. He went to Halle in 1779 to study at what was called the first modern university in Germany. Following the new principle of academic liberty, GutsMuths studied theology as well as physics, mathematics, philosophy, and history. He was especially influenced by a number of lessons on pedagogical methodology based on the principles of German educational reformer JOHANN BERNHARD BASEDOW.

Upon finishing his studies, GutsMuths returned to his occupation as a private teacher with the Ritter family. When the elder Doctor Ritter died GutsMuths assumed the responsibility for his children's upbringing and in that capacity followed the family to the new Philanthropic School in Schnepfenthal, Germany. The principal quickly noticed the young tutor's extraordinary pedagogical abilities and offered him a position at the school. GutsMuths remained there, with his wife and family, for the rest of his life.

GutsMuths was engaged as a teacher in the ordinary school subjects, but he won his international reputation as the founder of pedagogical GYMNASTICS when he took responsibility for gymnastics education at the school in 1786. His meticulously prepared book *Gymnastik für die Jugend* (Gymnastics for youth) was published 1793 as the first textbook in gymnastics (revised in 1804). The first five chapters of the book explain his theories of child rearing and the use of gymnastics as an instrument for raising children. The remaining chapters are concerned with the pedagogy of gymnastics, which GutsMuths divides into proper gymnastics, or exercises, various hands-on activities, including gardening, and social play. He believed that all gymnastics should take place outside and that a seven-year-old child ought to spend around ten hours a day in physical activity. The book's critical view of the prevailing culture places it in the German philosophical tradition of the ENLIGHTENMENT, especially as inspired by JEAN-JACQUES ROUSSEAU. GutsMuths wished to break with the teachings of the Middle Ages and replace the divine with nature.

Besides *Gymnastik für die Jugend*, GutsMuths published several shorter works on physical exercise. He also published two books in which he combined gymnastics with the German *Turnverein* (gymnastics club) movement, a movement that followed the ideals of German educator Friedrich Ludwig Jahn.

Posterity has seen GutsMuths as a person who worked incessantly for pedagogical gymnastics, but actually we see in his orientation towards the German *Turnverein* the same nationalistic and patriotic thoughts as can be found in Jahn's work. The fact that he was engaged as a teacher for more than fifty years at Schnepfenthal probably supported the impression of continuity in his work. GutsMuths died in May 21, 1839.

See also: **Interscholastic Athletics; Salzmann, Christian Gotthilf; Sports.**

BIBLIOGRAPHY

GutsMuths, Johann Christoph Friedrich. 1970 [1803]. *Gymnastics for Youth: or A Practical Guide to Healthful and Amusing Exercises.* Dubuque, IA: Brown Reprints.

JØRN HANSEN

Gymnasium Schooling

In the ancient world, the word *gymnasion* was applied to public places where young men exercised physically and were trained by teachers and philosophers, in particular in Athens at the Academy, which was associated with PLATO, and the Lyceum, associated with ARISTOTLE. Since the Renaissance, the term has been revived to designate educational institutions that refer expressly to the intellectual heritage of classical antiquity. In the Germanic countries, the Netherlands, Scandinavia, and Eastern Europe, *gymnasium* is the name for a senior secondary school that prepares students for the uni-

versity. Elsewhere in Europe and in the United States, however, the word gymnasium and its equivalents refer to the other element of the Greek *gymnasion*: a place for physical exercise.

Two periods are distinguished in the history of the classical gymnasium. From the sixteenth century, the word simply referred to the LATIN SCHOOL model that was developed by the humanists. This took various names: grammar school in England, *collège* in France, *colegio* in Spain, *Lateinschule* or gymnasium in the Holy Roman Empire. The French name was reminiscent of the university college, and indeed Latin schools were considered to be the first stage of higher education. In many countries the higher classes in the Latin schools, after the so-called humanities courses of grammar, poetry, and rhetoric, were part of the university system itself. The first truly Protestant gymnasium, created by Johann Sturm at Strasbourg in 1538, united a Latin school to a superstructure consisting of university-level chairs. Such chairs in arts, philosophy, and theology, and sometimes in law and medicine, prepared pupils in or near their hometowns for university level functions or academic degrees which they would go on to take at the full-fledged universities. In early modern Germany, the word gymnasium finally came to be used for the most elaborate form of a Latin school, with a complete range of classes, preparing the children of the literate citizens for the university and hence for the learned professions.

Neo-Humanistic Ideals

During the late eighteenth century, humanistic ideology underwent a radical change. The focus of classical education shifted from a philological approach and a conservative concept of erudition embedded in the society of orders toward a more dynamic vision of self-cultivation, linked up with a secular professional ethic in a society that wanted social and political change. As a consequence, the old, virtually closed "learned estate"' (*Gelehrtenstand*) was gradually replaced by a cultured bourgeoisie (*Bildungsbürgertum*,) characterized by functional expertise, a liberal spirit of self-cultivation, and a meritocratic ideology. After the era of the French Revolution, the German gymnasium was revived by the cultured bourgeoisie with a new, neo-humanistic scope: classical languages and literature, considered the main source of the new ideals of humanity and aesthetic purity, were henceforth the unavoidable rite of passage toward culture (*Bildung*), profession (*Beruf*) and office (*Amt*). This internal transformation of the classical education was legitimized by legislation. Indeed, the unitary school system of Prussia, designed in 1812 by Wilhelm von Humboldt (1767–1835) and Johann Wilhelm Süvern (1775–1829), culminated in the gymnasium, intended for what Humboldt called "a harmonious cultivation of the mind," though the body was certainly not neglected. The new gymnasium got a completely new curriculum, including modern languages, mathematics, and natural sciences. The nine-year course, for students aged ten to eighteen, was closed by an examination called the *Abitur*, the certificate of maturity, which was the prerequisite for matriculation at a German university.

The downfall of Latin as a language of science since the eighteenth century cleared the way for new functions. Henceforth the gymnasium could stress the intrinsic values of classical antiquity. It became a privileged tool for the intellectual, aesthetic, and spiritual education of the nineteenth-century cultured bourgeoisie. Yet in spite of its broad ambitions, it touched only a small elite—not more than 3 percent of the German population until World War II (whereas less than 1 percent matriculated at the universities). Research has shown that the highly selective practices of the prewar gymnasium had served the continuous self-reproduction of the intellectual elite though it admitted a small proportion of pupils from the middle classes. From the second half of the nineteenth century women were slowly admitted too.

During the nineteenth century, the Prussian gymnasium with its Humboldtian ideals heavily influenced the evolution of secondary education in the Germanic Empire and in the neighboring countries: the Austro-Hungarian Empire, Switzerland, the Netherlands, Scandinavia, the Baltic regions, and Russia. Its ideology also resembled the *belles lettres* paradigm in contemporary France, where the LYCÉE played a similar role with a still greater impact on the self-reproduction of the intellectual class. Yet social reproduction through the *lycée* seems to have been still stronger in the closed French prewar bourgeoisie than through the German gymnasium.

Institutional Change

The classical languages remain the core business of the neo-humanistic German gymnasium in the early twenty-first century. Its preparatory function for the university and its social prestige as a senior secondary school remain intact. Nevertheless the institution itself has gone through a long series of transformations over the centuries, due to the alternate pressures of church and state and the demands of changing social groups for a more utilitarian curriculum with fewer classical subjects. From a single branch of studies, the curriculum shifted slowly toward a "reformed upper phase" with a broad choice of courses. Moreover, it has had to share its tasks and privileges with competing schools. The *Progymnasium* taught only a six-year course, with a less demanding curriculum. After the German unification in 1871, university admission was also granted to the pupils of the *Realgymnasium*, which in addition to the modern languages taught Latin but not Greek, and of the *Oberrealschule*, which provided no classical instruction at all but only a modern languages and sciences curriculum. During the Third Reich, the elitist ideology of the gymnasium was easily co-opted by Nazi propaganda. The concept of *Bildung* was appropriated into the aesthetic, moral, and intellectual values of the Nazi state and the creation of an Aryan type. After World War II the German gymnasium went through a period of diversification and experimentation that was ended by the Federal Act of 1972.

See also: **Education, Europe.**

BIBLIOGRAPHY

Kraul, Margret. 1984. *Das deutsche Gymnasium, 1780–1980.* Frankfurt: Suhrkamp.

Müller, Detlef K., Fritz Ringer, and Brian Simon, eds. 1988. *The Rise of the Modern Educational System: Structural Change and Social Reproduction 1870–1920.* Cambridge, UK: Cambridge University Press.

Ringer, Fritz K. 1979. *Education and Society in Modern Europe.* Bloomington: Indiana University Press.

WILLEM FRIJHOFF

Gymnastics

The word *gymnastics*, the practice of which extends back thousands of years, has been used to refer to activities ranging from simple movements to extraordinary acrobatic feats. *Gymnastik für die Jugend* (1793), written by JOHANN CHRISTOPH FRIEDRICH GUTSMUTHS, is often cited as laying the foundations for a comprehensive system of exercises and as well as today's competitive sport. Drawing upon JEAN-JACQUES ROUSSEAU, contemporary physicians, and classical sources, GutMuths (a teacher at the Schnepenthal Philanthropinum) identified three components of PHYSICAL EDUCATION: manual arts; social games; gymnastic exercises, which included wrestling, running, swimming, leaping, balancing, and climbing. His ideas had a considerable influence on Friedrich Ludwig Jahn, who in 1810 began meeting pupils in a wooded area near their school. There they engaged in a variety of activities that included exercising on rudimentary apparatus. Jahn's *Die Deutsche Turnkunst* (1816) included sections devoted to the parallel bars, vaulting, and other movements that became the core of the German system, which made extensive use of equipment. The Swedish system (designed by Per Henrik Ling in the early 1800s) used comparatively little equipment and emphasized posture, sequential progression, proper breathing, and specific exercises for each portion of the body. Its educational and medical branches were adopted, and adapted, in many countries. Debates about which system was better were often intense and continued until sports became dominant in the curriculum.

Nineteenth-century teachers could draw upon small books like James H. Smart's *Manual of School Gymnastics* to provide classroom calisthenic drills. Turners (members of German gymnastic societies) who arrived in the United States following the 1848 German Revolution campaigned vigorously to make German gymnastics the basis of the curriculum. Outside the schools, Turnvereins (German gymnastic societies) and Sokols (Czech gymnastic associations) organized their own events. Others held that the Swedish system, introduced into the Boston public schools in the 1890s, was more appropriate, especially for children and females. Books like Wilbur Bowen's *The Teaching of Elementary School Gymnastics* (1909) set forth the strengths of each. In the 1920s Danish gymnastics (which offered more variety) were introduced into the American curriculum. Some attention also was given to stunts and tumbling (such as the forward roll and the handspring).

Competitive gymnastics consists of two forms: Modern Rhythmic Gymnastics, which uses balls, hoops, and similar light equipment; and Artistic (Olympic) Gymnastics. Team competition for women took place at the 1928 Olympics, but it was not until the 1952 Games in Helsinki that individual competition began. Television coverage of the 1960 Rome Olympics resulted in an upsurge of interest in a number of countries. Following the performances of diminutive Olga Korbut in 1972 thousands of young girls in the United States joined the rapidly growing number of private gymnastic clubs and became involved in the Junior Olympic program. Gymnastics requires strength, flexibility, coordination, discipline, and willingness to practice long hours. The nature of the apparatus is such that short stature and a light body is an advantage. Both the age and size of competitive gymnasts has been decreased as the sport became more competitive. Although many youngsters enjoy the challenges, and certainly the thrill of victory, considerable concern has been expressed about the effects of intense training on their bodies and their psyches.

See also: **Sports; Title IX and Girls' Sports.**

BIBLIOGRAPHY

Cochrane, Tuovi Sappinen. 1968. *International Gymnastics for Girls and Women.* Reading, MA: Addison-Wesley Publishing Co.

Gerber, Ellen. W. 1971. *Innovators and Institutions in Physical Education.* Philadelphia: Lea and Febiger.

Goodbody, John. 1982. *The Illustrated History of Gymnastics.* London: Stanley Paul.

Ryan, Joan. 1995. *Little Girls in Pretty Boxes: The Making and Breaking of Elite Gymnasts and Figure Skaters.* New York: Doubleday.

INTERNET RESOURCE

USA Gymnastics Online. Available from <www.usa-gymnastics.org>.

ROBERTA PARK

H

Hall, Granville Stanley (1844–1924)

A founder of the academic discipline of psychology in the United States and the first promoter of the scientific study of the child, Hall received a doctorate in philosophy at Harvard with William James. In 1888, he became president and professor of psychology at the new Clark University. At Clark, where he remained for the rest of his career, Hall trained such prominent child psychologists as ARNOLD L. GESELL, Henry H. Goddard, and Lewis M. Terman. He authored hundreds of books and articles, established several academic journals, helped organize the American Psychological Association, and brought SIGMUND FREUD and Carl Jung to Clark in 1909. Hall's ideas shaped CHILD PSYCHOLOGY from the 1880s through the 1910s.

Hall popularized an instinct psychology that stressed the importance of natural impulses and biological imprinting. He thought that a child's innate nature unfolded over time through an evolutionary process, in which the development of the child *recapitulated* the development of the human race. Young children were like "primitive races" who advanced as they grew, achieving the level of the most "civilized races" by adulthood.

This theory of human growth had practical applications. Parents who understood what behavior to expect at certain ages could guide their children appropriately. Hall argued that young children were like animals who should be treated with indulgence and freedom. He recommended that children be kept away from school until the age of eight, since formal schooling might harm a young child's development. Young children should roam the countryside to learn the ways of nature or satisfy their instincts in informal settings free from adult standards of proper behavior. Guided by their own natural impulses, children would pass through the stages of childhood to become self-controlled adults.

In the early twentieth century Hall turned his attention to ADOLESCENCE, a term he introduced into widespread use.

In his monumental study *Adolescence* (1904), he described a period of turmoil in which a child's instinctive, primitive nature struggled with more evolved characteristics. Hall concentrated on boys as he analyzed this critical stage of physical, mental, and emotional development.

Hall's ideas were widely disseminated and influenced the early child study movement, particularly the work of the National Congress of Mothers (later the Parent-Teacher Association), founded in 1897 as the first national group devoted to parent education. Hall was a frequent speaker at the organization's conventions and served as its chief scientific authority. Members of the group became participants in Hall's research, filling out detailed questionnaires about their children's behavior and speech for his research projects.

The instinct theory of child development came under attack in the 1920s as a new progressive orientation in social science stressed environmental over biological explanations of human development. Hall's research methods were challenged as unscientific, impressionistic, and sentimental. CHILD STUDY leaders in the 1920s adopted more rigorous scientific techniques and highlighted cultural influences on child development. By the 1920s, Hall's studies were largely discredited, though his ideas continued to have an influence on views of development as well as adolescence.

See also: **Child Development, History of the Concept of.**

BIBLIOGRAPHY

Ross, Dorothy. 1972. *G. Stanley Hall: The Psychologist as Prophet.* Chicago: University of Chicago Press.

Schlossman, Steven L. 1976. "Before Home Start: Notes toward a History of Parent Education in America, 1897–1929." *Harvard Educational Review* 46: 436–467.

DIANA SELIG

Halloween

The history of Halloween began with the ancient Celtic festival of Samhain, the last day of the Celtic year. The holiday was celebrated at the end of summer and the beginning of winter, as days became shorter and nights longer. The Celts believed that the dead returned on Samhain, and they created traditions to keep themselves safe from evil spirits, including dressing up in costume to fool the dead.

During the Middle Ages, the Catholic Church appropriated the Celtic festival of Samhain with the express purpose of absorbing pagan celebrations into the Christian cycle of holidays. The resulting All Saints' Day was officially moved to November 1 by Pope Gregory III in the eighth century. Also called All Hallows, the night before became known as All Hallows Eve, which later became Hallowe'en, and finally Halloween.

Other traditions contributed to the evolution of Halloween as an American holiday. The historian Lesley Bannatyne refers to Protestant English settlers of the eighteenth century importing the tradition of Guy Fawkes Day. Cited by numerous authors as a source for Halloween, celebrations of this holiday often took on an anti-Catholic theme, with celebrants burning effigies of the Pope as well as other major contemporary figures. The holiday began in 1605, when English Protestants foiled a plot by Catholics to blow up the Houses of Parliament in London. Celebrations also included pranks, masquerades, bonfires, and fireworks.

However, the Protestants, a large, influential group, frowned upon Halloween celebrations, effectively stopping any systematic observation of the festival in the United States until the nineteenth century. Elements of the European folk holiday remained, however. After the American Revolution, "play parties" became popular in the form of harvest celebrations for families.

Halloween evolved into a holiday for children in the nineteenth and twentieth centuries, as less frightening entertainments replaced commemorations of the dead. A large amount of printed ephemera about and for Halloween was produced at the end of the nineteenth century and the beginning of the twentieth, specifically for children. The earliest examples of this new genre were made by the lithographer Raphael Tuck, also known for the manufacture of paper DOLLS. The first quarter of the twentieth century also heralded the rise of businesses manufacturing products specifically for Halloween. Today Halloween is a major consumer holiday second in gross revenues only to Christmas.

Trick-or-treating, which began as a Thanksgiving tradition as early as 1881, became a major Halloween ritual in the 1920s. The phrase itself was first published in 1939 and has been used ever since. The "open house" tradition of welcoming trick-or-treaters (especially small children) became increasingly widespread in the 1930s.

For children Halloween is also traditionally an occasion to explore boundaries, often breaking rules or bypassing parental authority (whether symbolic or actual). In the past as in the present, this aspect of the holiday was often negative. By the 1930s the tradition of committing acts of vandalism on Halloween was a major concern of adults. Schools and civic groups across the country organized celebrations for children and teenagers in an effort to curb vandalism, a tradition that continues. Today Halloween is still a holiday primarily for children, which still includes age-old traditions such as dressing up in costumes and frightening masks and requesting candy favors.

See also: **Parades; Vacations.**

BIBLIOGRAPHY

Bannatyne, Lesley Pratt. 1990. *Halloween: An American Holiday, An American History.* New York: Facts on File.

Sklar, David J. 2002. *Death Makes A Holiday: A Cultural History of Halloween.* New York: Bloomsbury.

SHIRA SILVERMAN

Hammer v. Dagenhart

In *Hammer v. Dagenhart*, the U.S. Supreme Court declared the 1916 Keating-Owen Act, which restricted child labor through the Congressional power to regulate interstate commerce, unconstitutional. Keating-Owen prohibited the shipment of commodities across state lines if they were manufactured by firms employing children less than fourteen years of age, or in mines employing children less than sixteen years of age. When Keating-Owen became effective in 1917, a Child Labor Division under Grace Abbott was organized to enforce the law through the U.S. CHILDREN'S BUREAU directed by Julia Lathrop. Almost immediately, a Mr. Dagenhart, the father of two youths working in a mill in North Carolina, sued to stop the enforcement of the law. Dagenhart won a court injunction against the federal statute, and the North Carolina Attorney General appealed to the Supreme Court. In a 5–4 split decision, the majority rejected a lower court's reasoning that the statute was unconstitutional because it deprived parents such as Dagenhart of their property rights regarding their children. Instead, Justice William D. Day wrote that the statute attempted to achieve indirectly for the Congress what the Constitution did not grant them directly. The purpose of the federal statute was to regulate manufacturing in the states, and thus it had unconstitutionally used the commerce clause of the Constitution to intrude upon state's rights. Justice Oliver W. Holmes argued for the minority that the law was fully within the power of the interstate commerce clause, and the purposes and consequences of the Act relative to the states were irrelevant.

Keating-Owen and *Hammer* mark the first time the struggle over child labor moved before the highest judicial and political bodies of the nation. The result reveals the difficulties child labor reformers faced when confronting state's rights doctrine and laissez-faire justifications for unfettered corporate power. Even after the *Hammer* ruling, reformers continued to work for federal action because they understood that the economic pressure on state legislatures to make their states appealing to business interests made it impossible to curb the abuses of capitalism in a meaningful way through state law. After the Keating-Owen defeat, they tried to amend the act to meet the Court's demands. This was rejected in *Bailey v. Drexel* (1922). Next the NATIONAL CHILD LABOR COMMITTEE pushed for a child labor amendment to the Constitution in 1924, but this also failed. Reformers finally achieved a lasting and significant restriction of child labor in every state of the union with the 1938 Federal Labor Standards Act, and in 1941 the Supreme Court explicitly overruled *Hammer* in *U.S. v. Darby*. *Darby* was greeted with enthusiasm in progressive circles, but the *Hammer* defeat remained alive in the minds of reformers such as Edith Abbott, who responded by asking if the Court could repair the "stunted minds and broken lives" of the children who had been abandoned in the name of states' rights and free trade two decades before.

See also: **Child Labor in the West; Law, Children and the.**

BIBLIOGRAPHY

Lindenmeyer, Kriste. 1997. *A Right To Childhood: The U.S. Children's Bureau and Child Welfare, 1912–46.* Urbana: University of Illinois Press.

Trattner, Walter I. 1970. *Crusade for Children: A History of the National Child Labor Committee and Child Labor Reform in America.* Chicago: Quadrangle Books.

PATRICK J. RYAN

Harry Potter and J. K. Rowling

In the closing years of the twentieth century, few books for children enjoyed as much success, scrutiny, or controversy as the phenomenally popular Harry Potter novels. Part British school fiction, part mystery, part conventional fantasy, J. K. Rowling's planned, seven-part series concerns a boy named Harry who discovers that he was born a wizard and that a secret society of witches and wizards exists beneath the noses of the Muggle (or non-wizard) world. Orphaned under mysterious circumstances and branded with a strange lightning bolt on his forehead, Harry grows up with his neglectful relatives the Dursleys. On his eleventh birthday he is visited by Hagrid, a friendly, giant caretaker of Hogwarts Academy, a school for wizards that Harry is called to attend. There, he quickly becomes close friends with a bookish girl named Hermione and a comical friend Ron, as well as the enemy of a rich student named Draco. Through a number of noticeably darker adventures—each of Rowling's books describes one year at the school—Harry discovers not only the deeply

held secrets of the magic world, but also the facts of his own past, including the death of his parents at the hand of an evil wizard named Voldemort.

The novels are marked by increasing sophistication, depth, and length; the fourth book, one of the best-selling children's books in history, is nearly 800 pages. Packed full of mythic references and names, not to mention a broad cast of well-drawn characters, these smart books are noted for their complex mysteries that revolve around even the smallest detail. They feature clever objects and spells, fabulous creatures, secretive adults, a Gothic-style castle for a school, and a soccer-like sport called Quidditch that is played on brooms. Rowling frequently deals with such themes as prejudice (against those of mixed parentage), class (through the different dormitories one is assigned by The Sorting Hat), and ADOLESCENCE (as the young protagonists learn to control their powers).

By word of mouth and clever marketing, the first three books in the series, *Harry Potter and the Philosopher's Stone* (1997), *Harry Potter and the Chamber of Secrets* (1998), and *Harry Potter and the Prisoner of Azkaban* (1999) spawned a number of fan clubs and websites, filled up the best-seller list, and became a favorite of adult readers as well. Critics argued whether Rowling was merely rewriting old conventions in a new guise. Faith-based groups, meanwhile, challenged the novels' emphasis on witchcraft and the occult, making the first three titles the most frequently banned books of 1999. By the time the fourth book, *Harry Potter and the Goblet of Fire* (2000), was released, midnight sales and a rash of marketing had made Harry Potter a global phenomenon and a merchandising goldmine. The books, with an enticing world of flying brooms and invisibility cloaks, seemed to echo this drive for marketing. Yet Rowling's books are noticeably moralistic, often discouraging temptation by showcasing a number of alluring objects—a mirror of desire, a stone that gives eternal life—that are never fulfilling for the main characters.

Christopher Columbus's blockbuster film of the first book (2001), one of the highest grossing films in history, featured a near literal translation of the book to screen, employing an almost entirely British cast and a group of unknowns to play the three child leads. Its success guaranteed a franchise of films from the books. The fifth book, meanwhile, delayed by Rowling's own decision to spend more time with her family and to craft the plot, became a highly anticipated event. Scholastic capitalized on such reader anticipation with two supplementary books, *Fantastic Beasts and Where to Find Them* (2001) and *Quidditch Through the Ages* (2001), both marketed as textbooks from Hogwarts.

A former English and French teacher, born in 1966 in Chipping Sodbury near Bristol, England, Rowling wrote the first books primarily in cafés, while her infant daughter slept. Conceiving the series on a train ride, she formulated the plot

Harry Potter (Daniel Radcliffe) consults with Dumbledore (Richard Harris), the headmaster of Hogwarts Academy in *Harry Potter and the Sorceror's Stone*. The 2001 film adaptation of J. K. Rowling's first Harry Potter book became one of the highest grossing movies in history. THE KOBAL COLLECTION/WARNER BROS/MOUNTAIN, PETER.

of all seven books at once, in a burst of creativity, imagining full lives for all of her characters. Initially rejected by several publishers, the first book was eventually released in England, before being purchased by Scholastic in America. It was slightly revised, as the "Philosopher's Stone" of the original title was changed to the more fantastical "Sorcerer's Stone" in American editions, and some British slang was taken out. It was also eventually translated into nearly thirty languages. The books remain a publishing phenomenon and a significant touchstone of contemporary children's literature.

See also: **Children's Literature; Lord of the Rings and J.R.R. Tolkien; Series Books.**

BIBLIOGRAPHY

Fraser, Lindsey. 2000. *Conversations with J. K. Rowling.* New York: Scholastic.

Natov, Roni. 2001. "Harry Potter and the Extraordinariness of the Ordinary." *The Lion and the Unicorn* 25: 310–27.

Pennington, John. 2002. "From Elfland to Hogwarts, or the Aesthetic Trouble with Harry Potter." *The Lion and the Unicorn* 26: 78–97.

Routledge, Christopher. 2001. "Harry Potter and the Mystery of Everyday Life." In *Mystery in Children's Literature: From the Rational to the Supernatural*, ed. Adrienne E. Gavin and Christopher Routledge. New York: Palgrave.

Shafer, Elizabeth D. 2000. *Beacham's Sourcebook for Teaching Young Adult Fiction: Exploring Harry Potter.* Osprey, FL: Beacham Publishing.

Zipes, Jack. 2001. "The Phenomenon of Harry Potter, or Why All the Talk?" In his *Sticks and Stones: The Troublesome Success of Children's Literature from Slovenly Peter to Harry Potter.* New York: Routledge.

CHRIS MCGEE

Head Start

Head Start is a U.S. federal program that provides education and social services to low-income three- to five-year-old children and their families. Head Start began as a summer program for about 500,000 children in 1965 and by the early twenty-first century served almost 1 million people annually in a mixture of school-year and full-year programs. Head Start's programming and politics reflects Lyndon Johnson's efforts to build the Great Society in the 1960s. Unlike other Great Society programs, a coalition emerged to ensure Head Start's survival and expansion.

Head Start developed out of two trends in particular. First, the emerging academic interest in "compensatory education for cultural deprivation" taught that government intervention early in children's lives could help children overcome what many expert-advocates considered inferior parenting by poor and minority families, especially women. Second, the New Left sought to build a movement focused on civil rights and community action that would enable oppressed communities to take over government and social service institutions.

Expert-advocates and civil rights activists fought over Head Start's treatment of the parents of children enrolled in the program. Expert-advocates tended to want to educate parents, while civil rights activists wanted to empower them, and Head Start centers around the country displayed elements of both sides' desires. After arguing since Head Start's inception in 1965, the two groups reached a compromise in 1970 that required Head Start centers to create Policy Councils with parent majorities.

Neither expert-advocates nor civil rights activists correctly predicted how parents would actually experience Head Start. Head Start helped create a stronger sense of community among poor parents, especially poor mothers. As a result, parents advocated for themselves and their children more with local institutions and became a crucial part of the Head Start coalition, lobbying politicians on its behalf. This political organizing began without central coordination and led to the creation of the National Head Start Association, which organizes parents and Head Start employees to lobby on Head Start issues.

Despite disagreements over parent involvement, expert-advocates, and civil rights activists united in distrust for public schools and in their desire to use Head Start to reform the public school system. Throughout its history, members of the Head Start community helped establish broader changes throughout public education, pushing expanded early childhood education, comprehensive services and parent involvement.

This tense but effective coalition of expert-advocates, civil rights activists, and parents helped Head Start survive an era marked by academic and political challenges to many Great Society programs, including some studies that questioned its effectiveness and a brief attempt by the Nixon administration to eliminate it. By the late 1970s and 1980s, the coalition was aided by emerging research demonstrating the lasting benefits of Head Start in children it served. Research found that children enrolled in Head Start were less likely than their peers to be referred to special education or required to repeat a grade throughout their public school experience. Later studies found that children enrolled in Head Start were less likely than their peers to become pregnant as teenagers or become involved with the criminal justice system. Opponents could no longer argue that Head Start provided no benefit to children. The coalition continues to play a crucial role in its expansion and contemporary policy questions, such as how to increase academic standards in the pro-

gram, whether to move it from the Department of Health and Human Services to the Department of Education, and what are the appropriate means of assessing the program's effectiveness.

See also: **Education, United States.**

BIBLIOGRAPHY

Ames, Lynda J., and Jeanne Ellsworth. 1997. *Women Reformed, Women Empowered: Poor Mothers and the Endangered Promise of Head Start.* Philadelphia: Temple University Press.

Zigler, Edward, and Karen Anderson, eds. 1979. *Project Head Start: A Legacy of the War on Poverty.* New York: Free Press.

Zigler, Edward, and Susan Muenchow. 1992. *Head Start: The Inside Story of America's Most Successful Educational Experiment.* New York: Basic Books.

JOSH KAGAN

Healy, William (1869–1963)

William Healy can be credited with bringing the interpretative framework of psychology to the JUVENILE JUSTICE system, with designing the institutional structure for the practice of clinical child psychiatry and psychology, and with popularizing psychological interpretations of youthful misconduct through his clinics, writings, and public appearances. Unlike many of his contemporaries in the early twentieth century who blamed poor heredity and mental RETARDATION for juvenile crime and called for institutionalization, Healy argued for the intellectual and psychological normality of delinquents and made a strong case for the efficacy of psychological intervention strategies.

A physician by training, Healy began his work with delinquents in 1909 when he was employed by a group of Chicago reformers to direct the Juvenile Psychopathic Institute. These reformers, having inaugurated the JUVENILE COURT movement ten years earlier, wanted Healy to provide the new court with assessments of troublesome repeat offenders. At the same time, he was expected to use these cases to develop a general understanding of juvenile crime. Healy's results were published in 1915 as *The Individual Delinquent*, a compendium of social and environmental, psychological, and medical characteristics found in the youths he evaluated. Healy rejected unidimensional theories of causation, arguing instead for an eclectic approach. The task for the court and the clinic, he believed, was to determine the unique combination of factors that shaped each delinquent's individual personality. This profile could be deduced only through a thorough investigation of the delinquents and their families by a team of medical, psychological, and social-work professionals. As established by Healy, the process included efforts to elicit the child's "own story" (Healy's phrase for the psychiatrist's contribution to the evaluation).

Healy's views on DELINQUENCY as laid out in *The Individual Delinquent* were heavily influenced by the adolescent psychology of G. STANLEY HALL, the preventive mental hygiene programs of the psychiatrist Adolph Meyer, and the environmentalism of Progressive-era reformers. Increasingly, however, Healy was drawn to explanations of human behavior found in the works of SIGMUND FREUD. By applying psychoanalytic concepts of repression and the unconscious, Healy came to identify "mental conflicts" as the cause of much delinquency and adolescent misconduct. Like Freud, Healy was convinced that issues related to SEXUALITY usually caused these adolescent conflicts, and Healy's work helped to fortify the SEX EDUCATION movement of the 1920s and 1930s. Also like Freud, Healy located the source of personality and delinquency in family dynamics and in particular in the child's relationship with his or her mother. Healy's concurrence helped to give validity to the mother-blaming psychology that consumed child psychiatry after the 1930s.

In 1917 Healy became director of the Judge Baker Foundation of Boston, where he remained until retiring in 1947. Healy's clinic was originally designed to provide assessments of delinquents brought before the Boston juvenile court. By the 1930s the clinic evaluated and treated children from all walks of life who were experiencing a broad range of emotional or behavioral problems. In 1922, when the Commonwealth Fund, a wealthy private philanthropy interested in juvenile justice programs and research in child development, offered to support the establishment of a network of court-affiliated CHILD GUIDANCE clinics, Healy's Judge Baker Foundation served as the working model. At first these child guidance clinics were solely for delinquents, but during the 1920s the clientele came to include other troublesome youths—in trouble at school or difficult to live with at home, for example. During the 1920s and 1930s the parents of these nondelinquent adolescents learned about the teachings of child guidance through child-rearing manuals, popular magazines, and government publications, and William Healy contributed to all these venues.

See also: **Adolescence and Youth; Child Psychology.**

BIBLIOGRAPHY

Healy, William. 1915. *The Individual Delinquent: A Text-Book of Diagnosis and Prognosis for All Concerned in Understanding Offenders.* Boston: Little, Brown.

Healy, William. 1917. *Mental Conflicts and Misconduct.* Boston: Little, Brown.

Healy, William, and Franz Alexander. 1935. *Roots of Crime: Psychoanalytic Studies.* New York: Knopf.

Healy, William, and Augusta Bronner. 1926. *Delinquents and Criminals, Their Making and Unmaking: Studies in Two American Cities.* New York: Macmillan.

Healy, William, and Augusta Bronner. 1936. *New Light on Delinquency and Its Treatment.* New Haven, CT: Yale University Press for the Institute of Human Relations.

Jones, Kathleen W. 1999. *Taming the Troublesome Child: American Families, Child Guidance, and the Limits of Psychiatric Authority.* Cambridge, MA: Harvard University Press.

Schneider, Eric C. 1992. *In the Web of Class: Delinquents and Reformers in Boston, 1810s–1930s.* New York: New York University Press.

Snodgrass, Jon. 1984. "William Healy (1869–1963): Pioneer Child Psychiatrist and Criminologist." *Journal of the History of the Behavioral Sciences* 20:331–339.

KATHLEEN W. JONES

Herbart, J. F. (1776–1841)

Johann Friedrich Herbart, a German philosopher and educational theorist, is considered one of the founders of scientific pedagogy. Born May 4, 1776, in Oldenburg, Herbart started his study of philosophy in Jena in the spring of 1794. Johann Gottlieb Fichte and Friedrich Schiller, among others, were his teachers there. During this time Herbart critically analyzed Fichte's transcendental idealism. In 1797 Herbart left for Switzerland to become a private tutor for the Steiger family children, and recorded his findings on his work with them. These records are considered the first documents of Herbart's pedagogy. In 1802 he became a university lecturer at the University of Göttingen and in 1805 an associate professor of philosophy and pedagogy. In 1809 he accepted a call to the University of Königsberg (now Kaliningrad, Russia) to take over the chair currently being held by the philosopher Wilhelm Traugott Krug, a position that Immanuel Kant had previously held. In 1833, Herbart returned as a full professor to the University of Göttingen, where he lectured until his death on August 14, 1841.

Some of Herbart's main works on educational theory include *Ueber die ästhetische Darstellung der Welt als das Hauptgeschäft der Erziehung* (On the aesthetic representation of the world as the main subject of education), 1804, *Allgemeine Pädagogik aus dem Zweck der Erziehung abgeleitet* (General pedagogics derived from the purpose of education), 1806, and *Umriß pädagogischer Vorlesungen* (Outline of lectures on education), 1835, 1841. In *On the Aesthetic Representation of the World* Herbart discusses morality as the main purpose of education. As one of the proponents of realism, Herbart, in contrast to the supporters of German idealism, adheres to the recognizability of the objective world, meaning that the mind has to discern rules but does not create them. Thus Herbart understands morality as an ideal that one strives for by learning to assess and influence his or her will on the basis of objective perception in order to act in the interest of social existence. Herbart asks: How can the educator consciously support this learning process?

In *General Pedagogics* Herbart develops the means of education: *Unterricht* (instruction), and *Zucht*, which he later completes in *Outline of Lectures on Education. Unterricht* is to provide understanding. Therefore Herbart's theory of *Unterricht* stresses the material part of education concerning these dimensions: steps of instruction (structure), subject matter of instruction (choice of subject), and course of instruction (methods). *Zucht*, on the other hand, focuses the ethical ideal to act according to a better understanding. It refers to the personal attitude of the educator and the pupil toward each other. Both aspects of education, *Unterricht* and *Zucht*, lead to Herbart's idea of *erziehender Unterricht* (educating instruction). This idea gained influence on classroom activity and teacher training at the university level through his followers, the Herbartians.

Famous Herbartians included Karl Volkmar Stoy (1815–1885), Tuiskon Ziller (1817–1882), and Wilhelm Rein (1847–1929). Their efforts were focused on teacher training at the university level that aimed both at specialist training and pedagogical professionalism. In order to offer both theoretical educational studies and educational practice to students, they affiliated practice schools with teacher training colleges. Life at the practice schools included lessons, school trips, celebrations, gardening, sports, games, and self-government by the pupils. Stoy developed Herbart's systematic work on education into an acknowledged body of educational theories. Ziller added Herbart's theory on *Unterricht* and created within the framework of his didactics the *Formalstufentheorie* (theory of formal steps of instruction), the principle of *Konzentration* (concentration), and the *Kulturstufentheorie* (theory of cultural steps). It is thanks to Rein that Herbart became famous all over the world. His pedagogical teacher-training college and holiday courses at Jena gained international interest.

See also: **Education, Europe.**

BIBLIOGRAPHY

Cruikshank, Kathleen. 1993. "The Rise and Fall of American Herbartianism: Dynamics of an Educational Reform Movement." Ph.D. diss., University of Wisconsin.

Dunkel, Harold B. 1969. *Herbart and Education.* New York: Random House.

Kehrbach, Karl, and Otto Flügel, eds. 1989 [1887–1912]. *Johann Friedrich Herbart: Sämtliche Werke in chronologischer Reihenfolge,* 19 vols. Aalen, Germany: Scientia.

ROTRAUD CORIAND

High School

High school as it developed over the middle decades of the nineteenth century was diverse in its instantiations—as variable, in fact, as the cities that gave it birth. An array of secondary educational alternatives included everything from a few courses in the "higher branches" offered to a handful of students in a solitary room of a city's "union" school to Boston's precocious English Classical School, established in 1821. Between these extremes lay the ACADEMIES, commercial institutes, seminaries, and proprietary schools that dotted the landscape of midcentury American education.

Throughout most of the nineteenth century, indeed, until the 1880s, the high school was more easily defined by what it was not than by what it was: neither a college nor the classical GRAMMAR SCHOOL that prepared future collegians, the high school of the mid-nineteenth century both sprang from and was instituted in contradistinction to classical grammar schools, which prepared young people for college.

Development of the Nineteenth-Century High School

While high schools across the United States would continue to vary widely throughout the next seventy years in response to the highly specific needs of populations experiencing rapidly changing social conditions and political alignments, the very construction of a high school, whether in Kalamazoo or Philadelphia, demanded a shoring up of the school system that supported it. Age-grading and sequencing the curriculum became necessary to differentiate the offerings of the high school from its tributaries and to legitimize those offerings. This in turn was made easier by the adoption of standard textbooks and uniform high school entrance examinations. And since public schools largely justified their existence by offering education inexpensively, they hired the cheapest labor to teach their growing enrollments. Therefore, educated women, with few other avenues of employment open to them, soon replaced male faculty at the primary levels of public schooling. In some instances this ordering of the lower schools prepared the way for the building of a high school. In others, the "high" school, however modest its accommodations, preceded the reorganization of the lower schools or even the passage of COMPULSORY SCHOOL ATTENDANCE legislation. Yet all attempts to bring order and predictability were predicated upon the larger movement to centralize school bureaucracy locally.

By the end of the nineteenth century in the northeastern and midwestern United States this process had been largely completed, and the high school stood poised to become an extension of the American COMMON SCHOOL. Entrance examinations, widely employed during the middle decades of the century, were used to screen out students of lower aptitude and achievement in an effort to erect a perfect meritocracy. In one important respect this approach had been an unqualified success: before the turn of the century, once a student had entered the elite confines of the public high school, his or her grades were the best predictor of graduation; working-class pupils, whose chances of gaining entrance to high school were significantly diminished by their social background, performed just as well in high school as students of higher socioeconomic status. Their achievement after graduation, moreover, was rewarded in ways comparable to their graduate-peers across the social spectrum.

Committee of Ten

As high schools multiplied across the nation, one era came to a close and another beckoned. In response to this unruly expansion, the National Education Association convened the country's leading educators to suggest ways to rectify the uneven shape of the secondary school curriculum. "The Committee of Ten," chaired by Harvard University President Charles W. Eliot, issued a report in 1893 recommending that the secondary school curriculum rededicate itself nationally to the goal of "training and disciplining the mind through academic studies," thus creating a better fit between the subjects offered by the high schools and the colleges receiving their students. Yet, in effect, as Jurgen Herbst has observed, the Committee of Ten had "written an epitaph instead of a blueprint for the future" (p. 108).

Left out of the report was any consideration of the demand for a curriculum that was becoming more, rather than less, variegated: one which included not just the call for "industrial arts" training in the Prussian mode but also for "commercial" courses—training in the new technologies of business and commerce such as typing, stenography, sales, accounting, bookkeeping, and French and other modern languages which had been excluded historically from the classical curriculum. From its origins the high school, like its closest cousin, the academy, had offered an alternative to the classical training of the grammar school. It was to be practical in orientation and so was inclined to expand in this direction as its embrace of young people was enlarged. Indeed, by the time the Committee of Ten had issued its recommendations, most public high schools in the United States had abandoned the use of entrance examinations as a device to restrict enrollments.

Commission on the Reorganization of Secondary Education

Between 1900 and 1940 the ratio of seventeen year olds graduating from high school nationwide shot up from 7 percent to 49 percent. As the great boom in high school attendance got underway during the 1910s and 1920s, high schools across the nation assumed broad similarities however much they differed in their particulars. These similarities were enhanced by the next major report on the status and purpose of secondary education, which was issued by the Commission on the Reorganization of Secondary Education. Its Cardinal Principles (1918) stressed the importance of making secondary education available to the great majority of young people and dampened the emphasis of the Committee of Ten on strengthening connections between the high school curriculum and the mission of college education.

The Cardinal Principles laid the philosophical foundation for the adoption of the "comprehensive curriculum" and "tracking" during the 1920s and after—that is, the creation of curricular streams that channeled students according to aptitude, interest, and achievement into distinct courses of study judged to fit their individual abilities and inclinations. In practice, of course, this led to the reproduction of the very social structures that students experienced in the world outside the school, as principals, teachers, and career counselors often guided adolescents into tracks based upon their par-

ents' socioeconomic, racial, or ethnic backgrounds. As John Modell and J. Trent Alexander pointed out in 1997, in the "old regime" (high school before 1900) the school "reproduced the structures of the outside world by restricting admission." Under the new regime—high school as a mass institution—"schools reproduced the structures of the outside world through a variety of mechanisms that took place within the institutions themselves" (p. 23). Tracking was the curricular version of this device, indeed the major mechanism of sorting youths in the schools, but others arose in the form of the extracurriculum that emerged within the "new" high school of the 1920s and 1930s. The extracurriculum, which included every kind of student activity from sports to language clubs, was a way of engaging students in the values of high school outside the classroom. It was a means of extending enrollments by appealing to the interests of the average student, who a generation earlier would have "dropped out."

Postwar Developments

After World War II the great majority of adolescents attended and graduated from high schools. By 1967 graduation rates peaked at 76 percent and leveled off at around 75 percent for the remainder of the century. As high school graduation became normative, the financial consequences of not achieving a high school diploma became costly over the lifetime of those who failed to complete twelfth grade. The high school diploma had become a credential necessary both for employment after high school and for admission to college. On one hand, the expansion of higher education in the wake of the war fueled demand for this credential, and on the other, the collapse of the youth job market during the GREAT DEPRESSION and decline of the industrial sector of the U.S. economy and enlargement of the service sector after World War II discouraged leaving school early. Virtually as soon as high school became a mass institution, however, the problem of "warehousing" confronted educators. As greater numbers of adolescents entered high school for lack of economic opportunity, they were decreasingly likely, it seems, to find satisfaction in the school's offerings.

By the 1960s public high schools were criticized on a number of grounds: the bottom quintile of students who typically gravitated toward vocational offerings was incorporated into the comprehensive high school, but the skills imparted by the vocational curriculum had dubious application in the industrial workforce. The middle 60 percent, for whom a watered-down academic curriculum had been designed for "life adjustment," found the high school experience empty and irrelevant. And the top 20 percent of high school achievers, it was charged, were not being adequately prepared for the rigors of college. The most common criticism was that the social dimension of the high school experience was being overemphasized at the expense of academic achievement.

Roiling beneath the surface of these complaints was a more profound problem. If the Cardinal Principles early in the century had succeeded in shaping the high school into a meeting place for adolescents of diverse ethnic, socioeconomic, and racial backgrounds, the student culture was rent by very real out-of-school differences within the pupil population. In the wake of BROWN V. BOARD OF EDUCATION, the civil rights movement, and racial strife of the 1960s, middle- and working-class whites fled from inner-city high schools to new suburban schools. The effect of "white flight" was compounded by a plummeting birthrate among whites, so that by the 1980s it was commonplace for the composition of inner-city school populations to be composed of African-American and Latino students in excess of 90 percent. In addition to the detrimental social affects of such intensely segregated high schools, racial and ethnic segregation was accompanied by profound socioeconomic disadvantage. The separation of white suburban high school students from African-American and Latino central city students had erected a two-tiered, deeply unequal system of public schooling at every level.

Attempts to correct such imbalances have ranged from the use of vouchers in a handful of cities to the most pervasive approach, the creation of themed magnet high schools in inner-city districts. By attracting white students from the suburbs to take advantage of the specialized curricula of the magnets, the hope is to reintegrate the public high school. Thus far progress has been modest at best.

Despite its many problems, the high school became *the* institutional RITE OF PASSAGE for twentieth-century American youth. From a social standpoint it has provided the common basis for a youth experience that has included male and female, black and white, immigrant and native. It has served as an arena for the spread of youth styles and as an entry point for an expanding popular and YOUTH CULTURE. The high school, having largely abandoned its academic focus in the early twentieth century, found that by the twenty-first century, the search for academic retooling had become ever more difficult to achieve.

See also: **Education, United States; Junior High School; Vocational Education, Industrial Education, and Trade Schools.**

BIBLIOGRAPHY

Becker, Gary S. 1975. *Human Capital: A Theoretical and Empirical Analysis, with Special Reference to Education.* New York: National Bureau of Economic Research and Columbia University Press.

Coleman, James Samuel, Thomas Hoffer, and Sally Kilgore. 1982. *High School Achievement: Public, Catholic, and Private Schools Compared.* New York: Basic Books.

Fass, Paula S. 1989. "Americanizing the High School." In *Outside In: Minorities and the Transformation of American Education,* by Paula S. Fass. New York: Oxford University Press.

Grant, Gerald. *The World We Created at Hamilton High.* Cambridge, MA: Harvard University Press, 1988.

Herbst, Jurgen. 1996. *The Once and Future School: Three Hundred and Fifty Years of American Secondary Education.* New York: Routledge.

Krug, Edward A. 1964–1972. *The Shaping of the American High School.* 2 vols. New York: Harper and Row.

Labaree, David F. 1988. *The Making of an American High School: The Credentials Market and the Central High School of Philadelphia, 1838–1939.* New Haven, CT: Yale University Press.

Labaree, David F. 1997. *How to Succeed in School without Really Learning: The Credentials Race in American Education.* New Haven, CT: Yale University Press.

Modell, John, and J. Trent Alexander. 1997. "High School in Transition: Community, School, and Peer Group in Abilene, Kansas, 1939." *History of Education Quarterly* 37 (spring): 1–24.

Ogbu, John U. 2003. *Black American Students in an Affluent Suburb: A Study of Academic Disengagement.* Mahwah, NJ: Erlbaum.

Orfield, Gary, and Susan E. Eaton. 1996. *Dismantling Desegregation: The Quiet Reversal of* Brown v. Board of Education. New York: New Press.

Powell, Arthur G., Eleanor Farrar, and David K. Cohen. 1985. *The Shopping Mall High School: Winners and Losers in the Educational Marketplace.* Boston: Houghton Mifflin.

Reese, William J. 1995. *The Origins of the American High School.* New Haven, CT: Yale University Press.

Ueda, Reed. 1987. *Avenues to Adulthood: The Origins of the High School and Social Mobility in an American Suburb.* New York: Cambridge University Press.

STEPHEN LASSONDE

Hine, Lewis (1874–1940)

Lewis W. Hine was a pioneer of social documentary photography. His most sustained and influential body of work consists of over 5,000 photographs made between 1906 and 1918 for the NATIONAL CHILD LABOR COMMITTEE (NCLC) publicizing the prevalence and harshness of CHILD LABOR in the United States. Born and raised in Oshkosh, Wisconsin, Hine first took up photography around 1903 as an extension of his work as a teacher at the Ethical Culture School in New York City. A Progressive educator, he soon came to embrace the camera as a tool of "social uplift" a generation before the social-activist photographers and filmmakers of the 1930s coined the term *documentary.*

In 1904, Hine began taking photographs on Ellis Island, portraying, in a dignified and sympathetic fashion, a representative sampling of the great influx of immigrants from eastern and southern Europe. These images, made under difficult circumstances with bulky, primitive equipment, presented a powerful, humanist argument for open immigration at a time when nativist sentiment against the foreign-born was on the rise.

Hine's work for the NCLC took him to thirty-one states and the District of Columbia. He photographed from Maine to Texas, in the Plains states and the Far West, documenting children of all ages engaged in wage labor as textile workers, telegraph messengers, street vendors, newsboys, mine workers, glass workers, oyster shuckers, shrimp pickers, sardine packers, cigar makers, cigarette rollers, garment workers, lacemakers, and agricultural laborers. Hine's photographs were accompanied by meticulous field notes detailing the relevant sociological data: names and ages of the children, time and place of employment, hours worked, wages earned, length of employment, working conditions, and family circumstances.

As an impassioned middle-class reformer, he sought to convince an enfranchised liberal audience, by way of incontrovertible empirical evidence, of the harmful effects of child labor. At the time, both business leaders and working-class parents defended the social efficacy and economic necessity of child labor. Hine's photographs originally appeared on posters and in newspapers, bulletins, and periodicals advocating national legislation that would abolish most forms of commercial child labor and mandate a public-school education for all working-class children. However, despite compulsory education laws in most states, such policies were not enacted until the 1930s.

Hine worked mostly with a hand-held, wooden box camera, producing 4" x 5" and 5" x 7" glass-plate and film negatives from which he most often made contact prints, although enlargements were also common. Hine continued to make sociologically informed photographs for the remainder of his career, working for the American Red Cross in Europe during World War I and for the *Survey*, an early journal of social work. In 1930 he made a notable series of photographs documenting the construction of the Empire State Building. In this later phase of his career, Hine sought to portray in idealized terms what he came to see as the inherent dignity and heroic stature of the American worker and craftsperson.

As a freelance photographer without an independent income, Hine's work necessarily reflected the agendas of the clients for whom he worked. Just as Hine's NCLC photographs reflected the politics of that organization, so his 1933 photographs of the Shelton Looms, commissioned by its owner, represented the interests of management. That being said, Hine's child labor photographs were the result of a particularly fruitful and serendipitous conjunction of a talented and dedicated photographer with a well-organized and highly motivated social movement. Collectively, these images constitute an invaluable resource in the study of early-twentieth-century, working-class children in the United States. They have also served as a model and inspiration for documentary photographers.

See also: **Economics and Children in Western Societies: From Agriculture to Industry; Photographs of Children; Progressive Education.**

BIBLIOGRAPHY

Aperture. 1977. *America and Lewis Hine: Photographs 1904–1940*. Millerton, NY: Aperture.

"Lewis Hine." 1992. *History of Photography* 16 (summer): 87–104.

Rosler, Martha. 1989. "In, Around, and Afterthoughts (On Documentary Photography)." In *The Contest of Meaning: Critical Histo-*ries of Photography*, ed. Richard Bolton. Cambridge, MA: MIT Press.

Seixas, Peter. 1987. "Lewis Hine: From 'Social' to 'Interpretive' Photographer." *American Quarterly* 39, no. 3: 381–409.

Stange, Maren. 1989. *Symbols of Ideal Life: Social Documentary Photography in America, 1890–1950*. Cambridge, UK: Cambridge University Press.

Trattner, Walter I. 1970. *Crusade for the Children: A History of the National Child Labor Committee and Child Labor Reform in America*. Chicago: Quadrangle Books.

GEORGE DIMOCK

Historiography. *See* Comparative History of Childhood; History of Childhood.

History of Childhood

EUROPE
Benjamin B. Roberts

UNITED STATES
N. Ray Hiner
Joseph M. Hawes

EUROPE

With his 1960 *L'Enfant et la vie familiale sous l'Ancien Régime* (published in English in 1962 as *Centuries of Childhood*), PHILIPPE ARIÈS put the history of childhood on the map. Since then, this former *terra incognita* has become a well-trodden battlefield for historians and social scientists. In a nutshell, the childhoods that Ariès sketched in Europe's Middle Ages and early modern period were not happy. Childhood was a social construction that developed between around 1500 and 1800. According to Ariès, the major differences between contemporary childhood and childhood in earlier periods are a lack of sentiment for—that is, preparing children for adulthood (i.e., education) and making an emotional investment in them (i.e., affection, time, and attention)—and no separate activities assigned to children in the Middle Ages and early modern period. From birth to age seven, children were considered miniature adults: they dressed like adults and they were not sheltered from the adult world. By the age of seven, children were physically capable of helping their parents care for farm animals and work in the fields; cognitively, children had acquired the same vocabulary as their parents.

European medieval society was rural and its inhabitants resided in small villages and on farms. A formal education—learning how to read and write—was considered an unnecessary luxury for the majority of children, and after reaching the age of seven children were expected to follow in the footsteps of their parents as farmers and artisans. They only needed to learn these skills from their parents or from a master craftsman. The schools that did exist in the Middle Ages were a far cry from those that emerged in the nineteenth century, which children were required by law to attend. Medieval schools were attended not only by children. These one-room classrooms were for all age groups, from small children to middle-aged adults. The pupils learned at different levels and in the classical method, by reciting their lessons out loud. In addition to being noisy and difficult places for the pupils to concentrate in, classrooms were hard for teachers to manage. Discipline was physical and sometimes harsh. According to Ariès, both these conditions and the quality of education changed first under the auspices of the sixteenth-century humanists and then more fully over the course of the following three centuries. All this was accompanied by a growing affection for children.

Ariès detected a change in sentiment toward children in the seventeenth century, when painters started portraying children as individuals. In the Middle Ages, the only child painted was Jesus, who was portrayed as a stiff and unchildlike infant. According to Ariès, the seventeenth century was a significant benchmark in the attitude toward children in European history, and the beginning of modern childhood, which started to resemble twentieth-century childhood. With his negative conclusion about childhood in the past, Ariès launched a black legend into the historical community and the general public's mind.

The Black Legend

During the 1970s a wave of researchers investigated childhood from directions other than Ariès's but came to the same general conclusion. They agreed that childhood was a modern phenomenon but differed slightly on its exact discovery. Researchers probed and prodded the terrain of child ABANDONMENT, household structures, romantic LOVE between parents, and economic, social, and demographic factors in their quest to find affection for children in the past. In his 1974 *History of Childhood*, Lloyd deMause deduced that love for children did not exist in the antiquity, where child abandonment was common among the poor until the fourth century B.C.E. He also saw a landscape of CHILD ABUSE and mistreatment continuing until the very modern period. Jean Flandrin determined in his 1976 *Familles: Parenté, maison, sexualité dans l'ancienne société* that the notion of the nuclear family (father, mother, and children) in France, with its special focus on children, came in existence in the course of the nineteenth century. He based his work on terminology in dictionaries and encyclopedias. A main reason for paying more attention to children was the increased availability of BIRTH CONTROL, which started in the late eighteenth century. Parents realized that they could care for their children better if they had fewer of them.

According to the Canadian historian Edward Shorter (1995), romantic love, economic independence, and the nuclear family were the key ingredients of modern childhood. Romantic love between partners was necessary before parents could have affection for their children. This condition began to be met around 1750, when marriages were no longer prearranged for economic reasons. As a result, parents became more caring and concerned about their offspring. Free choice in marriage came about as a result of the rise of capitalism and the onset of the Industrial Revolution, which enabled young men to find work outside the family farm or business and to become economically independent of their families. This individualism allowed for couples to start their own nuclear families, consisting only of parents and children, and providing a haven for children from the world of adulthood, where parents could devote their time and energy to their children without the influence of the extended family and neighbors.

However, for the English historian Lawrence Stone (1977), the nuclear family doting over its children has a longer evolution. In the period from 1450 to 1800, Stone detects a transition in the structure of English families from an open lineage household—one with three or more generations and open to neighbors and distant family—to the closed, domesticated nuclear family. This consisted only of two generations, parents and children, with the parents giving a great amount of attention to their children. The closed, domesticated nuclear family came into existence parallel with what Stone terms "affective individualism," which allowed for personal choice in marriage partners and resulted in a growing affection for members of the nuclear family (including a recognition of the uniqueness of each), and for children in particular. Stone detected that the free market economy (and eventual Industrial Revolution) and other social factors—such as the ability of more people to leave rural communities, where they had previously been dependent on family and neighbors, and move to cities, where they were economically independent, and to marry a partner of their choice—were important stimulants for the closed, domesticated nuclear family.

To these economic and social factors, Stone adds that the eighteenth century also witnessed a demographic change. Mortality rates, especially those for children, had started to decline. This was an important factor, allowing parents to feel more affection toward their children. Before then, the emotional burden of childhood death was considered a reason for parents to be cool and distant towards their children.

In her 1981 *The Myth of Motherhood*, the French historian Elisabeth Badinter elaborated on Shorter's and Stone's economic and social analyses and concluded that the Industrial Revolution brought about a separation of spheres and tasks between fathers and mothers. In the bourgeois society of the early nineteenth century, men moved to the public domain of the workforce whereas women retreated to the household and dedicated their time to being mothers and homemakers.

In France, the mother no longer had to work outside the house and could breast-feed her children instead of farming them out to wet nurses in the countryside, which was a practice that black legend historians considered evidence of indifference. Badinter's bourgeois mother was able to give her children more attention and shelter them from the outside world. This idealized image of motherhood—and childhood—is often associated with the Romantic period, the 1830s and 1840s. However, Simon Schama (1987) discovered a paradise of childhood that already existed in the Dutch Republic during the seventeenth century among the middling sort. According to the iconographic interpretation and medical and pedagogical advice books, Dutch mothers of this period nursed their children themselves, showered them with love and affection, gave them toys, and provided them with a proper education according to their financial means. Childhood, according to these historians, was the gradual creation of the period from 1600 to 1850.

The White Legend

In the 1980s, the debate over childhood took a different turn. Historians focused on new sources and came up with different results. In his 1986 *Marriage and Love in England: Modes of Reproduction*, the English historian Alan Macfarlane showed demographic research indicating more continuity in household make-up and emotional investment in family members over a five-hundred-year period than the drastic changes detected by Stone. Macfarlane pinpointed the origin of the English nuclear family in the Middle Ages and argued, contrary to Stone, that the market economy and Industrial Revolution were a result of individualism and personal choice in marriage instead of being stimulants for them.

The notion of childhood as a modern phenomenon took another blow with the 1983 publication of Linda Pollock's *Forgotten Children: Parent-Child Relations from 1500 to 1900* and her 1987 *A Lasting Relationship: Parents and Their Children over Three Centuries.* Her conclusions, based on diaries and correspondence, were that parental affection and concern had remained steady factors from the late Middle Ages until the nineteenth century. According to Pollock, economic conditions such as prearranged marriages and demographic factors such as high mortality rates had less influence on affection in parent-child relations than black legend historians had claimed. When children were ill, parents showed great concern and used every means they had to cure them. However, the problem with sources such as personal documents is that they allow insight only into the higher echelons of society. The European masses could not read or write in the early modern period, so historians are left to speculate.

This new material stressing continuity in the early modern period reopened the discussion of antiquity and the Middle Ages. Despite having fewer sources to consult, historians have been innovative in their interpretations. In his 1988 *The Kindness of Strangers*, John Boswell readdressed child abandonment in late antiquity and argued that the custom of abandoning children at the doorstep of a monastery was not an act of indifference or lack of affection, as Lloyd deMause had concluded. It was usually done by the poor, who hoped their infants would grow up in the security of a monastery or be found and taken care of by kind strangers. In her 1990 *Childhood in the Middle Ages*, Shulamith Shahar examined medical treatises and finds that parents were quite concerned about the health of their offspring. Parental protection and care began during pregnancy, when mothers took precautions in their diet. Shahar, like Marfarlane and Pollock, drew positive conclusions about childhood; their stress on continuity in the history of childhood was responsible for creating a revisionist school, or white legend, in the debate.

Light Gray

In the early 1990s, the debate between historians of the white and black legends seemed to be deadlocked, because neither group was able to reach a general conclusion encompassing childhood in urban and rural environs, in all economic and social strata, and for all religious groups. The deadlock began to end after historians started investigating specific child-rearing practices, examining smaller social groups, conducting more longitudinal research, and experimenting with new interpretations. Louis Haas investigated the ruling elite of Renaissance Florence, studying early child care in medical treatises and personal documents and publishing *The Renaissance Man and His Children: Childbirth and Early Childhood in Florence, 1300–1600* in 1998. In regard to the use of wet nurses, Haas's evidence might prove historians such as Badinter to be correct. Florentine parents did have their infants farmed out to wet nurses living in the surrounding Tuscan countryside, but according to the personal documents Haas examined, parents were not at all indifferent toward their children. On the contrary, in most cases wet nurses were hired when mothers was incapable of producing milk. In addition, the milk of wet nurses in the countryside was considered to be healthier than the milk of mothers living in the city. Living in the country was thought to have a positive influence on the quality of a woman's milk and thus to be better for the child's health. The letters from Florentine fathers illustrated great affection for their children and active involvement in their upbringing. Similar results were found in the Dutch Republic during the seventeenth and eighteenth centuries. In his 1998 *Through the Keyhole: Dutch Child-Rearing Practices in the Seventeenth and Eighteenth Century*, Benjamin Roberts followed child-rearing practices in the correspondence of urban elite families over four generations. By examining the physical, cognitive, affective, and moral aspects of education and comparing them to medical and moral treatises, the author was able to detect continuity and change within families. The most significant change occurred in how children were educated. Parents in the course of two centuries changed school types and demanded different curricula for their offspring, but the physical care, moral lessons, and affection for children remained stable from one generation to the next.

In 1994, Ilana Krausman Ben-Amos published the innovative *Early Modern Adolescence and Youth* and in 1996 Paul Griffiths published *Youth and Authority in Early Modern England*. By examining youth through personal documents and legal records, Krausman Ben-Amos and Griffiths showed Ariès to be incorrect about the nonexistence of ADOLESCENCE prior to the nineteenth century, but at the same time these authors agreed that some of Ariès' conclusions were not unfounded. Early modern youths worked and lived outside the nuclear family and were entrusted with more independence than they are today; however, sending children into the world at an early age was not a sign of indifference, they argued, and can be regarded as a way to educate and prepare them for adulthood.

The lack of affection for children in the Middle Ages and the early modern period has been the most disputed of Ariès's arguments. However, Ariès's hypothesis about the lack of affection shown in the education of children is correct. Prior to the late nineteenth century, when school attendance became mandatory and CHILD LABOR was prohibited, educational opportunities were largely directed at a small sector of the population. Since 1960, the historiography of childhood has developed in many directions as new studies color in the numerous facets of childhood. New research into the formation of gender, personal identity, and SEXUALITY are now extending the lines on Ariès's map. By examining smaller, homogenous groups of similar economic, social, religious, and geographic background, historians are drawing more reliable conclusions and making less sweeping statements. The history of childhood is neither black nor white but somewhere in between—perhaps light gray.

History of Childhood beyond Ariès

The vast majority of European historians of childhood who have followed in Ariès's footsteps have worked on periods prior to 1900. Curiously enough, the century that the Swedish educator ELLEN KEY named the CENTURY OF THE CHILD has attracted much less attention. A few historians expanded their studies to cover the 1930s, but the years after 1945 have until very recently, as a general rule, been colonized by sociologists. As a consequence, their understanding of the rise of modernity as well as the welfare states has had a certain impact on the historians now studying the history of twentieth-century European childhood. The century is understood as having had a unique role in the understanding and the shaping of modern childhood. In the interwar years, new sciences, especially CHILD PSYCHOLOGY, supplemented the old medical knowledge about children and with the rise of the welfare state this knowledge has been spread to parents through infant-care programs, visiting nurses, and popular books on child rearing.

The rapid demographic changes of the twentieth century—with lower INFANT MORTALITY, lower fertility, and especially after World War II growing divorce rates and a rising number of mothers working in the paid labor market and away from home—have led historians to study changes in the roles of mothers as well as fathers and also to study the development of the day-care system.

The British historian Eric Hobsbawm has called the twentieth century the "Age of Extremes." It is an age that has seen more people killed in wars than any century before. It is therefore not surprising that war has become an important subject in the study of childhood. These studies examine state and interstate programs for orphaned or destitute children after World War I as well as the "war children" of World War II—children born in occupied territories to native mothers and German fathers or children born out of wedlock in Germany during the Nazi regime and placed in the so-called *Lebensborn* homes. Others deal with the children of the HOLOCAUST or with children who were born in Germany after the capitulation but fathered by American soldiers—the so-called Afro-German children.

With inspiration from the sociology of childhood, where children are understood as social actors in their own right, the British historian Harry Hendrick has raised the question of the absence of children's voices within the history of childhood. Because children live in an oral culture, the written sources are scarce—and despite its name, the history of childhood tends to deal with adults' views of children to a much larger degree than with the actual lived lives of children. This awareness is not new among European historians of childhood. The British historian Ludmilla Jordanova became famous by stating, in 1989, that there is nothing like "an authentic voice of children," meaning that history is a result of the historian asking and not of past children speaking in their own right. This did not prevent historians from trying to access the voices of children. The British labor historian Anna Davin made extensive use of memoirs in her work *Growing up Poor in London around 1900*, with the explicit purpose of giving children a voice in history. Another fruitful source of children's voices is letters to foster parents or to caretakers at children's homes.

What is new in the present debate is the insistence on bringing children back into the history of childhood by a more systematic use of sources like letters, diaries, and memoirs, and by using the growing range of twentieth-century sources where children have been filmed, videotaped, or questioned about their lives.

See also: **Comparative History of Childhood; Medieval and Renaissance Europe; Early Modern Europe; Enlightenment, The; Sociology and Anthropology of Childhood.**

BIBLIOGRAPHY

Ariès, Philippe. 1962. *Centuries of Childhood: A Social History of Family Life.* Trans. Robert Baldick. New York: Knopf.

Badinter, Elisabeth. 1981. *The Myth of Motherhood: An Historical View of the Maternal Instinct.* London: Souvenir.

Boswell, John. 1988. *The Kindness of Strangers: The Abandonment of Children in Western Europe from Late Antiquity to the Renaissance.* New York: Pantheon.

Cunningham, Hugh. 1995. *Children and Childhood in Western Society since 1500.* London: Longman.

Dekker, Jeroen, Leendert Groenendijk, and Johan Verberckmoes. 2000. "Proudly Raising Vulnerable Youngsters: The Scope for Education in the Netherlands." In *Pride and Joy: Children's Portraits in the Netherlands 1500–1700,* ed. Jan Baptist Bedaux and Rudi Ekkart. Ghent, Belgium: Ludion.

Flandrin, Jean-Louis. 1976. *Familles: Parenté, maison, sexualité dans l'ancienne société.* Paris: Hachette.

Griffiths, Paul. 1996. *Youth and Authority: Formative Experiences in England 1560–1640.* Oxford, UK: Clarendon.

Haas, Louis. 1998. *The Renaissance Man and His Children: Childbirth and Early Childhood in Florence, 1300–1600.* New York: St. Martin's.

Haks, Donald. 1988. "Continuïteit en verandering in het gezin van de vroeg-moderne tijd." In *Vijf Eeuwen Gezinsleven: Liefde, huwelijk en opvoeding in Nederland,* ed. H. Peeters, L. Dresen-Coenders, and T. Brandenbarg. Nijmegen, Netherlands: Sun.

Helmers, Dini. *'Gescheurde Bedden': Oplossingen voor gestrande huwelijken, Amsterdam 1753–1810.* Hilversum, Netherlands: Verloren.

Heywood, Colin. 2001. *A History of Childhood: Children and Childhood in the West from Medieval to Modern Times.* Cambridge, UK: Polity.

Krausman Ben-Amos, Ilana. 1994. *Adolescence and Youth in Early Modern England.* New Haven, CT: Yale University Press.

Macfarlane, Alan. 1986. *Marriage and Love in England. Modes of Reproduction 1300–1840.* London: B. Blackwell.

Mause, Lloyd de. 1974. *The History of Childhood.* New York: Psychohistory Press.

Peeters, Harry. 1966. *Kind en Jeugdige in het begin van de Moderne Tijd (ca. 1500–ca. 1650).* Meppel, Netherlands: Boom.

Pollock, Linda. 1983. *Forgotten Children: Parent-Child Relations from 1500 to 1900.* Cambridge, UK: Cambridge University Press.

Pollock, Linda. 1987. *A Lasting Relationship: Parents and their Children over Three Centuries.* London: Fourth Estate.

Roberts, Benjamin B. 1996. "Fatherhood in Eighteenth-Century Holland: The Van der Muelen Brothers." *Journal of Family History* 21: 218–228.

Roberts, Benjamin B. 1998. *Through the Keyhole. Dutch Child-rearing Practices in the 17th and 18th Century: Three Urban Elite Families.* Hilversum, Netherlands: Verloren.

Schama, Simon. 1987. *The Embarrassment of Riches: An Interpretation of Dutch Culture in the Golden Age.* New York: Knopf.

Shahar, Shulamith. 1990. *Childhood in the Middle Ages.* Trans. Chaya Galai. London: Routledge.

Shorter, Edward. 1975. *The Making of the Modern Family.* New York: Basic Books.

Stone, Lawrence. 1977. *The Family, Sex, and Marriage in England 1500–1800.* London: Weidenfeld and Nicolson.

BENJAMIN B. ROBERTS

UNITED STATES

The historiography of childhood is a vast and largely uncharted field. In an entry of this length it is not possible to do justice to the field as a whole. Accordingly we have chosen to emphasize the founders of the field, list some of the ways historians can approach the field (with examples of current work highlighted), and conclude with some discussion of what might be expected of the field in the future.

One of the first scholars to draw attention to the history of children was PHILIPPE ARIÈS, a French demographer and cultural historian. In *Centuries of Childhood: A Social History of Family Life* (1962), Ariès argued that childhood did not exist in the Middle Ages and since that time, adult-child relations had deteriorated. Ariès was convinced that in the sixteenth century when adults stopped seeing children as miniature adults and began to view them as helpless, vulnerable, and incompetent beings, the foundation was laid for the oppressive intervention of the state and the creation of separate institutions for children where they were subjected to harsh physical and psychological discipline. Ariès warned historians not to confuse "the idea of childhood" with affection, which was experienced in abundance by medieval children. Recent scholars have subjected Ariès' work to severe criticism, especially his heavy dependence on iconographic evidence, such as paintings, and his assertion that childhood did not exist before the early modern period. Even so, Ariès did as much as anyone to legitimize the history of children and can justly be called its founder. In addition, Ariès's contention that childhood as a social construct was part of the historical process seems undeniable and has helped to justify continued research into its historical development.

Another scholar who influenced the early development of the history of children was Lloyd deMause, who established the *History of Childhood Quarterly* and edited *The History of Childhood* (1974), one of the first major collections of scholarly work on the subject. DeMause, a vigorous advocate for a particular psychohistorical approach to the history of children, reached conclusions that directly contradicted those of Ariès. Whereas Ariès was nostalgic about the distant past, deMause was highly critical, arguing that "the history of childhood is a nightmare from which we have only recently begun to awaken." "The further one goes back in history," asserted deMause, "the lower the level of child care, and the more likely children are to be killed abandoned, beaten, terrorized, and sexually abused" (p. 1). From the infanticide characteristic of the earliest periods of civilization, deMause claimed that humanity has moved inexorably toward more humane treatment of children, especially among modern advanced parents and caregivers who seek the full development of children as persons. DeMause also argued that at critical points the state was vital to improving the care and nurture of children. Medieval historians, especially, have strongly condemned deMause's psychogenic theory as an unjustified attack on the humanity of those whom they study. In spite of this widespread criticism, much of which is justified, it is important to recognize that with his strong commitment to the humane treatment of children, deMause played a very important role in promoting interest in the history of children.

Peter Petschauer commented in the late 1980s that historians who had studied child rearing could be divided into two groups, "those who find tears and those who find smiles in the past" (p. 3). This is certainly an apt description of the work of Ariès and deMause, but at the turn of the twenty-first century historians of children seem increasingly reluctant to accept either the optimism of deMause or the nostalgic pessimism of Ariès. In fact, Linda Pollock's book, *Forgotten Children: Parent-Child Relations from 1500 to 1900* (1983), directly challenged Ariès's and deMause's claims that radical changes have occurred in parent-child relations in Europe and America. After drawing on sociobiological theory and reviewing almost 500 diaries and AUTOBIOGRAPHIES, Pollock observed that the evidence "does not support the evolutionary theories on the history of childhood" (p. 283). Parental care for children, she concluded, has been curiously resistant to change. Pollock's continuity thesis has itself been questioned, so the issue of adult-child relations, which generated so much of the early research on the history of children, remains unsettled among historians and seems unlikely to be resolved in the near future.

In retrospect, it is clear that much of the early, pioneering work in the history of children, though indispensable in stimulating interest in the field and establishing its legitimacy, suffered from a serious lack of definitional and theoretical clarity. If the history of children is to reach its full potential, more attention should be devoted to clarifying the nature of the subject and the questions that should be asked. For instance the concept of childhood may be viewed in at least three basic ways: as ideology or social construction, as experience, and as a set of behaviors. Childhood as ideology (the ideals and norms that society establishes for children) should not be confused with what children actually experience any more than an experienced teacher assumes that what is taught is necessarily learned. Beliefs about childhood clearly influence behavior and experience but is not coincident with either. Similarly, the behavior of children should not be confused with their experience or with childhood as an ideology. It would be naïve to believe that children reveal all of who they are in what they say and do. Thus, when historians declare that children in the past were miniature adults or that childhood did not exist in a certain period, what do they mean? Are they referring to what adults thought childhood ought to be, what children actually experienced, or what children actually did?

New Questions for the History of Children and Childhood

In 1985, N. Ray Hiner and Joseph Hawes proposed five basic questions that they believed should guide research in the history of children. The proposal was based on the assumption that although the questions that occupied early researchers in the field were important, they were not answerable in

their original form and needed to be refined. Thus, Hiner and Hawes designed these questions not only to guide research, but also to encourage continued thinking about how children in the past can be studied. Hiner and Hawes did not suggest that these questions actually determined the direction of scholarship or that they do not themselves need continued refinement, but they can serve as a convenient framework for assessing work in the field. These questions make it clear that the history of children is much broader than the history of childhood as a social construction or ideology. Below, we identify these questions and provide brief illustrations of how they can be used to organize and interpret information about children in the past.

1. What were the conditions that shaped the development of children? This question has been of special interest to social and demographic historians who have investigated the social indicators that determine the duration, scope, and intensity of childhood as a stage of life, the institutions in which children live, and the nature and patterns of relationships that occur within these institutions. One historian whose work emphasizes the importance of demographic factors is Robert Wells, whose *Uncle Sam's Family* sketches in demographic factors in American history.

2. What were the social, cultural, and psychological functions of children? Children, like members of all social groups, are assigned both implicit and explicit roles in American society and culture. Children are part of a larger system that places demands on them and shapes their behaviors in very precise ways that historians should investigate. An early and still relevant classic, Bernard Wishy's *Child and the Republic* is a fine example of this approach to the history of childhood. Another example of how societies define children's roles is provided by the classic study of colonial Plymouth, *A Little Commonwealth*, by John Demos.

3. What were the attitudes of adults toward children and childhood? In one sense, this is the easiest question for historians to answer primarily because adults left voluminous records about their attitudes toward children. However, care must be taken not to confuse attitudes or rhetoric with actual behavior. Still, knowledge of what adults thought about children, what they expected children to do and be, how childhood was constructed, is fundamental to creating a comprehensive history of children. While this may seem difficult terrain for the historian, the very complex history of the idea of ADOLESCENCE as developed by the historian Joseph Kett in his *Rights of Passage* illustrates one of the many ways historians may think and write about children in the past. Karin Calvert's *Children in the House* likewise examines changing models of children and is especially attentive to issues of gender.

4. What was the subjective experience of being a child in the past? This is a very difficult question for historians to answer in part because children, especially young children, have left relatively few records of their experiences. Yet with empathy, imagination, and careful attention to evidence, it is possible for historians to gain important insight into children's subjective worlds. Without this perspective, the history of children is not complete but because this is so difficult there are not many works which illustrate this point. An outstanding example here is the book by David Nasaw: *Children and the City.* Nasaw's imaginative use of a wide variety of sources shows both the importance of doing this work and the difficulty. William Tuttle has similarly tried to reconstruct American children's experiences during World War II in *Daddy's Gone to War.*

5. *How have children influenced adults and each other?* To understand this question, it is important not to confuse influence with power. Because children have obviously had little power, historians too often assume that most of the influence in adult-child relations flows in only one direction, from the adult to the child. However, all human relationships, even the most hierarchical, are inevitably reciprocal and dynamic. Although children have had little formal power, they have nevertheless exercised and continue to exercise great influence on virtually all aspects of American society and culture. The ways in which children influence adults are many and varied, but one of the most obvious and immediate occurs when a child is born. N. Ray Hiner has explored this dynamic in his articles on how children influenced the life and thought of Cotton Mather, a Puritan minister and early parent educator.

A sixth question might also be posed: *What institutions have been most important in defining children's lives and experiences?* Here could be included the many excellent studies of schooling, orphan asylums, family, and church and religion. Philip Greven's *The Protestant Temperament* is a deeply researched investigation into religion's role in forming children's contexts and Steven Mintz and Susan Kellogg's *Domestic Revolutions* provides important insights into the changing nature of the child's most basic site for development.

Unfortunately, history does not provide simple, definitive answers to these important questions about children in part because (1) these questions are themselves complex; (2) the sources for historical study of children are at times limited or unavailable; (3) history is a dynamic discipline constantly presenting new and challenging insights; (4) the history of children, though vigorous, is still a young, undeveloped field; (5) and perhaps most critically, because human experience is so full of variety children of the past, like adults, speak with many, sometimes confusing voices. As historians explore matters of race or class or gender, these inevitably create new paths in our studies of children. (For example, in the area of slavery, new work appeared in the 1990s, including Brenda Stevenson's *Life in Black and White: Family and Community in the Slave South* and Wilma King's *Stolen Childhood: Slave Youth in Nineteenth-Century America.*) However,

in spite of these limitations, historians have added greatly to our understanding of children during the last two decades.

The Influence of the "Powerless"

In what ways were children influential? One part of the answer is undeniable. All adults were once children, an experience that obviously shaped their development in complex ways. Yet, children's influence goes far beyond the *universality of childhood.* Children were influential in our past in at least four additional ways: (1) as members of families; (2) as members of a distinct population group; (3) as producers and consumers; and (4) as cultural and political symbols.

As members of families, children exercised great influence over the lives of their parents, siblings, relatives, and caregivers. One does not need to tell parents that the birth or adoption of a child changes the fundamental dynamics of a family. Our archives are full of documents that testify to this influence. Moreover, few parents would deny that most children learn how to get what they want from their parents and others. An example of this point is the marketing strategy of the McDonald's restaurant chain, which pitches its ads directly to children, supplements those ads with a cartoon character like Ronald McDonald, and designs its retail outlets in ways that cater to children and make them feel welcomed. Thus, McDonald's uses the ability of children to influence their parents both as a way to sell hamburgers and to make a handsome profit for stockholders. Throughout history, millions of parents and caregivers have by necessity and choice built their lives around providing for and caring for children. (The ways in which purchases of TOYS have been influenced and how this has changed is explored by Gary Cross in *Kids' Stuff.*)

As members of a distinct population group, children have shaped society in ways that go far beyond their individual families. For example, few in the twenty-first century can grasp fully the omnipresence of children during much of the past. Before 1800, at least half of the population in the United States was under the age of sixteen, and the average age of Americans did not exceed twenty-one until the twentieth century. An enormous amount of society's human and physical resources has been devoted to providing food, clothing, shelter, and education for children. Furthermore, because childhood mortality rates were often twenty to thirty times higher than they are in the twenty-first century, many children in the past died before they could replace the substantial investment that society made in their care and training. The collective influence of children was magnified when they were segregated by age in schools and other custodial institutions. One could argue with some justification that one of the most radical decisions ever made by American society was to confine large numbers of TEENAGERS together in limited spaces for extended periods in HIGH SCHOOLS. We live with the consequences still. (For a discussion of the beginnings and development of this phenomenon, see Paula

Fass's *The Damned and the Beautiful* and Thomas Hine's *The Rise and Fall of the American Teenager.*) Children's extraordinary collective influence can also be seen in the continuing effects of the BABY BOOM after World War II, which only temporarily raised the proportion of children in the population. Conversely, one can see in the early twenty-first century the powerful impact of declining birth rates on government programs, the economy, generational politics, and family dynamics.

As producers and consumers, children played a significant role in the development of the American economy. Because children constituted such a large percentage of the early American population, adult labor was relatively scarce, and children, often very young children, were expected to work. Preparation for work was a normal part of life for early American children. While the many individual tasks performed by children in households, fields, and shops of rural and small-town America were not in and of themselves highly significant, collectively they represented a vital contribution to the economy. Children also worked in the factories, mills, and mines of nineteenth- and early-twentieth-century America and thereby subsidized the industrialization of America by contributing to the production of cheap goods to compete in the growing international market. However, they did this at a very high cost in lost lives, ruined health, and lost opportunity for education and normal development. In spite of the intense campaign to eliminate CHILD LABOR, it had little effect until the 1920s when social pressure, regulatory legislation, new technology, and compulsory education laws combined to reduce child labor. As more children went to school than went to work, their primary economic role gradually shifted until the twenty-first century, when children's predominant economic role is to consume the extraordinary range of products that are created for them. (For these changes, see the collection of documents by Robert Bremner et al., *Children and Youth in America.*)

As cultural and political symbols, children have had a remarkable influence on a wide range of public issues. As children constituted proportionally less of the population and as their economic role shifted production to consumption, their psychological and cultural importance in families and in society intensified. Thus, children have often found themselves at the center of debates that express Americans' deepest feelings, hopes, and anxieties. Throughout American history, children have been central to debates about family, religion, crime, education, citizenship, slavery, gender, race, SEXUALITY, social justice, health, welfare, drug abuse, and day care, to name a few. A foundational work on how the sacralization of childhood greatly influenced the way society thought about children is to be found in Viviana Zelizer's path-breaking *Pricing the Priceless Child.* A more recent investigation of the cultural uses of the sacred child is Paula Fass's *Kidnapped: Child Abduction in America.*

The Future of the History of Children

The formation of the new Society for the History of Children and Youth in 2002 bodes well for the future of this relatively new academic field. What began in the 1960s as a small academic subspecialty has grown into a vigorous interdisciplinary enterprise that reflects more accurately the scope and importance of the subject. Not only historians, but also social scientists, literary and legal scholars, and educators, among others, have begun to realize that to study children is a fundamental and necessary step in understanding the human condition and that to study their history is essential to understanding human history itself.

See also: **Comparative History of Childhood; Sociology and Anthropology of Childhood.**

BIBLIOGRAPHY

Abbott, Grace, ed. 1998. *The Child and the State: Legal Status in the Family, Apprenticeship, and Child Labor,* 2 vols. Chicago: University of Chicago Press.

Ariès, Philippe. 1962. *Centuries of Childhood: A Social History of Family Life.* Trans. Robert Baldick. New York: Random House.

Bremner, Robert, et al., eds. 1970–1977. *Children and Youth in America: A Documentary History,* 3 vols. Cambridge, MA: Harvard University Press.

Calvert, Karin. 1992. *Children in the House.* Boston: Northeastern University Press.

Cross, Gary. 1997. *Kids' Stuff: Toys and the Changing World of American Childhood.* Cambridge, MA: Harvard University Press.

deMause, Lloyd, ed. 1974. *The History of Childhood.* New York: Psychohistory Press.

Demos, John. 1970. *A Little Commonwealth.* New York: Oxford University Press.

Fass, Paula. 1977. *The Damned and the Beautiful: American Youth in the 1920s.* New York: Oxford University Press.

Fass, Paula. 1997. *Kidnapped: Child Abduction in America.* New York: Oxford University Press.

Fass, Paula, and Mary Ann Mason, eds. 2000. *Childhood in America.* New York: New York University Press.

Finklestein, Barbara, ed. 1979. *Regulated Children/Liberated Children: Education in Psychohistorical Perspective.* New York: Psychohistory Press.

Graff, Harvey J. 1995. *Conflicting Paths: Growing Up in America.* Cambridge, MA: Harvard University Press.

Graff, Harvey J., ed. 1987. *Growing Up in America: Historical Experiences.* Detroit: Wayne State University Press.

Greven, Philip J., ed. 1973. *Child Rearing Concepts: 1628–1861: Historical Sources.* Itasco, IL: Peacock Press.

Greven, Philip J. 1977. *The Protestant Temperament: Patterns of Child-Rearing, Religious Experience, and the Self in Early America.* New York: Knopf.

Hawes, Joseph M., and N. Ray Hiner, eds. 1985. *American Childhood: A Research Guide and Historical Handbook.* Westport, CT: Greenwood Press.

Hawes, Joseph M., and N. Ray Hiner, eds. 1991. *Children in Historical and Comparative Perspective: An International Handbook and Research Guide.* Westport, CT: Greenwood Press.

Hiner, N. Ray. 1979. "Cotton Mather and His Children: The Evolution of a Parent Educator." In *Regulated Children/Liberated Children: Education in Psychohistorical Perspective,* ed. Barbara Finklestein, pp. 24–43. New York: Psychohistory Press.

Hiner, N. Ray. 1985. "Cotton Mather and His Female Children: Notes on the Relationship Between Private Life and Public Thought." *Journal of Psychohistory* 13 (summer): 33–49.

Hiner, N. Ray, and Joseph M. Hawes, eds. 1985. *Growing Up in America: Children in Historical Perspective.* Urbana: University of Illinois Press.

Hine, Thomas. 1999. *The Rise and Fall of the American Teenager.* New York: Bard.

Illick, Joseph E. 2002. *American Childhoods.* Philadelphia: University of Pennsylvania Press.

Kett, Joseph. 1977. *Rites of Passage: Adolescence in America, 1790 to the Present.* New York: Basic Books.

King, Wilma. 1995. *Stolen Childhood: Slave Youth in Nineteenth-Century America.* Bloomington: Indiana University Press.

Mintz, Steven, and Susan Kellogg. 1988. *Domestic Revolutions: A Social History of American Family Life.* New York: CollierMacmillan.

Nasaw, David. 1985. *Children of the City: At Work and Play.* New York: Oxford University Press.

Petschauer, Peter. 1989. "The Childrearing Modes in Flux: An Historian's Reflections." *Journal of Psychohistory* 17 (summer): 1–34.

Pollock, Linda. 1983. *Forgotten Children: Parent-Child Relations from 1500 to 1900.* Cambridge, UK: Cambridge University Press.

Stevenson, Brenda. 1996. *Life in Black and White: Family and Community in the Slave South.* New York: Oxford University Press.

Tuttle, William M. 1993. *Daddy's Gone to War: The Second World War in the Lives of America's Children.* New York: Oxford University Press.

Wells, Robert. 1985. *Uncle Sam's Family: Issues and Perspectives on American Demographic History.* Albany: State University of New York Press.

West, Elliott. 1996. *Growing Up in Twentieth-Century America: A History and Reference Guide.* Westport, CT: Greenwood Press.

West, Elliott, and Paula Petrik, eds. 1992. *Small Worlds: Children and Adolescents in America, 1850–1950.* Lawrence: University Press of Kansas.

Wishy, Bernard. 1968. *The Child and the Republic: The Dawn of American Child Nurture.* Philadelphia: University Press.

Zelizer, Viviana. 1985. *Pricing the Priceless Child: The Changing Social Value of Children.* New York: Basic Books.

N. Ray Hiner
Joseph M. Hawes

Hitler Youth

The youth organization of the National Socialist German Workers' Party (Nationalsozialistische Deutsche Arbeiterpartei–NSDAP) was founded in Munich in 1922 and included only boys. It was given the name Hitler Youth (Hitler Jugend) in 1926, when a parallel organization for girls (Schwesterschaften) was established, which was known from 1930 as the League of German Girls (Bund Deutscher Mädel–BDM). By the end of 1932 the Hitler Youth had no more than 108,000 members, but when the Nazi Party came to power in 1933, the organization's growth potential and functions were decisively altered. Other youth organizations

were prohibited, dissolved or taken over, and membership in the Hitler Youth rose to 2.3 million in 1933 and steadily increased in the following years: 3.6 million in 1934, 3.9 million in 1935, 5.4 million in 1936, 5.8 million in 1937, 7.0 million in 1938, and 8.7 million in 1939. From 1934 the Hitler Youth was the principal means by which the Nazi Party exerted its influence on German youth and was more important in this respect than the school system, which was not as fully controlled by the party. Its status in the Third Reich was emphasized in 1933 by the appointment of its leader, Baldur von Schirach, to the post of Youth Leader of the German Reich (*Jugendführer des Deutsche Reiches*), then by a law of 1936, which stipulated that the Hitler Youth, aside from parents and school, was the sole legitimate institution for rearing children, and finally by a law of 1939 introducing youth duty, which in effect made membership in the Hitler Youth mandatory for young men. Mobilization during World War II added further pressure to expand membership. In spite of these factors the Third Reich never managed to enroll all German boys in the Hitler Youth.

The task of the Hitler Youth was to politically indoctrinate and physically harden young people. Physical training played a paramount role, and the lure of camping trips, terrain sports, shooting practice, rowing, glider flying, and other activities was effective for recruitment. Its tasks were militarily organized, using uniforms, rank, and a division by age and geographical area. Ten- to thirteen-year-old boys were organized in the German Young People (Deutsche Jungvolk), while the Hitler Youth itself comprised boys and young men from fourteen to eighteen. Correspondingly, girls from ten to thirteen were enrolled in the Young Girls (Jungmädel), and girls and young women from fourteen to twenty-one in the League of German Girls. The organizations for both genders were organized hierarchically into regions at the top (*Obergebiete* and *Obergau*), counting up to approximately 750,000 members, which were successively subdivided down to the smallest units (*Kameradschaft* and *Jungmädelschaft*) with little more than ten members.

The Hitler Youth, like other of the Nazi Party's subordinate organizations, was amply represented at the annual Nuremberg Party Rallies, where thousands of young people had the opportunity to personally experience, even at a distance, the presence of the party leader. The leader cult was at the core of the Hitler Youth's training program, and Hitler himself considered it the foundation of his "Thousand Year Reign." He wrote in *Mein Kampf*: "A violently active, dominating, brutal youth—that is what I am after. Youth must be indifferent to pain. . . . I will have no intellectual training. Knowledge is ruin to my young men."

World War II brought new tasks to the Hitler Youth, both to the organization in general and to its specialized units, which had already captured youthful interest in flying, driving, sailing, gathering intelligence, patrolling, music,

A classroom of young boys give their teacher the Fascist salute, Germany, c. 1939.

and other activities. In 1940 Arthur Axmann was appointed Reich Youth Leader (*Reichsjugendführer*) and put in charge of committing youth to the war effort. The first assignments consisted in collecting blankets and clothes for soldiers and bones and paper for war production. As part of the mobilization for total war in the spring of 1943 combat units of Hitler Youth members, some of them no more than sixteen years of age, were formed. These units were sent into battle from the summer of 1944, often with huge losses due to inadequate training and experience. They surrendered to American forces in May 1945 along with the other German units.

See also: **Communist Youth; Fascist Youth; Organized Recreation and Youth Groups.**

BIBLIOGRAPHY

Koch, H. W. 1975. *The Hitler Youth: Origins and Development, 1922–45.* New York: Stein and Day.

JOHN T. LAURIDSEN

HIV. *See* AIDS.

Hobbies. *See* Collections and Hobbies.

Holocaust

The murder of Jewish children comported with the ideology of racial nationalism on which the Third Reich rested. Rooted in mythic notions of German national superiority, racial conflict as the key to history, and a vast empire ruled by a master race, this ideology identified Jews in particular as parasites in need of elimination. This anti-Semitism did not allow for distinctions according to religious commitment, social position, gender, or age: all Jews fit beneath a blanket condemnation. Adolf Hitler's central obsession was the removal of Jews from German lands, as well as from lands taken from "subhuman" Slavs and other Europeans by military conquest. A spirited debate continues about the sequence of decisions leading to the implementation of the "Final Solution to the Jewish Question," the Nazi plan not merely to remove but to kill every Jew in Europe. It is clear that by the beginning of World War II, in September 1939, however, the Nazis had already crossed the moral threshold with respect to murdering children. At least 6,000 children up to sixteen years of age with serious congenital or hereditary illnesses or physical deformities were killed in the Third

Reich's euthanasia program, which began at this time. Some of these children were subjected to painful experiments. Increasingly inured to the suffering of the young, the Nazis waged a war of extermination against their racial enemies. One should not be surprised that Jewish children were, in the words of Elie Wiesel—himself a youth of fifteen when he entered Auschwitz—"the first to suffer, the first to perish."

The Ghettos

The successes of the German military during the first three years of the war significantly increased the number of individuals under German control who could be exploited or tyrannized according to Nazi racial doctrines. Among these individuals were millions of Jews, who were subjected to the same kinds of persecutions that had led to the social death of Jews living in Germany in the 1930s: revocation of citizenship, reduction of food rations, confiscations, deprivation of schooling, restricted access to public institutions. Anti-Semitic propaganda was given free rein; Jews were ordered to display the yellow Star of David on their clothes. Condemned virtually to remain at home, Jews in occupied areas became isolated from their neighbors, who, with Nazi encouragement, withheld their sympathy or expelled Jews entirely from their orbit of moral responsibility. From Poland to France, from Holland to Greece, a regime of diatribe and harassment descended on Jewish communities. In the east, Nazi measures to render Jews vulnerable and contemptible included forcible removal from their homes to designated urban areas called ghettos. Isolating them in ghettos facilitated the seizure of their property. The policy also concentrated Jews for forced labor in the production of war supplies.

Jewish children experienced these persecutions in emotional and spiritual distress. Entries in children's diaries indicate a general inability among children to integrate ghetto life with their pre-ghetto existence and confusion about the moral reordering of their world. Many diarists could not understand why they were hated, why they had to be prisoners, why their fathers had been arrested, why their mothers had been beaten. In the ghettos, children confronted grave responsibilities. Every day, children were orphaned, as adults perished from hunger, disease, or execution, or were taken away for forced labor. ORPHANS begged for bread and potatoes or smuggled food by squeezing through gaps in the ghetto walls. Older children cared for younger siblings in this way. Some provided for their entire families. This harried existence had dreadful consequences. Children in particular suffered from overcrowding, hunger, improper sanitation, lack of medical care, and exposure to cold. In winter, thousands of children froze to death.

Social welfare organizations in the ghettos attempted to meet children's special needs. Children's kitchens were opened, as were CHILDREN'S LIBRARIES, and some children had access to schooling and cultural activities. In the ghetto at Theresienstadt, northwest of Prague, for example, children expressed themselves artistically. Some four thousand of their paintings and drawings were recovered. These included depictions of flowers and butterflies but also of executions, deportations at the railhead to Auschwitz, and queues for a ladle of broth. Most Jewish children, particularly those in large ghettos at places like Lodz, Warsaw, Minsk, and Riga, had little or no access to social welfare or cultural outreach programs. Their lives were consumed with meeting the everyday requirements of bare subsistence.

Hiding Children, Hunting Children

Tens of thousands of Jewish parents attempted to hide their children from the Nazis. When the ghettos were liquidated, parents hid them in pantries, coal boxes, toilets, walls, chimneys, floorboards—anyplace they might escape the Germans and their local collaborators. Forced laborers often hid their children in factories. Partisan bands fighting behind German lines ensconced children in woods, caves, bunkers, or family camps in the forests. Underground organizations tried to find refuge for Jewish children, too. Few non-Jewish individuals, however, were willing to endanger themselves or their families by hiding them. Those who agreed to help acted more from impulse than careful calculation. Girls found greater acceptance than boys did. Boys' Jewishness manifested itself physically through CIRCUMCISION, and it was not uncommon for the German police to demand that boys pull down their pants and expose their "race." Rescuers might conceal children around the clock in cellars, barns, even cupboards, or assign them false names and try to pass them off as non-Jews. Hundreds of children from across Europe found refuge in Christian children's homes and convents. Female religious orders in Poland, for example, especially if they ran ORPHANAGES or residential schools for girls, could be persuaded to hide Jews, sometimes on the understanding that the girls would be introduced to Christianity, other times to satisfy altruistic principles. An unusual episode of Christian heroism occurred at Le Chambon-sur-Lignon, France. Here the largely Protestant community concealed some four hundred Jewish children from German authorities, saving them from deportation and almost certain death. For all these hidden children of the Holocaust, privation and the trauma of losing parents and siblings were accompanied by loneliness and the mortal terror of being hunted.

The Nazis allowed precious few to escape. With their invasion of the Soviet Union in June 1941, they unleashed the full criminal power of the Third Reich against Jewish children. Hitler wanted the newly won territories in the east to be completely *Judenfrei*, free of Jews. All traces of Jewish existence were to be wiped out. Before the invasion commenced, Heinrich Himmler, the head of the SS and chief of the genocidal cohort, transmitted spoken orders to German military and SS commanders, which were interpreted broadly to authorize the extermination of Russian Jewry. Four mobile killing squads, or *Einsatzgruppen*, were organized to execute this task. Elements of the German military, reserve police battalions, and local auxiliaries, whose violence towards Jews was historic, assisted these units.

Although Jewish children were shot along with their parents as early as late July 1941, in many towns and villages only adult males were killed. Adult males were also the principle targets of pogroms (organized massacres of Jews), which local inhabitants in Belorussia and the Baltics initiated under German auspices. This evidence suggests that initially German killers were uncertain what to do with children. After shooting their parents, they often removed children to a nearby town or interned them in local buildings. They quickly abandoned this practice, however. Multitudes of screaming, starving, soiled small children with no one to care for them became a nuisance, and commanders began shooting them en masse. Some worried that allowing children to suffer in plain view was psychologically disruptive to their troops and thought it better to liquidate them on "humanitarian" grounds. Others acted on what they understood to be legitimate orders. Still others took their cue from Himmler, who justified the murder of children to avoid creating a generation of anti-German avengers. In any case, despite the initial hesitation, the mass murder of Jewish children rapidly became an integral part of the genocidal plan. By October 1941, at some execution sites, such as one outside Smolensk in the Soviet Union, the first to be shot were children, along with the sick, aged, and those who could not perform manual labor. Only later were their parents killed. The shooting of children at close range was particularly gruesome. Some killers shot children right next to their parents, who refused to abandon their boys and girls to face death alone. Spattered with blood and the brain matter of their victims, a handful of killers refused to continue. The great majority, however, became callused executioners, for whom the murder of children was routine activity. Before the death camps for gassing had even been constructed, almost a million Jews on the Eastern Front had been shot. Tens of thousands of these victims were defenseless children.

At the Wannsee Conference outside of Berlin in January 1942, Nazi officials met to systematize the genocide that was already underway. The Final Solution ordained that Jews from all over Europe be rounded up and evacuated to the east. Here they would be concentrated in transit ghettos before their murder at work camps or death camps. With extreme brutality, Jewish children were taken with the surviving members of their families to rail depots for deportation. Infants were shot on the spot, as were children found hiding or attempting to escape. Some children were snatched from their parents at deportation sites and were left to perish from hunger and the elements. Others were separated from their families and had to face the trials of deportation alone. From the fall of 1941 to the spring of 1945, more than 400 transport trains rolled to the work and death camps in the east.

Jammed into sealed cattle cars, many children were crushed to death or suffocated. Others starved or died of thirst.

Children in the Camps

When they disembarked, Jewish children encountered deadly peril. Those judged suitable for work were interned. Children as young as seven undertook heavy labor, such as carrying building materials or pushing overloaded carts. Some camp guards took Jewish boys for personal servants or for the traffic in children among pedophiles. Death visited young internees in numerous forms. Chronic malnutrition and exposure rendered children susceptible to infectious diseases. Many babies conceived in camps were forcibly aborted or had their heads smashed at birth by SS guards. At Auschwitz, some 3,000 twins underwent experiments conducted by the SS doctor Josef Mengele. These experiments included exposure to cholera and tuberculosis, operations without anesthetic, sterilization, and murder by phenol injection to the heart for the purpose of examining internal organs. In an attempt to create perfect "Aryans" from "inferior" racial stock, Mengele injected the eyes of some twins with chemicals in the hope of turning them blue. Few Jewish twins survived these horrific experiments. Few Jewish children survived internment at all. Those who did survive had generally been orphaned and continued to suffer after the war from penetrating psychological wounds and emotional disorders.

Most Jewish children, of course, were not interned in camps but were slaughtered upon arrival. All pregnant women, infants, and children deemed incapable of forced labor were sent for immediate gassing. As the commandant of Auschwitz explained, "Children of tender years were invariably exterminated, since by reason of their youth they were unable to work." Pressed against their mother's chests, some children did not die in the gas chamber and were burned alive in the crematoria. At Majdanek in 1943, the SS made sport of machine-gunning Jewish children in front of their parents. At Birkenau in 1944, Hungarian children, some of them still alive, were incinerated in great pits. Children were not always unaware of their imminent death. In October 1944, an eyewitness at Birkenau recorded the behavior of a large group of Lithuanian Jewish boys as they were herded into the gas chamber by SS guards: "Crazed with fright, they started running around the yard, back and forth, clutching their heads. Many of them broke into frightful crying. Their wailing was terrible to hear."

Between 1.2 to 1.5 million Jewish children died in the Final Solution—89 percent of all Jewish children living in German-occupied lands. They glimpsed the world, and then they were gone.

See also: **Frank, Anne; Holocaust, Jewish Ghetto Education and the; War in the Twentieth Century.**

BIBLIOGRAPHY

Dwork, Deborah. 1991. *Children with a Star: Jewish Youth in Nazi Europe.* New Haven, CT: Yale University Press.

Eisenberg, Azriel, ed. 1982. *The Lost Generation: Children in the Holocaust.* New York: Pilgrim.

Frank, Anne. 1995. *The Diary of a Young Girl: The Definitive Edition.* Trans. Susan Massotty. New York: Doubleday.

Holliday, Laurel. 1995. *Children in the Holocaust and World War II: Their Secret Diaries.* New York: Pocket Books.

Lagnado, Lucette Matalon, and Sheila Cohn Dekel. 1991. *Children of the Flames: Dr. Josef Mengele and the Untold Story of the Twins of Auschwitz.* New York: Morrow.

Marks, Jane. 1993. *The Hidden Children: The Secret Survivors of the Holocaust.* New York: Fawcett Columbine.

Sliwowska, Wiktoria, ed. 1998. *The Last Eyewitnesses: Children of the Holocaust Speak.* Evanston, IL: Northwestern University Press.

Valent, Paul. 2002. *Child Survivors of the Holocaust.* New York: Brunner-Routledge.

Volavková, Hana. 1993. *I Never Saw Another Butterfly: Children's Drawings and Poems from Terezin Concentration Camp, 1942–1944.* New York: Schocken.

Wiesel, Elie. 1982. *Night.* New York: Bantam.

JEFFREY T. ZALAR

Holocaust, Jewish Ghetto Education and the

Before World War II Jews enjoyed a rich cultural and social life throughout Europe. Despite pervasive anti-Semitism, Jews thrived and maintained their customs and traditions. Education had always been a cornerstone of Jewish life. But after the Nazis came to power in Germany in 1933, a series of laws were passed that gradually excluded Jews from business, civil service positions, universities, and all facets of professional life. On November 15, 1938—five days after a Nazi-organized night of widespread violence and vandalism against Jewish synagogues, stores, and businesses that came to be known as Kristallnacht (the night of broken glass)—Jewish children were barred from attending German schools. With the institution of Nazi decrees to end public education, the situation grew bleak. The effect on children was particularly harsh, as attested to by Naomi Morgenstern:

> Marisha, my best friend, invited me to come with her to school. We met in the morning and walked together with a lot of other children. . . . Marisha went through the gate [of the school], and I followed her, as the watchman greeted her. "Where are you going?" he asked me. "To school, to the first grade," I said proudly and continued walking. The watchman blocked my way. "No, not you." "But I am six already—really I am!" "You are a Jew," he said. "Jews have no right to learn. No Jews in our school. Go home!" I looked around. Marisha and the other children stood there listening. The school bell rang. Marisha, with the other children, ran into the building. I turned around, and walked away. Standing in the

street outside, I held on to the fence of the school. I watched Marisha. She entered the school building and disappeared. I did not cry. I thought: "I'm Jewish. There is no place for me. I stood there until no one stood in front of the school. Only me. The new school year had begun. But not for me." (p. 12)

After the start of World War II, the Germans began to segregate Jewish populations into ghettos, primarily in Nazi-occupied lands in Eastern Europe. Historian George Eisen noted that "the educational system in almost all ghettos became victims of similar decrees [as those in Germany]. With one swipe of the pen, schools were outlawed and Jewish learning, specifically that of children, was forbidden under threat of death" (p. 21).

Such decrees did not halt the establishment, mostly illegal, of a network of elementary and secondary schooling and even higher education. Evidence clearly indicates that elaborate networks of schooling were established in ghettos like Vilna, Lodz, and Warsaw. In the Vilna ghetto, for instance, the Jews established a regular school system. The religious schools in this ghetto were particularly comprehensive in that the curriculum included attention to secular subjects such as arithmetic as well as study of ancient Hebrew texts.

In Lodz, the first major ghetto established (on December 10, 1939) and the last to be destroyed, the educational system included at the start forty-seven schools from kindergarten through high school with a total enrollment of 15,000 children. Although conditions in these schools were unbearable (e.g., classrooms were unheated, textbooks and materials were in short supply, and illness was rampant), classes were held with few disruptions for the first two years of Nazi occupation. According to a chronicler of the Lodz ghetto: "For many of [these students], school was a ray of light amid darkness—an anchor and symbol of the continuation of 'normal' life" (Unger, p. 136).

Overt schooling, however, ceased in the autumn of 1941, as children aged ten and over were compelled to join the labor force. Clandestine schools continued in the Lodz ghetto despite gnawing hunger, backbreaking work, disease, and constant fear of deportation. According to one chronicler, "precisely because of these unbearable physical and psychological hardships—many ghetto residents sought refuge, albeit temporary, in other worlds far from day-to-day reality" (Unger, p. 133). One young resident, Dawid Sierakowiak, found this refuge in reading and study. He wrote in his diary on March 25, 1942: "I felt very bad today. I did some reading, but I find it hard to study anything, only several new words in English. One of the things I'm reading is a excerpt from the works of Schopenhauer. Philosophy and hunger—what an unusual combination" (Adelson, p. 120).

In Warsaw, the largest Polish ghetto, the first school year under German occupation began in October 1939. Occupation authorities allowed only elementary and vocational schools to open; they kept the secondary schools in the ghetto closed. Two months later, they closed all Jewish schools in Warsaw. Judenrate (Jewish Council) authorities made many unsuccessful appeals to the Germans to rescind this regulation. Lacking a legitimate educational system, the Jewish community began to establish an underground network of schools. Clandestine elementary schools operated mainly in children's kitchens under the aegis of various social agencies. However, only a tiny fraction of the ghetto's tens of thousands of school-aged children could actually attend them.

Another vast network of private schools was established in Warsaw primarily for high school students. Unemployed teachers from prewar faculties staffed these clandestine schools, known as *komplety* in Polish. In the Warsaw ghetto, some two hundred students also learned in at least eleven *yeshivot* (schools for advanced Hebrew studies). Most yeshiva students had no legal existence in the ghettos because they were not registered with the Judenrate. Their lack of official status meant that the students had no ration cards. Some more fortunate Jewish families supplied them with food in quantity, as did some welfare agencies. Students took turns begging on the street or soliciting food and money among people of means.

In many ghettos, clandestine schooling sometimes took the form of play. In an attempt to disguise a formal school structure, children, with the aid of educators, formed playgroups. In his brilliant study of children and play during the Holocaust, George Eisen described such playgroups:

The Youth Care organization of the [Theresienstadt] camp (Jugendfuersorge) formed several "play groups" which replaced the formal school structure. A prisoner remembered after the war that "lessons had to be camouflaged as games." In the guise of play, genuine school subjects such as history, math, and geography were taught. Children took turns in alerting their classmates and teachers to the approach of SS men. On a moment's notice, children and teachers magically transformed the classroom into a play scene. Even the smallest details of these activities had to be well rehearsed, for if anyone were caught it could mean death for children and teachers alike. (p. 84)

Conditions in ghetto schools were deplorable. Survivors, reminiscing about their experiences, recalled the horrible conditions in the Lodz ghetto. Dawid Sierakowiak noted in his diary "School is deteriorating. There are no teachers or classes. Everything is vanishing before our eyes" (Adelson, p. 120). Yet despite these horrendous conditions, learning became a form of spiritual survival and even resistance. David Weiss Halivni, in his memoir *The Book and the Sword: A Life of Learning in the Shadow of Destruction* (1996), described in detail how learning contributed greatly to his sur-

vival: "It was learning that made my life as a child bearable, insulated me from what was happening in the ghetto, . . . and it was learning that allowed me to resume my life after the Holocaust" (p. 175). Despite deplorable conditions, Jews established a network of schooling in many ghettos. The attention to the education of children and its impact on them as a means and expression of survival are remarkable testimonies of courage and determination.

See also: **Holocaust; Judaism; War in the Twentieth Century.**

BIBLIOGRAPHY

Adelson, Alan, ed. 1996. *The Diary of Dawid Sierakowiak.* New York: Oxford University Press.

Bitton-Jackson, Livia. 1999. *I Have Lived a Thousand Years: Growing Up in the Holocaust.* New York: Aladdin.

Butterworth, Emma Macalik. 1982. *As the Waltz Was Ending.* New York: Scholastic.

Durlacher, Gerhard. 1994. *Drowning: Growing Up in the Third Reich.* London: Serpent's Tail.

Eisen, George. 1988. *Children at Play in the Holocaust: Games Among the Shadows.* Amherst: University of Massachusetts Press.

Glanz, Jeffrey. 2000. "Clandestine Schooling and Education Among Jews During the Holocaust." *Journal of Curriculum and Supervision* 16, no. 1: 48–69.

Halivni, David Weiss. 1996. *The Book and the Sword: A Life of Learning in the Shadow of Destruction.* Boulder, CO: Westview Press.

Leapman, Michael. 2000. *Witnesses to War: Eight True-Life Stories of Nazi Persecution.* New York: Scholastic.

Milgram, Avraham, Carmit Sagui, and Shulamit Imbar. 1993. *Everyday Life in the Warsaw Ghetto.* Jerusalem, Israel: Yad Vashem.

Morgenstern, Naomi. 1998. *I Wanted to Fly Like a Butterfly: A Child's Recollections of the Holocaust.* Jerusalem, Israel: Yad Vashem.

Rosenbaum, Irving J. 1976. *The Holocaust and Halakhah.* New York: Ktav Publishing.

Rothchild, Sylvia, ed. 1981. *Voices from the Holocaust.* New York: American Library.

Roth-Hano, Renee. 1989. *Touch Wood: A Girlhood in Occupied France.* New York: Puffin Books.

Sommer, Jay. 1994. *Journey to the Golden Door: A Survivor's Tale.* New York: Shengold Publishers.

Tec, Nechama. 1984. *Dry Tears: The Story of a Lost Childhood.* New York: Oxford University Press.

Unger, Michal, ed. 1997. *The Last Ghetto: Life in the Lodz Ghetto, 1940–1944.* Jerusalem, Israel: Yad Vashem.

Volavkova, Hana, ed. 1994. *I Never Saw Another Butterfly: Children's Drawings and Poems from Terezin Concentration Camp, 1942–1944.* Jerusalem, Israel: Yad Vashem.

Weiss, Gershon. 1999. *The Holocaust and Jewish Destiny: Jewish Heroism, Human Faith, and Divine Providence.* Jerusalem: Targum Press.

Wiesel, Elie. 1982. *Night.* New York: Bantam Books.

JEFFREY GLANZ

Homeless Children and Runaways in the United States

The population of homeless children in the United States is estimated to range from five hundred thousand to more than two million. Historical studies of homelessness in general have concentrated on urban homeless men living on skid row. A 1996 National Rural Health Association study found rural homeless people so elusive that they refer to them as America's lost population. Large numbers of homeless and runaway children have always roamed the streets of every major city in the United States as well as the countryside, from small towns to remote rural areas.

The issues surrounding homeless children and runaways generally have been either ignored or altogether unknown; and, when the issues have been acknowledged, the discussion has most often focused on homeless families with children, not independent children with no homes to which they can return. The extent to which the populations of homeless children and runaways overlap is unknown, partly because there are no commonly agreed upon definitions of the terms *homeless* and *runaway*. Fortunately, there has been some research on homeless children in recent decades. Works such as Mark Nord and A. E. Luloff's "Homeless Children and Their Families in New Hampshire: A Rural Perspective," for example, have shown that childhood homelessness is a rural problem as well as an urban problem and that there are some significant differences between the two groups.

The History of Homeless and Runaway Children

Homeless and runaway children, although not specifically mentioned in early vagrancy laws, have existed since the early settlement of the United States. Throughout the country's history, the conditions of larger society, such as a frequently depressed industrial economy that struggled with overproduction and labor surpluses, resulted in family upheaval. Sara A. Brown (1922) lists reasons children ran away from home during the early twentieth century: death of parents, abusive home life, broken homes, feeblemindedness, DELINQUENCY, and poverty. The major difference between runaway children and homeless children was that runaways chose to leave their home for the reasons above while homeless children were victims of social and economic factors that left them without shelter for varying lengths of time.

As Gregg Barak has shown, treatment of homeless and runaway children was strongly influenced by the ideology of social Darwinism, particularly the EUGENICS movement. The eugenics movement was based on the belief that selective breeding and breeding control would rid society of the inferior genetic material that was responsible for crime, mental illness, and retardation. Sterilization laws were an important tool of the eugenics movement. If homeless or runaway children were determined to be feeble-minded, it was not uncommon for them to be institutionalized and sterilized.

The first state to pass sterilization laws was Indiana, in 1907. By 1944, thirty states had passed sterilization laws and forty thousand men, women, and children had been sterilized. Between 1945 and 1963, another twenty-two thousand people were sterilized. California sterilized the largest number at twenty thousand, followed by Virginia, with eight thousand. Virginia's sterilization program did not officially end until 1979. Homeless and runaway children and adolescents were the most likely to be sterilized.

Homeless and runaway children have been the victims of changing societal attitudes toward vagrancy over the years. Barak describes the early discussions and definitions of vagrancy laws, in which children were referred to as waifs and were included in the definition of hobos, tramps, vagabonds, beggars, and bums. The early definitions included terms such as wandering, deviating, devious, aberrant, undisciplined, twisted, freakish, and maggoty. Reform Darwinism, the ideology of the Progressive Era introduced around the turn of the twentieth century, carried somewhat kinder judgments of poor homeless children. Barak notes that the definition of the term *waif* changed to include words such as homeless, forlorn, abandoned, deserted, desolate, friendless, helpless, defenseless, indigent, and destitute.

However, along with the kinder definitions of poor homeless children came the distinction between the *deserving* and *undeserving* poor. The deserving poor were considered worthy of public assistance because the causes of their poverty were beyond their individual control. The undeserving poor, however, were poor due to their flawed characters and personal faults, and were thus unworthy of aid. It was believed that if the undeserving poor were given assistance, their numbers would simply increase.

A large percentage of Americans in the early twentieth century recognized that poor homeless people were victims not only of individual circumstances, but often and perhaps more importantly of institutional and structural arrangements. For example, many rural communities were accessible by automobile only during certain seasons of the year; therefore, social service agencies literally could not expand their services into remote areas in a consistent manner. However, any allowances made for causes external to the individual only went so far and were applied only to the socially defined deserving poor.

The distinction between the deserving and undeserving poor was applied to homeless and runaway children as well. Children who had lost their homes due to societal conditions fell into the category of deserving poor; runaway children who chose to leave their homes, for whatever reason, fell into the category of undeserving poor. Only deserving homeless children were viewed as unfortunate and in need of human services and caring intervention. Runaway children were viewed as vagrants and criminals deserving punitive forms of intervention from people trying to rid themselves and their

436

environment of spoiled goods. This attitude resulted in homeless children and runaways being abused and used as cheap labor by agriculturalists and industrialists.

Research indicates that people continued to discriminate against homeless children and runaways throughout the twentieth century. Johann Le Roux and Cheryl S. Smith examined attitudes toward urban homeless children and runaways and found that street children in the 1990s lived under a constant threat of violence and maltreatment. Some people regarded them as nuisances, and some regarded them as criminals.

Rural homeless and runaway children of the past had much in common with their counterparts of today as well. Their problems included distance from neighbors, school, church, stores, doctors, mail services, and telephones, bad roads, and a lack of social activities, wholesome recreation, and community school spirit. Brown reported in 1922 that of approximately five hundred thousand rural children under eighteen years of age in West Virginia, twenty-five thousand were dependent on people other than their parents for shelter, food, and clothing. Her study of 1,005 homeless children included children from broken homes, children who lived in hit-or-miss situations where they sometimes had homes for a while, children born out of wedlock, and feeble-minded children with feeble-minded parents. She described these children as unofficial wards of the community: some families provided for them, but those provisions were never totally predictable for the children.

In 2000, Peggy Shifflett reported the results of a study of contemporary adults who grew up between 1930 and 1960 as homeless children in a rural Virginia community. Homeless and runaway children in this community were called *field rabbits* because they roamed the roads with no attachment to their parents, and particularly their fathers. The adults reported that when they were homeless as children they were often beaten and forced to work, at minimal or no wages, for community families. Other families provided for their needs, and they knew from experience which families would feed them and give them a bed for a night. From this community, six adolescents were institutionalized and sterilized.

The Current Status of Homeless and Runaway Children

In 1989, the American Medical Association (AMA) called for research on the health-care needs of homeless and runaway children. They reported that they had no way of knowing the extent to which the populations of homeless children and runaway children overlapped, and noted that any attempt to distinguish between homeless and runaway children would be artificial since the health needs of both groups are likely the same. For the first time in the literature on homeless and runaway children the AMA had moved away from labeling poor children deserving and undeserving. However, the AMA's focus was still on urban children—the homeless and

runaway children who roam the streets of every major city in this country.

Janet Fitchen reported in her 1991 article that homelessness in rural America is still generally overlooked and ignored because it does not fit urban-based perceptions and definitions. Most Americans think of the homeless as living in boxes in alleys and sleeping on subway benches or in homeless shelters. Rural homeless people do not fit these images. In fact, few rural people are literally homeless in the sense of not having a roof over their heads. However, the roof they have may be only a car roof or a shed roof; it may be the leaky roof of a dilapidated farmhouse or an isolated shack with no running water, or the temporary roof of an old mobile home already full of relatives or friends.

Nord and Luloff reported in 1995 that there was a strong stigma associated with homelessness in rural areas. As a result, homeless children suffer from loneliness and depression. They are more likely to be diagnosed as retarded in school and relegated to SPECIAL EDUCATION classes for the learning disabled. Homeless children do attend school, but are inclined to drop out at age sixteen. Attention deficit disorder is the most frequent diagnosis, with emotionally disturbed bringing up a close second. Teachers often report homeless children as inattentive and sleepy in class. Most of these diagnoses result from inadequate sleep and poor nutrition.

The American Medical Association in 1989 summarized the health issues of homeless and runaway children as being the same as those faced by homeless people in general. The one exception is that older children tend to be healthier by virtue of their age and the shorter length of time they have been homeless. The health problems faced by homeless and runaway children can be grouped into six categories: nutrition, substance abuse, mental health, physical health, sexual health, and victimization.

Nutritional deficiencies are common. This situation has frightening implications for the health and well-being of children born to homeless adolescent females, among whom pregnancy is fairly common. Large numbers of homeless and runaway children drink regularly and up to one-half have diagnosable alcohol problems. The abuse of other DRUGS is also common. Homeless children are also afflicted with mental health problems, the most common of which are depression and self-destructive behavior, including SUICIDE.

The physical health of homeless and runaway children is challenged by exposure to the elements, lack of sleeping quarters, and the absence of a clean home. The most common problems reported are upper respiratory tract infections, minor skin ailments, and gastrointestinal tract problems. Sexual health problems include genitourinary disorders, pregnancy, and sexually transmitted diseases. Because homeless and runaway children are too young to work and lack marketable skills, they are often recruited by criminals involved in the illegal drug trade, prostitution, and pornography. They are either active participants in these activities or serve as recruiters of other vulnerable children.

Experts generally agree that homelessness among children is increasing in both rural and urban areas. The causes are social in nature. These children are often homeless along with their mothers and are victims of economic recessions, job loss, and high housing costs. Data on the extent of the problem is inadequate and can be found only in isolated case studies. Virtually nothing is known about the needs of racial and ethnic subgroups within the young homeless population or about what happens to these young people as they age.

See also: **Foster Care; Police, Children and the; Law, Children and the; Social Welfare; Street Arabs and Street Urchins.**

BIBLIOGRAPHY

American Medical Association. 1989. "Health Care Needs of Homeless and Runaway Youth." *Journal of the American Medical Association* 262: 1358–1362.

Barak, Gregg. 1991. *Gimme Shelter: A Social History of Homelessness in Contemporary America.* New York: Praeger.

Brown, Sara A. 1922. "Rural Child Dependency, Neglect, and Delinquency." In *Rural Child Welfare*, ed. Edward N. Clopper. New York: Macmillan.

Fitchen, Janet. 1991. "Homelessness in Rural Places: Perspectives from Upstate New York." *Urban Anthropology* 20: 177–210.

Le Roux, Johann, and Cheryl Sylvia Smith. 1998. "Public Perceptions of, and Reactions to, Street Children." *Adolescence* 33: 901–910.

National Rural Health Association. 1996. *The Rural Homeless: America's Lost Population.* Kansas City, MO: The National Rural Health Association.

Nord, Mark, and A. E. Luloff. 1995. "Homeless Children and Their Families in New Hampshire: A Rural Perspective." *Social Science Review* (September): 463–478.

Shifflett, Peggy A. 2000. "Rural Homeless Children." Paper presented at the Annual Conference on the History of Childhood, August 1–3, Washington, DC.

PEGGY A. SHIFFLETT

Homer, Winslow (1836–1910)

Winslow Homer was an American painter and engraver. After beginning his career as a freelance illustrator for magazines like *Harper's Weekly*, he turned to the subject of children in one-room schoolhouses, on farms, and at the seashore. By the 1880s he moved away from this theme of childhood, and began to paint the dramatic seascapes of Maine and the hunting and fishing scenes from the Adirondacks for which he is well-known.

Homer's pictures of schoolchildren depict both the interior and exterior of the rural red one-room schoolhouse.

Homer publicly exhibited or published eight paintings and two engravings of this subject between 1871 and 1874. The most well-known of these is a picture (of which there are two versions) of a group of boys playing the game of snap-the-whip. Others depict the young female teacher or children engaged in their lessons. The female teacher was a sign of the modernity of the pictures (the prevalence of female teachers was brought about by the Civil War), while the rural one-room schoolhouse was a nostalgic image for urban viewers. Importantly, the public school was seen as a uniquely American institution, and therefore the pictures were also seen as particularly national. Two of them represented the United States at the 1878 Paris Exposition.

During these years Homer also painted many farm scenes, featuring both children and adults. He depicted boys relaxing and engaged in summer activities (including crossing a pasture to go fishing, sleeping on the grass, eating watermelon, and fishing from a log). Many of these pastoral images also include young girls, and often a flirtatious exchange between the two. Henry James described these figures as "little barefoot urchins and little girls in calico sun-bonnets." Towards the end of the decade Homer painted a group of works which depicted young girls on the farm, or "shepherdesses," as contemporary critics called them.

Some of Homer's paintings were watercolors, including a large group from his 1873 summer visit to Gloucester, Massachusetts. These pictures depict children, especially boys, along the seashore: in the water on boats (including *Breezing Up*), on the beach, digging for clams, and looking out to sea. In Gloucester, where many fishermen were lost at sea in the 1870s, this last theme (as in pictures like *Waiting for Dad*) is especially poignant.

Homer's pictures are consistent with the growing interest in childhood in the late nineteenth century. Although they often depicted a sense of an earlier world, they were very different from the sentimentalized genre pictures of the period. As such, they received a mixed reception from contemporary critics. While some praised the subjects as particularly national and representative of the unique way of American life, others lambasted the subjects as coarse; while some saw his style as innovative and modern, others saw it as unfinished and crude. The mixed responses are typical of the changing standards of the art world in the 1870s; during the twentieth century some of these pictures of children were among Homer's best-known works.

See also: **Images of Childhood.**

BIBLIOGRAPHY

Carren, Rachel Ann. 1990. "From Reality to Symbol: Images of Children in the Art of Winslow Homer." Ph.D. diss., University of Maryland, College Park.

Cikovsky, Nicolai, Jr., and Frank Kelly. 1995. *Winslow Homer.* Washington: National Gallery of Art.

Conrads, Margaret C. 2001. *Winslow Homer and the Critics: Forging a National Art in the 1870s.* Princeton: Princeton University Press.

MELISSA GEISLER TRAFTON

Homeschooling

Schooling has historically often occurred both formally and informally at home. Most colonial children in the United States were homeschooled in what were called *Dame schools.* The children in each rural area would gather at a neighbor's kitchen table to read and reread the hornbook, a catechism, passages from the bible, *The Pilgrim's Progress,* and other improving material. This family-centered learning, along with APPRENTICESHIP, continued to be the primary mode of education until well into the nineteenth century.

For most of human history schools were exclusionary rather than inclusive. Latin GRAMMAR SCHOOLS were only for boys from wealthy families. Harvard was founded in 1634 for the young male graduates of the grammar schools. It was nearly two hundred years later, in 1827, that the first institution of higher education for girls opened. In most southern states, it was illegal to teach African-American slaves to read. Some of those who could not go to school were occasionally schooled at home.

In the early nineteenth century, COMMON SCHOOLS were opened to educate all, but many children did not attend. The growing industrial revolution of the late nineteenth and early twentieth century saw thousands of European immigrants coming to the industrial cities of the North. By the twentieth century, they were joined by a migration of blacks from the South. The children often did not attend school. They worked in the factories alongside their parents and other relatives. Together with child labor laws, compulsory attendance laws began to remove children from the factories. The state needed a safe place to warehouse children. School became a place you could go—if your family could spare you. In reality most children attended school only through the fourth to the sixth grades, after which they were needed to help support the family.

Access to schooling increased steadily from the middle of the twentieth century. HIGH SCHOOL attendance burgeoned following World War I and again after World War II. In 1954, the Supreme Court decided that African-American children should be allowed to attend local public schools instead of the separate schools they had been attending since the end of the Civil War. Desegregation of public schools was finally enforced in the 1960s by Presidents Kennedy and Johnson. Thus, by the end of the 1970s the United States saw high school graduation occurring for the largest percentage of its population ever before—or since. In response to this and other issues, the decade of the 1980s ushered in the era of school reform. One of those reforms was homeschooling. It has always been available to the privileged, some of whom were tutored at home. But when large numbers began to homeschool, district officials began to arrest parents, saying they were encouraging truancy. This led early homeschoolers to band together, to litigate, and to lobby.

Who was homeschooling at the turn of the twenty-first century, and why? The demographics are elusive. Detractors say only two hundred and fifty to three hundred thousand children are homeschooled. Supporters claim the number is closer to one and one-half million. A 1999 report from the Center for Educational Statistics in the U.S. Department of Education estimated that eight hundred and fifty thousand students nationwide were being homeschooled. Families choose homeschooling for a variety of reasons, but most are concerned either with ideology or with academic achievement. Ideologues, from fundamental Christians to New Agers, prefer the moral climate of their own homes and communities to that of school. Pedagogues are more concerned that their children will be academically handicapped if they are required to learn at the pace of classroom instruction.

Homeschooled children excel academically, despite the early concerns of educators and truant officers. Research shows that their test scores are at or above the norm, and the longer children are homeschooled the wider the gap between their test scores and those of conventionally schooled youngsters. The household income of homeschoolers in 1999 was no different from their conventionally schooled peers, but the homeschooling parents had higher levels of educational attainment. Another early concern, the socialization of homeschoolers, eventually dissipated as well. Homeschoolers form networks. They issue newsletters, have play groups, organize soccer teams, share resources, and interact in multiage social groups.

State statutes that regulate homeschooling come in three different categories. The most restrictive recognizes no exception to public school attendance except qualified private schools, but these statutes are rarely enforced. A second category gives implicit approval of homeschooling through language that allows "equivalent education elsewhere." A third is an explicit statute providing for home instruction and specifying some criteria and procedures. This last category allows superintendents to count the homeschoolers in their districts for the purpose of receiving state subsidies. Homeschooling remains controversial but has also become a much more ordinary choice and is now seen as one alternative among many in a society deeply concerned about educational achievement.

See also: **Education, United States.**

BIBLIOGRAPHY

Cremin, Lawrence A. 1970. *American Education: The Colonial Experience 1607–1783.* New York: Harper & Row.

Marrou, Henri I. 1982 [1956]. *A History of Education in Antiquity.* Trans. George Lamb. Madison: University of Wisconsin Press.

National Center for Education Statistics. 2001. *Homeschooling in the United States: 1999.* Washington, DC: U.S. Department of Education, Office of Educational Research and Improvement.

Simon, Joan. 1966. *Education and Society in Tudor England.* Cambridge, UK: Cambridge University Press.

Stevens, Mitchell L. 2001. *Kingdom of Children: Culture and Controversy in the Homeschooling Movement.* Princeton, NJ: Princeton University Press.

Van Galen, Jane, and Mary Anne Pitman. 1991. *Home Schooling: Political, Historical, and Pedagogical Perspectives.* Norwood, NJ: Ablex.

MARY ANNE PITMAN

Homework

Homework is not only a routine aspect of schoolchildren's lives, but also the key daily interaction between school and family. As such, it often leads to tension between family and school over control of children's time and over parents' role in education—particularly after the expansion of mass schooling during the nineteenth and twentieth centuries.

A vocal anti-homework movement emerged in the United States in the early twentieth century, asserting parental prerogatives and children's rights. One critic argued that "the cultural or recreational life of the family is seriously restricted or handicapped . . . by the school's invasion of the home hours" ("Home Study?" p. 69) while another pronounced that homework was a sin against childhood. The anti-homework position reflected the growing influence internationally of scientific knowledge about children's health and development. This in turn motivated a Progressive reform movement in education that rejected rote methods of teaching and learning in favor of individualized, "child-centered" approaches. Many educators argued that homework had no place in a Progressive educational regime, particularly in the elementary grades. During the first half of the twentieth century, school policies in many communities across the United States commanded the reduction or abolition of homework.

Nevertheless, throughout the era of mass education, most parents supported homework, at least in moderate amounts. They regarded homework not only as essential to academic achievement, but also as an important means for children to develop self-discipline and responsibility. Finally, some parents viewed homework not as an intrusion into family time but as a critical means of understanding how the school is educating their child. In the words of a parent from the 1930s, "Homework is a wonderful connecting link between the parents and the child's school life" ("Do You Believe in Homework?" p. 58). Two decades later, another parent made the point more bluntly: "Homework is our only way of keeping up with what goes on" in the school (Langdon and Stout, p. 370).

During the second half of the twentieth century, expert opinion increasingly came into line with parental views in support of homework. After the Soviet Union launched the Sputnik satellite in 1957, U.S. politicians, parents, and educators became concerned that the educational system required substantial improvement to match Soviet technological prowess. The resulting focus on science and mathematics reinforced challenges to PROGRESSIVE EDUCATION and sparked interest in using homework to support increasingly ambitious academic goals. By the 1980s, at least in the United States, a "back-to-basics" movement had largely replaced the earlier Progressive discourse in education. With it came a celebration of homework as vital to fostering academic attainment, moral virtue, and international economic competitiveness—and a strong endorsement of parental partnership in schooling.

Not all parents joined in the celebration of homework, however, particularly when its sheer quantity was overwhelming for their children or their family life. But in the United States the great majority of children never spent much time on homework. Despite small increases for high-school students in the post-Sputnik decade and for young children in the 1980s and 1990s, homework involved only a modest time commitment for most American students throughout the second half of the twentieth century. In the primary grades, despite the increases at the end of the century, homework occupied most children for only two hours *weekly*—an amount perhaps comparable to that given in other industrial nations. Meanwhile most U.S. high-school students spent around an hour *daily* on homework—substantially less than their counterparts in other advanced industrial nations. At the beginning of the twenty-first century, high-school students in many parts of Europe and Asia were spending substantial amounts of time on homework. In the United States, by contrast, an enormous gap was evident between a solidly pro-homework discourse and levels of homework practice that remained stubbornly low, even among college-bound students.

See also: **Education, United States.**

BIBLIOGRAPHY

Chen, Chuansheng, and Harold W. Stevenson. 1989. "Homework: A Cross-Cultural Examination." *Child Development* 60: 551–561.

"Do You Believe in Homework? Replies For and Against." 1936. *Parents Magazine* (January): 11, 14–15, 58–61.

Gill, Brian P., and Steven L. Schlossman. 1996. "'A Sin Against Childhood': Progressive Education and the Crusade to Abolish Homework, 1897–1941." *American Journal of Education* 105: 27–66.

Gill, Brian P., and Steven L. Schlossman. 2000. "The Lost Cause of Homework Reform." *American Journal of Education* 109: 27–62.

Gill, Brian P., and Steven L. Schlossman. 2003. "Homework and the Elusive Voice of Parents: Some Historical Perspectives." *Teachers College Record* 105, no. 5.

Gill, Brian P., and Steven L. Schlossman. 2003. "A Nation at Rest: The American Way of Homework, 1948–1999." *Educational Evaluation and Policy Analysis.*

"Home Study?" 1930. *Washington Education Journal* (November): 69–70, 82.

Langdon, Grace, and Irving W. Stout. 1957. "What Parents Think about Homework." *NEA Journal* 46: 370–372.

Larson, Reed W., and Suman Verma. 1999. "How Children and Adolescents Spend Time Across the World: Work, Play, and Developmental Opportunities." *Psychological Bulletin* 125, no. 6: 701–736.

Patri, Angelo. 1927. *School and Home.* New York: D. Appleton and Company.

BRIAN GILL
STEVEN SCHLOSSMAN

Homosexuality and Sexual Orientation

Traditional ideas about children and homosexuality depend upon a number of variables. One is what societal attitudes are toward same-sex activity among adults. This varied from culture to culture, but in Western societies where Christianity was dominant, such activity was regarded with considerable hostility. A second variable is what a culture determined should be the AGE OF CONSENT. Age of consent, the age at which individuals could legally come together in a sexual union, was for much of history something either for the family to decide or a matter of tribal custom. Probably in most cases this coincided with the beginning of PUBERTY, which is marked by physical developments that are clearly visible. In most cultures this was adjudged to take place between ages twelve and fourteen for girls and at a slightly older age for boys. Still another factor is how various societies break down sex and gender differences. In Western society there are only two different sexes or genders, while other cultures such as the Native American culture identify three, four, or even five, depending on how the individual researcher counts them. In some societies, those who do not conform to sex or gender stereotypes are regarded as special candidates to become a shaman or holy person. Sexual relations between two females are often regarded differently by a society than relations between two males, perhaps because in male-dominated societies what women did among themselves was not of much importance. In fact, much less is known about female relationships than about male, and much of what we do know about the female culture was disseminated through the eyes and voices of males for much of history.

In Western culture, much of what we know about youthful homosexuality comes from ancient Greece, where boys often entered into a relationship with an older man when they began to enter puberty. Studies suggest that this occurred earlier than was formerly believed, probably at an average age of about twelve. This early male initiation into sex was described in some detail by the classical writer Strabo in his account of the mock abduction and subsequent honeymoon of a youth coming of age. This consensual relationship between an adolescent and an adult male was institutionalized throughout Greek culture by the sixth century B.C.E. and survived well into the Roman period among some elements of society. Plutarch, in his *On the Education of Children* written in the first century of the common era, stated that though fathers might view the society of those who admired youth as an "intolerable outrage to their sons," he himself felt inclined to emulate such past followers as Socrates, Plato, Xenophon, and others in the practice.

The most influential force in changing such attitudes in the West was St. Augustine (354–430), the theological father of the Western Christian church. Augustine, who before his conversion had been living with a prepubescent girl to whom he was betrothed, became a strict advocate of celibacy after his conversion. He taught what became a basic doctrine of the Western Christian church, that the only justification for sexual activities was procreation. All nonprocreative sex was sinful. Essentially his idea of the sinfulness of homosexuality was written into Roman law and thus criminalized by the Emperor Justinian. Many religiously oriented groups in the Western world still adhere to this notion and for much of the twentieth century the American legal tradition was heavily influenced by it.

Despite the church's disapproval, homosexual activity did not disappear, and neither did same-sex relationships with and among children and adolescents. In the medieval Islamic world, as well as in medieval Judaism, there are a number of poems extolling same-sex relations with and among adolescents. Similar literary descriptions of adolescent homosexual relationships exist in the Chinese and Hindu traditions. In the West, both canon law and European civil law codes followed the Roman age of consent (twelve to thirteen) and generally regarded same-sex relations to be against the law. Thus most of our evidence of homosexual activity from this period comes through what law and society said about same-sex relationships, and does not necessarily indicate what individuals were actually doing. With the adoption of the Napoleonic legal code at the beginning of the nineteenth century in France, greater tolerance became possible, and more evidence of such relationships appears. The code established two standards, age and consent, to decide whether a sexual activity was criminal or not. Because the age of consent was thirteen, consensual same-sex acts were no longer criminal after that age. English and American common law were also revised in the nineteenth century, but same-sex relations were regarded with great hostility and homosexuality remained a crime until the last part of the twentieth century.

While hostility to homosexuality was well established in Western society for centuries, an important shift in attitudes occurred around 1900. Some physicians and other sex researchers began to claim that people were either homosexual or not. The idea that people could have a combination of both homosexual and heterosexual interests, which had been a common experience for some groups, was increasingly downplayed in favor of the new dichotomy. Further, homosexuality was now regarded by many as a disease, rather than simply a form of immorality. With this new approach, and with growing emphasis on the importance of heterosexual DATING and other activities for older children, concerns about signs of homosexuality among children increased. Parents and children themselves became increasingly anxious about homosexuality, and it became a major element of child rearing and socialization from the 1920s onward. While the most recent developments have loosened strictures about homosexuality, elements of this earlier tradition persist as well.

Children and Homosexuality

In the twentieth century more data became available and the study of childhood sexuality became systematized, although studies are very difficult to do except retrospectively, that is, through people's reported memories of their own childhood activities. We know that children learn early on what sex they are. In most cultures they are easily identified as a boy or girl by the clothes they wear and what their parents and others tell them. In fact, the sex of a newborn is usually the first question asked about it. Though children gain a gender identity sometime between one and two years old, they do not yet have a sense of gender constancy. A little boy may believe, for example, that at some later point in life he will be a girl. Even though the overwhelming majority of children soon realize this is an error, many keep wishing they were of the opposite sex and try to act like they are, and this seems to be a strong disposing factor for later transsexualism and homosexuality. Children's unwillingness to accept their assigned gender roles is often very difficult for parents and other adults to accept.

Most children, however, do learn a gender role, and this becomes their identification during preadolescence, which is considered to be roughly eight to twelve years old in Western cultures today. During this period they spend their time away from adults and generally in all-male or all-female groups if such groups are available. This homosociality, as it has been called, lessens the opportunities for heterosexual interactions at a period in which members of both sexes are learning the facts of life; it also facilitates homosexual behavior. Boys, for example, may participate in group MASTURBATION or exhibition of genitalia or competitive urinating contests, but such activities are not necessarily an indicator of later homosexuality. Preadolescent children who later become gay or lesbian are more likely to distinguish themselves not so much by their sexual behavior at this time but by gender nonconformity in a variety of nonsexual traits.

It is in this period of development that gender norms become much more strict not only in adult expectations but in

peer group pressures as well. Social disapproval is generally more severe for nonconforming boys than girls, perhaps because a degree of "masculine" aggressiveness might help a girl gain a leadership position in her peer group. The "feminine" boy, however, might find himself excluded not only from other boy groups but also from the girl groups and thrown into the group of other misfits that exist in childhood. Studies of male adult transvestites, however, find that they conformed outwardly to their male peers but then retreated in secret to don clothes associated with girls or play as if they were girls. It is also in this period that children begin to experiment sexually. Alfred Kinsey found that a large number of preadolescents (between ages eight and thirteen) engage in what he called homosexual sex play. Nearly half (48 percent) of the older males who contributed their histories reported having engaged in homosexual sex play in their preadolescence. In his study of females, Kinsey found 33 percent of the preadolescent females engaged in some sort of homosexual sex play and many reported that such experiences had taught them how to masturbate.

ADOLESCENCE, between ages thirteen and eighteen, roughly corresponds with biological events associated with puberty, including the onset of menses in girls and first ejaculation in boys. At this age in earlier periods in history, a person would be classified as an adult. Adolescence in our society can best be understood as a social construction, designed to describe the ever-widening gap between reproductive maturity and the age at which society is willing to grant men and women full adult rights and responsibilities. It also is a period in which homosexual identity is most clearly formed. Girls in particular form strong emotional FRIENDSHIPS in adolescence; interestingly, however, there is generally much less social concern about homosexuality in such relationships than there is about boys' friendships. Such relationships among girls are widespread and are an almost normative part of many girls' psychosexual development. It has been suggested that girls need the support, LOVE, and affection of intense friendships to help them survive in a male-dominated world. Many of these friendships have strong homoerotic overtones.

Since both sexes in preadolescence play almost exclusively with members of their own gender, homosexual behavior is far more common among younger children than it is later in adolescence. In a 1973 study by Robert Sorensen, of those reporting homosexual experiences, 16 percent of the boys and 57 percent of the girls had their first homosexual experience between six and ten years of age. By the time they had reached their thirteenth birthday, 78 percent reported having at least one such experience. The number of boys exceeded the number of girls as they went into their teens. This difference in the teens was also found by Edward Laumann and his colleagues in the 1990s. Kinsey described homosexual play in females as mutual insertion of objects (including fingers) into the vagina, mouth–genital contact, rubbing, and close examination. In the male he defined it as exhibition of genitalia, manual manipulation of genitalia in groups or between two individuals, anal or oral contacts with genitalia, and urethral insertions.

In the 1980s and 1990s there was growing public acceptance for homosexuality as well as increasing peer acceptance of varying gender identities among adolescents. Many high schools, particularly in urban areas, have clubs for gays and lesbians, and the stigma of being different has lessened. Critics are concerned that such open toleration will encourage more individuals to become gay or lesbian. Studies show, however, that many preadolescents and adolescents who express nonconformity in gender identity do not continue to do so as adults. Others who conformed to traditional views in childhood broke away to identify themselves as homosexual or lesbian adults. There are still many unknowns in the complex study of the formation of gender identity.

See also: **Gendering; Same-Sex Parenting; Sexuality.**

BIBLIOGRAPHY

Bullough, Vern L. 1976. *Sexual Variance in Society and History.* Chicago: University of Chicago Press.

Kinsey, Alfred, Wardell Pomeroy, and Clyde Martin. 1948. *Sexual Behavior in the Human Male.* Philadelphia: W. B. Saunders.

Kinsey, Alfred, Wardell Pomeroy, Clyde Martin, and Paul Gebhard. 1953. *Sexual Behavior in the Human Female.* Philadelphia: W. B. Saunders.

Laumann, Edward O., John H. Gagnon, Robert T. Michael, and Stuart Michaels. 1994. *The Social Organizations of Sexuality: Sexual Practices in the United States.* Chicago: University of Chicago Press.

Percy, William Armstrong. 1996. *Pederasty and Pedagogy in Archaic Greece.* Urbana: University of Illinois Press.

Smith-Rosenberg, Carol. 1987. "The Female World of Love and Ritual: Relations Between Women in Nineteenth-Century America." In *Growing Up in America: Historical Experiences,* ed. Harvey J. Graff. Detroit: Wayne State University Press.

Sorensen, Robert C. 1973. *Adolescent Sexuality in Contemporary America.* New York: World Publishing.

Tanner, James M. 1955. *Growth at Adolescence.* Oxford, UK: Blackwell Scientific.

Westermarck, Edward. 1922. *The History of Human Marriage,* 3 vols., 5th ed. New York: Allerton.

VERN L. BULLOUGH

Hull-House. *See* Addams, Jane.

Hygiene

By the close of the twentieth century, good hygiene had come to signify adherence to high standards of grooming, particularly personal cleanliness. This conception is a rela-

John Everett Millais's *Bubbles* (1886) was the basis of a popular Pears' Soap ad for many years. Children were often the focus of various crusades for cleanliness throughout the nineteenth and twentieth centuries. The Advertising Archive Ltd.

tively recent historical phenomenon, although hygiene as a health practice has its roots in antiquity. In classical Greece Hygeia was worshiped as the giver of health to all who followed a balanced physical regimen and lived in accord with her precepts. In this conception health came from maintaining both the internal harmony of the body and the equilibrium between the body and the environment in which it lived. One's well-being came from a holistic understanding of person and place. Through the European Renaissance the classical idea of hygiene as a set of routines aimed at keeping the individual in balance with the internal and external environment persisted. Prior to the modern period, however, almost all hygienic advice assumed that only the wealthiest members of society had either the leisure or the economic resources to follow hygienic rules. Nor was there much notion that children required any special hygienic attention. In the late classical period, the Greek physician Galen had given distinct advice about the hygiene of infants; otherwise most writing on hygiene and disease prevention remained primarily concerned with adults.

Evolving Ideas of Hygiene

Though many classical civilizations created strict regulations concerning domestic and personal cleanliness, the disposal of the dead, the elimination of human and animal waste, and other forms of public sanitation, these were not distinctly health routines. They were frequently rituals with deep religious meaning, like the Hebrew traditions of ritual baths, meant to purify the soul and not the body. Arabic writing incorporated the pursuit of health with religious purity. In his eleventh century *Almanac of Health*, Ibn Butlan, an Arab Christian, urged his audience to maintain good health through a personal regimen that included adherence to a diet that was determined by the individual's work and climate, regular exercise, sufficient sleep, daily washing, daily bowel evacuation, and weekly bathing. Central to his writing was the idea that balance in diet, exercise, and cleanliness was pleasing to God.

Christianity added an ascetic note to the hygienic. Medieval Christian writers introduced the persistent idea that good health required strict regulation of the appetites and disciplining of the body by diet and exercise. Hygiene routines became means of self-denial, aimed at living a temperate life. This conception paralleled the European medieval prejudice against public baths, which associated both classical and Muslim bathing practices with licentious sexuality and enfeebling luxury. Self-denial through strict hygiene (though not necessarily cleanliness) persisted as a theme in European and American writing well into the modern period. In early modern Europe this embedded Christian notion encouraged a cold bathing regimen for adults and children. JOHN LOCKE in *Some Thoughts Concerning Education* (1693) proposed a hardening hygiene for children of cold water, cold air, and light clothing to toughen the body and spirit. The promotion of cold water as healthful was central to the nineteenth-century hydropathic movement.

Beginning in the eighteenth century Western European society saw a transformation in manners that increasingly emphasized physical appearance, restraint, and personal delicacy related to bodily functions. French aristocrats developed rules of etiquette that required restriction of public spitting, use of handkerchiefs, and strict toilet practices. By the end of the eighteenth century, the middle classes were imitating elite standards of cleanliness because such standards were thought "mannerly" and their use distinguished one from the common and vulgar. Such manners were a social obligation and were not necessarily associated with health. In this era Enlightenment Christians attempted to uproot the medieval Christian sense that frequent bathing was self-indulgent by asserting that cleanliness followed the laws of nature and nature's god. The most often quoted assertion of this thinking was in John Wesley's December 1786 *Sermon 88 On Dress* in which he resurrected the ancient Hebrew doctrine of carefulness to support improved attention to appearance. He asserted, "Let it be observed, that

slovenliness is no part of religion; that neither this nor any text of Scripture, condemns neatness of apparel. Certainly, this is a duty not a sin. 'Cleanliness is, indeed, next to godliness.'"

Theories of Contagion

Even before any notion of germs became commonplace medical innovation created significant change in the understanding of hygiene. In the late eighteenth century theories of contagion began to emphasize the role of dirt in the spread of disease. These filth theories of contagion contributed significantly to linking visible dirt to infection. The development of the germ theory by Louis Pasteur, Joseph Lister, Robert Koch and others moved attention from visible to invisible dirt. Nonetheless, as Nancy Tomes in *The Gospel of Germs* has noted, general understanding of germs was often a superstitious caricature of the scientific theories concerning microorganisms and disease. People continued to associate visible filth with contagion well into the twentieth century, though they increasingly became concerned with eliminating unseen contamination as well.

One thing contagion and germ theory did was emphasize the degree to which individual health was dependent on the healthfulness of a person's surroundings. The health of individuals in society seemed to depend on a public commitment to cleaning, and middle-class people began by rigorously cleaning themselves and their homes. Acceptance of the germ theory, however, meant that cleaning oneself wasn't enough; fully preventing disease transmission required clean water, careful waste disposal, and improving the health of the poor. Public health measures related to improved hygiene became common in Western Europe and North America. These reforms included improvements in sanitation, provision of clean water, and the creation of a public bath movement that provided the poor with facilities for cleaning and attempted to convince them of the necessity of being clean. Such reforms often carried with them negative judgments and stereotyping of the working classes, the people Henry Peter, Lord Brougham, is reported to have first called "The Great Unwashed."

In the early to mid-twentieth century the general public seemed to become obsessed with hygiene. Hygiene continued to include a wide variety of practices such as diet, exercise, sexual abstention, and regular evacuation of the bowels (known as internal hygiene). The concept of hygiene was extended to even more aspects of personal and public life. This included the creation of new types of hygiene, such as mental hygiene, sexual hygiene, and the racial hygiene of the international EUGENICS movement. In an era of imperialism other nations came to be judged as civilized on the basis of their adherence to European and American standards of cleanliness. The irony of this is that Europeans and their American cousins, who were often filthy prior to the modern era, judged unworthy those Africans and Asians who had long practiced frequent bathing.

Public Hygiene

A number of factors contributed to the zealous adherence to hygiene practice in Western European and American society in the late nineteenth and early twentieth centuries. In public hygiene movements throughout Western Europe and North America the power of the state was used to enforce adherence to hygienic behavior, including rules prohibiting public spitting as well as building extensive sanitation and water infrastructures. One primary impetus in this process was the effort to educate the public through clinics, medical publications, and social-work associations, including settlement houses. New organizations of the industrial bureaucracy contributed as well. Insurance companies in the United States contracted with public-health nurses at the Henry Street Settlement in New York to oversee and reform the hygienic habits of their subscribers. Manufacturers of soap and other hygiene supplies used the modern media to sell products first by enlisting medical claims about the need to eliminate germs, and then by creating new disease concepts (such as the Listerine company's "halitosis"). Hygiene advertisers goaded people to bathe for health and to avoid the judgments of others about cleanliness and odor. In one example, a 1928 advertisement from the Cleanliness Institute, the educational branch of the Association of Soap and Glycerin Producers, asked, "What do the neighbors think of *her* children?"

Nurses played an important role in the spread and enforcement of hygiene rules in late-nineteenth- and early-twentieth-century Europe and the United States. Florence Nightingale supported theories of contagion, but not germ theory. Still, she and later nursing advocates made it clear that nurses, because of their medical expertise and womanly nature, were central to spreading proper methods of personal and domestic hygiene. Other British medical reformers Charles West and Ellen and Mary Phillips saw the establishment of hospitals for poor children, in which nurses provided most of the care, as an important means of improving environmental conditions for children.

A Focus on Children

Children were at the heart of a growing public obsession with hygiene. Major health and hygiene campaigns in the United Kingdom in the late nineteenth and early twentieth centuries had as their central focus the reductibn of INFANT MORTALITY, first through the Poor Laws and then through the National Health Insurance Act of 1911. Children also increasingly became the focus of much of the hygiene literature. Hygiene proponents used schools to spread the word about regulation of the body. The 1882 French primary school curriculum included instruction on proper toilet routine and washing. In the United States the Cleanliness Institute published and distributed materials for schoolteachers and schoolchildren on maintaining health through personal cleanliness. Instruction for teachers and mothers focused on the necessity of getting children to adhere to strict disciplin-

ing of the body so they might live healthy lives and fulfill their obligation to avoid offending others. This instruction was couched in medical, social, and political terms: children were taught to exercise, bathe, and eat in particular ways because it was good for their bodies, created social order, and because medical, educational, and social authority said so. This association between schooling and cleaning was so well established that the Kohler Corporation, one of the largest manufacturers of plumbing equipment in the United States, declared in a 1927 advertisement that the bathroom itself was the schoolroom of health.

Hygiene education carried with it the moralistic tone of the public health movement as a whole. In France children were taught that moral character was inextricably linked to hygiene habits. In the United States the Americanization Movement supported hygiene instruction as a means of converting European working-class immigrants into good Americans. Maintenance of social order seemed dependent on maintenance of high standards of hygiene, based on the manners of the white middle class. The hygiene lobby proposed a single standard of cleanliness that often failed to take into account individual differences in skin type or living conditions. In the United States this was particularly problematic for African Americans, both because of their physiological differences and because they often lacked the means for following the prescriptions of the hygienists. African-American leaders were well aware of this problem and offered instructions specifically geared toward the African-American community. The most famous of these was Booker T. Washington's "gospel of the toothbrush." Unfortunately, in the racial climate of the United States, even strict adherence to the rules of hygiene did not free African Americans from the stigma of being by nature dirty, because of the cultural association between whiteness and purity.

The Social Hygiene Movement

The association of cleanliness and hygiene with children and social fitness was certainly central to the international social (racial) hygiene movement. In her 1910 *Hygiene and Morality*, American nursing reformer and suffragist Lavinia Dock drew a connection between venereal disease incidence and the mistreatment and corruption of women and children. Not only did corrupted men infect their wives, but they also polluted what Dock called the germs of reproduction (that is, their sperm), thus creating deformed children. Finally, syphilis carriers created unhygienic conditions within the family that harmed their innocent offspring both physically and morally. Such attitudes encouraged increased intervention by the state into the personal practices of the populace.

The most radical of these efforts was the international social hygiene movement, arising from the pseudoscience of eugenics. Forced sterilization of the unfit was couched in hygienic terms that focused on preventing unclean and corrupt persons from continuing to pollute the species through reproduction. The concept of racial hygiene saw its greatest expression in Nazi Germany, but it did not originate there. It was in the United States that laws related to reproductive hygiene were first initiated. By the 1930s two to three thousand forced sterilizations of the mentally ill, retarded people, criminals, and racial minorities were performed in the United States each year. During the HOLOCAUST the Nazis used hygiene language as a code for what would later come to be called *ethnic cleansing* of the Jewish, Gypsy, homosexual, and other "undesirable" populations. Nazi propaganda was particularly focused on the control of women and childbearing as the means of eliminating racial corruption and creating the master race. The link between this and notions of hygiene are best seen in the euphemism of the shower/gas chambers and the experimentation with turning human fat into soap.

Commercialized Cleanliness

After 1945 the social hygiene movement was largely discredited, but the impulse toward greater and greater levels of cleanliness, particularly cleanliness in children, persisted. Schools remained the focus of much childhood education, but hygiene came to be narrowly defined as proper grooming to maintain personal cleanliness. Here, standards continued to escalate. In the United States, hygiene films for grade school and high school students became a staple of 1950s classrooms. These continued to promote cleanliness by combining scientific arguments about germs and skin and hair care with an emphasis on maintaining proper social standards. They also incorporated negative judgments about those who failed to adhere. Adolescents were particularly singled out for attention. High school students were warned that failure to follow strict grooming codes would lead to their becoming dateless social outcasts.

In the late twentieth century these messages increasingly came to be seen as ridiculous and outdated. In 1956 Horace Miner, distinguished professor of social anthropology at the University of Michigan, published an article called "Body Ritual among the *Nacirema*" in the *American Anthropologist*. In this he lampooned both jargon-ladened anthropological research and the American (Nacirema was "American" spelled backward) hygiene obsession. In this satire Miner targeted both the medical establishment for creating neuroses about health and cleanliness and parents for inculcating these neurosis in their children. In the radical sixties youthful rejection of these hygiene practices was a common feature of rebellion against parents and social authority. Around the same time purveyors of soap and children's books shifted tactics. They began emphasizing bathing as a means of relieving social tensions (a minor theme in the early-twentieth-century literature) and promoted bathing as a sensual and self-indulgent activity. Advice to parents proposed tricking reluctant tots into good habits by adding bubbles and toys. Children's literature depicted bath time as playtime.

Though hygiene came to be equated with good grooming in the late twentieth century, aspects of the health regimen of the ancients are reappearing in new forms. Proponents of aromatherapy and other New Age remedies are reemphasizing a holistic approach to hygiene. Still, this holistic attitude strikes a minor chord in the overall tone of preventive health care in Western society. Most of the activities associated with hygiene until the recent past are now specialized, distinct commodities. Postmodern society has divided care of the human body into separate components served by particular industries: the diet, exercise, soap, and cosmetic industries, as well as modern specialized medicine. Some critics call this process the commodification of the body. Yet, despite the intense selling of high levels of cleanliness and bodily discipline, public adherence to the standards authorities set shows marked unevenness. Even in the United States, where grooming practices encourage daily changing of clothes and bathing twice or more each day, hygiene routines that are less visible are often neglected. For example, studies in the 1990s indicated that cleanliness-obsessed Americans frequently failed to wash their hands after using public rest rooms.

Hygiene and Health

The impact of improved hygiene on health and comfort is difficult to deny. Several epidemiological studies have suggested that the decreased incidence of infectious disease and the dramatic decline in infant and child mortality that began in Western society in the late nineteenth century can largely be attributed to improvements in sanitation, water supply, and domestic and personal cleanliness. In the late twentieth century those nations that enjoyed the lowest levels of infectious disease were those that used the highest amounts of soap. This improvement has not been without cost, however. Increased attention to hygiene has also meant increased pressure on the natural environment. Even the most vocal proponents of maintaining high levels of cleanliness acknowledge that the degree of cleanliness in Western European and American society far exceeds what is necessary for health. This overcleaning has resulted in undue pressure on water supplies, chemical pollution of water and soil due to the use of soaps and other cleaning agents, and increased energy demands to heat water and wash clothing. Paradoxically, one cost of the advent of antibacterial soap and other products, such as Hygeia underwear, which manufacturers claim prevents the growth of bacteria, fungi, and yeast, may be the increased appearance of antibiotic resistant microorganisms.

Another possible irony in the success of hygiene campaigns is that improved domestic and personal cleanliness may also be associated with increased incidence of the so-called diseases of industrial society, particularly POLIO, allergies, and asthma. Under the regimen of the hygiene proponents, the best method for protecting children's health is to provide them with a clean, virtually germ-free environment.

The standard care for allergy-triggered asthma, for example, is removal of asthma triggers from the sufferer's environment. In the last decades of the twentieth century researchers in Italy, the United Kingdom, Switzerland, and the United States began to suggest that lack of exposure to microorganisms and dirt at an early age may result in the body's failing to produce natural resistance to foreign substances. This failure may be associated with the mid-twentieth-century polio epidemics and with the increased incidence of asthma. Epidemiologists meeting in 2001 at the Pasteur Institute cited these studies and those related to environmental pressures as signals that we need not reject hygiene altogether, but instead should seek more carefully targeted cleanliness standards. They proposed homing in on key behaviors such as frequent hand washing and strict cleanliness of food preparation areas. The presenters noted that we need germ-free environments only in hospitals and the residences of the seriously ill. Soap manufacturers and the general public do not seem as ready to make such a nuanced distinction, however, if the promotion and sale of antibacterial items is any indicator.

See also: **Children's Hospitals; Contagious Diseases; Epidemics; Mental Hygiene; Pediatrics; Vaccination.**

BIBLIOGRAPHY

Hoy, Suellen. 1995. *Chasing Dirt: The American Pursuit of Cleanliness.* New York: Oxford University Press.

Kühl, Stefan. 1994. *The Nazi Connection: Eugenics, American Racism, and German National Socialism.* New York: Oxford University Press.

Rosen, George. 1993. *A History of Public Health: Expanded Edition.* Baltimore, MD: Johns Hopkins University Press.

Tomes, Nancy. 1998. *The Gospel of Germs: Men, Women, and the Microbe in American Life.* Cambridge, MA: Harvard University Press.

Vigarello, Georges. 1988. *Concepts of Cleanliness: Changing Attitudes in France since the Middle Ages.* Trans. Jean Birrell. Cambridge, UK: Cambridge University Press.

Vinikas, Vincent. 1992. *Soft Soap, Hard Sell: American Hygiene in an Age of Advertisement.* Ames: Iowa State University Press.

Whorton, James C. 2000. *Inner Hygiene: Constipation and the Pursuit of Health in Modern Society.* New York: Oxford University Press.

JACQUELINE S. WILKIE

Hyperactivity

The pinpointing and treatment of hyperactivity in children forms a fascinating link between medical research and popular attitudes about and settings for the child. Scattered indications of new concern about hyperactive behavior began to accumulate in the second half of the nineteenth century. Hyperactivity formed part of a new interest in identifying and segregating "backward" children in the early twentieth century, particularly in western Europe. Medical research on brain dysfunctions accelerated in the 1920s and 1930s, but there was continued dispute about whether some special condition of hyperactivity existed. Drug treatment, first introduced in 1937, became more common after 1957. But it was only after 1970 that identification of hyperactive children, under the designation attention deficit disorder (ADD), became widely accepted. Amid controversy, treatment programs gained ground steadily through the 1990s.

Historical Background

Children's hyperactivity, to the extent it existed, was simply a question of DISCIPLINE until modern times and received no specific attention. Protestant clergymen and parents in the eighteenth and nineteenth centuries often resorted to physical discipline against children who could not sit still in long church services, but since this was seen as an expression of children's original sin and natural unruliness it did not come in for specific comment. We have no systematic indications of how what we would now call hyperactivity affected children's work performance.

A German children's book in the 1850s offered a character, "Fidgety Phil," who was the characteristic hyperactive child, unable to sit still. By this point stricter MANNERS for children included explicit injunctions about body control, which would implicitly single out children who had difficulties in this area. More regular schooling also created problems for hyperactive children. Still, a truly troubled child could still be pulled out of school and either sent directly to work or (in wealthy families) given private tutoring.

More extensive school requirements plus new medical research capabilities opened a new chapter in the identification of hyperactive children around 1900, particularly in England and Germany. Generally such children fell into a larger category of backward or mentally deficient children who could not perform well on standardized tests and/or who caused persistent behavior problems in school. Some of these children were placed in special schools or classes, where different kinds of instruction, focusing on specific tasks, could lead to improvements in learning capacity. By the 1920s experts began to realize that hyperactive children were often quite intelligent, and inclusion into a generic backward category began to diminish.

Research continued on brain dysfunction of children with hyperactive behavior problems, with increasing interest in the United States. A study by Charles Bradley in 1937 introduced the first possibility of medication, using Benzedrine. Widespread identification of a hyperactivity problem was still limited by a belief that a certain amount of unruliness in children was natural, that schools themselves were part of the problem, and that it was up to parents to figure out how to keep their children in hand.

Research, Diagnosis, and Treatment since 1957

Several developments, including the introduction of new psychostimulant medication, particularly the drug Ritalin in

1957, began to accelerate attention to and concern about hyperactivity. Fewer children were now encouraged to drop out before completing secondary school. With more mothers working, parental availability to help with hyperactive children declined; indeed parental interest in finding assistance intensified. With more children in day care facilities by the 1960s, opportunities to identify problems of hyperactivity at a younger age expanded. Increasing school integration in the United States exposed teachers to categories of children they might more readily define as behavior problems. Finally, teachers themselves faced new constraints in physically disciplining children, which put aggressive restlessness in a new light.

These various developments, along with effective medication, prompted a steady growth in the numbers of behaviors that were regarded as symptoms of attention deficit disorder—behaviors that in earlier decades might often have been regarded as normal. There were cautions: some observers worried about unduly frequent use of medicines that could have adverse side effects or induce dependency; some studies suggested that minority children were particularly likely to be cited as needing medication, with teachers using this option as a means of facilitating classroom control.

But acceptance of hyperactivity as a disease category gained ground steadily, and some schools required drug treatments for certain children as a condition of entry. Estimates in 1980 that 3 percent of all children suffered from ADD grew to 5 percent a decade later. Production of Ritalin soared 500 percent between 1990 and 1996. Popularizations of the ADD concept bolstered many parents, who could now point to a problem of brain function for behaviors that used to be blamed on poor home discipline. Supplementary measures, including therapy, special diets, and adult support groups, were deployed against hyperactivity, but medication continued to command the greatest attention.

BIBLIOGRAPHY

Armstrong, Thomas. 1996. "ADD: Does it Really Exist?" *Phi Delta Kappan* (February): 424–428.

Charles, Alan F. 1971. "The Case of Ritalin." *New Republic* (October): 17–19.

Fowler, Mary. 1994. *NICHCY Briefing Paper: Attention Deficit/ Hyperactivity Disorder*. Washington, DC: Government Printing Office, 1-S.

Smelter, Richard W., et al. 1996. "Is Attention Deficit Disorder Becoming a Desired Diagnosis?" *Phi Delta Kappan* (February): 29–32.

Swanson, James. 1995. "More Frequent Diagnosis of Attention Deficit-Hyperactivity Disorder." *New England Journal of Medicine* 33: 944.

PETER N. STEARNS

I

Illegitimacy. *See* Bastardy.

Images of Childhood

Reproductions of most of the images discussed in this entry can be found elsewhere in the encyclopedia. Please see the list of selected illustrations at the beginning of Volume 1 for specific page numbers.

Not all historians have agreed with PHILIPPE ARIÈS that childhood as we understand it did not exist before the Middle Ages. Yet his research opened up the possibility of examining childhood, including the modern Romantic idea of childhood innocence, as a social construction that changes along with the ongoing process of history. This can be applied to the history of art and visual culture. Visual representations of children can be interpreted as being not simply natural or transparently verifiable against some stable external reality, but rather as socially and discursively constituted out of shifting cultural and psychosexual paradigms. Since images of childhood are produced within particular cultural contexts and in response to specific historical moments, examining the changes in them over time does not mean abandoning the embodied historical child.

From the point of view of art history, visual images of children have often been marginalized or dismissed as a trivial, sentimental, or (given the sexual construction of femininity as infantile) feminized subgenre; frequently they have been interpreted as timeless or universal. According to Marcia Pointon, such pictures have frequently been seen as having simple and readily accessible topics, with the result that empathetic notions of shared human experience replace analysis. For this reason, depictions of children can say as much about their reception by adult spectators as they do about the childhood of their subjects. This is especially true for the early twenty-first century, when, as Anne Higonnet

has convincingly argued, the image of the child has become one of the most emotionally powerful and contradictory images in Western CONSUMER CULTURE. Intimations of innocence have been retained even as new meanings have been acquired having to do with political, sexual, and commercial forms of public and private power. With the recent development of children's studies, the category of age has been added to those of race, class, gender, and sexual orientation as a focus of critical inquiry. Providing a conduit for cultural anxieties and conflicting social values, visual images of childhood are seen as multivalent expressions of a Western, adult, middle-class search for identity. Interpreting them presents a challenge to map the social and psychological history of their production and reception.

Fifteenth and Sixteenth Centuries

The history of images of childhood in modern times begins with the revolution in pictures of the innocent child in the eighteenth century, yet children were certainly depicted before that time. They show up, for example, throwing snowballs in the margins of an early Northern Renaissance manuscript, "The Hours of Adelaide of Savoy," in *December: A Snowy Street*. Miniature images of children could similarly be found as marginalia in other fifteenth-century Flemish books of hours as well as in devotional images of the ages of man. Here, however, the image of children does not so much signify "childhood" in its own right as it refers symbolically to a specific time of year or season of human life.

Children retained a marginal social status even as the iconography of childhood was given a more central symbolic or allegorical emphasis in Renaissance images of the infant Christ, of cherubs, and of cupids. Leo Steinberg has discussed how the Christ child, and, in particular, his fleshly genitals, are made the compositional and iconographic focus of numerous Renaissance paintings of the Madonna and Child so as to signify tangibly the incarnation of God as man. Julia Kristeva has given a more psychoanalytic reading to what Steinberg interpreted doctrinally. Discussing Giovanni

Madonna and Child with Pear (c. 1500), Giovanni Bellini. In Bellini's painting, the Christ Child's sturdy body is a visual representation of Christ as "the Word made flesh." The Art Archive/Carrara Academy Bergamo/Dagli Orti (A).

eighteenth century. One can envision, in looking at the uninhibited variety of bodily positions, the "polymorphous perversity" that SIGMUND FREUD would later ascribe to INFANT SEXUALITY.

In sixteenth-century portraiture, children (who did not commission portraits) were more usually depicted with their parents than as separate individuals. Hans Holbein the Younger's *Edward VI as a Child* (1538) depicts its sitter as a tiny adult in the formal regalia and stiff pose of rule; it includes an elaborate inscription certifying his hereditary duties as heir to the throne. Rather than commemorating an individual child, the painting serves a social function that is more abstract, hieratic, and dynastic. Less formal portraits of children involved in everyday activities can be found in the work of Sofonisba Anguissola, who once painted her own self-portrait in the act of painting a tender kiss between the Madonna and Christ child (*Self-Portrait at the Easel, Painting a Devotional Panel*, late 1550s). Born into a provincial noble family that gave her a humanistic education, Anguissola painted her young sisters laughingly playing chess with their governess, whose presence attests to the artist's own higher social class, in *The Sisters of the Artist and Their Governess* (1555). According to Vasari, Anguissola's expressive and naturalistic black chalk drawing *Child Bitten by a Crayfish* (c. 1558) evidently impressed Michelangelo so much that he presented it as a gift to a friend, who later gave it, along with a drawing by the more famous Michelangelo himself, to the wealthy Florentine patron Cosimo I de' Medici. Anguissola thus achieved artistic recognition in giving a central focus in her work to children depicted in their own right. But she did so as a function of her marginal cultural position (despite her elevated social background and subsequent patronage by the Spanish court of Philip II) as a woman artist who did not produce the large-scale historical and religious works expected of male artists. As in the case of later artists like Berthe Morisot and MARY CASSATT, children could be seen as an appropriately feminized, domestic genre for a woman artist to portray.

The most elaborate sixteenth-century visual compendium of children, Pieter Brueghel the Elder's *Children's Games* (1560), exhaustively depicts over ninety different games, including blindman's buff, knucklebones, mumblety-peg, leapfrog, tug-of-war, piggyback, hide-and-seek, and mock marriage and baptismal processions. Despite the large size of the picture, the frenetic figures are so numerous as to become rather miniaturized in scale and detail. Some interpretations have linked the iconography of the scene allegorically to the seasonal or calendrical marginalia of illuminated manuscripts. Recent art historical accounts have debated playful and more moralizing meanings. On the one hand, realistic sixteenth-century details are depicted, including the caterwauling games, as well as the feminine costume worn by preadolescent boys, an allusion to early childhood's domestic construction. (Before the age of four boys wore dress-

Bellini's Madonnas as a visual (and tactile) recuperation of a preoedipal, prelinguistic maternal space, she emphasized the psychological passion, bodily (even erotic) connection, and emotional splitting between mother and child in his *Madonna and Child* (c. 1470).

Cherubs, that is, infant angels in the Christian iconography, often accompany the Christ child in Renaissance imagery, attesting to his innocent yet fleshly divinity. In Raphael's famous *Sistine Madonna* (1513), the cute pair of cherubs at the bottom (whose image would be extracted for a U.S. postage stamp in 1995) are multiplied into infinity in the heavenly clouds composed of cherub heads floating behind and above the levitating Madonna, Child, and saints. Less theological and more sensual, but equally winged and symbolic, are the omnipresent cupids who seem to overflow the frame of Titian's *Worship of Venus* (c. 1560). This fertile crop of cuddly baby flesh becomes a tangible index of the cupids' symbolic function as collective emanations of Eros. As they gather emblematic fruit, the *amorini* embody pagan desire, engaging in playful physical activities that are hard to see as entirely innocent, at least in comparison with the kind of childhood innocence that would be invented in the mides with aprons and bibs, as does, for example the boy with the hobbyhorse in the left central foreground of the picture; between the ages of five and eleven, they wore open frocks, as does the urchin on the barrel on the right; after that they adopted adult costume, like the short jacket with trousers worn by the boy with the hoop in the center). On the other hand, many interpreters, including Sandra Hindman, have read the picture as emblematic of folly, especially since various medieval and Renaissance humanist texts presented children as lacking in rational judgment. The topographical positioning of the uninhibited games, which are viewed from an omniscient perspective in proximity to civic architecture, may allude to the public virtues which correctly reared children should eventually be taught.

Seventeenth Century

Acknowledging the elusive and ambiguous meanings of Brueghel's games, as well as of related iconographies of children in seventeenth-century Dutch art, Edward Snow and Simon Schama have suggested that moralizing and more naturalistic interpretations need not be definitive or mutually exclusive. According to Schama, children were no longer necessarily regarded either as miniature adults or as vessels brimming with sin. As Mary Frances Durantini has shown, representations of children in seventeenth-century Dutch art were richly diverse, ranging from domestic genre scenes and family portraits to images of a more didactic nature. The growth of such pictures was facilitated by the early development in Holland of mercantile middle classes who favored art intended for their homes. From today's perspective, these images of children, produced in a democratic, largely Protestant, and capitalist republic, begin to look familiar. In seventeenth-century France and Spain, the lower-class beggar children found in the work of the brothers Le Nain, Bartolomé Esteban Murillo, and Jusepe de Ribera were conceptualized from the point of view of elevated social positions espousing virtuous poverty and picturesque sentiment. Ribera's plucky *Boy with a Clubfoot* (c. 1642–1652), who jauntily slings a crutch over his shoulder, is monumentalized in scale despite his physical disability. The paper he holds suggests the moralizing theme of charity as it asks the viewer for alms. In Holland, Jan Steen's pictures of spoiled or misbehaving middle-class children, such as *The Feast of Saint Nicholas* (c. 1665–1668) or the *Unruly School* (c. 1670) employ mischief and mirth to evoke a humanist and Calvinist lesson that childhood levity and free will are meant to lead to adult gravity and obedience.

Even in their most earthy and scatological manifestations, when they seem explicitly to break previous iconographic molds, Dutch images of children can retain potentially symbolic frames of reference. Card-playing and bubble-blowing children can be naturalistically playful at the same time that they function as iconographic reminders of vice or of the transience of life. Children with PETS, a topic that would multiply in the visual culture of later centuries, connected

Hans Holbein the Younger's 1538 portrait of Edward VI of England—dressed in the trappings of royalty—is less an image of an individual child than of a position in society, that of heir to the throne. Archive Photos, Inc.

children and animals with the natural realm. Judith Leyster's *Two Children with a Kitten and an Eel* (c. 1630s) combines teasing playfulness with potential symbolism, the kitten itself being an emblem of PLAY and the eel alluding to the proverbial slipperiness of life. That life's transience could be an especially sensitive issue in the case of mortal children and could often serve as a catalyst for their representation is evident in Gabriel Metsu's poignant painting *The Sick Child* (c. 1660).

Eighteenth Century

Pointon has charted further connections between CHILD MORTALITY and image-making in eighteenth-century England. As with later photographs of children, the captured image of the ephemeral child could serve on a psychic level as a visual fetish to acknowledge loss and to protect against it. It was during the eighteenth century that the idea of childhood innocence as a sheltered realm, fragile and susceptible to corruption, was elaborately invented and largely began to replace the notion of children as naturally immodest and uninhibited. Edward Snow, drawing upon Ariès, points out that even earlier, the idea of "weak" childhood innocence was not merely progressive or altruistic; it also had authoritarian implications about the strict supervision of the children it idealized. JEAN-JACQUES ROUSSEAU's enormously influential

In Gustave Courbet's *Studio,* subtitled *A Real Allegory,* (1855) the fact that the artist has managed to capture the attention and admiration of the child in the center of the painting is meant to signify the natural honesty of the realist painter and his art. Musée d'Orsay, Paris. The Art Archive/Dagli Orti.

book *Émile* (1762) presented the (male) child as free to express his "natural" inclinations, yet placed him under the controlling hand of a tutor. Without the guidance of education, a child's "natural" goodness could be corrupted by society. During the latter part of the eighteenth century, in the context of political revolution in France and Industrial Revolution in Britain, the idealized innocence of children was visually constructed by artists whose clients were aristocrats discovering Rousseauian sentiment and, increasingly, members of the industrial bourgeoisie pursuing a nostalgic withdrawal from industrial and political revolutions. A picture of presumed childhood innocence could, however, imply its unrepresented opposite, the power (physical, political, social, psychosexual) which threatens innocence.

In eighteenth-century Britain, which experienced the Industrial Revolution earlier than the rest of Europe, portraits of children could display them as luxury items, informally arranged as "dynastic" symbols of bourgeois parental (and particularly paternal) wealth. The elegantly dressed and remarkably clean children in William Hogarth's portrait *The Graham Children* (1742) probably served this purpose for their father Daniel, who commissioned the portrait not long after the king had given him a prestigious appointment as Apothecary of Chelsea Hospital. But the picture and its history are more complex than that. The smallest child on the extreme left (Thomas, an infant boy dressed in feminine attire) died between the time the picture was commissioned and completed. The innocent charm of the scene is tempered by the posthumous nature of the portrait: symbolic reminders of mortality are found in the clock directly above the baby, which features a cupid holding time's scythe, and by the cat avidly threatening the caged bird. (Even more menacing cats and a bird can be found somewhat later in the portrait of a more aristocratic child painted by Francisco Goya, a Spanish artist who had already seen five of his own children die young [*Manuel Osorio de Zuñiga*, c. 1788].)

In the case of Joshua Reynolds's portrait *Penelope Boothby* (1788), the pensive child sitter with oversized, frilly mobcap would be dead within three years, although her image would inspire later developments in the visual culture of childhood innocence. In portraits such as Thomas Gainsborough's *The Artist's Daughters Chasing a Butterfly* (c. 1756) and Joseph Wright of Derby's *The Wood Children* (1789), the elusive butterfly and the suspended cricket ball become signs of childhood's fleeting nature, even as the children are monumentalized in scale and set in idealized, Wordsworthian pastoral settings. Children could be further removed from present worries if they were dressed in antiquated costumes. Gainsborough dressed the preadolescent youth in his famous *Blue Boy* (c. 1770) in a seventeenth-century satin suit borrowed from a portrait by Anthony Van Dyck. By placing children in protected "natural" settings apparently removed from the menaces of death or industry, and in anachronistic, seemingly classless clothing, these eighteenth-century British artists effectively created what Higonnet has called the "modern Romantic child," a nostalgic sign of a past that for adults is always already lost.

For all the attempted "timelessness" of such images, several British portraits of "pure" childhood innocence harbor a colonial and racial ideology that reveals the Western nature and historical specificity of their construction. In an early example, Sir Peter Lely's *Lady Charlotte Fitzroy* (c. 1674), an Indian servant boy proffers a tray of fruit and kneels in homage to the young Charlotte. His dark skin is a foil to her fair whiteness, which is aligned with a classical relief in the background. According to James Steward, the presence of the Indian boy refers to the girl's higher-class position at a time when the place occupied by Indians in British society was comparable to that of African slaves. (For analogous images of affluent English girls with African child servants, see Bartholomew Dandridge, *Young Girl with Page* [c. 1720–1730], and Joseph Wright of Derby, *Two Girls and a Negro Servant* [1769–1770].) Steward suggests that in Reynolds's *The Children of Edward Holden Cruttenden with an Indian Ayah* (1759–1762), the ayah, who evidently saved the children's lives during an Indian uprising, serves the compositional purpose of pushing the lighter-skinned children forward, thus establishing her relationship of servitude to children who otherwise could be seen as lacking in power themselves.

In France, a less colonial but nonetheless political ideology could be present in pictures of happy or unhappy families which, as Carol Duncan and Lynn Hunt have argued, could mask or allude to oedipal conflicts surrounding the French Revolution's regicide. In the "family romance" of the Revolution, the recognition of the independent sphere of children was inspired not only by Rousseau, but also by the diminution of the father's traditional patriarchal role. In the most famous Revolutionary image of a child, Jacques-Louis David's painting *Death of Joseph Bara* (1794), an androgynous innocence is maintained even as the ephebic nude boy, whose genitals are conveniently hidden, is presented as a violated revolutionary martyr. *Bara* became a pubescent symbol of the state of childlike purity to which the Revolution aspired (but could not attain) during the Terror. In this invention of an unlikely Jacobin hero, David's modification of the adult Academic male body displaced child SEXUALITY to an implicit level of the political unconscious.

A more conspicuously depraved view of child sexuality and adult abuse of it was produced slightly later during the Revolutionary period in Spain by Goya in the etching "Blow" from the series *Los Caprichos* (1799). Here lecherous warlocks employ a child's buttocks as a pair of bellows to

Victorian imagery frequently subverted notions of children's innocence even while they claimed to celebrate it. Julia Margaret Cameron's photographs often mixed sensuality with a maternal affection toward her subjects, as in *The Double Star* (1864). (albumen; 11 x 95. Cm [4 3/8 x 3 3/4 in.]). Courtesy of the J. Paul Getty Museum, Los Angeles.

stoke the fire of carnality, even as fellatio is performed on another child. This purposefully irrational image of sadistic pedophilia exposed the dark underside of ENLIGHTENMENT ideals of innocence. In France, Jean-Baptiste Greuze had previously drawn less lurid symbolic connections between child innocence and its erotically charged Other. Unlike earlier, more uninhibitedly carnal rococo infants in the work of Boucher, Greuze's *Girl Mourning over Her Dead Bird* (1765) appealed to the philosophe Denis Diderot because of its moral didacticism. That sexual misconduct has taken place is symbolized by the open cage (lost virginity) and limp bird (spent passion). As Jennifer Milam has pointed out, the girl's evident remorse legitimized, but did not eliminate, the eroticism of the image. Childhood innocence, gendered as feminine, is here represented by its loss.

In Britain, innocence could likewise be gendered as feminine or could be more generic, even genderless. As Higonnet has argued, the pure white clothing of the girl in Reynolds's *The Age of Innocence* (c. 1788) is arranged so as to expose only those parts of the body least associated with adult sexuality. A sense of genderlessness was compounded by the feminine costume typically worn by young boys (compare Reynolds's girlish *Master Hare* of the same year, which displays more bare shoulder). The exception to protected yet vulnerable

Little Dancer Aged Fourteen (1878–1881), Edgar Degas. Degas' depiction of working-class child ballerinas was an exception to the Impressionists' primarily bourgeois representation of childhood. Degas drew attention to the dancers' hard physical training and their probable future in high-end prostitution. © Philadelphia Museum of Art/CORBIS.

cally criticize social injustice in the treatment of working-class children and thereby predict the reformist concerns of the nineteenth century. The image and accompanying text remove the blackened boy (a Rousseauian "noble savage") from idyllic nature and implicate parents, church, and king in the promotion and condoning of CHILD LABOR. Without specifically mentioning it, the image suggests in a picturesque way the ineffectiveness of reform legislation such as the Chimney Sweepers Act of 1788.

Nineteenth Century

Paradoxically, the codification, glorification, and diffusion of the Romantic cult of childhood innocence in the nineteenth century coincided exactly with an unprecedented industrial exploitation of children. A nostalgic regression of such mythic proportions can be interpreted as a social and cultural withdrawal from the urban-industrial as well as the political and scientific revolutions of the nineteenth century. Romanticism's exploration of the subjective self through the idealized state of the child sought a repository of sensitivities and sentiments thought to be lost or blunted in adulthood. While legal reforms (however ineffective they may have been initially) helped attract public opinion to the plight of factory children, capitalism discovered in middle-class children and their parents a ready-made consumer class. A burgeoning industry in children's TOYS, books, magazines, songs, clothes, and advice manuals for parents helped market the child as a symbol of progress and of the future. As state protection and the surveillance provided by its various institutions, including educational, medical, and legal, increasingly diminished the patriarchal power of fathers over their children, the bourgeois ideal of the family and of the protected place of the child within it was magnified. By the end of the century, primary school education was compulsory and free and child protection legislation was enacted. An ideal of sheltered childhood had become accepted by the middle classes and was finally extended, as a right, to poorer classes as well. Shifting attitudes towards working-class children could be seen in the writings of, among others, Charles Baudelaire, Victor Hugo, and Charles Dickens. PEDIATRICS was founded as a distinct field of medicine during the late nineteenth century, by which time there likewise had emerged in France a new so-called science of child rearing called *puériculture*. Nineteenth-century authors ranging from Jean-Marc-Gaspard Itard to Rodolphe Töpffer and Auguste Comte had meanwhile updated Rousseau's equation of childhood with cultural primitivism by comparing children to savages and by seeing them as representatives of the childhood of the human race as a whole, ideas that would later influence Freud. The constructed ideal of childhood innocence was, in many respects, a Victorian defense against advancing awareness of the sexual life of children and adolescents during the period when Freud himself was growing up.

innocence in Reynolds's numerous depictions of upper-class children was the working-class boy.

In *Mercury as a Cut Purse* (1771) and especially in *Cupid as a Link Boy* (1774), the fancy picture's trappings of classical myth allowed the artist to allude in a not so subtle way to adult vice. In London streets, link boys held torches that lit the route between front door and carriage; they were also exploited as aids to, and victims of, sexual liaisons. The erect, phallic shape of the boy's torch in Reynolds's painting, along with his lewd arm gesture and the mating dance of cats on a background roof, make him a less than innocent urban update of the mythological intermediary of love. (The boy's sexuality brings to mind Caravaggio's more titillating, if less victimized, *Cupid* of 1598–1599.) It was William Blake, in his etching and poem "The Chimney Sweeper" from his *Songs of Innocence and Experience* (1794), who would less unequivo-

The most famous Romantic portrait of childhood, *The Hülsenbeck Children*, by the German artist Philipp Otto

Children's Afternoon at Wargemont (1884), Pierre-Auguste Renoir. In this sunny domestic scene, Renoir depicts a feminized version of childhood. The girls are shown in a progression of feminine pursuits, from the doll play of the youngest child to her eldest sister's sewing. © Foto Marburg/Art Resource, NY. Nationalgalerie, Staatliche Museen, Berlin, Germany.

Runge (1805–1806), bursts with a tough, preternatural energy. The sheltered innocence of Reynolds's typical children gives way to an intense and looming monumentality that confers a new kind of mysterious, haptic power. As Robert Rosenblum has memorably described them, the Hülsenbeck children are given a primitive and plant-like vitalism. With a strong fist, the chubby-cheeked, barefooted baby boy in the wagon on the left grabs a sunflower stalk that seems to sprout with the same sap as he does; the stylized hair of his sister on the right resembles leaves; and the middle brother drives the others with a miniature horse whip. The three of them inhabit a utopian domain scaled to children, not to adults. Like growing Alices in Wonderland, they dwarf the picket fence that diminishes oddly into contracted space towards the seemingly miniature house on the right. The distant view of Hamburg on the left horizon includes the dye-works factory owned by their textile merchant father, reminding us that the growth of industry promoted the cult of the child by heightening a bourgeois desire to recuperate an imagined unity with nature. The Romantic artist seems to have envied

children's supposedly instinctual sensitivity to nature, imagined as unrepressed by civilization.

Although German Romanticism may have found an added impetus to depict children in a pietistic Christian revival, and specifically in Christ's injunction to become like a child to enter the kingdom of heaven, the French Romantic painter Théodore Géricault turned to something more sexually powerful and psychically uncanny (uncanny in the Freudian sense of the familiar becoming unfamiliar and disquieting). As Stefan Germer has pointed out, the spooky portrait *Alfred Dedreux as a Child* (c. 1814) makes its sitter tower over the horizon line, dominating the viewer with an alien gaze. Isolated within his surroundings and given oddly manneristic proportions, he no longer seems childish in the sheltered Reynolds sense, but more threatening, a potential wild child or savage trapped beneath his fancy suit. Just as strong but much less innocent than Runge's children is Géricault's *Louise Vernet* (c. before 1816), which is compositionally related to the *Alfred Dedreux* in terms of the child's loom-

Sphinx (1994), Judy Fox. The unnatural and contorted pose of Fox's child gymnast mirrors the ways in which children and childhood have often been manipulated to fit adult-constructed ideals. Courtesy private collection, New York.

a grisly *Saturn* symbolically devouring his children (1820–1823), the French Romantic Eugène Delacroix optimistically painted the French Revolution of 1830 as being led by a child. The title of his famous *Liberty Leading the People* (1830) refers to the allegorical female figure with bared breasts, but close inspection reveals that the first person to step over the barricade is actually the urchin to the right, a *gamin de Paris* of the type Victor Hugo would later immortalize in his novel *Les Misérables* (1862) as the character Gavroche. Another *gamin* (urchin) peers out from behind the barricade at the extreme left, grasping a dagger and a cobblestone (a potent symbol of insurrection) and wearing a pilfered *bonnet de police* (forage cap) of the infantry of the national guard (a militia which quickly opposed the king during the fighting). The more prominent urchin who brandishes pistols and carries an oversized ammunition bag stolen from the royal guard gives the composition an explosive force by leading the fray. As an emblem of the democratic future, he is a modern, urban, working-class boy wearing patched trousers and a blue-black velvet *faluche* (student beret). The latter, even if filched, serves as a sign of the bourgeois belief in education's promise of social reform. In the oedipal "family romance" configured in the composition, he plays the son to the maternal figure of Liberty; there is no single father figure, however, but rather several possibilities from both the working and middle class. Both politically and psychically, the boy is a symbolic *enfant de la patrie* (child of the nation) in the famous words of the French national anthem. His role would be played by the more neoclassical ephebe in François Rude's equally famous sculpture *La Marseillaise* (1836) on the Arc de Triomphe in Paris. From a different political perspective, even Paul Delaroche's medievalizing painting of two threatened boys, *Princes in the Tower* (1831), a scene inspired by Shakespeare's *Richard III* which was exhibited in the same Salon as the Delacroix, was suspected (probably incorrectly) of making a veiled comment on the recent unseating of a king. When revolution recurred in Paris in February 1848, the caricaturist Honoré Daumier made a lithograph portraying a perennial street urchin with stolen hat enjoying an oedipal bounce on the king's throne in the Tuileries Palace in *Le Gamin de Paris aux Tuileries* (1848).

In addition to political agency, the male child could become an emblem of artistic genius in the nineteenth century. In France, the childhood of famous Old Masters, including Giotto and Callot, regularly inspired Salon paintings, especially during the Romantic period. As Petra ten-Doesschate Chu has shown, nineteenth-century French artists' biographies followed standard "family romance" plots in which childhood was seen to foretell the future emergence of creative genius. Susan Casteras has mounted a related argument about pictures of boy geniuses in Victorian Britain, for example, Edward M. Ward, *Benjamin West's First Effort in Drawing*, (1849), or William Dyce, *Titian Preparing to Make His First Essay in Colouring* (1857).

ing position in a sublimely obscure landscape with none of Gainsborough's pastoral tranquility. Here the frank gaze at the beholder over a shoulder bared by a sliding dress may harbor a dangerous sexual power, symbolized by the oversized cat in her lap (very different from Leyster's kitten). Like Édouard Manet's later (adult) *Olympia* (1863), Louise Vernet is made to seem aware of a desiring gaze directed at her, without allowing herself to become its object. According to Germer, her knowing and rather confrontational gaze reverses the usual relations of power between image and viewer. If knowledge of sex was thought to separate children from adults, this is a child who seems to gain power over the adult viewer by ignoring that boundary.

In nineteenth-century France, male children could acquire a new political power in the imagery of democratic revolution. Gone was the monarchical stiffness of Holbein's *Edward VI* or the resigned victimhood of David's *Bara*. And whereas the Spaniard Goya famously depicted revolution as

During the realist period in France, at a time when authors like Rodolphe Töpffer were extolling the virtues of children's drawings, Gustave Courbet prominently featured two boys in his huge painting *Studio* (1855), one of them admiring a landscape painting in the center, the other one drawing on the floor to the right. In what Courbet called his "real allegory," the boys allude to the supposedly "natural," childlike naïveté and primitive, unmediated vision of the realist artist and perhaps to future generations of such artists. As Daniel Guernsey has argued, the central boy in particular serves as a Rousseauian "Émile" to Courbet's tutor as the artist teaches the child (as well as the Emperor Napoleon III, portrayed in travesty on the left-hand side of the painting) about the origins of social injustice and the restorative lessons of nature. The fact that this is a peasant child from the working class enhances Courbet's political agenda and aligns the figure with the more urban urchins in the Romantic work of Delacroix and in the naturalist work of Édouard Manet.

The Old Musician (c. 1861–1862), completed the same year that Hugo published *Les Misérables*, is the most monumental of several pictures of children from Manet's early career. In an allusive manifesto about social disenfranchisement that looks back to Courbet's *Studio*, it includes on the left various waifs and child misfits who conflate modern Parisian street urchins of the type celebrated by Hugo (as well as in popular visual culture) with more timeless art-historical references to Le Nain, Watteau, Murillo, and Velázquez. Further distancing the children from the street, Manet, like Courbet, also employs them as self-reflexive allusions to his own artistic practice. In this respect, they stand as visual reminders of the famous declaration by Manet's friend the poet and critic Baudelaire in his essay "The Painter of Modern Life" (1859–1863) that artistic "genius is nothing more nor less than *childhood recovered* at will." Yet there is a darker side to this romantic claim: as Nancy Locke has argued, Baudelaire's prose poem "La Corde" (1864) is colored with incidents from Manet's life, in particular the suicide of a child model, so as to comment on the ideological illusions involved in representation. In other prose poems, most notably "The Poor Child's Toy" (1863), Baudelaire created disquieting and ambiguous confrontations between rich and poor children.

A less unstable image of children's class differences can be found in Victorian Britain in John Faed's *Boyhood* (1849), a painting exhibited at the Royal Scottish Academy in 1850. Here a well-dressed boy is being rescued from the pugilistic belligerence of a poorer barefoot boy. Real class tension is effectively disavowed through the humorous combination of the exaggerated features of the red-faced and frightened rich boy, the handsome physiognomy and upstanding demeanor of the pugnacious poor boy, and the intervention of the old man, who is probably their schoolmaster. The caricatural presence of the old man, as well as the location of the bundle

of books at the poor boy's feet, helps assure the viewer of education's progressive potential to create middle-class harmony and unity. A comparable point was made later in France in Marie Bashkirtseff's enormously successful salon picture *The Meeting* (1884), which was painted during a period of public debate about free, compulsory children's education that followed the passing of the reformist Ferry Law of 1882. Here the proverbially mischievous *gamins de Paris* carry not the insurrectionary ammunition pouch of Delacroix's urchin, but a reassuring school satchel. Faed's scene is, by comparison, safely moved from city to countryside. And the image of boyish aggression in Victorian art often served, as Sara Holdsworth and Joan Crossley have noted, as a sign of the competitive spirit needed in business and empire.

The slightly darker skin of Faed's poor boy connects him back to Blake's chimney sweep and with other representations of so-called STREET ARABS. This latter term, employed in Britain since the mid-nineteenth century, effectively identified class with ethnicity, so that, as Lindsay Smith has explained it, a working-class child could function as a displaced form of the colonized Other. Like the swarthy gypsy boy in Manet's *Old Musician*, lower-class European children could now occupy the position previously held by Indian and African servants in eighteenth-century British child portraits. In the United States, the intriguing half-breed Native American boy strategically placed at the center of George Caleb Bingham's *Fur Traders Descending the Missouri* (c. 1845) could function, in concert with the more ominous bear cub on the left, as a racially hybrid sign of the interface between the mysterious wilderness and the supposedly civilizing influence of the French trapper on the right. In the urban context of Victorian England, race, class, and HYGIENE could be conflated in the representation of darker hair and skin, as can be seen in the figure of the homeless girl with a baby who figures prominently along with other "guttersnipes" in the central foreground of Ford Madox Brown's *Work* (1852–1865). Like the gypsy girl with an infant on the left in Manet's *Old Musician*, she has prematurely assumed the duties of womanhood, while her tattered and revealing red dress and position literally in the gutter seem to prophesy a future in the oldest profession. At a time when factory children were commonly referred to as "white slaves" in Britain, homeless street arabs were constructed as the Other of clean, white, middle-class children in photographs by Oscar Gustav Rejlander, as well as in comparably staged photographs promoting the "philanthropic abduction" campaigns of the evangelical reformer Thomas Barnardo in the 1860s and 1870s. Similar strategies would operate in the more grittily "documentary" photographs of American street arabs taken in subsequent decades in New York by Jacob Riis. By the latter part of the century, mass visual culture, such as British advertisements for Pears' Soap showing black children having their skin washed white with the product, had further disseminated the conflation of ideologies of race, class, and hygiene.

Meanwhile the hyperreal, Pre-Raphaelite clutter of William Holman Hunt's *The Children's Holiday* (1864) could speak in an elegant but claustrophobic way to the building momentum of commodification in middle-class children's fashions (the undepicted father of the portrayed children being a Manchester fabric manufacturer). It simultaneously addressed the retrenchment of bourgeois childhood's protected domain to a privatized, idyllic, and nonindustrialized nature dominated by a crisply sumptuous maternal figure from whom the immaculate youngsters seem to emanate. In what is perhaps the ultimate visual celebration of elite nineteenth-century childhood, American John Singer Sargent's *The Boit Children* (1882–1883), there is projected a more sensual mystery that has something to do with the painterly representation of gender. As David Lubin (1985) and others have argued, the Boit girls serve on one level as well-dressed and leisurely signs of their father's wealth and on another as evocations of female subjectivity (including sexuality) at various developmental stages. Biological destiny, perhaps symbolized by the birth-like positioning of the central figure's doll, seems to hover over the girls like the oversized oriental vessels that lurk in the shadows, miniaturizing the domestic interior (as well as the physical and mental space) these female children inhabit.

As Greg Thomas has shown, French Impressionism's representation of girls and dolls as analogous objects addressed the normative and increasingly commodified socialization of bourgeois feminine behavior. In light of literature (Victor Hugo's Cosette or the Comtesse de Ségur's Sophie) and industry (Pierre François Jumeau's mass-produced porcelain luxury dolls), Pierre-Auguste Renoir's *Children's Afternoon at Wargemont* (1884) clearly suggests, rather less mysteriously than Sargent's *Boit Children*, a cyclical maturation and reproduction of ideal feminine domesticity through doll play and other parlor accomplishments. Renoir's perpetuation of the feminized construction of childhood as a whole is indicated by his sumptuous portrait *Mme Charpentier and Her Children* (1878), in which the younger of what appear to be two elegantly dressed girls is actually a boy. The point is driven home further by a later portrait of his own small son (the future film director) engrossed in the decidedly distaff act of sewing, complete with a bow in his hair, in *Jean Renoir Sewing* (1898–1899).

Whereas Renoir freely chose to depict childhood as a modern life topic, Berthe Morisot and Mary Cassatt, his colleagues in the Impressionist movement, were, to a greater extent, relegated to depicting it by social expectations about appropriate subject matter for women artists. Yet, as Thomas argues, they found viable alternatives to the dominant representation of normative girlhood. Morisot, for example, painted the concentrated activity of her daughter as she shared a more boyish toy, perhaps a train, with her sun-dappled, bourgeois father in *Eugène Manet and Daughter at Bougival* (1881). Mary Cassatt turned conventional deport-

ment and etiquette on their respective heads in her *Young Girl in a Blue Armchair* (1878), something that may have contributed to the rejection of the picture at the 1878 Universal Exposition in Paris. The girl sprawls in a chair at loose ends both physically and psychologically. With legs apart, skirt thrown up to reveal petticoats, and one arm crooked behind her head almost in a parody of the pose of an odalisque (orientalist harem slave), Cassatt's child offers insight into the claustrophobic world inhabited by Victorian females and does so from a gendered perspective that differs remarkably from that of Cassatt's fellow American Sargent.

An exception to the Impressionist tendency to depict primarily bourgeois children was Edgar Degas's series of pictures concentrating on the hard work of child and adolescent ballerinas. Known as *rats* (in yet another analogy between children and animals) these working-class girls were transformed by the artifice of the dance. While acknowledging the eroticized reputation of the dancers promoted in popular visual culture, especially as regards their precocious relations with wealthy male "protectors," Degas more typically concentrated in his pastels on their repetitive labor, in which he saw analogies with his own serial work. Alternatively, in his realistic wax and multimedia sculpture *Little Dancer Aged Fourteen* (1878–1881), he drew upon the popular culture of dolls (in a remarkably different way from Renoir), anthropological mannequins, wax museums, and studies of "criminal" physiognomy in order to create a troubling indictment of the "degeneration" of the lower social orders as embodied in the scrawny girl. Although he rather fetishistically gave the sculpture actual hair and clothing, Degas for the most part de-eroticized the child.

Other artists of the later nineteenth century, following the precedent of Géricault's *Louise Vernet*, addressed child sexuality in repressed, coded, or more explicit fashion so that the seemingly contradictory states of childhood innocence and eroticism could be seen to coexist. As Lubin (1994) has discussed at length, the painting *Making a Train* by the English-born American artist Seymour Guy (1867) even raises the troubling possibility that innocence can be seen as erotic. The scene of the little girl (probably Guy's nine-year-old daughter, Anna) playing dress-up was evidently intended to contrast the innocence of the child's play with the vanity of grown women. Yet for adult viewers, the focus on the child's androgynous chest can bring mature female breasts to mind, with the difference serving as a stimulus to voyeurism. In Victorian Britain, a profusion of fairy paintings could, as Susan Casteras (2002) has pointed out, eroticize children and adolescents as a humorous invitation to viewers to experience vicariously, and thus to sublimate, illicit or transgressive behavior including gender masquerading and miscegenation (see, for example, Joseph Noël Paton, *The Quarrel of Oberon and Titania* [1849]). Such pictures subverted, even as they exploited it, the aura of innocence associated with Vic-

In the upheavals of the nineteenth century, children, particularly the dispossessed children "of the people," gained a new political significance. In Eugène Delacroix's *Liberty Leading the People* (1830), a street urchin brandishing his guns stands in the forefront of the picture, while the adult workers and members of the middle class follow behind. Musée du Louvre, Paris. © Archivo Iconografico, S.A./ CORBIS.

torian children's book illustrations of a type made famous later on by Kate Greenaway.

A frequently discussed example of this phenomenon in Victorian paintings and prints is the pedophilic innuendo of John Everett Millais's *Cherry Ripe* (1879), reproduced as a widely selling print in the *Graphic* Christmas annual in 1880. The image was based nostalgically on Reynolds's *Penelope Boothby*, but it moved the hands and the anachronistic black wrist cuffs to the genital area in an evocative reference to the hymen of its symbolic title. A more maternally erotic sensuality has been read by modern historians, including Carol Mavor, in the dreamily soft focus and invitingly haptic (nearly olfactory) flesh of Julia Margaret Cameron's photographs of children (see, for example, *The Double Star* [1864]). In a different vein, Diane Waggoner, through a close reading of images of Alice Liddell and her two sisters by LEWIS CARROLL, has analyzed visual strategies by which Victorian childhood, with its ambiguous mingling of purity and sexuality, was both fetishized and naturalized by photography. As both Mavor and Lindsay Smith have pointed out, interpretation of the fetishizing that informs, for example, Carroll's update of Reynolds in *Xie Kitchen as Penelope Boothby* (probably taken slightly before Millais' *Cherry Ripe*), or the class inflection of his earlier *Alice Liddell as the Beggar Maid* (c. 1859), or the orientalist frisson of his odalisque-like *Irene MacDonald* (1863) should take into consideration a historical moment in which, until 1885, the legal AGE OF CONSENT for girls in Victorian Britain was thirteen and abusive CHILD PROSTITUTION was rampant. This affected the representation of middle-class as well as lower-class children. Even more emphatically than in the eighteenth century, Victorian innocence implied its opposite.

That the ideological and psychic contradictions of the relationship between innocence and eroticism were not confined to Britain is suggested by the strategically positioned posterior of Jean-Léon Gérôme's boy *Snake Charmer* (late 1860s). Here orientalism and French colonialism became an excuse for a titillating gaze at child sexuality of a type that was disavowed publicly in the West but privately described by Gustave Flaubert in accounts of travels to North Africa with Maxime Du Camp. Even before Paul Gauguin traveled to the French colony of Tahiti seeking to experience, among other things, an exotic ideal of androgyny, he painted the *Naked Breton Boy* (1889), whose sunburned face and hands make him all the more naked and attest to his peasant, working-class status. As Patricia Mathews has described the picture, the viewer is positioned to stand over the boy, whose awkward, adolescent body, ambiguous expression, and prepubescent genitals (which the artist left in an unfinished state) add an erotic dimension. The loss of innocence as a charged topic for late nineteenth-century artists culminated with the Norwegian Edvard Munch's *Puberty* (1894–1895). Whether the depicted girl is frightened by or embraces her sexual awakening, symbolized by the phallic shadow behind her, it obviously oppresses and subsumes her with a specter of biological determinism. As Freud's contemporary, Munch was attuned to changing ideas about child sexuality that would burgeon more fully during the early twentieth century.

Twentieth and Twenty-First Centuries

To get an immediate sense of the post-Freudian paradigm shift in notions of child sexuality, one need only compare the late-nineteenth-century motif of girl with doll as represented by Sargent or Renoir with that found in early-twentieth-century child nudes by the German expressionist Erich Heckel (*Girl with Doll [Franzi]* [1910]) or the French independent painter Suzanne Valadon (*The Abandoned Doll*, [1921]). Innocence has been replaced by experience, but with a notable difference in the gendered perspectives of the artists. Heckel's girl, reclining on a Freudian couch with a reddish and rather vaginal arm rest, knowingly engages the viewer's gaze. The red-cheeked doll perched on the girl's nude thigh barely covers her genitals with its skirt and seems to gesture in the direction of the adult masculine legs cropped in the left background. More frankly than in Guy's *Making a Train*, the child's body is displayed as an erotic object for adult male delectation. In Valadon's rather Fauvist interior, a more pubescent girl discards her doll and, symbolically, her childhood as she turns away from the viewer to regard her own appearance in a mirror, a traditional emblem of vanity. The bow in her hair echoes that of the doll, perhaps alluding to the socialization of feminine adornment conditioned by doll play. The mother (or perhaps procuress) figure seems to initiate the girl into the realm of appearances. As Mathews has argued, Valadon's picture conveys a perspective on puberty that differs from that of Munch. Although the girl's ripening body may offer a voyeuristic pleasure to the viewer, the picture represents puberty from the girl's perspective as a process of acculturation that is as much socially constructed as biologically encoded.

In his *Three Essays on the Theory of Sexuality* (1905), Sigmund Freud himself had proposed the then controversial idea that children are not innocent in the conventional Victorian sense, but are sexual from birth and experience various stages of erotic experience (oral, anal, and genital) followed by a latency period between about age six and the beginning of puberty. Yet, as Alessandra Comini has discussed, artists in Freud's native Vienna mapped a terrain of childhood and adolescent torments that were initially bypassed by psychoanalysts. Egon Schiele and Oskar Kokoschka addressed the taboo topic of MASTURBATION and raised uncomfortable intimations of INCEST, most notably in Kokoschka's *Children Playing* (1909) and in Schiele's nude drawings of his twelve-year-old sister.

While reformist photography projected middle-class assumptions onto the representation of child labor, most notably in photographs taken for the NATIONAL CHILD LABOR

COMMITTEE between 1907 and 1918 by American LEWIS HINE, child sexuality still hovered, subliminally or not, in the Greek-inspired modernist abstractions of Edward Weston's famous pictorialist photographs of his nude son Neil in the mid-1920s. The eroticization of the female child continued to be exploited by male artists of the surrealist generation. The sadistically dismembered and fetishistic dolls made by the Polish-born sculptor Hans Bellmer conflated infantile and adult sexuality with disquieting violence. His more famous countryman, the reclusive Balthasar Klossowski, better known as Balthus, painted enigmatically aroused pubescent girls of a type that Vladimir Nabokov would name LOLITA in his 1950s novel. For example, *The Golden Days* (1944–1946) turns the motif of girl with mirror (found in a remarkably different way in Valadon's painting) into an unsettling image of narcissistic voluptuousness ripe for violation. The depicted girl may be attributed more than a modicum of sexual agency, but it is for the benefit of the adult male viewer's fantasies.

Meanwhile, as the post-Cubist tide of abstraction turned many twentieth-century artists away from the human figure, the popularity of the representation of children was supplanted in many respects by the cult of child art, now seen as a paradigm for primitivist modernism. To a certain degree, this was nothing new, as can be gathered from the boy drawing on the floor of Courbet's *Studio* or the stick figure drawn on the fence of Bashkirtseff's *Meeting*. Yet, as Jonathan Fineberg (1997) and others have noted, artists ranging from Wassily Kandinsky and Paul Klee to Joan Miró and Jean Dubuffet now wanted not to depict children but rather to paint like them in an attempted recuperation of their own lost inner child (a rather literal update of Baudelaire's "childhood recovered at will"). Painters' fascination with child art left the field of representing childhood increasingly open to photography and mass visual culture.

As Higonnet has pointed out, early twentieth-century illustrators like JESSIE WILLCOX SMITH and BESSIE PEASE GUTMANN kept alive Greenaway's nineteenth-century tradition of Romantic childhood innocence. Its perennial and pervasive marketability can be charted not only throughout twentieth-century advertising, but also in work since the 1990s by the enormously successful commercial photographer ANNE GEDDES, who has sold millions of greeting cards, calendars, notepads, children's books, and posters of cuddly kids in bunny or bumblebee costumes. This trajectory of prolonged cuteness has been tempered not only by the darker inflections of illustrators like MAURICE SENDAK, but also by developments in journalistic photography since the Great Depression. By mid-century, photographers including Americans Dorothea Lange and HELEN LEVITT had registered their concern with child welfare. African-American photographer Gordon Parks commented on racial discrimination through a poignant image of doll play, revealing it as a simultaneous instrument of socialization and hindrance to identity formation, in *Black Children with White Doll* (1942).

More recently, controversial photographers of childhood including Robert Mapplethorpe, Nicholas Nixon, and especially SALLY MANN have effectively documented, and aided the invention of, a paradigm shift away from Romantic innocence to what Higonnet terms "knowing childhood." Such photographs as Mann's *Jessie as Jessie, Jessie as Madonna* (1990) rivetingly suggest that the innocence and sexuality of children are not mutually exclusive and that bodily and psychological individuality can coexist with the state of being childlike. Likewise in recent years, photographer WENDY EWALD has facilitated children's taking photographs of their own complex identities, an all-too-rare example of child agency like that initiated in the early years of the twentieth century by Jacques Henri Lartigue (*Self-Portrait with Hydroglider* [1904]).

Meanwhile in a postmodern consumer world in which children's beauty pageants, waif models, and uncanny, ethnically diverse twin dolls have become mere tips of the iceberg in the commodified, sexualized visual culture of children, increasing numbers of sculptors, painters, and video and multimedia installation artists have joined photographers in returning to the representation of childhood in its current state of knowingness, not innocence. They address the way children are used to mold social patterns of consumption and desire so as to become powerful signifiers of the uncertainties of identity in global capitalist culture. Recent American exhibitions with titles like *My Little Pretty* and *Presumed Innocence* have featured works by artists including Janet Biggs, Dinos and Jake Chapman, Taro Chiezo, Larry Clark, Keith Cottingham, Kim Dingle, Todd Gray, Todd Haynes, Nicky Hoberman, Inez van Lamsweerde, Paul McCarthy, Tracey Moffat, Tony Oursler, Alix Pearlstein, Judith Raphael, Aura Rosenberg, Julian Trigo, and Lisa Yuskavage, who unabashedly and unsentimentally tackle the topic of children as both consumable objects and sexualized subjects capable of seduction or destruction. Charles Ray, in his mixed media sculpture *Family Romance* (1993) memorably created a new standard-issue nuclear family consisting of same-sized adults and children, all given the height of young adolescents. The increasingly indistinguishable interface of adult and child identities was likewise addressed by Dutch-born artist Inez van Lamsweerde in a series of computer manipulated digital photographs of girl models who were given the tight grins of adult males in a spooky prefiguration of images published four years later of the murdered child beauty queen JonBenét Ramsey (*Final Fantasy, Ursula* [1993]). Both artists mingled grotesque archaeological fragments of constructed childhoods past and present, including the Wordsworthian claim that the child is father of the man, the Freudian uncanny, and the disturbingly dark side of Disney. The quandary of being both adult and child was indelibly visualized by Judy Fox in her glazed terracotta statue *Sphinx* (1994). Offering something of a postmodern update of Degas's *Little Dancer*, the nude, life-sized body of the enigmatic young gymnast is poised in the physical and psychological contortions of a gesture of salute. Her uncanny knowingness likewise finds an ancestor in the eponymous hybrid monster of Greek mythology who destroyed those who could not answer its riddle. Such arresting images challenge us to decipher difficult and crucial questions posed by childhood today.

See also: **Boyhood; Children's Literature; Fashion; Girlhood; Madonna, Orthodox; Madonna, Religious; Madonna, Secular; Photographs of Children; Theories of Childhood; Victorian Art.**

BIBLIOGRAPHY

Ariès, Philippe. 1962. *Centuries of Childhood: A Social History of Family Life.* Trans. Robert Baldick. New York: Knopf.

Boris, Staci. 1997. *My Little Pretty: Images of Girls by Contemporary Women Artists.* Chicago: Museum of Contemporary Art.

Brooke, Xanthe and Peter Cherry. 2001. *Murillo: Scenes of Childhood.* London: Merrell.

Brown, Marilyn R., ed. 2002. *Picturing Children: Constructions of Childhood between Rousseau and Freud.* Burlington, VT: Ashgate.

Casteras, Susan P. 1986. *Victorian Childhood: Paintings Selected from the Forbes Magazine Collection.* New York: Abrams.

Casteras, Susan P. 2002. "Winged Fantasies: Constructions of Childhood, Innocence, Adolescence, and Sexuality in Victorian Fairy Painting." In *Picturing Children: Constructions of Childhood between Rousseau and Freud,* ed. Marilyn R. Brown. Burlington, VT: Ashgate.

Chu, Petra ten-Doesschate. 2002. "Family Matters: The Construction of Childhood; Nineteenth-Century Artists' Biographies." In *Picturing Children: Constructions of Childhood between Rousseau and Freud,* ed. Marilyn R. Brown. Burlington, VT: Ashgate.

Comini, Alessandra. 2002. "Toys in Freud's Attic: Torment and Taboo in the Child and Adolescent Themes of Vienna's Image-Makers." In *Picturing Children: Constructions of Childhood between Rousseau and Freud,* ed. Marilyn R. Brown. Burlington, VT: Ashgate.

Crutchfield, Jean. 1998. *Presumed Innocence.* Richmond, VA: Anderson Gallery, School of the Arts, Virginia Commonwealth University.

Dimock, George. 2001. *Priceless Children: American Photographs 1890–1925.* Seattle: University of Washington Press.

Duncan, Carol. 1973. "Happy Mothers and Other New Ideas in French Art." *Art Bulletin* 55: 570–583.

Durantini, Mary Frances. 1983. *The Child in Seventeenth-Century Dutch Painting.* Ann Arbor, MI: UMI Research Press.

Fineberg, Jonathan. 1997. *The Innocent Eye: Children's Art and the Modern Artist.* Princeton, NJ: Princeton University Press.

Fineberg, Jonathan, ed. 1998. *Discovering Child Art: Essays on Childhood, Primitivism, and Modernism.* Princeton, NJ: Princeton University Press.

Fuller, Peter. 1979. "Pictorial Essay: Uncovering Childhood." In *Changing Childhood,* ed. Martin Hoyles. London: Writers and Readers Publishing Cooperative.

Germer, Stefan. 1999. "Pleasurable Fear: Géricault and Uncanny Trends at the Opening of the Nineteenth Century." *Art History* 22, no. 2: 159–183.

Guernsey, Daniel R. 2002. "Childhood and Aesthetic Education: The Role of *Émile* in the Formation of Gustave Courbet's *The Painter's Studio.*" In *Picturing Children: Constructions of Childhood between Rousseau and Freud,* ed. Marilyn R. Brown. Burlington, VT: Ashgate.

Higonnet, Anne. 1998. *Pictures of Innocence: The History and Crisis of Ideal Childhood.* New York: Thames and Hudson.

Hindman, Sandra. 1981. "Pieter Brueghel's *Children's Games,* Folly, and Chance." *Art Bulletin* 63: 447–475.

Holdsworth, Sara, Joan Crossley, and Christina Hardyment. 1992. *Innocence and Experience: Images of Children in British Art from 1600 to the Present.* Manchester, UK: Manchester City Art Galleries.

Hunt, Lynn. 1992. *The Family Romance of the French Revolution.* Berkeley and Los Angeles: University of California Press.

Kristeva, Julia. 1980 [1975]. "Motherhood According to Giovanni Bellini." In *Desire in Language: A Semiotic Approach to Literature and Art,* ed. Leon S. Roudiez. New York: Columbia University Press.

Locke, Nancy. 2002. "Baudelaire's 'La Corde' as a Figuration of Manet's Art." In *Picturing Children: Constructions of Childhood between Rousseau and Freud,* ed. Marilyn R. Brown. Burlington, VT: Ashgate.

Lubin, David M. 1985. *Acts of Portrayal: Eakins, Sargent, James.* New Haven, CT: Yale University Press.

Lubin, David M. 1994. *Picturing a Nation: Art and Social Change in Nineteenth-Century America.* New Haven, CT: Yale University Press.

Mathews, Patricia. 1999. *Passionate Discontent: Creativity, Gender, and French Symbolist Art.* Chicago: University of Chicago Press.

Mavor, Carol. 1995. *Pleasures Taken: Performances of Sexuality and Loss in Victorian Photographs.* Durham, NC: Duke University Press.

Milam, Jennifer. 2001. "Sex Education and the Child: Gendering Erotic Response in Eighteenth-Century France." In *Picturing Children: Constructions of Childhood between Rousseau and Freud,* ed. Marilyn R. Brown. Burlington, VT: Ashgate.

Neils, Jenifer, and John Oakley, eds. 2003. *Coming of Age in Ancient Greece: Images of Childhood from the Classical Past.* New Haven, CT: Yale University Press.

Neubauer, John. 1992. "Visualizing Adolescence." In his *The Fin-de-Siècle Culture of Adolescence.* New Haven, CT: Yale University Press.

New Art Examiner. 1998. Special Issue, *Lolita* 25 (June): no. 9.

Pointon, Marcia. 1993. *Hanging the Head: Portraiture and Social Formation in Eighteenth-Century England.* New Haven, CT: Yale University Press.

Rosenblum, Robert. 1988. *The Romantic Child from Runge to Sendak.* New York: Thames and Hudson.

Schama, Simon. 1988. *The Embarrassment of Riches: An Interpretation of Dutch Culture in the Golden Age.* Berkeley and Los Angeles: University of California Press.

Schorsch, Anita. 1979. *Images of Childhood: An Illustrated Social History.* New York: Mayflower Books.

Smith, Lindsay. 1998. *The Politics of Focus: Women, Children and Nineteenth-Century Photography.* Manchester, UK: Manchester University Press.

Snow, Edward A. 1997. *Inside Bruegel: The Play of Images in Children's Games.* New York: North Point Press.

Steinberg, Leo. 1996 [1983]. *The Sexuality of Christ in Renaissance Art and in Modern Oblivion.* Chicago: University of Chicago Press.

Steward, James Christen. 1995. *The New Child: British Art and the Origins of Modern Childhood.* Seattle: University of Washington Press.

Thomas, Greg M. 2002. "Impressionist Dolls: On the Commodification of Girlhood in Impressionist Painting." In *Picturing Children: Constructions of Childhood between Rousseau and Freud,* ed. Marilyn R. Brown. Burlington, VT: Ashgate.

Waggoner, Diane. 2001. "Photographing Childhood: Lewis Carroll and Alice." In *Picturing Children: Constructions of Childhood between Rousseau and Freud*, ed. Marilyn R. Brown. Burlington, VT: Ashgate.

Wicks, Ann Barrot, ed. 2002. *Children in Chinese Art.* Honolulu: University of Hawai'i Press.

MARILYN R. BROWN

Immunization. *See* Vaccination.

Incest

The taboo surrounding incest has existed for thousands of years, but its social impact has shifted over time, reflecting changing notions of children, law, SEXUALITY, and the family. The historian must exercise caution in interpreting the role of incest in the United States because rhetoric does not always reflect reality. People rarely spoke about child sexual abuse prior to the 1970s; nevertheless incest clearly occurred. Society's responses to allegations of incest reflect the changing and often ambiguous role of children in society and are shaped by notions of gender, race, socioeconomic status, and ethnicity.

Colonial America through the Nineteenth Century

In the colonial period, children were economic assets to the family and essentially under paternal control. Their economic function was eclipsed as Victorian concepts of middle-class domesticity emerged in the nineteenth century. Children were recast as innately innocent and malleable, and mothers replaced fathers as the moral guardians of the home. This image of innocence underscored the perception of childhood vulnerability. During the Progressive Era, CHILD-SAVING professionals increasingly intervened in the family, subtly challenging parental authority and implying that faulty and inadequate PARENTING could harm children. The twentieth century saw the emergence of CHILDREN'S RIGHTS, often at the expense of parental authority.

Although rarely mentioned, there is mounting evidence that child sexual abuse occurred frequently throughout the last two centuries. Laws about statutory rape and incest reflect awareness that child sexual abuse existed, but their erratic enforcement suggests ambiguity about sexual abuse and society's role in child protection. Between the 1880s and 1900, for example, most states increased the AGE OF CONSENT from ten to at least sixteen, reflecting a common concern of the social purity movement that girls were vulnerable to sexual harm. Although almost every state outlawed incest, sexual acts between parent and child outside of intercourse fell under less stringent legal statutes.

Historians have argued that cultural practices may have facilitated sexual abuse in the home. Sleeping arrangements that placed adults in the same bed with children—such as occurred in the crowded conditions of nineteenth-century tenements, or the limited bed space in colonial and frontier homes—gave adults easy access to children, enabled children to witness carnal acts between adults, and may have facilitated incest. Myths about VENEREAL DISEASE transmission may have contributed to sexual abuse by reshaping taboos against incest into acts of desperation. According to one myth, which still occasionally surfaces as an excuse, intercourse with a virgin will cure a man suffering from a venereal disease. During the nineteenth century, men who invoked this explanation for sexual relations with minors were considered less predatory and legally culpable.

Late Nineteenth and Early Twentieth Century

During the Progressive Era the profession of social work was born; with it came increased scrutiny of the private lives of American families. When early social workers uncovered cases of incest, they frequently described the girls as seducers rather than victims. Considered sexually deviant, these girls risked incarceration in institutions for delinquent girls. Conversely, fathers who were named as perpetrators were rarely prosecuted; a promise to reform was considered sufficient. By the 1920s, children were often imbued with paradoxical qualities of being at once erotic and innocent, a tension epitomized in Nabokov's 1958 novel LOLITA.

Commonly held beliefs may have deflected suspicion away from parents. Victorian domestic literature frequently warned mothers to beware of salacious domestic workers caring for children. Accused of calming young charges by masturbating them and introducing sexual activity prematurely, domestic employees were often the first household members to be implicated when sexual abuse was suspected. Little evidence supports these accusations against nursery maids; yet the frequency with which the concern was raised reflects a simmering fear that sexual abuse could perturb the seemingly calm Victorian home. Similarly, when a child contracted gonorrhea and a parent was found to have the disease as well, infected sheets and toilet seats were blamed instead of the parent. The mistaken belief that children could catch gonorrhea from objects led sexual abuse to go unrecognized as late as the 1970s.

Historians have shown how twentieth-century rhetoric may have hidden more abuse than it exposed. The stranger-perpetrator, so threateningly portrayed in mid-twentieth-century media, diverted attention from more likely perpetrators in the home. Freud's notion of children's innate sexuality and his belief that memories of sexual abuse represented unconscious wishes stressed the erotic nature of children and caused many professionals to question the validity of memories of sexual abuse. Even as concern about sexual abuse grew throughout most of the twentieth century, most experts resisted the idea that incest might be common.

CHILD ABUSE burst into American social conscience in the last three decades of the twentieth century, but there were

Oskar Kokoschka's *Children Playing* (1909) raises disturbing questions about the relationship between the brother and sister depicted. Awareness of sexual abuse increased in the early twentieth century although both experts and the general public considered strangers to be the greatest threat and resisted the notion that incest might be more common than they believed. Wilhelm Lehmbruck Museum, Duisberg, Germany/Bridgeman Art Library. © 2003 Artists Rights Society (ARS), New York/ProLitteris, Zurich.

important antecedents, though initially they were focused on physical rather than sexual abuse. Organized social response to child abuse began in 1874 when a severely beaten girl was brought to the American Society for the Prevention of Cruelty to Animals and thus led to the founding of analogous societies to protect abused children. Her case typified nineteenth-century stereotypes: abused children came from immigrant, impoverished, intemperate, and marginalized homes. These stereotypes buttressed middle-class values, reinforced notions of middle-class domestic tranquility, and persisted for over a hundred years.

Other social movements helped set the stage for the late-twentieth-century discovery of incest. Feminism empowered women to expose domestic abuse and encouraged society to protect other victims, like abused children. The social activism of the 1960s and 1970s created a sympathetic audience for abused children. Increased sexual freedom gave society a vocabulary to discuss sexual abuse. In the early 1960s pediatricians, inspired by social activism and responding to increased professional interest in developmental and behavioral issues, began to identify and protect physically abused children. By the 1970s this medicalization of child abuse had expanded to include child sexual abuse as well, and medical evaluations became standard features of child sexual abuse cases. As society increasingly felt obliged to protect abused children, the paternal hegemony that dominated early American families had eroded and a variety of professionals gained authority in policing and protecting the family.

See also: **Law, Children and the.**

BIBLIOGRAPHY

Ashby, LeRoy. 1997. *Endangered Children: Dependency, Neglect, and Abuse in American History.* New York: Twayne Publishers.

Evans, Hughes. 2002. "The Discovery of Child Sexual Abuse in America." In *Formative Years: Children's Health in the United States, 1880–2000,* ed. Alexandra Minna Stern and Howard Markel. Ann Arbor: University of Michigan Press.

Freedman, Estelle B. 1989. "'Uncontrolled Desires': The Response to the Sexual Psychopath, 1920–1960." In *Passion and Power: Sexuality in History,* ed. Kathy Peiss and Christina Simmons. Philadelphia: Temple University Press.

Gordon, Linda. 1986. "Incest and Resistance: Patterns of Father-Daughter Incest, 1880–1930." *Social Problems* 33: 253–267.

Gordon, Linda. 1988. *Heroes of Their Own Lives: The Politics and History of Family Violence, Boston 1880–1960.* New York: Penguin Books.

Gordon, Linda, and Paul O'Keefe. 1984. "Incest as a Form of Family Violence: Evidence from Historical Case Records." *Journal of Marriage and the Family* 46: 27–34.

Jenkins, Philip. 1998. *Moral Panic: Changing Concepts of the Child Molester in Modern America.* New Haven, CT: Yale University Press.

Mason, Mary Ann. 1994. *From Father's Property to Children's Rights: The History of Child Custody in the United States.* New York: Cambridge University Press.

Odem, Mary E. 1995. *Delinquent Daughters: Protecting and Policing Adolescent Female Sexuality in the United States, 1885–1920.* Chapel Hill: University of North Carolina Press.

Pleck, Elizabeth. 1987. *Domestic Tyranny: The Making of American Social Policy against Family Violence from Colonial Times to the Present.* New York: Oxford University Press.

HUGHES EVANS

Indentured Servants. *See* Apprenticeship; Placing Out.

India and South Asia

India has the largest population of children in the world: some 300 million of its almost one billion people. Pakistan has 58 million children, Bangladesh 47 million, Sri Lanka 5 million, and Nepal 10 million, about 40 percent of the population in each case. Together the South Asian countries have some of the richest folklore and artistic creations for and about children in the world. Although the suggestion that childhood is basically a modern concept is a useful one, it does not tell us much about the empirical history and cultural systems of children in South Asia, either in a premodern past or for those who are not wholly "modern" in the conventional sense today. That work remains to be done, especially given the diversity of the region. All generalizations below need to be tempered with a view to this diversity.

The Love of Children
Studies of South Asian literature reveal a high regard for infancy and childhood, starting with rich descriptions of the physical looks, antics, and charms of children; going on to their emotional appeal; and including the multivocal symbolism of childhood, or how childhood means many different things, most of them wonderful. Philosophical perspectives see childhood as representing the highest, hidden truths for humans, as well as marking the fallacy of worldly life and its entanglements. The mythological figures of Hinduism revel in the chaotic PLAY of children, specifically boys. The term *play* (*leela*) for many Hindus describes the nature of God's work. Specially celebrated are the child-versions of Rama and Krishna in the many vernacular textual and performance versions of the Sanskrit epics *Ramayana* and *Mahabharata* (c. 300 B.C.E. to 300 C.E.). There is probably no

bigger corpus of poems about the naughtiness of a child than those by various poets about Krishna as an infant and young boy. In Tamil there is a genre that explicitly addresses God as a child and positions the author's voice as that of the mother. Adult saints or incarnations of godhood were and are often praised as being "childlike" in their innocence and proximity to the Ultimate Divine, such as Ramakrishna in the late nineteenth century and Anandmayi Ma in the mid-twentieth century. In totally secular literature too, there is an appreciation of childhood, as by the poet Rabindranath Tagore (1861–1941).

In the traditional Indian sciences, children are specially targeted. In the medical philosophies of Ayurveda the treatment of the child comprises one of the eight branches of medicine. The Indian/Hindu sciences of sociology and psychology discuss the graded stages of life and the relationships between the various ages. In modern times many memoirs, such as Mohandas Gandhi's *My Experiments with Truth* (1957), and novels, such as Mai Shree's 2000 work, that describe South Asian childhoods with empathy.

The Problem of Children
In modern South Asia over the course of the nineteenth and twentieth centuries, children have been seen as a problem in several ways. The urge for reform in colonial India often revolved around abolishing child marriages. Boys and girls were betrothed at any time from birth onward and could begin married lives from the age of ten or twelve onward. An early marriage meant frequent widowhood and among the higher castes there was a prejudice against widows remarrying, no matter how young the child-widow. A lack of formal education and overall gender discrimination was seen to be at the heart of the problem. Major reformers in the nineteenth century included Rammohan Roy (1772–1833), Isvarchandra Vidyasagar (1820–1891), and Jyotirao Phule (1827–1890), although they, like all the many other reformers of the time, did not think of themselves as working for the interests of children specifically.

The constitution of independent India, adopted in 1950, has taken an uncompromising stand in protecting children from many of these problems, and when practice lags behind theory, insufficient education is held accountable. The inefficacy of law is seen as related to another problem that arose in the middle of the twentieth century: overpopulation. The population of India went up from 238 million in 1901 to 439 million in 1961 and 844 million in 1991. Family planning was proposed as a solution, with national efforts to persuade people to have two or three children only. Apart from a brief interlude of coercion in India from 1975 to 1976 there have been efforts only to educate and persuade, unlike CHINA. However, the success of family planning efforts are belied by the growth rate of the population: 1.98 percent in 1961 and 2.28 percent in 1991. The answer lies partly in reduced INFANT MORTALITY rates, which vary all over the region, but had fallen for all of India from 129 per thousand in 1971 to 96 per thousand in 1986.

Another highly visible problem in recent decades is child labor. Many children work either as unskilled labor or as apprentices in skilled production. While unskilled child labor is due to the problem of poverty and the infrastructural bottlenecks in education and employment, APPRENTICESHIP is a complex system within which skills and ethical training are imparted and future employment guaranteed. Children working as apprentices in trades such as weaving and pottery making work in domestic settings and are not neglected or abused, although they certainly are not given the separate space, resources, and consumer goods taken as normative in the West.

Education and Socialization

In precolonial times there were several systems of education in South Asia, all local, community-based, and geared to specific purposes and futures. Diversity was the norm, and many factors, including caste, class, region, and religion decided the education that a child would receive. From the 1850s onward, home and community based schooling was gradually replaced by a centralized system of schooling. This was liberal and secular in its trappings and based on a unilaterally enforced British colonial understanding of the proper scope of knowledge, rather than on the extant plural understandings in South Asia. Because of its lack of resources and philosophy in the matter, the colonial state could not and would not provide total or compulsory education for children. The numbers being formally educated in South Asia have always remained small.

Elite children took to the new education with alacrity. Whereas some grew up to be distanced from the masses, most also learned their own histories and languages and became the nationalist intelligentsia of their countries. Today the problems of a system that is insufficient to educate all children continue, as well as those of inequality and division. Schools range from municipal schools for the poor to expensive private schools. In Pakistan the split is most dramatic, ranging between a *madrasa*-based religious education and a modern liberal education. Everywhere in South Asia, schooling is mechanical and uninspired, and at its best produces young people who can read, write, and count well, but not necessarily be creative or enterprising. The most popular type of schooling is in a liberal curriculum, English is seen as empowering, and the child is encouraged to pursue both as an investment for the family. But such is the lack of interest in the experience of the child, there is a dearth of modern, liberal educational resources, specifically of books, even as consumerism burgeons.

The community and the family are the main sources of socialization for children, where they learn of their religion, ethos, and identity. Muslim communities typically send their children to *madrasas*, domestic schools for learning the

Qur'an, for two to five years, before or together with formal schooling. Hindu communities have no formal religious education. Hindu children learn of their mythology from art, performances, festivals, popular everyday activity, and now the media. All children, with rare metropolitan exceptions, are socialized into an acceptance of interdependence with others, of negotiation about freedoms, and ultimately an age hierarchy.

Age is one of the most crucial hierarchies in South Asia, together with those of class and education. But gender is the fundamental dividing line in children's experiences across all regions, sects, and classes. Much of South Asia is patrilocal and all of it is patrilineal and patriarchal. Girls are encouraged to fit into a future of wifehood, housework, and mothering, each of which comes with complex rules. Muslim girls are taught to have "shame," to be private, and to adopt the veil from PUBERTY onward. Hindu girls are married to men and into families to whom they must adapt and configure themselves satisfactorily. Girls from the more liberal, educated classes, who are sent to mixed or all-girls' schools, are still socialized into roles deemed womanly. Boys of all sects and classes are encouraged to experiment, move around, and learn a skill or acquire a liberal education. The unemployment rate is high, meaning that not only do many boys grow up to be unemployed, they often retain a dependency on their parents well into adulthood. According to some psychoanalysts this dependency is responsible for a part of the economic backwardness and political problems of South Asia.

The games, activities, and media experience of children in South Asia are diverse and rich, even if specific spaces, consumption patterns, and identities are not considered essential for them as they are in the West. Children play a variety of local games, including the international favorites cricket and soccer, listen to a huge range of music, and are audience-participants in amateur theatricals, neighborhood celebrations, and small and large festivals. All this entertainment is free. According to their resources they also watch TELEVISION and MOVIES, although there are almost no programs or features specifically for children. There is little overt presentation of the SEXUALITY of children or adolescents. DATING and physical contact before marriage is publicly avoided in all classes and communities. Everyday violence is unknown.

For the most part, children in India and South Asia live in a rich communal world in which there are many fictive kin, and family members are around and available. These same kinspeople contribute to making it difficult for a child or adolescent to break with tradition and act autonomously, resulting in, perhaps, a dependency syndrome. Progress for children in South Asia requires a better system of education catering to the diversities of the region, as well as a more enlightened role for the community.

See also: **British Colonialism in India; Child Labor in Developing Countries; Islam; Japan.**

BIBLIOGRAPHY

Bose, Pradip. 1972. *Growing Up in India.* Calcutta: The Minerva Associates.

Carstairs, G. M. 1957. *The Twice-Born.* London: Hogarth Press.

Dasgupta, Amit, ed. 1995. *Telling Tales: Children's Literature in India.* New Delhi: Indian Council for Cultural Relations/New Age International Publishers.

Gandhi, Mohandas Karamchand. 1957. *My Experiments with Truth.* Boston: Beacon Press.

Kakar, Sudhir. 1979. "Childhood in India: Traditional Ideals and Contemporary Reality." *International Social Science Journal* 31: 444–456.

Kakar, Sudhir. 1981. *The Inner World: A Psycho-analytic Study of Childhood and Society in India.* Delhi: Oxford University Press.

Kumar, Nita. 2000. *Lessons from Schools: A History of Education in Banaras.* Delhi and Thousand Oaks, CA: Sage.

Kumar, Nita. 2001. "Languages, Families and the Plural Learning of the Nineteenth-century Intelligentsia." *The Indian Economic and Social History Review* 38, no. 1: 81–103.

Kumar, Nita. 2001. "Learning Modernity? The Technologies of Education in India." *Autrepart. Les Jeunes: Hantise de l'espace public dans les societes du Sud?* 18: 85–100.

Mahabharata. 1981. Trans. William Buck. Berkeley: University of California Press.

Menon, Navin, and Bhavna Nair, eds. 1999. *Children's Literature in India.* New Delhi: Children's Book Trust.

Miller, Barbara D. 1981. *The Endangered Sex: Neglect of Female Children in Rural North India.* Ithaca, NY: Cornell University Press.

Rahman, Mahmudar. 1970. *Humour in Urdu Children's Literature.* Karachi, Dacca: National Home.

Rajan, Chandra, trans. 1983. *Panchatantra: The Globe-trotting Classic of India.* New Delhi: Penguin.

Ramayana. 1976. Trans. William Buck. Berkeley: University of California Press.

Richman, Paula. 1997. *Extraordinary Child: Poems from a South Asian Devotional Genre.* Honolulu: University of Hawai'i Press.

Seymour, Susan C. 1999. *Women, Family, and Child Care in India: A World in Transition.* Cambridge: Cambridge University Press.

Sinha, Durganand, ed. 1981. *Socialization of the Indian Child.* New Delhi: Concept.

Srinivasan, Prema. 1998. *Children's Fiction in English in India: Trends and Motifs.* Chennai: T. R. Publications.

Statistics on Children in India: Pocketbook. 1995. New Delhi: National Institute of Public Cooperation and Child Development.

Tagore, Rabindranath. 1913. *The Crescent Moon.* London: Macmillan.

The English Writings of Rabindranath Tagore, vol. 1. 1961. New Delhi: Sahitya Akademi.

Vivekanand. 1953. *The Yogas and Other Works,* ed. S. Nikhalananda. New York: Ramakrishna-Vivekananda Centre.

NITA KUMAR

Indoor Games

While examples of board games still exist from ancient civilizations such as Egypt or Mesopotamia, indoor games involving manufactured TOYS did not become as common as homemade playthings among children until the nineteenth century. By the middle of the nineteenth century, changing definitions of childhood, as well as increased industrialization and urbanization, led to the beginnings of the modern toy industry in Europe and the United States, and to the rise of leisure.

However, leisure remained an occupation of the middle and upper classes. Working-class families, especially immigrants, rarely had the time or money to indulge in leisure activities. In addition, working-class children (and women) were a very important part of the industrial labor force until well into the twentieth century, with little time to play. Most evidence of play by working-class children is of outdoor games, or street play. Urban children living in overcrowded tenements had no space to play indoors, resorting instead to the street or the stoop.

By the 1830s, popular perceptions of childhood were completely different from those of the previous century. Children were considered pure and innocent, to be nurtured and protected. By the 1830s, conceptions of motherhood had also shifted. With industrialization, divisions of labor between men and women became more pronounced. According to the middle-class model, men went to work while women stayed home and took care of the children. This model was very different from that of the previous century, when many middle-class families were shopkeepers or artisans, working out of their own homes. In the eighteenth century, the home was still a major center for production, with a domestic economy involving all family members. In the nineteenth century, the domestic economy was transformed into a domestic haven.

Indoor games, within the controlled setting of the home, offered unparalleled opportunities for adults, whether parents, caregivers, or educators, to direct children's play. Historian Jay Mechling has observed that adults began trying to shape PLAY into a constructive form in the nineteenth century, often through toys. The KINDERGARTEN movement, based on a system of early childhood education developed by FRIEDRICH FROEBEL in the 1840s, advocated learning through play, especially in early childhood. However, evidence of spontaneous games, such as playing under the dining room table, singing, or dressing up the family dog, exists in anecdotal form in memoirs and fiction.

Board and Table Games

Early board games were manufactured in England in the late eighteenth century. American firms only began to produce board games around 1840. Prior to producing board games, most of the American manufacturers were already established as publishers of educational materials for children, such as maps or books. One of the first American manufacturers, W. & S. B. Ives of Salem, Massachusetts, published the card game Dr. Busby (or Happy Families) in the 1840s as a sideline for their stationery business. Milton Bradley first introduced the Checkered Game of Life in 1861, a year after starting a lithography business in Springfield, Massachusetts. Bradley went on to become one of the most successful manufacturers of board games in the United States. A proponent of the kindergarten movement, he published books and produced kindergarten "gifts." The gifts consisted of toys specified by Froebel. Other such companies included McLoughlin Brothers, Parker Brothers, and Selchow and Righter.

Many indoor games, including board games or card games, were educational in nature. Nineteenth-century board games, card games, and jigsaw puzzles often depicted contemporary events as well as educational themes. In her 1991 book on games, Caroline Goodfellow, an English toy expert, connected the rise of the middle class with an increased emphasis on educating children about national and international affairs. According to Goodfellow, the nineteenth century was an age of exploration and expansion, requiring more extensive preparation before children were ready to enter the adult world. Games such as the 1845 Game of the District Messenger Boy, manufactured by McLoughlin Brothers, taught children about commerce and trade. Such games also taught children about morality, elevating virtues such as honesty and initiative while showing the consequences of vice—failure and jail. Other games, such as the 1890 Around the World with Nellie Bly, also manufactured by McLoughlin Brothers, took current events and made them into a game.

Other Manufactured Toys

Most existing evidence of indoor play consists of manufactured toys, which became prominent immediately following the American Civil War. Although the toy-making industry in Europe (especially in England and Germany) was already solidly established by at least the eighteenth century, the mass production of toys was certainly a nineteenth-century phenomenon. Historians are divided on whether these toys (mostly cast iron and tin) were actually played with by children or whether they were less popular than handmade playthings or improvised games without toys (e.g., hide-and-seek) during the last quarter of the nineteenth century. What is known, however, is that the toy industry flourished.

TOY TRAINS and firefighting toys were especially popular with boys, beginning with cast iron sets from the 1870s, made by companies including Carpenter, Hubley, Ives, Kenton, and Pratt & Letchworth. As technology changed, so did toys: children played with scaled-down representations of the vehicles then in use.

DOLLS and dollhouses were especially important for girls. Over time, dolls have continued to be the toys most men-

tioned by girls. Recent scholarship has focused on negative aspects of doll play, most notably in the role of the doll in reinforcing stereotypes of femininity and domesticity. However, the positive aspects should not be understated, with many girls (and boys) playing with dolls in numerous ways—nurturing them, destroying them, and telling stories about them.

Mechanical toys are especially prominent in private and public collections of toys. Notoriously fragile, these toys were almost surely used only indoors. Most mechanical toys before the end of the nineteenth century are either French or German in origin, with the most famous examples produced by Fernand Martin of Paris or E. P. Lehmann of Brandenburg, Germany.

Toy Theaters

Toy theaters consisted of wooden stage sets and figures covered with lithographed images. Businesses producing toy theaters flourished in London, around the Covent Garden area, from the 1830s to the 1840s. Sets and figures were often based on plays then running at Covent Garden. By the 1850s, German manufacturers dominated the market.

In the beginning, toy theaters, like board games, were often produced by small publishers who sold numerous engravings or lithographs of popular plays. Toy theaters were typically middle-class entertainments, to be purchased and played with at home. Never manufactured extensively in the United States, toy theaters were likely to have been luxury imports. Today, the artistry of the printing is much prized by collectors.

Play Manuals

A number of instruction books about play were published for children in the nineteenth century. These books were generally filled with suggestions for both indoor and outdoor play, which consisted of activities and hands-on projects. One example, *The Boy's Own Toy-Maker: A Practical Illustrated Guide to the Useful Employment of Leisure Hours*, published by E. Landells in 1866, is almost entirely composed of suggestions for indoor amusements, with instructions for making paper and cardboard toys. Other books included chapters for both indoor and outdoor activities, including *The Boy's Own Book*, by William Clarke, published in 1829 and reprinted 1996. Clarke included numerous chapters on outdoor sports, as well as chapters on indoor activities such as tricks with cards and chemical amusements. Different games and activities are detailed in *The Girl's Own Book*, published in 1833 and reprinted 1992, by Mrs. L. Maria Child. Mrs. Child's suggestions include less vigorous games, most of which can be played either indoors or outdoors. Instructions for craft projects are for more "ladylike" pursuits, such as pressing flowers or dressing dolls. In the main, such books for children promulgated progressive notions of child rearing, encouraging moderation in all types of play, whether indoors or outdoors. These books mirrored the adult belief that children had to be trained to become model citizens through daily activities and amusements.

Most recreational books encouraged children to make their own toys in order to learn skills and promote creativity. Even today, commercially made playthings are often considered (by adults) to be inferior to the handmade toys of the past, continuing a debate that began as early as the late nineteenth century.

In some cases, there may in fact be a dramatic difference in toys and games from one generation to another. Shifts over time are especially important when studying indoor games, because this category of play has been so affected by the proliferation of manufactured toys, both for urban and rural children. In the 1993 *The Foxfire Book of Appalachian Toys and Games,* children from northern Georgia interviewed older residents about the past, compiling oral histories about toys and games. Most residents remembered making their own toys, especially dolls, and playing what folklorist Simon Bronner, in an introduction, calls "folk games." Indoor games were primarily for rainy days, when the weather prevented kids from going outdoors.

Games in Memoirs and Fiction

Memoirs of childhood from the nineteenth through the twentieth centuries rarely make direct references to indoor games. Play, while widely acknowledged by historians and sociologists as the primary activity of children, does not always seem to dominate childhood memoirs since they are works composed by adults about the past. The memoirs of urban writers differ radically from those of rural writers, and memoirs of middle-class childhoods are very different from the writings of authors who grew up in tenement buildings.

However, indoor games do appear in works of fiction from the nineteenth century. Particularly interesting is the work of Louisa May Alcott, best known for LITTLE WOMEN, published in 1868. Alcott described spontaneous indoor games in exhaustive detail, especially in her 1871 *Little Men* and her 1880 *Jack and Jill*. Like the authors of play manuals, Alcott emphasized the virtues of wholesome activities, such as crafts and cooking, but also mentioned commercially made toys such as dolls, building blocks, and miniature cooking stoves.

Studies of Games

By the end of the nineteenth century, children's play, especially games, were considered to be of such paramount importance to early development and growth that they warranted closer examination. Several major studies of children's play preferences are part of the historical discourse on toys and games. These studies collected data about toys and games in general, not about indoor games in particular.

In the earliest of these surveys, which was published in *The Pedagogical Seminary* in 1896, social scientist T. R. Cros-well sampled about 2,000 children in Worcester, Massachusetts, public schools. This extraordinarily detailed study asked questions differentiating between different types of amusements, which he classified according to their perceived functions. The resulting favorites, for both boys and girls, were predominantly outdoor games, with a few, such as dolls and doll carriages, that could be part of either indoor or outdoor play. In general, girls included more indoor games among their favorites than did boys, for whom physical activities were more important. In a 1991 article, cultural historian Bernard Mergen observed that the play of boys and girls, as evidenced by their choices of toys and games, was much more similar at the end of the twentieth century than in the previous century, and postulated that this change was due to the ubiquity of electronic media.

Indoor Spaces for Children

Nurseries became increasingly common throughout the nineteenth century as the middle class became an established part of the urban landscape. Separate spaces for children were made possible by the construction of larger houses, and by the removal of labor from the home to outside places of business. For upper-class families, entire suites of rooms, often with a bedroom for a live-in nanny, completely separated children from the everyday activities of adults. However, for both middle- and upper-class families, the nursery served the purpose of protecting children from what was considered the corrupt world of adults, as well as preparing them for later entry into the grown-up world.

By the end of the nineteenth century, most nurseries were filled with toys, probably both handmade and manufactured. Unfortunately, very few images exist of playthings within the context of children's rooms. Through the course of the twentieth century, separate rooms for children or spaces allocated for indoor play have become even more common for families from all social classes. However, the availability of space is still an issue for poor and working-class families, especially in cities.

Indoor Games as Family Entertainment

Certain indoor games were popular as amusements for the family as a whole. With the advent of gas lighting (among other factors), evening entertainments became more common. In 1992, Shirley Wajda observed in her essay on the stereoscope that Victorians in particular were dedicated to educational games designed for self-improvement. Parlor toys included magic lanterns (precursor to the modern slide projector) and lantern slides, as well as the stereoscope and stereographs. Board games, card games, and jigsaw puzzles also fall under the heading of family entertainment and had the same goal.

Table games are still primarily educational in focus at the beginning of the twenty-first century. Classic games like Monopoly, invented in 1935 by Charles Darrow, also reflect contemporary values and interests, affording families the opportunity to play together on several levels.

Electronic Games and Indoor Games as Commercial Enterprises

At the start of the twenty-first century, computer and video games are among the most popular pastimes for children and adults. According to most sources, the first computer game (Spacewar!) was invented in 1962 by Steve Russell; the first game played on a television screen was invented in 1967 by Ralph Baer; and the first arcade game (Computer Space) was invented in 1971 by Nolan Bushnell and Ted Dabney. Since the 1970s, electronic games have become increasingly popular. In 2001, the Interactive Digital Software Association reported sales of computer and video games amounting to nearly 6 billion dollars, not including educational software.

Parents and professionals have expressed a number of concerns related to electronic games. The violence depicted in games is a popular subject for research, due partly to several prominent cases linking computer games to crimes committed by children. To date, however, no substantial evidence has been found to support this theory. Another early concern was that the solitary nature of electronic games would somehow impair the development of social skills in children by limiting recreational activities with peers. While computer and video games are, by definition, indoor games, smaller handheld gaming consoles (such as GameBoy) were designed to be taken outside of the home.

While the market for computer games is primarily geared toward older children and adults, other businesses have turned their attentions to activities for smaller children. An interesting contemporary development is the creation of indoor play spaces for children within commercial enterprises. Several American entrepreneurs have created businesses for the indoor entertainment of young people in particular. Gymboree, for example, which also sells children's clothing, was one of the first companies to market music and physical activity classes for small children. Other businesses simply maintain an indoor play space, usually complete with climbing equipment and other recreational devices. Both are in the business of stimulating the child's development, either physically or mentally. Often, play equipment is elaborate enough, and the spaces large enough, that they serve as a simulation of the outdoors.

Collections of Indoor Games

Most major collections of toys are primarily repositories of indoor games. Collections of toys and games can be found at museums and historical societies around the world. Of particular interest in the United States are the Strong Museum in Rochester, New York, and the New-York Historical Society in New York City. The New-York Historical Society recently acquired the Arthur and Ellen Liman collection of games, which represents the largest publicly held group of American commercially manufactured board and table games. Other prominent museums include the Bethnal Green Museum of Childhood and Pollock's Toy Museum in London, England.

See also: **Children's Spaces; Street Games; Theories of Play.**

BIBLIOGRAPHY

Goodfellow, Caroline. 1991. *A Collector's Guide to Games and Puzzles.* Secaucus, NJ: Chartwell Books.

Mergen, Bernard. 1991. "Ninety-Five Years of Historical Change in the Game Preferences of American Children." *Play and Culture* 4: 272–283.

Mergen, Bernard. 1992. "Children's Play in American Autobiographies." In *Hard at Play: Leisure in America, 1840–1940,* ed. Kathryn Grover. Rochester, NY: Strong Museum.

Page, Linda Garland, and Hilton Smith, eds. 1993. *The Foxfire Book of Appalachian Toys and Games.* Chapel Hill: University of North Carolina Press.

Tibaldeo, Alessandro Franzini. 1991. *Guida ai Musei di Giocattoli d'Europa.* Milan: Odos Editions.

Wajda, Shirley. 1992. "A Room with a Viewer: The Parlor Stereoscope, Comic Stereographs, and the Psychic Role of Play in Victorian America." In *Hard at Play: Leisure in America, 1840–1940,* ed. Kathryn Grover. Rochester, NY: Strong Museum.

West, Elliott, and Paula Petrik, eds. 1992. *Small Worlds: Children and Adolescents in America, 1850–1950.* Lawrence: University Press of Kansas.

White, Colin. 1984. *The World of the Nursery.* New York: Dutton.

SHIRA SILVERMAN

Industrial Education.
See Vocational Education, Industrial Education, and Trade Schools.

Industrial Homework

Industrial homework refers to production of manufactured goods in private residences. The common arrangement is for factories to contract labor-intensive portions of their production out to networks of ethnically homogeneous families who live in a nearby neighborhood. Historically, industrial homework has been common in textiles, garment and needle work, cigar-making, and hand-made craft goods. Today, industrial homework remains common in all these sectors as well as more modern sectors such as consumer electronics. Similar homework arrangements are common in commercial agriculture involving pre-processing activities like stripping, shelling, and hulling. The employer saves money on space and utilities and assures cost-effective production by paying on a piece-rate. The more the household produces, the more it makes. Contracts between factories and households are often brokered by labor-agents who organize the networks of neighborhood production.

Industrial homework is infamous as a haven for CHILD LABOR. Wedded to preindustrial traditions where all able-bodied members of the household produced for the household's succor, and released from modern factory legislation providing for minimum working conditions, including minimum age requirements, children are an integral part of the industrial home workforce. Once industrial production leaves the factory, monitoring conditions of production becomes difficult. Once it enters the home, any remaining barriers to child labor are overcome.

Industrial homework is closely related to the "putting out" systems that have been associated with the "proto-industrial" phase of the Industrial Revolution. Originally, merchants contracted for production of goods with private households. Later, they organized "manufactories" where production could be organized under one roof, but where production technologies continued to use the traditional hand-craft methods. In colonial New England many of the first schools were "spinning schools" that taught farm girls the industrial arts of spinning and weaving so they could earn cash in the cottage industry network. As work gradually shifted to the factories, industrial homework remained an option for many employers whose product could be easily transported back and forth. It also remained an option to supplement the family income, especially among those who could not get out to work. Homeworkers invariably endured the lowest wages and the most irregular work—long hours during the busy season, no money during the slack season—of all workers in the commodity chain.

As child labor law and reform efforts emerge, the factories are the first to surrender their child workers. But eliminating children from the factories is no assurance that child labor has been eliminated in those industries where homework is prevalent. Often child labor is merely displaced from the factories back into the home production networks. Before RugMark—the global consumer labeling program in hand-woven carpeting, in which the International Labor Organization estimated over half-a-million children under fourteen were engaged—children were brought to the loom-sheds, the primitive "manufactories" of the industry. After RugMark, while consumers could be fairly well assured that labeled rugs were not made by children, many looms moved back to the children, in home-based worksites.

Because of the difficulties in regulating industrial homework, many in America's child labor reform movement concluded that to eliminate child labor from homework, homework itself must be abolished. But homework has never been effectively abolished, so regulation remains necessary. Industrial homework is the first and last refuge of child labor.

See also: **Economics and Children in Western Societies; European Industrialization; Work and Poverty.**

BIBLIOGRAPHY

Felt, Jeremy P. 1965. *Hostages of Fortune: Child Labor Reform in New York State.* Syracuse University Press.

Hall, George A. 1911. *What the Government Says About Child Labor in Tenements.* New York: National Child Labor Committee.

Hindman, Hugh D. 2002. *Child Labor: An American History.* Armonk, NY: M.E. Sharpe.

Howard, Alan. 1997. "Labor, History, and Sweatshops in the New Global Economy" In *No Sweat: Fashion, Free Trade, and the Rights of Garment Workers,* ed. Andrew Ross. New York: Verso.

Riis, Jacob A. 1890. *How the Other Half Lives: Studies Among the Tenements of New York.* New York: Scribner's.

UNICEF. 1997. *The State of the World's Children: Focus on Child Labour.* London: Oxford University Press.

U.S. Children's Bureau. 1938. *Prohibition of Industrial Homework in Selected Industries under the National Recovery Administration.* Washington, DC: Government Printing Office.

Van Kleeck, Mary. 1910. "Child Labor in Home Industries." *Annals of the American Academy of Political and Social Science* (July suppl.): 145–149.

HUGH D. HINDMAN

Infancy of Louis XIII

The infancy of Louis XIII of France is well documented, primarily in the detailed journal that his physician Jean Héroard kept from the dauphin's birth on September 27, 1601, until 1628. The royal infant did not grow up in daily contact with his parents, Henry IV and Marie de' Medici. Louis lived at Château Saint-Germain outside Paris, where he and the legitimate and bastard children of the king had their own little court. The main character in the upbringing of the infant was his governess, Françoise de Longuejoue, baroness of Montglat, whom the dauphin designated "Maman Ga."

Louis was a vigorous and temperamental child with a capacity for rapid learning. From infancy he was able to act in accordance with the *courtois* code of courtesy. At sixteen months old the dauphin began to hold his own *lever* ritual when rising in the morning, and within a short time the child also received princes, ambassadors, and noblemen in audience, performing the required gestures and phrases with proper politeness. The infant was fond of music and dance. He played the lute and the fiddle, among other instruments, and he danced all sorts of dances. To strengthen his morals he was taught from the influential collection of etiquette and morality *Les Quatrains,* by Guy du Faur, seigneur de Pibrac. When the dauphin lost his temper he was punished, mostly whipped. The dauphin's demonstrative playing with his genitals was much laughed about at the court at Château Saint-Germain and courtiers did not hesitate to joke about sexual matters when Louis was present.

When Louis was about seven years old he was drawn into a more adult and masculine sphere. In June 1608 he shed his child's skirt and began to wear the adult male costume, and in January of the following year he moved to the Louvre palace in Paris. A governor, Marquis Gilles Souvré, replaced "Maman Ga." Louis's intellectual education was now more systematic than before, and he was taught the noble arts of riding, shooting, and hunting. Simultaneously the indiscreet sex jokes ceased. When Henry IV was murdered on May 14, 1610, Louis, then eight years old, became king of France with his mother Queen Marie as guardian regent.

The American historian Elizabeth Wirth Marvick has seen Louis's early life experience as disastrous for his personal development: it left him, so she has claimed, at the Freudian anal stage. Taking the opposite point of view, Madeleine Foisil, the editor of Héroard's journal, sees Louis's early childhood as a happy experience in a supportive environment. Devoted letters written by the adult king to "Maman Ga" tend to support the latter interpretation. Heroard's journal has been used as a major source by PHILIPPE ARIÈS to support his argument that the idea of childhood is a modern-day novelty. The infancy of Louis XIII shows how noble infants in the early seventeenth century took part in adults' occupations and how sexual topics were not taboo for children.

See also: **Aristocratic Education in Europe; Early Modern Europe; Masturbation; Sexuality; Theories of Childhood.**

BIBLIOGRAPHY

Ariès, Philippe. 1962. *Centuries of Childhood: A Social History of Family Life.* Trans. Robert Baldick. New York: Knopf.

Foisil, Madeleine, ed. 1989. *Journal de Jean Héroard*, I–II. Paris: Fayard.

Marvick, Elizabeth Wirth. 1986. *Louis XIII: The Making of a King.* New Haven, CT: Yale University Press.

THOMAS LYNGBY

Infant Feeding

Feeding newborn babies is a fairly straightforward process, at least for the majority of mothers who are healthy and have adequate milk to nourish their young. Mothers worldwide have always breast-fed their babies. This has been considered the safest, easiest, healthiest, and least expensive means to ensure an infant's survival. Studies today show that breast milk contains certain antibodies, nutrient proteins, lipids, vitamins, and minerals to help a baby ward off various diseases, infections, and allergies. Until physicians and medical advisors began to investigate the subject and write about it, women carried on as tradition dictated, breast-feeding their infants by instinct to meet their babies' nutritional needs.

Early American Feeding Practices

Most mothers in the North American colonies breast-fed their infants. Details of these breast-feeding practices are scarce, however, since many women could not read or write, had little free time, or felt too constrained by the intimacy of breast-feeding to write about it. Using a wet nurse never became common practice among North American settlers as it had been among the European elite, due to different life styles, the frontier character of colonial settlement, and the paucity of wet nurses. Mothers intuitively understood that breast-fed babies had the best chance of surviving childhood. They also noted that breast-feeding helped to delay conception, providing a natural, even if not a completely reliable, means to space their children.

Of course, not all babies could be breast-fed by their mothers. Some women did not have enough milk or were too sickly or exhausted to feed their infants. A woman with swollen, impacted, or infected breasts found it too painful to have a baby suckle. If a mother died during childbirth, which happened far more often than it does today, a source of milk had to be found. A family might turn to a female neighbor, friend, or relative who was feeding her own baby or they might hire a wet nurse. Families also advertised in newspapers, stipulating the desired qualifications. Wet nurses were usually nursing their own or another baby or had just weaned their child. Many myths developed about nursing a baby. In cases where a baby needed a wet nurse, medical advisors warned parents that the type of woman hired to feed a baby was critical. For instance, parents were urged to avoid a wet nurse with red hair, for this apparently implied a volatile temperament that could affect the woman's milk.

In the antebellum South, elite women might use a slave woman to feed their babies, though this custom was less common than myth has led us to believe. When they did so, southern white mothers rarely expressed concern about a black woman feeding their infants, even though racial sensitivities affected other areas of southern life. In a few cases, white women fed slave babies when the slave mother had died or was unable to breast-feed her own newborn. The most important issue was to keep a baby alive. Slave mothers took their own babies to the field where they would hang them from a tree or lay them on the ground and breast-feed them as needed. Babies living on large plantations were often left in the care of an older slave woman, and mothers would rush back to the slave cabins to feed their infants.

Artificial feeding was always an option, usually a pragmatic response when other possibilities failed. If no woman was available to breast-feed, the baby was hand fed with what historians call artificial food. This often consisted of softened bread soaked in water or milk and fed from what was called a pap boat or pap spoon. Mothers fed their babies cow's or goat's milk, various teas, or clear soups from a suckling bottle or nursing can made of glass, tin, pewter, or other metal. They sometimes masticated table food in their mouths or mashed or strained adult foods for the babies—anything to feed hungry infants.

A few mothers made a conscious decision not to breast-feed their babies or nursed their infants for only a brief period of time, despite society's encouragement to breast-feed. Some women found it impossible to feed a baby and also help run the family business or work in the fields. Vanity influenced a handful of wealthy mothers who did not want to bother with the demands of nursing and who were eager to resume their social life. Husbands may have influenced the decision not to breast-feed since many people believed that it was inadvisable for a nursing mother to resume sexual relations. Hiring a wet nurse or hand feeding the baby were options in these cases.

By the mid- to late-nineteenth century, doctors became increasingly involved in obstetrics and infant care. Medical practitioners and advisors discussed numerous issues related to child rearing. They urged women to breast-feed their young, recognizing it to be the best way to keep a baby alive. One of the infant diseases that most concerned doctors and parents was cholera infantum, a severe form of diarrhea that affected especially those babies who were hand fed or who were being weaned from breast milk to artificial foods. Breast-feeding also fit the period's image of women and their central role as mothers. What made a better statement about a woman's commitment to her maternal duties than breast-feeding?

An issue that fostered debate among physicians and new mothers was whether to feed a newborn right after birth. The appearance of colostrum from a mother's breast fostered some uneasiness. To an observer, this watery liquid did not seem to provide adequate sustenance to ensure a newborn's survival. Lacking the scientific evidence we have today, people did not know that colostrum contains antibacterial ingredients and nutrients perfectly suited to protect a baby against certain diseases and infection. But wary mothers who could afford to do so might find another woman to feed their newborns temporarily until their breast milk flowed. Gradually, mothers and doctors began to accept the healthy aspects of colostrum.

Another concern was the proper age for weaning a baby off breast milk. As records reveal, up through the nineteenth century, many families had children spaced about two years apart, suggesting that the normal length for breast-feeding was about a year. Women often ceased breast-feeding when a baby's teeth came in, and nursing became uncomfortable. Mothers also stopped breast-feeding if they became pregnant, for they felt it could harm both the fetus and the infant to be simultaneously drawing vital sources from the mother. The timing of weaning also depended on the season of the year; the safest time was felt to be fall or spring in order to avoid the extreme temperatures of summer and winter. The process of weaning a baby from breast milk could be traumatic for both mother and baby. Mothers developed various strategies. Some covered their nipples and breasts with a nasty-tasting salve. Others left home for a few days, leaving the child in the hands of someone who hand fed it. Some sent the baby to a neighbor or nurse until the infant had become accustomed to artificial food and substitute liquids.

By the late nineteenth and early twentieth centuries, with the nation's increasing interest in children's health and well-being, doctors grew alarmed at the startlingly high INFANT MORTALITY rates in the United States, especially among the urban poor. A 1911 study of Boston showed that one in five infants who were bottle-fed died before they were a year old compared to only one in thirty babies who were breast-fed. Despite advances in scientific thinking related to infant feeding, especially knowledge about bacteria and pasteurization, doctors and social reformers still had to work hard to reduce high infant mortality. Urban health departments took a lead in establishing milk stations where poor mothers could obtain fresh, clean milk for their young. Cities passed laws requiring the inspection of dairies that delivered milk for urban consumption. In 1910 New York City passed a law stating that milk sold or distributed there had to be pasteurized; in 1912 it imposed a grading system on milk. Health departments sent agents to neighborhoods to advise mothers on proper infant care. Some communities set up milk banks where women could contribute their excess breast milk, which was then dispensed through a directory to needy infants. This system still exists through the Human Milk Banking Association of North America.

Advances in Artificial Baby Foods

Significant changes took place by the early twentieth century as more mothers began to depend less on breast-feeding and more on artificial foods and a modified form of cow's milk or infant formula. The reasons for this change are numerous, though historians debate the importance of each. For one thing, companies like Nestlé in Switzerland and Mellin's and Gerber's in the United States found safe, effective methods to process baby food. Companies hired chemists to develop baby formulas that would replicate mother's milk as closely as possible. Baby food producers eventually created and sold dozens of strained food and cereal products. They pitched their products to doctors and advertised widely in magazines.

Artificial baby foods and milk products became safer and more healthful. With an understanding of bacteria and sepsis, there was more emphasis on the need for sanitary bottles and pasteurized liquids, so infants would be less likely to get sick from artificial foods and unclean bottles. The development of rubber bottle nipples replicated the feel of mothers' breasts and made it easier to hand feed. As more women began to enter the paid work force, they welcomed the freedom and flexibility offered by artificial feeding. Further aiding the acceptance of artificial feeding was the development by baby food companies of pre-mixed, prepared formulas, soy milk products, and disposable bottles.

By the 1950s a majority of women in the United States no longer breast-fed their babies, a dramatic shift from past practice. A number of factors explain this change: the importance of PEDIATRICS as a medical specialty, the ready availability of manufactured formula and infant food, sanitary bottles, an increase in hospital rather than home births, the changing role of women as more moved into the public sphere and wage work, and the close relationship between food manufacturers and doctors. Baby food companies convinced doctors that babies would be healthy if artificially fed. By 1971 only 25 percent of mothers in the United States breast-fed their babies, and only 20 percent of those did so for more than six months.

However, change occurred again in the 1980s, and by 1990, 52 percent of mothers in the United States breast-fed their infants. Even as feminists encouraged women to pursue higher education and jobs outside the home to achieve self-fulfillment, they also encouraged maternal breast-feeding as a natural, healthful approach that was best for both mother and baby. Breast-feeding, they insisted, fostered bonding between mother and infant. Also, the LA LECHE LEAGUE, organized in 1956 by a group of Christian women, played a major role in raising awareness of the benefits of breast-feeding. Today, almost a third of mothers who breast-feed do so until their baby is six months old, paralleling a recommendation by the American Academy of Pediatrics that mothers should breast-feed their babies exclusively for six months, avoiding any supplemental liquids or food.

At the start of the twenty-first century, the number of mothers of all races and classes in the wage work force has created new challenges for those who feel that breast-feeding is best for babies. Almost 70 percent of mothers breast-feed their babies, at least for a month or two. Some companies and institutions have set up on-site day care centers and nurseries, giving mothers who work there the opportunity to breast-feed their infants. Most companies, however, leave it up to new mothers to handle childcare on their own. Mothers have found some flexibility by using a breast pump to produce maternal milk that their baby can drink when they are apart. But not all women do this. Other working mothers cut short breast-feeding and turn to artificial feeding or never start nursing in the first place.

Discussion about this important maternal duty continues. Physicians and mothers debate the advisability of feeding an infant on demand and at what age other foods should be introduced into the baby's diet. The suitability of breast-feeding in public fosters discussion, some of it heated. No matter what the debates, the majority of women will continue to ensure the good health of their newborns, through sensible, healthful sustenance, whether that means breast-feeding or giving the baby artificial foods.

See also: **Wet-Nursing.**

BIBLIOGRAPHY

Apple, Rima D. 1986. "'Advertised by Our Loving Friends': The Infant Formula Industry and the Creation of New Pharmaceutical Markets, 1870–1910." *Journal of the History of Medicine and Allied Sciences* 41: 3–23.

Arnold, Lois, and Miriam Erickson. 1988. "The Early History of Milk Banking in the U.S.A." *Journal of Human Lactation* 4: 112–113.

Barnes, Lewis A. 1987. "History of Infant Feeding Practices." *American Journal of Clinical Nutrition* 46: 168–170.

Blum, Linda. 1993. "Mothers, Babies, and Breastfeeding in Late Capitalist America." *Feminist Studies* 19: 291–311.

Cone, Thomas E. 1976. *200 Years of Feeding Infants in America.* Columbus, OH: Ross Laboratories.

Golden, Janet. 1996. *A Social History of Wet Nursing in America: From Breast to Bottle.* Cambridge, UK: Cambridge University Press.

Klein, Herbert S., and Stanley L. Engerman. 1978. "Fertility Differentials between Slaves in the United States and the British West Indies: A Note on Lactation Practices and Their Possible Implications." *William and Mary Quarterly* 35: 357–374.

McMillen, Sally G. 1990. *Motherhood in the Old South: Pregnancy, Childbirth, and Infant Rearing.* Baton Rouge: Louisiana State University Press.

Meckel, Richard A. 1990. *"Save the Babies": American Public Health Reform and the Prevention of Infant Mortality, 1850–1929.* Baltimore, MD: Johns Hopkins University Press.

Salmon, Marylynn. 1994. "The Cultural Significance of Breastfeeding and Infant Care in Early Modern England and America." *Journal of Social History* 28: 247–269.

Weiner, Lynn Y. 1994. "Reconstructing Motherhood: The La Leche League in Postwar America." *Journal of American History* 80: 1357–1381.

Young, James Harvey. 1979. "'Even to a Sucking Infant': Nostrums and Children." *Transactions and Studies of the College of Physicians of Philadelphia* 1: 5–32.

SALLY G. MCMILLEN

Infanticide. *See* Abandonment; Foundlings.

Infant Mortality

Of all the ways in which childhood has changed since premodern times, perhaps the most significant has been the dramatic decrease in the likelihood of dying during the first year of life. Although we can only estimate levels and trends of infant mortality prior to the most recent centuries, it seems probable that through much of human history 30 to 40 percent of all infants born died before they could celebrate their first birthdays. Today, in even the most underdeveloped and high-mortality regions of the world, barely a tenth do. And in the most developed and wealthiest regions less than 1 percent of infants fail to survive their first year. The vast majority of this sharp reduction in infant mortality took place in the twentieth century. Among today's highly developed nations, the major improvement in infant survival came prior to World War II. In the less developed nations, almost all the improvement has come since the war. In both sets of nations, mortality first dropped among older infants and then only later, if at all, among newborns.

Measuring Infant Mortality

The term infant mortality is generally understood to refer to the incidence of death among infants less than one year of age. When demographers attempt to chart the levels and trends of that mortality, they employ a number of statistics, most notably infant, neonatal, and post-neonatal mortality rates. These are standardized measures unaffected by differences in the proportion of infants in a given population. The infant mortality rate is the annual number of deaths among infants less than one year old per thousand live births. This measure is similar but not identical to what is called the infant death rate, which is the ratio of infant deaths to infants living and is somewhat higher. The neonatal mortality rate is calculated as the annual number of deaths of infants less than twenty-eight days old per hundred thousand live births. It is generally accepted that most of the deaths during this period are from *endogenous* causes; that is from congenital anomalies, gestational immaturity, birth complications, or other physiological problems. The post-neonatal mortality rate is computed similarly but describes the death rate of infants twenty-eight days to one year. In much of the world, the vast majority of deaths during this period continue to be from *exogenous* causes; that is, from injuries and from environmental and nutritional factors, especially as they interact with infectious disease like gastroenteritis and pneumonia. In the more highly developed nations, however, control of infectious disease and nutritional disorders has reached such a level that an ever-increasing proportion of post-neonatal deaths are attributable to *endogenous* causes.

Infant Mortality in the Developed Nations before the Twentieth Century

What we know about the historical mortality patterns of today's highly developed nations suggests that through the seventeenth century infant mortality averaged between 20 and 40 percent and fluctuated substantially from year to year, occasionally hitting extremely high peaks when EPIDEMICS, famines, and war created mortality crises for the general population. Highly dependent on levels of maternal nutrition and general health as well as on the local sanitary and disease environments, infant mortality also varied significantly from place to place. In isolated rural villages in seventeenth-century England and New England, as few as 15 percent of all infants born may have perished in their first year. At the same time, their counterparts born in seaports, where sanitation was poor and where there was commerce in people, goods, and infectious diseases, probably died at over twice that rate. In the Americas and in southern Europe the presence of malaria could push infant mortality to over 50 percent. So too could the introduction of new diseases. Following the arrival of Europeans and then Africans in the New World, the aboriginal populations of the Americas were decimated by exposure to diseases to which they had no acquired or inherited immunities. In short, nothing so characterized levels of infant mortality in the premodern era as their variability across time and place.

Some historians have theorized that parents in the premodern era did not bond with their young children until the children had passed the dangerous early years of life, yet this sixteenth-century woodcut, *Death Taking a Child,* by Hans Lutzelburger after Hans Holbein the Younger, clearly shows the anguish on the parents' faces as their child is taken away. Private collection/Bridgeman Art Library.

That variability continued into the early eighteenth century, when the yearly fluctuations began to decrease, the periodic peaks became less frequent, and the differences between localities diminished. In a few places, a slight secular downward trend took place, but for the most part the period saw the stabilization rather than the lowering of infant mortality. Contributing to the homogenization and stabilization of infant mortality rates were the concomitants of economic development. Improvements in transportation made travel to rural villages less difficult and time consuming, increasing the communication of diseases from place to place and thus decreasing the likelihood that isolated pockets of low infant mortality could exist. Better urban sanitation, improvements in housing, and the more even distribution of foodstuffs, the filling and draining of swamps, and, perhaps, a world-wide southward retreat of malaria all helped make it less true for infants that being born in certain years and certain places constituted a death threat that would be enacted within a year's time. Of course, variability by time and place did not disappear; it only decreased. Seaports and cities were still

TABLE 1

Probability of dying before age one in the developed world, c. 1900, selected nations

Location	Period	Probability of Death before Age 1[a] (percent)
Australia	1890–1900	11.0
Austria	1900–1901	23.0
Belgium	1900	19.5
Czechoslovakia	1899–1902	22.9
Denmark	1895–1900	13.4
England and Wales	1891–1900	15.6
France	1898–1903	17.2
Germany	1891–1900	21.7
Italy	1900–1902	16.7
Netherlands	1901	11.6
Norway	1891–1900	9.6
Russia (European)	1896–1897	27.7
Sweden	1898–1902	10.7
United States	1900–1902	12.4

[a]Based on published life table values.

SOURCE: Preston and Haines 1991, table 2.3.

more inimical to infant life than the countryside. And epidemics of smallpox, yellow fever, and other infectious diseases could still produce spikes of infant and general mortality. Additionally, considerable evidence exists that cultural differences in child rearing—particularly infant feeding practices—may have contributed significantly to higher rates in some areas than others.

The trend toward stabilization and conformity continued until the effects of early industrialization and urbanization began to be felt in the mid- to late eighteenth century. Industrialization brought increased wealth and higher living standards, but it also created industrial towns and massive cities which contained a significant underclass whose health was compromised by the social and biological pathologies that attend grinding poverty and filthy, overcrowded, disease-infested urban slums. For infants, it seems that initially the positive consequences of industrialization outweighed the negative ones. Although the evidence is not abundant, it is probable that infant survival improved in England through the third quarter of the eighteenth century and in western Europe and the United States during the forty years following 1790. It is also probable that by the middle of the nineteenth century, infant mortality rates were rising again as urbanization, industrialization, and the migration of workers and their families worsened sanitation and environmental pollution, made infant care more difficult, and increased the likelihood that pregnant women and infants would be exposed to dangerous diseases or toxins.

Indeed, late-nineteenth-century cities and industrial towns were deadly locales for infants, where 20 to 35 percent

of all those born died within twelve months and where summer epidemics of gastroenteritis and diarrhea turned densely packed neighborhoods into infant abattoirs. As the *New York Times* editorialized in 1876 after one particularly deadly July week in which over a hundred infants a day had died in Manhattan: "There is no more depressing feature about our American cities than the annual slaughter of little children of which they are the scene" (quoted in Meckel, p. 11). Growing public concern throughout the industrialized West over this annual slaughter helped precipitate a public health movement to improve infant health and survival. Along with a complex amalgam of socioeconomic, environmental, and medical developments at the end of the nineteenth century, that movement started infant and child death rates on the path of decline that they would follow through the twentieth century and into the twenty-first.

The Twentieth-Century Decline of Infant Mortality in the Developed World

As the twentieth century opened, infant mortality throughout much of the industrialized world had begun to drop. Nevertheless infant survival was still precarious, especially in eastern Europe. As table 1 shows, the probability of dying in infancy ranged from less than 10 percent in Scandinavia to over 22 percent in Austria, Czechoslovakia, and European Russia. In the United States the rate was approximately 12 percent. By the middle of the twentieth century it had declined significantly. In North America, northern Europe, and Australia it was less than 3 percent. In western Europe it was less than 5 percent and in eastern and southern Europe less than 9 percent. Much of that decline came among postneonates, initially from a reduction in gastroenteric and diarrheal disorders and then from control of respiratory diseases.

Behind this reduction lay several developments. Prior to the 1930s, declining fertility and better nutrition and housing, accompanied by a rising standard of living, played important roles in reducing infant mortality. So too did environmental improvements brought about by the publicly funded construction of sanitary water supply and sewage systems and the implementation of effective refuse removal, particularly in urban areas. Also crucial was the work of public health officials and their allies in medicine and social work in controlling milk-borne diseases and educating the public in the basics of preventive and infant HYGIENE. Indeed, in the first three decades of the twentieth century, all the industrial nations of the world were the sites of major public health campaigns aimed at dramatically reducing infant mortality.

For many of the same reasons that it declined during the first third of the century, infant mortality continued to fall during the second. However, beginning in the 1930s the development and application of medical interventions and technologies played an increasingly large role in driving down infant death rates. Particularly important were the development, production, and dissemination of effective immunizations and drug therapies to combat the incidence and deadliness of infectious and parasitic diseases. Also important were significant improvements in both the techniques and technologies available to manage or correct life-threatening diseases or health problems. Among the most important of these were the perfection and widespread us of electrolyte and fluid therapy to counter the acidosis and dehydration that is often a consequence of serious bouts of diarrhea and enteritis; the increasingly sophisticated preventive and therapeutic use of vitamins to aid metabolism and combat nutritional diseases; and the development of increasingly safe and effective obstetric and surgical techniques to facilitate problem births and correct the consequences of congenital malformations.

In the last third of the twentieth century, the decline of mortality among older infants slowed to a snail's pace. Among neonates, however, it quickened precipitously, falling over 50 percent in some developed nations. Driving neonatal mortality down was an intense international effort to develop and make widely available various sociomedical programs and specific techniques and technologies to increase the survival rate of neonates, who deaths had come to constitute the bulk of infant mortality in the developed nations. That effort resulted in the perfection of diagnostic techniques and drugs that have proven effective in regulating pregnancy and preventing premature labor, and in the development of sophisticated surgical, therapeutic, and intensive care techniques and technologies to correct congenital deformities and to counter the risks faced by low birth-weight and premature babies. It also resulted in significant improvements in both the quality and availability of nutritional, prenatal, and natal care. As a consequence of a century of profound decline in infant mortality, babies born in the late twentieth century in developed nations enjoyed a probability of surviving their first year unimaginable through most of human history.

Twentieth-Century Infant Mortality in Less Developed Nations

As the second half of the twentieth century began, life expectancy in the less developed nations of the world was not much better than it had been for centuries, largely because infant mortality remained astronomical. Some areas, of course, were less inimical to infant life than others. In LATIN AMERICA less than 13 percent of all infants born died each year, while in Asia over 18 percent did. Worst off was AFRICA, particularly sub-Saharan Africa, where infant mortality ranged above 20 percent. Indeed, in some sub-Saharan countries, over a third of all children born perished before they reached five years of age.

Over the next half century, infant mortality dropped dramatically in all these regions, though at different times and rates. In Asia, particularly China, it dropped earliest and fastest, declining from over 19 percent at mid-century to around 4 percent three decades later. Infant mortality also dropped significantly and relatively quickly in Latin Ameri-

TABLE 2

Infant mortality by world region, 1950–2000

Region	Infant Mortality Rate (Deaths before age 1 per 1,000 births)		
	1950–1955[a]	1980–1985[a]	2000
World	156	78	54
Africa	192	112	87
Asia	181	82	51
Europe	62	15	11
Oceania	67	31	24
Northern America	29	11	7
Latin America and the Caribbean	125	63	32

[a] Probability of dying before age one.

SOURCE: *Mortality* 1988, table A.2; U.S. Census International Database 2000, <http:/www.census.gov/ipc/www/idbnew.html>.

ca, halving by the mid-1980s. Even Africa, which remains the continent most dangerous to infant life, ultimately achieved over a 50 percent decline in the infant death rate. Indeed, at eighty-seven infant deaths per thousand births, the 2000 African infant mortality rate is lower than that in the United States on the eve of World War I.

Contributing significantly to this drop in infant mortality during the second half of the century has been an international movement to improve child health and survival that has been led primarily by two organizations created in the aftermath of World War II: the United Nations Children's Fund (UNICEF) and the World Health Organization (WHO). Through the 1970s, this international effort involved both specific medical and public health interventions aimed at improving nutrition, controlling the incidence of malaria, increasing the availability of immunizations, and promoting in poorer countries the development of health care and public health systems emulating those of wealthier countries. While efforts to purify water supplies generally had positive effects, the overall results of the effort were mixed, and in the early 1980s UNICEF and WHO embarked on a new community-based child survival program which sought to increase immunization and educate community members about proper sanitation, prenatal hygiene, breast-feeding, and the use of a newly developed and simple oral rehydration salt formula for treating infants with acute diarrhea. In combination with continuing efforts to make clean water available, this community-based program seems to have had considerable success. Between the mid-1980s and 2000, infant mortality throughout the world dropped by approximately 30 percent.

Not all infants, of course, have benefited equally from this drop in infant mortality in the less-developed regions. There is considerable variation not only between regions but

TABLE 3

Highest and lowest national infant mortality rates, 2000

	Infant Mortality Rate (Deaths before age 1 per 1,000 births)
Nations with lowest infant mortality rates	
Singapore	3.8
Finland	3.8
Sweden	3.9
Japan	4.0
Switzerland	4.8
Nations with highest infant mortality rates	
Afghanistan	137.5
Malawi	130.5
Angola	125.9
Somalia	125.8
Guinea	123.7

SOURCE: Kaul 2002, table A6-4.

also between different nations in the same region. In sub-Saharan Africa, which each year accounts for over 40 percent of the world's deaths of children less than five, infant mortality in the year 2000 ranged from a low of 58.8 per thousand in Kenya to a high of 130.5 in Malawi. Similarly, in western Asia, Iran had an infant mortality rate of 28.1 while neighboring Afghanistan suffered a rate of 137.5, the highest in the world. Even in the Americas, tremendous variation still exists. Only a relatively narrow stretch of water separates Cuba from Haiti, but an immense gulf exists between their infant mortality rates. In 2000 Cuba had a rate of 7.7 while Haiti had one of 96.3.

As in the past, the causes of infant mortality remain numerous and many: the communicable childhood diseases, diarrheal diseases and gastroenteritis from poor sanitation, pneumonia and other respiratory diseases, an environment infested with the parasites that cause malaria and other debilitating diseases, and the triangle of poverty, malnutrition, and lack of medical supervision that adversely affects the health of pregnant women and leads to gestational problems. Unlike the past, however, relatively effective means of dealing with these causes now exist. The incidence and deadliness of many of the communicable infectious diseases can be controlled by immunization and the use of antibiotics; the incidence of diarrhea and gastritis by improved sanitation, clean water, and use of rehydration therapies; and the incidence of gestational complications by prenatal care programs. All these, however, require resources and the willingness to use them. So long as some countries remain wretchedly impoverished and have governments which cannot or will not apply national resources to saving infants, the modern transformation of infancy from a period characterized by nothing so much as precariousness to one in which survival is almost a certainty will remain incomplete.

See also: **Contagious Diseases; Fertility Rates; Obstetrics and Midwifery.**

BIBLIOGRAPHY

Bideau, Alain, Bertrand Desjardins, and Hector Perez Brignoli, eds. 1997. *Infant and Child Mortality in the Past.* Oxford, UK: Clarendon Press.

Colletta, Nat J., Jayshree Balachander, and Xiaoyan Liang. 1996. *The Condition of Young Children in Sub-Saharan Africa: The Convergence of Health, Nutrition, and Early Education.* Washington, DC: World Bank.

Corsini, Carlo A., and Pier Paolo Viazzo, eds. 1997. *The Decline of Infant and Child Mortality: The European Experience, 1970–1990.* The Hague, the Netherlands: Martinus Nijhoff.

Crosby, Alfred W. 1991. "Infectious Disease and the Demography of the Atlantic Peoples." *Journal of World History* 2: 119–133.

El-Khorazaty, M. Nabil. 1989. *Infant and Childhood Mortality in Western Asia.* Baghdad, Iraq: United Nations Economic and Social Commission for Western Asia.

Kaul, Chandrika. 2002. *Statistical Handbook on the World's Children.* Westport, CT: Oryx Press.

Kunitz, Stephen J. 1984. "Mortality Change in America, 1620–1920." *Human Biology* 56: 559–582.

Livi-Bacci, Massimo. 2001. *A Concise History of World Population,* 3rd ed. Malden, MA: Blackwell.

Meckel, Richard A. 1990. *Save the Babies: American Public Health Reform and the Prevention of Infant Mortality.* Baltimore, MD: Johns Hopkins University Press.

Mortality of Children under Age 5: World Estimates and Projections, 1950–2025. 1988. New York: United Nations.

Owen, Norman G., ed. 1987. *Death and Disease in Southeast Asia: Explorations in Social, Medical, and Demographic History.* New York: Oxford University Press.

Preston, Samuel, and Michael Haines. 1991. *Fatal Years: Child Mortality in Late Nineteenth-Century America.* Princeton, NJ: Princeton University Press.

Schofield, Roger, and David Reher. 1991. "The Decline of Mortality in Europe." In *The Decline of Mortality in Europe,* ed. Roger Schofield, David Reher, and Alain Bideau. New York: Oxford University Press.

Stockwell, Edward G. 1993. "Infant Mortality." In *The Cambridge World History of Human Disease,* ed. Kenneth F. Kiple. New York: Cambridge University Press.

UNICEF. 1997. *State of the World's Children.* New York: Oxford University Press.

van der Veen, Willen Jan. 2001. *The Small Epidemiologic Transition: On Infant Survival and Childhood Handicap in Low Mortality Countries.* Amsterdam: Rozenberg.

INTERNET RESOURCE

U.S. Census International Database. 2000. Available from <www.census.gov>.

RICHARD MECKEL

Infant Rulers

Infant rulers are infants formally exercising supreme power, political or spiritual. Infant rulers have appeared in many cultures and civilizations. Their role and influence can be very different according to religious, political and social traditions. Infant rulers commonly appear in stable, hereditary power structures with generally recognized political and legal principles, but can also be found in elective political or spiritual systems. Special procedures are connected with Tibetan Buddhism, where future lamas are found among male infants believed to be reincarnations of late predecessors. In medieval and modern Europe the term *infant ruler* normally describes a royal child recognized as the legitimate head of state. Very often the political power is transferred to a regency or a supreme council governing in the name of the infant. This does not mean that the royal infant is a puppet in the hands of powerful adults. Being the focus of all attention infant rulers often dominate their surroundings socially and psychologically.

In later centuries infant rulers have been rarer, probably as a consequence of a rising average life expectancy. In principle, infant rulers are still a possibility in hereditary constitutional monarchies, where the monarch's role is primarily of symbolic and representative character. An infant as elective head of a modern state, as a president for example, seems not to be a serious possibility within the existing political and social order.

The function of an infant ruler is normally to be the representative of continuity, the visible symbol of the state and to legitimate power. In early medieval Europe, where a combination of elective and hereditary principles were characteristic of most Germanic states, insurgent groups very often legitimated rebellions by making an infant member of the ruling family the symbol of their cause. Rebellious parties exploited the commonly accepted view that every member of the royal family had a right to the throne and the crown land, a perception associated with the idea of kinship.

A state with an infant ruler might be regarded as weak and could be put under pressure by internal and external enemies. The infant ruler and his advisors might be dependent upon support from influential individuals and groups. In the period from 1163 to 1164, the party behind the seven-year-old Norwegian King Magnus Erlingsson achieved the support of the Church by granting it huge privileges. Ecclesiastical support could be expressed in coronations and anointments of an infant ruler or infant heir to the throne. One example is the coronation of the seven-year-old Knut VI as King of Denmark in 1170. Such ceremonies demonstrated that the infant was under divine protection and rebellion thus an act of insurgence against God. On the other hand the coronation of the nineteen-year-old Christian IV (1577–1648) in 1596 marked the end of his infancy and the regency.

The education of infant rulers did not differ much from the tutoring of heirs to the throne or from the upbringing of princely and aristocratic children in general. It normally reflected dominant social and cultural ideas and values of the contemporary society. In medieval Europe military qualifications were essential. The moral and Christian values in the upbringing of royal infants are reflected in the chivalric literature and in educational treaties such as the Norwegian *Speculum Regale* (The mirror of the king) from the thirteenth century which deals with the deeds and qualities of a Christian prince illustrated by historical and biblical ideals combined with reflections concerning other matters, such as the duties of court servants, military tactics, and chivalrous behaviour. Furthermore, the *Speculum Regale* presents common knowledge concerning the earth, the sun and the planets, the climate and geography of the Northern hemisphere.

The Christian and chivalrous ideas laid down in the *Speculum Regale* were in principle the ideological basis of European monarchies until the eighteenth century, but from the sixteenth century onward they were supplemented by humanism. The reading of classical literature and philosophy was an integral part of the education of the children of Henry VIII of England, including the boy king Edward VI, and Gustavus Adolphus of Sweden, who succeeded to the throne at the age of sixteen.

In the case of Christian IV of Denmark, nominally king in 1588 at the age of eleven, the aristocratic government excluded the Queen Dowager from the regency and from any influence on the education of the boy king. The purpose undoubtedly was to ensure that the infant ruler was brought up in the national tradition of the Danish aristocracy and to prevent him from being influenced by absolutist ideas. Apart from this, the education followed directions laid down by his father in instructions for his tutors. In most respects, Christian IV's education represented a traditional combination of Christian, chivalrous, and humanistic ideas. The moral and ideological basis was the writings of DESIDERIUS ERASMUS OF ROTTERDAM and Martin Luther. Pedagogically his chief tutor was inspired by the ideas of Johan Sturm. According to Sturm's ideas, great importance was attached to developing his written style both in Danish and Latin. From November 1591 to May 1593, he wrote more than 190 Latin letters as exercises. More than three thousand handwritten letters in Danish and German show that he could express even complicated matters with clarity. Mathematical and technical skills also played an important role in his education and he received training in shipbuilding as well as the building of fortresses.

Military leadership was the foundation of monarchy. As a consequence, men normally inherited before females. In 1632, King Gustavus Adolphus of Sweden was killed in military action leaving his six-year-old daughter Christina as the only heir to the throne. It was therefore decided that she should be educated just like a male infant. This was the only way to overcome the prejudices in society concerning female inferiority. She was trained in classical and modern languages, politics, history, mathematics, philosophy, and theology. "God knows what delight it is to me that her Majesty is not like a female, but a courageous person with a supreme intellect" wrote the chancellor Axel Oxenstierna later.

While there were some differences in the upbringing of royal infants between Protestant and Catholic parts of Europe these should not be overestimated. In general the education of the Catholic Louis XIV of France was based on the same combination of military, chivalrous, Christian, and humanistic ideas as the training of the Lutheran Christian IV some sixty years earlier. The reading of classical authors and lessons in modern languages, drawing, music, politics and history as well as the training of technical and engineering skills were in both cases the foundation of the infant ruler's instruction.

The health of infant rulers was always under strict surveillance. The diaries of the physicians of Louis XIV give a vivid impression not only of the medical treatment of symptoms of disease but also of the medical and psychological interpretation of the way in which the infant ruler reacted.

As a field of research the subject infant rulers is still uncultivated land. While much literature deals with individual infant rulers such as Louis XIV of France or Queen Christina of Sweden, the starting point in most of these cases is the political or social consequences of the regency or attempts to explain the political and social behavior of the adult monarch from influences and impressions received in the childhood. Few attempts have been made to introduce modern behavioral and pedagogical theories into the study of the bringing-up of infant rulers. In most cases the conclusions are based on general reflections made by historians without special insight into psychological and pedagogical disciplines. Comparative studies with examples from societies with different cultural and social values might prove to be useful, but comparisons between Western and non-European societies require considerable insight in ethnological and anthropological sciences. A typical eurocentric perception can be found in Bernardo Bertolucci's epic film *The Last Emperor*. Bertolucci interprets the life of Henry Pu Yi (1906–1967), the child who became emperor of China at the age of three, in a Freudian context and stresses the negative consequences of his growing-up in the huge palaces of the Forbidden City in Beijing for the development of his personality. Henry Pu Yi's personal inabilities are seen as the fruits of a feudal system that would inevitably be overruled by social revolution. Bertolucci is not a historian, but his portrait of the Chinese infant ruler follows the main tendencies in Western historiography.

The study of infant rulers in non-European societies can be complicated because of the difficulties in interpreting the sources themselves and the conceptions they reflect. This could be illustrated by supposed Egyptian infant rulers such as Thutmosis III and Tutankhamen. In much twentieth cen-

tury historiography it was believed that the co-regency between Queen Hatshepsut and Thutmosis III might be explained in the light of the minority of Thutmosis. The infancy reign of Tutankhamen seems to be an assumption based on a combination of evidence. His mummy belongs to a young person, and it is known that he reigned for about ten years. Unfortunately, his exact age at the hour of death is uncertain. The statements vary from eighteen to twenty-seven.

The bulk of literature concerning infant rulers is related to specific individuals in a certain political and social context. As a result it is a field of study which lacks a firm concept of itself and still has to develop a theoretical and methodological framework to understand and explain the psychological and mental impact of the role on the ruler.

See also: **Aristocratic Education in Europe; Infancy of Louis XIII.**

BIBLIOGRAPHY

Duneton, Claude. 1985. *Petit Louis dit Quatorzième: L'Enfance de roi-soleil.* Paris: Éditions Seuil.

Foisil, Madeleine, ed. 1989. *Journal de Jean Héroard*, I–II. Paris: Fayard.

Marvick, Elizabeth Wirth. 1986. *Louis XIII: The Making of a King.* New Haven, CT: Yale University Press.

STEFFEN HEIBERG

Infant Schools. *See* Nursery Schools.

Infant Sexuality

A child's SEXUALITY is normally understood to mean the precursors and parallels to adult sexuality which are found in childhood, although right up to the present time it is disputed whether one may ascribe sexuality to children at all prior to PUBERTY, and the topic has only with difficulty been approached scientifically, since any systematic investigation collides with legislation protecting children against sexual abuse.

While there has been, throughout history, an extensive literature concerning sexual relations of adults toward children, accounts of the sexual inclinations and sexual activities of children themselves remained sporadic until the eighteenth and nineteenth centuries, when a number of child-rearing manuals warned against the danger of children masturbating. Educators thus conceived ingenious methods of surveillance so that all instances of MASTURBATION could be eliminated from the outset by, for instance, installing small bells to reveal nighttime hand movements. In 1879, the pediatrician S. Lindner noted that even finger sucking could be a sign of premature sexual maturation and lead to masturbation. Signs of sexuality in children were as a rule regarded as morbid deviations caused by hereditary disposition and bad influences.

Freud's Theory of Infant Sexuality

Scientific theorizing about childhood sexuality began with new observations in embryology. The fact that every human being has to pass through a bisexual stage on the way to monosexuality was used to explain cases of biological hermaphrodites as well as certain sexual "deviations," particularly HOMOSEXUALITY, which was thought to be caused by incomplete or defective sexual differentiation, with remaining traits of the opposite sex continuing to be at work. This way of thinking included a rudimentary theory that infancy was the period when sexual differentiation takes place but is not yet complete. Beginning around 1890, several scientists put forth ontogenetic as well as phylogenetic hypotheses, in which the child's sexuality was viewed as a transitional phase on the way to adult sexuality. Of these, SIGMUND FREUD's theory of infantile sexuality soon became dominant.

Freud called the child's sexuality polymorphously perverse because it has certain similarities to adult "perversion" (sadomasochism, voyeurism, exhibitionism, fetishism, and homosexuality). It is spread across a plurality of activities, does not have procreation as its purpose, and is tied to bodily zones other than just the genitals. The most important of these so-called erogenous zones associated with pleasurable stimuli are the mouth, anus, and genitals, and Freud assumed that these three orifices successively play a major erogenous role in sexual development.

The simple version of Freud's developmental theory thus contains three successive phases: first is an oral phase during the first two years of life, when the oral sensations of pleasure are dominant. When the mother breast-feeds the child, the child experiences oral pleasure and subsequently sucks his or her finger in order to recover this pleasure. The nature of the breast-feeding determines the kind as well as intensity of oral sexuality. Second is the anal phase, in the third and fourth year, when the pleasurable sensations of the intestinal zone dominate. Anal sexuality is primarily linked to the pleasurable excitation arising through defecation and rectal hygiene and secondarily linked to pleasure associated with playing with excrement. Third is the phallic (infantile genital) phase, during the fifth year, when the genitals become central, though they are still lacking any procreative function. During the so-called latency period, which lasts until puberty, sexuality is less apparent, as its immediate expression is repressed or sublimated. It has, however, been pointed out that no sexual latency period is found in cultures without a restrictive sexual upbringing.

According to Freud, infantile sexuality is from the outset predominantly autoerotic (masturbatory), after which it, in the course of development, is linked to various so-called partial objects. Around the age of three to four, it finds an object in the parent of the opposite sex. When the erotic lust of the child connects with a possessive drive, the oedipal complex begins and the child will normally encounter obstacles along with prohibitions and possibly punishment. The oedipal conflict is typically expressed as obstinacy, antisocial activity, and demandingness. Children at this stage develop a special ability to do precisely what their parents consider most revolting, embarrassing, and offensive. The conflict-ridden material is itself culturally determined but is always thought to have its basis within the psychosexual register. In Western culture, it is often linked to TOILET TRAINING, the proscription of masturbation, and sexual roles. According to psychoanalytic theory, the struggle to renounce polymorphous sexuality and accept one sexual identity or the other causes the child both anxiety and envy. Overcoming the oedipal conflict is assumed to have wide-ranging significance for the child's gradual compliance with family and social norms.

Later Discussions

Theorists both within and outside the psychoanalytic community have at times tended to downgrade pre-genital sexuality and instead focus on the presence of genital sexuality from the time of birth. If a child was found to have a special interest in the oral or anal area, this was regarded by, for instance, Wilhelm Reich and Karen Horney as defective development and not, as Freud saw it, a part of normal sexual development. Alfred Kinsey, also a critic of Freud, in his seminal publications on human sexual behaviors (1948 and 1953), provided a detailed description of the child's genitalsexual reactions. Although he was later criticized for using manifest pedophiles as his source, he seems to have demonstrated that the child is physiologically capable of sexual activity comparable to adult sexuality, including the erection of penis and clitoris and orgasm through rhythmic muscular contractions in the genitals.

This, however, did not bring the discussion to a close. Perhaps the most important of the psychoanalytic hypotheses regarding infant sexuality is that it has to be evoked through object contact in order to be expressed, as Jean Laplanche and his collaborators stressed. According to this view, the body may be compared to a photographic plate, which can be exposed in a multitude of ways. A child with no physical contact, no touching, and no intense object relations does not get to know his or her bodily pleasure potential. René Spitz, who in the 1930s and 1940s did research on children placed in institutions, found that the lack of physical contact led to inactivity and in the long term to illness, while children with good bodily contact were sexually curious and actively masturbated. Freud's original intuitive understanding of infant sexuality as requiring some sort of "seduction" in order to come into play thus seems to be confirmed.

Following the youth revolution of the 1960s, the 1970s saw a renewed interest in the child's pre-genital sexuality, which many regarded positively, as an alternative to the tyranny of genital sexuality. Some theories of sexual politics considered pre-genitality truly revolutionary. The discussion of the child's sexuality became more structured, and it was held that since children harbored obvious sexual potentials, they should also have the right to exercise these in some form or other, although how and with whom remained an open question.

Beginning in about 1980, a reaction emerged against these approaches to the emancipation of infant sexuality. It was claimed from many sides that sexual abuse in childhood was occurring on a hitherto unknown scale and that a great deal of mental suffering was caused by early sexual abuse. Alice Miller, among others, blamed psychoanalysis for having overlooked this, and an at times hysterical campaign was waged against scientists who insisted on the natural sexuality of the child. The sexual games of children came into focus once more, since they were seen as being linked to abuse, even when the age difference between the children was small. That the strongest arguments for the sexual rights of the child often came from pedophile associations did not help the credibility of the argument.

Social Implications of Infant Sexuality

It is in no way the case that an overtly negative stance against infant sexuality will prevent infant sexuality from existing. Sexualization often goes hand in hand with prohibition, as Michel Foucault pointed out. The function of the prohibition is to hem in and intensify sexuality, after which it may be formed in a socially acceptable manner by enhancing the character traits that receive priority within a given society. This becomes clearer when one looks at cross-cultural studies. Entire cultures have been classified according to the fixations embedded in their handling of the problems of child rearing, as Ruth Benedict, MARGARET MEAD, and ERIK H. ERIKSON have shown.

Infant sexuality is never found in a purely natural form but is always defined in relation to socialization. Sexuality is most clearly exposed in societies where sexual relations between children and adults or among children themselves are instituted as a norm. In ancient Greece, boys were sexually initiated by adult males. In many so-called primitive societies, children are encouraged to practice sexual games, and their sexual initiation often takes places with older children (see Bronislaw Malinowski's research on the Trobriand Islands during World War I), but it may also take place with adult men (as shown by Gilbert Herdt's research in New Guinea during the 1970s). When a restrictive sexual morality prevails, as it did in Europe from the time of Rousseau, the explicit interest in children—their formation, manners, and illnesses—constitute a source for understanding how they are formed, for better or worse, as sexual individuals.

Anthropologist William Stephens (1962) found a connection between the severity of the demand regarding the mother's sexual abstention following childbirth (postpartum sex taboo) and the sexual exposure of the child when she, as compensation, throws all her love at the child. Something similar must be assumed regarding the development of the bourgeois family through the 1800s, when mothers were locked with their children within the sphere of intimacy. This close relationship generates a sexuality of friction. When physical lust is blocked, the sexual tension will instead appear as a high-strung sensibility, as a sentimental binding to the mother and to the childhood universe, or as "nervousness," the most noted form of illness in the Victorian period. This is richly illustrated in literature and in contemporary educational instructions, pathographies, childhood memoirs, and so forth.

Sexual emancipation has, during the twentieth century, gradually shifted from adult culture to YOUTH CULTURE to child culture. The sexual emancipation of youth gathered momentum following the youth revolution of the 1960s, when premarital sex became the norm rather than the exception; in the final decade of twentieth century, genital sexuality is breaking through to the realm of childhood, which cannot be explained solely by the fact that puberty has, during the last century, been brought forward from the age of fourteen to twelve. As adult sexuality becomes increasingly more visible to the child, sexuality becomes an explicit theme from the age of eight, and the presence of pornography in the public domain has allowed it to enter the children's room also. Despite efforts by puritan parents, sexually provocative clothes, in-depth knowledge of sexual matters, and games involving sexual roles are all communicated to young children by older children, by the media, and by an industry that has helped to make children's culture a poor copy of adult culture. This is arguably a more massive problem than the approaches of pedophiles, which has usually been the focus of suspicion in cases of premature sexual maturation. This is of particular concern because there seems to be a connection between children assuming adult roles inappropriate for their age and a longer struggle after puberty to overcome infantile personality traits.

See also: **Child Abuse; Child Psychology; Incest; Pedophilia.**

BIBLIOGRAPHY

Andkjaer Olsen, Ole, and Simo Køppe. 1988. *Freud's Theory of Psychoanalysis.* Trans. Jean-Christian Delay and Carl Pedersen with the assistance of Patricia Knudsen. New York: New York University Press.

Constantine, Larry, and Floyd Martinson. 1981. *Children and Sex: New Findings, New Perspectives.* Boston: Little, Brown.

Erikson, Erik H. 1950. *Childhood and Society.* London: Penguin.

Freud, Sigmund. 1905. "Three Essays on the Theory of Sexuality." *Standard Edition*, Vol. 3. London: Hogarth.

Laplanche, Jean. 1985. *Life and Death in Psychoanalysis.* Trans. Jeffrey Mehlman. Baltimore, MD: Johns Hopkins Press.

Sulloway, Frank. 1979. *Freud: Biologist of the Mind.* New York: Basic Books.

OLE ANDKJAER OLSEN

Infant Toys

The proliferation of infant toys, now marketed for every stage of development from birth to twelve months, is a fairly recent phenomenon. Until the twentieth century, TOYS made specifically for the entertainment of infants (mainly in Western societies) consisted almost solely of rattles, often made of expensive materials such as coral or silver. Other artifacts from the seventeenth and eighteenth centuries, such as walking stools, are more indicative of prevailing philosophies of child rearing than those of PLAY. Other cultures took care of their babies in different ways. Many Native American tribes placed their children in wooden cradleboards, SWADDLING the baby tight. Cradleboards could then be carried on the back or propped up next to the mother while she worked, presenting the baby with a wide array of visual stimuli. Small toys could also be hung from the hoop of the cradleboard. Patterns of child rearing also shared certain common characteristics across cultures. For example, toys for babies (whether coral rattles or woven ornaments) often served the dual purpose of entertaining the infant while warding against disease or accident.

The renowned folklorist IONA OPIE and her son, Robert Opie, in their book *The Treasures of Childhood* (1995), attribute the elaboration of playthings and games over time to the attainment of culture, which is historically delineated by the invention of rules and structures. In general, toys play a very important role in the socialization of children, promoting the values and expectations of the prevailing culture. The infant, then, engaged in acquiring basic physical and mental skills, is at the very beginning of this process of acquiring culture through play.

People as Playthings

In reality, toys are only a small part of a baby's daily life up to the age of one year. For a newborn, the earliest source of stimulation is the mother or primary caregiver. Since the 1960s many books have been published on infant play, most consisting of suggestions for activities and games for parents and babies such as singing songs, making the baby laugh, offering a variety of objects for the baby to examine, and popular games such as peek-a-boo. While it can be assumed that parents have everywhere entertained and interacted with their babies in these and similar ways, such books reflect how modern theories of child development became mainstream in the course of the twentieth century.

Changing Definitions of Childhood

By the mid-nineteenth century, new definitions of childhood promoted notions of learning through play. Child-rearing manuals from the nineteenth and twentieth centuries may be the best evidence of these more modern theories of child development. It is also possible that advice books served the purpose of suggesting toys for infants as well as aiding parents to make similar playthings with similar goals for stimulating the very young child. Certainly parents have made toys for babies out of a variety of materials since time immemorial. However, few if any examples of this ancient history exist. In particular, handmade toys rarely survive childhood and almost never reach museum collections.

Educators

By the beginning of the twentieth century, psychologists and educators had established a set of precepts almost identical to today's notions of child development. In 1934, when the psychologist Ethel Kawin published *The Wise Choice of Toys*, children's projected abilities according to age were a primary consideration in choosing toys appropriate to their interests and skills.

This new body of research (and conclusions) became increasingly part of the fabric of everyday life as accepted educational institutions such as the KINDERGARTEN incorporated it into their teaching activities. The kindergarten, in fact, as conceptualized by the German educator FRIEDRICH FROEBEL in the 1840s, was instrumental in transforming the field of early childhood education and influenced thinking about infancy as well. Froebel's idea that children learn best through play is still the basis for most scholarship on early childhood.

Stimulating Mental and Physical Development through Toys

Today play is considered to be a key part of the daily care of infants. Current child-rearing literature emphasizes the importance of early childhood development for achievements later in life. As a result, parents in industrialized societies often feel a real sense of urgency in stimulating their children enough, often through toys. The noted pediatrician T. Berry Brazelton observed in 1974 that this sense of urgency has been fueled by both toy manufacturers and child experts. So-called educational toys, in particular, are products of this trend. Lamaze toys (made by Learning Curve) and products made by the Baby Einstein Company are specifically marketed as playthings that contribute to an infant's physical and mental development. Baby Einstein, for example, produces a line of toys designed to stimulate precocious development through exposure to classical music.

Toys for babies are in the main discussed as tools to encourage the physical and mental development of very young children. For example, editions of one popular child care book produced by the American Academy of Pediatrics include lists of recommended toys for each developmental stage as well as possible activities.

Recommended Toys

In general, most recent child-rearing manuals recommend almost exactly the same types of toys for different stages of development. Mobiles, for example, are considered to be ideal toys for babies from one to three months, giving the baby a stimulating object to look at. Toys for the brand-new baby, then, are designed to gently stimulate developing senses of sight, hearing, and touch. Unbreakable crib mirrors are also very popular playthings for newborns, based on research showing that babies are interested in faces most of all. As the baby's vision develops, experts suggest the introduction of objects with high-contrast colors. Floor gyms are also popular toys, giving babies something to look at and reach for before they learn to sit up (between six and eight months). Throughout the first year, rattles, musical toys, and soft balls and toys are recommended to go along with babies' growing comprehension of the world around them. By the end of the first year, as infants learn to crawl and acquire more small motor skills, toys like stacking cups, plastic telephones, "busy boxes," board books, blocks, and push-pull toys are considered to be more appropriate.

However, babies, just like older children, do not always use toys in the recommended mode (according to adult designers). A young child, for example, may take the pieces of a stacking toy and pack them into a small bag to drag around the house rather than practicing the specific skill that the toy was manufactured for. In the same manner, an infant may find a use for a more advanced toy that has almost nothing to do with the original intent.

Changing Fashions in Toys

Certain traditional playthings have undergone major shifts in popularity due to changes in recommended child-rearing practices. The baby walker, for example, has lost the support of mainstream child care professionals because research has shown that babies prepare themselves for walking in other, more efficient ways. Other factors have also contributed to this trend, including the rise of concern about ACCIDENTS. Safety is an especially important concern in considering infant toys. Most safety recalls (now widely available through the Internet) concern products for infants and toddlers as the population most at risk from accidents.

Books as Toys

Books for babies are often grouped with toys. Inherent in this classification is the notion that babies spend the majority of their time engaged in play. Many authorities, most notably Brian Sutton-Smith, have contested the latter notion, asserting that very young children primarily explore and master important skills and that those activities are commonly perceived as play.

However, picture books (board books, in particular) do constitute a substantial body of material manufactured specifically for very young children. In the last decade, more and more picture book classics have been transferred to the more durable board book format. Other formats created for very young children are the bath book and the cloth book. The bath book, made of plastic, is intended for use in the tub, either for reading or for playing; the cloth, or stuffed, book, as in examples manufactured by Lamaze, are often written more simply than board books, with more movable features.

Many of these books are nearly indistinguishable from other stuffed toys.

Manufacturers of Infant Toys

Today there are a large number of companies that focus on toys for infants, designed for each stage of early development, as previously defined by child psychologists. Most of these businesses maintain websites with large sections devoted to parenting guides, which include information on how to select toys based on the growing skills of the baby and how to further stimulate those skills using their toys.

See also: **Child Development, History of the Concept of; Child-Rearing Advice Manuals.**

BIBLIOGRAPHY

Brazelton, T. Berry. 1974. "How to Choose Toys." Reproduced in *Growing through Play: Readings for Parents and Teachers*, ed. Robert D. Strom. Monterey, CA: Brooks/Cole.

Hewitt, Karen, and Louise Roomet. 1979. *Educational Toys in America: 1800 to the Present.* Burlington, VT: Robert Hull Fleming Museum.

Kawin, Ethel. 1934. *The Wise Choice of Toys.* Chicago: University of Chicago Press.

Opie, Iona, and Robert Opie. 1989. *The Treasures of Childhood: Books, Toys, and Games from the Opie Collection.* London: Pavilion.

Oppenheim, Joanne, and Stephanie Oppenheim. 2001. *Oppenheim Toy Portfolio Baby and Toddler Play Book*, 2nd ed. New York: Oppenheim Toy Portfolio.

Segal, Marilyn. 1983. *Your Child At Play: Birth to One Year.* New York: Newmarket Press.

Shelov, Steven P., ed. 1998. *Your Baby's First Year.* New York: Bantam.

Singer, Dorothy G., and Jerome L. Singer. 1990. *The House of Make-Believe: Children's Play and the Developing Imagination.* Cambridge, MA: Harvard University Press.

Strom, Robert D., ed. 1981. *Growing through Play: Readings for Parents and Teachers.* Monterey, CA: Brooks/Cole.

Sutton-Smith, Brian. 1986. *Toys as Culture.* New York: Gardner Press.

White, Burton L. 1985. *The First Three Years of Life.* New York: Prentice Hall.

SHIRA SILVERMAN

Inheritance and Property

Inheritance practices, associated as they are with death and with survival of family, name, and estate, reveal the mainsprings of human behavior at a time when people face their transitory nature. Approaches to this human necessity may be as various as the social groups they emanated from. Detailed studies may trace Latin, Celtic, German, and other influences, but they always reveal an extreme diversity of behaviors. In Brittany, for example, two communities, only ten miles apart, developed different inheritance customs.

Systems of Transmission

Comparative research on the subject is recent. To mention only France, it began with the ethnological approach of Claude Lévi-Strauss, who, beginning in 1949, explored the major role of family strategies. It continued with the historical and geographical comments of Emmanuel Le Roy Ladurie (1976) about Jean Yver's 1966 study of inheritance customs and with Pierre Bourdieu's sociological research, which opened new perspectives on BIRTH ORDER.

Two family transmission systems have been identified. The first one is more or less egalitarian, favoring kinship but resulting in divided up estates; the second one favors one privileged heir—male or female—and is apt to secure continuity for the house but is inegalitarian. Under both systems, transmission of family prestige and assets from a given generation to the following one is at stake.

Another feature of interest, illustrating the desire to provide a heir for the family when no satisfactory offspring is available, is adoption. Statutes of ADOPTION are as revealing of the mental and social factors governing inheritance as are the legal provisions governing estate transmission.

Inheritance practices were modified much less as a result of legal change than of demographic, economic, and social change. This confirms that these practices were deeply rooted in custom rather than in written law. It also explains why perturbations in the social climate, favoring, for instance, regional or overseas migrations of children, affected traditional family courses much more than did any legal clause. It may also explain other changes that took place when the legal basis stayed stable, such as the changing status and growing authority of women (as mothers and widows) in the Pyrenean family.

More or Less Egalitarian Inheritance Systems

Analysis of notarized property transfers and of land markets suggests clearly that so-called egalitarian societies did not shirk complex adaptations if they would result in smallholdings of reasonable size. Some big landowners developed ad hoc matrimonial strategies to avoid dividing up their land, but no child's share was reduced to zero. In many European societies, girls often got only movable property, leaving their brothers with the land and the means of production. In all Scandinavian countries, males inherited a property worth more than that which girls inherited—usually double the value.

There were pretensions to egalitarianism, as, for example, in Brittany according to a custom, written in 1539, which did not allow for any privilege to any child. Even an advantage given to a child before the death of the parents had to be compensated for in the global succession. But Breton peasants were seldom farm owners, so inheritance only concerned movables, which were easy to divide up. Things changed when land came to be more commonly owned.

Then the firstborn was privileged by being given a choice of the share he or she would take.

Many European rural areas practiced transmission of land, lease, or movables without gender or birth order discrimination. In those cases, marriage contracts were not necessary since marriage was not directly tied to succession and use of inherited assets. However, conflicts between brothers and sisters could appear when the successor delayed the agreed-upon payments after the succession was settled. This kind of egalitarian system did, in the end, help impoverish a population, especially in periods of population growth such as the nineteenth century.

At the beginning of the Industrial Revolution, the areas of egalitarian transmission were those where tenant-farming was predominant. But even then, some flexibility was possible since fathers were entitled to make a will. Not all fathers did, but those who did had to trust their notary's ability to accommodate their wishes to the law.

Inegalitarian Systems

Inegalitarian sharing out appeared as the result of a unified written law, theoretically inherited from Rome but very intricate when concrete sharing out had to be practiced: Who would be privileged? The males more than the females? The firstborn? The heir mentioned in a will? The boy or girl who had already received some share before the parents' death, thus being beneficiary of a *preciput*, or advantage? It would be simplistic to ignore the coexistence of local customs with written law.

Endowing a girl when she married or entered a convent was a common way to exclude her from a later sharing out. It was also used in countries that practiced egalitarian transmission, such as Normandy. Some old rights restricted the capacity of women to inherit even more than the dowry system did. The future of a family was reputed to be threatened when it depended on the female line: The saying "Girls mean the end of the father's family" (Julien, p. 441) was held to be true in more places than just eighteenth-century Provence.

Although so commonly mentioned in discussions of royal or feudal successions, the law of primogeniture was not frequently referred to in the legal documents. In France, it appears only in some customs of the Basque country and the surrounding Pyrenean valleys. But the father was entitled to choose his heir, and he usually chose the firstborn child, giving him a *preciput* by donation or will. It was rare for a family to wait until the head of the family died to fix the conditions of succession. Arrangements were usually made in the children's marriage contracts.

What happened when the father died before expressing a choice depended on custom. In seventeenth-century New York City, colonial parents could circumvent the laws of intestate succession and bequeath property according to their own desires, ignoring the English custom of primogeniture. But Pennsylvania and New England law allowed the eldest son a double portion of both real estate and personal property if there was no will, while granting his siblings only a single share, although most wills show equal grants to all sons. The *Statuts de Provence* gave Provençal sons equal shares of the patrimony, without consideration of birth order, reserving for the girls a "legitimate share" (a very reduced one) depending on the number of children in the family. When they were only two, the boy received five-sixth, the girl one-sixth. For two sons and one daughter, each boy received four-ninths and the girl one-ninth of the family assets, which was much less than the amount of the dowry she usually got when marrying. Such strategies involved some psychological and legal subtlety, since the interest of fathers was not to give rise to conflicts among the children. These inegalitarian customs were not limited to colonial North America and southwestern Europe. Giving a *preciput* was common in Picardy, Wallonia, and Luxemburg, contrasting with the strong egalitarian Flemish systems.

For all the countries with inegalitarian transmission systems, the French Civil Code of 1804, proclaiming equality in matters of family succession, created disruptions. But it allowed advantaging one of the children (up to one-third of the succession if there were two children, one-fourth if there were three, etc.), and it drew attention to the risk of land division, so that we now read it more as a compromise inherited from Parisian custom than as a revolutionary proclamation. The Code generated reactions that give the historian an opportunity to evaluate the resistance local customs posed to written law. For instance, as early as 1814, the German jurist Friedrich Karl von Savigny developed his thesis contrasting popular practice and law. Decades later, Frédéric Le Play, observing how traditional customs endured alongside the law, advocated a social reform enhancing the traditional custom of the stem family (when, at each generation, the married successor stays in residence with his parents in the family house) as an antidote to the harmful ideas of revolution, progress, land division, and proletarianization.

The influence of the French Civil Code was felt in many countries, including Spain and its American colonies, where *majorat*, the "right to inherit assets . . . under the condition that these assets would be kept in full and perpetually in the family" was suppressed in 1841 (Clavero, p.391). Social reality, contrary to what Le Play had predicted, actually helped this change: In stem family regions of Europe during the nineteenth century, the number of single people of both sexes who could not marry for want of a proper dowry led to a growing number of illegitimate births as the church lost most of its capacity to control sexual behavior; younger brothers and sisters refused to work in the natal house as unpaid servants; and after the 1860s, in the European middle uplands, from Norway to the Balkans and across all Mediter-

ranean countries, young people, especially boys, began to dream of a better life in the big cities or abroad, which often left only the lastborn child in the natal house, or girls more than boys. This transition to ultimogeniture is attested to in many places after the 1880s, as heiresses more often than heirs became farm heads.

The role of heiresses in Western Europe societies has been underestimated until recently. Historians and sociologists have long noted that heiresses were the main transmitters of family behavior models. But the fact that they happened to secure continuity for the house (be it the farm or the urban business) when it was needed was often considered nothing more than a deviation from the general model. But they did transmit, and the evidence is statistical: about 30 percent of family transmissions followed a female line (in the Pyrenees, Scandinavia, and in Austria) as early as the seventeenth century. And the proportion of inheriting females grew over time, eventually affecting more than half the inheritances in the parts of western Europe that were affected by emigration.

Replacing Missing Children or Missing Parents

The hazards of the family course and events, especially when life expectancy was short, generated many cases of missing children or missing parents. What happened, then, when a couple had no surviving child to inherit (and to take care of them in their old age)? Would they adopt?

Philippe Ariès writes, "It would be a distortion to interpret the attitude of traditional societies as one in which the child did not exist, did not count. On the contrary, he was physically necessary for the reproduction of a society that scorned adoption" (1980, p. 645). This suggests that Western societies valued blood filiation more than adoptive filiation. European societies had forsaken ancient practice, which considered adoption a standard method of transmission. In ancient Greek societies, adopted individuals were mainly male kin, whom the adoptive parents, deprived of a male descendant, adopted either during their lifetime or through a will.

In traditional western Europe, adoption did not play the same role it did in non-European societies, where adoption is not only a way to cope with demographic hazard but also an opportunity to integrate into one's family children born outside its social group, either native or foreign. Christianity seems to have preferred blood ties and direct transmission to legitimate or legitimated children, thus separating itself from many other societies known for their large circulation of children. In Asian societies, for example, adoption is recurrent and even desirable, so much so that the Japanese son-in-law becomes a true adopted son as soon as he enters the house. Adoption in JAPAN is essentially a substitution of ancestors. The adopted person must from then on worship his adoptive ancestors. In contrast, children entering a foster family in Europe are expected to behave respectfully, but they remain a member of their family by blood, even if at a young age they consider themselves members of their "milk-families."

Taking Charge of Underage Orphans

The problem of missing parents (or underage ORPHANS) was a recurrent one in the Western European and was subject to regulations emanating from ecclesiastic and civilian authorities—all the more so since, due to short life expectancy, orphanhood was common. Fostering orphans was generally delegated to somebody in the family—often the surviving parent in the case of semi-orphans—who would be designated as a guardian or curator subject to the control of a family council, sometimes with addition of an officer of the law. But fostering orphans day after day was one thing and preserving the patrimony another: How could dispersion of the family patrimony be avoided when the children were underage and had to be fostered?

Before the redaction of customary laws— that is, before the sixteenth century—the orphan's fate, at best, was sealed in a deed authenticated by a notary: a close family member received lease and guardianship, collecting the income of the orphan's real estate, acceding to ownership of the personal estate, and pledging to "feed, educate and maintain" the child, who in turn had to "serve" him or her. We sometimes find in such written deeds a provision that the child would receive back his or her real estate upon coming of age, with the condition that the income and personal estate had been sufficient to refund to the lessor his or her fostering expenses. The final and not surprising result was that the patrimony as a whole was more often than not absorbed in unverifiable expenses. The guardianship system may not have been that bad for the lessor, since we often note competition between candidates to care for one child or to "purchase" him or her for a certain time, although the theoretical aim of this competition was to secure maximal protection for the orphan's patrimony.

The institution of a family council, which would be in charge of naming and controlling the guardian, was not automatic. In fact, one finds evidence of such a council only when the orphan's interests were deemed worthy of specific attention—for instance in case of remarriage of the surviving parent or when the orphan became heir to an uncle or grandmother. Family council members were male kin plus the mother or grandmother if they were alive, and sometimes also male neighbors. They supervised fostering until the orphan reached age fifteen, when he or she usually could begin to earn a living.

Candidates to guardianship took into consideration the orphan's gender and age: a girl's work was thought to be of less value than the boy's; furthermore, the lessor would have to give her a trousseau when she married (but not a dowry, since that was a part of her patrimony). The younger the child, the later he or she became able to serve the lessor—

that is, to repay the costs of fostering. To preserve the child's patrimony, the lessor inherited the child's labor.

What were these children: temporarily adopted children, boarders, or simply small servants? They could go on living in familiar surroundings, but they were "eating their personal estate and the income of their real estate" (Desaive, p. 1987), with some hope of recovering their landed property. Only deep indigence could justify selling part of the orphan's patrimony—usually some badly maintained dwelling—and indigence was very often the case for widows who wanted to keep their children at their side. Widowhood meant a lower standard of living, so a widow had to promise the family council to take care of her children and to protect their portion of the patrimony whose usufruct she obtained.

It could happen that the guardians nominated by the family councils for these fostered children would be childless, so that fostering would be close to adoption, in fact if not in law. A Polish judicial writ from the district of Grabovice, dated 1729, says, "If it happens that a couple dies, whose husband is a farm-hand in the service of a peasant, it is the duty of the peasant to bring up their children. If a childless neighbor offers to take one of them at his home, he shall be allowed to" (Kula, p. 953). Taking in orphans was often one element in a strategy of family reproduction: Orphans filled the place of missing children and went where their hands were the most useful and where they had also a chance to become heirs as legatees through a will. There was therefore no need for adoption.

Preindustrial Fostering of Children

The orphan advancing in age represented a value which grew in relation to the value of his or her patrimony. According to Witold Kula, the European peasant saw the child as a charge until age ten; between ten and eighteen, the child's work more than covered the expenses of fostering. The work of boys and girls, however, was held to have different value and different seasonality, but a child of either sex had some prospective economic value, even in the absence of any patrimony.

If not abandoned and if not dependant on a community, the orphan child was transferred to the house of his guardian, foster parent, or "purchaser." His or her trustee—a childless aunt, an unmarried uncle—might choose this child as a beneficiary for the transmission of some assets, possibly adding in the registered will some provisions defining mutual and reciprocal commitments. The child might also be placed with some relative or neighbor (when at least ten years old) as a young apprentice or servant. This pattern of circulation of young children in the society can only be understood in the context of the family network: the young girl servant was more often than not a niece, a cousin, or a relative of some kind in the household where she served.

A family network was evidently what was missing when children were abandoned. Churches had cared for them since the earliest times and endeavored to find them substitute households. But at the end of the seventeenth century, in urban western Europe, the newly created hospitals had to deal with an increasing number of children who were abandoned at birth. While these children were taken care of, the administrator of the hospital looked for a foster family which would associate Christian hospitality with an anticipation of the gains the labor of the child would generate. For centuries, such placements were a constant in child welfare. When surviving infants were placed in foster families, the institution paid a pension that stopped as soon as the children reached age seven, at which age they were supposed to work and serve.

New conditions appeared with the beginning of industrialization, around 1800. Throughout Europe, textile manufacturers used CHILD LABOR, which was cheap. This opened another way to foster children: to exploit them. Most of the nineteenth century was a painful period for abandoned children. The church was still a force, but it was no longer the mighty institution it had once been, present in all sectors of public life, rural or urban. The state, however, did not yet coordinate the random efforts of communities to deal with abandoned children.

See also: **Abandonment; Bastardy; Family Patterns; Fertility Rates; Foster Care; Siblings.**

BIBLIOGRAPHY

Ariès, Philippe. 1962. *Centuries of Childhood: A Social History of Family Life.* Trans. Robert Baldick. New York: Knopf.

Ariès, Philippe. 1980. "Two Successive Motivations for the Declining Birth Rate in the West." *Population and Development Review* 6: 645–650.

Bourdieu, Pierre. 1972. "Les stratégies matrimoniales dans le système de reproduction." *Annales E.S.C.* 27: 1105–1125.

Clavero, Bartolome. 1974. *Mayorazgo: propriedad feudal en Castilla, 1369–1836.* Madrid: Siglo Veintiuno Editores.

Collomp, Alain. 1983. *La maison du père: famille et village en Haute-Provence aux 17e et 18e siècles.* Paris: Presses Universitaires de France.

Desaive, Jean-Paul. 1987. "Le bail à nourriture et le statut de l'enfant sous l'ancien régime en Basse-Bourgogne." *Bulletin de la Société des Sciences historiques et naturelles de l'Yonne* 118: 11–21.

Fauve-Chamoux, Antoinette, and Emiko Ochiai, eds. 1998. *House and the Stem-Family in EurAsian Perspective/Maison et famille-souche: perspectives eurasiennes.* Kyoto, Japan: Nichibunken.

Julien, Jean-Joseph. 1778. *Nouveau commentaire sur les statuts de Provence.* Aix-en-Provence, France: E. David.

Kula, Witold. 1972. "La seigneurie et la famille paysanne dans la Pologne du 18e siècle." *Annales E.S.C* 27: 949–958.

Le Play, Frédéric. 1875. *L'organisation de la famille selon le vrai modèle signalé par l'histoire de toutes les races et de tous les temps,* 2nd ed. Tours, France: Mame.

Le Roy Ladurie, Emmanuel. 1976. "Family Structures and Inheritance Customs in Sixteenth Century France." In *Family and Inheritance: Rural Society in Western Europe, 1200–1800,* ed. Jack Goody, Joan Thirsk, and Edward Palmer Thomson, pp. 37–70. New York: Cambridge University Press.

Lévi-Strauss, Claude. 1949. *Les structures élémentaires de la parenté.* Paris: Gallimard.

Lévi-Strauss, Claude. 1969. *Elementary Structure of Kinship.* Trans. James Harle Bell, John Richard von Sturmer, and Rodney Needham. Boston: Beacon Press.

Lévi-Strauss, Claude. 1983. "Histoire et ethnologie," *Annales E.S.C.* 38: 12–17.

Savigny, Friederich Karl von. 1840. *Traité de la possession, d'après les principes du droit romain.* Paris.

Savigny, Friederich Karl von. 1975 [1831]. *Of the Vocation of Our Age for Legislation and Jurisprudence.* Trans. Abraham Hayward. New York: Arno Press.

Yver, Jean. 1966. *Egalité entre héritiers et exclusion des enfants dotés. Essai de géographie coutumière.* Paris: Sirey.

ANTOINETTE FAUVE-CHAMOUX

In re Gault

In the landmark juvenile law decision *In re Gault* (1967), the Supreme Court established that children are persons within the scope of the Fourteenth Amendment, and as such, they are entitled to its procedural protections. The decision set forth the legal principle that although minors are not entitled to every constitutional protection afforded to adults, they are not entirely without constitutional protection. Perhaps the most famous statement to emerge from this Supreme Court decision was that made by Justice Abe Fortas: "Neither the Fourteenth Amendment nor the Bill of Rights is for adults alone."

Gerald Gault, a fifteen-year-old boy, was charged with making a lewd telephone call to one of his female neighbors. Following a hearing on the charge, the juvenile court judge determined that Gault's actions were a disruption of the peace and that he had exhibited a pattern of engaging in immoral behaviors. The judge committed Gault to the Arizona State Industrial School (a juvenile detention center) until the age of twenty-one. During this hearing, Gault was not offered the same procedural protections to which he would have been entitled had he been tried in an adult criminal court. His treatment, however, was consistent with the goals of JUVENILE JUSTICE during the first half of the twentieth century. During this era, juvenile justice was seen as reform rather than as criminal punishment; consequently, it was widely believed that the courts' reformative powers would be hampered if they were expected to apply the same constitutional rights to children as to adults. This approach, however, was not without controversy, and the Supreme Court voiced its disapproval in the *Gault* case.

The Court's decision in *Gault* established the principle that JUVENILE COURTS must observe standard procedures and provide specific protections guaranteed by the Constitution. The Court set forth several procedural requirements for juvenile DELINQUENCY proceedings. First, the juvenile and his or her parents must be given written notice of the particular charges brought against him or her, and this notice must be delivered within such time as to permit the juvenile to have a reasonable opportunity to prepare for the hearing. Second, the juvenile and his or her parents must be notified of the juvenile's right to be represented by an attorney, and they must be informed that the court will appoint an attorney if they are unable to afford one. The Court also held that juveniles, like adults, are entitled to the Fifth Amendment's privilege against self-incrimination, and, finally, that juveniles have the right to hear the sworn testimony against them and to confront that testimony through the cross-examination of witnesses.

The Court did not render an opinion regarding the key questions of whether a state must grant a juvenile a right to appeal a finding of delinquency or whether the state must provide an account (either a transcript or audio recording) of the court hearing. However, the Court's affirmative declarations were of far greater importance than these omissions. Because the Court acknowledged limits on the state's power to justify the regulation of juveniles through reliance on the doctrine of *parens patriae*, *In re Gault* was a watershed decision for juvenile rights. It is commonly cited as the most important CHILDREN'S RIGHTS case.

See also: **Law, Children and the.**

BIBLIOGRAPHY

Krisberg, Barry, and James F. Austin. 1993. *Reinventing Juvenile Justice.* Newbury Park, CA: Sage.

Mnookin, Robert H. 1985. *In the Interest of Children: Advocacy, Law Reform, and Public Policy.* New York: W.H. Freeman and Company.

Ramsey, Sarah H., and Douglas E. Abrams. 2001. *Children and the Law in a Nutshell.* St. Paul, MN: West Group.

Simonsen, Clifford E., and Marshall S. Gordon III. 1982. *Juvenile Justice in America.* New York: Macmillan.

Vito, Gennaro F., and Deborah G. Wilson. 1985. *The American Juvenile Justice System.* Newbury Park, CA: Sage.

AMY L. ELSON

Intelligence Testing

Treatments of modern measures of intelligence often begin with a discussion of the French psychologist ALFRED BINET (1857–1911). In 1905, Binet initiated the applied mental measurement movement when he introduced the first intelligence test. In response to a turn-of-the-century law in France requiring that children of subnormal mental ability be placed in special programs (rather than be expelled from school), Binet was called upon to design a test that could identify these children. Binet's first test consisted of thirty items, most of which required some degree of comprehension and reasoning. For example, one task required children to take sentences in which words were missing and supply the missing words that made sense in context (such sentence-

completion tasks are still used widely). Binet grouped his test items such that the typical child of a given age group was able to answer fifty percent of the questions correctly. Individuals of similar chronological age (CA) varied widely in their scale scores, or mental age (MA). The ratio of MA to CA determined one's level of mental development; this ratio was later multiplied by 100 to calculate what is now known as the intelligence quotient (IQ).

Binet's approach was successful: children's scores on his test forecasted teacher ratings and school performance. While Binet was developing this first test of general intellectual functioning, the English psychologist Charles Spearman (1863–1945) was conducting research to identify the dominant dimension responsible for the validity of the test's predictions.

The Hierarchical Organization of Mental Abilities
Spearman was the first to propose and offer tangible support for the idea that a psychologically cohesive dimension of general intelligence, g, underlies performance on any set of items demanding mental effort. Spearman showed that g appears to run through all heterogeneous collections of intellectual tasks and test items. He demonstrated that when heterogeneous items are all lightly positively correlated and then summed, the signal carried by each is successively amplified and the noise carried by each is successively attenuated.

Modern versions of intelligence tests index essentially the same construct that was uncovered at the turn of the twentieth century by Spearman, but with much more efficiency. For example, g is a statistical distillate that represents approximately half of what is common among the thirteen subtests comprising the Wechsler Adult Intelligence Scale. As noted by intelligence researcher Ian J. Deary, the attribute g represents the research finding that "there is something shared by all the tests in terms of people's tendencies to do well, modestly, or poorly on all of them." This "tendency" is quite stable over time. In 2001, Deary's team published a study that was the longest temporal stability assessment of general intelligence, testing subjects at the age of eleven and a second time at the age of seventy-seven. They observed a correlation of 0.62, which rose to over 0.70 when statistical artifacts were controlled.

Psychometricians have come to a consensus that mental abilities follow a hierarchical structure, with g at the top of the hierarchy and other broad groups of mental abilities offering psychological import beyond g. Specifically, mathematical, spatial-mechanical, and verbal reasoning abilities all have demonstrated incremental (additional) validity beyond g in forecasting educational and vocational outcomes.

g and the Prediction of Life Outcomes
Research on general intelligence has confirmed the validity of g for forecasting educational and occupational achieve-

ment. Empiricism also has documented general intelligence's network of relationships with other socially important outcomes, such as aggression, crime, and poverty. General intellectual ability covaries 0.70–0.80 with academic achievement measures, 0.40–0.70 with military training assignments, 0.20–0.60 with work performance (higher correlations reflect greater job complexity), 0.30–0.40 with income, and around 0.20 with obedience to the law. Measures of *g* also correlate positively with altruism, sense of humor, practical knowledge, social skills, and supermarket shopping ability, and correlate negatively with impulsivity, accident-proneness, delinquency, smoking, and racial prejudice. This diverse family of correlates reveals how individual differences in general intelligence influence other personal characteristics.

Experts' definitions of general intelligence fit with *g*'s nexus of empirical relationships. Most measurement experts agree that measures of general intelligence assess individual differences pertaining to abstract thinking or reasoning, the capacity to acquire knowledge, and problem-solving ability. Traditional measures of general intelligence and standard academic achievement tests both assess these general information-processing capacities. In 1976, educational psychologist Lee Cronbach noted: *"In public controversies about tests, disputants have failed to recognize that virtually every bit of evidence obtained with IQs would be approximately duplicated if the same study were carried out with a comprehensive measure of achievement"* (1976, p. 211, emphasis in original).

The Causes of Individual Differences in Intelligence

Both genetic and environmental factors contribute to the individual differences observed in intelligence. The degree to which individual differences in intelligence are genetically influenced is represented by an estimate of *heritability*, the proportion of observed variation in intelligence among individuals that is attributable to genetic differences among the individuals. By pooling various family studies of *g* (e.g., identical and fraternal twins reared together or apart), the heritability of general intelligence in industrialized nations has been estimated to be approximately 40 percent in childhood and between 60 and 80 percent in adulthood. This pattern is thought to reflect the tendency of individuals, as they grow older and more autonomous, to increasingly self-select into environments congruent with their unique abilities and interests.

Environmental contributions to individual differences in intelligence are broadly defined as all non-genetic influences. Shared environmental factors, such as socioeconomic status and neighborhood context, are those that are shared by individuals within a given family but differ across families; non-shared environmental factors, such as the mentoring of a special teacher or one's peer group, are those that are generally unique to each individual within a family. The majority of environmental influences on intelligence can be attrib-

utable to non-shared factors for which the specifics, thus far, are not well known. Family studies of intelligence have consistently documented that the modest importance of shared environmental influences in early childhood, approximately 30 percent, decreases to essentially zero by adulthood.

The Debate over Research on Intelligence

The above empiricism is widely accepted among experts in the fields of measurement and individual differences. Yet research pertaining to general intelligence invariably generates controversy. Because psychological assessments are frequently used for allocating educational and vocational opportunities, and because different demographic groups (such as those based on socioeconomic status or race) differ in test scores and criterion performance, social concerns have accompanied intellectual assessment since its beginning. Because of these social concerns, alternative conceptualizations of intelligence, such as Howard Gardner's theory of multiple intelligences and Robert Sternberg's triarchic theory of intelligence, have generally been received positively by the public. Measures of these alternative formulations of intelligence, however, have not demonstrated incremental validity beyond what is already gained by conventional measures of intelligence. That is, they have not been shown to account for any more variance in important life outcomes (such as academic achievement and job performance) than that already accounted for by conventional intelligence tests.

See also: **Age and Development; IQ; Retardation; Special Education.**

BIBLIOGRAPHY

Bouchard, T. J., Jr. 1997. "IQ Similarity in Twins Reared Apart: Findings and Responses to Critics." In *Intelligence: Heredity and Environment*, ed. R. J. Sternberg and E. L. Grigorenko. New York: Cambridge University Press.

Brand, Christopher. 1987. "The Importance of General Intelligence." In *Arthur Jensen: Consensus and Controversy*, ed. S. Magil and C. Magil. New York: Falmer Press.

Brody, N. 1992. *Intelligence*, 2nd ed. San Diego, CA: Academic Press.

Carroll, John B. 1993. *Human Cognitive Abilities: A Survey of Factor-Analytic Studies*. Cambridge, UK: Cambridge University Press.

Cronbach, L. J. 1975. "Five Decades of Public Controversy over Mental Testing." *American Psychologist* 30: 1–14.

Cronbach, L. J. 1976. "Measured Mental Abilities: Lingering Questions and Loose Ends." In *Human Diversity: Its Causes and Social Significance*, ed. B. D. Davis and P. Flaherty. Cambridge, MA: Ballinger.

Deary, Ian J. 2001. *Intelligence: A Very Short Introduction*. New York: Oxford University Press.

Gottfredson, Linda S. 1997. "Intelligence and Social Policy." *Intelligence* 24 (special issue).

Jensen, Arthur R. 1998. *The g Factor: The Science of Mental Ability*. Westport, CT: Praeger.

Lubinski, David. 2000. "Assessing Individual Differences in Human Behavior: Sinking Shafts at a Few Critical Points." *Annual Review of Psychology* 51: 405–444.

Messick, S. 1992. "Multiple Intelligences or Multilevel Intelligence? Selective Emphasis on Distinctive Properties of Hierarchy: On

Gardner's *Frames of Mind* and Sternberg's *Beyond IQ* in the Context of Theory and Research on the Structure of Human Abilities." *Psychological Inquiry* 3: 365–384.

Murray, Charles. 1998. *Income, Inequality, and IQ*. Washington, DC: American Enterprise Institute.

Neisser, U., G. Boodoo, and Bouchard, et al. 1996. "Intelligence: Knowns and Unknowns." *American Psychologist* 51: 77–101.

Snyderman, Mark, and Stanley Rothman. 1987. "Survey of Expert Opinion on Intelligence and Aptitude Testing." *American Psychologist* 42: 137–144.

Spearman, Charles. 1904. "General Intelligence Objectively Determined and Measured." *American Journal of Psychology* 15: 201–292.

APRIL BLESKE-RECHEK

International Organizations

In most cultures children are considered vulnerable and defenseless, and therefore deserving of special protection and treatment. However, throughout history millions of children have suffered or died due to starvation, disease, poverty, exploitation, or war. The emphasis on the protection of children started at the beginning of the twentieth century, and it is still evolving. The creation of international governmental organizations (IGOs), specifically the United Nations (UN) and its subagencies, religious groups, and nongovernmental organizations (NGOs), was propelled by the tragedy of the two world wars, primarily to provide humanitarian food and assistance to children in need. In 1950 there were only a handful of organizations working together to contribute to the improvement of the lives of children; today there are thousands.

The Emergence of IGOs

The League of Nations was established as an attempt to provide collective international security after World War I. However, the League's Covenant, adopted in 1920, did address some children's issues, such as providing humane labor conditions and halting the trafficking of women and children. The League failed to achieve its objectives, however, and disbanded when the victors of World War II created the United Nations in 1945.

The initial task of providing emergency aid to several hundred million people at the end of World War II, especially the housing and feeding of children, was given to the UN Relief and Rehabilitation Administration. In 1945, these functions were progressively transferred to newly created specialized UN agencies, such as the Food and Agricultural Organization (FAO), the World Health Organization (WHO), the United Nations Educational, Scientific, and Cultural Organization (UNESCO), and the International Refugee Organization (which became the UN High Commission for Refugees in 1951). The UN International Children's Emergency Fund (now called the United Nations Children's Fund, or UNICEF), was created in 1946 and, with offices in 126 countries, is now the principal UN agency for promoting and advocating CHILDREN'S RIGHTS. UNICEF works with UN agencies and NGOs to provide millions of children with food, medicine, and basic education.

Two new units created in the 1950s also work on programs targeting children: the United Nations High Commissioner for Human Rights (UNHCR) and the UN Development Programme (UNDP). UNHCR has helped an estimated fifty million people since it began operations in 1950, and it continues working with approximately 20 million refugees annually, 80 percent of whom are women and children. UNDP began in 1959, and is today one of the most important UN agencies. It provides multilateral and development aid to developing nations. Several IGOs, including UNICEF and UNHCR, and one NGO, the International Red Cross, have earned Nobel Peace Prizes for their efforts to promote and protect children.

Legal Instruments

There has been significant progress on children's rights issues since the League of Nations and UN were founded. IGOs and NGOs have worked together to help codify international laws and legal norms that define the legal rights of the child.

The first legal instrument specifically targeting children was the Minimum Age Convention in 1919. Two years later the League of Nations passed the International Convention for the Suppression of Traffic in Women and Children. The basic rights of children, including protection from exploitation, were first stated in the 1924 Geneva Declaration of the Rights of the Child, which was created to help Balkan children refugees.

After the League of Nations dissolved, the UN became the primary vehicle for the creation of international laws to protect the basic needs of children. This is done either through global conventions hosted by the UN or through UN General Assembly resolutions.

The Universal Declaration of Human Rights was adopted by the UN General Assembly in 1948. This declaration outlines basic political, economic, and social rights for all people. Among the children's rights that are included are those guaranteeing a free elementary education, an adequate standard of living, and social protections. These rights are meant to include those born out of wedlock, which is still controversial in many cultures.

A 1954 UN resolution and a 1962 treaty on marriage both declare that child marriages are illegal if the participants have not reached the age of PUBERTY. The Declaration on the Rights of the Child (1959) calls upon governments and civil society to provide children with access to education, health care and good nutrition. In 1965, the UN specified that the minimum age for marriage should be fifteen years old or older (with some exceptions).

In the 1970s, treaties and children's services began to reflect the child's perspective, rather than that of the parents or the state. For example, the UN Declaration on Foster Placement and Adoption (1986) gives children rights over their parents if their physical and emotional needs are not met. In 1988 the plight of child refugees unaccompanied by adults led UNHCR to establish its Guidelines on Refugee Children.

By far the most important treaty protecting children is the 1989 UN CONVENTION ON THE RIGHTS OF THE CHILD (CRC). This is the most ratified convention in the world, and it is the first to combine economic, political, civil, and social rights for children. Two optional protocols, one eliminating the sale of children, CHILD PROSTITUTION, and CHILD PORNOGRAPHY, and the other dealing with the involvement of children in armed conflicts, were added in 2002. It is estimated these new laws impact over 300,000 children serving as soldiers, servants, or sex slaves.

A UN review of the progress on children's rights during the 1990s shows progress in some areas and deterioration in others. Positive developments include millions of additional children in school; increasing gender equality, especially in education and health; the near eradication of POLIO; and children living longer and healthier lives. Violations of children's rights are increasingly gaining government and public attention, thanks to the passage of the CRC and the work being done by international organizations, NGOs, and the media. For example, multinational companies have faced public protests and boycotts as a result of their employment of child laborers.

However, at the beginning of the new millennium, 100 million children were still out of school (60 percent of them girls). Fifty million children were working in intolerable forms of labor, while 30 million more were being trafficked for sexual exploitation. In addition, 10 million children die annually from preventable causes; 150 million children suffer from malnutrition; and HIV/AIDS has infected millions of children. It is estimated that 30 million children will be orphaned by AIDS by 2010.

Despite efforts to provide assistance to children, and the many legal instruments that protect them, children living in poverty, in conflict zones, or in developing countries face many difficulties. Millions live in pervasive poverty, lacking access to proper sanitation, drinking water, education, or hope for a future. War, corruption, and foreign debt often prevent governments from financing the basic needs of children. Unfortunately, international organizations lack adequate funding to provide protection to all children.

See also: **Child Labor in Developing Countries; Child Labor in the West; Juvenile Justice: International; Soldier Children; War in the Twentieth Century; Work and Poverty.**

BIBLIOGRAPHY

United Nations. 2002. *We the Children: End-Decade Review of the Follow-up to the World Summit for Children.* New York: United Nations Publications.

Van Bueren, Geraldine, ed. 1993. *International Documents on Children.* Boston: Martinus Nijhoff Publishers.

Ziring, Lawrence, Robert E. Riggs, and Jack C. Plano. 2000. *The United Nations: International Organization and World Politics.* Orlando, FL: Harcourt College Publishers.

INTERNET RESOURCES

UNICEF. 2002. "About UNICEF." Available from <www.unicef.org/uwwide>.

UNICEF. 2002. "United Nations Special Session on Children." Available from <www.unicef.org/specialsession.html>.

United Nations. 1997. "Convention on the Rights of the Child." Available from <www.unhcr.ch/html/menu3/b/k2crc.htm>.

SONJA L. TAYLOR

Interscholastic Athletics

Interscholastic athletics emerged in the United States during the latter half of the nineteenth century, and like their collegiate level counterpart, they were organized and directed initially by students. The students at Worcester, Massachusetts High School inaugurated high school athletics when they formed a BASEBALL team in 1859. Students, eager for victory, recruited nonstudents for their teams, a practice that caused school administrators to take control of athletics. Although some New England boarding schools, public schools in Philadelphia and Buffalo, and private ACADEMIES in Chicago fielded teams during the 1860s, interscholastic athletics were not firmly established until the closing decades of the nineteenth century when social goals fostered by the Progressive movement gave athletics a useful purpose in America's high schools.

Social and Educational Benefits of Athletics

As Progressives labored to reduce turmoil in America's cities, they looked for a means of controlling youth whose affiliation with urban gangs resulted in deviant behavior. They believed athletics would keep youth occupied and hasten their transition into productive adults. An advocate of Progressive reform, LUTHER GULICK, Director of Physical Education in New York City, organized the Public Schools Athletic League in 1903. The PSAL sponsored interschool competition and self-testing fitness activities during the school day. So successful was Gulick's program that the PSAL prototype was duplicated in dozens of American cities, including Washington, DC, where Edwin B. Henderson adopted it for the District's segregated black schools. In 1905 Gulick and his assistant, Elizabeth Burchenal, organized the Girls' Branch of PSAL that emphasized noncompetitive activities. But in other cities at this time, namely Chicago and Los Angeles, girls athletics, particularly BASKETBALL, were highly competitive, though short-lived due to increasing social pressures to mold girls into refined young ladies in Chicago and to entice boys to stay in school in Los Angeles. High school athletics thus became the domain of boys. In extolling the educational benefits of athletics, educators not only defended the necessity of high school athletics, but they now had reason to expand physical education programs where they could assign athletic coaches for full-time administrative control.

National Tournaments, Intersectional Rivalries, and the Blossoming of Interscholastic Athletics

In the aftermath of World War I, interscholastic athletics experienced enormous growth. The number of athletic teams multiplied as high school enrollments increased. City and county leagues crowned champions in baseball, football, and basketball, states organized tournaments for major sports, and the National Federation of High Schools open its doors in 1920 to preserve the educational integrity of athletics.

Although intersectional competition in baseball and football dates to the early 1900s, New York and Chicago held seven intercity baseball championships during the 1920s. Intersectional rivalries in football were more widespread as teams from New England and Mid-Atlantic states played schools from the Midwest. Schools in Ohio, Indiana, Michigan, Illinois, and other states initiated rivalries with opponents in nearby states. From 1921 to 1924, Illinois high schools participated in nine intersectional contests each year that involved teams from Toledo, Cleveland, Louisville, Detroit, and Baltimore.

The University of Chicago sparked a trend of national tourneys when it hosted the National Interscholastic Basketball Tournament (NIBT) from 1917 to 1930. Catholic schools, excluded from NIBT, established their own tourney, NCIBT, at Loyola University in 1924. By 1928, thirty-two teams from around the country participated in this five-day event. Catholic schools declined NIBT's overtures in 1929, and a year later NIBT lost credibility when it denied an invitation to Phillips High School's all-black team, Chicago's Public League Champions that annually received an automatic bid. Black high schools held their own national basketball tournament at Tuskegee Institute, Tennessee A & I, and Hampton Institute in Virginia.

The Struggle of African-American and Female Athletes

African-American and female athletes endured an uphill battle to gain entry into interscholastic athletics. Excluded from the beginning, African Americans had to contend with such sanctioned segregation policies as they experienced in Indiana, for example, where the state association barred "colored" schools from participating in the state tournament from its inception in 1908 until 1942. Female athletes played

competitive interschool basketball early on, but soon feminine propriety and the prospect of future motherhood caught up with them. Physicians and educators feared sports damaged child-bearing organs, and female physical educators denounced competition as unladylike. During the 1920s, girls' high school basketball in North Carolina, for instance, was highly popular among white and African-American schools. But in North Carolina and elsewhere, female physical educators gained control of girls' athletics and replaced competition with a participation model that emphasized socialization and friendship. White schools followed suit, but most African-American schools continued with the competitive model. The feminist movement of the 1960s and the enactment of Title IX in 1972 reopened the doors of interscholastic competition for girls.

Commercialization, Specialization, and Exploitation

During the last quarter of the twentieth century, commercialism drove the course of high school athletics. National tournaments and intersectional contests returned on a grand scale. Post season all-star games and roundball classics abounded. Hundreds of high schools created Internet web sites that featured their athletic programs. In the 1980s *USA Today* began ranking the Top 25 boys and girls high school teams each season in sports such as basketball, football, baseball, and softball. Scouting services generate substantial revenue by identifying and tracking the most promising athletes for college recruiters. Some high schools, with financial support from footwear giants Nike and Adidas, recruited stellar athletes from other school districts. Increasing commercialism caused athletes to specialize in one particular sport in order to perfect their skills with the hope of someday landing a lucrative professional contract. Untold numbers resorted to steroids and other performance-enhancing substances to improve their lot of securing a college scholarship.

In many cities and towns across America, high school sports are at the center of the community. They provide entertainment, contribute to community building, and foster civic pride. But sometimes this creates an atmosphere where success in athletics becomes all-important, thereby forcing coaches to exploit young athletes. Nowhere was that more evident than in Texas high school football where H. G. Bissinger's *Friday Night Lights* revealed the clout of Odessa's Permian High School football program to supersede the school's educational mission. The overmatched underdog seeking stardom from a tiny hamlet, as portrayed in the film *Hoosiers*, had all but disappeared from interscholastic athletics by the dawn of the twenty-first century.

See also: **High School; Sports; Title IX and Girls Sports.**

BIBLIOGRAPHY

Bissinger, H. G. 1990. *Friday Night Lights, A Town, A Team and a Dream.* Reading, MA: Addison-Wesley.

Brown, Victoria Bissell. 1990. "The Fear of Feminization: Los Angeles High Schools in the Progressive Era." *Feminist Studies* 16: 493–518.

Cahn, Susan K. 1994. *Coming on Strong: Gender and Sexuality in Twentieth-Century Women's Sport.* New York: Free Press.

Grundy, Pamela. 2000. "From Amazons to Glamazons: The Rise and Fall of North Carolina Women's Basketball, 1920–1960." *Journal of American History* 87: 112–146.

Jable, J. Thomas. 1986. "High School Athletics, History Justifies Extracurricular Status." *Journal of Physical Education, Recreation and Dance* 57, no. 2: 61–68.

Miracle, Andrew W., Jr., and C. Roger Rees. 1994. "Sport and School Unity." In *Lessons of the Locker Room.* Amherst, NY: Prometheus Books.

Pierce, Richard B. 2000. "More than a Game, the Political Meaning of High School Basketball in Indianapolis." *Journal of Urban History*, 27: 3–23.

INTERNET RESOURCES

Johnson, Scott. 2003. "Not Altogether Ladylike, the Premature Demise of Girls' Interscholastic Basketball in Illinois." Available from <www.ihsa.org/feature/hstoric/earlybkg.htm>.

Pruter, Robert. 2003. "A Century of Intersectional Football Contests, 1900–1999." Available from <www.ihsa.org/feature/hstoric/intersec.htm>.

J. THOMAS JABLE

In Vitro Fertilization

In vitro fertilization (IVF) is a method of infertility treatment in which an egg and sperm are joined in a laboratory container ("in vitro" means "in glass"). This is in contrast to normal "in vivo" conception, in which fertilization occurs in the fallopian tube of a woman's reproductive tract. Scientist S. L. Schenk began animal IVF research in 1880, but it was not until 1959 that the first animal IVF was clearly documented by another scientist, Michael Chang. In 1978 Patrick Steptoe and Robert Edwards in England produced the first human IVF baby, Louise Brown, who became known as the world's first test-tube baby. The first IVF baby in the United States was born in 1981, largely due to the research work of Howard and Georgeanna Jones. The Joneses varied their technique from that of Steptoe and Edwards, and these newer techniques grew into contemporary IVF. In the United States alone, over thirty-five thousand babies were born through assisted reproductive technologies (ART) techniques in 1999. ART use has increased 54 percent between 1996 and 2000, the only years for which data is available. It is unclear if increase in use is due to actual increases in infertility over this time period, increases in knowledge and availability of services, or due to the aging of the large baby-boom cohort, many of whom delayed childbearing and reached their later and less fertile reproductive years during this time. Even so, ART is used by only 1 percent of all reproductive aged women, and by only 7 percent of all women who seek services for infertility.

Typically a woman's ovary produces one egg per month. Physicians who specialize in IVF use FERTILITY DRUGS to stimulate a woman's ovaries to produce multiple eggs. Eggs are then retrieved during an office procedure in which a needle is inserted into the ovary through the vagina. The eggs are then mixed with sperm in order to allow fertilization. After a period of growth and observation in the laboratory, a number of fertilized eggs, now known as embryos, are returned to the uterus of the woman who will carry the pregnancy. The embryo transfer is another brief office procedure in which embryos are deposited into a woman's uterus through a small plastic tube that is inserted in the cervix.

IVF was originally developed to treat infertility due to blocked or absent fallopian tubes in women under thirty-five years of age. The use of IVF has expanded considerably over the years, and it is now considered to be a treatment for ovulation dysfunction in women, male infertility, and infertility of unknown etiology. Some IVF facilities offer egg donation programs so women without ovaries or women whose advanced age or menopausal status makes successful conception impossible can achieve pregnancy. Embryos can be frozen and stored indefinitely for later use, for donation to other couples, or for transfer to the uterus of a surrogate mother. Embryos can also be screened for genetic disorders prior to transferring them to a woman's uterus.

The American Society for Reproductive Medicine publishes an annual report detailing success rates for IVF clinics in the United States. Success rates vary depending upon patient age, fresh or frozen embryo use and a variety of other factors. Data from 2002 shows that on average for every egg retrieval procedure a woman undergoes she has a 29.1 percent chance of delivering a live infant. There is currently no evidence of increased rates of birth defects in IVF babies, although recently, investigators have raised the possibility that placenta formation in these pregnancies is abnormal, which can lead to fetal growth problems.

IVF raises a host of medical, ethical, legal, sociological and religious questions and controversies. Medically, the techniques pose some risks to women. Fertility drugs can produce ovarian hyperstimulation syndrome (OHSS), which in rare instances can be life threatening. In addition, most IVF practitioners transfer several embryos into a woman's uterus in order to maximize the chance of successful pregnancy. This in turn carries a risk of twin (approximately 25 percent), triplet, and higher order pregnancies (approximately 5 percent). Multiple pregnancies carry increased risks to pregnant women compared to singleton pregnancies, and carry increased risk of premature delivery and associated newborn problems like cerebral palsy, blindness, and death. All of these consequences of IVF place enormous stress on families and on health care systems.

IVF is sociologically interesting because an IVF baby can have up to five "parents"—a genetic mother, a genetic father, a gestating mother, a rearing mother, and a rearing father. The separation of genetic, gestational, and rearing contributions to childhood raises questions about the meaning of parenthood and the family. Legal battles have arisen over "custody" of frozen embryos and of children born to surrogate mothers. Some religious groups prohibit IVF on the grounds that it separates sex and procreation. The issue of what to do with "leftover" embryos is also a source of intense controversy. When embryos are discarded or used for research purposes, as in the case of stem cell research, IVF becomes entangled in the intractable abortion debate in the United States.

IVF also raises questions related to issues of gender, race, and class. While some feminist scholars argue that IVF provides women with additional choices in life because it permits biological motherhood in otherwise impossible circumstances; others argue that it enforces women's conventional roles as reproducers and creates traffic in women's bodies. Some feminist critics argue that the medicalized discourse of "disease" that surrounds infertility prevents clear perception of the ways in which infertility is a socially constructed diagnosis. The racial dimensions of IVF are not well understood, and may relate, among other things, to the stereotype that excess fertility, not infertility, is the most salient black reproductive issue. Although black women in the United States have infertility rates one and one-half times higher than white women, white women use ART techniques at rates twice as high as those of blacks. IVF is inextricably linked to class, as the costs of IVF are exceedingly high—typically $10,000 per month—and not always covered by insurance, and even more rarely covered by public medical insurance.

See also: **Conception and Birth; Multiple Births; Surrogacy.**

BIBLIOGRAPHY

Brinsden, Peter, ed. 1999. *A Textbook of In Vitro Fertilization and Assisted Reproduction*, 2nd ed. New York: Parthenon Publishing.

Chandra, Anjani, and Elizabeth Stephen. 1998. "Impaired Fecundity in the United States: 1982–1995." *Family Planning Perspectives* 30, no. 1: 34–42.

Jones, Howard. 1991. "In the Beginning There Was Bob." *Human Reproduction* 6: 5–7.

Raymond, Janice. 1994. *Women as Wombs—Reproductive Technologies and the Battle Over Women's Freedom.* New York: HarperCollins.

Roberts, Dorothy. 1997. *Killing the Black Body—Race, Reproduction, and the Meaning of Liberty.* New York: Vintage Press.

Seoud, M., and H. Jones. 1992. "Indications for In Vitro Fertilization: Changing Trends: The Norfolk Experience." *Annals of the Academy of Medicine* 21: 459–70.

Society for Assisted Reproductive Technology and the American Society for Reproductive Medicine. 2002. "Assisted Reproductive Technology in the United States: 1998 Results Generated from the American Society for Reproductive Medicine/Society for Assisted Reproductive Technology Registry." *Fertility and Sterility* 77: 18–31.

Speroff, Leon, Robert Glass, and Nathan Kase, eds. 1999. *Clinical Gynecologic Endocrinology and Infertility*, 6th ed. Baltimore: Lippincott Williams and Wilkins.

INTERNET RESOURCES

American Society for Reproductive Medicine. Available from <www.asrm.org>.

CDC Reproductive Health. 2002. "2000 Assisted Reproductive Technology Success Rates—National Summary and Fertility Clinic Reports." Available from <www.cdc.gov>.

National Center for Health Statistics. "National Survey of Family Growth." Available from <www.cdc.gov/nchs/nsfg.htm>.

LISA H. HARRIS

IQ

IQ, or intelligence quotient, is a measure of intelligence that schools, children's homes, and other child-saving institutions have used since the 1910s to assess the intelligence of children for various diagnostic purposes. Welcomed and reviled in different social and political contexts in the twentieth century, especially in the United States, because its deployment has influenced the life chances of millions of children, the IQ and the tests that produce it had modest beginnings. French psychologist ALFRED BINET devised the first test of intelligence for school children in 1908 and 1911. He understood that intellectual capacity increased as children matured; his age scale, which he obtained as a norm of right over wrong answers about everyday artifacts and information for each year of childhood, was based on the Gaussian bell-shaped curve. The result gave the child's "mental age." If the child was three years old and her or his mental age was normal for a three year old, then the child was normal because his or her chronological and mental ages were the same. If the child's mental age was "higher" than her or his chronological age, then the child was advanced, or had a higher than normal IQ. If the situation were reversed, then the child was behind or retarded, with a lower than normal IQ for his or her age. There were several tests for each age, and Binet expressed scores as mental ages. His great insight was that mental age existed apart from, but was related to, chronological age. William Stern, of Hamburg University, devised the notion of the intelligence quotient—soon dubbed the IQ — by dividing the child's mental age by her or his chronological age. Thus a child of ten with a mental age of twelve would have an IQ of 120. One with a chronological age of five and a mental age of four would have an IQ of only 80, and so on.

The American psychologist Lewis M. Terman, of Stanford University, "Americanized" the Binet test, and Stern's notion of the IQ, in the 1910s. He standardized the Binet test on many small town, middle-class California school children of northwestern European, Protestant extraction, so that the norms for each age were synchronized with cultural knowledge best understood by such children—and their relatives, peers, and neighbors. In transforming Binet's test into the Stanford-Binet measuring scale of intelligence, or, more simply, the Stanford-Binet, Terman insisted that the test measured innate intelligence in individuals and in groups, and this assumption was not widely or seriously questioned by mainstream academic psychologists until the 1960s. The

Stanford-Binet became the model for subsequent IQ tests and tests of intelligence, in the United States for the next generation, thus influencing the lives of many children in America and abroad. From the 1920s to the 1960s, the IQ reigned supreme in education and social welfare institutions. Although it is true that in the 1920s there was a furious, if short-lived, controversy among social scientists over whether such tests constituted legitimate scientific measures of the "average IQ" of specific ethnic and racial groups in the population, only an ignored handful of researchers questioned whether an individual's IQ was innate at birth and stable thereafter.

After the 1960s, various constituencies and interest groups raised critical questions about IQ testing. Champions of civil rights and feminism claimed that defenders of segregation and institutionalized racism had used so-called average racial IQ scores to keep minorities and females from good schools, jobs, and neighborhoods. Some psychologists claimed that intelligence was too complex a phenomenon to be reduced to a simple ratio; most post–World War II tests, based on a model developed by the psychologist David Wechsler, argued that intelligence was the consequence of multiple factors and processes. Researchers in early childhood education insisted in the 1960s that IQs of preschool age children could and did respond to environmental stimuli and pressures by at least as much as the gap between many racial minorities and the white majority. As in the 1920s, a nature versus nurture debate took place over the next several decades without a definite conclusion. After World War II, most institutions, such as schools and child-saving organizations, tended to interpret IQ scores as mere indicators, to be used with many other indices to understand a child and her or his potentiality.

See also: **Child Development, History of the Concept of; Intelligence Testing.**

BIBLIOGRAPHY

Boring, E. G. 1950. *A History of Experimental Psychology*, 2nd ed. New York: Century Co.

Cravens, Hamilton. 1988 [1978]. *The Triumph of Evolution: The Heredity-Environment Controversy, 1900–1941*. Baltimore, MD: The Johns Hopkins University Press.

Cravens, Hamilton. 2002 [1993]. *Before Head Start: The Iowa Station and America's Children*. Chapel Hill: The University of North Carolina Press.

Cremin, Lawrence A. 1961. *The Transformation of the School: Progressivism and American Education, 1876–1955*. New York: Knopf.

Curti, Merle. 1980. *Human Nature in American Thought*. Madison: University of Wisconsin Press.

Hunt, J. McVicker. 1960. *Intelligence and Experience*. New York: The Ronald Press.

Stoddard, George D. 1943. *The Meaning of Intelligence*. New York: Macmillan.

Terman, Lewis M., et al. 1917. *The Stanford Revision and Extension of the Binet-Simon Scale for Measuring Intelligence*. Baltimore: Warwick and York.

HAMILTON CRAVENS

IQ Tests. *See* Intelligence Testing.

Isaacs, Susan (1885–1948)

The child-development theorist, educator, and psychoanalyst Susan Sutherland Fairhurst Isaacs, born in 1885, was the youngest of fourteen children, left school at fourteen, trained as a teacher, and in 1912 gained a philosophy degree from Manchester University. After a year doing research at the Psychological Laboratory, Cambridge, she lectured at Darlington Training College (1913–1914) and in logic at Manchester University (1914–1915). Between 1924 and 1927 she was head of Malting House School, Cambridge, an experimental school that fostered and observed the individual development of children, allowing extensive free play. From this experience she wrote several of her major works, which became classics of educational psychology, including *Intellectual Growth in Young Children* (1930) and *Social Development in Young Children* (1933). Two other important books were *The Nursery Years* (1929) and *The Children We Teach* (1932), about children from ages seven to twelve, followed by *Psychological Aspects of Child Development* (1935).

Isaacs trained and practiced as a psychoanalyst. In 1933 she became the first head of the Department of Child Development at the Institute of Education, University of London, where she established an advanced course in child development for teachers of young children. Between 1929 and 1940 she was also an "agony aunt" under the pseudonym of Ursula Wise, replying to readers' problems in child care journals. She married twice, first to William Brierley and second (in 1922) to Nathan Isaacs. Some of her papers are in the archives of the Institute of Education, London, and more material relating to her psychoanalytic practice and theory is at the Institute of Psychoanalysis.

Isaacs was a brilliant teacher, expositor, and clinician. Her most substantial theoretical contribution came out of her reconciliation between observational psychology and her recognition of the role of powerful forces of LOVE, FEAR, and hate in the minds of very young children. In the controversial discussions that shaped psychoanalysis in Britain she aligned herself with MELANIE KLEIN, believing that child analysis was possible and that the work of psychoanalysis was essentially conducted in the transference relationship between analyst and analysand, revealing the role of the unconscious. In Isaacs's words, "There is no impulse, no instinctual urge or response which is not experienced as unconscious *phantasy*" (1952, p. 83). She goes on to emphasize the importance of fantasy itself as a mechanism for dealing with the power of emotions: "phantasy soon becomes also a means of defence against anxieties, a means of inhibiting them and experienced in phantasies which give them mental life and show their direction and purpose."

Isaacs published widely in popular magazines and spoke frequently on the radio to spread ideas about the normalcy of anxiety, night terrors, behavioral manifestations of the unconscious at work, and the concept of child development being emotional and social as well as physical. She encouraged PLAY as a means of learning about the world and dealing with unconscious forces and set herself against the debilitating effects of mass educational testing. Generations of teachers in training were also encouraged to understand healthy emotional development as an end to their work.

See also: **Child Development, History of the Concept of; Child Psychology.**

BIBLIOGRAPHY

Gardiner, Dorothy. 1969. *Susan Isaacs.* London and Toronto: Methuen.

King, Pearl, and Ricardo Steiner. 1991. *The Freud-Klein Controversies, 1941–45.* London: Tavistock/Routledge.

Steiner, Ricardo. 1989. "Activities of British Psychoanalysts during the Second World War and the Influence of their Interdisciplinary Collaboration on the Development of Psychoanalysis in Great Britain." *International Review of Psychoanalysis* 16.

DEBORAH THOM

Islam

Any child of Muslim parents is considered a Muslim, and Islamic law contains precise and detailed provisions regarding children. Islam is the system of beliefs, rituals, and practices traced back to the Prophet Muhammad (c. 570–632 C.E.), who reportedly started his mission in Arabia in 610 C.E. Islamic law is contained in the Muslim holy book, the Qur'an (or Koran), as revealed to Muhammad. The Qur'an contains 114 *suras*, or chapters, that were revealed to Muhammad over the course of twenty-three years. There are over one billion Muslims in the world, who inhabit forty predominantly Muslim countries and five continents, traversing a diverse geographical and cultural area. As Islam spread and established itself in these diverse areas, some of the many local cultures and customs became assimilated into Islamic practices. Thus, there may be slight variations on classical Islamic practices from country to country. There are also variations between the two major sects of Islam: the Sunnis and the Shi'is (also spelled *Shiite*).

Islamic Law

Islamic life is determined by the *Shari'a* (the Way), which is Islamic law, although in the strict sense of the word it is much more than law, as it contains prescriptions for every aspect of life, ranging from rituals, customs, and manners to family law—including the treatment and rights of children. The primary source of the Shari'a is the Qur'an, which is considered to be the direct and unmediated word of God. Although there is only one Shari'a, there are slight differences in the constitution of the Shari'a amongst the Sunnis and Shi'is. These differences are due on the one hand to different interpretations of the Qur'anic text, known as *tafsir* (sing.), and on the other to legal interpretations, or *fiqh* (sing.), by the jurists. This exercise is known as science of the law (*usul al-fiqh*).

According to the Sunni jurists, four principal sources (known as legal indicators) provide the basis for the Shari'a: the Qur'an (the word of God as revealed to the Prophet Muhammad); the Sunna of the Prophet (Muhammad's words, actions, and habits); *ijma* (consensus among Muslim jurists on a particular subject or the consensus of the Muslim community); and *qiyas* (reasoning by analogy), in which jurists develop new laws based on the Qur'an or the Sunna. The primary sources for the Shari'a used by the Shi'is are also the Qur'an and the Sunna of the Prophet, as well as the Sunna of the Imams, who are the descendants of the Prophet and who, for the Shi'is, also carry the spiritual mantle of the Prophet. The historical differences between Shi'i and Sunni Islam affect the structure and method by which they formulate laws from original sources. In place of *qiyas*, the Shi'i *faqih*, known as *mujtahid*, uses a method of legal inference called *ijtihad*, which is essentially a personal soul searching and reasoning. These variations are also due to the cultural differences of the diverse areas which Islam encompasses. However, the major provisions for the rights of children are the same within all the sects of Islam as they are based on the Qur'an and the Sunna.

Before the advent of Islam in Arabia, children not only had no rights but newborn babies were frequently buried alive, either because of poverty or because they were female and considered a burden. There are several Qur'anic verses on this subject: "And when the birth of a daughter is announced to one of them, his face becomes black and he is full of wrath." (Qur'an XVI: 58); "And kill not your children for fear of poverty—we provide for them and for you. Surely the killing of them is a great wrong." (XVII: 31); "And when the one buried alive is asked for what sin she was killed . . ." (LXXXI: 8–9). These verses support the fact that the custom of infanticide was practiced in pre-Islamic Arabia.

A Child's Upbringing

In Islamic societies the main purpose of marriage was, and still is, procreation, which is an obligatory religious duty. The advent of a child is not only welcomed and considered a blessing, it is also regarded as essential for strengthening the marriage bond, for the perpetuation of the line of descent, and for enlarging the community of the faithful. A house in which no child is born is seen to lack God's blessing. Childlessness frequently results in divorce, or at least the addition of another wife (as polygyny is permitted in Islam) who is able to bear children, as the inability to do so is always considered to be the fault of the woman.

There are various rituals associated with the birth of a child, and it is the duty of the father or legal guardian to see

These boys read the Qur'an by lamplight at a school in Kabul, Afghanistan, in November 2001. Religious education is an important component of Islam and *makhabs* (Qur'anic schools) exist in all Islamic countries. © Reuters NewMedia Inc./CORBIS.

that they are fulfilled. The first of these dictates that when the child is born the Muslim call to prayer is whispered in both its ears. The parents choose the child's name, but if there is a disagreement it is the father who chooses the name. On the seventh day after the birth a ceremony known as *aqiqa* takes place, during which a sheep is slaughtered and the child's hair is cut. Another rite, considered by some to be an aspect of incorporating the child into the community of the faithful, is male CIRCUMCISION. This can take place at any age ranging from seven days to fifteen years, depending on the local culture, and is usually accompanied by festivities. Female circumcision does not exist in the Qur'an and there is no evidence that the Prophet recommended it. In the Muslim areas where it is practiced, as in parts of northeastern Africa, it is the consequence of local pre-Islamic practices.

In Islam, childhood is considered a special period in an individual's life. The different stages of childhood are well

defined, and there is a rich vocabulary for them in Arabic. For example, the general term for the child is *walad*; the baby in the mother's womb is called *janin* (fetus); at birth, *tifl*; and at completion of seven days, *sadigh*. A baby who has not yet been weaned is called *sabiyy* if male and *sabiyya* if female. A boy is called *ghulam*; a young man, *habab*. Once he attains the faculty of discernment and is able to differentiate between good and evil, he has reached the stage of *tamyiz*. There are other terms for the various stages until the child reaches maturity. For instance a child who dies before adulthood is *farat*.

Physical maturity in either sex establishes majority (*bulugh*) in Islamic law. There is a difference of opinion in the legal schools about the exact age, but it ranges from nine for girls to eighteen for boys, although for girls the age of menstruation is generally acceptable. If there is doubt, however, a statement by the person that he or she has reached PUBERTY is adequate. Before reaching majority, a minor is not legally recognized, does not have social responsibilities, and is under the care of a parent or guardian.

Duties of Parents

Islam considers children to be vulnerable and dependent beings. Therefore, Islamic law provides diverse rules for the protection of their body and property. According to these rules both parents have well-defined duties toward their children before they reach the age of maturity. In Islamic countries the patrilineal system of descent is the norm, so these duties are incumbent upon an established paternity resulting in mutual rights of INHERITANCE, guardianship, and maintenance. Any child born within wedlock is considered legitimate, and provisions have been made regarding paternity in cases of divorce or the death of the father. Due to the importance of patrilineal descent, adoption is not permitted in Islam (Qur'an XXXIII: 4–5), although before the advent of Islam it was practiced in Arabia. Muslims are enjoined to treat children of unknown origin as their brothers in the faith.

The father of a child should provide the mother with the necessary material for the child's growth and survival. The baby has the right to food, clothing, and shelter (Qur'an II: 233). The father should also see to the child's education (both secular and religious). Should the child's father be dead or unable to provide for the child, and if the child does not have any inherited property, then providing for the child becomes first the duty of the paternal grandfather, then other paternal relatives, and finally any other living relatives.

It is the responsibility of the mother to take care of the child during infancy. The mother must breast-feed the child at least up to the age of two (Qur'an II: 233), although even in present-day Islamic countries breast-feeding usually continues as long as the mother has milk. If a mother is unable to nurse, it is permitted to employ a wet nurse who is in good health and of good character (it is believed by some jurists that traits are inherited through human lactation)(Qur'an II: 233, LIV: 6). If the family cannot afford a wet nurse, frequently a neighbor or a friend who has recently given birth may fulfill the role.

If there is a dispute between parents, it is generally agreed that mothers have the right of custody for the first few years of a child's life. If a mother dies, custody reverts to a female relative, preferably in the mother's line. However, aside from these facts, the different schools of *fiqh* hold dissimilar opinions on this matter.

Children also have well-defined rights in respect to inheritance. Provisions have been made within the Qur'an and the Shari'a for the inheritance rights of both female and male offspring. In pre-Islamic Arabia, women and children had no inheritance rights. In Islam, boys inherit two times the amount that girls inherit. There are also provisions for the inheritance rights of parents (Qur'an IV: 11, 12).

The child is also entitled to a guardian. This may be the father, or it may be someone the father appoints to protect the child's property interests. Under Islamic law a child, as a minor, is not permitted to enter into any contractual arrangement. It is therefore the duty of the guardian to ascertain that any intended contract is to the child's advantage.

Religious Education

The religious education of the child is the responsibility of the parents, with boys being educated by their fathers, and girls by their mothers. Through the initial rituals at birth, the child is incorporated into Islam, and the basic principles of the faith are explained when the child starts talking. However, the systematic religious education of the child does not begin until the age of *tamyiz*. In the past, this education frequently began by sending boys to the *maktab* (Qur'anic school), where they learned the recitation of the Qur'an and instruction on the performance of religious commandments. Female children did not go the *maktab*, although female *maktabs* were available in some countries. Girls frequently received their religious instruction at home from their mother and were taught household work. However, although *maktabs* exist in all Islamic countries today, religious instruction is also incorporated into the general curriculum of modern state education, and special religious books have been written for children. In some Islamic countries, such as Turkey, schools are coeducational, while in others, such as Saudi Arabia, any kind of schooling for girls is of recent origin, and children are taught in separate male and female facilities.

The ritual five daily prayers, which constitutes one of the five pillars of Islam, do not become incumbent upon the child until she or he reaches his or her majority. (As explained above, although different schools of law hold diverse opinion on the actual age of majority, fifteen is generally considered the age that separates the minor from the major.) Corporal punishment is permitted for children who do not fulfill their religious obligations or who show signs of unacceptable traits or behavior. In addition, children have duties toward their parents. They are enjoined to be kind, obedient, and respectful toward their parents, and to look after them in old age (Qur'an: XVII: 23; XXIX: 8; XXXI: 14, 15; XXXXVI: 15).

The Family

It must be remembered that Islam encompasses many different cultures, so it is difficult to generalize about the rights of children in present-day Islamic countries. But it can be seen that within Islamic law there are definite rights and duties granted to children. Although most modern-day Islamic societies have incorporated parts of the Shari'a into their constitution, they have not necessarily incorporated all rights accorded to children by Islam. However, there is one institution in most Islamic societies that is of great importance in the upbringing of children, the extended family system.

The number of people living in one household varies according to the economic status of the family. But the minimum number would include grandparents in addition to the nuclear family and any unmarried siblings. This often results in early indulgence of the child. The child spends a considerable amount of time with its mother and is breast-fed on demand. It also receives much affection and pampering from its mother, father, older siblings, and other members of the extended family.

In spite of differences from country to country, there are certain cultural norms regarding children that are shared by most Islamic societies and have continued from the past to the present. These include the importance of the group over the individual, the importance of children (particularly sons) to continue the line of descent, and responsibility for parents in old age.

See also: **Africa; Bible, The; Middle East.**

BIBLIOGRAPHY

Awde, Nicholas, ed. and trans. 2000. *Women in Islam: An Anthology from the Qur'an and Hadith.* London: Curzon Press.

Fernea, Elizabeth Warnock, ed. 1995. *Children in the Muslim Middle East.* Austin: University of Texas Press.

Holy Qur'an. Arabic text, translation, and commentary by Maulana Muhammad 'Ali. 1991. Lahore, Pakistan: Ahmadiyyah.

Momen, Moojan. 1985. *Introduction to Shi'i Islam: The History and Doctrines of Twelver Shi'ism.* New Haven, CT: Yale University Press.

Ruthven, Malise. 1997. *Islam: A Very Short Introduction.* Albany: State University of New York Press.

SHIREEN MAHDAVI

Israel

The modern state of Israel was founded in 1948 and, in the early twenty-first century, has a population of over 6 million people. Of these 6 million, over 2 million (36.7 percent of the population) are children. However, the history of childhood in Israel, like the history of Israel itself, extends to earliest days of human civilization.

In the land of Israel, part of the ancient "fertile crescent," one can find some of the oldest evidence of agriculture and early signs of town life. The Biblical figures of Abraham, Isaac, and Jacob, the forefathers of the Jewish people, lived in the area about 2000 B.C.E. and later the twelve tribes of Israel settled the land. Judea prospered under King David and his successors between 1000 and 600 B.C.E. After being conquered and dispersed by the Babylonians, Persians, and Greeks, Judea again became independent under the Hasmonean Jewish Kingdom from 165 to 63 B.C.E. Then, within a century, the land was occupied by the Romans. Rome suppressed revolts in 70 and 135 C.E., and renamed Judea Pales-

tine, after the Philistines who had inhabited the coastal land before the Hebrews arrived. The Romans dispersed Jews to all parts of the Roman Empire.

Arab invaders conquered the land in 636. Within a few centuries, Islam and the Arabic language became dominant and the Jewish community reduced to a minority. During the eleventh to thirteenth centuries, the country became a part of the Seljuk, Mamluk, and Ottoman empires, although the Christian Crusades provided a temporary break in the dominance of Islamic culture between 1098 and 1291.

As the Ottoman empire collapsed in World War I, Britain took control of the Palestine Mandate (comprising present-day Israel and Jordan). The Balfour Declaration in 1917 pledged support for a Jewish national homeland in that area, but the British gave 80 percent of the land to Emir Abdullah in 1921, and Jordan was created. Jewish immigration, which began in the late nineteenth century, swelled in the 1930s as Jews fled the rise of Nazism in Germany. After the turmoil of World War II, the United Nations General Assembly voted to partition what was left of Palestine into separate Arab and Jewish states. In 1948, Britain withdrew from the country and Israel declared itself an independent state. The Arab world rejected the new state and Egypt, Syria, Jordan, Lebanon, Iraq, and Saudi Arabia invaded, but were defeated by Israel. In separate armistices signed with the Arab nations in 1949, Jordan occupied Judea and Samaria (sometimes called the West Bank of the Jordan) and Egypt occupied the Gaza Strip, although neither granted Palestinian autonomy. Subsequent wars expanded Israeli territory but created recurrent tensions with Arab states and with the large Palestinian minority within Israel's borders.

Conditions for Childhood

Childhood in Israel has been shaped by several factors. From Jewish tradition came, among other things, a strong emphasis on education that was maintained even by secular Jews. Following the experiences of the Jewish people in Europe, where Jews had sometimes been seen as unduly passive victims of outside attacks, many Israeli leaders developed a desire to alter some aspects of the traditional socialization of children, particularly to create a greater emphasis on physical prowess and assertiveness. These qualities also fit the role of agriculture in Israel, with its demand for physical labor, and the need to maintain military service and preparedness. Childhood in Israel was also quite diverse, as Jewish immigrants not only from Europe but also from North Africa and the Middle East brought different customs and habits (including different levels of religious commitment) and as substantial Muslim and Christian minorities also coexisted. Finally, particularly amid mounting internal violence after 2000, fear and insecurity played a growing role in children's experience in both Jewish and Arab communities.

Judaism

The Jewish faith does not claim that the Jews were the first to worship one God. The Jewish tradition is based on *the law of the sons of Noah*, the law that is the foundation of an universal ethical religion (including the worship of God; bans on murder, theft, INCEST and sex aberrations, eating "the limb of the living" or cruelty to animals, and blasphemy; and the establishment of justice, i.e., courts, judges, and a system of equity).

The ten commandments, an expansion of the above, were given by God at Mount Sinai to the Jewish people to guide them in their everyday life. Historically, JUDAISM never separated belief from performance, so in the Torah (the written law, or Bible, and the oral law, or Talmud) gives the Jew vision and purpose in life, a feeling of supremacy and special purpose in life for the superior mission he must accomplish. With the superior strength of Torah he overcomes failures during his lifetime. From this it can be seen that the Torah, rather than a history book, is the guidebook for life from which Jews must draw their power. A great sage of Judaism, Rabbi Hillel, who lived in the second century B.C.E., put it very plainly to a convert who asked to be taught all the Torah while standing on one foot. Hillel told him: "Love your neighbor as yourself. All the rest is commentary. Go now and learn."

Childhood in Judaism is considered a period of joy and purity that should be valued. The Talmud describes childhood as "a garland of roses." For every Jewish boy, childhood lasts from birth to the age of thirteen years, but after his BAR MITZVAH at age thirteen he is considered a man. At this age he begins to be responsible for his own actions and obliged to perform and fulfill mitzvot (good deeds). For a Jewish girl the age of reason begins at the age of twelve years.

Childhood in Israel

The educational system was established in 1948 in the new state of Israel in order to serve the Jewish population returning to their homeland. The system focused on culture, language, and ideology in order to create a new and strong Jew. In this period the kibbutz movement, which focused on the group and not the family, was very important. Growing from socialist theories, the kibbutz downplayed the traditional family. Children lived by themselves in children's houses, grew up collectively, and had very little family life. Long seen as the most distinctive aspect of Israeli childhood, the kibbutz movement was designed to instill strong community values and to promote hard work and efficiency, particularly in commercial agriculture. Children socialized in the kibbutzim were found to have less individualism and emotional fervor than children raised in traditional families, but their combination of schooling and work activities helped build the Israeli economy in the nation's early decades. Growing urbanization and the spread of more individualistic and consumer-oriented values increasingly undermined the kibbutz movement. In the early twenty-first century only 2 percent of children live in kibbutzim and even on remaining kibbutzim, children often live with their parents and have an in-

creasing array of consumer items such as televisions. In the late twentieth and early twenty-first centuries Israeli society has changed from agriculture to high-tech industry and the kibbutz population has declined. The kibbutz childhood was an experiment that got the attention of many important researchers in child development in the twentieth century, but has been mostly abandoned as an idea in the twenty-first century. This change can be seen in the draft of soldiers to elite units. Years ago the best soldiers came from the kibbutz population, but in recent years the elite has shifted to the modern Orthodox population and the child of the kibbutz is no longer in demand.

Israeli society is mainly Western oriented with many contacts and relationships with the United States. This consumer-oriented society has influenced children growing up in Israel. TELEVISION, Burger King, and whatever is the hit in America will quickly be introduced to the Israeli child. Israeli children have been avid consumers of MTV and other Western fads and fashions. But even with that influence, childhood is not the same for every child. The religious Jewish child in a settlement or in an ultra-Orthodox neighborhood of Jerusalem (where children grow up without television at all) will live a life integrated with the history of Israel, a life different from that of a secular Jewish child in Tel Aviv living the life of Western civilization, which again is different from that of a child in a Druze village or an Arab village.

CHILD ABUSE, family violence, and school violence, while always a part of life, have only emerged as a concern in Israel in the 1990s. With massive immigration from the former Soviet Union and Ethiopia, rates of reported family violence have risen. The increasing internal conflict and terrorist action that started in 2000 has killed more than one thousand persons (including children, mothers and fathers and grandmothers and grandfathers). The experience will have long-term effects and psychological consequences on children growing up in Israel. Terror has been part of the scene in Israel for many years, but the latest period has brought the terror closer to home, with many more victims.

Research and clinical experience have shown that in Israel today four groups of children are at a disadvantage: children living in poverty (25 percent of the children in the Israeli population), the Arab minority, immigrant children, and disabled children. In these areas the government will need to focus in order to make childhood in Israel better for all children.

BIBLIOGRAPHY

Aburbeh, Myriam, Ronit Ozeri, Ethel-Sherry Gordon, Nechama Stein, Esther Marciano, and Ziona Haklai. 2001. *Health in Israel. 2001 Selected Data.* Jerusalem: Ministry of Health.

Ben-Arieh, Asher, Yaffa Tzionit, and Zoe Beenstock-Rivlin. 2001. *The State of the Child in Israel. A Statistical Abstract.* Jerusalem: Israel National Council of the Child.

Efrat, Galia, Asher Ben-Arieh, John Gal, and Muhammed Haj-Yahia. 1998. *Young Children in Israel.* Jerusalem: Israel National Council of the Child.

JOAV MERRICK

J

Jahn, Friedrich Ludwig. *See* Gymnastics; Physical Education.

Japan

In studying the history of children in Japan, as in studying the history of children in other parts of the world, it is possible to distinguish between the history of childhood and the history of children. Investigating the history of childhood involves tracing the history of the idea, or rather, ideas, about children. Mothers, fathers, relatives, and religious, political, and other leaders, in addition to children themselves, have held ideas about what a child is and how children should behave. These ideas have been spoken and also written in pamphlets, magazines, newspapers, and books and have appeared in plays, films, and radio and TV programs. On the other hand, the history of children can be defined as the history of children's attitudes and experiences. In other words, the history of childhood is a history of norms, a history of notions of what a child should be, while the history of children attempts to grasp the lived experience of children. Because family, children, and childhood are cherished ideals for many people, there is sometimes resistance to the idea that childhood and children's experience have varied across space and time. Although the history of childhood and children in Japan is in its early stages, a survey of existing data and research presents solid evidence of changing ideas of childhood and changing children's experiences in Japan since roughly the seventeenth century.

Although Japanese prehistory shades into history around the sixth to eighth centuries C.E., this article focuses on childhood in Japan from the seventeenth to the early twenty-first centuries. These four hundred years span three historical periods: the early modern (or Tokugawa) period, from 1600 to 1868; the modern (or pre–World War II) period, from 1868 to 1945; and the contemporary (or postwar) period, from 1945 to the present. The history of childhood or children in earlier eras is not included due to limitations of space and the scarcity of existing research.

Like other historical projects, the history of children in Japan requires sources. As in other countries, it is easier to find material about Japanese children than by Japanese children. The difficulty of finding sources is one of the limiting factors for research on children's attitudes. On the other hand, adult observations on the situation of children are not hard to find, and many youths and adults have recorded memories of their childhoods. Therefore, material on the history of childhood is easier to find than sources for the history of children.

Five major issues are crucial to a basic understanding of the history of Japanese childhood and children over the past several centuries: (1) shifting definitions of childhood; (2) continuity and change in Japanese lifecycle rituals; (3) the changing importance of children in Japanese families (or households); (4) substantial continuity in Japanese child-rearing techniques; (5) the modern proliferation of schools and other children's institutions. The emphasis here is on the history of Japanese childhood because the history of children has been much more difficult to uncover.

Definitions of Childhood

Probing the history of childhood in Japan leads to a very basic question: What is a child? In advanced industrial societies today, children are economically dependent on their parents, and many are expected to be students until their early twenties. Legally, children may be required to live with their parents, attend school, and stay out of the labor force. However, in early modern Japan, most children were workers rather than dependents, and many children never attended school. Children in poor and ordinary families labored in peasant, merchant, and artisan households. They were valued for their contribution to the family livelihood as workers, especially in farm households. Despite increasing enrollment in schools of various types in the early modern period, most children were not students. Formal education was generally required for samurai sons who would inherit official positions in the warrior hierarchy, and it was highly useful for children working in merchant households and for the sons of peasant leaders. Tutoring or school education also functioned as a marker of status for the sons and daughters in the families of samurai and wealthy peasants and merchants. Yet the majority of children learned necessary social and vocational skills in households—in their natal households if they resided at home, in their adoptive households if they had been taken in by another family as successors, or in their masters' households if they had been placed out as servants or apprentices.

The transition to modern notions of the child as an economically dependent student took place in Japan's modern period with the implementation of a national school system and laws requiring four, then six, and finally nine years of compulsory education. Leaving home to attend school for many hours each day greatly reduced children's labor in the home at both economically productive and housekeeping chores. Today, according to the 1997 *Japan Almanac*, although only nine years of education are required, high school graduation rates are 96 percent of eligible children, while 45 percent of high school graduates go on to attend two- or four-year colleges.

Lifecycle Rituals

RITES OF PASSAGE mark various stages of Japanese childhood. They have not been extensively studied by Western scholars, but the available evidence indicates that since the early modern period these ceremonies have varied by region, social status, and economic status. Lifecycle rituals have changed over time as well; much of the information presented here is from the modern and contemporary periods. In general, NAMING ceremonies involving household members or the larger community took place within about a week after birth. Thereafter, the newborn was presented to the guardian deity, or *ujigami*, at the local shrine, often thirty-one days after birth for boys and thirty-three days after birth for girls, but sometimes as long as fifty to a hundred days after birth. Midwives, neighbors who breast-fed an infant, wet nurses, nannies, or a couple in another household sometimes became lifelong ritual parents to a child. In some regions, the first full BIRTHDAY was celebrated, but not later birthdays, or a feast with decorations was held on *sekku*, the doll festival on the third day of the third month for girls, or the carp kite festival on the fifth day of the fifth month for boys. May 5 is now a national holiday known as Children's Day, or *kodomo no hi*. On November 15, the *shichi-go-san*, or Seven-Five-Three Celebration, children of these ages are dressed in their best clothes, usually in traditional costumes, and taken to shrines. In the early modern period, a major rite for children, especially boys, was coming of age. This generally occurred around age fifteen. In some regions, not age but the

ability to perform work tasks was the main qualification for attaining adult status. Upon entering adulthood, children might change names, clothes, and hairstyles. In the modern period, eligibility for conscription at age twenty also became a marker of adulthood, although conscription ended when the armed forces were abolished in 1945. In the contemporary or postwar period, children are often taken to shrines after birth and for the Seven-Five-Three Celebration, ceremonies mark the entry and exit from preschool and elementary, middle, and high school. The legal age for voting and drinking is twenty, although the marriage age is lower, eighteen for boys and sixteen for girls. On January 15, Adults Day, or *seijin no hi* young women reaching age twenty may visit shrines wearing kimono.

The Changing Importance of Children in the Household and Family

In Japan household goals and structure are closely related to conceptions of childhood and the treatment of children. Both children's experiences and notions of childhood have shifted as the goals and structure of Japanese households changed over the centuries. In the early modern and modern periods, when the overriding goal was the eternal continuity of the *ie*, or stem family (one couple from each generation in a household), children were essential to households as future heirs and heads of households. Lineal, or blood, continuity was not required; Japanese households could be carried on by adoption of kin or nonkin—for example by adoption of a boy, or of a daughter's husband, or even of a married couple. Occupations were hereditary, so children born to or adopted into a household, or brought in as servants or apprentices, were valued as successors, heirs, and laborers for samurai, peasant, artisan, and merchant families. The treatment of children varied according to their status as permanent or temporary household residents. The heir often received more attention and better food and clothing than non-inheriting sons and daughters, who were destined to leave the household for employment, adoption, or marriage.

From the end of the nineteenth century, as the ideal of a companionate family, stressing affective relations between husband and wife and parents and children, began to replace the household goal of everlasting continuity, the importance of children decreased in the home. As workplace and home separated and state bureaucracies and corporations replaced family enterprises from the early twentieth century, the need for children as heirs, successors, and laborers declined. At the same time, children came to be defined primarily by their role as students rather than as productive workers. The government aimed to mold children into loyal, self-sacrificing citizens of a modern, powerful nation-state. But in Japan's advanced industrial society of the contemporary period, the main life goal, or *ikigai*, of many Japanese, especially of the younger generations, is shifting from continuing the stem family or self-sacrifice for the company to consumption, leisure, or self-fulfillment. As the age at marriage increases, divorce rises, the proportion of women who never marry increases, and the birthrate falls, Japanese society is becoming less family- and child-centered. Despite politicians' laments about national decline, demographic analysis shows Japan to be an aging society, with a corresponding fall in the proportion of children in the population.

Child-Rearing Methods

Despite changes in family and individual goals, and in family structure, there has been significant continuity in child-rearing techniques. True, some early modern and modern physical punishments, such as locking children in storehouses and moxibustion (igniting a powder on the skin), have fallen into disuse, but patterns of indulgence of infants and toddlers followed by steadily tightening behavioral expectations for older children and youths remain. Babies still sleep with (or even between) their parents, are breast-fed on demand, are carried on the backs of their caregiver with head facing forward, and are toilet trained by following the child's natural elimination schedule. Cultivating the child's dependence on the mother's affection, approval, and care is still a major means of controlling older children, as opposed to scolding, physical punishment, or withdrawal of privileges. In general, children focus on their homework, extracurricular lessons, or play, and do little household or remunerative work.

Schools and Other Children's Institutions

A fifth major issue in the history of childhood is the proliferation of children's institutions. In the early modern period, children were born, cared for, and educated in households. In that period, many types of schools developed in both rural and urban areas. The number of schools and the social range of children attending school expanded. Not only the children of the ruling warrior and commoner elites, but increasingly the children of lower-ranking warrior families and the children of merchant and farm households also attended schools. In the upper ranks of society, girls as well as boys received educations through tutoring, formal schooling, or household service. Ronald Dore estimates that at the end of the early modern period, overall LITERACY rates were around forty percent. Children were even more likely to attend school in the modern and contemporary period. According to a 1997 Asahi Shinbun almanac, in 1960, 58 percent of children advanced to HIGH SCHOOL, but the rate was 96 percent in 1995. In that year, 13 percent of high school graduates (2 percent of males and 25 percent of females) went on to junior colleges, and 32 percent (41 percent of males and 23 percent of females) to four-year colleges. The corresponding 1960 figures were 2 percent and 8 percent. Furthermore, in the modern and contemporary periods children live and are cared for in households, but they are increasingly educated in various types of schools rather than at home. In addition, especially from the modern period, specialized institutions such as ORPHANAGES, reformatories, clubs, camps, mother-child shelters, mother-child guidance centers, milk depots, and day care centers have developed to care for children.

The history of childhood in Japan exhibits a fascinating combination of change and continuity. Prepared by prior interest in schooling, particularly in the early modern period, the Japanese made the transition to mass compulsory schooling quickly after 1872. Work obligations for children declined, particularly as emphasis not only on schooling but on school success expanded. By the 1950s, conversion to a low birth rate also shaped childhood. From the late 1970s, the spread of consumerism also had a strong impact on children, with participation in international musical fads and leadership in the development of electronic games for children. Yet Japan has preserved both continuity in child-rearing methods and considerable emphasis on group norms for children, as opposed to the more individualistic socialization that is standard in the United States. From day care and preschool onward, education tends to emphasize the importance of links with other children and of conforming to peer standards and achievement of national and corporate norms.

See also: **China; Comparative History of Childhood; India and South Asia.**

BIBLIOGRAPHY

Asahi Shinbun. 1996. *Japan Almanac 1997.* Tokyo: Asahi Shinbun-sha.

Beardsley, Richard K., John W. Hall, and Robert E. Ward. 1959. *Village Japan.* Chicago: University of Chicago Press.

Doi, Takeo. 1973. *Anatomy of Dependence.* New York: Kodansha International.

Dore, Ronald P. 1965. *Education in Tokugawa Japan.* Berkeley: University of California Press.

Early Childhood Education Association of Japan, ed. 1979. *Early Childhood Education and Care in Japan.* Tokyo: Child Honsha.

Embree, John. 1935. *Suye Mura: A Japanese Village.* Chicago: University of Chicago Press.

Goodman, Roger. 1990. *Japan's "International Youth": The Emergence of a New Class of Schoolchildren.* Oxford, UK: Clarendon Press; New York: Oxford University Press.

Hendry, Joy. 1986. *Becoming Japanese: The World of the Pre-School Child.* Honolulu: University of Hawai'i Press.

Jolivet, Muriel. 1997. *Japan: The Childless Society?* Trans. Anne-Marie Glasheen. New York: Routledge.

Katsu, Kokichi. 1988. *Musui's Story: the Autobiography of a Tokugawa Samurai.* Trans. Teruko Craig. Tucson: University of Arizona Press.

Lewis, Catherine. 1995. *Educating Hearts and Minds: Reflections on Japanese Preschool and Elementary Education.* Cambridge, UK: Cambridge University Press.

Marshall, Byron. 1994. *Learning to Be Modern.* Boulder, CO: Westview Press.

Nakane, Chie. 1972. "An Interpretation of the Size and Structure of the Household in Japan Over Three Centuries." In *Household and Family in Past Time: Comparative History in the Size of the Domestic Group Over the Last Three Centuries*, ed. Peter Laslett, pp. 517–543. Cambridge, UK: Cambridge University Press.

Ochiai, Emiko. 1996. *The Japanese Family System in Transition: A Sociological Analysis of Family Change in Postwar Japan.* Tokyo: LTCB International Library Foundation.

Rohlen, Thomas. 1983. *Japan's High Schools*. Berkley: University of California Press.

Smith, Robert J., and Ella Lury Wiswell. 1982. *The Women of Suye Mura*. Chicago: University of Chicago Press.

Smith, Thomas C. 1977. *Nakahara: Family Farming and Population in a Japanese Village, 1717–1830*. Stanford, CA: Stanford University Press.

Tonomura, Hitomi. 1990. "Women and Inheritance in Japan's Early Warrior Society." *Comparative Studies in Society and History* 32: 592–623.

Uno, Kathleen. 1991. "Women and Changes in the Household Division of Labor." In *Recreating Japanese Women: 1600–1945*, ed. Gail Lee Bernstein, pp. 17–41. Berkeley: University of California Press.

Uno, Kathleen. 1999. *Passages to Modernity: Motherhood, Childhood, and Social Reform in Early Twentieth-Century Japan*. Honolulu: University of Hawai'i Press.

White, Merry. 1994. *The Material Child: Coming of Age in Japan and America*. Berkeley: University of California Press.

Yamakawa, Kikue. 1992. *Women of the Mito Domain: Recollections of Samurai Family Life*. Trans. Kate Wildman Nakai. Tokyo: University of Tokyo Press.

KATHLEEN UNO

Japanese Art, Contemporary

The signs of Western childhood play a very prominent role in post–World War II Japanese popular art, which has become increasingly global in its reach. This imagery, which is loosely called *anime*, takes many forms, including animated films, books, still drawings, playing cards, clothing, accessories, and toys.

Begun in reaction to the events of World War II, *anime* have been described as both evidence of Japanese cultural vitality in the face of trauma and an escape from it. The great *anime* pioneer Osamu Tezuka codified the genre in the 1960s, establishing an *anime* facial type and a distilled drawing style that eschews fluid realism and emphasizes metamorphosis. Overall, the look of *anime* has been dubbed "superflat." Classic examples of *anime* film include *Princess Mononoke* (1997) by Hayao Miyazaki (the highest-grossing Japanese film of any genre) and *Ghost in the Shell* (1995).

The salient characteristic of Japanese popular art within the history of childhood is its wholesale adoption of distinctly Western conventions for representing the ideal of innocent childhood— hybridized with traditionally Japanese *manga* comic drawings and mainstream Western cartoons. Most importantly, the large, round-eyed facial features of the stereotypically innocent child quickly became the standard mode of representing *anime* heroes and heroines, despite their clear racial difference from Japanese facial features. The complete roster of Western childhood toy and costume imagery also reappeared in *anime*, and, intensified, has spread through Japanese popular culture to become a popular esthetic, sometimes called *kawaii*.

Kawaii can be translated as "cute," "cool," "pretty," and "sweet," but also "smart" and "elaborate." But although the Western image of childhood is often translated into Japanese culture in a hyper-cute mode, just as often *anime* are about extremes of sex and violence (and also often deal with post-nuclear environmental issues). The stereotype of the Western schoolgirl, for instance, dressed in white blouse, pleated plaid skirt, socks, and flat shoes, has become a highly sexual image in Japanese popular art. The many people, referred to as *otaku*, who are preoccupied with *kawaii*, *anime*, and *manga*, are hardly all children, but rather a growing group of all ages that has spread outward from JAPAN.

Since the mid-1990s, the globalization of culture in general, and, more particularly, trends in contemporary high art to adopt the styles of popular art, have brought attention to Japanese popular art on a new scale. The work of leading *otaku* artists such as Yoshimoto Nara and Takashi Murakami are now widely exhibited in the West in galleries and museums. Western artists, moreover, have begun to incorporate *anime* imagery into their traditions, causing the stereotypes of childhood to reappear where they came from in radically new modes. A group of artists led by the award-winning French conceptual artist Pierre Huyghe, for instance, created a series of works made between 1999 and 2002, collectively titled *No Ghost Just a Shell*, based on an *anime* girl character called Annlee. These works addressed a range of distinctly adult concerns. As with other aspects of a postmodern, global culture, the signs of what was once considered inherently natural, in this case innocent childhood, have been detached from their content.

See also: **Comic Books; Globalization; Images of Childhood.**

BIBLIOGRAPHY

Aoki, Shoichi, ed. 2001. *Fruits*. London: Phaidon.

Brophy, Philip. 1997. "Ocular Excess: A Semiotic Morphology of Cartoon Eyes." *Art and Design* 12 (March/April): 26–33.

Higuinen, Erwan. 2000. "Au pays de l'anime." *Cahiers du Cinéma* 543 (February): 36–39.

Hoptman, Laura. 2002. *Drawing Now: Eight Propositions*. New York: Museum of Modern Art.

Kravagna, Christian. 1999. "Bring on the Little Japanese Girls! Nobuyoshi Araki in the West." *Third Text* 48 (autumn): 65–70.

Murakami, Takashi. 2000. *SuperFlat*. Japan: Madra.

ANNE HIGONNET

Jealousy and Envy

Since the nineteenth century, parents, psychologists, and educators have expressed concern over children's envy and jealousy. Envy and jealousy are often conflated today, but in the nineteenth and early twentieth centuries the two emotions elicited different responses from child experts and moralists who believed them to be quite distinct. *Envy* described the feelings experienced by one who longed for the belongings or attributes of another. In contrast, *jealousy* referred to the emotion experienced when an individual felt that a relationship or possession was threatened. While envy was frequently associated with material longings, jealousy was more often linked with LOVE.

Long viewed as a deadly sin, envy first became a source of worry for many in the United States during the last half of the nineteenth century. In the midst of a rapidly expanding consumer economy, moralists worried that Americans were becoming too covetous and materialistic. Educators, ministers, and pioneering psychologists expressed particular concern over the envy that children were displaying. They repeated Judeo-Christian condemnations of the emotion and told youngsters that they must learn to be contented with what they had rather than envying the belongings of their playmates. God had placed people in the condition he believed best for them; to long to be in different circumstances was to question God's wisdom. This message was repeated ceaselessly in children's schoolbooks, sermons, and stories, as well as in parenting advice.

By the 1910s and 1920s, many child-rearing experts had ceased thinking of envy as a sin. They still regarded it as a problem; however, believing that children who did not learn to conquer the emotion in youth might grow up to be unsuited for the corporate world which increasingly demanded cooperation and teamwork. Therefore, envy among children still had to be addressed. The experts suggested that the way to do this was not to force children to repress their envy and live with deprivation, but instead to give them the things they desired. If they envied their classmates' clothing or playthings, they should be provided with similar items.

While restrictions on envy generally relaxed in the twentieth century, rules governing jealousy became more rigid. Peter Stearns (1989) describes how attitudes towards the emotion changed. In preindustrial Europe and America, jealousy was not as harshly condemned as it would be in later years. Many authors claimed that jealousy arose naturally from love and the desire to protect a cherished relationship. Jealousy was considered a manly emotion, intimately connected to honor. Because it was seen as natural and even laudable, very little attention was paid to the question of how to limit jealousy in children.

In the early 1800s, attitudes towards jealousy began to change. Many commentators and moralists regarded jealousy as antithetical to true love. Ideally, love was so encompassing and total that jealousy need never arise. Women, in particular, were told to control the emotion in themselves, and the selfishness on which it was based. But while the emotion was becoming both feminized and stigmatized, scant attention was paid to it in child-rearing literature. Conventional wisdom held that real jealousy did not plague children—it only became a problem in adolescence and adulthood when romantic feelings were developing. Children might squabble and fight, but family love and unity were supposed to be strong enough to offset these problems.

By the late nineteenth century, however, child experts deemed jealousy a problem. During this period, family size decreased and maternal attention increased, causing more intense competition between SIBLINGS for affection and attention. Experts often framed their discussion of jealousy in terms of sibling rivalry, a problem first identified in the 1890s. They concluded that sibling rivalry was widespread in middle-class families, and that girls were more prone to the emotion than boys. As a result, throughout most of the twentieth century, child-rearing literature frequently addressed the problem of sibling rivalry and jealousy. Advisors suggested that children who did not overcome jealousy ran the risk of being maladjusted as adults and incapable of sustaining satisfying relationships. They advised parents to address the problem of jealousy by giving their jealous children extra love and TOYS. While concern with sibling rivalry subsided in parenting literature after the 1960s, parents continued striving to distribute affection and playthings evenly, in order to minimize sibling rivalry and jealousy.

The modern approaches to children's jealousy and envy reflect not only the changing nature and structure of family life, but also the powerful influence of CONSUMER CULTURE. The contemporary solutions to these childhood problems are based on the belief that material goods can bring contentment, and that it is better to indulge longings than to repress them.

See also: **Anger and Aggression; Child-Rearing Advice Literature; Emotional Life; Guilt and Shame.**

BIBLIOGRAPHY

Foster, George. 1972. "The Anatomy of Envy: A Study in Symbolic Behavior." *Current Anthropology* 13: 165–202.

Matt, Susan. 2003. *Keeping Up With the Joneses: Envy in American Consumer Culture, 1890–1930.* Philadelphia: University of Pennsylvania Press.

Schoeck, Helmut. 1969. *Envy: A Theory of Social Behavior.* Trans. Michael Glenny and Betty Ross. New York: Harcourt Brace.

Spielman, Philip M. 1971. "Envy and Jealousy: An Attempt at Clarification." *Psychoanalytic Quarterly* 40: 59–82.

Stearns, Peter. 1989. *Jealousy: The Evolution of an Emotion.* New York: New York University Press.

Stearns, Peter. 1998. "Consumerism and Childhood: New Targets for American Emotions," In *An Emotional History of the United States*, ed. Peter Stearns and Jan Lewis. New York: New York University Press.

Stearns, Peter. 1999. *Battleground of Desire: The Struggle for Self-Control in Modern America.* New York: New York University Press.

SUSAN J. MATT

Judaism

Jewish conceptions of childhood have undergone considerable transformation from the biblical era to the present. The practical challenges posed by child rearing have elicited a wide range of approaches to CHILD CARE, DISCIPLINE, and education, while also raising important questions concerning the role of gender, the scope of parental authority, and the nature of parent-child relations. The evolution of these issues reflects the impact of ethnic, cultural, and regional factors in Jewish history, and also bears unmistakable traces of the ever-changing role of religious ritual in Jewish life. No aspect of childhood has remained immune to these forces or indifferent to the dynamic influence of neighboring cultures.

Conceptions of Childhood

Research conducted by Jewish historians over the last thirty years, similar to most general studies devoted to childhood, stands largely in opposition to the theories advanced by French historian PHILIPPE ARIÈS. Ariès argued that childhood as we know it today did not exist in medieval society, owing to a lack of "awareness of the particular nature of childhood." Only with the approach of modernity was childhood "discovered." Countering these claims, Judaic scholars have assembled overwhelming evidence, culled from ancient and medieval Jewish sources, attesting to distinct developmental phases of childhood within Judaism and a clear appreciation of the child as such. As understood within Jewish society and culture, childhood refers broadly to all stages of life that precede adulthood, at which point an individual attains economic independence and assumes family or communal responsibilities. Abundant evidence in the Talmud indicates that the transitional stages, which include infancy, childhood, ADOLESCENCE, and youth (young adulthood), were widely acknowledged within ancient Judaism.

Several ritual ceremonies denote critical moments in the development of the child. CIRCUMCISION, a ceremony that takes place on the eighth day after birth, marks the entrance of the male child into the covenant of ISRAEL. In the Talmudic age it served additionally to set Jewish males apart from others in the Greco-Roman world. An intricate new ritual created in northern France and Germany during the twelfth century marked the initiation of boys at the age of five or six into Hebrew studies. Dressed in his best clothes, the boy was escorted to the synagogue and was fed eggs, fruit, and cakes of honey. The letters of the Hebrew alphabet were written on a slate and read to the boy. Then the letters were covered with honey, which the boy licked. Staged during the festival of Shavuot (Pentecost), the ceremony symbolically incorporated the child into the ranks of the Jewish people by reenacting the Torah covenant that was created at Mount Sinai. It was also intended as a rite against forgetfulness and as a means to open the heart. Some scholars have suggested that this initiation, insofar as it contains elements resembling the Christian Eucharist devotion, was designed as a counter-ritual to challenge the claims of the majority faith. Bread, wine, and honey likely were included in the Jewish ceremony simply because they represented knowledge and were commonly used to teach the alphabet. The initiation ceremony later found its way to distant Jewish communities in the Mediterranean basin and eastern Europe during the seventeenth century.

The BAR MITZVAH ceremony commemorates a boy's reaching the age of religious majority: thirteen years and one day. No comparable ritual marked a girl's attainment of her majority (twelve years and one day). The bar mitzvah first arose in Germany during the eleventh century, though it only became popular two centuries later. Thirteen had been established as the male age of religious obligation during the previous century; in the new ritual the boy's father was called to the Torah to declare that he was now relieved of responsibility for his son's misdeeds. Although minors had been technically permitted to participate in the full range of ritual commandments before their bar mitzvah, they were nonetheless dissuaded from performing certain rites until they attained their religious majority. Fourteenth-century sources describe a boy being called to the Torah for the first time on the Sabbath that coincided with or followed his thirteenth birthday; in sixteenth-century Poland, the ceremony developed into a bona fide RITE OF PASSAGE.

For all practical purposes, however, a young person did not become a full-fledged member of the community until he was much older than age thirteen. The precise age at which this occurred varied according to time and place. Furthermore, in many communities, unmarried men regardless of age were not eligible for certain synagogue honors; for example, religious authorities in eighteenth-century Metz refused to authorize unmarried men as ritual slaughterers. Marriage by itself could not definitively confer adult status, however, in part because child marriages were still prevalent in the early modern period. Seeking to harmonize the Talmudic tradition of "at eighteen to the marriage canopy" with the social and cultural desirability of marriage at a younger age, the authoritative *Shulhan Arukh* code of 1566 stated: "It is the duty of every Jewish man to marry a wife in his eighteenth year, but he who anticipates and marries earlier is following the more laudable course, but no one should marry before he is thirteen." The phenomenon of young men who married even at the age of ten was not unknown in early modern Europe. In some instances where the age at marriage was significantly higher, limitations were still imposed on relative newlyweds. According to an enactment of the Council of Lands in Poland in 1624, no note signed by a man within two years after his marriage had any validity; this period was subsequently extended to three years. Similarly, the council barred the extension of a loan to any person who was either under the age of twenty-five years or who had not been married for at least two years.

Care of Children

In sharp contrast to ancient Greece, where the practice of leaving newborns to die of exposure was not uncommon, Jews of antiquity emphatically rejected infanticide as murder. Philo of Alexandria, a leading Jewish philosopher of the first century, forcefully articulated the importance of caring for all infants. His revulsion against infanticide (he called it "a violation of the laws of nature") went hand-in-hand with the Judaic view of procreation as a divine command. Eventually this teaching would enter the mainstream of Christian thought as the Roman Catholic Church subsequently outlawed infanticide in the fourth century. Child ABANDONMENT would nonetheless persist as an acute social problem well into the modern age, tolerated by the Church so long as there was an economic argument for it.

The care given to young Jewish children reflected Judaism's overwhelmingly positive attitude toward childhood. According to ancient rabbinic law as recorded in the Talmud, a father was obligated to redeem his (first-born) son, circumcise him, teach him Torah, teach him a trade, obtain a wife for him, and according to one other opinion, to teach him to swim as well. No provision for child maintenance was mentioned explicitly in this list of parental obligations because the moral obligation to care for one's children was so elemental. Only after the Bar Kokhba Revolt (132–135 C.E.), in an era when Roman law developed in a parallel fashion, *mishnaic* law was recast so as to offer greater protection for children. The father's obligation to feed his children became a matter of law, and the prerogative to sell a son as security was abolished, though this legal advancement was not applied as fully to daughters. Even so, in times of severe economic hardship some parents felt compelled to offer their sons and daughters for sale.

Most sources describe the ideal medieval home as a gentle regime resting on mutual affection between parent and child. Ethical writings of the Middle Ages, such as the thirteenth-century German *Sefer Hasidim*, emphasized the obligations of mothers to keep their infants clean, well fed, and protected from the elements. Unlike other cultures that showed a clear preference for adult children, Judaism was partial to infants. This is evident in Jewish tomb inscriptions, where more attention was paid to the deaths of young children than was the case in ancient Egypt and Rome. Similarly, the anguish expressed upon the death of a child by Rabbi Judah Asheri of fourteenth-century Spain and others, consistent with the advice offered by *Sefer Hasidim* about showing sensitivity to parents who have lost a child, confirms the depth of attachment to children. Consistent with this is the imagery of *Midrash Rabbah* (on Psalm 92:13), which portrays playfulness between parents and their young children in the most positive terms.

Medieval sources also point to the growing involvement of Jewish fathers in their child's upbringing, as is evident in both the Ashkenazic and Sephardic cultural orbits. Fathers are depicted as becoming increasingly aware of intensity of love for an infant rather than an older child. Perhaps for this reason, the ethical literature was alert to the tensions between the competing demands of child care on the one hand and adult responsibilities on the other, and therefore underscored the priority that fathers were expected to give to their own Torah learning. Parents were nonetheless cautioned against indulging the child in an overabundance of affection. Excessive indulgence, it was argued, would undermine the goal of training children to fear their parents. This oft-repeated concern, which can be traced to a fourteenth-century Spanish moralistic work, *Menorat Ha-Ma'or*, also confirms that such expressions of affection were commonplace.

Discipline

In the biblical era corporal punishment was commonly viewed as the primary means of DISCIPLINE, as exemplified by Proverbs 13:24, "Spare the rod, despise the child." In the Talmudic age the strap replaced the rod, and by all accounts, strict punishment was meted out both in the home and at school. From the third century on, however, a reduction of physical punishment was favored; instead, alternative disciplinary measures were employed. For example, in response to the problem of the inattentive student, the specific recommendation of the Talmud was to "place him next to a diligent one" rather than to impose physical punishment. Parents and teachers were advised to exercise patience and sensitivity. Medieval sources point to a reality that was frequently at variance with the picture emerging from these Talmudic prescriptions. Although *Sefer Hasidim* was equivocal about corporal punishment, Rabbi Moses ben Maimon (Maimonides) (1135–1204) and Rabbi Solomon ben Aderet (1235–1310) acknowledged the right of the parent or teacher to strike a boy in the course of his studies. The fourteenth-century Sarajevo Passover Haggadah and the Coburg Pentateuch show teachers with whips, and a number of early modern sources, such as the *Brantshpigl*, advised teachers to gauge the severity of the punishment in accordance with the pupil's age.

Education

Owing to the primacy of ritual in traditional Judaism, instruction of children focused on the attainment of ritual literacy as its central goal. In the Talmudic era, boys attended elementary school or studied with a tutor from the age of five, six, or seven until the age of twelve or thirteen. A network of schools operated in the Land of Israel by the second century. School children learned to read the Torah and to write; at age twelve they studied *Mishnah*. No formal instruction in secular courses such as mathematics, Greek, or GYMNASTICS, was included in the Jewish school curriculum in this period. Initially, the houses of study excluded children from the lower strata of society, but by the third century education was made available to children of all classes. Girls were, by and large, excluded from the elementary schools, however, though some Talmudic sources suggest that fathers taught their daughters informally.

In the medieval period there was no system of communally funded elementary schools in northern France or Germany. Schooling was a private arrangement between parents and teachers. By contrast, the Jews of Spain and Italy maintained a more formal educational structure; moreover, in southern France there are references to elementary schools, though it is unclear whether these were schools or synagogues. Conditions in Italy were likely exceptional. Women gave elementary lessons in reading and writing to girls and boys, often in the teacher's home; the most striking example was the establishment of a special elementary school ("Talmud Torah") for girls in Rome in 1475.

Quite apart from formal schooling, great emphasis was placed on ritual education within the home and the synagogue. Each of the Jewish festivals provides an opportunity for children to acquire an understanding of the religious ideals of Judaism within a national and historical perspective, while at the social level the holidays foster shared values and a strong collective identity. The Passover *seder* offers perhaps the most outstanding paradigm of informal education in the entire Jewish calendar. The narration of the exodus from Egypt follows a question-and-answer format and uses rituals and symbols specially created to hold the interest of the children and to deepen their experience. Talmudic in origin, these strategies stress the importance of adapting both the supporting materials and the level of discussion to the child's ability to understand.

The importance attached to ritual literacy was also emphasized in less formal settings. The seventeenth-century Polish mystical-ethical work *Shnei Luhot Ha-Berit* emphasized the importance of teaching the child from the age of two or three, as this was seen to be the critical period for acquiring proper moral virtues, such as fear of one's father. The author, like the author of the *Brantshpigl*, went so far as to assign great importance to the role of mothers in rebuking their children, "even more than the father." Although children were formally exempt from reciting the *Shema* (daily credo) and from putting on *tefillin* (phylacteries), they were nonetheless obligated in prayer, *mezuzah* (scriptural verses attached to the door posts of the home), and grace after meals for training purposes. Nevertheless, at each successive stage in the child's development a new level of ritual involvement was added, and children were thus taught to observe certain commandments as soon as they were old enough to perform them. When a boy reached the age of three, he was given *tzitzit* (ritual fringes) to wear, and by the age of five, he was taught to recite the *Shema*. At the age of nine or ten the oaths that a child might take were considered valid. Girls and boys at this age were also encouraged to fast for several hours on Yom Kippur, with the time period increasing by one hour each year "so that they may be versed in the commandments" and so that when they reached the ages of twelve and thirteen, respectively, they would be ready to observe the full day of fasting.

Developments in the Early Modern and Modern Periods

The sixteenth century opened an era of escalating intergenerational tension. Challenges to parental authority in numerous Jewish communities became especially pronounced in the age of the PROTESTANT REFORMATION, and this trend would continue through the modern period. Numerous Jewish communities in the 1520s and 1530s prohibited marriages that were contracted without parental consent. Nevertheless, several distinguished rabbinic authorities at mid-century upheld the independence of young people to choose their marriage partners. Misgivings about the instability of youth and juvenile DELINQUENCY found expression in a variety of communal initiatives, including the creation of publicly funded schools and legislation establishing compulsory education. Other efforts sought to curb the freedom sought by adolescents from parental authority, especially in the realm of sexual conduct.

Revolutionary changes in society's attitude toward children were felt conspicuously within Jewish communities as well. Since the Renaissance era, thinkers had placed ever-increasing emphasis on the power of nurture over nature. The European ENLIGHTENMENT, and its Jewish variant, the Haskalah movement, favored the image of a child's mind as a *tabula rasa* on which teachers could write suitable information. Modern Jewish schools, founded in Berlin and other centers of Haskalah in the late eighteenth and early nineteenth centuries, drew heavily on the new pedagogical theories advanced principally by J. B. BASEDOW and J. H. PESTALOZZI. Their emphasis on a systematic approach to education that was attuned to the individual needs and talents of each child exerted enormous influence on Jewish educational reformers such as Naphtali Herz Wessely (1725–1805). Ambitious efforts to provide vocational training to children of poor Jewish families were part of the same modernization project. In the traditional *heder* (Jewish elementary school) of Eastern Europe, however, the modern spirit was much less in evidence. Throughout the nineteenth and early twentieth centuries, corporal punishment continued to be severe.

Powerful currents of religious modernization in the nineteenth century not only dominated the ideology of religious reform, but also substantively influenced the leadership of traditional Judaism. Among the most pressing issues was the recasting of educational and religious opportunities to include girls. Early in the century, most modern Jewish schools in Germany and France had been designed to educate both girls and boys. At the 1856 Paris rabbinical conference, a new ceremony for the blessing of newborn girls was created and adopted. The most widely implemented innovation in

France and Germany was the confirmation ceremony. Adopted by traditionalist rabbis, the ceremony was conducted for boys and girls who had passed examinations in Hebrew reading and in the catechism designed for Jewish students.

In the same spirit of egalitarianism, bat mitzvah ceremonies for girls proliferated in Conservative and Reform congregations in the United States in the twentieth century. In the second half of the century, such ritual celebrations also found acceptance, albeit in a more limited manner, in the Orthodox movement. There is also an increasing trend among vastly different Orthodox streams to provide Jewish elementary (and higher) education for girls that is virtually identical to that of boys. Dynamic forces at work in the State of Israel, as well as developments in the United States, are setting the pace for these trends.

See also: **Catholicism; Christian Thought, Early; Holocaust; Holocaust, Jewish Ghetto Education and; Islam.**

BIBLIOGRAPHY

Ariès, Philippe. 1962. *Centuries of Childhood: A Social History of Family Life.* Trans. Robert Baldick. New York: Vintage Books.

Baron, Salo W. 1942. *The Jewish Community: Its History and Structure to the American Revolution.* 3 vols. Philadelphia: The Jewish Publication Society.

Berkovitz, Jay. 2001. "Social and Religious Controls in Pre-Revolutionary France: Rethinking the Beginnings of Modernity." *Jewish History* 15: 1–40.

Biale, David. 1986. "Childhood, Marriage, and the Family in the Eastern European Jewish Enlightenment." In *The Jewish Family: Myths and Reality,* ed. Steven M. Cohen and Paula E. Hyman. New York: Holmes and Meier.

Blidstein, Gerald. 1975. *Honor Thy Father and Mother: Filial Responsibility in Jewish Law and Ethics.* New York: Ktav Publishing.

Cooper, John. 1996. *The Child in Jewish History.* Northvale, NJ: Jason Aronson.

Goitein, Solomon D. 1978. *A Mediterranean Society: Vol. 3.* Berkeley, CA: University of California Press.

Hundert, Gershon D. 1989. "Jewish Children and Childhood in Early Modern East-Central Europe." In *The Jewish Family: Metaphor and Memory,* ed. David Kraemer. New York: Oxford University Press.

Kanarfogel, Ephraim. 1992. *Jewish Education and Society in the High Middle Ages.* Detroit. MI: Wayne State University Press.

Kraemer, David. 1989. "Images of Childhood and Adolescence in Talmudic Literature." In *The Jewish Family: Metaphor and Memory,* ed. David Kraemer. New York: Oxford University Press.

Marcus, Ivan. 1996. *Rituals of Childhood: Jewish Acculturation in Medieval Europe.* New Haven, CT: Yale University Press.

Schimmel, Solomon. 1976. "Corporal Punishment of School Children: The Teacher's Tort Liability in Jewish Law." *Jewish Education* 45: 32–40.

Stow, Kenneth. 1987 "The Jewish Family in the High Middle Ages: Form and Function." *American Historical Review* 92: 1085–1110.

Ta-Shema, Israel. 1991. "Children of Medieval Germany: A Perspective on Ariès from Jewish Sources." *Studies in Medieval and Renaissance History* 12: 263–380.

Weissbach, Lee Shai. 1987. "The Jewish Elite and the Children of the Poor: Jewish Apprenticeship Programs in Nineteenth-Century France." *Association for Jewish Studies Review* 20: 123–142.

Yarborough, O. Larry. 1993. "Parents and Children in the Jewish Family of Antiquity." In *The Jewish Family of Antiquity,* ed. Shaye J. D. Cohen. Atlanta: Scholars Press.

JAY R. BERKOVITZ

Junior High School

The first junior high school opened its doors in Berkeley, California in 1910, and by 1920 over 800 junior high schools, each containing grades 7 through 9, had opened across the country. Outspoken advocates for the establishment of junior high schools like Leonard Koos, Thomas Briggs, and William Smith generally agreed on a core group of aims they attributed to a school specifically designed for students ages eleven to fifteen. These aims included:

> enriching and strengthening the curriculum and instruction offered in junior high schools in ways suitable to the age group
>
> recognizing and accommodating the special nature of early adolescence and individual differences in aptitude, interest, and ability
>
> staffing the schools with teachers specially prepared to work with young adolescents.

Some advocates also believed that the junior high school would encourage students, many of whom would halt their education at the end of the eighth grade, to stay in school for an extra year.

The push to introduce a more rigorous and varied curriculum earlier in students' public schooling began in 1888 with Charles Eliot's speech to the National Education Association (NEA) in which he argued college freshmen were not being adequately prepared during their years in public school. In their 1893 report, NEA's Committee on Secondary School Studies recommended beginning study of academic subjects in the upper elementary grades. Beginning in 1906, Carnegie units became the focus of college entrance requirements and secondary school academics. Each Carnegie unit required seat time of 40 to 60 minutes per day, five days a week, for one school year. Fourteen Carnegie units were required for college entrance, and those units started accumulating in ninth grade. Most junior high schools included ninth grade and adopted an organizational structure that supported acquiring Carnegie units. That structure was exactly like that adopted in the nation's high schools and eliminated practices like instruction across academic disciplines and flexible schedules that junior high advocates believed essential to responding appropriately to young adolescents' needs.

The idea that adolescence is a discrete phase of human development originates in the psychological studies of the early twentieth century and particularly the work of G.

STANLEY HALL. Hall argued that adolescence was a time of rapid, significant changes in virtually every aspect of human development, including physical, mental, social, emotional, and moral. Junior high advocates called for practices, like individualized instruction, that recognized and responded to the needs of young adolescents in the midst of the "storm and stress" Hall described. In reality, junior high schools did not individualize instruction, instead ignoring the learning trajectory of each child and sorting students into academic, vocational, or remedial tracks from which the students could rarely move regardless of their intellectual development.

Most junior high school teachers were prepared in programs that supported high school-like curriculum, instruction, and organization. Without structures and practices tied to young adolescent development and without specialized preparation for teachers, the junior high school that advocates envisioned did not survive the crush of the high school's traditions, setting up the push, begun in the 1960s, for a new school structure for young adolescents: the middle school.

See also: **Adolescence and Youth; Grammar School; High School.**

BIBLIOGRAPHY

Briggs, Thomas H. 1920. *The Junior High School.* Boston: Houghton Mifflin.

Hall, G. Stanley. 1905. *Adolescence: Volume I.* New York: Appleton-Century.

Koos, Leonard. 1927. *The Junior High School.* Boston: Ginn and Company.

Scales, Peter. 1992. *Windows of Opportunity: Improving Middle Grades Teacher Preparation.* Carrboro, NC: Center for Early Adolescence.

Smith, William. 1927. *The Junior High School.* New York: Macmillan.

Tyack, David, and William Tobin. 1993. "The 'Grammar' of Schooling: Why Has It Been So Hard to Change?" *American Educational Research Journal* 30: 453–479.

P. GAYLE ANDREWS

Juvenile Court

The first official juvenile court was established in Cook County, Illinois, in 1899. By 1920, juvenile courts existed in almost every major city in the United States. Juvenile courts provided separate proceedings and facilities for criminal, neglected, and dependent youths under eighteen, and focused on prevention, diagnosis, and rehabilitation. The court originated as part of a larger movement in the nineteenth century to segregate children from the adult criminal system. Urban reformers had worried that the poor living conditions in many American industrial cities were causing deviant behavior. They advocated separate institutions and organizations that would remove troubled youths from bad environments and train them to become productive citizens. By the late nineteenth century, however, many Progressive reformers were critical of these earlier methods. Encouraged by new psychological and sociological studies, reformers promoted earlier intervention in children's lives. Through the juvenile court, reformers believed court authorities could alter bad behavior by taking into account each child's individual experiences. Since its inception, the juvenile court has served as both a humanitarian enterprise and a tool for social control.

Broadly conceived, juvenile courts intervened in the lives of children and their families. Courts adopted the medieval English doctrine of *parens patriae*, in which the state acted as parent in cases when the child's welfare was threatened. Judges conducted cases informally, as civil rather than criminal proceedings, and had a great deal of discretion to act in the child's best interests. Typically, judges appointed probation officers to investigate the child's family, living conditions, and health, and to determine if the child needed to appear in court or to be referred to social services. Children awaiting hearings often were placed in detention centers. There, the child would be segregated according to his age, sex, and medical condition, and evaluated. When the case came to court, the judge could use all the information gathered up to that point, as well as his own informal interactions with the child and the parents, to render his decision. Usually, judges ruled in favor of probation. However, if a case was serious and the judge could find no other recourse, the child could be committed to a state reformatory.

Although many people heralded the juvenile court as a humanitarian achievement, others were more critical. Early critics complained that juvenile courts did not adequately implement their intended procedures and programs. Courts often were overwhelmed with their caseloads, and were unable to provide sufficient attention to the children in their custody. In many instances, courts relied on overworked volunteers as probation officers, and continued to use jails and punitive measures rather than rehabilitative treatments.

Others criticized juvenile courts for wielding too much power over children and parents. Children were labeled delinquent not only for criminal offenses, but also for statutory offenses and for being dependents. Juvenile courts had no juries, no rules of evidence or of witnesses, and no due process. Judges also discouraged defendants from seeking attorneys. This meant judges commanded a disproportionate amount of discretion. Meanwhile, as numerous juvenile court scholars have noted, courts interfered with the authority of parents, and were frequently the location of class and cultural conflicts between court officials and families. Although in many instances parents used juvenile courts to assert their own authority over their children, some scholars have suggested that the Progressive juvenile court served as a mechanism of social control over both parents and children, and over the lower classes, minorities, and immigrants.

The 1960s brought about the most significant changes to the juvenile court since the beginning of the century. Civil libertarians argued that juvenile courts often discriminated against youths according to class, race, and ethnicity through discretionary rulings and institutional commitments. Moreover, they contended that youths faced punitive incarceration similar to adult offenders without the same constitutional rights in the courtroom. Within a ten-year period, the Supreme Court handed down five major decisions—most famous of these was IN RE GAULT (1967)—which, together, restructured the juvenile court. These rulings provided greater due process and formalized proceedings, and narrowed judicial discretion. At the same time, many states legislated the removal of status offenders from the courts, mandated attorney involvement, modeled juvenile court proceedings after criminal courts, and placed more juvenile offenders in noninstitutional facilities. Ironically, since the late 1970s, as juvenile courts became more oriented towards CHILDREN'S RIGHTS, their proceedings also became more criminalized. Americans increasingly expressed greater concern about youth violence, and juvenile courts responded with tougher procedures and by trying more adolescents as adults.

The 1899 Chicago juvenile court has been influential internationally. Many industrialized and some developing countries have used the American juvenile court model as the basis for their own courts, incorporating judicial discretion and a social welfare approach. While each country's juvenile court is unique to that nation's culture, they all struggle with many of the same dilemmas regarding children's rights, racial and ethnic discrepancies, and rehabilitative versus punitive methods of controlling delinquency.

See also: **Delinquency; Juvenile Justice.**

BIBLIOGRAPHY

Platt, Anthony M. 1969. *The Child Savers: The Invention of Delinquency.* Chicago: The University of Chicago Press.

Rosenheim, Margaret K., et al., eds. 2002. *A Century of Juvenile Justice.* Chicago: The University of Chicago Press.

Ryerson, Ellen. 1978. *The Best-Laid Plans: America's Juvenile Court Experiment.* New York: Hill and Wang.

Schlossman, Steven L. 1977. *Love and the American Delinquent: The Theory and Practice of "Progressive" Juvenile Justice, 1825–1920.* Chicago: The University of Chicago Press.

Schneider, Eric C. 1992. *In the Web of Class: Delinquents and Reformers in Boston, 1810s–1930s.* New York: New York University Press.

LAURA MIHAILOFF

Juvenile Justice

INTERNATIONAL
Diane E. Hill

UNITED STATES
Victor L. Streib
C. Antoinette Clarke

INTERNATIONAL

In the late nineteenth century, a movement began in Europe and the United States that acknowledged the role played by social and economic conditions in setting children in conflict with the law. This resulted in the establishment of separate judicial proceedings for juveniles in many parts of the world by the beginning of the twentieth century, with uneven success and public support. Although interwoven with other human rights issues, such as a child's right to education, and to structural injustices—particularly racism and poverty, with its criminal wake of drug-dealing, prostitution, and theft—juvenile justice administration as a topic of international human rights concern did not fully emerge until the last quarter of the twentieth century.

The League of Nations' 1924 Declaration of the Rights of Children, followed by the United Nations' declaration (1959), recognized the issue of CHILDREN'S RIGHTS as a topic of international concern. However, neither document addressed the rights of children in conflict with the law or whether the young should be differentiated from adults in justice administration. The UN's 1955 Standard Minimum Rules for the Treatment of Prisoners stipulated that young offenders should not be imprisoned and, if they were, that they be separated from incarcerated adults. It was not until 1980 that the UN's Congress on the Prevention of Crime and Treatment of Offenders resolved to comprehensively address the unique needs of juvenile offenders.

Following this initiative, in 1985 the UN adopted the Standard Minimum Rules for the Administration of Juvenile Justice, or Beijing Rules. Recognizing the juvenile's evolving social, physical, and psychological development, the Beijing Rules sought to couple rehabilitation with judicial correction proportionate to a juvenile's personal circumstance and offence. Subsequently, the nonbinding UN Rules for the Protection of Juveniles Deprived of Their Liberty and the UN Guidelines for the Prevention of Juvenile Delinquency, or Riyadh Guidelines, were adopted by the UN in 1990. Contributing to forming international norms that applied child-centered values to juvenile DELINQUENCY and criminality, these documents prescribed that society interact with its troubled youth as valuable members and not as objects to be socialized or controlled.

However, the most significant instrument establishing juvenile justice as a topic of international concern is the 1989 UN CONVENTION ON THE RIGHTS OF THE CHILD (CRC). Entering into force in 1990 as the most well-received human rights treaty in history, it obligates its 191 ratifying states—only Somalia and the United States have yet to ratify—to alter their domestic legislation to comply with its provisions and regularly report their compliance to the CRC's monitoring mechanism, the Committee on the Rights of the Child. Importantly, the CRC generalized seventeen as the maximum age for juvenile status, a dividing line between children and adults that has remained the international norm.

Although some of the CRC's general provisions are relevant to children in conflict with the law, Articles 37 and 40 specifically address juvenile justice issues. Article 37 upholds the dignity owed a young offender as a human being, prohibits torture and degrading treatment or punishment, and abolishes capital punishment and life imprisonment without possibility of release for people under eighteen. Imprisonment of a child is proclaimed a measure of last resort to be applied for as little time as possible. Reflecting the 1966 International Convention on Political and Civil Rights, the young offender must be separated from incarcerated adults if detained or imprisoned.

Article 40 advocates the reintegration of the child as a constructive member of society. It echoes the 1948 Universal Declaration of Human Rights in proclaiming a child's right to due process and presumption of innocence until proven guilty, to have access to legal assistance, and to obtain an expeditious trial. Besides requiring states to establish a minimum age below which children cannot be deemed criminally culpable, Article 40 calls for children to be handled without resort to judicial proceedings whenever possible and offered alternative correction programs which might involve counseling, probation, FOSTER CARE, education, and vocational training proportionate to their circumstances and offenses.

Regional treaties also significantly contribute to the shaping of international rights norms for juvenile justice administration. The 1969 American Convention on Human Rights prohibited the death penalty for those under the age of eighteen and prescribed the separation of young offenders from adults. It also specified the right to a speedy trial before "specialized tribunals" mindful of the offender's status as a minor. In 1999, the Organization of African Unity's African Charter on the Rights and Welfare of the Child (1990) went into force as the first regional charter subsequent to the CRC that specifically addresses the administration of juvenile justice (Article 17) from the CRC's child's rights perspective. The 1954 European Convention for the Protection of Human Rights and Fundamental Freedoms (ECHR) stipulated few children's rights relevant to youth in conflict with the law, prompting the Council of Europe to adopt the comprehensive European Convention on the Exercise of Children's Rights in 2000.

Although much has been done in the last few decades to strengthen the rights of children in justice systems around the world, urgent human rights issues remain. Many countries, especially those most impoverished, lack a specific ju-

venile justice system or insufficiently support the existing system's infrastructure, resulting in overcrowding, unsanitary conditions, and the detention of minors with adults. Countries are challenged to fund rehabilitation programs and training programs for juvenile system personnel (who are often of a different cultural and economic background from the offenders), and coordination of relevant services of child psychologists, social workers, and lawyers is lacking. A country's wealth is not necessarily an indicator of a thriving juvenile justice system or immunity from inefficient legal processes that lead to lengthy delays and confinement of a child pending indictment or trial. In 2002, Human Rights Watch reported the lack of legal representation and systemic guarantees to fair hearings for young offenders in the United States, along with Brazil, Bulgaria, Guatemala, India, Jamaica, Kenya, Pakistan, and Russia. In detention facilities, children can face prolonged separation from their families, denial of legal assistance, and sentences that are incommensurate with the offense.

Another profound problem is physical abuse, including corporal punishment, meted out by police or staff. The Committee on the Rights of the Child has noted incidences of torture, flogging, or whipping visited upon youth offenders in LATIN AMERICA, AFRICA, and other areas. Youth detention also occurs as a remedy for perceived social problems such as sodomy or for family problems such as unruliness. Moreover, increasing crime at the end of the twentieth century in such countries as the United States and AUSTRALIA led to the establishment of mandatory sentencing rather than allowing the judge discretion to consider a juvenile offender's individual situation.

Underscoring the pressing nature of these human rights needs is a lack of domestic legislation that integrates the international norms of the CRC and other UN rules and guidelines regarding juvenile justice administration, as manifested in some formerly colonized countries that have retained colonial-era legislation. Some countries, like Vanuatu, have experienced conflicts because the application of new domestic legislation has been challenged by traditional law and custom. Tribal leaders and community chiefs, skeptical of the Western values the CRC seems to represent, expressed concern that the Convention's provisions might alienate children from their traditional values and customs and accelerate youth delinquency.

In complying with the CRC, many states assign its juvenile justice provisions low priority since the plight of young offenders attracts far less sympathy and support for scarce resources. Besides creating or strengthening juvenile justice administration, the young offender's right to education is generally neglected by states in contrast to their willingness to expand education for other children. The lack of sympathy this reveals is often exacerbated by the mass media's proclivity to link types of crime with young offenders in the public's imagination, and to frequently distort the pervasiveness of juvenile delinquency in society. The Riyadh Guidelines specifically urge the media to "portray the positive contribution of young persons to society" since it has a substantial influence on the public will for either punitive or rehabilitative change in the juvenile justice system.

Global diplomacy is also affected by differences between national juvenile justice systems. Extradition treaties between countries must account for different views concerning the death penalty. This is especially true in relations with the United States, since it is one of the few countries that permits this sentence for those who commit capital crimes before age eighteen. Contravening the emerging international norm, twenty-three states within the United States still allow the death penalty for convicted youth under eighteen or life imprisonment without possibility of parole. Since 1985, only Bangladesh, Iran, Iraq, Nigeria, Pakistan, Saudi Arabia, the United States, and Yemen have executed offenders younger than eighteen. Other international difficulties emerge with detained children who are in conflict with immigration laws in Australia, the United States, and Germany, among others. Abuses against certain minorities also bridge national borders, as illustrated by the Roma's plight in Italy, Slovakia, and the Czech Republic. An effective and integrated approach to address global increases in cross-border youth prostitution and drug-dealing is a continuing topic of international concern for juvenile justice administration.

See also: **Abduction in Modern Africa; Child Labor in Developing Countries; Child Labor in the West; Child Pornography; Child Prostitution; Soldier Children: Global Human Rights Issues.**

BIBLIOGRAPHY

Feld, Barry C., ed. 1999. *Readings in Juvenile Justice Administration.* New York: Oxford University Press.

Shoemaker, Donald, ed. 1996. *International Handbook on Juvenile Justice.* Westport, CT: Greenwood Press.

United Nations. 1985. *Standard Minimum Rules for the Administration of Juvenile Justice (The Beijing Rules).* G.A. Res. 40/33, 40 U.N. GAOR Supp. No. 53 at 207, U.N. Doc. A/40/53.

United Nations. 1989. *Convention on the Rights of the Child.* G.A. Res. 44/25, U.N. GAOR, 44th Sess., Supp. No. 49, U.N. Doc. A/44/49.

United Nations. 1990. *Guidelines for the Prevention of Juvenile Delinquency (The Riyadh Guidelines).* G.A. res. 45/112, annex, 45 U.N. GAOR Supp. (No. 49A) at 201, U.N. Doc. A/45/49.

United Nations. 1990. *Rules for the Protection of Juveniles Deprived of their Liberty.* G.A. res. 45/113, annex, 45 U.N. GAOR Supp. (No. 49A) at 205, U.N. Doc. A/45/49.

United Nations. 2002. *Report of the Committee on the Rights of the Child.* U.N. GAOR, 57th Sess., Supp. No. 41, U.N. Doc. A/57/41.

INTERNET RESOURCES

Annan, Kofi. A. 2003. "We the Children: Meeting the Promises of the World Summit for Children." Available from <www.unicef.org/specialsession/about/sg-report.htm>.

Cothern, Lynn. 2002. "Juveniles and the Death Penalty." Available from <www.ncjrs.org/html/ojjdp/coordcouncil/index.html>.

Defence for Children International. 2003. Available from <http://defence-for-children.org/>.

Human Rights Watch. 2003. "Juvenile Justice." Available from <www.hrw.org/children/justice.htm>.

Human Rights Watch. 2003. "World Report 2003." Available from <www.hrw.org/wr2k3/>.

United Nations. 1989. *Convention on the Rights of the Child,* U.N. Doc. A/44/49. Available from <www.unhchr.ch/html/menu2/6/crc/treaties/crc.htm>.

United Nations. Office of the High Commissioner for Human Rights. Committee on the Rights of the Child. 2003. Available from <www.unhchr.ch/html/menu2/6/crc/>.

DIANE E. HILL

UNITED STATES

The American judicial system operates on the premise that "children have a very special place in life which law should reflect" (*May v. Anderson,* 1953). A prime example of this "special place" for children who are offenders is the U.S. juvenile justice system, with responsibility for protecting the general public from juvenile offenses while observing an intricate network of legal rights and procedures for those caught up in the system.

Major Eras of Juvenile Justice

Social welfare. The social welfare era (pre-1899) of American juvenile justice had its roots in centuries-old English common law. Derived from the royal prerogative, the early common law gave the English Crown the right and responsibility to protect persons deemed legally incapable of caring for themselves. Protection of children, however, was normally confined to families of the landed aristocracy, with an eye toward securing financial reward for the Crown itself. After the American Revolution, the states assumed for themselves the authority held by the Crown, but they extended protection beyond the landed gentry.

Throughout most of the United States' early history, children were viewed as legal incompetents in family and financial matters until they reached the age of majority (age twenty-one for most of U.S. history). The law remained generally unconcerned with affairs within the family and recognized almost absolute parental authority over children. Supported by religious and educational views that emphasized corporal punishment, parents and educators were free to use whatever means they deemed appropriate to break or to beat down disobedient children. Courts rarely interfered with parental and school disciplinary practices. This "hands-off" approach to problematic behavior by children generally characterized governmental approaches until the early and middle decades of the 1800s.

In nineteenth-century America, the Industrial Revolution forced people to live in close proximity to each other and to confront the social challenges that came with the urban lifestyle. The changes that were taking place were especially significant with respect to children, and states quickly recognized the need to deal with children who were considered incorrigible or who posed a problem to their families or to the community.

In direct response to these concerns, the state of New York and later the city of Philadelphia established Houses of Refuge. These privately funded houses were designed to provide custody for children who had committed criminal offenses or who were found to be runaways or vagrants. These institutions were essentially established to save children from a life of crime and the consequences of incarceration with adults. By the end of the nineteenth century, concern for these children became widespread and similar institutions to house all wayward children were created in a number of major cities. This concern served as a basis for the creation of juvenile courts, through which states could intervene officially on behalf of children who had committed criminal acts.

Socialized juvenile justice. The socialized juvenile justice era (1899–1966) began with the advent of the JUVENILE COURT, a product of the social and political movements from the 1890s through the early 1900s. These movements have been characterized alternatively as Progressive child-welfare movements reaching out to rescue children from the harsh criminal justice system or as mechanisms to impose middle-class values upon poor and powerless children. Whatever the motives for its creation, the juvenile court idea took root and spread throughout the country. By 1912, about half of the states had juvenile courts, and by the end of the twentieth century juvenile courts existed in every state.

Until 1966, the juvenile justice system operated under a concept of law and justice fundamentally different from other American judicial systems. Instead of reacting to violations of law or providing a forum for resolution of legal disputes, the socialized juvenile justice system attempted to intervene before serious violations of law occurred. This approach involved predicting the future behavior of a child rather than deliberating over evidence of a child's past criminal acts. It was designed to offer approximately the same care, custody, and discipline that a loving parent would offer to a child. Acting in the capacity of a foster parent, the state assumed the nearly unchallengeable authority of a parent over a child.

All of the basic functions were performed in the socialized juvenile justice system that are performed in the current system, albeit in a much more informal and perfunctory manner. The socialized system simply left presentation of the child's side of the case to the same police officer or probation officer responsible for presentation of the state's side of the case.

Defendants' rights. The defendants' rights era (1966–1990) began when the Supreme Court examined the social-

ized era and expressed a "concern that the child receives the worst of both worlds: that he gets neither the protections accorded to adults nor the solicitous care and regenerative treatment postulated for children" (*Kent v. United States*, 1966). In 1967 the Supreme Court imposed the requirements of constitutional due process upon the juvenile court's adjudication hearing in IN RE GAULT, including the right to defense counsel for the juvenile, the right to notice of the charges and hearings, the right to confront and cross-examine opposing witnesses, and the right to remain silent and not to testify against oneself.

These basic procedural rights were bolstered in 1970 when the Supreme Court decided that delinquency cases must be proven beyond a reasonable doubt by the state, the same level of proof required in adult criminal cases (*In re Winship*, 1970). Since the general rules of evidence from criminal court also are followed in juvenile court, these juvenile adjudication hearings became almost indistinguishable from criminal trials, except that the Constitution does not require that juvenile cases be decided by juries (*McKeiver v. Pennsylvania*, 1971).

These procedural requirements had a profound effect upon the juvenile court process. Assurance of representation by a defense attorney meant that the hearings were converted from informal conferences into adversarial contests, often quite similar to criminal trials. Proof requirements increased the focus upon the elements of each offense charged and decreased the emphasis upon the individual child.

Retribution and responsibility. The juvenile justice system entered a retribution and responsibility era in 1990. The defendant's rights of juvenile offenders remained generally intact, but in the early 1990s American society became much more focused on juveniles being held responsible and suffering retribution for their offenses. This meant that more cases were transferred from juvenile to criminal court and the discretion given to prosecutors to file juvenile cases directly in adult criminal court was increased. This was a complete reversal of the original impetus for the creation of the juvenile justice system in the early 1900s, which was to remove children from the punitive criminal justice system in order to provide them with treatment and rehabilitation.

A relatively new type of statute, known as blended sentencing or extended juvenile jurisdiction, is also becoming more popular as an effort to merge critical functions of the juvenile justice system and the adult criminal system. Blended sentencing allows the adult criminal judge or the juvenile judge to impose both a juvenile sentence and, subsequently, an adult sentence for those juvenile offenders who should be incarcerated beyond the age of majority. This type of legislation is seen as a way to detain juveniles who may be too young for imprisonment in adult jails at the time of the offense but who should not be released in just a few years. Typically, the adult sentence is stayed pending good behavior while serving the juvenile sentence. However, for particularly heinous crimes, such as murder or rape, the sentence becomes effective immediately after the juvenile reaches that state's age of majority. Variations of blended sentencing statutes range from the juvenile receiving either an adult sentence or a juvenile sentence to the juvenile receiving one combined sentence consisting of both juvenile and adult incarceration. A contiguous blended sentence allows the juvenile court to impose a juvenile sanction that may remain in force beyond the age of the court's extended jurisdiction.

In other modern legal systems, the youthfulness of juvenile offenders typically is an explicit factor in both the processes pursued and the sentences imposed, but few other countries have officially separate juvenile courts as found in the United States. Generally, the offenses and special needs of children are handled much more informally elsewhere, and American sanctions imposed on juvenile offenders are much more severe than almost anywhere else in the world.

Juvenile Offenses and Correctional Alternatives

The concept of children as offenders encompasses the instances in which persons under the juvenile court age limit (usually age eighteen) commit acts that harm or threaten to harm the persons and/or property of others or, in some cases, of themselves. Most of these acts would be crimes, but they are not treated as such because the actors are children.

Traffic offenses were originally treated no differently from other juvenile offenses. However this practice has come under considerable criticism, and the trend is to relegate less-serious traffic offenses to traffic court. The teenage driver is treated just as an adult driver would be, except that the teenager may have more restrictions placed on their driver's license and they may lose their driving privileges more easily than would an adult driver. More serious traffic offenses, such as reckless homicide, tend to remain in juvenile court and are processed as regular delinquency cases. Some jurisdictions allow the trial proceedings to be held in either the juvenile court or the traffic court, but the Supreme Court has made it clear that trials in both courts for the same offense would be unconstitutional (*Breed v. Jones*, 1975).

Status offenses cover a range of noncriminal behaviors by children and may account for up to one-half of the total work load of juvenile courts. Status offenses are comparatively vague, all-encompassing behaviors, such as habitual truancy, that could easily be interpreted to include the behavior, at some time, of every child. As a result, juvenile courts have essentially unchecked power to find almost any child guilty of a status offense. Juvenile courts also have the power to order almost the same punishment for status offenders as for delinquents, ranging from probation while continuing to live at home to placement in a secure institution far from home. Thus, status-offender jurisdiction remains broad and sweeping as compared to the comparatively narrow delinquency jurisdiction.

An act of DELINQUENCY is defined generally as a violation of a state or local criminal law, an act that would be a crime if committed by an adult. Some states have limited this broad definition of delinquency by excluding the most serious and/or the most minor criminal offenses. Such jurisdictions will exclude, for example, any criminal offense punishable by death or life imprisonment. At the other end of the scale, some jurisdictions exclude such minor crimes as traffic offenses and fish and game law violations. Some acts of delinquency are law violations that apply only to children. Violations of curfew laws by minors is the most common example, but others include possession of air guns or drinking alcohol. Correctional alternatives for delinquents range from community probation to institutionalization for several years.

The most serious criminal offenses, such as murder, rape, and robbery, typically result in the teenager being prosecuted in adult criminal court, either after having been transferred from juvenile court or having been filed directly in criminal court from the beginning. In most jurisdictions, juvenile offenders convicted of such serious criminal offenses can and do receive the harshest adult sentences, including life in prison and even the death penalty. These most severe American sentences are nearly unmatched by other modern societies. Prison sentences in the United States generally are much longer than would be found for the same offenses elsewhere, and most other nations have eliminated the use of the death penalty for juvenile offenders. By the early twenty-first century, only the United States, especially in the state of Texas, continued to execute offenders for crimes committed as juveniles.

Juvenile Justice Process

When children within the age limits of juvenile court jurisdiction commit acts of delinquency or status offenses, the juvenile justice system usually has the authority to process them accordingly. It is not unusual for juveniles and their parents to voluntarily contact the police juvenile officer or the juvenile probation officer without an arrest or a request to appear. Most often the family is referred to other social service agencies for the assistance they request, but in some cases official court action is deemed appropriate.

The arrest of a child is not significantly different from the arrest of an adult. Considerable physical force can be used to effect the arrest, up to and including deadly force if absolutely necessary, although this is rare. Along with the arrest, there is a wide variety of police investigative activities necessary to gather evidence for use in the case being prepared against the juvenile. This may involve, for example, search of the child's person, home, car, or school locker. The police must give the required warnings prior to custodial questioning, which include the right to remain silent and the right to have an attorney present during questioning—though there is some ambiguity in the law on this point (*Fare v. Michael C.*, 1979). Some states prohibit questioning of children if their parents are not present, while other states require that the child first consult with an attorney before being allowed to make any statement.

If there are no parents to take the child, if the child's parents refuse to take the child, or if the situation is so serious that release seems inappropriate, the child may be detained pending further proceedings. The decision to do this is first made on the spot by a juvenile probation officer, but soon thereafter a detention hearing is held before a juvenile court judge. The policy of denying pretrial release to juveniles to prevent interim offenses was approved as constitutionally acceptable by the Supreme Court in 1984 (*Schall v. Martin*).

The next step is the intake hearing, which is the first stage of the juvenile court process. Here potential cases are screened for appropriateness for further, more formal action. Typically, the juvenile probation officer meets with the child and parents to discuss the police charges. The child is asked to give his or her side of the story, and everyone tries to determine whether or not formal court action will be necessary to resolve the matter.

If the case is not diverted at the intake hearing, the probation officer initiates a formal juvenile court petition under the authority of the juvenile court judge, establishing a formal prosecution of the juvenile in a court of law. The juvenile petition alleges that the child violated certain specific laws on a certain date in a certain place in a certain manner. Status-offender petitions are somewhat less specific but also allege the violation that is the basis of the case, and very serious juvenile offenses might be filed in directly adult criminal court.

In juvenile court a trial is referred to as an adjudication hearing, although it is quite similar in procedure to the criminal court trial. The prosecuting attorney presents the evidence for the state tending to prove that the juvenile committed the offenses alleged in the petition, and the defense attorney counters with evidence tending to cast doubt on that evidence. In almost all states the adjudication hearing is presented to the juvenile court judge alone, who returns the verdict and decides upon the proper sentence or disposition. Juvenile hearings are almost always closed to the public and press.

If the child has been adjudicated to be a delinquent or a status offender, then the juvenile justice process moves into the sentencing, or dispositional, stage. During the period between the adjudication hearing and the disposition hearing, the probation officers prepare a social history or presentence report. In addition to the probation officer's social history report and disposition recommendation, the juvenile court considers evidence and disposition recommendations presented by the juvenile's attorney, the parents, and anyone else knowledgeable about the child.

The dispositional alternatives available to the juvenile court judge in delinquency and status-offender cases are various forms of probation and institutionalization. Generally, younger juveniles with minimal previous offenses who have not committed very serious offenses tend to be placed on probation, while institutions are reserved for older juveniles with past records and those who have committed more serious offenses. The juvenile offender's record is kept confidential; and it may even be sealed and ultimately expunged from all official records, as if the offense never happened.

See also: **Children's Rights; Law, Children and the; Police, Children and the.**

BIBLIOGRAPHY

Feld, Barry C. 2000. *Cases and Materials on Juvenile Justice Administration.* St. Paul, MN: West.

Feld, Barry C. 2003. *Juvenile Justice Administration in a Nutshell.* St. Paul, MN: West.

Fox, Sanford J. 1970. "Juvenile Justice Reform: An Historical Perspective," *Stanford Law Review*, 22: 1187–1239.

Mack, Julian W. 1909. "The Juvenile Court." *Harvard Law Review* 23: 104–122.

VICTOR L. STREIB
C. ANTOINETTE CLARKE

Juvenile Publishing

One of the consequences of the formation of the new, white middle class in the Northeast in antebellum America was the lengthening of childhood. Children's longer dependency within the family helped create and support institutions, namely private and public schools that provided children with skills and knowledge for the new white-collar occupations. But the rising sons of the middle class could not spend all their time at study, and hours apart from school became playtime, increasing the need for suitable recreations for adolescents. Besides typical boyish pranks, organized sports, and junior political and reform activities, boys and, to a lesser extent, girls between twelve and eighteen published their own newspapers in which the youngsters practiced for adulthood in a world all their own.

Juvenile newspapers all over the Northeast sprang up during the 1840s and 1850s as their youthful editors scavenged used type, cast-off composing sticks, and put their mothers' abandoned cheese presses back into service. Some teenage pressmen depended on their mechanic skill and copied their machines from engravings of Benjamin Franklin's press. However they were able to gather the tools of their trade, the young editors became part of a vast amateur recreation; on March 16, 1846, the editor of the Boston *Germ* noted that the city boasted eight juvenile papers and Worcester an equal number. Amateur newspapers continued to be a feature of boys' and, on occasion, girls' teen years until 1867, when the invention of the Novelty Press and its later imitators, such as the Cottage, Lowe, and Kelsey Presses, brought publishing within financial reach of an even larger number of children. Selling for between fifteen and fifty dollars, depending on the style, the presses guaranteed professional results, albeit at a slow speed. For those young people who had the economic wherewithal, the presses provided the means to test their literary and journalistic talents and organizational abilities.

The advent of the small, toy press, moreover, ushered in the golden age of amateur publishing during the 1870s. Because subscription lists were large and because exchanging papers was an important element in amateur journalism, the hobby spread from the Northeast across the nation, creating a mass culture for adolescents who shared the experience of reading the same stories and debating the same issues. Louisa May Alcott, for example, had the March girls engaged in writing and editing an amateur paper, *The Pickwick Portfolio*, in *Little Women*, and L. Frank Baum, the author of *The Wonderful Wizard of Oz*, started his literary career with an amateur newspaper, the *Rose Lawn Home Journal*. Although many of the papers of the 1840s and 1850s generally imitated their adult counterparts by reprinting selections from other periodicals, the juvenile papers of the 1870s were firmly committed to original work. Bereft of stylistic sophistication—metaphor, symbol, character development, and, sometimes, plot—the amateur papers and miniature novels provided a forum for young people's thinking as they used a toy to mark the longer time between childhood and adulthood. Because they were novice writers, the authors often copied or, more precisely, plagiarized plots and characters created by their favorite adult authors: Captain Mayne Reid, Horatio Alger and, especially, Oliver Optic. Nevertheless, in their so-called adaptations of adult work, the amateur editors made significant alterations in characterization and plotting to suit their own perceptions.

The National Amateur Press Association

In 1876 the amateur authors founded the National Amateur Press Association, holding their first convention in Philadelphia. Aside from allowing the editors to meet one another, the association furnished endless opportunities for reportage and editorials about the politics of the organization and amateur publishing in general. In their discussions of membership requirements, organizational protocols, and publishing problems, the young editors confronted difficult issues. Although the amateur press editors did not reject their parents' views in toto, they experimented with different relationships with women—relationships that included female autonomy and sexuality. They also grappled with race when the amateur editors discovered that several among their number were African American. Finally, they undertook the transformation of public policy, sparring with the U.S. Post Office when an increase in postal rates and reclassification of their papers threatened their newspaper exchange program.

The amateur newspapers and novels produced by novelty press owners show that nineteenth-century ADOLESCENCE was much more complex than socialization explanations involving structural shifts or parental exertions. The stories written by the young journalists capture young men and women in the mutually educative process of interpreting for themselves the complicated array of relationships in their society and freeze them in the act of exploring the possibilities of their own perceptions. Not only do these amateur journals demonstrate the pervasive influence of contemporary children's authors, but they also reveal a new set of values about gender and suggest how young men and women recast middle-class standards to shape the ideology of their own generation. The amateur papers also constitute one of the few places in which children and adolescents speak in their own voices.

New Publishing Forms

Amateur publishing persisted by fits and starts after the first generation of amateur publishers passed from the scene. An article in *St. Nicholas*, the popular children's periodical, revived the hobby in 1882 and attracted a new group of adolescents to amateur publishing. Never as popular as it was during the nineteenth century, amateur publishing fell on hard times in the early twentieth century but experienced a renaissance in the 1930s, largely as a result of a recruitment program sponsored by the Kelsey Press Company in concert with several amateur publishers. The demographics of amateur publishing had, however, changed; by the 1930s, amateur publishing was an adult pastime. The National Amateur Press Association, the organization created by the young people in the mid-nineteenth century, also maintained its existence, although its membership after 1930 also consisted largely of adults, and continued its program of annual meetings and paper exchanges. The advent of the Internet and World Wide Web ushered in an entirely new form of amateur publishing. Although web browsers and HTML editing software replaced the composing sticks, type trays, and presses of amateur publishing, the spirit of a teenage pastime lives on in the numerous adolescent websites and *blogs* (Web-based journals, diaries, or accounts) that populate the Web.

See also: **Autobiographies; Children's Literature.**

BIBLIOGRAPHY

Harrison, George T. 1883. *The Career and Reminiscences of an Amateur Journalist and a History of Amateur Journalism*. Indianapolis, IN: George T. Harrison.

Horton, Almon. 1955. *The Hobby of Amateur Journalism, Part One*. Manchester, UK: Almon Horton.

Kett, Joseph F. 1977. *Rites of Passage, Adolescence in America, 1790 to the Present*. New York: Basic Books.

Mergen, Bernard. 1982. *Play and Playthings, A Reference Guide*. Westport, CT: Greenwood Press.

Petrik, Paula. 1989. "Desk-Top Publishing: The Making of the American Dream." *History Today* 39: 12–19.

Petrik, Paula. 1992. "The Youngest Fourth Estate: The Novelty Printing Press and Adolescence, 1870–1876." In *Small Worlds:*

Children and Adolescence, 1850–1950, ed. Elliott West and Paula Petrik. Lawrence: University of Kansas Press.

Spencer, Truman J. 1957. *The History of Amateur Journalism*. New York: The Fossils.

PAULA PETRIK

K

Keene, Carolyn

Carolyn Keene was the pseudonymous author of the Nancy Drew and Dana Girls series of juvenile mystery books about young girl detectives. In the late 1920s, Edward Stratemeyer, the founder of the Stratemeyer Writing Syndicate, a producer of juvenile SERIES BOOKS (including The Rover Boys, The Hardy Boys, Tom Swift, and The Bobbsey Twins), created the penname Carolyn Keene, which was to be the name of the author of a new series based on a teenage heroine named Nancy Drew. Stratemeyer himself wrote the first three plot outlines, including detailed character profiles, while hired ghostwriters fleshed out the finished texts. The character of Nancy Drew represented a new phenomenon in juvenile literature. She was an independent, clever young woman who solved complicated mysteries, with the occasional help of two female friends.

Two weeks after Stratemeyer's death in May 1930, the first Nancy Drew books were published by Grosset and Dunlap. His two daughters Harriet, age 37, and Edna, age 35, then formed a partnership to continue their father's writing empire. The sisters wrote detailed chapter-by-chapter plot outlines for the next fifteen Nancy Drew adventures, as well as outlines for their father's other successful series. They sent them to ghostwriters, but maintained exclusive control over their stories and final published manuscripts.

The Dana Girls book series, about two sister detectives, was introduced by Harriet and Edna in 1934, also under the penname Carolyn Keene. This series continued intermittently until 1979.

In 1942, Harriet Stratemeyer Adams assumed full control of the Stratemeyer Writing Syndicate, which she ran from offices in New Jersey for the next forty years (until her death in 1982 at the age of eighty-nine). She herself wrote the story outlines for Nancy Drew books numbers 19 through 23, and she wrote books number 24 through 58 in their entirety.

Harriet Adams was eventually recognized around the world as the real Carolyn Keene. Her role in important series like The Hardy Boys, The Bobbsey Twins, and Tom Swift Jr. was less well known. Beginning in 1956, Adams, with the help of other Syndicate employees and editors, began rewriting the Keene books to shorten and modernize them, and to delete ethnic stereotyping and dialect.

Adams had graduated in 1914 from Wellesley College, where she was editor of the school newspaper. After graduation, she was offered a full-time job as a writer with the *Boston Globe* and the *New York Times*, but Edward Stratemeyer refused to let his daughter go out to work. He told her that if she wanted to write, she could work at home for him, editing manuscripts for his series books. It was not until her father's death in 1930 that she and her sister were able to become directly involved in the work of the Stratemeyer Syndicate.

In 1984, two years after Harriet Adams's death, Simon and Schuster bought the Stratemeyer Writing Syndicate, and the Nancy Drew series of books continue to be written by a stable of their writers, still under the penname Carolyn Keene.

See also: **Children's Literature.**

KIMBERLEY STRATEMEYER ADAMS

Kerschensteiner, Georg (1854–1932)

Georg Kerschensteiner was born and raised in Munich, Germany. His family background was poor, and his childhood was filled with chaos and contradiction. He was arrested at the age of eight for gang theft, yet he was also educated at the Holy Spirit Seminary and demonstrated an aptitude and interest in art, books, nature, and technique. Kerschensteiner gained experience in teaching through a combination of in-service classroom training, a position as an assistant schoolmaster, and the pursuit of ongoing studies in science and math. Praxis, experience, and participation are central tenets of Kerschensteiner's theory of education, along with order, obedience, and responsibility. As had his predecessor JOHANN PESTALOZZI (1746–1826), Kerschensteiner also recognized that children want to develop and express themselves.

Kerschensteiner considered the value of an individual's work to be directly related to its importance to the state. The most valuable citizens worked in positions that used their full capacities. Teaching methods were transformed from trade and craft to qualified and skilled work processes that also trained the pupil's thinking, emotions, and will. The ongoing industrialization and struggle for democratic reforms in Germany are not explicitly reflected in his theory, however. Kerschensteiner believed that skilled work processes support and create capacities to learn, to explore, to investigate, and to act; these jobs also require punctuality, care and precision, task prioritization, and self-reliance. He found that organizing education into workshops and laboratories helped his students learn specific activities and also helped build character and self-reliance through praxis and reflection.

As director of education he reformed the Munich school system in 1900, grounding the vocational school on his confidence in the students' self-activity, sense, and experience. He claimed that vocational and general education must also be recognized as providing equal opportunities for the personal and social development of a student. Parallel with his work as school director he became lecturer at Munich University in 1904, and then he systematically transformed his experience and knowledge into theoretical writing. His body of work qualified him as an honorary professor at Munich University. He also served in the German Parliament from 1912 to 1919 as an elected representative of the liberal Progressive People's Party.

Kerschensteiner promoted the concept of National State Citizenship in a time and place where parliamentary governments were immature and unstable: wars, revolutions, industrialization, and class struggle were ingredients of everyday life in his Europe. Kerschensteiner revealed that education for citizenship is historically defined and shaped. Other educators, such as the American JOHN DEWEY (1859–1952) and the Soviet educator Nadezhda Krupskaya (1869–1939), also connected work and activity to the process of learning; practicing manual skills while studying bodily and aesthetic topics enhances students' imagination and reflection. Ideas of empowerment, state, and citizenship help to illuminate the differences. Dewey focused on learning by doing to empower students to be versatile, experienced citizens who would participate in democratic development. Krupskaya wanted to empower students through polytechnic education to overcome a class society and master the development of a social-

ist state. Kerschensteiner thought that teachers could use skilled work to educate responsible future citizens who would contribute to the state through their work and knowledge of their civic obligations. These three ingredients—work, civic duty, and social rights—remain the key building blocks in the construction of a functioning citizenship through education.

See also: **Education, Europe; Vocational Education, Industrial Education, and Trade Schools.**

BIBLIOGRAPHY

Kerschensteiner, Georg. 1912. *Der Begriff der Arbeitsschule.* Leipzig and Berlin: Teubner.

Kerschensteiner, Georg. 1912. *Der Begriff Staatbürgerlichen Erziehung.* Leipzig and Berlin: Teubner.

Kerschensteiner Georg. 1917. *Das Grundaxiom des Bildungsprozesses und seine Folgerungen für die Schulorganisation.* Berlin: Union Deutsche Verlagsgesellschaft.

INTERNET RESOURCE

UNESCO on Georg Kerschensteiner. Available from <www.ibe.unesco.org/International/Publications/Thinkers/ThinkersPdf/kerschee.PDF>.

KNUD JENSEN

Key, Ellen (1849–1926)

Ellen Key, a feminist writer and pedagogue, grew up on an estate manor in southern Sweden. Her father was a liberal politician and her mother came from an influential aristocratic family. She received a thorough education at home, which was completed with a journey to the Continent, accompanying her father who was undertaking a study of NURSERY SCHOOLS and houses of correction in Germany. As a teenager, Key founded a SUNDAY SCHOOL for the children of the estates' servants and laborers; she also served as the school's first teacher.

Her main interest, apart from teaching, lay in literature. She was a voracious reader of English literature in particular and wrote essays and articles on George Eliot and Elisabeth Barrett Browning in the feminist journal *Tidskrift för hemmet* (Home journal). She also functioned as her father's secretary during his terms in the Swedish parliament and familiarized herself with liberal politics, although she later developed strong sympathies for the burgeoning workers' movement. In 1880, she began teaching at a private girls' school founded by an acquaintance. Here, she introduced new methods of teaching and attempted to organize the staff into large blocs. Throughout her life she maintained a critical attitude toward the established tradition of teaching several subjects in one class simultaneously.

During the 1880s and 1890s, Key lectured at the Stockholm Workers Institute, a Swedish variant of the Institution of Mechanics, founded by a liberal writer and physician. Her subjects dealt mostly with European literature and the history of ideas. Key nurtured a vision of a society consisting of citizens capable of discussing political and cultural matters in an atmosphere of full intellectual freedom. She also regarded aesthetics as an important part of any society. Inspired by John Ruskin and William Morris, she developed ideas about what she termed "the beauty of daily life" (*vardagsskönhet*), which would not only produce a happier population but also a more morally refined one. In Key's mind, unsightliness eroded the ethical character of human beings. An understanding of aesthetic beauty needed to be learned, and to this end Key published several pamphlets on home furnishing and arranged exhibitions, addressed directly to the working class.

From 1900, she earned her living as a writer and lecturer. Her main works are *Barnets århundrade* (1900; Century of the child) and *Lifslinjer* (1903–1906; Lifelines). The first book met with a rather skeptical response in Sweden but was received as a success in Germany, being republished in seventeen subsequent editions by the time of her death. According to Key, the twentieth century would prove to be the CENTURY OF THE CHILD. Children would be the focal point of political reform and their status in society would change dramatically. Key had a utopian perception of the coming century and projected her own ideas and ideals into the future. Each child has the right "to choose its parents," Key wrote, meaning that the child has a right to a good home and a proper education. In Key's view, a proper education was one that encourages children to develop their own "personalities": "Let them have their own will, let them think their own thoughts." She felt the school must not be allowed to "murder" the individuality that is inherent in every child.

In her second book, *Lifslinjer*, Key described the changing family structure to which she looked forward. In the future, she stated, women will enjoy the same rights as men in both the family and society. And, she argued, women must exercise these rights in order to turn society in a more nurturing direction, since women have a natural capacity for care and nurturing that men often lack. Part of the ideology of the Swedish welfare state was inspired by Key's perception of society as an extended family.

The theoretical basis for Key's feminist ideas, as well as her pedagogy, is comprised of evolutionism in its nineteenth-century form, having closely studied Charles Darwin and Herbert Spencer. In the theory of evolution, Key thought she found (especially in Spencer) a solution which met the requirements for creating a secularized morality. According to this philosophy, the individual's aspirations must be judged after taking into consideration the effects these will have on the lives of future generations. Like Spencer, Key was convinced (incorrectly, it would prove) that characteristics acquired by the individual during his or her lifetime would be inherited by future generations. The lifestyle adopted by the individual would determine its future.

This theory of the heredity of acquired characteristics was to revive interest in problems of upbringing. For Ellen Key, who had been interested in questions of upbringing since her youth, evolution in its Spencerian form provided a stimulus for continued involvement in the subject. The individual was "fashioned" by its environment. But upbringing was concerned with more than the fashioning of one individual; it also created characteristics which were to be inherited by generations to come. When choosing how to live, the individual must consider the future, since each choice confronts the individual with the task of formulating his or her own utopia.

The problems which evolutionism raised would become particularly important for women. According to Key, women lived in a period of transition, in the gap between what she called two "consciousnesses." If women chose to enter the labor market under the same conditions as men, there was a risk that the woman-type might change, become more "masculine," which would be devastating for future society. Key was very critical of the women's rights movement in Sweden. She formulated her criticism in a widely debated book, *Missbrukad kvinnokraft* (1896; Misused womanpower), criticism which later recurred in her great writings of the turn of the century. On the one hand, she accused the women's movement of not being radical enough in regard to sexual and political freedom for women, while on the other, she limited the female labor market by advocating special "natural workfields" for them, mainly consisting of the teaching and nursing professions.

Ellen Key spent her last years in Strand, a large home she herself designed and had built on the shores of Lake Vättern in central Sweden. Having earned quite a reputation through her works, she was constantly visited by European writers and critics. In her will, Key left Strand to female workers, to be used by them as a place for retreat and study.

See also: **Age and Development; Child Development, History of the Concept of; Education, Europe; Social Welfare.**

BIBLIOGRAPHY

Hacksell, Siv, ed. 2000. *Ny syn på Ellen Key: 32 texter av 23 författare.* Stockholm. Essays about Ellen Key.

Key, Ellen. 1896. *Missbrukad kvinnokraft.* Stockholm.

Key, Ellen. 1900. *Barnets århundrade. Studie av Ellen Key.* Stockholm.

Key, Ellen. 1903–1906. *Lifslinjer 1–3.* Stockholm.

Key, Ellen. 1976. *Hemmets århundrade: Ett urval av Ronny Ambjörnsson,* ed. Ronny Ambjörnsson. Stockholm.

Lengborn, Thorbjörn. 1976. *En studie i Ellen Keys tänkande främst med utgångspunkt från Barnets århundrade.* Stockholm.

RONNY AMBJÖRNSSON

A scene from an early kindergarten in New York City, 1879. © Bettman/CORBIS.

Kindergarten

The kindergarten was developed in the nineteenth century by FRIEDRICH FROEBEL, a German reformer and educator. He built upon the ideas of JOHANN HEINRICH PESTALOZZI, a Swiss follower of JEAN-JACQUES ROUSSEAU's belief in the inherent goodness of children. During the 1830s and 1840s, Froebel made a case for the importance of music, nature study, stories, and play as well as symbolic ideas like children sitting together in the kindergarten circle. He advocated the use of "gifts" (or materials, largely geometric) and "occupations" (or crafts), which the teacher taught the children to manipulate. In 1837 Froebel opened the first kindergarten in Blankenburg, Germany. He also established a training school for women, whom he saw as the ideal educators of young children. Because of Froebel's unorthodox ideas, the Prussian government banned the kindergarten in 1851, but the kindergarten idea spread not only to other European countries but also to North America, the Middle East, Asia, and Australia. After 1860, the kindergarten also returned to Germany, where today it serves children aged three to six.

Johannes and Bertha Ronge, who left Germany after the revolutions of 1848, took Froebel's ideas to England and founded a kindergarten in London in 1851. Women helped to set up private kindergartens for middle-class Britons between 1850 and 1870. By 1890 the kindergarten had been incorporated into some publicly funded British schools but did not achieve universal success, and between 1900 and World War I, reformers turned their attention to private kindergartens ("free kindergartens") for the poor, which charged little or no tuition. Ultimately, the kindergarten supplemented and transformed but did not replace other modes of early childhood education in Britain. There was a similar development in France, when the *salles d'asiles* of the 1830s were replaced by the first infant schools fifty years later. The French opted for an eclectic method, where schoolwork was combined with kindergarten activities. This also characterizes the present-day *écoles maternelles*.

Kindergarten in the United States

The kindergarten was much more influential in the United States and in the northern part of Europe. In the United States Margarethe Schurz founded the first kindergarten in Watertown, Wisconsin, in 1856. Her German-language kindergarten impressed Elizabeth Peabody, who opened the first American English-language kindergarten in Boston in 1860. The National Education Association began a kindergarten department in 1874, and teachers founded the International Kindergarten Union in 1892.

Before 1890, the kindergarten was most prevalent in private institutions, including free kindergarten associations, social settlements, charities, parochial schools, and orphanages. These half-day, free kindergartens were often funded by philanthropists to educate the three- to six-year-old children of working-class parents, many of them immigrants, who crowded the cities. During the late nineteenth and early twentieth centuries, the kindergarten did not teach academic skills like reading and writing but instead sought to educate the whole child, a goal that encompassed a large range of social welfare and educational activities from helping to clothe, feed, and clean children to teaching urban children about nature study. Training schools specifically for kindergarten teachers (then called kindergartners) were organized separately from normal schools for elementary school teachers.

St. Louis was the first American public school system to adopt the kindergarten, in 1873, under Susan Blow. After 1890, the kindergarten entered school systems in larger numbers; often, boards of education began housing and funding previously existing free kindergartens. By 1900 public-school kindergarten students outnumbered private-school kindergarten students by almost two to one, with 225,000 children, or about 6 percent of the kindergarten-aged population, attending kindergarten.

By World War I, the major American urban school systems all had kindergartens. In 1920 about 510,000 children, or about 11 percent of the kindergarten-aged population, attended kindergarten, with public-school students outnumbering private-school students by almost nineteen to one. Once publicly funded, the kindergarten was open primarily to five year olds only, and people argued that it should be concerned with academic and social preparation for the first grade. Teachers now taught two sessions a day rather than one, leaving them little time for home visits and mothers' meetings, important elements of the earlier American kindergarten.

During the late-nineteenth and early-twentieth centuries, kindergarten teachers differed on how strictly to follow Froebel's teaching plan. Some teachers were particularly influenced by the American psychologist G. STANLEY HALL and the emerging CHILD STUDY movement. Hall praised Froebel's work but believed in the importance of "free play," an idea that influenced kindergarten teachers Patty Smith Hill and Alice Temple. The American philosopher and educator JOHN DEWEY, too, argued that Froebel's work was valuable, but he criticized the abstract nature of the Froebelian system. Beginning in the 1910s, the American kindergarten was influenced also by the ideas of the Italian physician and educator MARIA MONTESSORI, who stressed developing the child's initiative. Although Froebel's influence remained present in the existence of the kindergarten circle and other aspects of the program, by the 1930s the kindergarten in the United States was very different than that envisioned by Froebel.

The Modern Kindergarten

Kindergarten enrollments in the United States fell from 1930 to 1940, as many school districts cut back their funding (though other school districts simultaneously adopted the kindergarten). Public kindergarten enrollments then grew almost 150 percent from 1940 to almost 1.5 million children in 1954. Class sizes ranged from twenty to forty-nine students, and some states passed laws to lower the enrollment (to twenty-four per class in New Jersey, for example). Kindergartens also increased the age requirement of the kindergarten, accepting children whose fifth birthdays fell on or before November.

In 1965 between about 50 percent and 85 percent of five-year-olds attended kindergarten, more than 2 million of them in public schools in over forty states, most of which made state funds available for that purpose. The HEAD START program, begun in 1965, both served as a substitute for kindergarten for some five-year-olds and helped promote further kindergarten establishment.

By the 1980s kindergartens in the United States had moved away from child-centered education to academic preparation for first grade. Between 82 percent and 95 percent of five-year-olds attended kindergarten. In 1986 Mississippi became the last state to offer public kindergartens. As of the 1980s, ten states required children to attend kindergarten, and most states required teacher certification in elementary education, fewer in kindergarten or early childhood education. Today, about four million children in the United States attend kindergarten, over three million of those in public schools.

In Germany and Scandinavia the kindergarten for children between the ages of three and seven has developed from an institution caring for children of poor parents and single mothers to an integrated part of the life of nearly all children. This shift began in the 1970s after many mothers entered the paid labor market. There is a variety of kindergartens in Europe—private, public, and, especially in Germany, religious institutions. Kindergartens are separate from the school system, although recently there have been efforts to bring them into a closer relationship. In many communities the kindergartens are integrated with day-care centers for very young children as well as with after school activities for older children.

See also: **Child Care; Nursery Schools.**

BIBLIOGRAPHY

Beatty, Barbara. 1995. *Preschool Education in America: The Culture of Young Children from the Colonial Era to the Present.* New Haven, CT: Yale University Press.

Borchorst, Anette 2002. "Danish Child Care Policy: Continuity Rather than Radical Change." In *Child Care Policy at the Crossroads: Gender and Welfare State Restructuring,* ed. Sonya Michel and Rianne Mahon. New York: Routledge.

Ross, Elizabeth Dale. 1976. *The Kindergarten Crusade: The Establishment of Preschool Education in the United States.* Athens: Ohio University Press.

Shapiro, Michael Steven. 1983. *Child's Garden: The Kindergarten Movement from Froebel to Dewey.* University Park: The Pennsylvania State University Press.

Spodek, Bernard, Olivia N. Saracho, and Michael D. Davis. 1991. *Foundations of Early Childhood Education: Teaching Three-, Four-, and Five-Year-Old Children.* Englewood Cliffs, NJ: Prentice Hall.

Wollons, Roberta, ed. 2000. *Kindergartens and Cultures: The Global Diffusion of an Idea.* New Haven, CT: Yale University Press.

ELLEN L. BERG

Kipling, Rudyard (1865–1936)

The poet, essayist, and fiction writer Rudyard Kipling was born in Bombay, the child of English parents. Although cherished by his parents, he also developed strong bonds with the Indian servants who tended him, to the extent that his first language was Hindustani. In 1871, however, Kipling was sent to England to be educated. He was boarded with an unfeeling foster family, an experience he later used as the basis for "Baa, Baa, Black Sheep" (1888). In this short story young Punch is so ill-used by his caretaker that no amount of later love can take away his knowledge of "Hate, Suspicion and Despair." Nevertheless, Kipling also credited this period with the development of qualities that would later serve him as a writer, such as keen observation of people and their moods. In 1878 Kipling entered the United Services College in North Devon. This furnished the material for *Stalky Co.* (1899), the story of three schoolboys who form an alliance that enables them to outwit peers and adults. Immediately after finishing school, Kipling returned to India, where he worked as a journalist for seven years. It was during this time that he began to write and publish fiction.

Although a number of Kipling's books are categorized as children's literature, it might be more accurate to say that he wrote for a dual audience. For example, his *The Jungle Book* (1894) and *The Second Jungle Book* (1895) work on several levels: as simple adventure tales, as mystical coming-of-age stories, and as thoughtful explorations of the relationship between individuals and their societies. While children can read and enjoy these books, there is also much in them for adults to ponder.

Many readers have criticized Kipling for his imperialist views. In his famous poem "The White Man's Burden" (1899), for example, Kipling urges English readers to accept the responsibility of civilizing people of other countries. However, another poem, "The Two-Sided Man" (1913), shows a different aspect of Kipling:

Something I owe to the soil that grew—
More to the life that fed—
But most to Allah Who gave me two
Separate sides to my head.

The presence of "two separate sides" characterizes much of Kipling's work. The novel *Kim* (1901) is the story of a young Irish orphan living in India, torn between his roles as a secret agent for the British government and as a disciple of a holy lama. By presenting India as a diverse society harmoniously united under British rule, *Kim* justifies imperialism. On the other hand, Kim's great love and respect for the lama implies that Kipling questioned British assumptions about the inferiority of native peoples. Similarly, *Just So Stories for Little Children* (1902) both depicts sexist stereotypes (a henpecked husband triumphs over his wife) and celebrates female intelligence (a small girl invents writing). If Kipling reinforces many of the conventional views of his time, he also often subverts them.

Kipling's texts have been adapted for film, including *The Jungle Book*, which was adapted and released by Alexander Korda Films in 1942 and animated by Walt Disney Productions in 1967. *Kim* was adapted and released by Metro-Goldwyn-Meyer in 1950. Kipling's writings also have been adapted for theater, radio, and television.

See also: **Children's Literature.**

BIBLIOGRAPHY

Kipling, Rudyard. 1990. *Something of Myself*, ed. Thomas Pinney. New York: Cambridge University Press.

Pinney, Thomas. 1990. Introduction to *Something of Myself*, by Rudyard Kipling, ed. Thomas Pinney. New York: Cambridge University Press.

Plotz, Judith. 1992. "The Empire of Youth: Crossing and Double-Crossing Cultural Barriers in Kipling's *Kim*." *Children's Literature* 20: 111–131.

JENNIFER MARCHANT

Klein, Melanie (1882–1960)

Born Melanie Reizes into a middle-class, Jewish family in Vienna, Austria, where she received a grammar-school education, Melanie Klein married Arthur Klein in 1903 and had three children before the family moved to Budapest in 1910. In 1914 she began treatment for depression with the Hungarian psychoanalyst Sandor Ferenczi, who encouraged her intellectual interest in psychoanalysis. Klein began by psychoanalyzing her own children, and she presented one of the earliest papers on child analysis to the Budapest Psychoanalytic Society in July 1919 when she became a member.

In 1921 Klein left her husband and took their children to Berlin, where she joined the Berlin Psychoanalytic Society. With the support of its president, Karl Abraham, Klein developed her method of child analysis: the psychoanalytic play technique, which treated children's play activity as symbolic of unconscious fantasies. When Abraham died suddenly in 1926, Klein lacked professional support in Berlin, so she moved to London to join the British Psychoanalytical Society. Its members were very enthusiastic about her PLAY technique, and most took Klein's side in her 1927 debate about child analysis with ANNA FREUD, another pioneer in the field. In that debate, Klein and her followers advocated a deep analysis of Oedipal fantasies, while Anna Freud argued that analysis should instead seek to strengthen the child's ego.

Klein's psychoanalysis of children led her to develop theories that challenged the Freudian account of child development; for example, she proposed the existence of an early infantile superego and an innate aggressive drive. Her most important contribution, however, was the idea that an infant has a primary object relationship with its mother. Freud had asserted that the infant feels love for its mother only because she satisfies its basic physiological needs. On the other hand, Klein argued in her 1932 book *The Psychoanalysis of Children* that the infant is predisposed to seek a relationship with its caregiver independent of any other needs, and that this relationship is represented within the psyche as a complex world of objects. Klein and her followers developed this idea into object-relations theory, which emphasizes the importance of the mother-infant bond in shaping adult personality. These ideas later influenced the British developmental psychologist JOHN BOWLBY, who trained with Klein, to form his theory of infant attachment.

Klein also proposed the existence of two fundamental phases in child development: the paranoid-schizoid and the depressive positions. The concept of the paranoid-schizoid position, which suggests that the infant mind is dominated by psychotic defense mechanisms such as splitting, sparked a second debate with Anna Freud in the early 1940s who, as a new and powerful member of the British Psychoanalytical Society, argued that Klein's ideas were incompatible with traditional psychoanalysis. The so-called Controversial Discussions were resolved when the Freudians and Kleinians agreed to separate training programs for their groups. Klein's famous 1961 case study *Narrative of a Child Analysis* was published shortly after she died of cancer in 1960. Her papers were placed in the Wellcome Institute for the History of Medicine in London.

See also: **Child Development, History of the Concept of; Child Psychology.**

BIBLIOGRAPHY

Grosskurth, Phyllis. 1986. *Melanie Klein: Her World and Her Work.* New York: Knopf.

Hinshelwood, Robert D. 1989. *Dictionary of Kleinian Thought.* London: Free Association Books.

King, Pearl, and Ricardo Steiner, eds. 1991. *The Freud-Klein Controversies 1941–45.* London: Routledge.

Segal, Hanna. 1979. *Klein.* London: Karnac.

GAIL DONALDSON

L

La Leche League

In 1956 seven women organized the La Leche League to defend the traditional practices of breast-feeding and natural childbirth. From its beginnings as a small discussion group in the Chicago suburb of Franklin Park, Illinois, the League grew rapidly and by 1981 sponsored 4,000 support groups, a monthly newsletter, and a telephone hotline. The group promoted its ideology through the sales of millions of books, leaflets, and the best-selling *Womanly Art of Breastfeeding*, first published in 1958.

League founders were white, middle-class, Catholic women who believed that babies and small children required the continuous presence of their mothers. The League ideology of "good mothering through breastfeeding" was intended to encourage an intensive, maternal-centered family practice. This ideology competed with two social developments during the twentieth century that profoundly transformed family life—the medicalization of childbirth and early child development, and the rising number of working mothers.

Since the start of the twentieth century infant feeding had become increasingly subject to scientific scrutiny. By the 1890s food manufacturers had developed complex formulas to substitute for mother's milk, and by the 1920s commercially canned baby food had been adopted by American consumers as well. Physicians and scientists popularized the use of these infant foods through advice books and magazines designed to promote elaborate methods of INFANT FEEDING, where babies would be weighed before and after formula feeding, which was to take place on rigid schedules. If breast-fed, they were to be weaned to formula by three to seven months of age. By the 1950s, at the time of the League's founding, breast-feeding rates in the United States had fallen from a nearly universal practice at the beginning of the century to about 20 percent.

Childbirth, too, became increasingly the province of medicine, as more mothers turned to hospital rather than home birth. Whereas some 95 percent of births took place at home at 1900, by 1940 about 50 percent of women and by the mid-1950s about 95 percent of women chose to have their children in hospitals, where many births involved the use of forceps, pain-killing drugs, and other interventions.

A second force challenging traditional styles of mothering was the growing tendency of mothers to seek employment outside of the home. From the 1950s on, an increasing number of mothers of children under the age of six worked, and from the 1970s, more and more mothers of infants entered the labor force as well.

The League's challenge to scientific and medical authority on the subject of motherhood resonated with thousands of women and anticipated the women's health movement that developed in the 1970s, while at the same time questioning the practice of mothers of young children working outside of the home. But the league, while arguing that it was in the best interest of children if their mothers were home full-time, still recognized contemporary practice and offered advice and encouragement to working mothers wishing to breast-feed their babies. By the 1970s breast-feeding rates began to rise, reaching some 60 percent by the mid-1980s, and 67 percent by the turn of the twenty-first century. At the turn of the twenty-first century, the La Leche League sponsored over 3,000 monthly breast-feeding support groups around the world and supported a Center for Breastfeeding Information.

See also: **Mothering and Motherhood.**

BIBLIOGRAPHY

Apple, Rima. 1987. *Mothers and Medicine: A Social History of Infant Feeding, 1890–1950.* Madison: University of Wisconsin Press.

Blum, Linda M. 1999. *At the Breast: Ideologies of Breastfeeding and Motherhood in the Contemporary United States.* Boston: Beacon Press.

Torgus, Judy, and Gwen Gotsch, eds. 1997 [1958]. *The Womanly Art of Breastfeeding*, 6th rev. ed. Schaumburg, IL: La Leche League International.

Weiner, Lynn Y. 1994. "Reconstructing Motherhood: The La Leche League in Postwar America." *Journal of American History* 80: 357–1381.

INTERNET RESOURCE

La Leche League International. 2003. Available from <www.lalecheleague.org>.

LYNN Y. WEINER

Latin America

OVERVIEW
Elizabeth Anne Kuznesof

COLONIALISM
Nara Milanich

WARS IN CENTRAL AMERICA
Anna L. Peterson

OVERVIEW

Publications on the history of childhood in Latin America only date since the 1980s. In fact, most pertinent sources are about something else: the development of institutions such as education or social welfare, or the history of women. Ironically, this neglect of childhood as a historical subject exists while scholarly focus on the historical role of the family as a political, economic, and social force continues to be strong, especially for Argentina, Brazil, Colombia, and Chile.

Children and the Family

Since the colonial period (1492 to approximately 1826), children have constituted a large proportion of the population of Latin America, and continue to be vital to the work force. One possible explanation for this scholarly neglect is that colonial Spanish and Portuguese law codes determined that the care and nurturing of children were private functions, and fell into the corporate sphere of the family. As a result, children who appear in historical documents were seldom members of "legitimate" families; most often they were children of the popular classes. Thus scholars have normally discussed abandoned and orphaned children, children enlisted in military service, children thrust into institutionalized workshops as "apprentices," or caught up in the criminal justice system. Other topics include prescriptive ideas about children's upbringing, and discussions of laws relating to children. In the nineteenth and early twentieth centuries, scholars, legislators, and politicians were also preoccupied by the levels of infant and child mortality, child labor, juvenile DELINQUENCY, and issues related to public education.

From a historical and legal perspective, the family in Latin America is represented consistently as the fundamental unit of society, and as a nuclear unit that is essentially patriarchal, based on a system of monogamous marriage, and focused on reproduction. This vision is retained from the sixteenth to the twentieth century in spite of the remarkable diversity in family and household forms that existed and exist in Latin America. The family as constructed through law can be seen as the codification of an elite world vision, concerned with the legality of family ties, the legal definition of marital and paternal power, the legitimacy of offspring, and the regulation of family wealth. The remarkable fact is that the majority of children born in Latin America since 1492 were not born in such families. Thus most children have been defined as in some sense marginal, and in need of social control by some institution.

In a rare edited volume focused on childhood in Latin America since the colonial period, Tobias Hecht argues that the lives and histories of children must be studied for an understanding of society at large. He observes that familiar aspects of Latin American history can be seen in a new light through an examination of the experiences of children and notions about childhood. For example, he suggests that boys aged eight through seventeen, including forty percent or more of transatlantic crews, had an important role in the Conquest. In addition, Europeans commonly viewed the condition of Indians as similar to that of children, who were "only potentially, but not actually, rational beings" (Hecht, p. 10). Thus Europeans argued that Indians were better off under the tutelage of Spain. Their "childishness" provided a rationale for the Conquest. Similarly, in the early twentieth century, intellectuals blamed poor parents for the "moral abandonment" of their children and for being "childish" or unworthy parents, a verdict sometimes leading to loss of custody.

Rights and Obligations

The very definition of childhood in Latin America evolved over time through a continuous dialogue concerning the duties and responsibilities of parents and children toward each other, and the responsibilities of the state toward children. In the colonial period the parent-child relationship was seen as an aspect of the corporate family, embedded in the patriarchal property rights of legally constituted families. At that time, focus was on the parental obligations from early childhood up to age seven, which was considered the age of reason. The first period, from birth to age three, was designated infancy and distinguished by the child being sustained by human milk, either from the mother or a wet nurse. Children were generally left with their mothers during infancy if their fathers died, because of the need for mother's milk. In the second phase, from ages four to seven, the child remained with the parent, with little being expected of her or him. Education in the sense of learning obedience, manners, and prayers was emphasized. From age four the child was taken to mass.

In this second period the father was responsible for providing sustenance, whether the child was of legitimate or illegitimate birth. He had the legal right of *patria potestad*, which included the obligations to feed, clothe, discipline, educate, select occupations, and sanction the marital plans of children. In return, children were to obey parents and work without wages. In order to have a legal heir, fathers had to acknowledge paternity; otherwise the single mother had to support her children alone, though mothers were denied the legal rights of *patria potestad*.

Fathers who felt little obligation to children existed at all levels. During the colonial period orphaned children were usually the responsibility of grandparents or their parents' siblings. Abandoned children, estimated at between 10 and 25 percent of births, were also cared for by families.

From age seven the child was seen as having reason and as morally responsible for his or her acts. The child was required to study, work, confess, and follow the rituals of CATHOLICISM. Girls were expected to be modest. At age seven the little boy could go to primary school or work for a salary in somebody's house while he learned a skill or profession. The little girl at that age could begin to help with domestic tasks, learn to sew and do embroidery, and very rarely might be taught to read and write by a cleric or teacher. Until age ten, children could not be legally punished for crimes. Families assumed any penalties for crime. After age ten girls and boys had to sleep separately. According to colonial law, girls could be married at twelve and boys at fourteen.

After age seven a child's labor was believed to have value and judges emphasized the rights of an orphaned child from age seven to receive a salary and not to be exploited for free labor. However, there was no real discussion about what kind of work was appropriate for that age, or how many hours the child should work. In the eighteenth century the state began to exert influence as levels of child ABANDONMENT grew. In the nineteenth century mothers began to argue for child custody and *patria potestad*, usually with little success.

In the late eighteenth and early nineteenth centuries we see the emergence of an ethic of protection of children, including adolescents, with an emphasis on their fragility and assumed innocence, as well as on the importance of education. Early nineteenth-century governments began to assist abandoned children through ORPHANAGES and poor houses, though many beneficent societies were associated with the Catholic Church or lay brotherhoods. In Mexico, families in hard times would sometimes "abandon" a child for some weeks or months at an orphanage, and then reclaim the child when the family had more resources. For older children, orphanages often functioned as workhouses where the children remained until they were sent out for foster care, often as servants.

The concept of ADOLESCENCE and a specific notion of how children ages twelve through nineteen should be treated were linked to the dramatic economic and social developments in late-nineteenth-century Latin America. This development extended life expectancy and created expanded employment opportunities dependent on longer schooling. For example, the substantial sector of service occupations that developed in increasingly urbanized communities were an important source of new employment, particularly for children and women.

By the late nineteenth century, discourse based on ENLIGHTENMENT views of education as a means to foster civic responsibility were displaced by a growing penal consciousness, intent on the prevention and punishment of crime. An ideology focused on children's protection was transformed into a preoccupation with order and social control. Nineteenth-century legislation very often targeted the social control of abandoned or orphaned children, since unruly vagrant youths were seen as potentially dangerous to society. In Brazil, the child began to be referred to as a *minor*, with the term carrying an implication of danger and a tendency toward crime. The Brazilian Criminal Code of 1830 determined that a child between seven and fourteen could be sent to jail if the judge determined that the child understood his or her crime. Otherwise the child was sent to a juvenile correction house to age seventeen. Similarly, the Criminal Code of 1890 emphasized responsibility as related to a consciousness of duty, right and wrong, and the ability to appreciate the consequences of acts. This kind of emphasis implicitly argued that schooling rather than age determined the level of a child's responsibility.

Education

Until the first decades of the twentieth century, the definition of *education* was essentially identical with that of *work*. Much "education" took the form of APPRENTICESHIP or some kind of specific job. For adolescents in the lower classes this "education" was often provided through a kind of child-circulation, in which young people from poorer families were sent to serve in the homes or businesses of more elite families. By the early twentieth century, efforts were made to limit the types and hours of labor for children under fourteen, and to specifically reinforce formal education for children. The 1890 code in Brazil specified that children under nine years of age were mentally incapable of criminal behavior; those between nine and fourteen could be jailed if they understood their crime.

High child mortality in the late nineteenth and early twentieth centuries helped to return the discussion somewhat to questions of child protection, though the criminal potential of unruly children continued to preoccupy jurists. Legislators refocused on childhood as the key to the future. Intellectuals spoke of investing in children, and argued that society was protected through the protection of children.

Nevertheless, in Brazil and Chile, special JUVENILE JUSTICE systems were created in the 1920s to deal with "minors." Although legislators wished to rehabilitate delinquent children, they did not make education a priority because they saw education as a "dangerous weapon" (Hecht, p. 176). It was recognized that education was an antidote for criminality; a minimal education was desirable to make "minors" into useful workers. Legislators debated the challenge of how to create an educated population that would also be docile and hardworking. Because the laws focused on marginal children, legislators did not consider developing a national policy of quality education accessible to all. Children continued at the margins in terms of social policy, still seen as a threat to law and order.

Mandatory schooling for children ages seven to fourteen was instituted in most of Latin America in the first decades of the twentieth century, though once again the felt need for social control of an otherwise disruptive population was a major incentive. In addition, many lower-class families were unconvinced that education would improve the lives or economic choices of their children. While school attendance and LITERACY have improved in most countries, child labor continues to compete actively with schooling in the minds of many families and children. Families with minimal incomes often view the salaries of children as vital to family survival strategies. Observers in several Latin American countries argue that childhood as a stage of life is denied to a large proportion of their children; however, it might be more accurate to say that the childhood experienced by poor children is distinct from that of the elite.

See also: **Brazil; Child Labor in Developing Countries; Sociology and Anthropology of Childhood.**

BIBLIOGRAPHY

Blum, Ann. 1998. "Public Welfare and Child Circulation, Mexico City, 1877 to 1925." *Journal of Family History* 23, no. 3: 240–271.

Hawes, Joseph M., and N. Ray Hiner, eds. 1991. *Children in Historical and Comparative Perspective: An International Handbook and Research Guide.* New York: Greenwood Press.

Hecht, Tobias, ed. 2002. *Minor Omissions: Children in Latin American History and Society.* Madison: University of Wisconsin Press.

Kuznesof, Elizabeth. 1991. "Sexual Politics, Race, and Bastard-Bearing in Nineteenth-Century Brazil: A Question of Culture or Power." *Journal of Family History* 16, no. 3: 241–260.

Kuznesof, Elizabeth. 1997. "Who Were the Families of 'Natural' Children in 19th Century Rio de Janeiro, Brazil: A Comparison of Baptismal and Census Records." *The History of the Family: An International Quarterly.* 2, no. 2: 171–182.

Kuznesof, Elizabeth. 1998. "The Puzzling Contradictions of Child Labor, Unemployment, and Education in Brazil." *Journal of Family History* 23, no. 3: 225–239.

Mezner, Joan. 1994. "Orphans and the Transition to Free Labor in Northeast Brazil: The Case of Campina Grande, 1850–1888." *Journal of Social History* 27, no. 3: 499–515.

Salinas Meza, Rene. 1991. "Orphans and Family Disintegration in Chile: The Mortality of Abandoned Children, 1750–1930." *Journal of Family History* 16, no. 3: 315–329.

ELIZABETH ANNE KUZNESOF

COLONIALISM

In his classic 1946 study *The Masters and the Slaves,* Gilberto Freyre traced the formation of the Brazilian social order through what he called a "domestic history" of the patriarchal plantation household he saw as the center of colonial society. For Freyre, children and childhood were central to this domestic history and, by extension, to the formation of Brazilian civilization and psyche. Consequently, he devoted considerable attention to such issues as child-rearing practices and coming-of-age rites, education, SEXUALITY, and socialization.

Freyre's work became part of the Brazilian canon, but it did not set the agenda for future historical work. It was not till the late 1990s that historians took the first tentative steps toward addressing the history of childhood in Latin America, and most focused on the nineteenth and twentieth centuries. The dearth of research on children and childhood in colonial America makes any attempt at a comprehensive overview of the topic a difficult, even hazardous, endeavor. Consequently, this entry will highlight several emerging themes in the historiography rather than provide an all-inclusive survey of the topic.

Colonial Latin American Childhoods

Given that *children* and *childhood* are themselves culturally and historically bound constructs, we might begin by asking who was a child in colonial Latin America and how was childhood defined and demarcated? In a society stratified by sex, class, and color, the answers to such questions depended fundamentally on a young person's gender, social position, race, and legal status as free or enslaved. For example, girls were deemed to reach physical and social maturity faster than boys and for a number of purposes were granted legal majority earlier; on the other hand, because they were regarded as inherently vulnerable to corruption, charitable assistance for girls was more widely available and frequently more extensive than for boys. Meanwhile, definitions and experiences of childhood were necessarily contingent on caste. A case in point is the expansive definition of legal minority that governed INHERITANCE law and the exercise of parental authority. According to Spanish law codes, the age of majority was twenty-five—and for certain legal purposes, unmarried children were beholden to paternal authority as long as their fathers were alive. Similarly, the late eighteenth-century Royal Pragmatic on marriage held that prospective brides and grooms identified as white or Spanish had to obtain paternal permission to marry until they turned twenty-five.

This protracted legal minority had relevance only among limited segments of colonial society: those from propertied families or those identified as Spanish. Very different life chronologies applied to the poor, the non-white, and the enslaved. Chantal Cramaussel's research on late-seventeenth-century baptismal registries from northern New Spain, for example, shows that captive Indian children over age ten were classified as adults. Renato Venâncio, in turn, has noted that eighteenth- and nineteenth-century Brazilian censuses recorded slave children over age three along with their occupations. It is difficult to say how such administrative designations translated into practice. What is clear is that perhaps the most widely observed milestone in the everyday lives of free colonial plebeians came at age six or seven. It was at this age that youngsters were deemed capable of performing useful labor and were often put to work.

This is not to say, however, that plebeians and slaves did not have a childhood. As in many societies historically, in colonial Latin America, childhood and labor were not defined as mutually exclusive. In fact, in some Amerindian cultures, the former was actually defined *in terms of* the latter: the Incas and peoples of central Mexico not only viewed children as productive members of family, community, and state but actually classified people into age groups according to the work they were capable of performing. Childhood for the poor and nonwhite was simply less clearly differentiated from adulthood in terms of the expectations and activities associated with it. This suggests that in colonial Iberoamerica, there were "childhoods" that varied across social groups rather than a single, universal childhood experience.

The characteristics of these different childhoods have only just begun to be explored, but a few observations are possible. The first, of course, is that labor was central to the experience of most children, the exception being the sons and daughters of a privileged minority. Long before the presence of young people in factories captured the attention of social critics in early-twentieth-century Mexico City or Buenos Aires, children in colonial Latin America performed valuable domestic, artisanal, and agricultural labors. The brief glimpses of their everyday lives afforded by sources like judicial and census records often find them busy herding animals, spinning, performing agricultural tasks, or laboring in the infamous bakeries of colonial cities. Insofar as minors were expected to contribute to the household economy from an early age, the colonial period provides antecedents for the experiences of children and the meanings of childhood among low-income sectors in Latin America today.

Child Circulation

Another significant aspect of childhood is the fact that many minors were reared outside of their natal households. The widespread ABANDONMENT of children to FOUNDLING homes is merely the most visible facet of this phenomenon. Many poor children resided as *agregados* (attached people) or as *criados* or *conchabos* (servants) in the homes of unrelated caretakers. Their presence was characterized by a broad constellation of arrangements, from informal fostering and ADOPTION to APPRENTICESHIPS and domestic service. The experiences of these minors contrast with those of elite children, who lived within a restricted private sphere of immediate kin. Living and laboring under the tutelage of unrelated caretakers also served as the sole means of education for many minors.

In some instances, parents voluntarily gave up children they could not or would not care for. Circulation reflects the burden that child rearing could entail for the impoverished majority of colonial society. It also reflects the stigma attached in some social groups to out-of-wedlock birth, even as illegitimacy was endemic across colonial society. In other instances, coercion was at work. In frontier societies such as southern Chile and northern New Spain, intractable wars with native peoples fueled a lively traffic in indigenous children. In southern Chile, and probably elsewhere, the sale of children as war booty eventually gave way to the routine abduction by local authorities of poor youngsters whose parents were deemed morally, ethnically, or economically unfit.

These myriad forms of child circulation reflect the value of minors as laborers in peasant economies, artisanal trades, and urban households. The economic role of child *criados* seems to have been particularly important in areas where slaves were either scarce or too expensive for modest households. But the presence of minors in non-natal households had significance beyond the value of their labor. Sometimes children became the heirs of their caretakers, suggesting the importance of these practices to the construction of kin relations. Children were also a form of currency within the patronage networks on which colonial society was based. María Mannarelli has shown how the circulation of abandoned children among households in seventeenth-century Lima bound individuals of all social levels and ethnic and racial groups. Moreover, the rearing of young *criados* may have acquired particular significance in societies in which many individuals served as the clients, dependents, and servants of others. What better way to guarantee the lifelong loyalty of a subordinate than to rear him or her from "tender youth"? This is precisely what households of all social ranks sought to do, grooming parentless, abandoned, orphaned, poor, and illegitimate youngsters as dependents, with an eye not only to their present labor but also to the prospect of long-term dependence.

Children and Imperial States

Particularly in the first centuries of the empire, the Iberian states' interest in their minor subjects was limited. Civil law was concerned with the rights of the young in their role as inheritors, but such issues obviously had little relevance to the lives of the majority of young people. Broader and potentially more interventionist preoccupations with children's health and labor, child-rearing practices and education, and the development of correctional institutions and protective legislation would come into full flower only in the nineteenth and early twentieth centuries. It does appear, however, that Portuguese authorities were more activist both in their oversight of child welfare and in their use of children for certain state purposes than were the Spanish. For example, in Portugal and Brazil one crucial role of the probate judge, the *juiz de órfãos*, was, as the name suggests, to oversee the welfare of the community's ORPHANS. No such official existed in Spain or Spanish America. The Portuguese crown also put into practice a system in which orphans were used to colonize its far-flung empire. Future research is necessary to confirm the impression of contrasting Spanish and Portuguese postures towards children, as well as to explain it.

Both crowns began to assume greater interest in child welfare in the late eighteenth century. Their newfound concern coincided with beliefs about the significance of population increase to the wealth of nations; an ENLIGHTENMENT preoccupation with charity and education; and an identification of children and their welfare with modernity. A series of imperial dispositions improved the legal and social condition of orphaned and abandoned children, and that quintessential institution of Enlightenment modernization, the foundling home, spread throughout the region. While ORPHANAGES had been founded sporadically since at least the early seventeenth century, they multiplied rapidly in eighteenth-century colonial urban centers, becoming the most visible public initiatives directed at children in colonial and republican Latin America. They also enjoyed a striking endurance: many functioned into the twentieth century, and the one in Santiago, Chile, continues to operate at the beginning of the twenty-first century. Because of the documentation they generated, foundling homes and their wards are the single best-studied aspect of Latin American childhood.

The Symbolic Significance of Children and Childhood

Childhood had an important symbolic function in colonial society. Cultural encounter, domination, and amalgamation, as well as political authority, were expressed and understood through the lens of childhood. For example, European interpretations of native peoples were refracted through early modern notions of children and childhood. Both critics and defenders of Amerindians portrayed them as childlike and childish. Whether willful and irrational, as critics charged, or unsullied in their innocence, as defenders countered, native peoples required the guidance and protection of paternal overlords. Meanwhile, indigenous children became the objects *par excellence* of missionaries' efforts to Christianize and acculturate native peoples. While Amerindian adults were often dismissed as intransigent in their barbarism, their children were seen as pliant and receptive to the faith.

Children also became symbolically associated with processes of *mestizaje*, or racial mixture. The eighteenth-century *pinturas de castas*, pictorial representations of *mestizaje*, produced primarily in New Spain, portray two parents of different racial or ethnic identities together with the product of their union, the mixed-race (*casta*) youngster. In such representations, children became the concrete embodiments of racial and cultural miscegenation. The association is evident in public discourses beyond the canvas as well. As Bianca Premo has pointed out, Bourbon commentators associated disorder and danger, DELINQUENCY and crime not just with the urban *castas* but with mixed-race youths specifically. But if the progeny of mixed unions personified danger, in other contexts they embodied the potential to consolidate the socio-racial order. Kathryn Burns documents how the founding fathers of sixteenth-century Spanish Cuzco paid particular attention to the acculturation of their mestiza (mixed Spanish and Indian) daughters. The rearing of young mestizas as Hispanicized wives, mothers, servants, and nuns was regarded as crucial to the reproduction of Spanish pedigrees and hegemony in the city. The experience of Cuzco's mestizas also reveals how the social roles and symbolic significance of mixed-race young people—indeed, how childhood as social construction and social experience in general—were deeply gendered.

Finally, political authority itself in Iberoamerica was understood through discursive analogies based on family relations. The king was a father who guided his subject-children, and *patria potestad*, the principle of paternal authority that was a hallmark of civil law, was an organizing principle of political order. Little wonder, then, that early-nineteenth-century independence struggles were expressed in parallel metaphors as a process of coming of age, in which the colonies reached maturity and sought to emancipate themselves from an outgrown political minority.

See also: **Brazil.**

BIBLIOGRAPHY

Burns, Kathryn. 1999. *Colonial Habits: Convents and the Spiritual Economy of Cuzco, Peru.* Durham, NC: Duke University Press.

Cramaussel, Chantal. 1995. "Ilegítimos y abandonados en la frontera norte de la Nueva España: Parral y San Bartolomé en el siglo XVII." *Colonial Latin American History Review* 4: 405–438.

Dean, Carolyn. 2002. "Sketches of Childhood: Children in Colonial Andean Art and Society." In *Minor Omissions: Children in Latin American History and Society,* ed. Tobias Hecht. Madison: University of Wisconsin Press.

Del Priore, Mary. 1999. *História das crianças no Brasil.* São Paulo: Editora Contexto.

Freyre, Gilberto. 1956. *The Mansions and the Shanties: A Study in the Development of Brazilian Civilization.* New York: Knopf.

Hecht, Tobias, ed. 2002. *Minor Omissions: Children in Latin American History and Society.* Madison: University of Wisconsin Press.

Kuznesof, Elizabeth Anne. 1998. "The Puzzling Contradictions of Child Labor, Unemployment, and Education in Brazil." *Journal of Family History* 23: 225–239.

Lavrin, Asunción. 1994. "La niñez en México e Hispanoamérica: Rutas de exploración." In *La familia en el mundo iberoamericano,* ed. Pilar Gonzalbo Aizpuru and Cecilia Rabell. Mexico City: Universidad Autónoma de México.

Lipsett-Rivera, Sonya, ed. 1998. Special Issue on Children in the History of Latin America. *Journal of Family History* 23, no. 3.

Lipsett-Rivera, Sonya. 2002. "Model Children and Models for Children in Early Mexico." In *Minor Omissions: Children in Latin American History and Society,* ed. Tobias Hecht. Madison: University of Wisconsin Press.

Mannarelli, María. 1993. *Pecados públicos. La ilegitimidad en Lima, siglo XVII.* Lima: Ediciones Flora Tristán.

Marcílio, Maria Luiza. 1998. *História social da criança abandonada.* São Paulo: Editora Hucitec.

Meznar, Joan. 1994. "Orphans and the Transition to Free Labor in Northeast Brazil: The Case of Campinas Grande, 1850–1888." *Journal of Social History* 27: 499–515.

Milanich, Nara. 2002. "Historical Perspectives on Illegitimacy and Illegitimates in Latin America." In *Minor Omissions: Children in Latin American History and Society,* ed. Tobias Hecht. Madison: University of Wisconsin Press.

Premo, Bianca. 2002. "Minor Offenses: Youth, Crime, and Law in Eighteenth-Century Lima." In *Minor Omissions: Children in Latin American History and Society,* ed. Tobias Hecht. Madison: University of Wisconsin Press.

Twinam, Ann. 1999. *Public Lives, Private Secrets: Gender, Honor, Sexuality, and Illegitimacy in Colonial Spanish America.* Stanford, CA: Stanford University Press.

Venâncio Pinto, Renato. 1999. *Famílias abandonadas.* São Paulo: Papirus Editora.

NARA MILANICH

WARS IN CENTRAL AMERICA

Poverty, land hunger, and political repression have long characterized much of Central America. These social ills disproportionately affect the region's children, many of whom suffer from hunger, illiteracy, infectious disease, and inadequacies in housing, formal education, and health care. Children often work from an early age in order to supplement family incomes. Especially in El Salvador, Nicaragua, and Guatemala, poverty, social inequalities, and a closed political process have generated opposition movements and, in response, repression by government and economic elites. During the 1970s and 1980s, these conflicts erupted into full-scale civil war. Guerrilla armies and militant popular movements directly challenged authoritarian governments, and in post-1979 Nicaragua counterrevolutionaries tried to oust the Sandinista government.

Children suffer as disproportionately from political violence as they do from poverty. In 1995 the United Nations Children's Fund (UNICEF) reported that more civilian children than soldiers are killed in contemporary wars and that half of all refugees in the world are children. This holds true for Central America, where millions of civilians were displaced from their homes during the 1980s, including 30 percent of El Salvador's population. In addition to death and displacement, the Central American Human Rights Commission (CODEHUCA) reports that war's direct effects on children include permanent injury, loss of parents and other relatives, destruction of home and land, and loss of family income. War also damages many children psychologically. Researchers have noted, for example, the prominent place of soldiers, airplanes, and corpses in the drawings of refugee children. In El Salvador, Guatemala, and Nicaragua, the psychological, economic, and cultural damage created by the political violence of the 1970s and 1980s continued even after the wars officially ended. Some researchers attribute the growth of juvenile violence and gangs in many parts of Central America in the 1990s to the social dislocation, economic hardship, and desensitization to violence resulting from the civil wars.

Children's victimization is not without political significance. Different parties in Central America have utilized images of suffering children to channel indignation toward the enemy that has hurt them. However, children are not only passive victims of political violence. In this region, as in other parts of the world, children as young as seven or eight have participated in both government and opposition armies. Despite governments denials, international observers repeatedly confirmed that boys under fifteen, often forcibly recruited, were serving in the Salvadoran and Guatemalan government armies.

Many boys and girls also participated in guerrilla movements as combatants and also, for younger children, as couriers or lookouts. However, most of these joined voluntarily. Especially in conflicted rural areas, joining the opposition often seemed preferable to the risks of civilian life. Guerrilla participation carried benefits, including not only protection and food but also social support structures, education, and respect. Further, many young people felt strong commitments to the political opposition, based on family, ethnic, or regional loyalties, ideological and religious beliefs, or personal experiences of violence.

While young guerrillas often received respect and affection from others in their movement, authoritarian governments usually called them delinquents, arbitrary opponents of law and order. The association of youth and political opposition created a climate, especially in Nicaragua and El Salvador, in which any youth was seen as potentially subversive and thus a legitimate target of government reprisal. Nicaraguans recalling the repressive period prior to President Anastasio Somoza's defeat in 1979, for example, often assert that "It was a crime to be young."

In sum, popular perceptions in Central America during the 1970s and 1980s understood children as primarily victims of the civil wars but also as active agents, either heroic combatants or dangerous subversives. This agency was rarely affirmed by humanitarian organizations or scholars, who generally condemn all political participation by children. Their critiques rest on an assumption that children can only be victims, never victimizers; only acted upon, never actors. While these assumptions undergird vital efforts to protect children, they also reinforce a culturally and historically limited vision of children's needs, interests, and capacities, even of the nature of childhood itself. Images and experiences of Central American children, in other words, challenge the mainstream Western view of childhood as a time of innocence, ignorance, and isolation from the moral and political conflicts of the adult world.

See also: **Soldier Children: Global Human Rights Issues; War in the Twentieth Century.**

BIBLIOGRAPHY

CODEHUCA. n.d. *Los niños de la década perdida: Investigación y análisis de violaciones de los derechos humanos de la niñez centroamericana (1980–92) (The children of the lost decade: Investigation and analysis of violations of human rights of Central American children [1980–92]).* San José, Costa Rica: CODEHUCA.

Marín, Patricia. 1988. *Infancia y guerra en El Salvador (Childhood and war in El Salvador).* Guatemala City: UNICEF.

Peterson, Anna L., and Kay Almere Read. 2002. "Victims, Heroes, Enemies: Children in Central American Wars." In *Minor Omissions: Children in Latin American History and Society,* ed. Tobias Hecht. Madison: University of Wisconsin Press, 215–231.

UNICEF. 1995. *Annual Report.* Paris: United Nations Children's Fund.

ANNA L. PETERSON

Latin School

The term *Latin school* covers a variety of educational options throughout European history. At present, it persists only in Great Britain, as a general term for secondary schools offering an academic type of education. On the continent, the former Latin school developed into the modern GYMNASIUM in the Germanic and Scandinavian countries and the LYCÉE in France, or was replaced in the course of the nineteenth century by other forms of secondary education.

The Latin school has its roots in the Middle Ages, when literate people were predominantly clerics and had to know Latin in order to perform religious services. Initially Latin schools were set up by cathedral chapters, convents, parishes, or other ecclesiastical bodies for choirboys and future clerics destined for the service of church and state. Roughly from the fourteenth century secular authorities followed suit. Kings, princes, local lords, or town councils founded Latin schools in the interest of a better education for their subjects, for the development of intellectual skills, and to provide support for their administrations. By 1500, Latin or grammar schools existed all over Europe, either under a cleric, called the *scholaster,* or under a secular headmaster, who was often controlled by a board. The pupils were exclusively male, and mostly between six and eighteen years old, depending on age of entry and individual achievement.

In the early modern period two major developments—the spread of LITERACY and the differentiation of teaching institutions—determined the position of the Latin schools within the rising educational system, either as a secondary school or as the first step in higher education. When literacy became a more common requirement in the urbanizing societies of the West, elementary schools were founded, or split off from the Latin schools, for teaching literacy and numeracy in the vernacular tongue. Henceforth, the Latin school limited itself to the classical languages: Latin and, after the rise of humanism, Greek. Since Latin was the lingua franca of the learned world of Europe, the Latin school was for many pupils a first step to the university. Until the late nineteenth century the universities were reserved for a small elite, generally not more than two percent of the males aged eighteen to twenty-four, but Latin schools may have taught several times this number. This was still a small percentage of the youth, even in the major cultural centers, but it did provide a Latin-based education to a substantial elite.

Birth of the School Class

At the turn of the fifteenth century, a historical change occurred when a new curriculum was introduced by headmaster Joan Cele (d. 1417) in the flourishing Dutch Hanseatic towns of Zwolle and Deventer. Instead of rewarding individual progress, it distinguished between eight group levels of achievement, called *ordines,* or classes, numbered from the eighth (the lowest class) to the first (the highest). A fixed part of the curriculum was assigned to each class. Subjects included grammar, poetry, rhetoric or eloquence, and dialectic (which made up the old *trivium* of the arts faculty, as a result of which the Latin school was often called the Trivial school), and in the higher classes logic, moral philosophy, and elements of the *quadrivium,* which included physics, arithmetics, music, and geography. For each level particular authors were selected. The most widely used throughout the centuries were probably Cicero, Caesar, Ovid, Pliny, Sallust, Terence, Virgil, and Horace in Latin (along with a few neo-Latin works like Erasmus's *Dialogues*); and Xenophon, Homer, and the dramatists in Greek.

With the help of the printing press, standardized textbooks like the Latin grammar of Despauterius (c. 1460–1520) allowed for a truly European curriculum. Erasmus's dialogues on social behavior (*De civilitate morum puerilium*), used as a textbook throughout Europe and published in countless editions and in several translations since its first publication in Latin at Basle in 1530, have durably marked Europe's manners. Many humanists have either highly praised or fiercely criticized their education. Erasmus, who studied at Deventer under the famous Alexander Hegius (c. 1433–1498), rejected both the pedantry of the schoolmasters and the leveling effect of the school system on the boys' intelligence. Soon important reforms were proposed like that of the more practical method for the teaching of dialectics by the French Huguenot Petrus Ramus (1515–1572).

Tuition and Boarding

The new Latin schools attracted thousands of pupils and spread quickly over Northern Europe. Until the sixteenth century, pupils had wandered around as vagrants. François

Rabelais's *Pantagruel* (1532) and the diaries of the Platter boys from Basle give a marvellous insight into that moving adolescent world, described by Le Roy Ladurie in his *Beggar and the Professor*. This changed in the sixteenth century. Since many pupils came from far away, boarding houses were set up, either outside the school or by transforming the Latin schools into boarding schools. These were called colleges or *pensionnats* in France, or PUBLIC SCHOOLS (Winchester, founded in 1382, was the first) in England. After its introduction in Montaigu College at Paris in the late fifteenth century, the new collegiate system became known as the Parisian style. Through the Jesuit order it swept the Catholic world from Portugal to Lithuania, with the Jesuit college at Rome becoming the Catholic model. Through Strasbourg (Johann Sturm) and Geneva (John Calvin) it reached the Protestant world too, although in the Holy Roman Empire the day school remained more popular than the college. From a material necessity the boarding school soon developed into a pedagogical tool for the moral education of the youth. In the eighteenth century, attending a boarding school became a status element of the higher classes. In these closed communities, young boys assimilated social skills, good manners, and group values, and were efficiently prepared for entrance into the male networks of the ruling class.

Initially schoolmasters were church officials for whom teaching was only a part-time job. Full-time teachers at Latin schools had often been taught themselves in the arts faculty. In Protestant Europe, the teaching job soon became an alternative to the clerical profession, until teaching developed during the eighteenth century into a full profession in itself. As such, it required adequate training and examinations (such as the first systematic and compulsory professional examination in Europe, the French *agrégation*, instituted in 1766 and still in existence today). In the Catholic countries, new religious orders (Jesuits, Oratorians, Piarists) devoted themselves to the education of youth, and founded or took over a huge number of Latin schools. The Jesuits drew up a general rule of study (the *ratio studiorum*, 1599), combined teaching and moral education in their boarding schools, developed school drama, and introduced a very successful pedagogy of emulation among the pupils. They were imitated throughout Europe, by the Protestants as well, for example at Francke's *Paedagogium* in Halle (1696), with its emphasis on the merits of self-achieved talent.

During the sixteenth to eighteenth centuries, virtually every town had its Latin school, small or great. Teaching was not free, but since the schools were generally endowed fees were moderate, and scholarships did exist. The Latin schools served essentially to reproduce the social elites below the aristocracy, but they also enabled some gifted impecunious pupils to climb into the learned professions. In some countries at the beginning of this period students sang in the churches, and had official permission to beg in the streets in order to help pay their way.

Curriculum and Reform

Ideally, a school had six grade levels (classes) of humanities. The two or more top classes of semi-university level were realized only in the greater *collèges de plein exercice* or *gymnasia academica*. But each level could require more or less than a year's work, according to the school regulations and the pupil's capacity. School regulations varied greatly but there was a tendency toward regional or national unification. In Germany an examination called the *Abitur* (1788) and the *baccalauréat* in France (1808) were finally standardized as formal prerequisites for admission to the university.

Curricula in the Latin school turned entirely around the mastery of Latin, spiced with some Greek. Latin was the teaching language; Latin eloquence, poetry, and dialectic formed both the tool and the ideal of the classical education; and pupils were supposed to speak Latin with each other. Imitation of classical rhetoric was supposed to transfer classical values to the pupils: clarity of language equaled clarity of thought. Yet Christian values constantly interfered. Church attendance and catechization were compulsory. The Jesuits promoted religious school congregations and the Protestants strongly advocated an alloy of piety, eloquence, and erudition. Modern languages had to be learned after school time or in other schools, such as the private schools that flourished in the eighteenth century. The Czech refugee bishop JOHANN AMOS COMENIUS (1592–1670) tried with some success to introduce multilingual and visual teaching methods through his textbooks *Janua linguarum* and *Orbis pictus*. Natural sciences and mathematics were only taught in the philosophy classes, and were not common before the eighteenth century reforms.

During the later eighteenth century the reform of the Latin school became a national issue everywhere in Europe. It was included in the ENLIGHTENMENT reform of the educational system, which started from the conviction that it was the state's responsibility to properly educate its citizens: a cultural elite and a skilled bureaucracy were the two pillars of a well-ordered state. The new meritocratic ideals sapped the old society of orders and enhanced education as a tool of self-achievement. The expulsion of the Jesuits from most of the countries of Europe in the mid to late eighteenth century made reform urgent, but radical measures really had to wait for the great revolutionary wave that swept away the institutions of the ancien régime. After the Restoration period of the early nineteenth century, Latin schools reemerged with a new impetus throughout Europe, often with a curriculum adapted to the new order, except in Britain, where schools were still tied by their foundation statutes. However, they came under the pressure of modernization everywhere and were gradually replaced by the neo-humanist gymnasium or the secondary school with its modern language and science curriculum that we know today.

See also: **Aristocratic Education in Europe; Desiderius Erasmus of Rotterdam; Education, Europe.**

BIBLIOGRAPHY

Ariès, Philippe. 1962. *Centuries of Childhood: A Social History of Family Life.* Trans. Robert Baldick. New York: Knopf.

Chatellier, Louis. 1989. *The Europe of the Devout: The Catholic Reformation and the Formation of a New Society.* Cambridge, UK: Cambridge University Press.

Davis, Robin. 1967. *The Grammar School.* Harmondsworth, UK: Penguin.

Grafton, Anthony, and Jardine, Lisa. 1986. *From Humanism to the Humanities. Education and the Liberal Arts in Fifteenth- and Sixteenth-Century Europe.* Cambridge, MA: Harvard University Press.

Heafford, Michael. 1995. "The Early History of the Abitur as an Administrative Device." *German History* 13: 285–304.

Houston, Robert A. 2002. *Literacy in Early Modern Europe: Culture and Education 1500–1800.* Harlow, UK: Longman.

Huppert, George. 1984. *Public Schools in Renaissance France.* Urbana: University of Illinois Press.

La Vopa, Anthony J. 1988. *Grace, Talent, and Merit: Poor Students, Clerical Careers, and Professional Ideology in Eighteenth-Century Germany.* Cambridge, UK: Cambridge University Press.

Le Roy Ladurie, Emmanuel. 1997. *The Beggar and the Professor: A Sixteenth-Century Family Saga.* Trans. Arthur Goldhammer. Chicago: Chicago University Press.

O'Day, Rosemary. 1982. *Education and Society, 1500–1800: The Social Foundations of Education in Early Modern Britain.* London: Longman.

Roach, John. 1986. *A History of Secondary Education in England, 1800–1870.* London: Longman.

Tinsley, Barbara Sher. 1989. "Johann Sturm's Method for Humanistic Pedagogy." *The Sixteenth Century Journal* 20: 23–40.

WILLEM FRIJHOFF

Laura Spelman Rockefeller Memorial

The Laura Spelman Rockefeller Memorial was founded October 18, 1918 by John D. Rockefeller Sr., in memory of his deceased wife, and was terminated as a legal entity on January 3, 1929. The Memorial's mandate was the promotion of the welfare of women and children worldwide. In the 1920s the foundation was one of the major American supporters of applied social science research. By 1922, the Memorial's trustees gave away some $13 millions, of which $50,500 went to scientific research, the rest largely to traditional Rockefeller charities in the New York area. In January 1922, the Memorial had some $74 million at its disposal, and the Trustees decided that the Memorial needed an overall plan for its dispersal. They were committed to social betterment through science, and believed they needed foundation professionals to help them. That May they lured Beardsley Ruml from the Carnegie Corporation as the Memorial's director. Ruml and the Trustees worked out three major programs for the Memorial, including general social science, interracial relations, and child study and parent education. They appointed Lawrence K. Frank program officer for child study and parent education.

The program's underlying assumptions were simple. Parents and teachers were directly responsible for the care of children. Such care often suffered from ignorance of CHILD CARE and nature; hence research would advance child welfare and educate parents and teachers in the best means of child nurture. Besides research, essential activities included disseminating such information to parents and teachers, training professional researchers, teachers, and administrators, and conducting experiments to determine the best methods of parent education.

Between 1922 and 1928, Frank created the entire professional scientific subculture of child development and parent education. He crisscrossed the country by train to interview prospective personnel for centers in research and parent education. He and the Trustees did not enroll volunteers. Instead they anointed particular groups and cadres after often long evaluations. They gave money to an existing research center, the Iowa Child Welfare Research Center, at the University of Iowa, and established other research centers—usually called institutes of child welfare—at Teachers College, Columbia University, Yale University, the University of Toronto, the University of Minnesota, and the University of California at Berkeley. Each center had a core of researchers dedicated to certain scientific problems; each center was to develop a statewide program in parent education, including research, teaching, and popularization. There were other centers of parent education research and teaching at various land grant or liberal arts institutions, including the University of Georgia, the University of Cincinnati, and Iowa State College of Agriculture and Mechanic Arts. These public institutions complied more with the Memorial's plans than the private ones; Teachers College closed its institute when the Memorial's funds ran out in 1936, and Yale insisted on creating an Institute of Human Relations from its Institute of Psychology, neither of which functioned as a genuine interdisciplinary home for Yale professor ARNOLD GESELL, who preferred to work by himself. The institutes at Minnesota and Berkeley continued to operate into the twenty-first century; the Iowa Station lost its intellectual primacy in the 1950s and was closed in the 1970s.

Frank also helped create a Committee on Child Development of the National Research Council, which in the 1930s became the professional society of child development researchers. In addition, he helped fund journals for the nascent field, a program of National Research Council fellowships for 160 graduate fellows to take advanced study, and even a scheme with PARENTS MAGAZINE to generate dividends to the research centers for new investigations; although the magazine never paid a dividend on the Memorial's substantial investments. A small professional scientific subculture was thus inserted into American higher education, thanks to the Memorial's largess, and often over the protests of faculty in traditional psychology and other social science departments.

When the Memorial was closed in 1929, the bulk of its resources were allocated to the social sciences division of the Rockefeller Foundation. Other foundations intervened to support child development and parent education in the Great Depression and later, but clearly without the Memorial, the field's history would have been much less assured.

See also: **Child Development, History of the Concept of; Child Saving; Child Study; Parenting; Social Welfare.**

BIBLIOGRAPHY

Cravens, Hamilton. 1985. "Child-Saving in the Age of Professionalism, 1915–1930." In *American Childhood: A Research Guide and a Historical Handbook.* ed. J. M. Hawes and N. Ray Hiner. Westport, CT: Greenwood Press.

Cravens, Hamilton. 1993. *Before Head Start: The Iowa Station and America's Children.* Chapel Hill: University of North Carolina Press.

Laura Spelman Rockefeller Memorial. 1993. *The Laura Spelman Rockefeller Memorial, Final Report.* New York: Laura Spelman Rockefeller Memorial.

HAMILTON CRAVENS

Law, Children and the

As British colonists began peopling North America, political philosopher Thomas Hobbes voiced the stark traditional English view of the legal status of children: "For the child like the imbecile and the crazed beast there is no law." Over three hundred years later, United States Supreme Court Justice Harry Blackmun reached a very different conclusion. In a decision that granted a minor the right to an abortion without parental consent, Blackmun asserted: "Constitutional rights do not mature and come into being magically only when one attains the state-defined age of majority. Minors, as well as adults, are protected by the Constitution and possess constitutional rights." In the years between these dramatically different declarations, age had become increasingly significant in American law. However, the legal status of children had not simply improved steadily over that time. More critically, the law increasingly had become a primary source of identity, status, and power for American children. It did so as children gradually acquired a separate and distinct legal identity.

Central to the creation of law for children at any particular time and over time has been the ideal of youthful dependence. Though exact conceptions of youthful dependence have changed significantly since the first colonial settlements, in every era of the American past children were assumed to be less competent and more vulnerable than adults. Since immaturity was assumed to render them incapable of making competent decisions about critical aspects of their lives, lawmakers concluded that children should not be as legally accountable as adults for their market, criminal, or other acts. Denying children the legal powers and liabilities

of adults also meant that the law entrusted parents, the state, and other adults with significant legal authority over them. Consequently, the line between child and adult became the most critical legal boundary for young Americans. It has been, though, an uncertain marker because of the diversity of American children. Within the legal category of minors, children varied according to age, race, gender, capacity, and other critical factors and these variations complicated legal policies. Since the seventeenth century, the law dealt with this reality by devising particular policies for particular actions by particular groups of children. Thus, for instance, within the larger legal category of children, minors of various ages have had the legal power to wed before reaching majority. Taken together laws for children expressed the persistent conviction of legal policy makers that minors were a special class of citizens who required a different set of legal policies than adults.

Colonial Americans created a foundation for the law by transferring English policies to their new settlements. Fundamental changes then occurred in the first part of the nineteenth century when a comprehensive code for children was first devised. Other significant changes were made in the late nineteenth and early twentieth centuries when the role of the state in children's lives was increased in significant ways. A second era of substantive change occurred late in the twentieth century. The result of these eras of legal change is a multilayered set of judicial decisions, statutes, and legal customs that has made the law more and more consequential in the lives of American children.

Early America

Although never as completely outside of the bounds of law as Hobbes's declaration suggests, children in early America did find themselves enmeshed in a traditional European legal order. Children were part of a patriarchal system in which the household was to replicate the larger polity. Thus the father, like the king, served as head of the family while the wife and children were classified as subordinates. And in an era in which the definition of childhood meant that infants were treated as a distinct group but other children were considered more as members of the adult world, early integration of the young into the larger social order was the primary object of the law. In this system children were bound to their families and communities through webs of reciprocal duties and responsibilities, many of which were codified and enforced through the law. The most profound of these relationships fell under the traditional doctrine or legal rule of *parens patriae*, which made the monarch or the state the principal protector of children and other dependents. It was, and continues to be, the fundamental legal basis for all state intervention on behalf of children.

Colonial legislatures transferred the English legal system and its fundamental assumptions and policies about the young to the New World with relatively few changes. At its heart was the notion of legal reciprocity: children exchanged their labor for parental care. Parents, primarily fathers, assumed the responsibility to maintain and educate their offspring and to give them a suitable start in life. In exchange, fathers were granted the right to the custody of their children and in turn the right to a child's labor. Mothers had relatively few legal rights to their children's custody or labor. Equally important, the imposition of English rules governing the age of majority made it the primary legal dividing line between children and adults. Set according to English custom at twenty-one, the age of majority was the designated point at which a youth shed the disabilities of childhood and assumed the full rights and responsibilities of adulthood.

Majority marked off childhood as a distinct legal category and made children legal dependents, but it could not encapsulate all youthful legal actions. Instead, the law crafted rules for specific actions, such as the right of girls to wed at twelve and boys at fourteen or the criminal innocence of children under the age of seven. In this way, following English policies meant establishing both a clear legal line between children and adults and also secondary lines within childhood for particular legal acts. This combination of uniformity and specificity laid the basis for the legal treatment of American children well into the future. It also ensured that legal contests would be waged over what a minor could or should be able to do and what he or she could not or should not do.

INHERITANCE is an apt illustration of the transfer of English legal policies to the new world. English rules were dominated by a determination to keep property in the family. Its most revealing policies were primogeniture and entail. The former dictated that the family estate was to be bequeathed to the eldest son; the latter severely restricted the right of a child to sell or otherwise diminish the family estate. Both envisioned the filial duty of family maintenance and the right of the parent to control the child. These rules were followed in much of colonial America, particularly in the South. However egalitarian ideas in the New England colonies led to the creation of a new policy: partible inheritance. It allowed a parent to divide his estate among his offspring and suggested the emergence of new ideas of sibling equality. Critically, all of the inheritance rules expressed the traditional English belief that child welfare was best secured through property arrangements. Those with property had greater security and also greater independence. The inheritance rules also underscored the primal belief in parental responsibility, especially that fathers should support their children. The implications of these practices were clear in the Chesapeake colonies, where officials established special orphan courts because the high death rate due to malaria left countless children without parents. The purpose of the courts was to protect the person and property of the ORPHANS. These courts recognized that children had interests of their own and used property as the children's most important welfare protection and most fundamental legal right.

A similar mix was evident in one of the most significant colonial legal policies toward the young, APPRENTICESHIP. It rested on a contract in which masters pledged training and support in exchange for a child's personal service. Fathers and, upon their death, mothers could indenture their children voluntarily because the right to an offspring's services carried with it a corollary authority to assign those services to another. The master then stood *in loco parentis*, receiving the child's services in return for parental support, nurture, and education. Indentures could also be forced upon a child by poor-law authorities after a finding of parental neglect or failure. These became the primary legal recourse of an emerging American approach to orphans, child poverty, abuse, and neglect. As in England, the practice was designed to teach children occupations and trades and to inculcate in them the habits of industry and thrift so that they would become self-supporting citizens. The system aimed to relieve the community of their support. The law governing apprenticeship thus typified English rules designed to integrate children into the adult world at an early age.

A similar approach emerged in the transfer of another traditional policy to the colonies. BASTARDS, as Anglo-American law had long classified children born out of wedlock, traditionally faced legal repression and discrimination. Statutes, doctrines, and customs used matrimony to separate legal from spurious issue. The latter suffered the legal status of *filius nullius*, the child and heir of no one. For centuries under English law, the bastard had no recognized legal relations with his or her parents, and no claims to inheritance, maintenance, or family membership. Nor did the illicit couple have any rights or duties toward the child. The English reluctance to help bastards was evident in their refusal to follow civil law and allow legitimation by the subsequent marriage of the parents. The only major reform in the law came with the inclusion of bastards in the Elizabethan Poor Law of 1601 and the demand that parents aid in their upkeep. Bastardy law had two primary purposes: repelling challenges to established family organization, especially property distribution, and preventing the public from being saddled with the costs of rearing children born out of wedlock. Beyond their streamlining of paternity hearings, colonial Americans made few alterations in the law.

Innovation in colonial laws regarding children was perhaps most evident in the creation of the most abject form of child legal dependency—SLAVERY. The need of colonists for labor coupled with the settlers' racism led to a fundamental modification of English law. Beginning late in the seventeenth century, lawmakers altered the legal pedigree of African-American children by decreeing that they would assume the status of their mothers, not their fathers. This shift helped ensure their continued enslavement. Slave children were also denied basic legal rights to family membership, could be sold at any time, and had the fewest legal protections of any children in the colonies. Though the adoption of slavery created the most dependent legal status of all colonial children, it was less anomalous legally than it would be later in the history of the United States, because the young were to be found in a number of dependent legal statuses, from apprenticeship to indentured servitude.

Colonial legal policies represented a transatlantic transfer of traditional European policies codifying the dependent status of the youth. They were premised on the belief that child welfare was best promoted by the creation of webs of reciprocity that made families and, when they failed, communities responsible for children. In exchange, both were given extensive rights to govern the young. Policies like the age of majority established a European base for laws that would continue to govern children's lives far into the future. In this regime, children had few independent legal rights or powers and age was relatively unimportant as a source of distinctive legal rules. Thus in many ways the law was simply less significant in the lives of colonial children than it would be for later generations.

After the Revolution

In the years after the American Revolution the laws governing children were transformed in fundamental ways. Legal change was both a cause and a product of larger changes in the place of children in American society. New family beliefs and practices treated children more than ever before as distinct individuals with special needs. An individualization of the household implicit in the new view of the family led to an understanding of children as particular kinds of people with distinct rights and duties and relationships with the state. Age became a more important demarcation of legal rights and responsibilities, a development that challenged the Hobbesian view of children as beyond the reach of the law.

Determining a new legal place for the young became a major challenge for the antebellum legal order. It was one addressed primarily in the states because under reigning American conceptions of federalism the states had primary jurisdiction over children and families. As the principal definers of children's legal status, state judges and legislators struggled to find a way to treat children somehow as distinct individuals and yet not adults in a system that tied legal power to individual autonomy. The result was to emphasize children's needs. This approach found its most revealing expression in a new doctrine that would dominate legal debates about children into the twenty-first century: *the best interests of the child*. Early in the nineteenth century judges and other policy makers developed this doctrine by reinterpreting the *parens patriae* power of the state to include a newfound sense of children as having distinct interests recognizable by the law. The legal doctrine contained the assumption that children had their own needs and that others, most appropriately parents, and when they failed, judges or other suitable public or private officials such as the overseers of the poor,

must determine them. At the same time, this doctrine supported the emerging notion of the family as a private institution that should be granted significant autonomy by deferring to family privacy and parental rights. In this way, the new rule sanctioned broad discretionary authority to determine the interests of children only in the event of family conflict or failure.

The best interests of the child doctrine emerged most directly out of child custody disputes between warring parents. Those disputes, in turn, were fueled by new ideas about child rearing and gender roles. A sense of children as vulnerable and in need of nurture coincided with a growing faith in the nurturing power of mothers to make the mother–child bond the most important connection in the family. One result was the determination of more and more women to keep their children when their marriages failed and the equally critical decision of more and more courts to grant them that wish. State and federal judges used the best interests of the child doctrine to make maternal preference the basic rule of American custody law. And they created subsidiary doctrines to support this reallocation of parental rights, most notably the *tender years rule* dictating that the custody of young children and girls must be given to mothers. The custody laws' innovations redefined children's welfare to stress nurture and maternal care rather than property holding and thus ensured that most children of failed marriages would stay with their mothers. Equally important, the new custody rules led to the creation of ADOPTION, which authorized the legal construction of a family based on choice rather than blood ties. Beginning with Massachusetts in 1851, by end of the century almost every state had added adoption to its children's code. Though legal battles were waged over the inheritance of adoptees and their new parents, the idea that child nurture warranted this kind of new custodial relationship won wide approval and thus diminished the legal power of blood ties in children's lives.

The early-nineteenth-century reorientation of custody law also began to influence traditional children's legal policies like apprenticeship and bastardy. The importance of mother–child bonds and the notion of the home as a nursery and refuge undermined the attractions of apprenticeship at the same time that the creation of public schools in the north also undercut the role of apprenticeship as a training device. Voluntary indenture narrowed to a method of vocational training for youths and young men. Involuntary indenture, however, remained a basic poor-law relief tool, though it existed uneasily with the new ideals of custody law. The primary concern remained reducing the burden of poor relief for local taxpayers, not child welfare. The differing fates of these two forms of indenture graphically illustrate the corrosive effect of dependency on the legal rights of the young. Laws for middle-class and upper-class children stressed the private common-law rights of parents and freedom from state interference, but the laws for poor children used dependency to abridge individual rights and to sanction broad public controls. And nowhere was that more evident than in the fate of free black children. Poor-law indentures, especially for blacks, came to resemble involuntary servitude as several states eliminated the educational requirements of their indentures and granted masters the right to indenture black children regardless of parental finances. When coupled with the complete denial of rights to slave children, these policies used the law to create an American system of apartheid for black children and suggest how race as well as class restrictions were being embedded in the laws governing American children.

The impact of the best interest of the child standard was more visible in bastardy law. Beginning in Virginia in the 1780s, state after state rewrote its laws to express the new conviction that children should not be punished for the sins of their parents and that they should be in families whenever possible. Statutes and judicial decisions declared the offspring of a couple who wed after its birth to be legitimate. They did the same for the children of annulled marriages. And even if parents failed to wed, state lawmakers lessened the penalties of illegitimacy by creating a new legal household when they turned the customary bonds between the bastard and its mother into a web of reciprocal legal rights and duties. Similarly, judges and legislators conferred reciprocal inheritance rights on bastards and their mothers and other kin. Through such policies illegitimate children began to have their own rights and responsibilities. Even so, American bastardy law never jettisoned two traditional influences: fiscally conservative local officials anxious to control child support costs, and a deeply ingrained prejudice against extramarital sexual relations. Indeed, protection of taxpayers' pocketbooks reinforced a general legal conviction that proper child nurture required guardians capable of providing adequate material support and thus determined that children with parents who relied on poor relief for sustenance probably did not benefit from the new custody rights.

The emerging conviction that children required special legal rules also affected those deemed unruly, neglected, and delinquent. They became part of the reform of criminal justice and punishment in the era with the creation of specialized institutions for the young: houses of refuge. Beginning in New York in 1824, houses of refuge were constructed throughout the country to provide wayward or neglected youngsters with special treatment aimed at making them grow into responsible adults. Predicated on the *parens patriae* power of the state, the jurisdiction of a house of refuge was purposely broad. Children were confined in these institutions on the basis of crime, vagrancy, disobedience, or parental neglect. Lumping children at risk together in this manner received judicial sanction in 1838 when the Pennsylvania Supreme Court rebuffed a father's challenge to the incarceration of his daughter without a trial. In EX PARTE CROUSE the court contended that "[t]he basic right of children is not to

liberty but to custody. . . . We know of no natural right exemption from the restraints which conduce to an infant's welfare" and thus equated the legal status of children at risk with their physical and social dependency. The justices went on to argue that placement in the house of refuge was treatment, not punishment, and that the public had a right to act when parents failed. The decision voiced a clear distinction between children and adults, while it blurred many differences among children by lumping together all juveniles deemed at risk.

As a result of developments like these, the legal place of American children was transformed during the years between the Revolution and the Civil War. The new laws expressed rules and assumptions of a legal order more explicitly stratified by age than ever before. They made the primary line between adulthood and childhood even more of a legal divider between rights and needs, autonomy and dependence. Children, like other dependents in a society fundamentally divided by class, race, and gender, were designated special legal individuals, and the legal officials created special policies like these for them. As childhood came to constitute a separate legal category, the law moved further from the Hobbesian view of youthful legal powerlessness.

Industrial America

In the turbulent years after the Civil War, the law regarding children underwent further change as it was selectively redrawn to include a greater role for state regulation of the young. A new assertion of public power and public interest in families challenged the now powerful American tradition of family autonomy: the right of families to be left alone and of parents to raise their children as they saw fit. That challenge was prompted by a growing sense among the middle and upper classes that families were in crisis. Beginning in the 1870s fears about disordered families stirred an intense national debate about the fate of children. Concern about abuse, DELINQUENCY, and neglect led to demands for greater state intervention based on the *parens patriae* doctrine. The resulting expansion of the role of the state in children's lives also expressed a growing faith in law as a tool for changing children's lives.

Self-styled child-savers took the lead in extending youthful dependence as they and their legislative allies filled states' codes with new regulations that substantially enlarged the legal definition of risks facing children. Each addition, from bans on entering dance halls or skating rinks and prohibitions against joining the circus or purchasing alcohol, to specific criminal penalties against CHILD ABUSE or neglect, represented a risk that now had to be prescribed. Each was premised on the assumption that childhood was a distinctive and vulnerable stage of life and that public regulation of child rearing had to be expanded to protect the young. These assumptions in turn were drawn in part from a new conviction that older children should be more precisely segregated into their own legal category of ADOLESCENCE. Much of the debate and controversy of the era focused on this newly designated group of children and the determination that their childhood must be prolonged by keeping them in their families to gain more extensive preparation for adult roles. The intent, if not the full result, of changes like these was to use the law to increase children's dependence on adults and to remove the young from the adult spheres of the marketplace and the civic community. This logic was evident in the successful campaign to raise the legal age of marriage from the old common-law standards of twelve for girls and fourteen for boys to sixteen and eighteen respectively. Protective legislation like this also challenged an earlier faith in parental supervision of their offspring by circumscribing parental authority and creating a more direct legal relationship between children and the state.

The new concerns of the era were evident in the prolonged campaign to use the law to ban CHILD LABOR. Children filled many of the new places in the factories of industrial America and swarmed into urban streets selling everything from newspapers to artificial flowers. Child savers sought to redefine childhood by excluding work from the lives of children for the first time in the country's history. They turned to law as their tool of reform. By 1900, seventeen states restricted the age, hours, and conditions of youthful employment. But reformers wanted a national ban, as in Europe, where by the end of the nineteenth century nearly all countries had passed laws that prohibited or restricted child labor. They faced numerous opponents: manufacturers, particularly southern textile owners, who wanted young workers; working-class and immigrant parents and their allies who defended child labor on the grounds of the income that it brought to poor families; farmers who wanted the seasonal labor of children; and other critics who resented the intrusion by the government into their family work traditions. Resistance represented a recognition that child labor reform sought to sever the traditional common-law notion of family reciprocity in which children exchanged their labor for parental support. In an effort to entrench child nurture as the fundamental duty of families, child labor legislation attempted to restrict parental rights to children's services yet continued to insist on parental support for children. Reformers succeeded in securing congressional action in 1916 and again in 1920, only to have the Supreme Court declare the acts unconstitutional each time. They also failed to secure a national amendment. Despite these setbacks national restrictions on child labor were finally approved in 1941 when the Supreme Court upheld the Fair Labor Standards bill that prohibited the employment of children under sixteen in industries engaged in interstate commerce and young people under eighteen in dangerous occupations. As a result, the law provided yet another definition of childhood by restricting the place of the young in the workplace and by creating a growing thicket of regulations for youthful workers that regulated when, where, and how long they could work.

Reformers had more immediate success in another attempt to use the law to redefine childhood: compelling children to go to and to stay in school. The campaign took place in the states, since education was thought to be a state, indeed a local concern. Compulsory education laws were championed as another way of taking children out of the workforce and prolonging childhood. They proved to be a popular reform; thirty-two states had COMPULSORY SCHOOL ATTENDANCE laws by 1900, and by 1918, with their passage in Mississippi, all the states had them. As its advocates intended, compulsory education and the increasing curricular and disciplinary authority of teachers and school officials further regulated parental authority over children and made schooling a critical component of the legal definition of childhood and children's experience.

No development of the era more fully epitomized the new approaches to children and the law than the creation of the JUVENILE COURT. Advocates of special courts for children argued that adult standards of criminal responsibility should not be applied to children because the young lacked the moral understanding and judgment of adults. They demanded a separate JUVENILE JUSTICE system that emphasized rehabilitation, not punishment. These sentiments led them to advocate a legal trade-off: children forfeited due process rights to have an attorney, to face a clear charge, to an open hearing, and other criminal law protections in exchange for rehabilitation. The idea proved very appealing. Chicago created the first court in 1899 and by the 1920s every state had authorized the establishment of juvenile courts in major cities. Though critics complained that the new tribunal forced children to sacrifice too many rights, judges disagreed and accepted it as a legitimate exercise of the states' *parens patriae* powers. According to the Pennsylvania Supreme Court, "Every statute which is designed to give protection, care, and training to children, as a needed substitute for parental authority and performance of parental duty, is but a recognition of the duty of the state, as the legitimate guardian and protector of children where other guardianship has failed. No constitutional right is violated." Equally important, the courts' reliance on foster families and adoption rather than institutional placements whenever possible and their abandonment of apprenticeship also demonstrated how a nurture-based definition of child welfare had been embedded in the law.

The most radical departure of the era was the creation of a special set of legal rights for children. Devising rights for children proved difficult because the existing concept of rights was designed only for adults who could assert their own claims directly against the state. Children could not do this, nor did reformers want them to. Instead they fashioned an idea of paternalistic rights that defined CHILDREN'S RIGHTS in special age-bound terms of needs and parental failure instead of the individual autonomy associated with adult legal rights. Reformers did so by recasting education, socialization, nurture, and other fundamental needs of children as rights. In this way children's rights acquired a restrictive meaning. Children did at times assert more adult-like rights. Newsboys, for instance, organized a successful strike against New York press magnets based on their belief in their rights as workers. And sons and daughters used the juvenile court to renegotiate authority within their families by seizing the right to lodge complaints against abusive parents. Nevertheless, in most cases it was not children, but parents, reformers, or bureaucrats who asserted the newly proclaimed children's rights. For example, United States Supreme Court decisions in the 1920s such as *Meyer v. Nebraska* (1923) and *Pierce v. Society of Sisters* (1925) used children's rights to schooling to construct a constitutional foundation for parents' control of their children's education. Thus the initial conception of children's legal rights was steeped in paternalism; it translated children's needs into rights without jettisoning their dependent status. Such rights were unusual because they could not be exercised or waived by their holder. In this way, paternalistic rights institutionalized the irresolvable tension between treating the young as family dependents or as autonomous individuals.

In this era, most legal policies for the young devised in the previous period remained in place, but revisions used the law to increase the presence of the state in children's lives and to create a more direct relationship between children and the state. The result was greater legal surveillance of children and yet also the emergence of the first legal rights for young Americans. These two seemingly contradictory developments suggest both the depth and significance of the legal developments of the era.

Liberal America

The law regarding children took another dramatic turn in the last half of the twentieth century. Basic legal rules and practices underwent enough changes to warrant comparisons with the transformations of the early nineteenth century. At the core of the era's changes were two new realities. First, the federal government, and particularly the federal courts, assumed a powerful role in setting legal policies for America's young people. Consequently, many of the endemic tensions in American law that had plagued state lawmakers in the nineteenth century began to bedevil federal lawmakers in the twentieth. Second, rights for children underwent a major redefinition. In an era dominated by rights struggles, children's legal rights became a movement. For the first time children's plight in America was explained as a consequence of the lack of adult rights: an assertion challenging the long-standing belief that the denial of adult rights to children required no justification. The impact of the twin developments was evident in almost every legal category as the laws governing children moved even further from their Hobbesian roots.

Particularly revealing were changes in the laws of child custody, a critical issue in an era when almost half the na-

tion's children would live in families torn asunder by divorce. Amid broad changes in gender roles and beliefs, the central tenet of custody rules—maternalism—came under attack both as an ideal and as a policy as support for the presumed superior ability of mothers to raise children eroded. Consequently, basic custody doctrines like the tender years rule, which presumed that infants and young children were best cared for by their mothers, were eliminated or had their significance reduced in nearly all states. Similarly, the Uniform Parentage Act recommended that the claims of mothers and fathers be balanced equally. Though most awards of physical custody still went to women, the new rules enabled more fathers to secure custody than ever before. They also led to new custodial arrangements such as joint custody, shared custody, and divided custody. Because of the magnitude of divorce, the custody changes significantly increased the likelihood that young Americans would encounter the law.

Similarly momentous changes occurred in the laws governing illegitimacy. A series of Supreme Court decisions in the 1960s and 1970s remade the law amid rising rates of illegitimate births, problems with unpaid child support by putative fathers, concerns about the psychological impact of illegitimacy on children, increasingly reliable paternity tests, and reevaluations of the social utility of illegitimacy as a means of policing sexual misconduct. The court made illegitimacy a constitutionally suspect classification and granted children new rights to be treated as individuals and not punished for the sins of their parents. They did so in cases in which the court ruled that there existed no rational basis for denying illegitimate children the right to recover for the wrongful death of their mothers and in which it directly repudiated the age-old policy of using illegitimacy to check immorality and sexual promiscuity by declaring that states must have more convincing arguments than the "promotion of legitimate family relations" to support such policies. Equally dramatic, courts began to give custodial rights to unwed fathers for the first time in addition to their traditional obligation of support. And the 1973 Uniform Parentage Act urged states to jettison the concept of illegitimacy entirely and equalize the inheritance, wrongful death, and workers' compensation rights of all children. However, neither illegitimate children nor unwed fathers won rights as extensive as their legitimate and married peers. The court narrowed but retained the law's long-standing moral commitment to matrimony by limiting the rights of illegitimate children and their parents. Critically, like the continued resistance to giving greater custody rights to step- or foster parents, the retention of discrimination based on birth meant that blood ties continued to be the most important legal bond for children.

Children also acquired new national protections in the era. During the 1950s child abuse was rediscovered as a result of the identification of battered child syndrome. Accordingly, every state revised its laws on child abuse to include more stringent penalties and reporting requirements. Congress also passed child abuse prevention measures for the first time and created a national reporting system. Child sexual abuse, a little-recognized problem in previous eras, became prominent as a threat to the nation's young. Panic over sexual abuse led virtually all states to rewrite their abuse and neglect statutes to specify particular penalties for this crime. These legislative actions and the accompanying national concern about child abuse led to the conviction that children had a legal right to a life free from abuse.

Developments like these demonstrate the growing importance of the rights of children in this legal era. Statutory changes, judicial decisions, and even a constitutional amendment significantly increased juvenile rights, particularly for adolescents. The federal courts, especially the Supreme Court, played a key role in recasting children's rights. Since the 1930s the courts had been increasingly receptive to claims of individual liberty and due process rights. They applied those concerns to children beginning in 1954 with BROWN V. BOARD OF EDUCATION. The unanimous decision not only declared segregated schools unconstitutional, but it presented the ruling in terms of children's rights: "In these days it is doubtful that any child may reasonably be expected to succeed in life if he is denied the opportunity of an education. Such an opportunity, where the state has undertaken to provide it, is a right which must be made available to all children." Children's rights expanded further in a series of cases that gave children constitutionally protected rights they could assert against the state and even against their parents. IN RE GAULT (1967) granted youths coming before juvenile courts procedural rights such as the right to counsel and thus restored some of the rights lost when the juvenile courts had been created. TINKER V. DES MOINES (1969) ruled that high school students had the constitutional right to freedom of speech. Decisions like these applied adult models of rights to children. And those rights were increased by corresponding statutory changes such as medical emancipation laws and lowered drinking ages. Finally, the TWENTY-SIXTH AMENDMENT lowered the voting age to eighteen and thus redefined the civic rights of adolescents. Tellingly, "age-blind" rights became the goal of children's rights advocates, who argued that children should have the same rights as adults. Indeed, some even called for the abolition of minority status, which was likened to slavery and coverture.

However, the legal changes of the era did not eliminate the use of age as a means of determining legal rights. Instead resistance arose to the notion of autonomous children's rights and thus renewed the debate over the legal status of the young. Even the Supreme Court consistently qualified its assertions of children's rights. In *Tinker* Justice Potter Stewart had insisted that the rights of children were not "co-extensive with those of adults." And in *Ginsburg v. New York* (1968) the court upheld limits on access to obscene materials to those over seventeen, with one justice declaring: "I think

that a State may permissibly determine that, at least in some precisely delineated areas, a child—like someone in a captive audience—is not possessed of that full capacity for individual choice which is the presupposition of First Amendment guarantees." Such caveats underscored the persistence of legal policies that assumed the dependent status of children and the paternal power of the state. And amid fears of mounting risks to the young—parental abuse, TEEN PREGNANCY, SUICIDE, DRUG addiction, gang membership—the children's rights movement itself faced growing opposition. Critics argued that more rights put children at risk instead of helping them. They challenged the premise that autonomous adult rights were the most effective means of raising and resolving children's problems. Indeed a growing number of opponents charged that increased rights had undermined child welfare by fostering adversarial family relations and undermining necessary parental and school authority.

These concerns led to another round of legal change in the last decades of the twentieth century. States began to revise some of their earlier endorsements of greater rights for children. For instance, Michigan, which in 1971 had lowered the minimum age for purchasing alcoholic beverages from twenty-one to eighteen, raised the age back up to twenty-one seven years later. Similarly, state legislators sought to impose greater restrictions on the right of young women to obtain abortions without parental consent. And in response to increases in violent juvenile crime, states rejected rehabilitation in favor of policies that made it easier for prosecutors to try adolescents who commit serious crimes as adults and to sentence them to adult prisons. Doing so erased not only rights but previous protections that resulted from age-defined dependency.

Fears about children viewing obscene materials led to the Communications Decency Act of 1996 and Children's Online Protection Act of 1998, which sought to protect children by asserting the rights of parents and other adults to control what they see, by prohibiting the use of the Internet for sending indecent material to children, and by imposing responsibilities on those who use the Internet to protect minors. Though declared unconstitutional because of vague and overreaching terms, attempts to limit juvenile computer access continue. As a result of such policies, children continued to have a separate age-based body of law even as they gained new adult-like legal rights.

Conclusion

In 1993, the Illinois Appellate Court offered its reading of the history of children and the law in the United States. The judges declared: "Fortunately, the time has long past when children in our society were considered the property of their parents. Slowly, but finally, when it comes to children even the law rid itself of the Dred Scott mentality that a human being can be considered a piece of property 'belonging' to another human being. To hold that a child is the property of his parents is to deny the humanity of the child." This judicial declaration certainly captured a part of that history, particularly the growth of distinctive laws and especially legal rights for the young. And it suggests how fundamental the legal changes have been since Hobbes placed the young beyond the law. However, the progressive vision of constant improvement in the legal condition of children masks the persistence of conflict and controversy and ignores the complicated relationship between children and the law. Greater legal autonomy for American children has not always meant better lives or even recognition of their humanity, though it has meant the law assumed a greater and greater presence in the lives of children. Consequently, at the dawn of the twenty-first century age continues to be a fundamental dividing line in the law. And that will surely be the case in the future as well.

See also: **Age of Consent; Beyond the Best Interests of the Child; Divorce and Custody; Youth Gangs.**

BIBLIOGRAPHY

Costin, Lela B., Howard Jacob Karger, and David Stoesz. 1996. *The Politics of Child Abuse in America.* New York: Oxford University Press.

Felt, Jeremy. 1965. *Hostages of Fortune: Child Labor Reform in New York State.* Syracuse, NY: Syracuse University Press.

Grossberg, Michael. 1985. *Governing the Hearth: Law and the Family in Nineteenth Century America.* Chapel Hill: University of North Carolina Press.

Hawes, Joseph M. 1991. *The Children's Rights Movement: A History of Advocacy and Protection.* Boston: Twayne.

Odem, Mary E. 1995. *Delinquent Daughters: Protecting and Policing Adolescent Female Sexuality in the United States, 1885–1920.* Chapel Hill: University of North Carolina Press.

Pleck, Elizabeth. 1987. *Domestic Tyranny: The Making of Social Policy Against Family Violence from Colonial Times to the Present.* New York: Oxford University Press.

Polsky, Andrew. 1991. *The Rise of the Therapeutic State.* Princeton, NJ: Princeton University Press.

Ryerson, Ellen. 1978. *The Best-Laid Plans: America's Juvenile Court Experiment.* New York: Hill and Wang.

Trattner, Walter I. 1970. *Crusade for Children: A History of the National Child Labor Committee and Child Labor Reform in America.* Chicago: University of Chicago Press.

Zelizer, Viviana A. 1985. *Pricing the Priceless Child: The Changing Social Value of Children.* New York: Basic Books.

MICHAEL GROSSBERG

Levitt, Helen (b. 1913)

Helen Levitt was born and raised in Brooklyn, New York. She briefly apprenticed with a portrait photographer, but rejected commercial work (and formal study) for a more intuitive approach to the medium. Inspired by French photographer Henri Cartier-Bresson, whom she met in 1935, Levitt acquired a Leica camera in 1936. She worked mainly in the densely populated streets of Harlem and the Lower East Side, especially in the summer, for this is where and when she found activity on sidewalks and front stoops at its most vibrant. The Leica's small size, her use of a right-angle viewfinder, and a sharp eye allowed her to capture her subjects quickly and inconspicuously.

Levitt spent almost her entire life in New York City, although a trip to Mexico in 1941 resulted in a significant body of work. She also worked on films, including *In the Street* (1945–1946; released in 1952), a short documentary done with James Agee and Janet Loeb. This film partly prompted Agee's important essay on her work, *A Way of Seeing*, first published in 1965. She was awarded a Guggenheim Fellowship in 1959 (renewed in 1960) and worked in color for much of the 1960s and 1970s. Levitt's approach is more lyrical than documentary. Though she established herself as an artist during the Depression, spent time in working-class neighborhoods, and admired the work of Walker Evans and Ben Shahn, her images are not didactic constructions exposing poverty or social injustice, though they do reveal sensitivity to issues of gender and race. Rather, they call our attention to the poetry of everyday human movements and interactions—with an eye to both laughter and sorrow.

Much of Levitt's work features children, caught playing in vacant lots, dancing in the streets, wearing masks, embracing, exploring, with or without the presence of adults. Although frequently seen at close range (leaving parts of bodies outside the frame), they almost never acknowledge the photographer. Levitt moved swiftly through their world, searching for signs of nobility and joy: a little boy comforts a friend, a girl struggles to lift her younger brother; others have fun with baby carriages, crepe paper, and boxes. *In the Street* is a nonscripted film featuring similar actors and activities. Yet Levitt's work occasionally hints at darker forces, though veiled in play: a boy peeks under a girl's skirt, children clutch toy guns and engage in mock battles. A similar juxtaposition of comedy and tragedy informs her photographs of chalk drawings and inscriptions, mostly done by children, which range from hilarious versions of pinup models to dark and threatening messages. In Mexico City, Levitt also photographed children. While some of the children in these Mexican pictures are absorbed in their games, others appear timid or distant, more burdened by responsibility or poverty than their U.S. counterparts.

Levitt's best-known images of children from the late 1930s and 1940s are contemporary with research on child psychology and children's art, also of interest to the surrealists. Yet the influences back and forth were generally indirect, results of a shared fascination with the complexity and contradictions of childhood and modern urban life. In her work, we see how easily games can veer into threats, how dreams collide with reality, and how adversity breeds creativity as much as tragedy. Though they are among the most complex and insightful images ever created of childhood, Levitt's photographs never attained popular fame (like those by Evans or Dorothea Lange), in part because they evade easy didactic or saccharine readings.

See also: **Images of Childhood; Photographs of Children.**

BIBLIOGRAPHY

Levitt, Helen, and James Agee. 1965. *A Way of Seeing.* New York: Viking Press.

Levitt, Helen, and Robert Coles. 1987. *In the Street: Chalk Drawings and Messages, New York City, 1938–1948.* Durham, NC: Duke University Press.

Levitt, Helen, and James Oles. 1997. *Mexico City.* New York: Center for Documentary Studies in association with W.W. Norton.

Phillips, Sandra S., and Maria Morris Hambourg. 1991. *Helen Levitt.* San Francisco: San Francisco Museum of Modern Art.

JAMES OLES

Life Course and Transitions to Adulthood

The idea of the life course is relatively new, a concept, like that of human evolution, that reflects the modern tendency to think of everything (species, nations, individuals) as developing through time in a certain irreversible sequence. Today, we think of stages of life in the same way we think of periods of history, as separate and distinct, each with its own peculiar qualities. We think of adulthood (a term that was not used until 1870) as being far removed from the ages that precede it. In the modern understanding of development through time, childhood and youth often seem like foreign counties, to which we can connect only through memory.

Nostalgia for childhood is a unique feature of modern culture. Prior to the nineteenth century, people yearned for certain places but not for certain pasts. They did not feel separated from either their own individual pasts or the pasts of the societies to which they belonged. Both life and history were imagined to be short, containing everything that had existed or would ever exist. Different stages of life were, like different eras of history, variations on a similar theme. Children and adults were simply bigger and smaller versions of one another. In the traditional representations of the ages of man, elderly people were often given childlike qualities. It was not that there was no recognition of differences between children and adults, but rather that there was no inclination to emphasize or institutionalize them in the ways that modern Western middle-class cultures have done. It is not that the biological and psychological processes of aging have changed, but rather that our understanding of what it means to age has altered.

Prior to the nineteenth century, age groups mixed together in ways that make modern age-conscious societies

In *The Abandoned Doll* (1921), by Suzanne Valadon (French, 1865–1938), a girl turns away from her mother to focus on her own image in a mirror. The doll that lies abandoned on the floor indicates her readiness to leave behind her childhood and become an adult. (Oil on canvas. 51 x 32 in. National Museum of Women in the Arts. Gift of Wallace and Wilhelmina Holladay. © 2003 Artists Rights Society (ARS), New York/ADAGP, Paris).

very uneasy. In the early twenty-first century, as the problematic character of age segregation has become more apparent, we have come to have a greater appreciation of these premodern sensibilities. We were first alerted to these by PHILIPPE ARIÈS's 1962 *Centuries of Childhood.* Today we are even more aware of the limitations of notions like the "life course" and "adulthood," understanding that they cannot be applied to every historical period, but belong specifically to a modern sensibility which may even now be in the process of changing. It is useful therefore to think of three distinct eras in the history of the Western transitions to adulthood: the premodern, modern, and late modern.

Premodern Transitions to Adulthood

In preindustrial Europe and North America much less attention was paid to distinctions between ages. Life was not perceived as a series of distinct, sharply defined stages organized in a certain uniform age-graded sequence. Schooling was far from universal, with pupils entering and exiting at a wide variety of ages. At the universities, young boys sat in classes alongside adult males. The sequences of a woman's life differed from that of a man's, and transitions also varied by economic status among both sexes. The age of majority, the legal transition to adulthood, varied not only by region but status group. In a world where who you were born to was far more important than when you were born, elite males assumed military and civilian office at very young ages. The AGE OF CONSENT differed from place to place and there were no age limits on entry into or exit from most occupations. The age of marriage varied widely and there was little sense of being "too young" or "too old" in a society where most people did not know their own age with any great precision. Precocity was honored, but so too was seniority. There were no mandatory retirement ages, but, on other hand, there were no special protections provided for either the young or the old. Everything depended on one's ability to perform rather than on age criteria.

The unimportance of age criteria was related to the demographic and economic conditions of a preindustrial society. Prior to the nineteenth century, high death rates were compensated for by high FERTILITY RATES. Average life expectancy in Western societies remained below fifty, though there was considerable variation by status. There was considerable mortality at every stage of life, but the greatest uncertainty was in childhood, where one-quarter of all children died before the age of one, and half were dead by age twenty-one. As a consequence, fertility rates remained high; and inability to control the number of living children left many parents in a situation where they could not support their surviving offspring much beyond early childhood. Rates of poverty comparable to today's developing countries contributed not only to high levels of child labor within families, but to the vast circulation of children among households, usually from the households of the poor to those of the propertied classes. In some European regions, as many as three-quarters of children had left home by their mid-teens. The notion that preindustrial society consisted of multigenerational families rooted in a particular place by a small farm or business is a nostalgic fantasy with no basis in reality.

The preindustrial, prewage economy was household rather than family based. The possession of an economically viable household was a virtual prerequisite for marriage. Couples waited for a household to become available, one of the reasons the age of marriage was relatively late and rates of marriage relatively low by modern standards. Slaves and those too poor to acquire a household were often prevented from marrying, though many cohabited clandestinely. But only those with the status of a master or mistress of a household were accorded the full status of maturity. The other members of the household, even those who were of the same or older ages, remained "boys" or "girls," terms that defined their subordinate place in the household hierarchy rather than indicated their actual age. Indeed, in a society that saw

itself as a static great chain of being organized in spatial terms of high and low rather than in temporal terms of early and late, an aged retainer addressing the teenage head of the household as "sir" or "madam" made perfect sense.

The uncertainty of life, together with extremes of economic and social inequality, account for the lack of universal age categories in the premodern West. Space rather than time organized generational relations inside and outside households. Furthermore, there were no powerful organizations interested in, much less capable of, organizing society by age criteria. European states still depended on mercenary armies, so there was no need to set ages of military service. Political power was a privilege of the propertied, so age was irrelevant to it as well. It would not be until the introduction of universal male citizenship during the American and French Revolutions that voting age became the issue it has remained ever since. As long as LITERACY remained a luxury, largely irrelevant to the functioning of the economy, states had no interest in organizing schooling. Sumptuary laws— that is, laws governing what certain classes and groups of people could and could not wear—existed, but they were aimed at maintaining the existing social hierarchy rather than maintaining the order of age groups. Children and adults drank, ate, smoked, worked, and played alongside one another without heed to the age and gender distinctions that modern society later learned to regard as natural and therefore sacrosanct. In such a world, transitions from one age to the next were rarely marked and the terms for childhood, youth, adulthood, and old age were vague and general. Before the nineteenth century only the elites marked birthdays, and then only toward the end of life. Both boys and girls passed into youth without specific rites of passage.

Religious ceremonies like CONFIRMATION and BAR MITZVAH were of much less significance then, and were not tied so closely to specific ages. In the absence of schools, there were no graduation ceremonies; in the absence of the draft, no age-related military RITES OF PASSAGE existed. The one great rite of passage was marriage, publically celebrated by the community on the occasion of the creation of a new household. It clearly marked a momentous transition for both the man and woman involved, but it was less age than status related. It was less a transition to a stage of life called *adulthood* (the word itself did not yet exist) than an elevation to a higher place in the social hierarchy, a spatial rather than a temporal realignment. The new bride and groom were perceived not as older, but higher, the thing that mattered most in a world still organized by space rather than time.

Modern Transitions to Adulthood, 1870–1970

The concurrent industrial and democratic revolutions of the late eighteenth and early nineteenth century not only changed the course of history but placed change at the center of modern consciousness. Older notions of a static great chain of being gave way to a dynamic view of the world in which individuals, nations, and species were seen as developing through linear time, following certain universal irreversible sequences. In a process which Martin Kohli has called *chronologization*, a normative life course, with certain set stages and turning points, came into being, first among the middle classes and ultimately for society at large. By the middle of the twentieth century, not only the clocks and calendars, but the lives of Europeans and North Americans had become synchronized to a remarkable degree.

The lowering of the death and birth rates made chronologization possible. With the lowering of mortality, life became more predictable and for the first time in human history longevity became a reasonable expectation for everyone. Now aging became a personal responsibility, yet another of life's many challenges. With an extended horizon of expectation, men began to plan their lives around a series of distinct stages leading from childhood to school, adult careers, and eventual retirement. Women's lives were planned around marriage and child rearing. Once child mortality rates fell, fertility also declined. This, combined with the conquest of poverty, allowed families to dispense with child labor.

In the course of the Industrial Revolution, the household ceased to be a productive unit. Men's work in urban areas moved outside the household, which now took on the characteristics of the modern "home," a separate sphere associated with women and children. Adequate wages and salaries brought home by male breadwinners meant that children no longer circulated from the households of the poor to those of the rich. Children stayed at home for longer periods and went to school, which became compulsory in the second half of the nineteenth century. In the first half of the twentieth century, their dependency on home and family was extended still further, creating the stage of life we now know as ADOLESCENCE. Middle-class males were the first to experience adolescence, but by the twentieth century a female variation had come into being. After World War II, when university education became more general, yet another new stage of life—young adulthood—became normative in the Western world.

Chronologization meant not only fixed ages for school entry, but age-graded curricula, classrooms, and promotion procedures. Children not only learned their time tables, but began to "act their age" as defined by new theories of child development, which established norms for each stage of life from infancy onwards. Birthdays became for the first time an important family occasion. In the course of the twentieth century, both childhood and adolescence were increasingly subjected to scientific and medical inquiry. In the age of new mass education, both precocity and retardation were stigmatized; and in the era of the nation-state, male adolescence moved in lock step through school into the cohort of draft-eligible youth. While it was not until World War I that

states commandeered women's time, the female life course also underwent its own form of chronologization. By the twentieth century, marriage was becoming not only more universal, but virtually compulsory. Women of all classes and ethnic groups began to feel the pressure to marry and have children at a certain age. To marry too early or too late was to forfeit their claim on true womanhood.

In the modern era, the stages of life became increasingly marked by official and unofficial rituals. Schools provided an increasingly complex set of entry and graduation ceremonies. Religions provided confirmation and bar and bat mitzvah ceremonies to mark the transition from childhood to the newly invented status of adolescence. For boys going away to school furthered the process of both maturation and masculinization, but becoming a man often involved even more rigorous tests involving sports and military service. Upper-middle-class girls remained longer in the feminized orbit of home, making their transition to young womanhood through a series of rites culminating in the coming-out ball, placing them in the category of marriageable females. But the ultimate test of true womanhood was marriage leading to motherhood. Those who failed it, childless wives as well as spinsters, were condemned to feel inadequate and immature. The single male could still prove his masculinity in the world outside the family, but for women biology was regarded as destiny.

In industrial society, access to maturity had been democratized. No longer associated exclusively with heads of households, maturity was now seen as a time of life rather than a place in a social hierarchy. Yet it had its own norms and locales, notably the suburban single family home, the symbol of male earning power and female domesticity. By the 1950s marriage and home ownership had come to be *the* major transition to adulthood. For females, it was the wedding itself which formed the horizon of expectation; for males, it was the first mortgage which confirmed maturity. In any case, never before had marriage meant so much to so many as it did in the 1950s and 1960s, when marriage rates reached a historic high throughout the Western world. Equally telling is the fact that cohabitation was at an all time low, an indication of just how important being married was to the adult sense of self at the time.

By this time, Western societies had become extraordinarily age segregated. Class, gender, and ethnic life-course differences remained, but what is striking is the degree to which the life course had been divided into a series of discrete age groups, set apart not just temporally but spatially from one another. Children were now confined to their own worlds, complete with their own special foods, clothing, and forms of play. They were kept apart from adolescents, who now had a distinctive YOUTH CULTURE, complete with its own dress and music. Marriage automatically separated men and women into yet another set of separate worlds, identified with the suburbs, while for the growing body of elderly people there were now separate retirement communities. These novel forms of age apartheid were reinforced by a variety of laws regulating age-appropriate behavior and by the current psychological and medical theories of the life course, which defined anything but the prescribed sequence of life stages as abnormal. Those who did not conform to the strictly gendered and sexed rules of child development were stigmatized as deviant and consigned to the newly invented categories of the "retarded," "juvenile delinquent," or "homosexual."

The division of life into a series of radically different stages generated among adults a sense of being cut off from their own pasts. The yearning for "lost" childhood appeared first among middle-class men and gradually spread across class and gender to become a part of modern popular culture. Having failed to locate paradise in remote parts of the world, Western culture relocated it to the time of childhood. In a secular age which had ceased to believe in eternity, childhood became proof of immortality, the one thing that remained the same when everything else was constantly changing. Childhood became the most photographed and memorialized of all life's stages. "We fend off death's terrors, snapshot by snapshot," observes Anne Higonnet, "pretending to save the moment, halt time, preserve childhood intact" (p. 95). Even though families had fewer children, they became ever more child-centered. Family time came to be organized around children's meals, birthdays, and school holidays. The calendar was restructured in a similar way, with Christmas, Easter, and Hanukkah becoming child-centered holidays. While ostensibly organized for children, these occasions reflected adult desires to preserve their own remembered childhoods. By the mid-twentieth century, this effort to connect with and preserve an imagined past had become a driving force of Western CONSUMER CULTURES. Ironically, the cult of childhood only reinforced the distance between adults and children, thus intensifying the nostalgia for "lost" childhood.

Late Modern Lives, 1970s and Beyond

From the late 1960s onward, the rules and institutions of chronologization began to be questioned. Young people chafed against age restrictions on consumption and voting; older folks balked at mandatory retirement, or sought to retire early. This was partly the result of changing demographics: the average life span had been extended by as much as twenty-five years since the beginning of the century, radically raising the proportion of elderly people while reducing the proportion of children and juveniles. The three stages of life—childhood, adulthood, and old age—that once seemed natural and immutable were now challenged. Earlier maturation of children was reflected in the emergence of the "preteen," and adolescence was extended by education and late marriage into the twenties and even early thirties. At the other end of the life course the term "young-old" has appeared, and we distinguish between those still capable of living an active life (what Laslett calls the Third Age) from those who are not (the Fourth Age). The concept of adulthood itself has come under pressure with evidence of the increasing occurrence of the so-called midlife crisis.

Changes in the economy were also at work in the post-1970 reassessment of the life course. Western capitalism had begun to restructure itself by moving its industrial processes to Third World countries, reserving for itself the key managerial and service-sector occupations. Deindustrialization of Europe and North America meant that many well-paid traditionally male jobs disappeared. In order to maintain family standards of living, married women moved into full-time work in massive numbers. But most of the new jobs were not lifelong careers. To remain employable, adults now had to retrain, which meant going back to school. Education, once something associated with the young, became a lifelong affair, with huge implications for the structure of the life course and age relations. But the new economy, organized around consumption as well as production, has also affected children and adolescents. They have been drawn into consumption at ever earlier ages, encouraged to emulate older age groups in everything from food and drink to fashion and leisure activity, including SEXUALITY. Precocity is once again encouraged, producing what one psychologist has described as the *kinderdult*, half child/half adult, who no longer belongs to any conventional age category. To pay for these new tastes, juveniles have also been drawn into employment in numbers that have not been seen since the nineteenth century. In an era when the gap between the rich and poor has increased dramatically, more children are also working out of necessity. Indeed, in many impoverished Third World countries the vast majority of children have no experience of a childhood free from labor.

Childhood has lost its association with innocence as experiences once associated with older age groups become more accessible through the electronic media to very young children. The boundaries of adolescence have also been blurred, moving both earlier into the so-called preteen years and later into the extended period of semi-dependency that characterizes young women and men whose educations now extend into their late twenties through professional training and graduate school. Over the past twenty years the average age of marriage has been delayed by several years for both men and women. Women are staying in school longer and establishing themselves in careers before deciding to marry. Men who once had the earning power to marry early are also delaying the decision. Rates of cohabitation have shot up over the past thirty years, and marriage and parenthood have been decoupled as the rate of single parenthood grows and married couples postpone parenthood to ever later ages. Marriage, which was once the universal gateway to adulthood, can no longer serve that purpose. The markers of maturity have become more various, as single mothers contend with married women for adult status in an era that is much more tolerant of unwed parenthood. In a similar way, gays and lesbians claim adulthood with marriage and partnership rituals once reserved only for heterosexuals. The very notion of adulthood has been called into question, transformed from a state of being into a series of passages, and thus, like other late modern stages of life, a state of perpetual becoming. Even old age has lost its static character, becoming plastic and performative. Older people are urged to think and act young. Rules of good aging, such as retirement at a designated age, that only a short time ago seemed so natural and self-evident are being challenged at every age level.

The institutions which once policed the boundaries of age no longer show much interest in doing so. Schools are not as rigorous about ages of entry and exit as they once were. The curriculum is less age-graded and students are more likely to be allowed to learn at their own pace. Young offenders are now more likely to go to adult jails as the ages of criminal responsibility become less rigid. Religions still offer a range of rites of passage, but they do not insist that their members go through them. Even marriage rites are not so strictly enforced as they once were and some churches even offer ceremonies adapted to homosexual partners. The state has also ceased to regulate age in the ways that it once did. It still polices sumptuary practices with respect to reading, movie-going, drinking, and smoking, but has deregulated retirement and rules of seniority to a considerable extent. Furthermore, nation-states have come to rely on professional armies, making draft age much less important than it once was. And since the military services are no longer sex segregated, joining the army or navy is no longer the mark of manhood it once was.

In this era of GLOBALIZATION, with its massive migrations of people, the cultural standards of aging have become much more diverse. A whole new raft of rites of passage have been introduced by new immigrants to both Europe and North America. Our calendars are now full of new holidays which underline the heterogeneity of our current understandings of what it means to be a child or an adult. In short, the notion of a single universal life course is no longer viable. The notion that aging is culturally and socially variable, that it is a system of meaning rather than a set of natural facts, is now increasingly accepted in the social and psychological sciences as well as in popular culture. People may hold firmly to notions of childhood or adulthood that seem right for them, but they have also come to accept that other versions of the life course may be right for other people. But while aging has fallen into that realm of personal preference, it is still seen as the personal responsibility of each person to age well. The late modern period has also seen something of a convergence of the male and female life courses. With so many women entering into higher education and full-time employment, their lives have become more closely synchronized with those of men.

Women typically delay marriage and motherhood, waiting until they feel settled in careers before bearing children. The arrival of the first child need not disrupt women's careers if there is sufficient maternal (or paternal) leave and if good child care is available, as is the case in many European countries, especially Scandinavia. But older differences linger where these child-care supports are missing, as in the United States, where the working woman is faced with many difficulties. While men have become somewhat more involved with household and parenting in the late modern period, it is still rare that they become full-time housekeepers or parents. Even in Scandinavia, fathers have been reluctant to take the full parental leave they are entitled to because they fear losing their place on the career track. Thus men's and women's lives tend to go out of synch when children arrive. The problem is worst in the United States, but gender differences are still evident everywhere, reflected in the startling growth of single parent families across the Western world.

The Future of the Life Course

Since the 1970s, notions of universal human development have been challenged. It is no longer possible to think of all societies as developing through time in the same linear sequence, some ahead, others behind. Modernization theories, which assume a backward "underdeveloped" world which must model itself on supposedly more advanced "developed" Western countries in order to achieve modernity, are now discounted in favor of notions of multiple paths and multiple modernities, although globalization also produces uniformities. In this global age, we have the opportunity to understand societies on their own terms, recognizing spatial differences and thus avoiding the fallacy of organizing everything into dichotomies of traditional versus modern, backward versus advanced, early versus late, infantile versus mature.

In a similar way, it is now possible to see that individual lives do not develop in a uniform linear manner. We accept a greater range of variation in terms of physical, mental, and psychological growth, but equally important we no longer segregate age groups as rigidly as we once did. While it is true that many of the old age-segregated institutions still exist, we can expect them to be challenged in the future. Schools without walls and college internship programs are evidence of how temporal as well as spatial boundaries are eroding. The notion of the old-age home and the segregated retirement community are also being questioned. The suburb, once a ghetto for families with children, is becoming more diverse as well. There are many walls to break down before our society becomes as age-heterogeneous as premodern society, but the process of rethinking age segregation has begun in both the United States and Europe.

In the era of the service economy, seniors rub shoulders with teenagers at work as well as in leisure activities. Adults going back to school find themselves sharing classrooms with younger people. Sports have become a good deal less age segregated as well. Older people are not only allowed but encouraged to remain physically active. As the distinctions between different ages become increasingly blurred, we can expect many of the old rites of passage to change and even disappear. This may already be happening at the boundary between childhood and adolescence, but it is surely the case at the borderland between youth and adulthood. Yet, it would be unwise to announce the demise of such things as the wedding ceremony, for, while this may not take the same uniform character as it did a few decades ago, people are finding a whole raft of new rites to express the meanings of their lives. In addition to the traditional wedding ceremony there are now a variety of rites suitable to cohabiting men and women as well as to gay and lesbian partners. As adulthood is now more a state of becoming, punctuated with frequent changes, a whole series of rituals dealing with mid-life crises (including divorce) have appeared on the scene. This should not surprise us, for it is in those moments of life that are the most ambiguous and uncertain that people have always turned to ritual to reassure them of the meaning of what they are doing. As the life course becomes ever more fluid, it is safe to predict a proliferation of rituals meant to deal with this condition.

We have come to see that what we call the life course is a product of culture rather than nature. Life is not so much a script we follow as one we as individuals and as societies write as we go along. The premodern script was a religious one; the modern script was dictated by the social and medical sciences, but today we are encouraged to craft our own life narratives. This freedom brings with it great responsibilities, however. We need to acknowledge that people not only think *about* age, but think *with* age, giving meaning to lives that would otherwise seem hopelessly confused. We need to listen carefully to the ways other cultures, including those of our own past, talk about aging, for this constitutes an invaluable source of wisdom from which we can draw in facing our own existential dilemmas.

See also: **Age and Development.**

BIBLIOGRAPHY

Ariès, Philippe. 1962. *Centuries of Childhood.* New York: Knopf.

Brandes, Stanley. 1985. *Forty: The Age and the Symbol.* Knoxville: University of Tennessee Press.

Brumberg, Joan. 1997. *The Body Project: An Intimate History of American Girls,* New York: Random House.

Chudacoff, Howard. 1989. *How Old Are You? Age Consciousness in American Culture.* Princeton, NJ: Princeton University Press.

Cole, Thomas. 1992. *The Journey of Life: A Cultural History of Aging in America.* Cambridge, UK: Cambridge University Press.

Cook, Daniel. 2000. "The Rise of 'the Toddler' as Subject and as Merchandising Category." In *New Forms of Consumption: Consumers, Culture, and Commodification,* ed. Mark Gottdiener. Lanham, MD: Rowman and Littlefield.

Ehrensaft, Diane. 2001. "The Kinderdult: The New Child Born to Conflict between Work and Family." In *Working Families: The Transformation of the American Home,* ed. Rosanna Hertz and Nancy Marshall. Berkeley: University of California Press.

Gillis, John. 1974. *Youth and History: Tradition and Change in European Age Relations, 1770–Present.* New York: Academic Press.

Gillis, John. 1985. *For Better, for Worse: British Marriage, 1600 to the Present.* New York: Oxford University Press.

Gillis, John. 1996. *A World of Their Own Making: Myth, Ritual, and the Quest for Family Values.* New York: Basic Books.

Graff, Harvey. 1995. *Conflicting Paths: Growing Up in America.* Cambridge, MA: Harvard University Press.

Higonnet, Anne. 1998. *Pictures of Innocence: The History and Crisis of Ideal Childhood.* New York: Thames and Hudson.

Keniston, Kenneth. 1972. "Youth: A 'New Style of Life.'" *American Scholar* 39, no. 4: 631–654.

Kohli, Martin. 1985. "Die Institutionalisierung des Lebenslaufes." *Vierteljarhesschrift fuer Soziologie und Sozialpsychologie* 1: 1–29.

Laslett, Peter. 1991. *A Fresh Map of Life: The Emergence of the Third Age.* Cambridge, MA: Harvard University Press.

Lowe, Donald. 1982. *History of Bourgeois Perception.* Chicago: University of Chicago Press.

Modell, John. 1989. *Into One's Own: From Youth to Adulthood in the United States.* Berkeley: University of California Press.

Myerhoff, Barbara. 1978. *Numbering Our Days.* New York: Simon and Schuster.

Myrowitz, Joshua. 1985. *No Sense of Place: The Impact of Media on Social Behavior.* New York: Oxford University Press.

Orme, Nicholas. 2001. *Medieval Children.* New Haven, CT: Yale University Press.

Pleck, Elizabeth. 2000. *Celebrating the Family: Ethnicity, Consumer Culture, and Family Rituals.* Cambridge, MA: Harvard University Press.

Robson, Catherine. 2001. *Men in Wonderland: The Lost Girlhood of the Victorian Gentleman.* Princeton, NJ: Princeton University Press.

Rothman, Ellen. 1987. *Hearts and Hands: A History of Courtship in America.* Cambridge, MA: Harvard University Press.

Scheper-Hughes, Nancy, and Carolyn Sargent, eds. 1998. *Small Wars: The Cultural Politics of Childhood.* Berkeley: University of California Press.

Sheehy, Gail. 1995. *New Passages: Your Life Across Time.* New York: Random House.

JOHN R. GILLIS

Lindbergh Kidnapping

The kidnapping of Charles Augustus Lindbergh Jr. on the evening of March 1, 1932, shocked the world and became one of the best known and most notorious crimes in modern history. The child's father, Charles A. Lindbergh, was probably the most famous man in the world at the time—a hero for completing the first solo flight across the Atlantic Ocean on May 22, 1927. Lionized wherever he went and married to the charming, talented and wealthy Anne Morrow in 1929, their tragedy became a measure of the precarious social and economic times in which they lived, and emblematic of the powerful role that childhood played in the modern American imagination.

The baby, who was pictured in papers around the world after he disappeared, was twenty months old at the time of his ABDUCTION. During the six weeks which followed, the state police, the Federal Bureau of Investigation (FBI), private detectives, and hundreds of thousands of people around the world tried to find the child, for whom a ransom demand of $50,000 was paid on April 2, 1932. But the child was never recovered alive. On May 13, his partial remains were discovered not far from the house in New Jersey from which he had been taken. The hunt for the child then gave way to a massive hunt for his abductor.

The story of the arrest, trial and execution of Bruno Richard Hauptmann for the kidnapping and murder of the Lindbergh child has become one of the most well-known crimes in American history, not least because of the controversy that still surrounds the final disposition of the case in 1936. The event has often been featured on radio and television programs, and the outcome of the case against Hauptmann continues to generate revisionist interpretations. But the kidnapping and its resolution were important only because the crime itself was so horrifying and considered a direct attack on the substance of American institutions and culture. The audacious disappearance of the "nation's child" as the baby was called at the time, became a terrible blow to the country's sense of security in precarious depression times, and a reminder of the threats to law and order in the early 1930s. It was used in the press to remind parents about the importance of their children and to confirm their commitment to family safety and well-being. The crime had major consequences in law and became the basis for the passage of the first federal kidnapping statute ("the Lindbergh Law") which made kidnapping a capital offense. It was also instrumental in the reorganization and reinvigoration of the FBI. For much of the rest of the twentieth century, the kidnapping of the Lindbergh baby would help to define the horrors of child loss for modern parents as it became a touchstone of a media increasingly sensitive to parents' anxieties about their children.

BIBLIOGRAPHY

Berg, A. Scott. 1998. *Lindbergh*. New York: Putnam.

Fass, Paula S. 1997. *Kidnapped: Child Abduction in America*. New York: Oxford University Press.

Milton, Joyce. 1993. *Loss of Eden: A Biography of Charles and Anne Morrow Lindbergh*. New York: Harper Collins.

PAULA S. FASS

Literacy

Precise knowledge about levels of literacy in different times and different places is notoriously difficult to ascertain, for two major reasons. First, it is not always clear what should count as "literacy": what level of ability at reading or writing should we designate as literate? The concept of functional literacy has been developed to deal with this semantic problem: the term *functional literacy* was originally coined by the U.S. Army during World War II, and denoted an ability to understand military operations and to be able to read at a fifth-grade level. Subsequently, the United Nations Educational, Scientific and Cultural Organization (UNESCO) has defined functional literacy in terms of an individual possessing the requisite reading and writing skills to be able to take part in the activities that are a normal part of that individual's social milieu.

However these definitional problems may be resolved, it is clearly problematic to specify the degree of literacy of a particular period, place, or population. The second problem is that our evidence for the historical distribution of levels of literacy is limited, based in the main on marriage registers and other legal documents. In using this evidence to generate best guesses about literacy levels, we pay special attention to the ability of bride, groom, and witnesses to sign marriage registers, and other individuals to sign other legal documents. Such evidence may lead to an overestimation of literacy levels; individuals may be able to sign but have little else in the way of literacy skills. Conversely, the same evidence may lead to an underestimation of literacy skills; writing requires a productive proficiency that reading does not, and therefore those who cannot sign may be able to read, and yet would be in danger of being classified as illiterate. With these warnings in place, what can we say about the historical character of literacy in the West?

Before the PROTESTANT REFORMATION, education was very closely controlled by the Catholic Church, and was limited to elite groups—men in holy orders. Further, literacy in Latin rather than in vernacular languages was the goal of these elites. However, by the middle of the sixteenth century, while many schools and teachers still maintained links to organized religion, a number of new schools arose due to the efforts of private individuals, parishes, guilds, and the like. This secularization of education meant that literacy was less and less the preserve of elite social groups; the deliberate spread of (first Latin, and then vernacular) literacy throughout the social body played an important role in the maintenance of religious orthodoxy, both Catholic and Protestant, but it also came to be seen as a political tool for state building, for the maintenance of morality, and for equipping the population with valuable skills. DESIDERIUS ERASMUS (c. 1469–1536) and Martin Luther (1483–1546) were especially important in drawing attention to such political and governmental possibilities. James Bowen, in *A History of Western Education*, estimates early sixteenth-century literacy rates in England to have been less than 1 percent; yet by the reign of Elizabeth I (1558–1603) he suggests it was getting close to 50 percent. The Reformation, then, was a major spur to education and to literacy, but we must be aware that while the starting point for this education was religious knowledge

Seven Ages of Childhood (1909), illustration by Jessie Willcox Smith. By the early twentieth century, literacy rates in many Western countries were near 100 percent. Reading, especially parents reading to their children, became seen as an integral part of family life. © Blue Lantern Studio/CORBIS.

and morality, it also aimed at other sorts of useful knowledge.

However, the situation was not the same across all of Europe, and Protestant countries generally had better literacy rates than Catholic ones. In France, for example, a government-inspired study of historical rates of literacy published in 1880 showed that for the 1686–1690 period, 75 percent of the population could not sign their names. As Carlo M. Cipolla shows in *Literacy and Development in the West*, literacy rates for Catholic Europe as a whole were roughly in line with these statistics from France. Protestant Europe fared much better, with literacy rates of maybe 35 to 45 percent. In addition, Cipolla makes it clear that within these statistics we can see great variation by class and geography: the urban bourgeoisie had literacy rates of at least 90 percent, as compared to a rate of 10 percent for rural peasants. Furthermore, literacy rates differed between the sexes: a 1880 government study in France shows that between 1686 and 1690 the female literacy rate (based on ability to sign) was just 14 percent, while the male rate was 36 percent.

In England, the growth in the number of schools and in the literacy rate—during and after the Reformation—went hand in hand with the growth of the book trade. Richard Altick has shown that in the Elizabethan period, despite deliberate attempts to limit quantities, school texts (grammars, primers, and so forth) were allowed a print run of up to twelve thousand copies per year. Popular enthusiasm for reading and writing coexisted with official suspicion that such skills, if they became too widespread, would lead to social discontent and disorder. Toward the end of the eighteenth century, the charity school movement in England and Scotland (especially associated with the Society for Promoting Christian Knowledge) concentrated on trying to increase literacy levels among the poor. The aim of these schools was to ensure that literacy skills were sufficient for Bible study, but they also aimed to inculcate in the poor acceptance of their low status in life. These schools were also important actors in the process of nation building, explicitly teaching only in English and striving to eliminate the Gaelic language from Scotland.

From the Reformation until the nineteenth century, popular education and literacy education were virtually synonymous. While the elite had the opportunity to gain other skills and knowledge, schooling for the masses mostly concerned itself with learning to read. Moreover, reading meant reading the Bible. What was at stake was the desire for the general population to become what Ian Hunter has termed socially trained and spiritually guided. Learning to read was a step on the way to the production of a new type of person who was morally developed but also economically productive, and it was primarily through the reading of religious and moral texts that this was achieved.

Over the course of the nineteenth century, the state slowly assumed more and more control of the schools, in a period which culminated in the introduction of compulsory education in most of the Western nations (for example, in the United States between 1852 [Massachusetts] and 1918 [Mississippi], in Prussia in 1868, in England in 1870, and in France in 1882). In England, the 1861 Newcastle Report had stopped short of recommending compulsory education, but noted that about 2.5 million children were receiving some schooling, and that literacy rates were 67 percent for men and 51 percent for women. The Newcastle Report was typical of the era: even as the arguments over the rights and wrongs of compulsory education in the context of a liberal state were taking place, state intervention into these matters was increasing, at the very least in terms of collecting statistics and adjudicating on issues and problems.

In the United States in the nineteenth century, the COMMON SCHOOLS pioneered the notion of a free, compulsory, and secular education. Fundamental to this endeavor was the attempt to guarantee an educated populace who could partake in political, social, and economic life. Schooling and civics, then, grew together. Education in literacy was still the core concern in the common schools and in the public schools which succeeded them, but by now schooling was concerning itself with other subjects, including history, geography, arithmetic, and bookkeeping. HORACE MANN (1796–1859) was a crucial figure in the shift toward this compulsory public schooling system in the United States. Mann traveled widely, especially through Europe, and tried to implement the best features of overseas systems in the nascent Massachusetts system. Mann served as secretary of the first ever state board of education, established in Massachusetts in 1837, and lived to see that state implement the first compulsory education system in the United States. While it took some time for compulsory education to be fully implemented for both boys and girls and for all sectors of society, the early years of the twentieth century saw literacy rates in many Western countries approach 100 percent.

See also: **Compulsory School Attendance; Education, Europe; Education, United States.**

BIBLIOGRAPHY

Altick, Richard. 1957. *The English Common Reader.* Chicago: Chicago University Press.

Bowen, James. 1981. *A History of Western Education.* 3 vols. London: Methuen.

Cipolla, Carlo M. 1969. *Literacy and Development in the West.* Harmondsworth, UK: Penguin Books.

Hunter, Ian. 1994. *Rethinking the School: Subjectivity, Bureaucracy, Criticism.* London: Allen and Unwin.

Vincent, David. 1989. *Literacy and Popular Culture: England 1750–1914.* Cambridge, UK: Cambridge University Press.

GAVIN KENDALL

Literature. *See* Children's Literature.

Little League. *See* Baseball.

Little Women and Louisa May Alcott

Born November 29, 1832, in Germantown, Pennsylvania, Louisa May Alcott is best known as the author of *Little Women* (1868), a children's novel about the four March sisters, based on the experiences of her own family. Her father, BRONSON ALCOTT, was a well-known transcendentalist who failed in his career as a schoolteacher and afterward made little money to support his family. Her mother, Abigail May Alcott, took in sewing, did domestic work, and became a charity agent to help make ends meet. "Louy" and her three sisters, on whom the March girls were closely modeled, grew up in poverty but with a rich domestic life. Alcott always felt a strong sense of duty toward her family. She never married, instead devoting herself to supporting her relations through her successful writing career.

Before she began writing, Alcott was the subject of a book of observations by her father. In 1831 Bronson Alcott began a journal in which he recorded the development of his first daughter, Anna. Louisa entered its pages the following fall. Bronson continued his observations for five years, filling 2,500 manuscript pages with details of his daughters' development. His portrait of Louisa is strikingly similar to her creation, Jo March. Young Louisa was headstrong, physical, and aggressive—a difficult child.

Alcott wrote many novels and short stories for children, including *Flower Fables* (1855), *Good Wives* (1869), *Little Men* (1871), *Eight Cousins* (1875), *Rose in Bloom* (1876), *Jack and Jill* (1880), and *Jo's Boys* (1886). She also wrote adult fiction, including *Moods* (1865) and gothic thrillers under various pseudonyms. Her children's fiction differed in tone from much of the literature that appeared before it; her characters were more realistic, and her message was less moralistic and overtly didactic. Although Alcott's works have been criticized for presenting a sentimentalized depiction of Victorian domesticity, her stories also include characters who challenge societal norms. The tomboy Nan Harding from *Little Men*, who like Jo March and Louisa herself rejects Victorian standards of girlhood, becomes a doctor and never marries. Alcott also challenged the practice of corporal punishment, creating an indelible scene in *Little Men* where the kindly schoolteacher, Mr. Bhaer, punishes a misbehaving student by compelling the youth to beat Mr. Bhaer himself. Alcott's novels support coeducation, and her fictional Plumfield School even opens its doors to a black student.

Alcott's conceptions of childhood were shaped by her father and the other transcendentalist writers with whom she was intimate. As a child, Alcott took nature walks with Henry David Thoreau. She borrowed books from Ralph Waldo Emerson and composed her first short stories for his children. Like her mentors, Alcott adopted the romantic belief that children were intuitively wise and good. She believed the purpose of education was to develop children's consciences and to help them to become self-reliant.

Alcott was a hearty youth who was raised on a strict vegetarian diet and subjected to cold-water baths in the early morning. A short stint nursing Union soldiers during the Civil War, however, ruined her health. Calomel treatments for a case of typhoid fever left her with mercury poisoning that caused muscle aches and hair loss. She died at the age of fifty-five on March 6, 1888, three days after the death of her father.

See also: **Children's Literature.**

BIBLIOGRAPHY

MacDonald, Ruth K. 1983. *Louisa May Alcott.* Boston: Twayne.

Payne, Alma J. 1980. *Louisa May Alcott: A Reference Guide.* Boston: G. K. Hall.

Stern, Madeleine B. 1950. *Louisa May Alcott.* Norman: University of Oklahoma Press.

RACHEL HOPE CLEVES

Locke, John (1632–1704)

English thinker John Locke insisted both that children are potentially free and rational beings, and that the realization of these crucial human qualities tends to be thwarted through imposition of the sort of prejudice that perpetuates oppression and superstition. It was, Locke believed, upbringing and education that stymied development of children's humanity when the older generation, itself enmeshed in prejudice, preferred to maintain the status quo rather than to examine whether their lives qualified as truly human through the rational and free action characteristic of autonomous individuals. Locke argued that when an older generation imposes unquestioned beliefs and ways of action on its youth, the outcome is bondage rather than actualization of freedom.

The problem of the actualization and preservation of human freedom and rationality occupied Locke in all of his major works, from the *Essay Concerning Human Understanding* (1690) and the *Two Treatises of Government* (1690), through his four letters *Concerning Toleration* (1689, 1690, 1692, 1704), *The Reasonableness of Christianity* (1695), *Some Thoughts Concerning Education* (1693), and the posthumous *Of the Conduct of the Understanding* (1706). Both the promise of and danger to childhood emerged in each of these influential writings on philosophy, politics, religion, and education.

The Tabula Rasa

Locke characterized a newborn child's mind as a blank sheet of paper, a clean slate, a tabula rasa. Implicit is a doctrine of egalitarianism, well-known from the fourth paragraph of the *Second Treatise of Government*: There is "nothing more evident, than that Creatures of the same species. . .born to all the same advantages of Nature, and the use of the same faculties, should also be equal amongst one another without Subordination or Subjection. . . . " This egalitarianism is one of the aspects of the modern view of human nature, so different from the Platonic or medieval outlooks with their inborn inequalities foundational to nature- or God-ordained hierarchies in society, church, and state. For Locke, there are no natural obstructions that would block development of children's native potential for acting freely and rationally. True, some possess more agile intellects or stronger wills than others; but all are innately equipped to become persons capable of freely following their own reason's pronouncements, that is, to become autonomous beings.

Egalitarianism is one of two consequences of the doctrine of the tabula rasa. The second is vulnerability. Young children are at risk because through their senses their environment inscribes on their minds all sorts of beliefs and practices. Reason would disapprove of most of these. But even if the inscriptions are rational, the young child's mind is still incapable of discerning them to be so; for all the child knows these so-called truths may be falsehoods. Hence their presence saddles the child with prejudice, and action based on prejudice will tend to be confining instead of liberating. So when he proclaimed all human beings equal from birth, Locke also had in mind the precarious position of children, their equal vulnerability to being habituated to wrong patterns of thought and behavior. Locke viewed prejudice as the root of evil. It is contracted especially through children's forced exposure to myopic parents or teachers and the self-serving powers of church and state. Thus early upbringing and education, guided by prevailing custom rather than by reason, can be disastrous as it rivets to the mind that which has the appearance of truth or goodness but which, once believed or enacted, blocks development of one's humanity.

For Locke, the only natural disposition all children and adults share is that which makes them pursue pleasure and avoid pain. In this pursuit or avoidance they are not naturally inclined to either good or evil. Originally, human beings occupy a position of neutrality: Children are born neither "trailing clouds of glory" (as Wordsworth would have it a century later) nor burdened with original sin (as Augustine proclaimed before the dawn of medieval times). To be human, children must acquire the inclination to act on what is true and good, and each must acquire it for herself or himself. Because there is neither original depravity nor original inclination to knowledge or goodness, the egalitarianism of the tabula rasa has moral import: to be human, each must personally stake her or his claim to truth and goodness. But because they cannot do so during the years of early childhood, this thorough egalitarianism remains coupled with thorough vulnerability. Each generation, itself imposed upon by the one that preceded it, tends to be more than willing to impose on children such principles and practices as will enhance their own power. And so each new generation is vulnerable to the bondage of prejudice, as custom habituates children into compliance with prevailing beliefs and practices.

The Role of Mathematics

How to escape the bondage of prejudice and develop childhood potential? Though central to these acts, children depend for their instigation on sensitive adults for whom life itself militates against prejudice. Oppressive social, religious, and political structures chafe and irritate these adults, forcing them to examine their legitimacy, which in turn reveals their irrational and hence immoral principles. During such examinations, sensitive persons will introspect and become aware of the workings of their rational minds and recognize that rational procedures are most clearly revealed in mathematics where prejudice—unlike in religion or politics—has no purchase. When such enlightened persons guide children, actualization of childhood potential becomes possible. As Locke writes in the sixth and seventh paragraphs of the *Conduct of the Understanding*, "mathematics . . . should be taught . . . not so much to make them mathematicians, as to make them reasonable creatures," for "having got the way of reasoning, which that study necessarily brings the mind to, they might be able to transfer it to other parts of knowledge."

Early upbringing guided by the prevailing custom of overprotecting and spoiling children will not equip them with the habit of self-discipline needed to give mathematical studies the focused attention they demand. Hence, in the early parts of *Some Thoughts Concerning Education*, Locke propounds a regimen that will make for strong and disciplined children. His instructions are very specific: children's winter clothes should be as light as their summer clothes; their shoes should be thin to let in water, and their feet should be washed daily in cold water; they must spend much time in the open air without a hat whether in wind, sun, or rain and little time by the heat of the hearth; they must not overeat, and their diet should be very plain with little sugar, salt, or spices, no wine, and lots of dry brown bread; they should get plenty of sleep on a hard bed, but rise early. With this routine "there will not be so much need of beating children as is generally made use of"; their growing self-discipline will tend to make the rod superfluous. For "the principle of all virtue and excellency lies in a power of denying ourselves the satisfaction of our own desires where reason does not authorize them," a power "to be got and improved by custom, made easy and familiar by an *early* practice" (para. 38).

Mastery in mathematics allows children to recognize and use the procedures of reason, to discern and reject prejudice where it occurs (so cleaning the slate of its irrational inscriptions), and to develop a life in which their own will and reason begin to determine them. It allows children to develop into autonomous, useful individuals who will understand "the natural rights of man," "will seek the true measures of right and wrong," and will apply themselves "to that wherein [they] may be serviceable to [their] country" (para. 186–187).

See also: **Child Development, History of the Concept of; Education, Europe; Enlightenment, The.**

BIBLIOGRAPHY

Gutman, Amy. 1987. *Democratic Education.* Princeton, NJ: Princeton University Press.

The Golden Days (1944–1946), Balthus. A contemporary of Nabokov, Balthasar Klossowski, known as Balthus, depicted seemingly sexually aware pubescent girls of the type Nabokov would later describe in *Lolita*. Hirschhorn Museum and Sculpture Garden, Smithsonian Institution. Gift of the Joseph H. Hirschhorn Foundation, 1966. Photo by Lee Stalsworth.

Locke, John. 1960 [1690]. *Two Treatises of Government*, ed. Peter Laslett. Cambridge, UK: Cambridge University Press.

Locke, John. 1975 [1690]. *An Essay Concerning Human Understanding*, ed. P. H. Nidditch. Oxford, UK: Clarendon Press.

Locke, John. 1989 [1693]. *Some Thoughts Concerning Education*, ed. John W. Yolton and Jean S. Yolton. Oxford, UK: Clarendon Press; New York: Oxford University Press.

Locke, John. 1996. *Some Thoughts Concerning Education; and Of the Conduct of the Understanding*, ed. Ruth W. Grant and Nathan Tarcov. Indianapolis: Hacket Publishing Company.

Schouls, Peter A. 1992. *Reasoned Freedom: John Locke and Enlightenment*. Ithaca, NY: Cornell University Press.

PETER SCHOULS

Lolita

Lolita began as a novel and has become a code-word for the attractions of sexual girlhood. The novel titled *Lolita* was written by Vladimir Nabokov between 1949 and 1955, and published in France in 1955 and in the United States in 1958. Nabokov was born in Russia in 1899 and emigrated to the United States in 1940 after living in Europe since the Russian Revolution. He taught at Stanford University, Wellesley College, and Cornell University until the financial success of *Lolita* allowed him to stop teaching and move to Montreux, Switzerland, where he died in 1977. *Lolita* tells the story of Humbert Humbert, a middle-aged man who falls desperately in love with a young girl, Lolita, whom Nabokov famously described as a "nymphet." Humbert Humbert marries Lolita's mother in order to get close to her. After Lolita's mother's death, Humbert Humbert's passion is consummated during the course of an epic car trip, which ends in tragedy.

While Nabokov claimed his real subject matter was the esthetics of extreme erotic desire, the ostensibly pedophilic content of his novel rendered it scandalous. The book manuscript was first rejected by four United States publishers, then published, in English, by Maurice Girodias's Olympia Press in France, and finally in an American edition by Putnam in 1958. The novel elicited outraged protests against its content, which did not lead to censorship in the United States, but caused the Olympia Press edition to be banned by the French Ministry of the Interior, at the request of the British Home Office. Having already generated brisk illicit sales, *Lolita* soared to the top of the United States' best-seller lists once it was officially published. Three days after publication, 62,500 copies were in print, and by 1964 the novel had sold 2.5 million copies in the United States alone. By the mid 1980s, *Lolita* had sold about 14 million copies around the world.

Lolita's notoriety was magnified by its translation into film. The famed director Stanley Kubrick created his screen version in 1962, starring James Mason as Humbert Humbert, Sue Lyon (then fifteen years old) as Lolita, Shelley Winters as Lolita's mother Charlotte Haze, and Peter Sellars as Humbert's rival Clare Quilty. The film's screenplay was written by Nabokov himself. The film proved as controversial as the novel had been. After much debate and some editing of the film, it was released, but rated for adults only.

Kubrick's *Lolita* provided an image that resonated as widely as the novel's title. In an early scene, Lolita, reclining on the grass in a two-piece bathing suit, casts a sultry gaze at Humbert Humbert over her sunglasses. This image became conflated with a publicity still for the film showing a close-up of Lolita looking over red heart-shaped sunglasses while sucking on a red lollipop. Merged in the popular imagination, these two images have come to stand for *Lolita*, and, by extension, for the entire issue of whether precocious sexuality is an abusive adult fantasy, or the reality of incipient adolescence.

A sign of *Lolita*'s ongoing relevance was the remake of the film by Adrian Lyne in 1997. The new film's screenplay was by Stephen Schiff and starred Jeremy Irons as Humbert Humbert and Dominique Swain as Lolita (with a body double widely announced to be playing Lolita's sex scenes). Though Lyne had proved himself to be a commercially successful director in the past, he had great difficulty finding a U.S. distributor for the film. The problem of SEXUALITY in and with young girls, "nymphets," remains a troubled cultural terrain and the ambiguities of *Lolita* that connect PEDOPHILIA with sexual precocity incorporate and reflect that terrain.

See also: **Images of Childhood; Theories of Childhood.**

BIBLIOGRAPHY

Boyd, Brian. 1991. *Vladimir Nabokov: The American Years.* Princeton NJ: Princeton University Press.

LoBrutto, Vincent. 1997. *Stanley Kubrick: A Biography.* New York: D. I. Fine Books.

Nabokov, Vladimir. 1964. "Interview: Vladimir Nabokov" *Playboy* 11 (January): pp. 35–41, 44–45.

Nabokov, Vladimir. 1991 [1955]. *Lolita.* Rev. ed., annotated and introduced by Alfred Appel, Jr. New York: Vintage Books.

Phillips, Glen D., and Rodney Hill. 2002. *The Encyclopedia of Stanley Kubrick.* New York: Facts on File.

ANNE HIGONNET

Lord of the Rings and J. R. R. Tolkien

John Ronald Reuel Tolkien amused his four children with bedtime stories, tales, and pictures, and his love of storytelling led to the creation of *The Hobbit*, begun in 1930 and published in 1937. Written for children, the book introduced Middle Earth and its inhabitants, primarily hobbits, dwarves, elves, a wizard, and men. The great Ring of Power central to *The Lord of the Rings* is secondary in *The Hobbit*'s story of the conquest of a dragon and the capture of his hoard of gold. A main theme of *The Lord of the Rings*, that of small folk doing great deeds, is presaged in Bilbo Baggins, the hobbit who begrudgingly leaves his comfortable home, confronts challenges and dangers, and acquires the Ring. Upon the success of *The Hobbit*, illustrated by Tolkien, his publishers requested a sequel, and Tolkien began *The Lord of the Rings*.

Although Tolkien is most famous for his *Lord of the Rings*, his prolific writing career began in childhood and was lifelong. His poetry, tales, critical essays, linguistic work, and translations and editions of medieval literature appeared in magazines, scholarly journals, encyclopedias, and other publications. Tolkien's consuming passion, however, was the creation of a myth for England, the *Silmarillion*, which he began in 1917 as "The Book of Lost Tales." Although he worked on it his entire life, it was never completed. It was edited posthumously by Tolkien's son Christopher and was published in 1977.

Tolkien began *The Lord of the Rings* in 1937. A medievalist, he drew on Norse and Old and Middle English literature to populate his imaginary world. Middle Earth, which is imbued with verisimilitude, is home to many types of beings, each with its own culture, history, and language. Tolkien continuously revised his epic tale of confederated free peoples saving their world from subjugation, and the subsequent passing of an age before it was finally published in the mid-1950s. Originally a single work, *The Lord of the Rings* was divided by the publisher into three volumes, now known as the Trilogy: *The Fellowship of the Ring* (1954), *The Two Towers* (1954), and *The Return of the King* (1955). Seemingly a simple tale of good against evil, *The Lord of the Rings* also encompasses the themes of technology versus nature, fate, free will and moral choice, power, mortality, cultural diversity, heroism, and human potential, the complexities of which engage adult readers. Although many people read *The Lord of the Rings* in their youth, they experience it differently upon rereading the books as adults. Rather than just enjoying the tale of adventure and quest, they also become involved in the larger issues and are more aware of its dark nature.

The Lord of the Rings offers to everyone the escape, recovery, and consolation that Tolkien perceived as an elemental function of the fairy tale, as well as the hope that the most unassuming person can become a hero through bravery, loyalty, and love. Perhaps the story's greatest appeal to all readers is the presence of the magical: not sleight of hand but the shimmering light of the majestic elves, the wisdom and sight beyond mortal vision, and the power of words, all seemingly lost to the modern world. Historical context also plays a role in readers' attraction to *The Lord of the Rings*; for example, the cult-like response in America on college campuses upon the (unauthorized) publication of the books in 1965 coincided with a cultural movement characterized by a desire for peace and empowerment in a time of disillusionment.

The Hobbit and *The Lord of the Rings* have been translated into many languages and media, including radio, audio recordings, and film. Director Peter Jackson made an award-winning movie version of *The Lord of the Rings*, in three segments following the volume order; the first was released in 2001 and the others followed in consecutive years. Reactions were mixed among viewers who were familiar with the books. Some, particularly adolescents, objected to the plot changes, while others felt the films were as faithful as possible, and many praised them for sparking a new interest in the books.

See also: **Children's Literature.**

BIBLIOGRAPHY

Carpenter, Humphrey. 2000. *Tolkien: A Biography*. Boston: Houghton Mifflin.

Hammond, Wayne G., and Christina Scull. 2000. *J. R. R. Tolkien: Artist and Illustrator*. Boston: Houghton Mifflin.

Tolkien, J. R. R. 2000. *The Letters of J. R. R. Tolkien*, ed. Humphrey Carpenter. Boston: Houghton Mifflin.

DINAH HAZELL
GEORGE W. TUMA

Love

Parents' attachment to and affection for their children are perhaps the most profound emotional experiences of human existence. Infancy and childhood require an extraordinary level of parental involvement and typically call for the parent or caretaker to sacrifice resources, comfort, and even safety in the interests of the child. Contemporary evolutionary theory views affection for children and parental attachment as biologically motivated behavior, fundamental to the survival of the species. Some psychological theories also place the experience of parental love and attachment at the center of emotional development. As children develop, other important emotional relationships grow out of the experiences of affection and attachment that they had as children.

The Ancient and Medieval World

Culture has inevitably grown up around attachment behavior, investing it with meanings and also shaping the behavior to conform to other human needs. Although examples abound in the Bible and in Greek literature of the love of parents for children, these do not necessarily resemble contemporary standards for love. For instance, in 2 Samuel, King David mourns for his dead, rebellious son, Absalom. But his general, Joab, rebukes David for his sadness, reminding David of the danger his men had incurred to defeat Absalom.

Evidence from Rome depicts an upper class that poured out affection for dead infants and children. Yet the experience of childhood may have been filled with relatively few moments of abiding tenderness. Roman fathers could reject children at birth, allowing them to be exposed and die. Roman medical literature has little to say about childhood illness, and children in Roman letters and memorials were often praised for adult characteristics. This does not indicate a Roman ignorance of stages of child development—children played freely in their early years and received many toys from fond relatives. But upper-class Romans may have cared more for the adult to be than for the child. Roman children began life and continued through childhood within a dense network of relationships in which the biological parents often were not the primary caregivers and may not have been the primary givers of love and affection. As they grew, boys had to learn the Roman values of citizenship and generally received a relatively extensive education under harsh masters. Even so, there is evidence that by the first century B.C.E. parental affection for young children had wider acceptance and that during the early imperial period some Romans came to see the family as their principal source of identity.

Historians in the two decades following PHILIPPE ARIÈS's groundbreaking 1960 work generally applied Ariès's insights to the affectional bonds of medieval and early modern households. According to Ariès parents loved their children, but not so much for themselves as for the contribution these children could bring to the household. High infant and childhood mortality meant that families feared to invest much time, affection, and attention in small children who might not survive. Even names were reused, either family names or the names of dead siblings. WET-NURSING meant mothers had little opportunity to become attached to their infants, and SWADDLING and inattention meant that the very young received little opportunity to bond with mothers. Similarly the lack of privacy foreclosed opportunities for purely family activities. Between ages seven and fourteen both boys and girls could expect to be apprenticed to another family, thus ending family closeness altogether. Childhood ended quickly, and youths became miniature adults, with versions of adult roles and responsibilities. Thus, the household economy completely absorbed the bonds of affection.

More recent historians have stressed continuity rather than a sharp change in child rearing from medieval to early modern times. Evidence exists back to antiquity of the recognition that childhood was a distinctive phase in human development and worthy of special attention. Children's TOYS, evidence of grief for dead infants, and new insights into practices such as wet-nursing all point to a more affectionate family environment. One study of rural France found mothers fussing over young children and grieving at the loss of children through death or separation. Important changes in child raising accompanied economic and intellectual trends from the late Middle Ages. These included extended schooling, the renewed importance of classical models for education, and a newly vital embrace of marriage and family life. These trends tended to reinforce the importance of warmth and affection in the home.

Early Modern and Modern Times

By the eighteenth century the general features of the modern affectionate or sentimental family had become widely disseminated in child-rearing literature and the values of close family ties and affection began to be taken for granted among middle- and upper-class families in western Europe and the British North American colonies. JOHN LOCKE's 1693 *Some Thoughts Concerning Education* became a fundamental text of the new family ideal. Locke believed that children were distinct from adults in having few if any concepts, and that the education of children should be central to family life. He urged parents (he wrote to fathers) to use physical punishment as little as possible, but rather to shape behavior through esteem and disgrace. Locke's work became an important point of departure for ENLIGHTENMENT writers who encouraged sentimental relationships within the family.

By the early nineteenth century, the affectionate family, with recognizably contemporary attitudes toward parental love, had taken firm root among the middle classes in western Europe and the northern United States. The economic functions of the family had largely withered away and in their place powerful affectionate bonds had grown up. Even with continuing high INFANT MORTALITY, parents recognized each new child as an individual and as worthy of a unique relationship. Children received new and distinctive names. Mothers nursed their own children and both parents attempted to spend time playing with children and nourishing the bonds of affection. Boys and girls would still have gender-neutral clothing until age seven, but the ages of childhood were valued as intrinsically important. Extended schooling limited, sometimes even replaced, APPRENTICE-SHIPS for boys, and girls generally remained in the home. Within the larger middle-class homes, private parlors allowed the family to spend time together away from outsiders. The love of family members for one another, and particularly of parents for their children, became the central concern of the family.

Gender, Class, Ethnicity, and Region

The workings of the affectionate family varied by gender, social class, ethnicity, and region. Among the important economic and social changes in the United States and western Europe was the separation of work from the home. Middle-class fathers, as breadwinners, were absent from the home for most of the day, six days a week. This reduced or eliminated many of the relations that fathers would have with their children within a household-based economy such as a farm or artisan's workshop. Fathers still strived to serve the family and still enjoyed their children and gave them warm regard, but their time for this was limited.

The role of the middle-class mother became far more important. During the nineteenth century, motherhood assumed a vitally important role, becoming the epitome of all love and the highest example of devotion. Mothers, especially as they gained assistance from maids and other servants, could devote ever larger periods of time to raising children, a calling that became central to the self-identity of middle-class mothers. Literature was filled with examples of maternal sacrifice and love. Evidence from letters in the nineteenth century, and from surveys in the early twentieth century, show that both male and female children had fonder memories of mothers than of fathers. But boys had eventually to separate from mothers to pursue independent lives. Girls, on the other hand, could grow to womanhood within a realm of motherly affection that was extended through relations to other female relatives, friends of the mother's, and age-contemporary friends who were part of the extended female network.

In the pre–Civil War American South, the sentimental family bound by affection and centered on the rearing of children appeared in a modified form among upper-class white families. Here the fathers may well have taken more of a role in the life of the children, and these families may have given greater scope to affection. But southern parents also demanded that children acquire a sense of family pride and honor, and take on roles that were often more prescriptive than those found in the North. Consequently, these families have been described as warm and affectionate but with careful control of emotional displays.

African-American families in the South prior to the Civil War maintained affectionate ties in spite of the hardships of slavery. Frederick Douglass recalled his mother's visits to him, even though she had to travel many miles at night, after her work. The vulnerability of the slave family to being broken by the sale of its members, and the harsh conditions of slavery, meant that many children developed kinship ties to aunts, uncles, grandparents, and fictive kin within the slave community. These ties spread the child-rearing tasks and also the bonds of affection throughout the community. Even so, after the war one of the most common reasons for the almost universal movement of freed men and women was the desire to find spouses and children and reunite families.

Working-class white families in the nineteenth century had little in common with middle-class families. Children in industrializing America had to work and contribute to the family economy from an early age. Affectionate ties within the family always competed with the material needs of the family. Fathers may have been even more distant than in middle-class families. A primary source of tension within working-class families was the demand for children's wages. In immigrant families, especially those from southern and eastern Europe, traditions of patriarchy meant that fathers preferred sons and the family focus was not on raising and adoring children but on serving fathers and catering to male children. Combined with the pressing demands for the entire family to work, this limited affectionate play and the warmth of family life.

The Twentieth and Early Twenty-First Century

The twentieth century brought a range of changes to the affectionate family. With the growing prosperity of the middle class, fathers could budget more time for activities with children. This still left the bulk of child rearing and family chores with mothers, but fathers at least had more opportunities for affectionate play with children. Growing prosperity also meant that successful working-class families began to resemble middle-class families, with their affectionate ties. Mandatory school laws and the limited success of CHILD LABOR laws meant that more working-class children were experiencing extended childhoods similar to those of children of the middle class.

A peer culture also developed among adolescent youth in the twentieth century. With extended schooling, and with the popularity of SUMMER CAMPS, many more children found themselves with age peers for much more time. Some conflicts grew out of this development, with adolescent children convinced that parents had little understanding of and affection for them. Mothers found it more difficult to continue the long tradition of female bonds among girls and young women.

Motherhood and mother love also came in for criticism. By the 1920s, social scientists and journalists began to attack mother love as a dangerous, even suffocating, emotional attachment. While maternal affection continued to characterize home life, at least middle-class mothers often found themselves fearing that their desire to coddle or praise or worry over children might have long-term harmful effects. After World War II this trend was partially reversed, with the renewed cultural emphasis upon the affectionate family, but suspicion of mother love continued as a motif in American culture throughout the twentieth century.

As indicated by biological and psychological theories that place parental affection for children at the center of human evolutionary survival and emotional development, love of children has become transcendent in contemporary America. Child-centeredness is taken for granted, with the only de-

bate being around the proper means of aiding children in their development. At the same time, late-twentieth- and early-twenty-first-century Americans recognize the possibilities for abuse disguised as love for children. Revelations of the sexual exploitation of children in child-care facilities and religious institutions, and the recognition of dysfunctional family life as an important social issue, have made the proper form of love, care, and affection for children a pressing issue. Because of its importance in contemporary culture, love for children will continue at the center of vital debates on social and moral issues.

Love by Children

The history of children's love is obviously more obscure than that of parental love. As sentimental love became more highly emphasized, it was usually assumed that children would respond in kind. But not all children proved as loving as their parents hoped. One feature of ADOLESCENCE often involved a period in which active affection was less forthcoming, which could be confusing to child and parent alike. Sociologists have speculated that a longer-term result of the growing emphasis on love for children involved a need for children (perhaps particularly girls) to fall in love in order ultimately to separate themselves from their parents (particularly their mothers). The ramifications of the history of love and childhood deserve further attention.

See also: **Emotional Life; Fathering and Fatherhood; Mothering and Motherhood.**

BIBLIOGRAPHY

Ariès, Philippe. 1962. *Centuries of Childhood: A Social History of Family Life.* Trans. Robert Baldick. New York: Alfred A. Knopf.

Buss, David M. 1988. "Love Acts: The Evolutionary Biology of Love." In *The Psychology of Love*, ed. Robert J. Sternberg and Michael L. Barnes. New Haven, CT: Yale University Press.

Clement, Priscilla Ferguson. 1997. *Growing Pains: Children in the Industrial Age, 1850–1890.* New York: Twayne.

Dixon, Suzanne. 1992. *The Roman Family.* Baltimore, MD: Johns Hopkins University Press.

Greven, Philip. 1977. *The Protestant Temperament: Patterns of Child-Rearing, Religious Experience, and the Self in Early America.* Chicago: University of Chicago.

Griswold, Robert L. 1993. *Fatherhood in America: A History.* New York: Basic Books.

Hawes, Joseph M. 1997. *Children between the Wars: American Childhood, 1920–1940.* New York: Twayne.

Herlihy, David. 1985. *Medieval Households.* Cambridge, MA: Harvard University Press.

Ladurie, Emmanuel Le Roy. 1988. *Montaillou: The Promised Land of Error.* Trans. Barbara Bray. New York: Vintage.

Macleod, David I. 1998. *The Age of the Child: Children in America, 1890–1920.* New York: Twayne.

Ozment, Steven. 2001. *Ancestors: The Loving Family in Old Europe.* Cambridge, MA: Harvard University Press.

Rawson, Beryl. 1991. "Adult Child Relationships in Roman Society." In *Marriage, Divorce, and Children in Ancient Rome*, ed. Beryl Rawson. Oxford: Clarendon Press.

Reinier, Jacqueline. 1996. *From Virtue to Character: American Childhood, 1775–1850.* New York: Twayne.

Shaver, Philip, Cindy Hazan, and Donna Bradshaw. 1988. "Love As Attachment." In *The Psychology of Love*, ed. Robert J. Sternberg and Michael L. Barnes. New Haven, CT: Yale University Press.

JOHN C. SPURLOCK

Lycée

Created as state schools in France in 1802, the *lycées* educated the future French elite for more than a century. They were intended for boys only, recruited pupils mainly from higher classes, and offered a general education, extended to all secondary classes, with no immediate occupational application. Today's *lycées* are restricted to the last three years of secondary education and to some higher education classes, but their curriculum has been extended to technical and VOCATIONAL EDUCATION and they welcome almost all boys and girls. This transformation has been accompanied by deep changes in the *lycées'* organization, education, and pedagogical practices.

The Classical Lycée

Napoleon Bonaparte created the *lycées* in order to put the education of future officers, administrators, engineers, and professionals under state control. They took the place of the *écoles centrales* of 1795, which had failed to fill the gap caused by the suppression of universities and the collapse of the old *collèges* during the French Revolution. The creators of the *lycée* were inspired by the model of the collèges, including the presence of religious education and practices. The *lycées* were closed boarding schools with a military-type discipline, welcoming scholarship students as well as paying boarders and day pupils.

Whereas the *écoles centrales* had an encyclopedic curriculum, the birth of the *lycées* marked a return to the humanistic model of education, which meant classical studies and the domination of Latin. The first curriculum, however, left a lot of room to science education, which was carried on afterwards because the *lycées* prepared some of their pupils for the entry examination to the *École polytechnique* and other schools of scientific higher education. Up to the 1880s, pedagogical methods were based on memorization and imitation, and involved a lot of written exercises, whose handing out and correction occupied a large part of teachers' courses. The pupils therefore had considerable personal work to perform, which boarders did under the supervision of tutors, who supervised boarders at all times, except during classes.

The Lycées' Modernization

The humanistic model was questioned as early as the first half of the nineteenth century when the curriculum started becoming specialized. In the bigger *lycées*, physics, history and geography, living languages, art, gymnastics, and natural science gradually became subjects in their own rights with specialized teachers, despite the attempt by minister Hippolyte Fortoul (1851–1856) to break with the return to ency-

clopedism. A special education intended for pupils in need of more modern and practical courses developed beside classical studies. From 1880, republican authorities backed up the cause of the modernization of the curriculum and pedagogy. The role of Latin was reduced, despite fierce resistance from supporters of the classics, and new pedagogical methods requiring observation, experimentation, and personal reflection on the part of the pupils gradually imposed themselves. The 1902 reform put modern education at the same level as classical studies, and replaced the traditional two-hour classes with modern one-hour courses.

These changes created anxiety for many teachers. They regarded their new role—which implied a more direct contact with the pupils—as a threatening confusion between teaching and tutoring functions, and a fall in the status to the teaching profession. This unrest persisted throughout the twentieth century. In fact, the status and working conditions of tutors improved considerably after 1880. They were better educated and the decline in the number of boarders led the authorities to reform their task. Generally, whereas the teachers who had tenure, holders of the *agrégation*, reached their best social position ever around 1900, the lot of all the teaching profession improved massively, even in the *collèges communaux* (municipal secondary schools). The bigger *collèges communaux* were gradually converted into *lycées*, so the number of *lycées* for boys rose from 36 in 1820 to 110 in 1900 (when there were 39 *lycées* for girls) receiving about 32 percent of secondary education pupils (*collèges communaux* received 21 percent; and private secondary schools received 47 percent).

Lycées for girls, created in 1880, developed a secondary education distinct from that of boys until 1924. GIRLS' SCHOOLS did not teach Latin, which led the way to a remarkable development of the teaching of French literature. Girls' secondary education did not include the *baccalauréat*, the final examination on which the admission to higher education depended, but many girls managed to take it nevertheless.

From the Education of the Elite to Mass Education

Public secondary education became entirely free in 1934, but the *lycées* actually switched from the education of the elite to mass education after World War II. Post-elementary schooling rapidly spread to all social classes, and all types of post-elementary schools, like the higher primary schools (1941), the primary higher courses, the technical schools and the schools for apprentices (1959), gradually merged into a sole second *degree* derived from secondary schools thanks to institutional reforms. From 1963, the *lycées* lost their first four classes, which were converted into new lower secondary schools called *collèges*. *Collèges* were unified in 1975 (*le collège unique*) as was the first grade of the *lycées* a few years later.

Since then, the specialization in technical or vocational education has been assigned to the last two classes of the *ly-*

cées. General and technical education have both led on to the *baccalauréat*, as well as vocational education since 1985. But the equality between all secondary courses is more formal than real. The specialization in vocational or technical education has often been considered a failure. The abilities by which pupils are judged did not change much after the beginning of the twentieth century, and the way these abilities were measured favored pupils from higher social and cultural backgrounds. The extinction of tutoring, in the 1960s, probably made things worse.

Therefore, the *lycées'* democratization was not completed by the end of the twentieth century. The proportion of French pupils reaching the *baccalauréat* level soared up to three quarters by the mid 1990s, which represented a great leap forward in a few decades. But, at the beginning of the twenty-first century, the probability of reaching the best courses was still strongly connected with pupils' social background, and girls, though generally more successful than boys academically, were a minority in courses like science which led to the best higher studies.

See also: **Education, Europe; Gymnasium Schooling; High School.**

BIBLIOGRAPHY

Anderson, Robert D. 1975. *Education in France, 1848–1870.* Oxford: Oxford University Press.

Baker, Donald N., and Patrick J. Harrigan, eds. 1980. *The Making of Frenchmen: Current Directions in the History of Education in France, 1679–1979.* Waterloo: Historical Reflections Press.

Belhoste, Bruno. 1989. "Les caractères généraux de l'enseignement secondaire scientifique de la fin de l'Ancien Régime à la Première Guerre mondiale." *Histoire de l'éducation* 41: 3–45.

Chervel, André. 1998. *La culture scolaire. Une approche historique.* Paris: Belin.

Compère, Marie-Madeleine. 1985. *Du collège au lycée (1500–1850).* Paris: Gallimard-Julliard.

Compère, Marie-Madeleine, and Philippe Savoie, eds. 2001. *L'établissement scolaire. Des collèges d'humanités à l'enseignement secondaire, XVIe–XXe siècles.* Special issue of *Histoire de l'éducation* no. 90.

Margadant, Jo Burr. 1990. *Madame le Professeur. Women Educators in the Third Republic.* Princeton, NJ: Princeton University Press.

Mayeur, Françoise. 1977. *L'enseignement secondaire des jeunes filles sous la Troisième République.* Paris: Presses de la Fondation nationale des sciences politiques.

Müller, Detlef K., Fritz Ringer, and Brian Simon, eds. 1989. *The Rise of the Modern Educational System: Structural Change and Social Reproduction, 1870–1920.* Cambridge, UK: Cambridge University Press.

Prost, Antoine. 1968. *Histoire de l'enseignement en France, 1800–1967.* Paris: Armand Colin.

Prost, Antoine. 1992. *Éducation, société et politiques. Une histoire de l'enseignement de 1945 à nos jours.* Paris: Éditions du Seuil.

Savoie, Philippe. 2000. *Les enseignants du secondaire. Le corps, le métier, les carrières. Textes officiels. Tome 1: 1802–1914.* Paris: INRP–Economica.

PHILIPPE SAVOIE

M

Madonna, Orthodox

At the council of Ephesus, in 431 C.E., the Church confirmed that Mary, the mother of Jesus, could bear the title *Theotokos*, meaning "Bearer of God." In doing this, the Church encouraged the emergence of a public cult of the Virgin. In the course of the fifth century a number of churches dedicated to the Virgin were built in Rome, Constantinople, and Jerusalem. During the sixth and seventh centuries the feasts of the Annunciation, Purification, and the Nativity and Dormition (or "falling asleep") of Mary were established. In the seventh century the Virgin came to be perceived as the supernatural protector of the city and its head: the emperor in Constantinople, the pope in Rome.

The political power vested in the figure of the Virgin found a visual expression in the formation of the Maria Regina image that emerged in the second half of the sixth century and became prominent in the eighth century, especially in Rome. The Maria Regina representation shows the Virgin dressed as a Byzantine empress with a crown, pearl necklaces, and a silk sash or *loros*. She sits on a gem-encrusted throne and supports the child Jesus on her lap. Both figures are displayed in a directly frontal attitude, addressing the viewer with their gaze. In the Maria Regina images the imperially dressed figure of Mary functions metaphorically as a "living throne" to the divine figure of Christ. However, these hierarchic images, manifesting the presence of supernatural power on earth, do not explore the maternal and filial link between mother and child.

Only during the period of Iconoclasm (730–843) was a new emphasis placed on the relationship between the Virgin and Child; the neutral term *Theotokos* was gradually supplanted by the appellation *Meter Theou*, or "Mother of God." This new title emphasized the maternal link between Mary and Christ. The emotionally intense love between the mother and child that developed in the ninth-century texts was not immediately manifested in the visual culture, however.

Only by the late tenth century did new emotionally evocative images of the mother and child appear, such as that in Tokali Kilise, Cappadocia, Turkey. These images show the child Jesus lovingly placing his arm around his mother's neck, while the Virgin inclines her head, pressing her cheek to that of her son. With one arm she cradles Christ, while with the other she gestures towards him, addressing the prayers of the viewer to Christ (the icon of the Vladimir Virgin in Moscow is an example).

These representations place an equally strong emphasis on the unfaltering love of the child, who actively reaches out to his mother, embraces her by the neck, and brings his lips close to her face. By depicting Christ's love, these images present the source of Mary's power, for it is because Christ loves his mother beyond measure that he would grant his blessing to her pleas on behalf of humanity. The images of the playful and loving child Jesus thus explain that the salvation of humankind rests in Christ's unfaltering love for his mother.

Along with the affection of the child, these images also convey the idea of motherly sacrifice. The Virgin beseeches Christ, but she also presents and offers him to the viewer. Her raised, gesturing hand symbolizes this act of offering. Her grip is loosened, allowing the viewer into the image to be part of the mother-and-child embrace. Thus, the Byzantine icons of Mary and Christ present an image of a double sacrifice: the mother offering her son, and the Son offering his life for the salvation of humanity.

The best pictorial expression of these ideas is revealed in one of the most powerful icons in the Byzantine and Orthodox world: the Hodegetria. By the twelfth century this icon was perceived as the supernatural protector of the capital (Constantinople), the emperor, and the empire. The panel displayed the image of the Virgin and child on the front side, and the Crucifixion on the back. The obverse side presents an image of the incarnation of the Logos (word) in the form of the Christ child carried in his mother's arm. He receives the pleas of Mary on behalf of humanity and responds with a blessing. The Crucifixion on the reverse side displays the fulfillment of the promise in Christ's sacrifice. Christ's body sags lifelessly from the cross, and Mary's hands are empty, one pressed to her chest as a sign of her loss and suffering and the other still raised in a gesture of intercession. The Virgin's sacrifice is here poignantly expressed: the sacrifice of her motherly love and the death of her child is the price offered for the salvation of humanity.

See also: **Images of Childhood; Madonna, Religious; Madonna, Secular.**

BIBLIOGRAPHY

Carr, Annmarie Weyl. 1993–1994. "The Presentation of an Icon on Sinai." *Deltion tes christianikes archaiologikes hetaireias* 17: 239–248.

Kalavrezou, I. 1990. "Images of the Mother: When the Virgin Became Meter Theou." *Dumbarton Oaks Papers* 44: 165–172.

Peltomaa, L. M. 2001. *Medieval Mediterranean: Peoples, Economies, and Cultures, 400–1453: Vol. 35. The Image of the Virgin Mary in the Akathistos Hymn.* Leiden, the Netherlands: Brill.

Pentcheva, Bissera. 2001. "Images and Icons of the Virgin and Their Public in Middle Byzantine Constantinople." Ph.D. diss., Harvard University.

Vassilaki, M., ed. 2000. *Mother of God: Representations of the Virgin in Byzantine Art.* Milan: Skira.

BISSERA V. PENTCHEVA

Madonna, Religious

The term *Madonna*, which comes from the Italian for "our lady," is a title of respect for the Virgin Mary commonly applied to works of art, especially those images that feature mother and infant, known familiarly as Madonna and Child. The Virgin Mary appears so frequently in Christian art that many are surprised to learn how rarely she is mentioned in the four Gospels. Her artistic identity is a compilation of scripture, tradition, faith, and interpretation. Particularly significant is the Protevangelium (or Infancy Gospel) of James, a mid-second-century apocryphal manuscript that describes Mary's childhood and Jesus' early life, neither of which is narrated in the Bible.

Traditions continued to evolve over the centuries, reflecting liturgical practice, popular belief, and scriptural exegesis. Collections of popular tales can be found in the thirteenth-century *Legenda aurea* (Golden legend) by Jacobus de Voragine, and in the nineteenth-century *Legends of the Madonna* by Anna Jameson. Nor were developments confined to the Middle Ages. The decades of the late sixteenth and seventeenth centuries (known as the Counter-Reformation or post-Tridentine period) following the division of the Western Church into Protestant and Catholic denomina-

tions, saw the rise or reform of many aspects of Marian devotion, as well as renewed demand in Catholic regions for works of art featuring the Madonna. Two important elements of Marian doctrine, the Immaculate Conception (referring to Mary's birth free of the stain of original sin) and her Assumption into heaven, were only defined as dogma (required truth faith) by the Catholic Church as recently as 1858 and 1950, respectively, although the feast days of the Immaculate Conception and Assumption date respectively from the thirteenth and seventh centuries.

It is not uncommon for the Madonna to be depicted without her child, in scenes that narrate events before Jesus' birth—such as the Immaculate Conception, the Annunciation (when Gabriel brings news that Mary will bear the son of God), and the Visitation (when Mary's miraculous pregnancy is recognized by her cousin Elizabeth)—or events that take place after his death, such as Pentecost (the descent of the Holy Spirit onto Mary and the apostles) or the Assumption of the Virgin. At times, the Madonna may be shown alone, outside of a narrative context, especially in a devotional image (a figure intended to evoke prayers and elicit veneration for the individual represented). For example, cult statues of Mary need not include her child, if honoring her role as intercessor in heaven on behalf of those who address prayers to her. However, because Mary's significance in Christianity is linked directly to her role as Jesus' mother, it is more common to find her represented as the young mother of an extraordinary infant than as a solitary woman.

Origins of Marian Art

Images of the Madonna and Child have not always been characterized by the warm, loving exchanges characteristic of familiar works of art. Initially the two protagonists displayed a regal and formal bearing many today characterize as distant and austere. The earliest known depiction of Mary comes from the Catacomb of Priscilla, a late-second-century or early-third-century underground burial site in Rome. The wall painting depicts a woman nursing a baby, seated beside a bearded man who stands pointing to the sky. Scholars identify this man as either Isaiah or Balaam, two Hebrew prophets whose writings were interpreted to prefigure Jesus' birth.

In early Christian art Mary was portrayed as an orant (figure in prayer), a mother, or enthroned in the manner of an empress, borrowing from Greco-Roman conventions of prestige. As a new religion, it was prudent for Christianity to use an artistic vocabulary already in place and understood by the public to express unfamiliar ideas. Images that conveyed Mary's high status encouraged viewers to hold her in equal or higher regard than secular rulers. Pagan audiences in late antiquity never would have confused the Madonna with their fertility goddesses, who wore elaborate costumes, not the simple veil of an ordinary woman; nor did Mary embody their destructive powers. Pagan goddesses kept apart from humans, but Mary was accessible. Through her, Christians could approach her imposing son and his austere father, much as mothers and wives of the remote and all-powerful Roman emperors served as intercessors for their subjects.

Marian depictions became more frequent in the fifth century, after her status was elevated by the Council of Ephesus in 431 C.E., which honored Mary with the title *Theotokos*, a Greek term meaning "God-bearer." The first church to be dedicated to her, the Roman basilica of Santa Maria Maggiore (St. Mary the Great), was consecrated in 432 C.E., and not long after copies of the *Hodegetria* icon (Greek for "she who leads the way") were circulated widely throughout the Roman Empire, showing Mary as a solemn, regal mother holding the infant Jesus in her left arm and pointing to him with her right, while her son held up his hand in blessing. This Byzantine format was repeated for centuries in Western art.

Gradually, a more loving, less formal relationship unfolded between mother and child. Mary's head inclined more toward her son, while the infant began to twist in his mother's arms, their cheeks touching or gazes meeting. The somber child became a squirming baby, and Mary a tender mother. The throne and crown that had initially been incorporated to portray Mary in the guise of an empress became identified in medieval art as aspects of her role as Queen of Heaven and *Sede sapientia* (seat of wisdom). By the late thirteenth century, greater naturalism began to replace the rigid postures that had been employed earlier to convey prestige and respect, and artists strove to portray the strong maternal bond between mother and child. In Gothic paintings, the isolation of figures against a gold ground retained a sense of formality, but the adaptation of descriptive backgrounds in the Renaissance concluded this transition.

Emergence of the Mothering Madonna

Aesthetic trends toward more representational art in the late-medieval and early-modern period coincided with a corresponding philosophical shift that viewed humanity as a metaphor for the cosmos, and the natural world as a mirror of the divine. Religious thought, influenced by the teachings of the newly founded Franciscan order, likewise began to focus more on Jesus' humanity than his divinity. Christianity holds that, as the son of God, Jesus was both fully divine and fully human, with his mother, the Virgin Mary, contributing his human nature. Whereas divinity had been expressed through images of a regal Queen and an adult Savior, the doctrinal emphasis on humanity was best illustrated through images of a maternal Madonna and Child.

Developments in religious practice also supported this change. *Devotio moderna*, a late medieval form of worship popular in Northern Europe, emphasized personal identification with Mary's grief and Jesus' suffering. Its practitioners used works of art as tools to inspire meditation and prayer. The presentation of the Christ child as a baby in his mother's

The image of *Maria lactans*, the nursing Madonna, which became common during the fifteenth century, emphasized the human relationship between the Virgin Mary and her child. *The Virgin and Child before a Firescreen* (c. 1440), follower of Robert Campin. The Art Archive/National Gallery London/Eileen Tweedy.

arms not only reminded worshipers of Jesus' human birth, but also helped foster a feeling of connection, through their own experiences of childhood or parental nurturing. At a time of high INFANT MORTALITY, such scenes evoked both sorrow and sympathy. Thus, theology, philosophy, and popular custom all found confirmation in these images of an infant God in his mother's arms.

Sentiment versus Scripture

The Madonna and Child pairing appealed greatly to Renaissance artists, writers, and preachers. Mary was increasingly portrayed as the compassionate, protective mother of a gifted, precocious child. Though the Madonna retained her customary red dress and blue mantle (red symbolizing passion and true love, blue heaven and spiritual love), her son was now shown naked or scantily clothed, fully revealing his male genitalia. Leo Steinberg, in his influential book *The Sexuality of Christ in Renaissance Art and in Modern Oblivion*, argues against the tendency to dismiss this as a natural display of maternal pride or casual reflection of contemporary childcare. He links the frequently exposed infant genitalia to the Renaissance emphasis on the doctrine of the incarnation—God's presence on earth in human form—translated artisti-

Our Lady of Guadalupe (c. late 17th century) is the most significant image of the Madonna created in the New World. Her likeness, first created in colonial Mexico, has been adopted as a source of Hispanic pride throughout the Western Hemisphere. The Art Archive/Pinacoteca Virreinel Mexico City/Dagli Orti.

cally into a young boy who embodied the Gospel phrase, "the Word made Flesh." Mary's role as instrument of the incarnation was celebrated in Nativity scenes and in devotional images of *Maria lactans*, the nursing Madonna, a form that emerged in the mid-fourteenth century and gained popularity in the fifteenth century.

Clergy praised images of the Virgin breast-feeding her son and urged women to follow her example, rather than send children out to wet nurses. Jean de Gerson (1363–1429) of Paris preached that mother's milk was not only natural infant's food but also the beginning of a Christian education. Nevertheless, during the Reformation, Protestants objected to scenes of Mary nursing her child on religious grounds, claiming these works asserted Mary's power over Jesus because they showed his dependency on her for nourishment. The Puritan minister William Crashaw (1572–1626) called it degrading to depict Jesus as a small baby subservient to a woman. Such imagery, he complained, would not let Christ

grow up into a miracle-working male, equal in size and stature to God the Father.

Many Protestants felt that the Roman Church gave Mary too much prominence; the most radical accused the Church of Mariolatry—a form of idolatry based on exaggerated importance of Mary's role in Christianity. Though many believers probably did esteem Mary too highly, this was due more to the popular appeal of the Madonna as an ever-loving, ever-forgiving mother than to a deliberate effort on the part of the Church to diminish Christ's stature. In Catholic teaching, only God is entitled to worship; the Madonna, as a saint, may be venerated (paid homage) and asked to intercede on behalf of the faithful, but not worshipped. From its inception, the Church had taken pains to distinguish the use of art in worship from the worship of idols, defining religious art as a tool for teaching the illiterate, a means of honoring the saintly, and a way to remember the salvation story. Prayers were to be addressed not to a statue or painting, but to the personage represented by it, with the works of art serving to aid the inner eye to mentally re-create sacred experience.

Non-Western Adaptations

Missionaries to non-Western lands brought works of art along on their journeys. Jesuits in seventeenth-century JAPAN set up *Namban* painting academies to produce European-style paintings in local techniques and with Asian features. The Madonna and Child was by far the image most requested by newly converted clients. To explain the Virgin Mary to native audiences, Europeans compared her to Amaterasu, the Shinto sun goddess, because of an artistic resemblance to the Madonna. Despite visual similarities, Amaterasu was not an appropriate match, for her powers were natural, not moral. The Japanese Buddhist goddess of compassion, Kannon (known as Kuan Yin in China), would have been a better equivalent had missionaries based their comparison on doctrine rather than visual appearance.

In AFRICA, mother-child figures were already a familiar part of ritual art, which helped facilitate the transfer of Christian meanings onto traditional forms. Hybrid items such as Kongo crosses attest to the assimilation of native and imposed religious traditions, as well as the acceptance of Christianity by African converts. Nigerian-American poet Ifeanyi Menkiti has written about how Africans venerate the Madonna as an active patron and advocate, rather than a passive vessel for the incarnation, a perspective influenced by the dynamic roles of indigenous female deities.

Conversion was an official goal of European colonizers in the Hispanic new world, where clergy accompanied soldiers on missions of exploration. Unlike Protestant colonists in Anglo-settled North America, Spanish colonizers viewed natives as souls to be saved rather than as savages to be eradicated, resulting in a higher number of coerced conversions but a greater survival rate among the indigenous population.

There was also a degree of covert cultural survival as well, as native religious traditions were adapted and subsumed into Christian ones.

The most significant new-world Madonna is Our Lady of Guadalupe, the name given to the 1531 apparition of the Virgin Mary to a Nahuatl Indian convert in Tepeyac, just outside of Mexico City. Many identify Our Lady of Guadalupe as the Christianization of an Aztec goddess whose ancient temple lay on the hill of Tepeyac, citing the similarity between the names *Guadalupe* and *Coatlicue*, the Aztec goddess of earth and death (though today she is associated with the mother goddess *Tonantzin*). Few realize, however, that Our Lady of Guadalupe was also the name of a wonder-working black Madonna from Spain whose cult clergy had tried to promote in Mexico, only to find natives associated the miraculous powers of blackness with male deities rather than female. Hence, to conform to popular belief and win over the indigenous population, a black Madonna was lightened rather than a Caucasian Madonna darkened. Despite this history, Our Lady of Guadalupe, known affectionately as *la Morenita* (little brown one), has been adopted as an emblem of cultural and religious affiliation and as a symbol of Hispanic pride, for her perceived mixed-race skin tone. Her strong devotion among Americans in the twenty-first century is testimony to the enduring influence of the Madonna as a cultural and religious figure.

See also: **Images of Childhood; Madonna, Orthodox; Madonna, Secular.**

BIBLIOGRAPHY

Ashley, Kathleen, and Pamela Sheingorn. 1990. *Interpreting Cultural Symbols: Saint Anne in Late Medieval Society.* Athens: University of Georgia Press.

Atkinson, Clarissa W. 1991. *The Oldest Vocation: Christian Motherhood in the Middle Ages.* Ithaca, NY: Cornell University Press.

Bailey, Gauvin A. 1999. *Art on the Jesuit Missions in Asia and Latin America 1542–1773.* Toronto: University of Toronto Press.

Belting, Hans. 1994. *Likeness and Presence: A History of the Image before the Era of Art,* trans. Edmund Jephcott. Chicago: University of Chicago Press.

Bossard, Alphonse, et al. 1985. *Dictionary of Mary.* New York: Catholic Book Publishing.

Boyer, Marie-France. 2000. *The Cult of the Virgin: Offerings, Ornaments, and Festivals.* New York: Norton.

Brown, Raymond E., Karl P. Donfried, Joseph A. Fitzmyer et al., eds. 1978. *Mary in the New Testament.* Philadelphia: Fortress Press.

Bynum, Caroline Walker. 1991. *Fragmentation and Redemption: Essays on Gender and the Human Body in Medieval Religion.* New York: Zone Books.

Carroll, Michael P. 1986. *The Cult of the Virgin Mary: Psychological Origins.* Princeton, NJ: Princeton University Press.

Cunneen, Sally. 1996. *In Search of Mary: The Woman and the Symbol.* New York: Ballantine Books.

Durham, Michael S. 1995. *Miracles of Mary: Apparitions, Legends, and Miraculous Works of the Blessed Virgin Mary.* San Francisco, CA: HarperSanFrancisco.

Gold, Penny Schine. 1985. *The Lady and the Virgin: Image, Attitude, and Experience in Twelfth-Century France.* Chicago: University of Chicago Press.

Grabar, André. 1968. *Christian Iconography: A Study of Its Origins.* Princeton, NJ: Princeton University Press.

Graef, Hilda. 1963–1965. *Mary: A History of Doctrine and Devotion,* 2 vols. New York: Sheed and Ward.

Heldman, Marilyn E., ed. 1993. *African Zion: The Sacred Art of Ethiopia.* New Haven, CT: Yale University Press.

Jacobus de Voragine. 1993. *The Golden Legend: Readings on the Saints,* trans. William Granger Ryan. Princeton, NJ: Princeton University Press.

Jameson, Mrs. (Anna). 1852. *Legends of the Madonna as Represented in the Fine Arts.* London: Longman, Brown, Green, and Longmans.

Katz, Melissa R., ed. 2001. *Divine Mirrors: The Virgin Mary in the Visual Arts.* New York: Oxford University Press.

Levi D'Ancona, Mirella. 1957. *The Iconography of the Immaculate Conception in the Middle Ages and Early Renaissance.* New York: College Art Association of America/Art Bulletin.

MacGregor, Neil, with Erika Langmuir. 2000. *Seeing Salvation: Images of Christ in Art.* New Haven, CT: Yale University Press.

Miles, Margaret R. 1985. *Image as Insight: Visual Understanding in Western Christianity and Secular Culture.* Boston: Beacon Press.

Os, Henk van, et al. 1994. *The Art of Devotion in the Late Middle Ages in Europe, 1300–1500.* Princeton, NJ: Princeton University Press.

Ousterhout, Robert, and Leslie Brubaker, eds. 1995. *The Sacred Image East and West.* Urbana: University of Illinois Press.

Pelikan, Jaroslav. 1996. *Mary Through the Centuries: Her Place in the History of Culture.* New Haven, CT: Yale University Press.

Peterson, Jeanette Favrot. 1992. "The Virgin of Guadalupe: Symbol of Conquest or Liberation?" *Art Journal* 51, no. 4 (winter): 39–47.

Réau, Louis. 1957. *Iconographie de l'Art Chrétien.* Paris: Presses Universitaires de France.

Russell, H. Diane. 1990. *Eva/Ave: Woman in Renaissance and Baroque Prints.* Washington, DC: National Gallery of Art.

Schiller, Gertrud. 1971. *Iconography of Christian Art,* trans. Janet Seligman. Greenwich, CT: New York Graphic Society.

Steinberg, Leo. 1983. *The Sexuality of Christ in Renaissance Art and in Modern Oblivion.* New York: Pantheon.

Stratton, Suzanne L. 1994. *The Immaculate Conception in Spanish Art.* New York: Cambridge University Press.

Trens, Manuel. 1947. *María, iconografía de la Virgen en el arte español.* Madrid: Editorial Plus Ultra.

Warner, Marina. 1976. *Alone of All Her Sex: The Myth and Cult of the Virgin Mary.* London: Weidenfeld and Nicolson.

MELISSA R. KATZ

Madonna, Secular

For centuries, the Virgin Mary has been the most visible woman in history. She has been the subject of countless works of art, music, literature, and theology, and many great architectural monuments have been erected in her name. In

Adoration (c. 1897), Gertrude Käsebier. Käsebier was one of a number of artists at the turn of the twentieth century who produced romanticized images of mothers and children. *Adoration* draws upon a long tradition of Madonna and Child imagery but lacks any overt religious symbolism, in accordance with the preferences of an increasingly secular American audience. Courtesy George Eastman House.

poetry, sermons, and musical compositions. The predominant representation of Mary as a nurturing parent has helped to foster a collective identification of womanhood with motherhood.

Conversely, societal dependence on women for reproduction of the species has encouraged people to view the Madonna primarily through her biological role as mother rather than her theologically valid status as virgin. Cloistered nuns identified not only with Mary's virginity, but also with her motherhood—defining themselves as spiritual mothers sharing in the care and rearing of the Christ child. The destiny of women not bound for convents was marriage, the purpose of which, as understood by church and society, was to produce children. The production of children—whether to work in the fields, perform trades, inherit wealth, or nurse aging parents—was essential to society's well-being, and it was in this realm that women's contributions were perceived.

Childless women were considered cursed, and infertility was grounds for divorce. Barren women prayed to the Madonna to help them conceive, just as pregnant women asked her for a safe delivery, and mothers for the continued health of a child. Mary's gentle, forgiving persona made her more approachable and less intimidating to both sexes, but her maternal experience forged an especial bond with women, who could draw upon their experiences of pregnancy, birth, and nurturing to deepen their spiritual empathy with the Virgin Mary.

Depictions of the Madonna as a gentle, caring mother gave comfort and a sense of purpose to women who were fulfilling their Christian and civic duty through motherhood. Madonna and Child imagery also reinforced patriarchal values that confined women to the domestic sphere, projecting a model of appropriate female behavior that was as much social as religious. This interweaving of religious and secular spheres gave rise to the expression Secular Madonna to indicate a strong projection of values and expectations onto ordinary women, based on the selfless love of the Virgin Mary.

The Angel of the House

In reality, the Secular Madonna was based less on the Biblical figure of Mary than on male fantasies of female submission. The characteristics of the Secular Madonna included ceaseless sacrifice for the welfare of others, ungrudging service to the needs of all around her, self-denial to the point of erasure, constant devotion to home and family, and a docile, uncomplaining disposition. This indulged the child's natural narcissism and desire to be the center of the mother's existence, if not the entire home's. Needless to say, the true Secular Madonna hardly existed outside of FAIRY TALES, fiction, and artworks, but that did not stop her impact from being felt by flesh-and-blood women. Though present from the time of Patient Griselda—the submissive victim of spousal abuse in Boccaccio's *Decameron* and Chaucer's "Clerk's Tale" in the *Canterbury Tales*—the Secular Madonna

our own century, she remains the woman whose face has appeared most frequently on the cover of *Time* magazine, an ambiguous comment on women's achievement, recognition, and historical visibility. As both a religious and cultural figure, she represents an ideal paradigm, one whose characteristics have been defined largely by men to be practiced by women. Mary's chastity, modesty, humility, and obedience have been held up as a model to Christian and non-Christian women alike, yet the aspect that most distinguishes her—perpetual virginity before, during, and after giving birth—renders it impossible for any living woman to meet this standard of perfection.

Biology as Destiny

Perhaps nowhere has Mary's influence on secular culture been greater than in defining the mother-child relationship. This is due no doubt to the extensive depiction of the image known familiarly as Madonna and Child in Christian art, where Mary is portrayed as a lovely and loving young mother to the infant Jesus. While primarily a visual image circulated in paintings, sculpture, and printed form, the theme of Madonna and Child has been the subject of religious dramas,

The North-West Passage (1874), by John Everett Millais exemplifies the image of the Secular Madonna as an ideal of female submission. The young woman at the feet of her much-older husband is a picture of uncomplaining devotion, willing to follow wherever he might lead her. The Art Archive/Tate Gallery London/Eileen Tweedy.

reached her zenith of cultural influence in the nineteenth century, when she was bolstered by the idealism of the Romantic movement and the earnestness of the Victorian era. Her children were sentimentalized as innocent creatures whose moral and civic development rested on their mother's guidance, and whose defects and deviations stemmed from faulty parenting.

Visual and literary portraits of female goodness as based in maternal solicitude and sacrifice furthered transmission of Western cultural messages. From innocent peasants to long-suffering maidens to angelic wives, artists portrayed women as paragons of virtue, more ethereal than earthly. Nor was the fantasy restricted to male artists; the Victorian photographer Julia Margaret Cameron produced dozens of images of models representing the Virgin Mary and portraits of women exemplifying her ideal of universal goodness and maternal devotion. Though little-known today, Coventry Pat-

more's immensely popular and influential poem *The Angel of the House* glorified the status of wife and mother. Published in installments from 1854 to 1863, it followed the progress of the wedded bliss of its heroine, Honoria, based on Patmore's first wife Emily Andrews, who bore six children and died young in 1862.

Equally telling were the fates assigned to women who failed to embody the attributes of the Secular Madonna. Any sign of carnality was treated as a harbinger of evil, with punishment befalling both the woman and her child, either socially, through poverty and ostracism, or symbolically, through illness or deformity. Works about seduced maidens such as Thomas Hardy's *Tess of the d'Urbervilles* (1891), in which Tess's illegitimate baby dies, and Augustus Egg's *Past and Present* (1858), a triptych depicting an unfaithful wife who ends up a homeless suicide, portrayed the dire consequences for women who strayed from the path of perfection.

Not surprisingly, a double-standard operated for male phi-landerers, with no similar restrictions placed on their behavior nor such stern repercussions.

Then, as now, standards for women were set so high as to engender levels of stress that affected sensitive children, or frustrations that led to suppressed resentment or outright rejection of the children themselves. Just as the Virgin Mary's miraculous purity, freedom from sin and sex, and perpetual virginity make it impossible for any living woman to match her ideal, so today's generation of women—told by the media that fulfillment lies in balancing marriage, child rearing, community involvement, and a successful career, all while retaining a desirable weight—are doomed from the start to fall short of their goals.

The New World Madonna

Less virulent than the British form though no less sentimental, the American concept of the Secular Madonna was no less effective in shaping global attitudes toward women, regardless of ethnicity or religious affiliation. This variant was rooted in the image of mother and child, often to the exclusion of the father, as attested to by the works of MARY CASSATT, whose success as an artist was due largely to her talented treatment of suitable female subjects. Men were restricted to the role of family provider, their nurturing instincts eclipsed by the mother's, and regarded as suspect. (The stern father was a remnant of pre-Enlightenment notions of PARENTING, when child rearing centered on DISCIPLINE and correction.)

Coinciding with the era of European colonization of Asia, Africa, and the Americas, the notion of the Secular Madonna spread worldwide and became a social force whose influence was felt independently of race, religion, or nationality. Immigrants to the New World assimilated sex roles as well as social mores, while missionaries encouraged non-Western societies to adopt Western conventions of gender as well as creed. Rarely was the influence mutual. Traditional African societies regarded motherhood as a domestic duty that benefited the entire community, valuing women's contributions more than Western societies. In Asian gerontocracies, mothers were expected to sacrifice their welfare for their children's, and adult children to fulfill responsibilities for their parents. Western values rejected such a quid pro quo—maternal sacrifice was an end in itself, unrewarded by filial obligations.

Scenes of idyllic childhood are found in the works of American women artists such as photographer Gertrude Käsebier, illustrator BESSIE PEASE GUTMANN, and author Laura Ingalls Wilder. Children, too, were romanticized as angelic creatures, innocent, sweet-smelling, and as bound to their mother as she was to them. Despite their lack of haloes, a spiritual bond was believed to exist between mothers and offspring, much as Mary's relation to Jesus had transcended the limits of biology. Indeed, in a period of animosity toward Catholics—who primarily made up the lower-class immigrant population of the mid-nineteenth century—the lack of haloes and other ostentatious symbols of religion made such images more palatable to a primarily Protestant middle-class audience in a proudly secular nation.

The broad appeal of Madonna imagery detached from overt signs of religion has fostered its endurance to the present day, often in subtle ways that go unrecognized by mainstream audiences. Its firm adoption by the media, particularly as a marketing strategy, furthers the message not only that women are primarily mothers and caregivers but also that their physical, emotional, and psychological well-being is expressed through family nurturing. From commercials that encourage guilt on the part of mothers who fail to give enough (of themselves, as well as of the product in question) to television programs and films that feature gender stereotypes only superficially modernized for the new millennium (both benign, as in *The Simpsons* cartoon series, and insidious, as in the film *Fatal Attraction*), we are saturated with expectations of female behavior derived from a 2,000-year-old Jewish maiden named Mary.

This generational transmission, however secularized, is due in part to the intrinsic role played by children in defining the Secular Madonna, perpetuating the fantasy of a perfect (and perfectly) loving mother. As long as children are encouraged to see themselves as central to the mother's existence, and mothers are conditioned to place family needs above their own, future generations will continue to accept the notion of a woman's natural inclination to selfless love. Both mothers and offspring are complicit in the acceptance and perpetuation of the myth of the Secular Madonna, with its uneasy mix of historical desires, biological roles, psychological needs, and deeply rooted cultural expectations for both men and women.

See also: **Gendering; Madonna, Orthodox; Madonna, Religious; Mothering and Motherhood; Victorian Art.**

BIBLIOGRAPHY

Atkinson, Clarissa W. 1991. *The Oldest Vocation: Christian Motherhood in the Middle Ages.* Ithaca, NY: Cornell University Press.

Carroll, Michael P. 1989. *Catholic Cults and Devotions: A Psychological Inquiry.* Kingston, ON and Montréal, QB: McGill-Queen's University Press.

Cunneen, Sally. 1996. *In Search of Mary: The Woman and the Symbol.* New York: Ballantine Books.

Katz, Melissa R., ed. 2001. *Divine Mirrors: The Virgin Mary in the Visual Arts.* New York: Oxford University Press.

Maeckelberghe, Els. 1994. *Desperately Seeking Mary: A Feminist Appropriation of a Traditional Religious Symbol.* The Hague, Netherlands: Pharos.

Marsh, Jan. 1987. *Pre-Raphaelite Women: Images of Femininity.* New York: Harmony Books.

Miles, Margaret R. 1989. *Carnal Knowing: Female Nakedness and Religious Meaning in the Christian West.* Boston: Beacon Press.

Musacchio, Jacqueline Marie. 1999. *The Art and Ritual of Childbirth in Renaissance Italy.* New Haven, CT: Yale University Press.

Parsons, John Carmi, and Bonnie Wheeler, eds. 1996. *Medieval Mothering*. New York: Garland Publishing.

Pelikan, Jaroslav. 1996. *Mary Through the Centuries: Her Place in the History of Culture*. New Haven, CT: Yale University Press.

Thurer, Shari L. 1994. *The Myths of Motherhood: How Culture Reinvents the Good Mother*. Boston: Houghton Mifflin.

Warner, Marina. 1976. *Alone of All Her Sex: The Myth and Cult of the Virgin Mary*. London: Weidenfeld and Nicolson.

Yalom, Marilyn. 2001. *A History of the Wife*. New York: HarperCollins.

MELISSA R. KATZ

Magnet Schools

Magnet schools, sometimes referred to as alternative schools or schools of choice, are public schools that provide an alternative to mandatory school assignment and busing by offering parents a choice among several school options with specialized curricular themes or instructional methods. The term *magnet* gained popularity in the 1970s when policy makers were designing desegregation plans in an effort to make them more attractive to parents, educators, and students. Magnet schools were established to promote racial diversity, improve scholastic standards, and provide a range of programs to satisfy individual talents and interests.

Since 1976, when federal courts accepted magnet schools as a method of desegregation (*Morgan v. Kerrigan*), their number has increased dramatically. By the 1991–1992 school year, Corrine Yu and William Taylor found that more than 1.2 million students were enrolled in magnet schools in 230 school districts. During the 1999–2000 school year there were more than 1,372 magnet schools across the United States. In some states, such as Illinois, a National Center for Educational Statistics (NCES) study found that 12 percent of all students attend magnet schools.

Magnet schools are typically established in urban school districts with large student enrollments (over ten thousand). According to the U.S. Department of Education, 53 percent of large urban school districts include magnet school programs as part of their desegregation plans, as compared to only 10 percent of suburban districts. For example, NCES reports that in the City of Chicago Public School District, 45 percent of all public schools are magnets, serving 48 percent of the student body. Over half of all magnet programs are located in low socioeconomic districts. Although they can involve all grade levels, Yu and Taylor and Roger Levine found that more than half of the nation's magnet programs serve elementary school students, and only 20 percent of magnets serve the high school level. The most common type of magnet school is one that emphasizes a particular subject area, such as math and science, computers and technology, or a foreign language. Other programs offer a unique instructional approach, such as Montessori or Paideia.

Magnet school programs are popular, as measured by the fact that over 75 percent of all districts with magnets have a greater demand for student slots than they can fill; Rolf Blank, Roger Levine, and Lauri Steel found that half of these districts maintain long waiting lists. With this level of demand, most districts manage the admissions process using a lottery format. Others rely upon a first-come, first-served arrangement. Only about one-third of all magnet programs use a selective admissions policy; these usually involve either a minimum test score requirement or in a performing arts magnet, performance in an audition.

In many instances, districts have supported magnet schools with a considerable investment of resources. On average, expenditures per student are 10 percent higher in districts with magnets; almost three-fourths of magnet programs have additional staffing allowances as well. Some magnet programs are funded through state desegregation funds. Most are funded under three-year grants through the federal Magnet Schools Assistance Program (MSAP), which began awarding grants in 1985. These funds are made available to districts that are either implementing magnet programs voluntarily or that are acting on court-ordered desegregation. The MSAP plays a critical role in magnet school creation and expansion efforts nationwide. Currently, the program provides about $100 million each year to support magnet school programs; between 1985 and 1998, some 379 MSAP grants ($750 million) were awarded to 171 school districts in 35 states and the District of Columbia, according to Phyllis DuBois and her colleagues. In December 2001, the U.S. Department of Education awarded $37.2 million in MSAP grants to 24 school districts.

Magnet Schools and School Improvement

Research results are mixed as to the effectiveness of magnet schools. Adam Gamoran's 1996 study on student achievement compared students in magnet schools with those in Catholic schools, nonreligious private schools, and public comprehensive schools and found some advantages for magnet school students in achievement in reading and history. Similarly, Robert Crain found that career magnet schools in New York City helped raise students' reading scores. Other researchers, including Patricia Bauch, Ellen Goldring, and Claire Smrekar, have found that magnet schools provide more opportunities for parental involvement and effective communication between home and schools. In fact, studies by Mary Driscoll and Valerie Martinez, Kenneth Godwin, and Frank Kemerer have shown that parents who exercise choice report higher levels of satisfaction with their schools than do those who don't choose their children's schools. Mary Haywood Metz's studies of specific magnet schools indicate they tend be more innovative in terms of distinctive curricula and unique student–teacher relationships. However, larger-scale studies using national data contradict these findings. According to Lauren Sosniak and Carolyn Ethington's 1992 study, magnet and nonmagnet schools use similar curricula and modes of instruction. Smrekar and Goldring found that magnet schools do seem to afford teachers more autonomy and involvement in decision making, as choice advocates predict.

Magnet Schools and Racial Balance

Several large urban school districts in the nation stand at the crossroads of sweeping changes in the use of magnet schools as tools for racial desegregation. In a series of major rulings in 1999 (*Capacchione v. Charlotte-Mecklenburg Board of Education, Eisenberg v. Montgomery County Public Schools, Tuttle v. Arlington County School Board, Wessman v. Gittens*), federal courts repudiated school district efforts to maintain race-conscious admission policies in order to promote and ensure racial diversity through magnet schools. Under the precedent established in a 1995 Supreme Court ruling (in *Adarand v. Pena*, a case that involved a federal program that awarded a percentage of construction contracts to minority owned construction companies), race conscious programs that involve promoting diversity through strategies construed to involve "racial balancing" are constitutionally suspect and are subject to "strict scrutiny."

This elevated constitutional bar includes a two-pronged test that compels districts to prove that their racial classification scheme "furthers a compelling state interest" and is "narrowly tailored" (*Adarand v. Pena*). Consequently, unless school districts are currently under court order to remedy the effects of past racial discrimination in their systems, magnet school admissions policies must be race neutral. This standard of racial neutrality applies to school districts declared "unitary," where a federal court has ruled that a district has complied in good faith with desegregation decrees to eliminate dual school systems that discriminate between children on the basis of race. In order to gain a grant of "unitary status," districts must provide proof that they have acted "in good faith" to eliminate the vestiges of past racial discrimination in public education programs. More and more large urban school districts, including Dade County in Florida, are seeking and securing unitary status in federal court.

See also: **Charter Schools; Homeschooling; Private and Independent Schools; School Choice; School Desegregation; School Vouchers.**

BIBLIOGRAPHY

Bauch, Patricia, and Ellen Goldring. 1998. "Parent–Teacher Participation in the Context of School Restructuring." *Peabody Journal of Education* 73: 15–35.

Blank, Rolf, Roger Levine, and Lauri Steel. 1996. "After Fifteen Years: Magnet Schools in Urban Education." In *Who Chooses? Who Loses? Culture, Institutions, and the Unequal Effects of School Choice*, ed. Bruce Fuller, Richard F. Elmore, and Gary Orfield. New York: Teachers College Press.

Crain, Robert L. 1992. *The Effectiveness of New York City's Career Magnet Schools: An Evaluation of Ninth Grade Performance Using an Experimental Design.* Berkeley, CA: National Center for Research in Vocational Education.

Driscoll, Mary E. 1992. "Changing Minds and Changing Hearts: Choice, Achievement, and School Community." In *Choice: What Role in American Education?* Symposium conducted by the Economic Policy Institute, Washington, DC.

DuBois, Phyllis, Bruce Christenson, Marian Eaton, and Michael Garet. 2001. *Evaluation of the Magnet Schools Assistance Program, 1998 Grantees: Year 1 Interim Report.* Washington, DC: U.S. Department of Education.

Eaton, Susan, and Elizabeth Crutcher. 1996. "Magnets, Media, and Mirages." In *Dismantling Desegregation: The Quiet Reversal of Brown v. Board of Education*, ed. Gary Orfield and Susan Eaton. New York: New Press.

Gamoran, Adam. 1996. "Student Achievement in Public Magnet, Public Comprehensive, and Private City High Schools." *Educational Evaluation and Policy Analysis* 18: 1–18.

Levine, Roger. 1997. "Research on Magnet Schools and the Context of School Choice." Paper presented at the Citizens' Commission on Civil Rights Issues Forum: Magnet Schools and the Context of School Choice: Implications for Public Policy, April, Washington DC.

Martinez,Valerie, Kenneth Godwin, and Frank Kemerer. 1996. "Public School Choice in San Antonio: Who Chooses and with What Effects?" In *Who Chooses? Who Loses? Culture, Institutions and the Unequal Effects of School Choice*, ed. Bruce Fuller, Richard F. Elmore, and Gary Orfield. New York: Teachers College Press.

Metz, Mary Haywood. 1986. *Different by Design: The Context and Character of Three Magnet Schools.* Boston: Routledge and Kegan Paul.

Orfield, Gary. 2001. *Schools More Separate: Consequences of a Decade of Resegregation.* Cambridge, MA: The Civil Rights Project, Harvard University.

Smrekar, Claire, and Ellen Goldring. 1999. *School Choice in Urban America: Magnet Schools and the Pursuit of Equity.* New York: Teachers College Press.

Sosniak, Lauren and Carolyn Ethington. 1992. "When Public School 'Choice' Is Not Academic: Findings from the National Education Longitudinal Study of 1988." *Educational Evaluation and Policy Analysis* 14, 35–52.

Steel, Lauri, and Marian Eaton. 1996. *Reducing, Eliminating, and Preventing Minority Isolation in American Schools: The Impact of the Magnet Schools Assistance Program.* Report prepared for the Office of the Undersecretary, U.S. Department of Education, Washington, DC.

Steel, Lauri, and Roger Levine. 1994. *Educational Innovation in Multiracial Contexts: The Growth of Magnet Schools in American Education.* Palo Alto, CA: American Institutes for Research.

Yu, Corrine M., and William L. Taylor. 1997. *Difficult Choices: Do Magnet Schools Serve Children in Need?* Washington, DC: Citizens' Commission on Civil Rights.

INTERNET RESOURCE

National Center for Education Statistics. 2001. *NCES Statistical Analysis Report.* Available from <www.nces.ed.gov/pubs2001/overview.>

CLAIRE E. SMREKAR

Manners

There has not been a great deal of scholarship on manners and childhood (historians of manners have focused more on

The girl in Mary Cassatt's *Young Girl in a Blue Armchair* (1878) sprawls in a chair with legs apart and petticoats displayed, not the model of proper deportment for a nineteenth-century young lady—something that may have contributed to the picture's rejection at the 1878 Universal Exposition in Paris. Mellon Coll., Nat. Gallery of Art, Washington, DC, USA/Bridgeman Art Library.

class and gender relations), but a historical trajectory can nevertheless be traced in the numerous discussions of proper conduct that have circulated in the West since the Middle Ages. The path has been mostly continuous, despite each generation's sense that manners have changed—usually for the worse—for the succeeding generation. This continuity reflects basic biological and developmental constraints on the construction of childhood. It also upholds historians' recent revision of the notion advanced in the 1960s and 1970s that views of childhood have changed dramatically over time, from medieval and early modern "miniature adults," for example, to Victorian innocents. While changes in the larger society and culture have affected PARENTING styles and rules for youth, expectations for proper behavior in children have changed little. The stability of manners for children reminds us of the stubborn reality of their physical and mental immaturity. Children are not born with proper behavior; they need to be taught the rules. Above all, they need to be taught self-control. And children's physical and intellectual weakness relative to adults has led to continuous demands that

they defer to their elders. Thus, although the story of manners and inequality has changed along with the larger social order, the social inferiority of children has a long history. There appears to have been only one exceptional period: that of the post–World War II baby boom. But this exception only proves the rule, as recent decades show a reversion to tradition.

While this entry focuses on the history of manners for children as manifested in America, many of the patterns are more general. Indeed, differences in manners between America and western European societies are often overstated. Whether acknowledged or not (and in some periods Americans actively denied it), Americans have looked to tutelage from Europe for most of their history. Continuity and the pan-Western applicability of manners for children are seen first in one of the earliest manners books for children printed in America, Eleazar Moody's *The School of Good Manners*. While compiled by Moody, a Boston schoolmaster, in 1715, much of this work was adapted from a 1595 English version of a French courtesy work of the 1560s. There were at least five other English editions in the seventeenth century before Moody's American adaptation. And Moody's work was published over and over again—in at least thirty-four editions between 1715 and 1846. The book also appeared under other titles.

The Seventeenth Century to the Civil War

The many different editions of this work give us a sense of the prevailing rules for proper behavior in children from the seventeenth through the mid-nineteenth centuries. Above all, they were to defer to their elders, especially their parents. They were to show their reverence in various ways, such as bowing whenever they encountered adults and refraining from interrupting them. They needed to master their bodies by standing up straight, avoiding any fidgeting, and restraining their tongues. Moody and his imitators spent a good many words instructing children in table manners. Among other things, they advised children to come to table with their hands and face washed and their hair combed. They were to wait for all to be seated before sitting themselves. They were not to express any likes or dislikes concerning the food. They were to wait for others to begin eating, and then eat slowly and carefully. They were to sit up straight, and keep their elbows off the table.

The continuity in manners for children indicated by the persistence of these rules conflicts with the notion that the eighteenth century saw great change in the status of children. The ideas of JOHN LOCKE and JEAN-JACQUES ROUSSEAU are supposed to have revolutionized parent–child relations. These ENLIGHTENMENT ideas did change the advice given to parents on how to behave with children. Parents were urged to be a bit more loving in their demeanor than they had been in the past. This change was subtle, for discussions of proper parental behavior in seventeenth-century America (mostly from the pens of New England Puritans) had not been starkly authoritarian. Still, this evolution in proper parental behavior may have modified the tenor of children's relations with adults. More important in changing the context for children was the liberation of youth from their formerly shared inferior status. Lumped together with children in the seventeenth century, from the mid-eighteenth century on youth were increasingly asked to behave like adults. This development yielded tangible results for children in the nineteenth century. Antebellum conduct works described a middle-class world of adults in which youth were accepted on equal footing, but from which children were banished. While youth were given the same advice as adults on how to make and receive parlor visits, for example, children were best left at home. Parents were even discouraged from allowing their children to make an appearance when they entertained. With middle-class housing growing increasingly substantial and differentiated in the nineteenth century, instructions to keep the children's nursery or playroom "back stage" became explicit. To be sure, nineteenth-century art and literature often portrayed middle-class children as angelic innocents. But these portrayals do not appear in manners advice, unless one interprets children's banishment from society as a means of protecting their innocence.

The Post–Civil War Era

While children were not taught how to behave in adult society, they still needed to learn the old rules in order to keep their place, whether at home or at school. The fact that Moody was a schoolmaster is reflective of another important continuity in the history of manners for children: from the seventeenth century to the present, parental admonition has been thought to require reinforcement in the classroom. Early nineteenth-century schoolbooks included chapters on manners and politeness, often copied from Moody's compilation. These were surely more influential in the northern states, where common schooling was more widespread. But their influence spread along with both settlement and schooling to the West. In the post–Civil War era, some new states actually passed laws providing for the instruction of manners in schools. And a 1911 survey of public schools suggested that the majority were teaching manners. In more recent decades, a whole industry has sprung up providing audiovisual materials for the teaching of etiquette in schools. To be sure, the context for this instruction changes. In the late nineteenth and early twentieth centuries, the perceived need for manners in the curriculum was undoubtedly a by-product of fears generated by the cresting tide of European immigration. In the early twenty-first century we are more likely to look to schools to carry out business left unfinished by harried single parents or two-career couples. The changing social and cultural context makes the need seem urgent and new, but the reality is that Americans have always looked to schools to help teach children manners.

The post–Civil War era did see some significant changes in American manners. Antebellum authors had pretended to be departing from European ways in prescribing a code of behavior more fitting for a republic, although in fact there were few differences in the rules they gave from those prevailing in Great Britain, whether for children or adults. After the Civil War, the authors stopped attempting to appear so democratic, and indeed, as befitted this rapidly industrializing society with its growth of inequality, they grew unabashed in their pursuit of European or "aristocratic" ways. New etiquette writers inscribed these changes in new works. But they did not write new advice for children. While Moody's work was not reprinted after mid-century, continuity is reflected in the incredible longevity of a contemporaneous work, *Youth's Behavior*, better known as "George Washington's Rules of Civility." As a youth, Washington had copied out one hundred and ten maxims from this book, which, like Moody's, was a seventeenth-century English version of a late-sixteenth-century French work. While it did not have as great a circulation as Moody in the eighteenth and early nineteenth centuries, it had even greater staying power. *Youth's Behavior* differed from Moody in important ways, but offered similar advice on deference to superiors, control of the body (especially speech), and proper behavior at table. These rules continued to be cited well into the twentieth century. Samuel Goodrich, author of the popular Peter Parley series, quoted extracts in his 1844 work *What to Do and How to Do It.* Sarah Josepha Hale quoted nearly thirty of the precepts in *Happy Homes and Good Society* (1867). Amy Vanderbilt recommended them as late as 1952.

The Early Twentieth Century

There were many new works for children published in the twentieth century, but these, too, display a remarkable continuity of expectations. Gelett Burgess revived an old practice of setting rules to rhyme in his popular *Goops and How to Be Them* (1900). Burgess began with table manners, and gave all the ancient injunctions about not talking while eating or eating too fast. He reiterated the old advice to respect elders, joking "When you're old, and get to be, Thirty-four or forty-three; Don't you hope that you will see, Children all respect you?" Gelett's work is stamped with a certain late-Victorian fastidiousness. It devoted separate pages to the need for cleanliness, neatness, tidiness, orderliness, and punctuality. It begged children to refrain from "Disfiguration" (drawing on fences and walls), and playing in Sunday clothes. This combination of traditional rules with a new push for cleanliness and order persisted in the 1920s. It is seen in Margaret Bailey's *The Value of Good Manners* (1922), where she named cleanliness and tidiness as the first requirements for well-mannered children. And she held out for deference to elders, disagreeing with those who would suggest that it was passé. She thus gave rules that are found in Moody: when adults entered the room, for example, children were to rise and offer their seats.

Even authors who thought they were coming up with something new were actually giving old advice. Lillian Eichler (1924) and Margery Wilson (1937) both claimed to be offering "the new etiquette," but their advice was strikingly traditional. Eichler stated, "The new etiquette does not attempt to stifle the child's personality. But it does attempt to stifle the bad habits . . . [of] rudeness, disobedience, untidiness, bad table manners, and lack of courtesy" to parents and elders. While her pleas that children should not be repressed sounded new, her specific injunctions for children were old. As had authors before her, she stressed the importance of table manners, and gave the same basic instructions to "eat slowly and carefully, and keep the mouth shut while chewing." The nineteenth-century banishment of children from adult social life persisted as well, with her claim that children should not be included in formal dinners. Moody could have penned her advice for informal dinners, where she claimed that children "must not seat themselves until all the elders have been seated. They must come to the table with hands and nails scrupulously clean, hair brushed, clothes neat. They must not show greediness at table, dis-

pleasure because of some dish they do not like, or delight because of some dish of which they are particularly fond. They must not begin to eat before the others or leave the table before the elders have finished dining." Margery Wilson gave the same advice, and added precepts on correct speaking and greeting of adult guests that also echoed Moody.

There were some new notes sounded in advice to parents in these early-twentieth-century works. More often than in the past parents were reminded that they taught manners best by setting an example for their children, and that they should respect their children's rights. But what parents were encouraged to teach their children had changed little. At the same time that books of manners kept to the old standards, however, it is likely that changes in other social areas, especially in popular culture, began to have an effect on the actual behavior of children and youth. New, less formal signals about carriage and POSTURE, dress and language, and other matters began to stream out of movies, magazines, and school peer culture by the 1920s. While these changes had a greater impact on youth, soon new child-rearing manuals would also begin to emphasize greater informality in parent–child relations.

The Postwar Period

In advice books to parents, a revolution in manners for children is first evident following World War II. After something of a hiatus during the Depression and war years of the 1930s and 1940s, etiquette works began to pour forth again in the late 1940s and 1950s. The reigning arbiter of manners in this period was Amy Vanderbilt, whose *Complete Book of Etiquette* appeared in at least ten editions between 1952 and 1970 alone. One notices a change right away in Vanderbilt's discussion of table manners. She is silent on the age-old admonition that children should be taught not to express their dislike of various foods, instead telling parents not to dictate what a child should eat. Instead of teaching children to be silent until addressed, she recommended encouraging children to converse at table, so long as they did not monopolize the conversation. Compared to the past, her expectations of children are surprisingly relaxed: if a child made a scene at the dinner table, she simply recommended gently removing him, for his own comfort, and urged parents not to expect too much of their children in terms of manners. In places Vanderbilt suggests that adults conform to children's lack of manners, as in her suggestion that because children like eating with their fingers, parents should give them plenty of opportunities to do so with snacks and picnics and in fact should join in, rather than give lectures on manners. Vanderbilt assured parents that manners could not be taught through "constant nagging," but rather children would naturally want to know how to behave properly. She suggested, moreover, that there would be something wrong with a child who was perfectly behaved. Some experts have dubbed this new approach an "informality" of manners.

Where did this change come from? Many observers of postwar child rearing have pointed to an author who was even more ubiquitous than Amy Vanderbilt: DR. SPOCK. In addition to numerous English editions between 1945 and 1960 (and at least six editions since), his *Baby and Child Care* was published in twenty-four languages, including Croatian, Tamil, Armenian, and Urdu. While not as starkly child-centered as Vanderbilt, Spock's suggestions were similar. One of his brief sections on manners, for example, bore the reassuring header "Good Manners Come Naturally." He maintained that if parents were considerate of each other, their children would simply "absorb" good manners. He did think parents needed to do some actual teaching of manners, but rather than the old emphasis on the necessity of showing respect for elders, he claimed parents needed to teach manners because they owed it to their children to make them likeable by others. In all, however, he recommended a relaxed stance, regarding what formerly would have been seen as unacceptable behavior as a phase of development. He described how six to eleven year olds typically displayed bad manners—in their speech, at table, and in their comportment. But rather than advising parents to combat this development, he lauded it as an essential part of growing up. He assured parents that good manners would soon resurface on their own.

By the end of the baby boom, the pendulum began to swing back to tradition. This is evident in *Eleanor Roosevelt's Common Sense Book of Etiquette* (1962). Like other twentieth-century writers, she urged parents to respect their children's individuality and to show them courteous behavior, but she was equally emphatic that parents had an obvious duty to teach their children manners. While parental example was the most effective, kind instruction would also be necessary. Roosevelt's advice in specific situations was likewise a mix of postwar relaxation and a revival of older patterns. She opined, for example, that children should be encouraged to speak freely and have their dislikes respected at table, but maintained that children should show respect for their elders and learn table manners. Echoing Moody, she claimed that children should rise when elders entered the room and not sit down until the adults were seated. They were never to come to table without clean hands and face and combed hair.

After the Baby Boom

Roosevelt's ideas gave a glimpse of things to come when books addressing manners for children began to pour from the presses in the 1980s. But the immediate impact of the postwar relaxation in the teaching of manners to children was a marked hiatus in the production of instructions as the BABY BOOM GENERATION came of age. Their parents had been advised not to worry too much about manners, so the rising generation was without much lore to pass on. Very few works addressing manners for children appeared in the decade from the late 1960s through the 1970s. Virtually the only manners for children materials produced in this decade

were some film strips for use in schools and a couple of episodes of a television show for children, *Mr. Roger's Neighborhood*. The dearth of books discussing manners for children in the late 1960s and early 1970s is not surprising given the cultural revolution taking place in the West at that time with the feminist and youth movements. But a long-term view shows two things. First, the anti-manners sixties and seventies were produced by child-rearing trends in the postwar decades, and second, the experiment could not last. As the boomers became parents and confronted their own uncivilized progeny, they began to look for help.

Manners writers in the 1980s and 1990s reflect the perplexities of their readers in their tone and format. Two of the most popular writers, Judith Martin (a.k.a. Miss Manners) and Mary Mitchell (a.k.a. Ms. Demeanor), both adopt the question and answer format of their newspaper columns in their books, as if to suggest that today's audience is in urgent need of answers to real and pressing etiquette problems. They both also employ humor to a degree not witnessed in earlier etiquette books. Perhaps this is to deflect the self-consciousness of anti-ritual baby boomers in their quest for social certainty. That the boomers have a serious desire to teach their children manners despite their own deficiencies is shown by the rise of a new industry of manners schools and camps. PARENTS MAGAZINE—a doctor's office staple—has also published a steady stream of articles on how to teach manners to children. Even colleges are helping parents apply the finishing touches with special "dine and act fine" etiquette-lesson dinners for prospective job applicants.

What are children taught by all these agencies of manners instruction? By and large, the traditional rules. The only new spin is a nod, for the first time, to the multicultural character of American society. This usually takes the form of repeated acknowledgements that European-American standards for behavior are not the only standards present in American society, let alone the world. But this has not led to any lesser adherence to the old standards. Thus, after a typical twentieth-century nod to the idea that parents should not expect their children to be polite if they themselves are rude, Miss Manners launches into the old admonitions. Children should be encouraged to listen to rather than talk much before adults. They should address adults formally with proper titles unless invited to do otherwise. Family dinners should be employed to teach children table manners. Children should wait until their parents begin eating, should refrain from expressing their dislikes or playing with their food, should use their utensils and napkins properly, and should not leave the table without permission.

Mary Mitchell soft-pedals on deference to elders, advising children to feel free to initiate conversation with adults, and claiming that parents deserve respect because they are human beings and parents, not because they are older. But she, too, coaches parents in traditional table manners, reminding them, among other things, to teach children to sit up straight and refrain from eating too fast or talking with their mouths full. Elizabeth James and Carol Barkin's *Social Smarts: Manners for Today's Kids* (1996) is similar to Mitchell's work in acknowledging cultural differences while dispensing traditional European-American table manners rules, but is more traditional than Mitchell on respect for elders. Busy parents at the turn of the twenty-first century can also supplement their own instruction with that of their child's favorite cartoon characters, as manners are now taught in books and videos by the Berenstain Bears, Clifford (the Big Red Dog), Winnie the Pooh, Barney, and the Muppets. And parents can rest assured that these works teach the tried and true rules for children: polite address and posture, table manners, cleanliness. While the baby boom generation is ambivalent about the need for respect for elders, life with their own children has taught them that manners do not in fact "come naturally."

See also: **Child Development, History of the Concept of; Child-Rearing Advice Literature; Hygiene; Theories of Childhood.**

BIBLIOGRAPHY

Bailey, Margaret Emerson. 1922. *The Value of Good Manners: Practical Politeness in the Daily Concerns of Life.* Garden City, NY: Doubleday, Page.

Burgess, Gelett. 1968 [1900]. *Goops and How to Be Them: A Manual of Manners for Polite Infants Inculcating Many Juvenile Virtues Both by Precept and Example.* New York: Dover.

Caldwell, Mark. 1999. *A Short History of Rudeness: Manners, Morals, and Misbehavior in Modern America.* New York: Picador.

Eichler, Lillian. 1924. *The New Book of Etiquette.* Garden City, NY: Nelson Doubleday.

Goodrich, Samuel Griswold. 1844. *What to Do and How to Do It, Or Morals and Manners Taught by Examples, by Peter Parley.* New York: Wiley and Putnam.

Hale, Sarah Josepha. 1867; rev. ed. 1889. *Happy Homes and Good Society.* Boston: Lee and Shepard.

Hawkins, Francis. 1646. *Youth's Behaviour, or, Decency in Conversation Amongst Men. French by Grave Persons for the use and Benefit of Their Youth. Now newly turned into English by Francis Hawkins.* London: W. Lee.

Hemphill, C. Dallett. 1999. *Bowing to Necessities: A History of Manners in America, 1620–1860.* New York: Oxford University Press.

James, Elizabeth, and Carol Barkin. 1996. *Social Smarts: Manners for Today's Kids.* New York: Clarion Books.

Martin, Judith. 1982. *Miss Manners' Guide to Excruciatingly Correct Behavior.* New York: Atheneum.

Martin, Judith. 1984. *Miss Manners' Guide to Rearing Perfect Children.* New York: Atheneum.

Mitchell, Mary. 1994. *Dear Ms. Demeanor: The Young Person's Etiquette Guide to Handling Any Social Situation with Confidence and Grace.* Chicago: Contemporary Books.

Moody, Eleazar. 1754 [1715]. *The School of Good Manners.* New London: Green.

Roosevelt, Eleanor. 1962. *Eleanor Roosevelt's Common Sense Book of Etiquette.* New York: Macmillan.

Schlesinger, Arthur. 1946. *Learning How to Behave: A Historical Study of American Etiquette Books.* New York: Macmillan.

Spock, Benjamin. 1945. *Baby and Child Care.* New York: Simon and Schuster.

Vanderbilt, Amy. 1952. *Amy Vanderbilt's Complete Book of Etiquette.* New York: Doubleday.

Washington, George. 1926. *Rules of Civility and Decent Behavior in Company and Conversation,* ed. Charles Moore. Boston: Houghton Mifflin.

Wilson, Margery. 1937. *The New Etiquette: The Modern Code of Social Behavior.* New York: Frederick A. Stokes.

C. DALLETT HEMPHILL

Mann, Horace (1796–1859)

A prominent statesman, Horace Mann is best remembered as a pre–Civil War educational reformer who was instrumental in the creation of the Massachusetts system of public education. A statue of Mann stands before that state's capitol today as evidence of his importance. Mann was also a successful lawyer, a member of both the Massachusetts General Court and the U.S. Congress, the president of a fledgling college, and a humanitarian reformer.

Mann was born in Franklin, Massachusetts, and he grew up in a poor and puritanical environment. He received the typical schooling of the time, consisting of brief periods in the district school under ill-equipped teachers, but he seems to have devoured the town library's collection. He was admitted to nearby Brown College in 1816 at the age of twenty (which was older than customary) as a sophomore. He graduated as valedictorian of his class and returned to the college a year later to serve several terms as a tutor. He read law intermittently with a local barrister, attended the Litchfield (Connecticut) Law School, and was admitted to the bar in 1823. Four years later, in 1827, he was elected to the lower house of the state legislature from Dedham, where he had set up his practice, commencing a thirty-year career devoted, as he put it, to the "benefit of mankind." In 1830 he married Charlotte Messer, the daughter of Asa Messer, president of Brown and Mann's early mentor. After his wife's death two years later Mann resigned his seat and moved from Dedham to Boston to continue to practice law. He was elected to the state senate in 1834 as a representative of Boston.

Although he had been born in modest circumstances, Mann became a member of the Massachusetts establishment. His second wife, whom he married in 1843, was Mary Peabody, sister of Elizabeth Peabody, an inveterate reformer. Mann had initially stood for office as a National Republican, and he later became a Whig. In the legislature his stances were those of a moralistic reformer. His maiden address was a defense of religious freedom, while his next argued that the support of railroads would lead to prosperity, which in turn would lead to the intellectual and moral betterment of the populace. He was an ardent supporter of the temperance movement, was instrumental in the establishment of the first state institution for the mentally ill, and was a moderate abolitionist. It was for his efforts on the behalf of common schools, however, that he is most remembered today.

Massachusetts had, as early as 1647, mandated the support of schooling by local communities, but by the nineteenth century the state's schools, dependent on local sources, were in a sorry state. Inspired by reports of educational reform in Europe and a growing national movement, and prodded by eminent citizens such as Edmund Dwight, James G. Carter, Josiah Quincy, Charles Brooks, and the governor, Edward Everett, the legislature passed a bill on April 20, 1837, authorizing the creation of a state board of education. Mann accepted the secretaryship a month later, vowing that from that moment to "let the next generation be my client." For the next twelve years he served that client with dedication.

The board, in actual fact, had virtually no power; its role was the collection and dissemination of information about the state of the schools. Mann lectured widely on educational topics to citizens and teachers, and he utilized his twelve annual reports to publicize and advance his cause. His first report, in 1837, served to introduce the reformist agenda, including the need for good schoolhouses, competent teachers, committed school boards, and widespread public support. His twelfth and final report, in 1848, was by far the most thoughtful, and it provided his valedictory—an anthem in support of public education. Other reports addressed issues such as language instruction, teacher training, music and health education, compulsory attendance, the necessity of school libraries (as well as free public ones), and the economic benefits of better schools. In his seventh report (1843), Mann summarized his observations of schools in Europe, lauding especially the Pestalozzian techniques he had seen demonstrated in the schools of Prussia, but the angered response of an association of Boston schoolmasters led to a lengthy and acrimonious exchange.

To Mann, good, publicly financed COMMON SCHOOLS would never succeed without an informed and concerned citizen body and without good teachers. Local authorities had to rekindle their commitment under the supervision and urging of the central government. Good teachers had to be trained in the newest pedagogical techniques that emphasized motivation and encouragement, rather than DISCIPLINE, and recognized the individuality of each child. The curriculum had to be designed for every child in the commonwealth, and it should encompass all that was necessary for the creation of upright, responsible citizens. Mann believed that schools were vested with intellectual, political, and, most importantly, moral authority—the morality of the liberal, nonsectarian, Protestant elite of the day.

In 1839 the first public normal school (for training teachers) was opened in Lexington, Massachusetts, and two others

soon followed. However, partisan politics threatened the board's existence when the democratic governor, preaching economy, advocated returning control of the schools to the localities. But the board survived, and Mann continued as its secretary until he resigned in 1848, when he was appointed to John Quincy Adams's seat in Congress. He was elected in his own right later the same year, and was re-elected as a Free Soil advocate. He served in Congress until 1852, the year in which he was defeated in the race for the governorship of Massachusetts.

Although he had given scant attention to higher education previously, Mann was intrigued, during a lecture tour through the West, at the descriptions of a projected nonsectarian, coeducational college in Ohio, and in 1853 he accepted the presidency of the not-yet-completed Antioch College in Yellow Springs. Despite near financial disaster, faculty opposition, and an innovative honor code, the college survived, and the first class of sixteen students (including three women) graduated in 1857. Mann declined offers to become the head of other institutions of higher learning and remained at Antioch until his death in August, 1859. His final address to that year's graduating class was both a challenge to them and a summary of his life: "Be ashamed to die until you have won some victory for humanity."

See also: **Compulsory School Attendance; Pestalozzi, Johann Heinrich; Urban School Systems, The Rise of.**

BIBLIOGRAPHY

Cremin, Lawrence A., ed. 1957. *The Republic and the School: Horace Mann on the Education of Free Men.* New York: Teachers College Press.

Mann, Mary Peabody. 1867. *Life of Horace Mann, By His Wife* Boston: Walker, Fuller.

Messerli, Jonathan. 1972. *Horace Mann: A Biography.* New York: Knopf.

EDITH NYE MACMULLEN

Mann, Sally (b. 1951)

Sally Mann's photographs of her three children, produced between approximately 1984 and 1996, opened up new and influential possibilities for the visual representation of childhood. Rejecting sentimentality, Mann's camera captured scenes tinged with SEXUALITY, danger, and ferocity. Mann's work first came to wide public attention in 1992 with the publication of *Immediate Family*, a book of sixty photographs of Mann's children, Emmett, Jessie, and Virginia, taken in and around the family home in rural Virginia. Some critics saw suggestions of abuse and exploitation in the pictures; others argued that Mann was revealing a more honest vision of childhood. Mann's work was frequently cited in the heated debates on CHILD PORNOGRAPHY of the 1990s, yet, unlike other photographers such as Robert Mapplethorpe, Mann was never threatened with prosecution. In fact, after the publication of *Immediate Family*, Mann was awarded a grant from the National Endowment for the Arts.

A consummate technician, Mann photographed her children with a large-format camera. Her black-and-white prints are pristine and richly tonal. While her photographs contained suggestions of spontaneity, many were carefully staged. Mann's work consciously quoted earlier, iconic photographs of children by artists such as Edward Weston, Charles Dodgson (LEWIS CARROLL), and Julia Margaret Cameron. This strategy inserted her photographs within an exalted historical context, while at the same time highlighting Mann's own innovations. In *Fallen Child* (1989), the naked body of Mann's youngest daughter, Virginia, cuts a luminous swath across a grassy lawn. Virginia lies face down, her arms tucked underneath her. Tendrils of curly blond hair splay out around her head like a halo, making reference to Cameron's photographs of children dressed as angels. The camera is positioned over Virginia's prone body, as if the viewer has stumbled across her. She is both a child, perhaps an injured one, and an angel fallen to earth. What at first appear to be tiny dark scratches on Virginia's back are in fact grass clippings. Before our eyes, she becomes a child, engrossed in the game of rolling on freshly cut grass. One can read *Fallen Child* as an art-historical joke, a statement on CHILD ABUSE or loss of innocence, or a meticulously crafted formal composition.

Mann was born in Lexington, Virginia, in 1951. She received a B.A. from Hollins College, as well as a master's degree in writing from the same institution. From 1971 through 1973 Mann studied photography at the Praestegaard Film School in Denmark. She also studied at the Aegean School of Fine Arts and the Ansel Adams Yosemite Workshop. Mann has received grants for the National Endowment for the Arts and the National Endowment for the Humanities. Her photographs are in the collections of the Museum of Modern Art, the Metropolitan Museum of Art, and the Whitney Museum of Art, among others. Mann lives and works in Lexington, Virginia.

See also: **Images of Childhood; Victorian Art.**

BIBLIOGRAPHY

Ehrhart, Shannah. 1994. "Sally Mann's Looking-Glass House." In *Tracing Cultures: Art History, Criticism, Critical Fiction*, ed. Miwon Kwon. New York: Whitney Museum of American Art.

Higonnet, Anne. 1998. *Pictures of Innocence: The History and Crisis of Ideal Childhood*. London: Thames and Hudson.

Mann, Sally. 1992. *Immediate Family*. New York: Aperture.

Weinberg, Jonathan. 2001. *Ambition and Love in Modern American Art*. New Haven, CT: Yale University Press.

A. CASSANDRA ALBINSON

Masturbation

In the early seventeenth-century French court, the infant Louis XIII, according to the royal physician's diary, was constantly displaying and touching his penis, a habit courtiers seem to have found amusing. Nearly two centuries later, in 1793, one of the indictments brought against Marie Antoinette by the Revolutionary Tribunal was that she had encouraged the dauphin to masturbate. A major change in attitudes emerged during the first decades of the eighteenth century: previously, "self-abuse" was considered just one among the sins of lust.

Concern and Control

An anonymous text entitled *Onania, or, the Heinous Sin of Self-Pollution, and All its Frightful Consequences in Both Sexes consider'd with Spiritual and Physical Advice to those, Who Have Already Injur'd Themselves by This Abominable Practice. And Seasonable Admonition to the Youth of the Nation, (of both Sexes) and Those Whose Tuition They Are Under, Whether Parents, Guardians, Masters, or Mistresses*, first published in London sometime during the first two decades of the eighteenth century, became a best-seller throughout Europe. While laying emphasis on the extreme sinfulness of self-pollution, *Onania* also alleged seriously deleterious effects on health, claiming it caused specific genital ailments and undermined the whole system, causing fits, consumption, and infertility (in both sexes). This new emphasis on adverse physical effects was not unconnected with the patent remedy the pamphlet promoted. Masturbation thus first became a concern in connection with relatively mature individuals, with disposable income available to purchase both *Onania* and the remedy, though anxieties over youth were also present. Some historians have argued that the rise of masturbation paranoia reflected anxieties within Protestant culture, cut off from old sources of moral authority, but masturbation fears were at least as prevalent in Catholic nations, possibly reflecting anxieties generated by political, social, and economic change.

The theme was taken up by numerous authors in the same world of commercial quackery, and then became the subject of a work by the highly respected Swiss physician Samuel Tissot, first published in Latin in 1758, and two years later in French as *L'Onanisme, ou Dissertation physique sur les maladies produit par la masturbation*. Tissot located the adverse effects in contemporary theories of physiology and bodily economy, suggesting that a small amount of seminal fluid was equivalent to a many times greater quantity of blood, and that the expenditure of nervous energy destabilized the bodily mechanism. However, he did not propose a patent remedy but lifestyle practices which would become standards: cold baths, exercise, regular evacuation of the bowels, sleep only in moderation (no lying in bed), and conscious effort to keep the thoughts pure.

These efforts to control a practice considered potentially lethal soon affected child-rearing practices, with the prophylactic inculcation of good habits and the prevention of those tending to lead to masturbation. It is debatable whether concerns over childhood masturbation arose from increasing interest in the moral and physical welfare of children and more interventionist child-rearing practices, or whether these practices were the outcome of a belief that greater surveillance of children was necessary to prevent the development of "secret habits." Probably the two phenomena were self-reinforcing—increased surveillance might reveal previously unsuspected practices, leading to even closer attention. There was also a growing tradition of stories about children inducted into masturbation by servants and nursemaids.

The masturbatory hypothesis provided an explanatory model for many conditions for which the medical profession of the day could find no other diagnosis and for which they could do nothing. By the early nineteenth century self-abuse was beginning to be blamed not only for physical and nervous ailments, but also for mental disorder. By the mid-century, in Britain and North America in particular, a particular form of "masturbatory insanity" was identified. This was strongly associated with ADOLESCENCE, and in some cases may have been *dementia praecox*.

The major focus of masturbation anxieties in the nineteenth century was the male in adolescence and young adulthood. There were sporadic manifestations of concern over females but compared to the pervasive antimasturbation rhetoric directed at men and its policing by medical and pedagogic authorities, these were the exception. Particularly for middle- and upper-class youth it was hard to avoid learning of the evils of self-abuse, whether from school sermons or quack literature and the horrifying waxworks in anatomical museums. A number of devices were manufactured and sold for the control of masturbation and nocturnal emissions. It is not however clear to what extent these were applied to children by concerned adult guardians, rather than being employed by worried postpubertal males. This awareness of the dangers of masturbation ratcheted up a further degree in the later nineteenth century. A range of well-meaning organizations and individuals disseminated tracts warning against the dangers of self-abuse and also against succumbing to the horror stories of quacks, associating this with advocacy for cultivating a type of manhood fit for national and imperial purposes. This torrent of warnings about a practice which early investigations already suggested was almost universal among adolescent boys could have serious psychological effects.

A Loosening of Controls

By the end of the nineteenth and the beginning of the twentieth centuries, it was being argued by many medical authorities that (except in "excess") masturbation was less harmful than the common fears about the damage that the practice might have caused. However, older views still circulated in such works as the 1908 *Scouting for Boys* by Boy Scout found-er ROBERT BADEN-POWELL. And well into the late twentieth century, manuals of advice to young people, while reassuring them that masturbation was not harmful, nonetheless recommended that they should try to refrain from it. It was also presented as a problem in CHILD-REARING ADVICE LITERATURE, though with the rise of increasingly humane ideas preventive measures were recommended rather than punitive approaches. Nonetheless, relatively late in the twentieth century and well into the "permissive era," people still reported traumas caused by parents or nurses threatening to "cut it off if you don't stop that!" and students reportedly attributed various ailments to masturbation.

Masturbation is still an uncomfortable subject. Questions on individual, rather than mutual, masturbation were omitted from the British Sexual Attitudes and Behaviour Survey of the early 1990s. Joycelyn Elders was dismissed from her post as U.S. Surgeon General in 1994 because she recommended including discussion of masturbation (as safe a sex practice as one could wish) in school sex education programs. This continuing ambivalence doubtless still affects children and young people.

See also: **Infancy of Louis XIII; Sexuality.**

BIBLIOGRAPHY

Comfort, Alex. 1967. *The Anxiety Makers: Some Curious Preoccupations of the Medical Profession.* London: Nelson.

Gilbert, Arthur N. 1975. "Doctor, Patient, and Onanist Diseases in the Nineteenth Century." *Journal of the History of Medicine and Allied Sciences* 30: 217–234.

Hall, Lesley A. 1992. "Forbidden by God, Despised by Men: Masturbation, Medical Warnings, Moral Panic, and Manhood in Great Britain, 1850–1950." In *Forbidden History: The State, Society, and the Regulation of Sexuality in Modern Europe: Essays from the "Journal of the History of Sexuality,"* ed. John C. Fout. Chicago: The University of Chicago Press.

Hare, E. H. 1962. "Masturbatory Insanity: The History of an Idea." *Journal of Mental Science* 108: 1–25.

Stengers, Jean, and Anne Van Neck. 2001. *Masturbation: History of a Great Terror,* trans. Kathryn Hoffman. London: Palgrave.

Spitz, René A. 1953. "Authority and Masturbation: Some Remarks on a Bibliographical Investigation." *Yearbook of Psychoanalysis* 9: 113–145.

Stolberg, Michael. 2000a. "Self-Pollution, Moral Reform, and the Venereal Trade: Notes on the Sources and Historical Context of 'Onania' 1716." *Journal of the History of Sexuality* 9: 37–61.

Stolberg, Michael. 2000b. "An Unmanly Vice: Self-Pollution, Anxiety, and the Body in the Eighteenth Century." *Social History of Medicine* 3: 1–2.

LESLEY A. HALL

Mead, Margaret (1901–1978)

Margaret Mead was born into an academic family in Philadelphia, Pennsylvania, on December 16, 1901. She attended

Barnard College and received her doctorate in cultural anthropology, working with Ruth Benedict and Franz Boas at Columbia University. Mead spent her entire professional career as a curator at the Museum of Natural History in New York City. Between 1924 and 1936, she did fieldwork in eight different cultures and wrote extensively about most of them for the rest of her life. From the start of World War II, Mead directed most of her work toward public affairs. Mead died in New York City on November 15, 1978.

While studying cultural anthropology with Boas, Mead went to Samoa to document the influence of culture on ADOLESCENCE. *Coming of Age in Samoa* (1928) became a classic for its news that adolescence is more a cultural preoccupation than a biological imperative:

> The adolescent girl in Samoa differed from her sister who had not reached puberty in one chief respect, that in the older girl certain bodily changes were present in the older girl which were absent in the younger girl. There were no other great differences (p. 196).

Mead also reported that the young women of Samoa suffered much less constraint and neurosis in matters related to sex. Mead's book, with its open discussion of the SEXUALITY of adolescent girls and its conscious inversion of contemporary morals, became a major text of the mid-twentieth century. Coming of age would never be the same again.

Mead used much the same argument to take a stand on the gender issues of her time. She wrote that "we know of no culture that has said, articulately, that there is no difference between men and women except in the way they contribute to the creation of the next generation" (1949, p. 8). For Mead, there are biological differences between males and females, but how these differences make a difference is greatly dependent on the cultural environment in which they are staged, interpreted, and made consequential.

In subsequent fieldwork, Mead studied younger children in New Guinea and toddlers in Bali. In each case, she delivered a cultural analysis of the child-rearing process by documenting "those sequences in child-other behavior which carry the greatest communication weight and so are crucial for the development of each culturally regular character structure" (Mead and Macgregor, p. 27). Documented differences in crucial "sequences in child-other behavior" from other cultures challenged Western categories of child development, gender, and desire. Whether in popular magazines or on television shows, Mead used human variation to disrupt heartfelt American biases about what was natural and inherent.

Mead wrote more than twenty books, some technical, most not. As the public face of anthropology, she celebrated a comparative method based on intense fieldwork. For Mead, anthropology was a clearinghouse for moral affairs.

She tried every available device for eliciting, recording, and representing patterns of interaction and interpretation among the people she studied. With Gregory Bateson, she pioneered the photographic documentation of life and learning in different cultures. Culture and character could be filmed because they are relentlessly worked on by persons teaching and learning together. From Bali, Mead offers a nice image:

> Where the American mother attempts to get the child to parrot simple courtesy phrases, the Balinese mother simply recites them, glibly, in the first person, and the child finally slips into speech, as into an old garment, worn before, but fitted on by another hand. (Bateson and Mead, p. 13)

People fit into each other as into garments, with give-and-take leading to fragile but consistent outcomes. In nine photographs covering two minutes of a mother/son interaction, Bateson and Mead show how the Balinese practice "awayness," a give-and-take in which participants arrange ways to be together, but unengaged, to be in each other's presence—even touching—but unavailable. In her notes on the photographs, Mead points to a communicatively weighty sequence in child-other behavior in a "culturally regular character structure" marked by awayness: the mother calls the child to her, stimulates the child (photos 1–2), then attends elsewhere (photos 3–8), until both mother and child look out on the world, bored and away (photo 9).

Mead remains a source of celebration and controversy. Soon after her death, Derrick Freeman (1983) claimed the young Mead had been fooled by her Samoan informants: in Freeman's view she was naïve and driven to confirm Boas's position that culture, not biology, was primary in the organization of behavior. Where Mead saw sexual license, Freeman counted rape; where Mead saw generosity and detachment, Freeman found jealousy and aggression; where Mead saw cooperation, Freeman found hierarchy and ambivalence. The ensuing Freeman/Mead controversy has been resolved strongly in her favor. Lowell Holmes worked in Mead's village decades after she left Samoa and stated:

> Despite the greater possibilities for error in a pioneering scientific study, her tender age (twenty-three), and her inexperience, I find that the validity of her Samoan research is remarkably high. . . . I confirm Mead's conclusion that it was undoubtedly easier to come of age in Samoa than in the United States in 1925.

Late-twentieth- and early-twenty-first-century controversy attacks Mead less for the quality of her science than for her commitment to a science tied to Western colonialism and imperialism. Nonetheless, leading anthropologists, such as Clifford Geertz and James Boon, continue to praise her work, her methods, and her fierce effort to use anthropology to confront social problems from a new perspective.

See also: **Sociology and Anthropology of Childhood.**

BIBLIOGRAPHY

Bateson, Gregory, and Margaret Mead. 1942. *Balinese Character: A Photographic Analysis.* New York: New York Academy of Sciences.

Bateson, Mary Catherine. 1984. *With a Daughter's Eye.* New York: William Morrow.

Freeman, Derrick. 1983. *Margaret Mead and Samoa.* Cambridge, MA: Harvard University Press.

Holmes, Lowell. 1987. *Quest for the Real Samoa.* New York: Bergin and Garvey.

Mead, Margaret. 1928. *Coming of Age in Samoa.* New York: William Morrow.

Mead, Margaret. 1930. *Growing Up in New Guinea.* New York: William Morrow.

Mead, Margaret. 1949. *Male and Female.* New York: William Morrow.

Mead, Margaret. 1972. *Blackberry Winter: My Earlier Years.* New York: William Morrow.

Mead, Margaret. 1977. *Letters from the Field.* New York: Harper and Row.

Mead, Margaret and Francis Macgregor. 1951. *Growth and Culture.* New York: G.D. Putnam and Sons.

Sullivan, Gerald. 1998. *Margaret Mead, Gregory Bateson, and Highland Bali: Fieldwork Photographs of Bayung Gedé.* Chicago: University of Chicago Press.

RAY McDERMOTT

Measles. *See* Contagious Diseases; Epidemics; Vaccination.

Media, Childhood and the

By the time children reach the age of eighteen, they have spent more time with various forms of media than at school. This has been the case in industrialized countries since the 1950s, and the fact is often cited in debates on children and media. The popularity of the citation testifies to the central position the media hold both in children's lives and in adult perceptions.

The Dual Nature of Media

Modern media developed in tandem with modern childhood from the eighteenth century on. The media—from inexpensive magazines and "dime novels," to film and RADIO, and on to TELEVISION, computer media, and cell phones—are at once a set of concrete technologies and a set of symbolic, meaning-making processes. Most media are commodities that need to be bought in order to be used; they are used mainly outside of work and school; and they require a modi-

cum of leisure time and money. As technologies, media serve to differentiate children according to access and application. But media also serve, for children, as a way to connect to other people, periods, and places, because they communicate messages that may transcend time and space. So media at once serve to divide and to unite children.

Media communicate information and entertainment by means of signs: letters, talk and sound, still and moving images, and mixtures of these. As such, media are not only a neutral window to the world, they are also and at the same time a shaping of the world through factual and fictional accounts. All signs need interpretation in order to make sense. Learning to understand letters and talk requires training, and in the case of reading the training is often of a formalized kind that historically develops with schooling. Conversely, the ability to decipher images and sound are integral parts of children's perceptual capacities from infancy, even if it takes experience with media to recognize, for example, genre characteristics. These differences play into children's abilities to make use of media, and, more importantly, they play into adults' reactions and their abilities to regulate these uses.

The historical relations between childhood and media thus develop in two interlaced dimensions, namely children's concrete and often divergent uses of a variety of media, and adult reactions to and debates about this development. These debates are public forums that form the institutional and normative framework within and against which actual content and uses are set. Hence the historical development of public debate on childhood and media is fundamental to an understanding of how the relations between actual children and single media evolve.

Media Debates

Every time a new mass medium has entered the social scene since the eighteenth century, it has become the focus of public debates on social and cultural norms. These debates serve to highlight, negotiate, and possibly revise these very norms. Participants in these debates are mostly middle class, often professionally engaged in education or cultural politics or personally involved in ethical or religious causes. Early on, the objects of debate were mostly defined in terms of class (the lower classes, the mob, the mass). But from the late nineteenth century on, they increasingly became defined in terms of age as more and more children entered what may be defined as a modern concept of childhood, in which economic production is severed from reproduction, including upbringing.

Public debate on media in general, and media and children in particular, follows strikingly similar routes throughout history. The North American media scholar Joli Jensen, in her 1990 book *Redeeming Modernity: Contradictions in Media Criticism* calls these routes the discourses of optimism and pessimism, respectively. It is significant that the dis-

Media—from mass-produced broadsides to computers and cell phones—has been a part of modern childhood since the eighteenth century. © Ed Bock/CORBIS.

course of optimism, voiced by proponents of the new medium in question, is primarily linked to aspects of the new medium that may be associated with rationality, while the discourse of pessimism, voiced by critics of the very same medium, is linked to aspects that equally readily may be associated with emotionality. The new medium becomes a metaphor for discussing and debating wider sociocultural issues in relation to childhood and, by implication, to adult life.

Print Goes to Town

A little time to oneself, a bit of private spending money or parents' provision of the medium at hand are the preconditions for children to use media. Other preconditions may include the ability to read, since print media are the earliest and were for a long time the most popular media available to children.

The first medium to reach a juvenile audience was not aimed at the young. Ballads, broadsides, and chapbooks with emotionally charged and politically subversive tales, printed on coarse paper with crude woodcuts, had a wide readership in the eighteenth century. The French Revolution of 1789 created widespread fears of social insurrection, and religious groups and educationalists in countries such as Germany, Britain, and the United States warned against the perceived

threats posed by these popular fictions. In Britain, cheap "repository tracts" were published by Evangelical groups as an antidote to the commercial fare. Decked out as sheep in wolves' clothing to look like chapbooks, they were often given away as prizes to poor children in the newly established SUNDAY SCHOOLS and other places of moral reform.

This early media development highlights three important aspects of public debate on childhood and media. First, modern media is universal in the sense that it has the ability to deliver all kinds of information and entertainment to large numbers of people very quickly. Much of children's media fare was not aimed at the young, and that is still the case. Second, the wider issues that modern media raise highlight struggles for power in the sense that the debates focus on the regulation of groups other than the ones involved in the debate. Children have often been among the first to adopt new media whose application challenges the received cultural standards, and adults, through their discussions, lay claim to and seek to redefine cultural norms and sociocultural competencies. Third, the attempts to counteract bad media content with good hinges on a view of children as more vulnerable and hence more malleable than adults. The debates set up and help sustain a division between juvenile and adult perception, which much popular media fare seems to undermine. All three aspects tend to focus upon issues of violence or crime, which are linked to boys, and issues of sex, which are primarily linked to girls.

Throughout the nineteenth century, the combined forces of industrialization and urbanization created the basis for a wider juvenile readership. In most industrialized countries, children's books were aimed at middle-class readers of both sexes, while inexpensive serialized novels and magazines were brought out on a weekly or fortnightly basis from the 1830s on, catering to working-class and lower-middle-class boys with their crime, mystery, and adventure stories. Their heyday was before World War I. Investigations carried out in Britain in the 1830s demonstrated that three-quarters of working-class homes possessed books, and LITERACY was sought after by many children. By the late nineteenth century, the magazine market had been diversified to include very young readers and middle- and working-class girls.

Popular print media for children continued to cause controversy through the first half of the twentieth century, with the most explicit debate carried out in the early 1950s when so-called horror comics were introduced. Their most vicious critic was the American psychiatrist Frederic Wertham, the title of whose 1953 book, *Seduction of the Innocent*, summed up the prevalent view. Still, from the 1900s on, widespread anxiety over children's popular reading was beginning to be balanced by other, more optimistic, voices. Some teachers and librarians praised the beneficial effects of reading as a solitary experience of introspection and elevation of taste, much to be preferred to a new medium which was then beginning to vie for the attention of the young.

Public Pleasures

The major media that have reached young audiences since the beginning of the twentieth century are auditory or audiovisual in nature, from film, radio, records, and CDs on to television, videos, and the computer. Unlike popular literature, these media do not share their means of expression with media approved as art (e.g., the book) or information (e.g., the serious newspaper). Unlike popular literature, these media allow children to develop abilities to listen, watch, and move rhythmically beyond the confines of formal training.

From its inception in 1896, film was a true mass medium, and children and young people made up a sizeable part, and at times a majority, of its audience. In Britain immediately after World War I, juveniles accounted for about 30 percent of the cinema audiences, and in 1939 the renowned sociologist Seebohm Rowntree, in his comprehensive study of the city of York, stated that more than half of the cinema audiences were children and young people. In the United States, studies in the early 1930s showed that children and adolescents made up 30 percent of American cinema audiences and that early elementary school-age children saw a MOVIE twice a month, whereas adolescents saw one once a week on average.

Unlike reading, movie-going is a social event, and cinemas are public places whose attractions are visibly publicized on posters and billboards—characteristics that quickly made them objects of the debate over the regulation of juveniles' use of public space. This debate was most intensely focused on adolescents, many of whom lived in cramped conditions and found in cinemas an attractive space for romance that was not necessarily confined to the screen.

For younger children, cinema clubs and special screenings were set up between the world wars in many towns and cities, a practice that combined the monitoring of viewing through special programs with commercial promotion through product tie-ins. For example, in the United States the DISNEY company in 1931 started hugely popular Mickey Mouse cinema clubs, where young members not only enjoyed a weekly Mickey Mouse cartoon and feature film, but also joined in reciting the club creed and singing "The Star-Spangled Banner," as well as participating in contests whose prizes were Disney toys. This fusion of public and commercial regulation was widely accepted and must be understood in the context of the prevalent views on media at the time.

Film and Media Effects Theory

After World War I, many Germans entertained the opinion that they had lost the war not on the battle field but in the press, and both in Europe and North America propaganda became a focus of intense professional interest between the wars. This interest was based on the widely held assumption that the media had direct and measurable effects on people—effects that could be turned to both beneficial and harmful ends.

In the history of childhood and media, this assumption combined with the view of children as malleable creatures, which had developed in the late eighteenth century. To this combination was added the fact that film is an audiovisual medium, which makes it more prone to being judged by its resemblance to external reality than are print media. So the question of film's impact on children became focused upon the issue of imitation: Would children emulate sex or violence in real life if they were exposed to sex and violence on the screen? Moreover, realism became a norm by which other media expressions were judged. The assumption of direct media effects merged with realism as an aesthetic norm. From this, debates ensued about whether children would be better served by fact than by fiction. Answers to this question played into the ways in which public debate tends to validate rational aspects of the media, aspects that readily lend themselves to informational genres. In contrast, the emotional aspects—aspects that are associated with fictional accounts—are downgraded.

Proponents of film applied the norm of realism in arguing for its educational potential. Film was called "the working-man's [sic] university," a "theater of democracy" and "the Esperanto of the eye" — all indications that film was for everyone and required no formal training.

In both Britain and the United States, the 1920s and 1930s saw major investigations into children and film, investigations that were framed by the effects tradition which a now-burgeoning media research field helped institutionalize. In Britain, the first enquiry was set up in 1917 by the National Council of Public Morals. Its 1925 report, *The Cinema in Education*, did not validate the accusations leveled against film for its debauching effects. In fact, it put the blame for juvenile DELINQUENCY on social conditions.

In many European countries in the 1930s, the debates on film and childhood were increasingly inflected by nationalist, even racist, overtones as Hollywood gained superiority over European film companies. In Britain, perhaps the most extreme example of this is *The Devil's Camera*, written in 1932 by two journalists, R. G. Burnett and E. D. Martell, who accused mainly Jewish financiers in Hollywood of undermining British strength and stamina in the young. In Germany, the dual development of rapid modernization and inflation after World War I impoverished the academic and administrative middle classes as well as many self-employed people. As the cultural elite lost its social stronghold, its opposition to new cultural artifacts intensified. A well-known film critic, Herbert Jhering, writing in 1926 equated American film with a mental militarism that seduced the masses—a curious historical irony given the contemporary strengthening of the Nazi movement.

Europe had a strong tradition, begun in the nineteenth century, of public regulation and reform for the public good, which made many adults turn to educational films as an antidote to the perceived ill-effects of the commercial output, and public funding of special films for children continues to be a mainstay of cultural policy in several European countries. Not so in the United States, where pressure groups furthered self-regulation measures by the industry.

In 1928, the Reverend William H. Short and his Motion Picture Research Council commissioned a series of studies to be financed by the philanthropic Payne Study and Experiment Fund. Their resulting eight volumes, published in 1933 and 1934, are among the most detailed investigations of movie-going and the main findings corroborate the findings of their British colleagues. In addition, the studies show that films were important to the young not so much because children directly emulated their content but because films created interpretive frameworks for understanding their personal problems and aspirations.

Religious groups especially continued to campaign against the medium of the popular film, and in 1934 the Hays Code, which was written by an influential Republican, William Harrison Hays, was made mandatory. It was the film industry's self-imposed code of conduct, monitored by the Motion Picture Producers and Distributors of America, and was aimed at scenes of perceived indecency and violence. The Hays Code thus gave credence to the propaganda underlying the effects theory, not the more nuanced results of empirical research.

The division between European public regulation and industrial regulation in the United States continued when television gained ground in the 1950s.

Media Domestication

Unlike film, television in Europe and the United States developed in the privacy of the home. And unlike reading, watching it was a family affair well into the 1970s in the United States and the 1980s in Europe, when multiple sets became the norm. In other parts of the world, television has remained a collective and often public affair, demonstrating that contexts of use depend on wider social traditions and options—including access to electricity.

With the advent of television, an audiovisual medium became an everyday experience in the lives of the very young to an unprecedented degree. The day's flow of programs were divided into slots, graded according to gender and generation, and serving to regulate children's daily routines as no medium had done before. Most TV networks developed children's sections that produced both informational and entertaining programming. Cartoons became an absolute and longstanding favorite with children until they reached ADOLESCENCE.

In the United States, television, like film, developed as a commercial enterprise within broadcasting networks, with public broadcasting playing a negligible role in program development and viewing. In Europe, television, like radio, evolved as a public-service medium—an institution that catered to the public good, independent of both the state and the commercial media industry. John Reith, the legendary first director of the British Broadcasting Corporation (BBC), professed that the aim of public service should be to "inform, educate and entertain" all groups of society, including children, with programming that had a decisive focus on the first two aspects well into the 1970s. Children's sections, along with the news and drama sections, remained the main pillars in public-service broadcasting until the late 1980s, when the combined forces of statutory deregulation, computer media, and intensified global media commodification served to inaugurate new alliances between public and private media sectors.

From the early days of television, institutional differences meant that most European children were addressed as future citizens, whereas American children were addressed as future or even present consumers. These differences played into public debate and research priorities. The notion of citizenship is closely bound up with nineteenth-century ideals of public communication and reform based on print media, and so television's ability to reach children even before they went to school or were able to read had many European educators, politicians, and parents question the relations between books and television: was viewing ousting reading as a pastime?

This displacement thesis, where one form of leisure eclipses another, became a central element in media investigations, and its importance was reinforced by the subsequent introduction of a spate of new media technologies through the 1980s (videos, Walkmans, satellite television) and 1990s (computers, Gameboys, Discmans, cell phones), making comparison with, and possibly displacing, older media technologies an immediate cause of debate. In 1958, the British psychologist Hilde Himmelweit and her colleagues published *Television and the Child*, whose main results demonstrated that television, being a novelty, to some extent displaced reading and "doing nothing," but that the displacement was most pronounced for activities serving similar functions. With its social-psychological approach, the study pioneered a new trend in media studies, which asked what individual children did with media rather than what media did to children.

This uses-and-gratifications approach resonated with media scholars in North America, where it remains the main research tradition. In tune with postwar views on children as consumers, it focused on individual needs and active choice, thereby stressing children's independence as long as this independence was exerted within the commercial domain. A study published in 1961 by Wilbur Schramm and his colleagues, *Television in the Lives of Our Children*, largely corroborated Himmelweit's findings and framed future discussions on children and television in terms of parental guidance and safe scheduling. In the 1980s, these discussions gained new impetus from, but were not radically challenged by, the introduction of video recorders, which facilitated children's viewing of a wider range of films.

Transgressing Boundaries

Both Himmelweit and Schramm, as well as later studies, showed that most of children's television viewing did not consist of children's programs. Still the most prevalent medium in children's lives, television acts as a leveler of age, gender, and ethnic boundaries. With television, the relationship of childhood and media has come full circle: the medium reaches nearly everyone, just as the earliest print media did. The main themes in the debate about that relationship has also come full circle in that media culture now reaches all children and does so both in public and private spaces: are children to be protected from or educated by the media? Are media a cause of cultural optimism or pessimism?

The media situation at the beginning of the twenty-first century in many ways radicalizes earlier concerns and contradictions. The introduction of satellite television and computer media in the 1980s and especially the exponential growth of the Internet in the 1990s brought a new urgency to old questions about children's autonomy as independent beings or their protection as vulnerable minors in relation to their exposure to media violence and sex. The different routes pursued by European and North American broadcasters in addressing children were undermined by a commercial computer and Internet industry of potentially global reach, and it threw into relief the dilemmas involved in addressing children as future citizens, as beings in need of protection, or as present consumers in charge of the joy stick, the remote control, and the parental purse.

The development toward global and commodified media production equally threw into relief the historical changes in the debates on childhood and media. In the nineteenth and first half of the twentieth centuries, the debates addressed specific media output, focusing on its ill effects, often in shrill voices that bordered on panic, making the discourse of pessimism the most clearly heard. Since then, the debates have become more diffuse and short-lived, mixing the discourse of pessimism with a discourse of optimism, which has focused on media as resources and children as possessing rights.

This has made the dilemmas no less complex: should media be defined as commodities or a public good? What are CHILDREN'S RIGHTS in regard to media? Commercial media producers lay claim to a definition of children as mediawise, rational consumers who should be able to buy whatever media output producers make available. Public-service interests stress the 1989 UN CONVENTION OF THE RIGHTS OF THE CHILD, which stipulates the child's rights to privacy (article 16), freedom of expression, and access to a diversity of media (articles 13 and 17), which it defines as part of the public domain.

The early debates were played out against, and played into, a sociocultural context in which the boundaries of gender and generation were as well defined as the hierarchies of culture and taste, making the stakes easy to define, oppose, and defend. Later debates operate within, and lay claim to, sociocultural contexts where it is no longer feasible to uphold such hierarchies—not least because of media culture itself, which has become more complex and differentiated. From the late 1990s on, media producers began incorporating prospective opposition into their marketing strategies. This is seen, for example, in the promotion of controversial music groups whose "explicit lyrics" are highlighted and in advertisements for television concepts such as the reality show *Big Brother* that focus on the special attractions allegedly found in a blurring of public and private boundaries.

The development of mobile media, through which children may reach and be reached by images, sound, and print at nearly all times and places, operates within a socio-cultural context where discourses of pessimism and optimism, protection and rights, citizenship and consumerism, are the important stakes. No longer confined to the intimate sphere of the home or the regulations of broadcasting and film censorship, the mobile media generation of children faces a future in which they have to tackle old, adult concerns under radically new circumstances.

See also: **Advertising; Comic Books; Consumer Culture; Theories of Childhood.**

BIBLIOGRAPHY

Barker, Martin, and Julian Petley, eds. 1997. *Ill Effects: The Media/ Violence Debate.* London: Routledge.

Dale, Edgar. 1935. *Children's Attendance at Motion Pictures.* New York: Macmillan.

deCordova, Richard. 1994. "The Mickey in Macy's Window: Childhood, Consumerism, and Disney Animation." In *Disney Discourse: Producing the Magic Kingdom,* ed. Eric Smoodin. New York: Routledge.

Denning, Michael. 1987. *Mechanic Accents: Dime Novels and Working-Class Culture in America.* New York: Verso.

Drotner, Kirsten. 1988. *English Children and Their Magazines, 1751–1945,* 2nd ed. New Haven: Yale University Press.

Drotner, Kirsten. 1999. "Dangerous Media? Panic Discourses and Dilemmas of Modernity." *Paedagogica Historica* 35, no. 3: 593–619.

Gilbert, James. 1986. *A Cycle of Outrage: America's Reaction to the Juvenile Delinquent in the 1950s.* New York: Oxford University Press.

Himmelweit, Hilde, et al. 1958 *Television and the Child: An Empirical Study of the Effects of Television on the Young.* New York: Oxford University Press.

Jacobs, Lewis. 1968 [1939]. *The Rise of American Film: A Critical History.* New York: Teachers College Press.

Jowett, Garth. 1976. *Film: The Democratic Art.* Boston: Little, Brown.

Kaes, Anton. 1987. "The Debate about Cinema: Charting a Controversy (1909–29)." *New German Critique* 40: 7–33.

Livingstone, Sonia, and Moira Bovill, eds. 2001. *Children and Their Changing Media Environment: A European Comparative Study.* Mahwah, NJ: Erlbaum.

Richards, Jeffrey. 1984. *The Age of the Dream Palace: Cinema and Society in Britain, 1930–1939.* London: Routledge and Kegan Paul.

Rowntree, B. Seebohm. 1941. *Poverty and Progress: A Second Social Study of York.* London: Longmans, Green, and Company.

Schramm, Wilbur, et al. 1961. *Television in the Lives of Our Children.* Stanford, CA: Stanford University Press.

Vincent, David. 1983. "Reading in the Working-class Home." In *Leisure in Britain, 1780–1939,* ed. James K. Walton and James Walvin. Manchester. UK: Manchester University Press.

Wertham, Frederic. 1953. *Seduction of the Innocent.* New York: Rinehart.

West, Mark I.. 1988. *Children, Culture, and Controversy.* Hamden, CT: Archon Books.

KIRSTEN DROTNER

Medieval and Renaissance Europe

The narratives of traditional political history written by historians from the north and west of Europe confidently set the boundaries of the beginning of the medieval period at the fall of Rome in 476 C.E. and ended the period of the Renaissance either in 1492, with Christopher Columbus's voy-

Children appear, throwing snowballs, in the margins of a fifteenth-century illustrated manuscript, "The Hours of Adelaide of Savoy." The Art Archive/Musée Condé Chantilly/Dagli Orti (A).

age to the Americas, or in 1527 with another sack of Rome, this time by the troops of Charles V, the Holy Roman emperor. At both extremes, a narrow geographic focus also made the precision of these dates seem more convincing than it really is. At the beginning of the period, the focus on the north and west of Christendom, where medieval civilization eventually flourished about 1000 C.E., for the most part led historians to neglect the geography of the Roman Empire itself, wrapped as it was around the Mediterranean Sea. Thus the continuing vitality of the Byzantine Empire, so Roman that its inhabitants styled themselves *Romanoi,* never gained as much attention as it deserved. Political and military history also exaggerated the cultural conflict between ISLAM and the Christian West, even as Islamic civilization appropriated the fruits of Greek science and philosophy and retransmitted them to the Latin West toward the end of the eleventh century.

At the other chronological extreme, the sack of Rome appeared to mark the end of the independence of Renaissance Italian city-states, even though the struggle between the Papacy and secular powers throughout the High and late Middle Ages made the entire Italian peninsula so vulnerable to invasion and constant warfare that political independence failed to have much meaning. As Renaissance humanism came to be seen as the center of the movement known as the

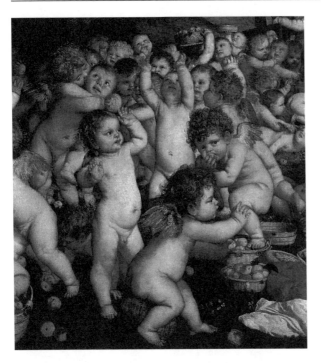

The Worship of Venus (c. 1560) [detail], Titian. The profusion of chubby baby Cupids in Titian's painting embody a decidedly non-Christian sensuality that would be at odds with later conceptions of childhood innocence. Prado, Madrid, Spain/Bridgeman Art Library.

Renaissance, the geographical boundaries of Renaissance culture came to be understood as extending across the Alps into France, Germany, and England, as well as to Bohemia, Hungary, Poland, and Spain. The Renaissance is now considered to end at about 1600, with some literary historians willing to extend the chronological boundary as late as the 1640s to encompass the English poet John Milton (1608–1674) and the English Civil War (1642–1648).

Periodization of the History of Childhood

For the purposes of the history of childhood, the more important debates concerning chronological definitions have centered around what distinction, if any, can appropriately be made between the Middle Ages and the Renaissance. The American historian Charles Homer Haskins, in *The Renaissance of the Twelfth Century* (1927), sought to claim for the twelfth century the cultural achievements traditionally attributed to the Renaissance: individualism, love for classical antiquity, and the origins of science. In the 1970s, this attack on the originality of the Italian Renaissance was flanked by an attack from feminists, led by Joan Kelly-Gadol's article "Did Women Have a Renaissance?" (1977), and from social and economic historians, who noted that daily lives as experienced in the premodern economy and society remained established in identifiable cyclical patterns that stayed virtually unchanged from the urban revival of the eleventh century until the beginning of the Industrial Revolution in the mid-eighteenth century.

Such attempts to diminish the status of the Italian Renaissance as an important period for the fashioning of the modern age, though exaggerated, certainly had the beneficial effect of forcing Renaissance scholars to define more carefully what was distinctive about this period. What has resulted is a much more sophisticated understanding of the relationship between medieval and Renaissance learning, a relationship that involved a shift in emphasis from the scientific disciplines of the seven liberal arts (arithmetic, geometry, astronomy, and music) to the humanistic disciplines (grammar, rhetoric, and logic). In particular, the content of humanistic instruction placed an emphasis on the skills and subjects required for active participation in urban politics and society: history, poetry, and moral philosophy.

Between the works of Haskins and Kelly-Gadol appeared PHILIPPE ARIÈS's monumental *Centuries of Childhood* (1962). Ariès accepted the traditional boundaries between Middle Ages and Renaissance, but argued that the Renaissance ushered in a new attention to children and their education, an attention that curtailed the freedom of children themselves. Using examples from medieval paintings that he saw on weekends as part of his itinerant government job, Ariès argued that the Middle Ages had no separate conception of childhood: that children were depicted as little adults. As in art, so in life, Ariès believed: children were expected to assume adult roles quite precociously, and little or no attention was paid to the special needs of children until the educational revolution of humanism in sixteenth-century France began to regiment and DISCIPLINE the moral lives of children. Indeed, high INFANT MORTALITY, in Ariès's view, blunted any real parental affection when emotional investment in children came at such a high personal cost. Although that view is no longer prevalent among historians, much of the history of childhood in the Middle Ages and Renaissance is still being written as though Ariès's very provocative ideas still frame the entire debate.

Defining the Stages of Childhood

The chronological boundaries and terms for the stages of children's lives in the European past were quite different from those that prevail in the early twenty-first century. In the early seventh century the writer Isidore of Seville divided childhood into two equal periods of seven years each, a basic division and terminology that legal sources largely repeated. The first seven years was defined by the child's inability to speak, with *speak* meaning, in this case, the child's ability to express thought with grammatical correctness. This expressivity marked the beginning of the age of reason around the age of seven. Most importantly, it marked the age at which schooling began, just as the age of fourteen marked the end of formal schooling and the beginning of ADOLESCENCE, a period that formally ended at the age of twenty-eight. At fourteen a child formally entered the adult world and could contract matrimonial obligations. Criminal culpability began somewhere in the middle of this period of *pueritia*, or childhood, which was marked by the increasing ability to distinguish right from wrong. Although the exact age at which this was considered to occur juridically varied from one set of town statutes to another, in general the law prescribed half the adult penalty for crimes committed by children between the ages of ten and fourteen, with the full adult penalties applying once the child reached fourteen years of age. The death penalty for children under fourteen was rare, but not unknown. This aside, however, the actual use of these definitions and terms for various stages of childhood varied by writer, by location, and by period.

Sources of Evidence

Ariès's use of evidence from art history underscores a fundamental problem faced by all historians of medieval childhood: a lack of sources, or at least a lack of the traditional sources such as family and personal diaries. Family and personal diaries begin to emerge in the fourteenth century, especially in Italy, and some historians have seen in the relative lack of reference in such works to the lives and upbringing of children a lack of interest in children as individuals even in the early Renaissance. More recently, however, it has become clear that even for the late Middle Ages and Renaissance, these sources are not personal or family diaries in the modern sense, but family account books that chronicle the life of the family as an economic unit and as a claim to political office and high social status.

Thus for the entire period of the Middle Ages and Renaissance in Europe, historians have relied on inference from archeological evidence, literary evidence, and evidence from institutions such as monasteries and hospitals, plus a few autobiographical accounts, in order to reconstruct the realities of medieval and Renaissance childhood. If describing "normal" childhood in a stable family setting is the historian's goal, the set of sources available produces very frustrating results, because historians come across children in court documents, ORPHANAGE records, and literary accounts of ABANDONMENT, so that children in the context of household and family play a less significant role in the evidence than they might have in reality. Even sermons and other literature from the Church fathers refer to children in the Biblical context—the abandonment of Moses and the Slaughter of the Innocents are favorite themes, as are the stories of miracles involving the healing of sick children. Similarly, medieval preaching about children, as well as images in late medieval art, dwelt on the miraculous intervention of saints to prevent children from accidental injury or death.

Continuities in Medieval and Renaissance Childhood

Differences in geography and time aside, certain common features of medieval and Renaissance childhood provide a sense of continuity across the premodern era, stretching from antiquity to the nineteenth century. According to prevailing beliefs, conceiving a child required both the right timing and the right setting in order to produce the desired result. In this, the imagination of the mother, or the visual images with which the couple was surrounded, played an important role in determining the physical characteristics as well as the character of the child. Similarly, food ingested by the mother, according to popular and medical belief, influenced the outcome of the child. During the Renaissance, *deschi da parto*, or birth trays, as well as various ceramics presented as gifts to the child's parents, repeated heroic themes as well as other messages meant to influence the upbringing by parents and mental absorption by the child.

For the period after the child's birth, virtually all authorities recommended maternal breast-feeding. Those same authorities conceded the infrequency of maternal breast-feeding by emphasizing the importance of choosing a wet nurse whose character would be transmitted through breast milk to the child. Following Ariès, some historians have argued that WET-NURSING was a form of emotional distancing from the cruel realities of high infant mortality. More recently, however, issues of family strategy have become more prominent in the historical literature, suggesting that because breast-feeding inhibited fertility, mothers sent children out to wet-nurse in order to reduce the amount of time between pregnancies and to maximize a woman's potential for childbearing.

In Mediterranean societies in particular, family strategies also revolved around male preference, so that wet nurses were somewhat more likely to neglect female infants than male infants. The polyptychs, or censuses, of Saint-Germain-des-Prés, an abbey near Paris, in the Carolingian era (768–814) show more males than females, with the difference in gender ratios most pronounced for the smallest landholdings. During the Renaissance, this disparity in treatment by gender is evident in the mortality records of FOUNDLING hospitals, a disparity that began to disappear only in the eighteenth century. Medical anthropologists have argued that male preference is a consistent feature of environmentally stressed societies, in which parents pay more attention to male children precisely because of their greater biological vulnerability during the first year of life.

Infanticide, Abandonment, Institutions

High infant mortality, infanticide, and abandonment also represented continuities in the history of childhood during this period, although historians sharply disagree about how widespread the latter two practices were. Infant mortality in premodern societies seems to have ranged from approximately 17 percent among elites in the best of economic conditions to 50 percent among the poor and in charitable institutions—still considerably less than the infant mortality rates of 80 to 90 percent common in foundling hospitals in eighteenth- and nineteenth-century Europe. In precarious economic circumstances, and during epidemics, both infant and child mortality reached appallingly high levels.

Infanticide and abandonment were clearly related to one another, not in the sense that they were necessarily equivalent, but in the sense that parents justified (and sometimes rationalized) abandonment as the only humane alternative to starvation. As early as the mid-fourth century, orphanages and foundling hospitals were established in the Byzantine Empire, deliberately imitating Roman law. Indeed, Roman law established in Byzantium an elaborate system of guardianship for vulnerable children, in which abandonment to an institution was the last resort after networks of kinship and clients had been exhausted. Later Byzantine emperors and ecclesiastical patriarchs established and supported foundling hospitals for the abandoned children of prostitutes, although these institutions were specifically designated as orphanages at their inception. A number of Byzantine orphanages became renowned for their musical training, a tradition either reinvented or rediscovered in Renaissance Italian foundling homes as well.

In this respect, early medieval Byzantium, a relatively urbanized society compared to the more rural north and west of Europe, had a greater variety of alternatives and institutions for abandoned children. The north and west of Europe, at least from about 500 to 1000 C.E., was prey to invasion, famine, and widespread rural poverty. For an age in which both adults and children were at risk, there is nonetheless archeological evidence that parents struggled to keep alive even their sickly and deformed children, crafting makeshift clay feeding bottles for children unable to take the breast. Nor did high infant mortality necessarily weaken the bond between parents and infants. In fourteenth-century France, records from the Inquisition suggest the agony of a mother who could not bear to abandon her infant to join the heretical Cathar movement, and who ultimately had to order that the child be taken out of the room.

The closest analogue in early medieval western Europe to orphanages and foundling hospitals was oblation, the practice of giving children, especially male children, over to the monastic life. Although genuine religious motivations were at the heart of this practice, it is also quite clear that for some parents, having an older child reared and educated in the monastic setting arose from considerations of economic necessity and family strategy as well. As was true for charitable institutions in the later Middle Ages, monasteries adopted the terminology of family to construct a form of fictive kinship and familial closeness in monasteries and convents as well.

As medieval society in the Latin West became more urbanized in the eleventh century, structures and forms of abandonment changed as well. Although western Europe would not develop foundling homes until the early fifteenth century, large general hospitals as well as more specialized institutions took in orphans and foundlings in addition to their other patients and pilgrims. A series of frescoes in the hospital of Santa Maria della Scala in Siena, Italy, depicts the various forms of assistance that this large general hospital provided for abandoned children.

Just as was true for medieval convents and monasteries, the vocabulary and organization of hospitals for children sought to replicate what families normally did. Thus both general and specialized hospitals in the Middle Ages and Renaissance sent infants out to wet nurses both in city and countryside. In late medieval Italy, for example, entire towns in remote mountainous areas developed microeconomies of wet-nursing. As families did, these hospitals sent boys out to be schooled and apprenticed to a trade. Girls were taught to weave and sew, tended to remain inmates of these hospitals much longer, and often left the hospital with a dowry intended for the convent or for marriage. Over the course of the sixteenth century, many institutions required girls to keep track of their production of cloth, for which their dowries received partial credit, with the remainder going to underwrite the institution's expenses. Both boys and girls might be available for informal adoptions that usually involved working as servants for the families in which they were placed.

Affection and Exploitation

The high levels of infant and child mortality, as well as high levels of abandonment, have led some historians (often, in the Ariès tradition) to argue that the emotional lives of children were highly restricted at best and that parents lacked affection for children. Most historians of childhood would now agree that medieval and Renaissance parents displayed the same range of emotion toward children that one finds in the present: CHILD ABUSE and exploitation then, as now, were present but not necessarily representative. Rituals of BAPTISM and godparenthood, as Louis Haas showed in *The Renaissance Man and His Children* (1998), welcomed the infant into both the immediate family and into larger networks of kin, neighborhood, and community. Humanist pedagogy during the Renaissance, first in Italy and then in the north, emphasized the role of families as ministates in which children trained for adult roles in public life. Consequently, the training of children became the basis for the revival of classical visions of discipline and the early modern state both in the Catholic and PROTESTANT REFORMATIONS.

Yet the boundaries concerning appropriate social and sexual behavior were certainly drawn differently from those of contemporary times. In Renaissance Florence, for example, as shown in Michael Rocke's *Forbidden Friendships* (1996), the activities of the Officials of the Night revealed an extremely widespread network of same-sex encounters between older men and younger boys—encounters that often reflected nonsexual networks of patronage, clientage, and assistance. Sexual encounters between adult men and teenaged boys were tolerated with greater latitude than encounters between two adult males. It was just such issues that Catholic and Protestant reformers sought to address by melding religious and political discipline. Precisely at this point in the middle of the sixteenth century one may begin to discern modern outlines of childhood.

In continuing the educational innovations of the Renaissance, the Catholic and Protestant Reformations did not address economic exploitation, which continued to be a matter of survival for rural families; consequently, children within the family took on important economic roles. Barbara A. Hanawalt's examination of coroners' records from medieval England, in both *The Ties That Bound* (1986) and *Growing Up in Medieval London* (1993), showed high rates of accidental death, especially by drowning and by falling into fires. Similar dangers awaited laboring children and apprentices in medieval London. Indeed, to some extent, the new charitable initiatives of early modern Europe fostered the economic exploitation of institutionalized children as de facto wards of the early modern state. Even regular APPRENTICESHIPS often subjected young adolescents not only to hard work but also to very strict discipline.

The deaths of children in this period, however, were never taken lightly. Although Italian Renaissance diaries often record the deaths of children rather laconically, this has more to do with the function of diaries as accounts of family finances and family prestige, than with any lack of affection for children. Even in the case of tax records, in which during certain times large numbers of female children appear to have gone missing, the gaps are accounted for by the deliberate falsification of these records by taxpayers in order to make their daughters appear younger and therefore more marriageable. Personal correspondence from the period shows that parents placed a high value on the lives of their children and felt an extreme sense of loss for them when EPIDEMICS and other calamities took their lives. Moralists instructed parents to bring up and educate children according to the children's individual characteristics and abilities.

If in many respects medieval and Renaissance childhoods resemble those of the twentieth and twenty-first centuries, the cultural context of medieval and Renaissance childhood was so strikingly different that the superficial similarities are often misleading. What appears initially as a lack of attention to children has more to do with the nature of the sources, as well as with the integration of children at a very young age into functioning communities of honor, SEXUALITY, extended family, neighborhood, and work. The economic functioning of family life and child rearing did not completely submerge affection. In the case of inheritance practices, rigid rules concerning INHERITANCE often worked to the long-term protection and advantage of children. At the same time individual families often had to tread a very fine line when bonds of affection and the family's economic, social, and political survival pulled in opposite directions.

See also: **Early Modern Europe; Enlightenment, The.**

BIBLIOGRAPHY

Alexandre-Bidon, Danièle. 1997. *Les Enfants au Moyen Age: Ve–XVe siècles.* Paris: Hachette.

Ariès, Philippe. 1962. *Centuries of Childhood.* Trans. Robert Baldick. New York: Knopf.

Boswell, John. 1988. *The Kindness of Strangers: The Abandonment of Children in Western Europe from Late Antiquity to the Renaissance.* New York: Pantheon.

Crawford, Sally. 1999. *Childhood in Anglo-Saxon England.* Gloucestershire, UK: Sutton Publishing.

Gavitt, Philip. 1990. *Charity and Children in Renaissance Florence: The Ospedale degli Innocenti, 1410–1536.* Ann Arbor: University of Michigan Press.

Grendler, Paul. 1989. *Schooling in Renaissance Italy: Literacy and Learning, 1300–1600.* Baltimore, MD: Johns Hopkins University Press.

Haas, Louis. 1998. *The Renaissance Man and His Children: Childbirth and Early Childhood in Florence, 1300–1600.* New York: St. Martin's Press.

Hanawalt, Barbara A. 1986. *The Ties That Bound: Peasant Families in Medieval England.* New York: Oxford University Press.

Hanawalt, Barbara A. 1993. *Growing Up in Medieval London.* New York: Oxford University Press.

Haskins, Charles Homer. 1927. *The Renaissance of the Twelfth Century.* Cambridge, MA: Harvard University Press.

Hausfater, Glenn, and Sara Blaffer Hrdy, eds. 1984. *Infanticide: Comparative and Evolutionary Perspectives.* New York: Aldine.

Kelly-Gadol, Joan. 1977. "Did Women Have a Renaissance?" In *Becoming Visible: Women in European History*, ed. Renate Bridenthal, Claudia Koonz, and Susan Stuard. Boston: Houghton Mifflin.

Kertzer, David. 1993. *Sacrificed for Honor: Italian Infant Abandonment and the Politics of Reproductive Control.* Boston: Beacon Press.

King, Margaret. 1994. *The Death of the Child Valerio Marcello.* Chicago: University of Chicago Press.

Kuehn, Thomas. 2002. *Illegitimacy in Renaissance Florence.* Ann Arbor: University of Michigan Press.

Miller, Barbara. 1981. *The Endangered Sex: Neglect of Female Children in Rural North India.* Ithaca, NY: Cornell University Press.

Miller, Timothy. 2003. *The Orphans of Byzantium: Child Welfare in the Christian Empire.* Washington, DC: Catholic University of America Press.

Musacchio, Jacqueline. 1999. *The Art and Ritual of Childbirth in Renaissance Italy.* New Haven, CT: Yale University Press.

Niccoli, Ottavia. 1995. *Il seme di violenza: Putti, fanciulli e mammoli nell'Italia tra Cinque e Seicento.* Bari, Italy: Laterza.

Orme, Nicholas. 2001. *Medieval Children.* New Haven, CT: Yale University Press.

Ozment, Steven. 1983. *When Fathers Ruled: Family Life in Reformation Europe.* Cambridge, MA: Harvard University Press.

Ozment, Steven, ed. 1990. *Three Behaim Boys: Growing Up in Early Modern Germany: A Chronicle of Their Lives.* New Haven, CT: Yale University Press.

Rocke, Michael. 1996. *Forbidden Friendships: Homosexuality and Male Culture in Renaissance Florence.* New York: Oxford University Press.

Schultz, James. 1995. *The Knowledge of Childhood in the German Middle Ages, 1100–1350.* Philadelphia: University of Pennsylvania Press.

Shahar, Shulamith. 1990. *Childhood in the Middle Ages.* London: Routledge.

Taddei, Ilaria. 2001. *Fanciulli e giovani: Crescere a Firenze nel Rinascimento.* Florence, Italy: Leo S. Olschki, Editore.

Trexler, Richard. 1998. *The Children of Renaissance Florence.* Asheville, NC: Pegasus Press. Originally published as *Power and Dependence in Renaissance Florence.* Binghamton, NY: Medieval and Renaissance Texts and Studies, 1993.

PHILIP GAVITT

Megan's Law(s)

Megan's Law is a generic term for a statute providing for community notification of the whereabouts of convicted sex offenders following their release from prison. Such a statute is generally coupled with a law requiring the registration of released sex offenders. The girl whose name become synonymous with this legislation, seven-year-old Megan Kanka, was raped and killed in 1994 by Jesse Timmendequas, a twice-convicted sex offender who had moved in across the street from her home in suburban Hamilton, New Jersey. That Timmendequas had been diagnosed as a "repetitive-compulsive sexual offender" and incarcerated in New Jersey's treatment center for sex offenders at Avenel gave shape to the outrage provoked by his crime. If Americans still saw sex offenders as "sick," they no longer believed that experts could treat and rehabilitate them. That loss of faith diminished the concern with the childhood origins of sex offending, with how to prevent men from becoming offenders, that had emerged in the 1930s. Evidence that offenders had themselves been victims as children was in the 1990s increasingly dismissed as the "abuse excuse." If experts and courts could not protect children from sex offenders, then that task fell to the community, almost inevitably represented as composed of parents. This argument rested on the untested notion that if his neighbors had known about Timmendequas, they could have prevented his crime, and it involved a radical move to public participation in the task of surveillance previously given to police departments or other public agencies.

Campaigns for community notification laws relied on the political and symbolic power of the innocent child. Attaching the name and the image of a child victim, either Megan Kanka or a local child, to the law tapped emotions already aroused by a broader anxiety about the "disappearance" of a sheltered, innocent childhood, and made opposition, and even reflection, politically difficult. This was influenced in part by the widespread fear and alarm that had been increasingly attached to "stranger" ABDUCTIONS since the 1970s. Rallying around the innocent child, a grassroots movement succeeded in having community notification and/or sex-offender registration laws adopted by all fifty states, and by the federal government, by 2002.

Despite widespread adoption, Megan's laws remained highly controversial. Critics argued that the laws were punitive rather than regulatory, and therefore contravened constitutional protections against cruel and unusual punishment and ex post facto laws, as well as violating offenders' right to privacy. In practice, critics claimed, the laws encouraged vigilantism, and made the rehabilitation of offenders virtually impossible. Megan's laws were also charged with diverting attention from the majority of sex crimes, those committed within families. From that perspective, the laws were part of a backlash against the focus on INCEST and CHILD ABUSE that feminists had helped promote since the 1960s. In February 2002, the U.S. Supreme Court agreed to decide whether Alaska's notification law amounted to extra punishment in violation of the Constitution's ban on ex post facto laws. The Court upheld the law in March 2003.

See also: **Law, Children and the; Pedophilia; Sexuality.**

BIBLIOGRAPHY

Cole, Simon A. 2000. "From the Sexual Psychopath Statute to 'Megan's Law': Psychiatric Knowledge in the Diagnosis, Treatment, and Adjudication of Sex Criminals in New Jersey, 1949–1999." *Journal of the History of Medicine and Allied Sciences* 55: 292–314.

Davis, Peter. 1996. "The Sex Offender Next Door." *The New York Times Magazine* July 28: 20–27.

Jenkins, Philip. 1998. *Moral Panic: Changing Concepts of the Child Molester in Modern America.* New Haven, CT: Yale University Press.

INTERNET RESOURCE

Parents for Megan's Law. 2000. "Megan's Law Clearinghouse." Available from <www.parentsformeganslaw.com>.

STEPHEN ROBERTSON

Menarche

Menarche, the onset of menstruation, marks an important physical, psychological, and social transition in the lives of young women. The physical transition is preceded by bodily changes in which the breasts develop, body weight increases, and overall body shape changes, resulting in fuller hips. The psychological transition is less well charted, but the fact that a girl's first period marks the beginning of her ability to bear children suggests that it is a meaningful event. The social transition, and the rituals that surround it, vary across cultures and through time. Sexual maturation is of great social moment, since all societies have an interest in reproduction.

Historians have explored the meaning of these transitions in the past, but conclusions are limited by paucity of sources. The historian Vern Bullough's overview suggests that classical writers found menarche to occur between the ages of twelve and fourteen, while medieval authorities put the onset on menstruation at fourteen. Nineteenth-century and early-twentieth-century studies sometimes put the age slightly later, between fifteen and sixteen.

During the twentieth century the age of girls at menarche declined in the West. The median age at menarche in North America, estimated to be around 15.5 years in 1850, decreased by three to four months each decade after 1850, but has remained relatively stable since the 1970s when it reached 12.5 years. Similar trends have occurred in other Western countries and are attributed to rising standards of living, improved nutrition, higher levels of female LITERACY, and less hard labor for girls. A declining age at menarche was also evident in China during the closing decades of the century.

Contemporary studies indicate the continued variability of the age of menarche. Agta women foragers of Cagayan province, Luzon, in the Philippines, typically experience menarche at 17, Haitian women experience it at 15.37 years, while in the United States the mean age is now 12.3 years. Such studies also point to the differences between rural and urban groups, indicating that physical labor may lead to later onset of menarche.

Using medical texts, letters, and diaries, American and British historians have sought to understand the psychological import of sexual maturation. Nineteenth-century American physicians regarded menarche as a "crisis point" in the development of middle-class girls. The historian Joan Jacobs Brumberg has charted the growing emphasis on HYGIENE, rather than fertility, in twentieth-century understandings of menarche. By studying oral histories, twentieth-century historians have noted that in the past mothers often found it difficult to communicate with their daughters about the meaning of menarche. Girls were often unprepared for menstrual bleeding when it first occurred, and they were consequently fearful. Since the mid-twentieth century, sanitary product companies have sought to provide information, and they have become an increasingly important source of education about bodily maturation for girls.

The social transition brought about by menarche has been subject to scrutiny by anthropologists who seek to delineate the cultural practices—from community celebrations to seclusion and genital cutting—that accompany the advent of menarche across cultural groups. But however the advent of menarche is marked, it is commonly understood as the time when a girl becomes a woman, and is therefore subject to new codes of behavior. Menarche could thus be a time of ambivalence for the individual, a time when the freedom of childhood is relinquished for the benefits of maturity. Historically, the emphasis in many cultures on a woman's virginity prior to marriage meant the imposition of strict social controls over young women between the time of menarche and the advent of marriage.

See also: **Adolescence and Youth; Girlhood; Puberty; Rites of Passage; Sex Education; Sexuality.**

BIBLIOGRAPHY

Brookes, Barbara, and Margaret Tennant. 1998. "Making Girls Modern: Pakeha Women and Menstruation in New Zealand, 1930–1970." *Women's History Review* 7, no. 4: 565–581.

Brumberg, Joan Jacobs. 1993. "'Something Happens to Girls': Menarche and the Emergence of the Modern American Hygienic Imperative." *Journal of the History of Sexuality* 4, no. 1: 99–127.

Bullough, Vern L. 1983. "Menarche and Teenage Pregnancy: A Misuse of Historical Data." In *Menarche, the Transition from Girl to Woman*, ed. Sharon Golub. Lexington, MA: Lexington Books.

Thomas, Frederic et al. 2001. "International Variability of Ages at Menarche and Menopause: Patterns and Main Determinants." *Human Biology* 73, no. 2: 271–290.

BARBARA BROOKES

Mental Hygiene

Mental hygiene, the public-health perspective within psychiatry, was influential from 1910 until about 1960. Since World War II, mental hygiene ideas became increasingly incorporated into mainstream psychiatry, in particular through the community health movement of the 1960s. The mental hygiene, or mental health, movement thereafter ceased to exist as a separate movement.

Instead of focusing on the treatment of MENTAL ILLNESS, mental hygienists emphasized early intervention, prevention, and the promotion of mental health. Mental hygienists were interested in children because they were convinced that mental illness and mental disorder were to an important extent related to early childhood experiences. Their interest in prevention made them focus their public-health education activities on reaching parents to inform them about the latest scientific insights in child development and child rearing. Mental hygienists also viewed the educational system as a suitable location for preventive activity and became involved in programs for teacher education and educational reform.

Origins of the Mental Hygiene Movement

The National Committee for Mental Hygiene was founded in New York in 1909 by a number of leading psychiatrists and Clifford W. Beers (1876–1943), who had been institutionalized in several mental hospitals after a nervous breakdown. He described his experiences and the deplorable conditions in mental hospitals in his autobiography *A Mind That Found Itself* (1913). The National Committee aimed to improve conditions in mental hospitals, stimulate research in psychiatry, improve the quality of psychiatric education, develop measures preventing mental illness, and popularize psychiatric and psychological perspectives. Although mental hygiene originated within psychiatry, mental hygiene ideas also inspired social workers, teachers, psychologists, sociologists, and members of other professions. Consequently the mental hygiene movement became interdisciplinary in nature.

The basic ideas of mental hygiene were derived from the dynamic psychiatry of Adolf Meyer (1866–1950). According to Meyer, mental illness and mental disorder were the outcome of the dynamic interaction of individuals with their environments. Inspired by evolutionary theory and the philosophy of pragmatism, Meyer interpreted these conditions as inadequate responses to the challenges of everyday life or as forms of maladjustment. Investigating an individual's life history enabled psychiatrists to trace the origins of maladjustment and to intervene therapeutically. In Meyer's views, the treatment of early forms of maladjustment could prevent more serious problems later on. His ideas also contained suggestions for preventive measures.

During the 1920s, SIGMUND FREUD's psychoanalytic ideas became increasingly influential in the United States.

Psychoanalysis emphasized the importance of early childhood experiences and their impact on mental health later in life. Mental hygienists became convinced that preventive intervention was best directed at growing children and those individuals who had the most extensive contact with them: parents and teachers. Initially mental hygienists emphasized the importance of therapeutic intervention in the emotional problems of young children. They later also emphasized the importance of fostering mental health in all growing children.

Starting in the 1920s, mental hygienists promoted a therapeutic perspective toward the everyday problems of children. The National Committee was instrumental in the establishment of CHILD GUIDANCE clinics. Initially these clinics were associated with JUVENILE COURTS. They were modeled upon the clinic of WILLIAM HEALY (1869–1963), who had been the first director of the Juvenile Psychopathic Institute in Chicago, which was associated with the juvenile court there. In 1917 he became the director of the Judge Baker Foundation in Boston. According to Healy, juvenile delinquents needed to be investigated individually by a team consisting of a psychologist, a psychiatrist, and a social worker in order to ascertain the child's abilities, home background, emotional life, motivations, and intelligence. On this basis an individualized treatment plan could be developed and implemented. During the 1930s child guidance clinics came to focus less on diagnosing and treating juvenile delinquents and more on the therapeutic treatment of the emotional problems of children from middle-class families. Child guidance clinics increasingly treated parents and children who came for help on their own initiative.

During the 1920s academic research on children became increasingly respectable and well organized as a consequence of the funding provided by the LAURA SPELMAN ROCKEFELLER MEMORIAL, a large philanthropic organization that supported research in child development at several academic institutions. The aim was to investigate the development of normal children and to popularize the findings of this research. Inspired by this research, a number of leading mental hygienists argued that preventive activity should no longer be focused on detecting early signs of maladjustment but instead on tracing aberrations in normal child development. Consequently preventive activity was potentially directed at all children instead of only those children who were troublesome to parents and teachers. During the 1930s a few leading mental hygienists developed educational programs aimed at fostering mental health in schoolchildren.

Mental Hygiene and the Educational System

Mental hygienists viewed the educational system as a promising venue for preventive activities because it could potentially reach all children. During the 1930s they successfully influenced teacher education programs to include developmental psychology. Initially they wanted to raise awareness among teachers about the ramifications of educational practices—particularly methods of maintaining control and punishment for transgressions—for mental health. A number of educational reformers became interested in mental hygiene to provide a rationale for educational reform by claiming that the curriculum needed to be organized in conformity with insights in child development. In addition, many Progressive educators viewed the school as the place where children were trained for adjustment; they viewed the school as the preparation for life. The life adjustment movement in education claimed that the school should train the whole child and not just his or her intellect. Educational reformers criticized the traditional academic curriculum for its emphasis on mental discipline and rote learning, which they saw as irrelevant for most children. They advocated instead a variety of educational initiatives such as vocational training and project learning. The influence of these ideas on education was profound: the development of the personality became one of the central goals of education.

The influence of mental hygiene ideas after World War II was illustrated by the pervasive interest of parents, especially mothers, in child-rearing literature. Critics have argued that this literature made mothers unnecessarily worried about the well-being of their children, and the influence of mental hygiene ideas on education was countered at times by an emphasis on the teaching of basic academic skills. In the 1990s the influence of psychiatric and psychological ideas on educational practice has been criticized as one of the causes of educational decline in North America.

See also: **Child Development, History of the Concept of; Child Psychology; Child-Rearing Advice Literature; Delinquency; Hygiene.**

BIBLIOGRAPHY

Beers, Clifford W. 1913. *A Mind That Found Itself: An Autobiography,* 3rd ed. New York: Longmans, Green.

Cohen, Sol. 1983. "The Mental Hygiene Movement, the Development of Personality and the School: The Medicalization of American Education." *History of Education Quarterly* 23: 123–148.

Dain, Norman. 1980. *Clifford W. Beers: Advocate for the Insane.* Pittsburgh: University of Pittsburgh Press.

Jones, Kathleen. 1999. *Taming the Troublesome Child: American Families, Child Guidance, and the Limits of Psychiatric Authority.* Cambridge, MA: Harvard University Press.

Meyer, Adolf. 1948. *The Commonsense Psychiatry of Adolf Meyer: Fifty-Two Selected Papers Edited, with Biographical Narrative, by Alfred Lief.* New York: McGraw-Hill.

Pols, Hans. 2002. "Between the Laboratory and Life: Child Development Research in Toronto, 1919–1956." *History of Psychology* 5, no. 2: 135–162.

Richardson, Theresa. 1989. *The Century of the Child: The Mental Hygiene Movement and Social Policy in the United States and Canada.* Albany: State University of New York Press.

HANS POLS

Mental Illness

Mental illness is a series of disorders and diseases that affect the intellectual, emotional, and psychological makeup of individuals. Causation is wide ranging (from organic and genetic maladies to environmental triggers; from poor nutrition and poverty to psychological trauma) but many times unknown. Because of the myriad of disorders under the label of mental illness, a generalized "cure" has not been developed. Measures to ameliorate the effects of the spectrum of disorders include therapy of various forms, counseling, and pharmacological interventions.

Mental illness does not exist in a social vacuum, independent of the context of time and place. Its assumed etiology (causes) and manifestations are reflections of the social setting in which it exists. The twentieth century saw a large increase in the number of individuals exhibiting symptoms of mental illness. Whether this resulted from better reporting methods, shifting levels of category description, or a generalized increase in the number of individuals afflicted is still open to debate. It is apparent, however, that children at the turn of the twenty-first century were suffering from an epidemic of mental illness. More children in the United States in 2003 suffered from psychiatric illness than from AIDS, leukemia, and diabetes combined. The solutions proposed to the problems caused by mental illness in children reflect the underlying assumptions of society. That these solutions have changed over time similarly reflect that American society itself has reshaped its intellectual presuppositions throughout history.

Religious Causes in Colonial America

Traditionally, emotional and psychological problems in children were viewed through the prism of religion. Children experiencing visions, hearing voices, or enduring seizures were seen as individuals touched by either God or Satan. Etiology was considered as otherworldly; therefore, alleviation of the disorder would come through supplication to the Deity. This was in the form of prayer, Scripture reading, and personal admission of sin and guilt.

The Salem, Massachusetts, witchcraft crisis of 1692 provides the most familiar example of how childhood mental illness was perceived and dealt with during the colonial American era. Dozens of young women were involved in a wide-ranging frenzy of accusations of witchcraft, punctuated by visions, spells, physical maladies, and the belief that Satan was actively working to control individuals in and around Salem Village. Historians have argued over the "actual" cause of these happenings, positing economic, cultural, psychological, and medical explanations. What is known, however, is that contemporaries had only one explanation—the young women participating in the naming of witches were not mentally ill in the modern sense of the term: they were victims in the ongoing battle between God and Satan for the

souls of mankind. Cotton Mather, the influential Puritan clergyman, expressed this belief most clearly in his book *Wonders of the Invisible World*, published in 1692. Mather and other Puritan leaders saw young women, because of their age and dependent condition, as especially susceptible to the hallucinations and physical assaults caused by this cosmic battle. Prayer for the afflicted, as well as punishment for those bewitched by Satan himself, were seen as cures for the physical and mental ailments of the girls involved in the witchcraft hysteria.

Shift to Social Causes in the Eighteenth Century

By the eighteenth century, the hysterical outbursts associated with witchcraft and Satanic possession subsided, lending credence to the belief that social, rather than religious, causes led to the maladies. Incidences of childhood mental disorders were not as visible, or seemingly as prevalent, during this period. Childhood was viewed as a time of unrequited joy, when children did not face the problems and toil of adult life. Adults exhibiting overt signs of mental disorder were treated in differing ways depending on their class and status in society. Upper-class individuals who showed signs of mental problems were usually cared for within the family and labeled as strange or eccentric. Members of the lower class who gave signs of mental disorder often were not able to take care of themselves or their families and were "warned out" of communities or placed in poorhouses, with other undifferentiated categories of dependent individuals. Separate institutions for the mentally ill were developed in the late colonial or early national period throughout the United States and treated their patients (often called inmates) with a combination of primitive medical care (such as purging or bleeding), forced work to give the mind discipline, and moral care based on the treatment plans developed by the French physician Philippe Pinel (1745–1826). Few children, however, were admitted to these new institutions (often called asylums, as their founders saw them as refuges from the problems of an increasingly complex society). Children appeared more often as the victims of familial mental disorder, as wards forced to depend on private and religious philanthropies or the state to raise them.

Gendered Differentiation in the Nineteenth Century

The nineteenth century saw an increasingly gendered differentiation in the maladies that comprised the spectrum of mental disorder. The Industrial Revolution that swept over western Europe and the United States in the first half of the nineteenth century was both a cause and consequence of the emerging separation of the sexes by occupation and position. Dubbed the notion of "separate spheres," this vision of society was one in which men worked outside the home as providers and women ran the household as protectors of the domestic sphere. Changing perceptions of women's emotional, intellectual, and sexual makeup accompanied this paradigm shift. Seen as needing male protection to survive, women were classified into a larger category of dependent individuals, a category that also included children. By the middle of the nineteenth century, women and young girls were exhibiting a series of mental maladies that doctors and social critics tied to the specific problems of female anatomy and emotionalism. Running the emotional gamut from depressive melancholia to hyperemotional hysteria, these disorders could be acute or chronic, incapacitating or simply bothersome. Attempts at cures ranged from bed rest, asylum stays, and dietary changes to medical interventions such as water treatments and purgatives. Most regimens were not successful, but many women recovered to live what seemed to be "normal" lives.

These disorders were inordinately centered in young women of the upper and middle classes who were among the first of their sex to achieve higher levels of formal education, an education that may have been in strong conflict with the prevailing assumptions of female dependency. By the last quarter of the century, medical doctors had developed a name for these emotional illnesses—*neurasthenia*, or a weakness of the nervous system. Popularized by the American neurologist George Beard and the American physiologist S. Weir Mitchell, the term became a catchall category for the mental problems associated with feminized nervous energy. That young upper-class males also began to be diagnosed with the disease (for example, the American psychologist and philosopher William James was incapacitated for almost a year with nervous problems) led doctors to decry the feminization of American culture. A strident dose of "the strenuous life" was recommended to cure "weak" young males of this malady.

Neurasthenia was not seen as a problem among young people from the working class. The emotional problems these people exhibited were thought to arise from their inferior intellectual makeups or their genetic background. With the advent of massive streams of immigrants from southern and eastern Europe in the last twenty years of the nineteenth century, the composition of the American working class took on an increasingly foreign character. Medical doctors (almost exclusively from white American backgrounds) viewed foreigners as inferior and unable to handle the problems associated with complex modern societies. The lack of assimilation into mainstream American society, the petty crime that many young immigrant males seemingly engaged in, and the perceived inability of young immigrant women to rise to standards of appropriate feminine behavior all contributed to notions of immigrant inferiority. The increasingly foreign composition of state institutions for those with mental problems seemed to validate that belief. These mental problems among immigrants were not thought to be curable, as they were believed to be manifestations of inherited, and therefore, unchangeable traits.

Twentieth Century: Competition among Social, Psychological, and Medical Paradigms

By 1900, childhood and ADOLESCENCE were clearly viewed as separate stages of life, with their own problems and possibilities. The development of separate public institutions designed around the needs of children became a key component of Progressive-era changes during the first two decades of the twentieth century. Historians debate whether JUVENILE COURTS and specialized facilities for young offenders that arose during this period were instruments of social reform or social control. What is not at issue, however, is the notion that children were to be treated differently because they had different needs and concerns. Because of this seminal shift, historian Theresa R. Richardson, following the lead of reformer ELLEN KEY, has called the twentieth century "THE CENTURY OF THE CHILD."

With this transition, doctors began to examine the issue of childhood diseases as a separate category of analysis. The mental disorders of children were not immune from this alteration. Simultaneously, the development of psychology as a discrete discipline saw the bifurcation of the understanding of what caused and what constituted mental disorders. The neurasthenic problems were increasingly viewed as emotional or intellectual problems, rather than somatic illnesses (those affecting the body). They could be cured or alleviated through therapy and counseling, not medical intervention. The more serious mental illnesses, often labeled around the catchall phrase of insanity, still remained the purview of medical doctors, who were marginalized as employees of large state institutions. Insanity appeared incurable, but by the 1920s and 1930s doctors experimented with such invasive techniques as electroshock therapy and lobotomy surgery with decidedly mixed results. Finally, problems that had been categorized as mental disorders, particularly those associated with young boys such as theft and truancy, were increasingly viewed as social, rather than medical, disorders. As such, they became issues for social workers and JUVENILE JUSTICE officials, rather than psychologists or medical doctors.

The social, psychological, and medical paradigms competed for control over the issues of mental disorder in general, and childhood mental illness more specifically, throughout the twentieth century. By approximately 1975, the success of the medical model in establishing hegemony over the field of what became known as mental illness was a seminal moment. The medicalization of problems in adjusting to social situations led to a reliance on both over-the-counter and prescription pharmaceuticals to solve disorders previously assumed to be social in nature. New advances in genetics revealed the importance of biological characteristics in the development of such disorders as drug addiction and alcoholism. Finally, the *Diagnostic and Statistical Manual of Mental Disorders* of the American Psychiatric Association drastically increased the type and number of mental disorders from 112 in the first edition, published in 1952, to 374 in the fourth edition, published in 1994. Many of these newly defined disorders deal specifically with mental illnesses of childhood. As the twenty-first century began, childhood mental illness was defined as a major social problem. Solutions and cures appeared difficult to come by, as contentious arguments continued over the efficacy of medical interventions and the true nature of childhood mental disorders.

Exacerbating the issues surrounding the medicalization of childhood mental disorders are concerns over both the increasing number of children exhibiting these illnesses and of the class, racial, and gendered nature of these problems. Whereas some disorders, such as conduct disorders and oppositional defiance, occur overwhelmingly in young males, others, especially eating disorders such as ANOREXIA and bulimia, are mainly female in character. The epidemics of attention deficit hyperactivity disorder (ADHD) and autism similarly show significant male components, whereas anxiety disorders occur largely in females. Physicians and researchers search for stronger connections between genetics and disorders such as childhood schizophrenia, while rates of teen SUICIDE continue to increase. Teen violence—despite high-profile cases such as the Columbine High School shootings in middle-class, white, suburban Littleton, Colorado, in 1999—is overwhelmingly centered in poor, minority, urban neighborhoods. Physicians report that minority youths receive approximately one-third the support given to white youths suffering from similar mental health problems. National Institutes of Health reports show that in 2001, one out of ten children and adolescents suffered from a mental disorder severe enough to cause some level of impairment, yet only about 20 percent of those affected received needed treatment. The issue of mental illness in children will remain a pervasive national concern to Americans well into the twenty-first century, as citizens debate the nature of these disorders and their relationship to broader social trends.

See also: **Child Psychology.**

BIBLIOGRAPHY

Gijswijt-Hofstra, Marijke, and Roy Porter, eds. 2001. *Cultures of Neurasthenia: From Beard to the First World War.* Amsterdam: Rodopi.

Lutz, Tom. 1991. *American Nervousness, 1903: An Anecdotal History.* Ithaca, NY: Cornell University Press.

Richardson, Theresa R. 1989. *The Century of the Child: The Mental Hygiene Movement and Social Policy in the United States and Canada.* Albany: State University of New York Press.

Safford, Philip L., and Elizabeth J. Safford. 1996. *A History of Childhood and Disability.* New York: Teachers College Press.

INTERNET RESOURCES

"Childhood Mental Health." Available from <www. childhooddisorders.com>.

"Mental Disorders in America." Available from <www. nimh.nih.gov/publicat/numbers.cfm>.

STEVEN NOLL

Middle East

Children under the age of fifteen constitute the majority of the population today in most Middle Eastern countries. This burgeoning population is challenging many long-accepted assumptions about children's needs, development, and future. In this entry we will outline the old cultural ideal of childhood and then turn to the new conditions which bring this ideal into question.

Childhood and family patterns have, until recently, been similar across religious and ethnic lines: the extended family was the fundamental unit of the society; the patrilineal model was basic to that family ideal; and childhood was seen as a time, not of play, but of learning and training for the duties and responsibilities of adulthood. Some significant differences also obtained: the ban on divorce among Christians, for instance, in contrast to Jews and Muslims, meant that the world of the child, as well as of the adult, was not always the same. But overall, similarities were greater than differences.

In the predominantly agrarian societies of the past, the primary social unit across the Middle East was the extended family, which might range in size from twenty to two hundred people, related on both sides of the marital connection, and which operated together for survival. Within this kin group, each child received identity, affection, discipline, role models, and economic and social support, ideally from birth to death. In exchange the family required conformity and loyalty from all members, beginning in early childhood. The crucial test of allegiance came at the time of marriage, when the son or daughter either acceded to or rebelled against the wishes of the family. Marriage in this system was not officially perceived as an emotional attachment between individuals (though this might develop later) but as an economic and social contract between two family groups, which was to benefit both. Although marriage was a crucial step in tying individual members to the group, it was the birth of children that conferred full adult status on both the man and the woman. Only after the birth of children were the newly married man and woman considered full members of their particular family and adult members of the wider society. Such attitudes toward marriage and children are found in Christian and Jewish groups, but within ISLAM they are intensified. "When a man has children he has fulfilled half of his religion, so let him fear God for the remaining half," states one of the *hadith*, or sayings of the Prophet Muhammad. Children have always been valued in Middle Eastern traditions, not only for economic and political but also for religious reasons.

The Jewish, Christian, and Muslim family systems are patrilineal; that is, in the reckoning of one's descent, kin-group membership passes through the male line on the father's side. A girl is a member of her father's family, but unlike her brother, she cannot pass that membership on to her children. In the Islamic tradition, male and female descendants of the same father inherit from him, and continue to carry his name throughout their lives. A daughter never takes her husband's surname for example, but retains, like a son, the name of the father. The patrilineal system is hierarchically organized, with the oldest male ideally holding publicly accepted authority over his descendants, and acting as the primary economic provider of the group. He remained head of the group and controller of its economic resources, including the labor of its members, as long as he lived. Without issue, and particularly male issue, the kin group as traditionally constituted could not continue. Children were on the lowest rung of the group in terms of power. But their presence was crucial, for they were the generational link to the family unit, the key to its continuation, and the living person that tied the present to the past and to the future. Hence great pressure was placed on newly married couples to produce children, particularly sons, who could carry the name and take over the burden of supporting the family. Daughters were also important, to help mothers and grandmothers and as potential brides for men within the larger kin group, but sons were of primary importance.

Specific instructions about the care and training of the child are found in Jewish, Christian, and Muslim texts. Many ethnographies document attitudes toward small babies—great indulgence, on-demand breast-feeding, and affectionate behavior from mothers, fathers, older siblings, and relatives. This pattern included early toilet training, often before the age of one year, and either long-term breast-feeding or abrupt weaning, the latter taking place when the next child was born. Weaning marked the end of parental indulgence and the beginning of socialization into specific gender roles. The prophet Muhammad is reported to have said, "Be gentle to your children the first seven years, and in the following seven be firm." Jewish attitudes might be summarized as "The rod and reproof give wisdom, but a child left to himself causes shame to his mother" (Prov. 29:15). DISCIPLINE began long before the age of seven. Girls as young as four or five were expected to share responsibility for a younger sibling; small boys would be given responsibilities such as caring for animals in rural areas; in urban areas, the boy would be asked to run errands or help in the family business. Such expectations are still common.

Socialization for other societal norms of behavior began almost as soon as the child was conscious of others. These included respect for food, for religion, for the kin group, hospitality to guests, and above all, respect for and obedience to the authority of the father. According to the Egyptian sociologist Hamed Ammar, a Muslim, a good child is one who is a *muaddab*, polite and disciplined, and conforming to the values of the group. The goal of child rearing was to instill and develop reason, which was seen to be necessary for successful adult life. Jewish and Christian families had similar expectations. The child's period of socialization was also marked by ritual events, such as ceremonies surrounding

birth and NAMING; CIRCUMCISION for all boys and some girls; and successful completion of religious schooling, whether Judaic, Christian, or Muslim. Religious socialization took place in the home for both boys and girls and also in local religious schools. Although circumcision of boys was more or less universal, circumcision of girls was not. Female circumcision has no religious justification in Judaism, Christianity, or Islam, but is a traditional cultural practice found mainly along the Nile, among both Christian and Muslim groups. Girls in North Africa had a different RITE OF PASSAGE, an ear-piercing ceremony, held when the child was four or five years old.

The cultural ideals of the past meant, in sum, the primacy of the group over its individual members; the importance of children, especially sons, to continue and maintain the group; and the dominance of the father. Religious ideology reinforced this ideal. It began to be questioned at the end of the eighteenth century, with invasions by European powers, colonial rule, and then resistance and revolution followed by independence and the emergence in the mid-twentieth century of modern nation states.

The nineteenth and early twentieth century were periods of political and economic upheaval. European colonial rulers denigrated traditional patterns: language, traditional technology, folklore, modes of subsistence, religion (Islam, the majority religion in the area, was seen as "the stagnant hand of the past"), and social structure. However, Western influence did not, as had been expected, disrupt the patrilineal model of family or the perception of childhood as a time of learning and preparation for adulthood. Rather, as colonialism became stronger and men found their authority diminished, the family became the last refuge where traditions of child rearing, socialization for male and female gender roles, and parental authority could still operate. The only exception was the institution of the kibbutz, or collective farm, in the area which would become the state of ISRAEL in 1948. Early Jewish immigrants had, as early as the 1920s, set up kibbutzim as conscious alternatives to the old patriarchal system that operated in the European countries where the immigrants had grown up. The kibbutz was organized so that not only economic activities were collective, but so also were child rearing, PARENTING, and schooling. The experiment continues in Israel today, though less than 5 percent of the population now live and work on kibbutzim.

In the modern nation-states of the contemporary Middle East, several important factors may eventually affect the traditional family system, and therefore the traditional view of childhood. The patriarchal system remains firmly in place, though movements continue for increased equality for women. Such movements, however, are focused not on destroying the family, but on giving more equality to men and women within the family. The introduction of universal free public education, mostly secular in nature, has resulted in an impressive climb in LITERACY rates (80 percent in Kuwait; 90 percent in Israel; 60 percent in Egypt; 90 percent in Jordan; 70 percent in Iraq). A middle class is rapidly developing in almost all countries, and the majority of people now live in cities, not rural areas. But unemployment plus spiraling inflation has led millions of men to migrate for work outside their countries and millions of women to work outside the home. Fathers are thus absent for crucial years in their children's lives, and mothers, too, are away for most of the day. Parental authority is thus no longer omnipresent. On the other hand, children are still being socialized for female and male roles. The high cost of living has led to children staying longer in their parents' residence, often contributing to family income. Young people are being forced to delay marriage, largely for economic reasons, which in turn is bringing down national birth rates. TELEVISION is everywhere, putting children and teenagers in touch with the outside world. All of these factors may lead to future change in the concept of childhood and the practices of child rearing for both boys and girls, but this has yet to be documented.

BIBLIOGRAPHY

Ammar, Hamed. 1954. *Growing Up in an Egyptian Village.* London: Routledge and Kegan Paul.

Fernea, Elizabeth, ed. 1995. *Children in the Muslim Middle East.* Austin: University of Texas Press.

Meijer, Roel, ed. 2000. *Alienation or Integration of Arab Youth: Between Family, State, and Street.* Richmond, UK: Curzon Press.

Rugh, Andrea. 1997. *Within the Circle: Parents and Children in an Arab Village.* New York: Columbia University Press.

Talman, Yonina. 1972. *Family and Community in the Kibbutz.* Cambridge, MA: Harvard University Press.

ELIZABETH WARNOCK FERNEA

Midwifery. *See* Obstetrics and Midwifery.

Milne, A. A. *See* Children's Literature.

Montessori, Maria (1870–1952)

Maria Montessori was born in Chiaravalle, Italy, on August 31, 1870. She was one of the most famous figures in the diverse and frequently contradictory formation known as the Progressive education movement. As was the case in other fields at the time, it was a male-dominated movement and Montessori was its most prominent woman leader. A first-wave feminist who, when young, had spoken at women's conferences, she overcame many social obstacles to become an internationally renowned public figure. Among the potential barriers to her success was the fact that she was a sin-

gle parent. Throughout her life she managed to conceal from the general public the fact that she had a son. She was driven by an unshakable belief in the correctness of her educational opinions and beliefs and was highly skilled in communicating them to international audiences. The strength of her convictions about the efficacy of her methods, while adding to her persuasiveness, paradoxically undermined her ambition to see her practices widely adopted. This failure was also partly due to the necessity to generate income from her method and apparatus in order to live. Unable to sanction any version or representation of her methods other than those over which she had complete control, the movement she inspired repeatedly split when she disowned it.

Although Montessori's impact was perhaps greatest in the field of early childhood education, where PROGRESSIVE EDUCATION was at its most coherent, as she outlined in her *The Advanced Montessori Method* (1917), she hoped that her method would be implemented in schools for older children. Like other child-centered educators, such as JOHANN PESTALOZZI, FRIEDRICH FROEBEL, and JOHN DEWEY, she made a unique contribution to the formulation of the general principles and practices that currently inform the field of early childhood education.

In 1896 Montessori became the first woman graduate of a medical school in Italy. In 1897 she joined the staff of the psychiatric clinic attached to the University of Rome and as part of her work she visited mental asylums and came into contact with children who at that time were referred to as "feebleminded." This encounter led her to an examination of the work of the French physicians Jean-Marc-Gaspard Itard and Édouard Séguin who, earlier in the nineteenth century, had written about children with physical and mental disabilities. Having formed the opinion that the problems encountered by such children required a pedagogical rather than a medical solution, Montessori then embarked on a study of the work of the Romantic educationalists Pestalozzi, Froebel, and JEAN-JACQUES ROUSSEAU, as well as other less well known educational theorists. In addition, she studied anthropology, particularly the versions taught by Cesare Lombroso and Giuseppe Sergi. From this mix of study and experience she concluded that, given the right scientific approach, the children of the poor, including the disabled, were all educable and that by this means social reform could be achieved.

For two years, from 1900 to 1902, she held a position at the Orthophrenic School, an institute responsible for the training of teachers in schools for physically and mentally disabled children. During this time, she developed her own apparatus based on that of Itard and Seguin to assist children's learning. From 1904 until 1908 she lectured at the University of Rome in anthropology and education. Her lectures were published in a book entitled *Pedagogical Anthropology* (1913). While the content of this book is dated it contains ample evidence of Montessori's social reforming impulses, and her commitment to "scientific pedagogy" and social regeneration. Overall, her work is characterized by a combination of positivism and spirituality or even mysticism, mixed with Roman Catholicism, feminism, and theosophy.

During this period, the focus of her work changed from a concern with the physical condition of individuals to their social condition. In this respect the trajectory of her thinking was similar to that of social reforming women in many countries such as Kate Douglas Wiggin of the free KINDERGARTEN movement in the United States and Margaret McMillan, the pioneer of nursery schools in England.

Montessori's involvement in attempts at social reform intensified in 1907 when her *Casa dei Bambini* (Children's House) was opened in a model dwelling in a slum in the San Lorenzo district of Rome. There she was able to experiment with the educational methods and apparatus that she had developed with children with disabilities. Many visitors to the *Casa dei Bambini*, and to the other schools she opened subsequently, were astonished by the success of her approach.

In 1912, an English edition of her book on her work at the *Casa dei Bambini* was published. Entitled *The Montessori Method*, this book made her internationally famous. In it she outlined the origin of her pedagogical apparatus which was used for sense training and which, she claimed, made possible, "the method of *observation* and *liberty*." Observation by the teacher, individualism, and autoeducation were the watchwords of the Montessori method. The latter meant that by means of carefully graded apparatus the children would educate themselves in a prepared environment with little help from a teacher.

By 1913, the year of her first trip to the United States, Montessori's fame had spread widely and both the educational and mainstream press were full of reports of her work. From then until the end of the 1920s, Montessori occupied a prominent place in education debate and policy. Although many schools adopted some of her ideas, few implemented them in their entirety. During this period Montessori travelled widely and provided training courses for teachers in many countries.

In 1924, she accepted government support for her methods in Italy from the fascist dictator Benito Mussolini. Ten years later when she refused to concede further to the demands made by Mussolini, he ordered that all the Montessori schools in Italy be closed. The same fate befell her schools in Germany, Austria and Spain as Nazi and fascist governments came to power. As the threat of war intensified, Montessori began to devote her efforts to a campaign for world peace.

During World War II, Montessori was stranded in India when the British authorities in India interned her son, Mario, as an enemy alien. They had gone there at the invitation of the Theosophical Society just as the war broke out. When the war ended, Montessori resumed her work of training teachers, lecturing and publication. Her later books, which include *The Absorbent Mind*, consist mainly of notes of her lectures. Montessori died in 1952 near The Hague in the Netherlands. Her ideas still attract followers in education and the *Association Montessori Internationale* (AMI), founded in 1929 continues to promote them.

See also: **Age and Development; Child Development, History of the Concept of; Education, Europe.**

BIBLIOGRAPHY

Beatty, Barbara. 1995. *Preschool Education in America*. New Haven, CT: Yale University Press.

Brehony, Kevin J. 2000. "Montessori, Individual Work and Individuality in the Elementary School Classroom." *History of Education* 29, no. 2: 115–128.

Chattin-McNichols, John. 1992. *The Montessori Controversy*. Albany, NY: Delmar.

Cohen, Sol. 1968. "Educating the Children of the Urban Poor: Maria Montessori and her Method." *Education and Urban Society* 1, no. 1: 61–79.

Cohen, Sol. 1969. "Maria Montessori: Priestess or Pedagogue?" *Teachers College Record* 71, no. 2: 313–326.

Cunningham, Peter. 2000. "The Montessori Phenomenon: Gender and Internationalism in Early Twentieth-Century Innovation." In *Practical Visionaries: Women, Education and Social Progress, 1790–1930*, ed. Mary Hilton and Pam Hirsch. New York: Longman.

Kramer, Rita. 1968. *Maria Montessori: A Biography*. Oxford, UK: Basil Blackwell.

Martin, Jane Roland. 1994. *Changing the Educational Landscape: Philosophy, Women, and Curriculum*. New York: Routledge.

Montessori, Maria. 1912. *The Montessori Method*. Trans. Anne E. George. New York: Frederick Stokes.

Montessori, Maria. 1913. *Pedagogical Anthropology*. Trans. Frederic Taber Cooper. London: Heinemann.

Montessori, Maria. 1914. *Dr Montessori's Own Handbook*. London: Heinemann.

Montessori, Maria. 1917. *The Advanced Montessori Method*. Trans. Arthur Livingston. New York: Frederick A. Stokes.

Montessori, Maria. 1967. *The Absorbent Mind*. Trans. Claude A. Claremont. New York: Holt.

Rohrs, Hermann. 1982. "Montessori, Maria." *Prospects* 12, no. 4: 524–530.

INTERNET RESOURCE

Association Montessori Internationale. 2002. Available from <www.montessori-ami.org/ami.htm>.

KEVIN J. BREHONY

Mortality. *See* Grief, Death, Funerals; Infant Mortality.

Mortara Abduction

On the evening of June 23, 1858, in Bologna, papal police broke into the home of a six-year-old Jewish child, Edgardo Mortara, and snatched him from his distraught and bewildered parents. According to Inquisition authorities in Rome, the family's Catholic housekeeper testified that she had had Edgardo secretly baptized when he fell ill at the age of one. The kidnappers had the law on their side, for the abduction of Edgardo, which was the most infamous example of several such cases in nineteenth-century Italy, was sanctioned by canon law, which maintained that a child once baptized was forbidden to be reared in a Jewish home. Edgardo was spirited away to the Catechumens and his Catholicization began immediately. Frantic efforts to have the child released came to naught; his parents were repeatedly told, however, that they could be reunited with their son provided they themselves converted. Despite the storm of international protest, both popular and diplomatic, Pius IX refused to relent and in fact raised Edgardo as his own "son." Pio Edgardo Mortara joined the priesthood in 1873. A celebrated preacher, he failed, despite consistent efforts, to induce his parents to convert. Mortara died in a Belgian abbey on March 11, 1940.

Beyond the immediate family tragedy occasioned by the kidnapping, the event had profound historical implications. Men such as Count Camillo Cavour, the architect of Italian unification, and Napoleon III of France, both of whom sought to destroy the temporal authority of the Papal States, used the affair to agitate against Rome. Protestants across Europe and the United States were incensed by the injustice and mobilized against the obscurantism of the Catholic Church. Both the failure of world Jewry's protests to free the boy and the abduction itself only underscored Jewish vulnerability. The Mortara Affair made Jews aware of the need for a central body to represent their interests. In 1860 in Paris they founded the Alliance Israélite Universelle (Universal Jewish Alliance). Its motto, taken from the Talmud, was "All Israel is responsible for one another." The organization actively sought to combat discrimination against Jews wherever it occurred. When Pius IX was elected pope in 1846, liberal Catholic circles had hoped that Pius would lead a liberalizing trend and reverse the conservative thrust of his predecessor, Gregory IX. Pius's first two years fulfilled their expectations but the political upheavals of 1848 saw him reverse policy, and his thirty-two-year-long pontificate, the longest in Church history, waged a relentless battle against the forces of modernity. The Mortara Affair is emblematic of this stance, as was Pius's issuance of the Syllabus of Errors in 1864, which, among other things, condemned freedom of speech and religious tolerance. In September 2000, Pope John Paul II beatified Pius IX.

The kidnapping of Edgardo Mortara was not the act of an all-powerful church. Rather, it was a last-gasp effort to assert its shrinking temporal authority. While Edgardo was lost to his family and community, the long-term effect of the abduction was to diminish the power of the Papacy, for it galvanized those forces promoting liberalism, nationalism, Italian unification, and anticlericalism. In 1870 Italian troops entered Rome and the temporal power of the popes, which had lasted for a thousand years, came to an end.

See also: **Abduction; Catholicism; Judaism.**

BIBLIOGRAPHY

Kertzer, David I. 1997. *The Kidnapping of Edgardo Mortara.* New York: Knopf.

JOHN M. EFRON

Mothering and Motherhood

It is common sense that all mothers love and care for their children. Or at least it is comforting to believe this is true in all times and places. Yet news broadcasts flash crimes such as teenage mothers abandoning infants in restrooms, mothers burning cigarettes into their children's flesh, mothers starving their children to death, and the like. Although this short entry cannot consider motherhood and mothering (the tasks of caring for children) in all times and places, it offers evidence from several eras and continents to suggest historical and cultural variations in motherhood and mothering. In other words, operating on the premise that both motherhood and mothering are socially constructed, this entry looks at how both ideas about what a mother is and should be and ideas about how mothers should care for their children have varied over time and space. It focuses primarily on agricultural and industrial societies of the nineteenth and twentieth centuries. (Some references for continents not covered in the text appear in the bibliography.)

Motherhood

For analytic purposes, it is possible to distinguish several types of motherhood based on social recognition and function—birth motherhood, social motherhood, and care-giving motherhood. First, the birth mother is the person who physically gives birth to the child. Since the development of new reproductive technologies, the concept of birth mother has become more complicated, for if another person donated the egg, the child in the womb may not be the biological offspring of the birth mother. Second, in some societies the social mother, the person who is married to the head of a household or listed on a registration form, is recognized by the people of the community as a child's mother, even though she might not be the birth mother. Third, the aspect of motherhood involving child-rearing tasks such as feeding, bathing, dressing, watching over, TOILET TRAINING, and teaching basic MANNERS to a child may be called care-giving motherhood. Of course persons other than the mother can perform child-rearing tasks. In the United States in the early 2000s, many but not all people expect that the birth mother,

Sistine Madonna (1513), Raphael. In Western art and culture, the Madonna has served as a powerful image of ideal motherhood, one of selfless love and devotion. The Art Archive/Gemaldegalerie Dresden/The Art Archive.

social mother, and care-giving mother be the same person, but this has not necessarily been the case in all times and places.

In some cases, the birth mother is known as a surrogate mother, a woman who carries or gives birth to a child, with society then recognizing the social mother as the child's mother. New procedures allow the implanting of a woman's fertilized egg in the womb of another woman who carries and gives birth to the baby. Surrogate mothers, however, have existed in societies without advanced medical technologies. Set in Korea in a past era when ADOPTION was frowned on and when carrying on the father's lineage was the highest family goal, the film *The Surrogate Mother* (1986) describes the secretive life of a lower-class birth mother during her hidden pregnancy. After the child is brought to the home of the wealthy but barren social mother, the birth mother is driven out of the community in secret at night, to be forgotten and never to see her child again. And all the while, helped by her servants, the social mother fakes pregnancy by stuffing pillows under the high-waisted native Korean dresses and agonizes that the deception might be uncovered.

In U.S. society today, it is generally expected that the birth mother will serve as the care-giving mother of an infant. In many societies past and present, however, it is thought normal or socially acceptable for persons other than the biological mother to be the primary caregiver for infants and older children. Other possible main caretakers for children, besides the birth or social mother, include grandmothers, SIBLINGS, wet nurses, governesses, foster mothers, live-in or commuting BABY-SITTERS, or even apprentices or grandfathers. In JAPAN from the nineteenth to early twentieth century, live-in baby-sitters (*komori*) carried tended infants or babies on their backs all day and slept by them at night, freeing farm mothers to participate in agricultural labor. They brought infants to the mother to nurse. Commuting baby-sitters did the same but did not sleep with their charges at night. Boy apprentices sometimes carried babies on their backs all day.

Mothering

In examining motherhood, the complexity and cross-cultural variability of the tasks of mothering become visible. Mothering takes many years of labor providing physical care to a growing child. A bare minimum of care includes feeding, clothing, and guarding the safety of infants and children, but beyond these mothering usually includes keeping children clean and healthy and efforts to educate or socialize children to earn a living and to fit into the family, the community, and religious and other institutions as well as the larger society and nation.

Although only the woman who carries a child during pregnancy can give birth and often only the woman who is registered as a child's mother is recognized as the mother by society, as mentioned, the tasks of care-giving motherhood—feeding, bathing, watching over, sleeping by, and training a child—can be and are done by persons other than the birth or social mother. In other words, when broadly defined as carrying out such tasks, "mothering" can be performed by nonmothers.

Ideas about motherhood and mothering do not exist in a vacuum. Ideas about what a mother is, how mothers should think, and what mothers should do are influenced by ideas about attitudes and behavior toward children and expectations concerning other possible caregivers and socializers. Other caregivers may include fathers, sisters, brothers, aunts, uncles, GRANDPARENTS, GODPARENTS, neighbors, and others in kin or residential groups, communities, and the larger society. They may also include institutions such as boarding schools, ORPHANAGES, day-care centers, KINDERGARTENS, schools, and reformatories. Also, activities besides caring for infants and children can have an impact on notions of motherhood and mothering. In particular, economic activities—farm, handicraft, and service work in agricultural societies, and manufacturing, clerical, technical, research, and service work in industrial societies—may demand large amounts of time that compete with minding children.

When the family is a unit of production and women's labor is crucial to its survival, there may be low expectations for mothers to devote themselves to care-giving motherhood or the tasks of mothering—the physical care, minding, and socialization of children. That is, although proximity of domestic (or reproductive) labor such as child rearing and housekeeping to public or social (or productive) labor such as farming, petty manufacturing, trading, or retailing in household enterprises might seem to ease mothers' participation in both types of labor, in fact the long hours of labor required for farming, secondary employments, cooking, washing, and other necessary tasks can severely limit the time that adult women can spend on CHILD CARE. While the birth mother is indispensable to the continuity of family, community, people, or nation, and while the social or political order generally requires children to have a social mother then and now, neither the state nor society can require a woman to be a care-giving mother if her family circumstances do not allow it. When others assume daily child-care tasks, this frees women from the burdens of care-giving motherhood to perform other vital activities. In this way, in agricultural communities care-giving motherhood or mothering activities might not be central to women's lives or ideals of womanhood, at least for certain classes or social groups.

As the workplace separates from the home in industrial societies, mothers' participation in productive and reproductive labor becomes more problematic. Yet as the work of mothering becomes more difficult for wage-earning women in industrial societies, new ideals of female domesticity can emerge and spread among nonworking, middle-class women, such as expectations of closer mother–child bonds, mothers devoting more time to children and child rearing, and higher standards of children's cleanliness, socialization, nutrition, education, and leisure. The next sections present a few concrete examples of motherhood and mothering in agricultural and industrial societies in varied eras and places.

Motherhood and Mothering in Agricultural Societies

In agricultural societies, much of the labor producing a family's subsistence is expended on the land—whether as unpaid labor on the family's owned or rented fields or as farm labor for wages in someone else's fields. When fields are cultivated primarily by family members, especially when household size is small, a mother's farm work is often indispensable. In this case, however, expectations that a mother will serve as the sole or even the primary caregiver for infants may be absent.

Although trade and manufacturing increased steadily over time, until the late nineteenth century, the United States was predominantly an agricultural nation. According to Laurel Thatcher Ulrich, author of the 1980 book, *Good Wives*, in northern New England in the colonial period (1650–1750) there was very high regard for birth mother-hood as the genesis not only of children but also of grand-children and more distant descendants in a time of high IN-FANT MORTALITY. The patriarchal social order, which valued strictness and obedience, tended to frown on women as care-giving mothers, regarding motherly love and indulgence as fostering disrespectful children. Tenderness and affection expressed toward infants gave way to DISCIPLINE, obedience, and religious training as children grew older. Also, Ulrich argued that mothers tended not to "focus intense care and concern" (p. 157) on a single child in their own household, although they were willing to help keep an eye on their neighbors' offspring. In the preindustrial United States, there existed other variations in conceptions of motherhood and mothering that were influenced by regional, religious, ethnic, economic, and other factors.

In stem families, households containing one couple of each generation, in Japanese villages from the eighteenth to the mid-nineteenth century, authority over children, especially over the heir to the headship and property, belonged to the older generation. (This was also the case in urban enterprise households.) In households of poor and average means, so great was the need for mothers' labor at agriculture and handicrafts that child care was generally left to anyone but the biological mother. Therefore, older children, grandmothers, grandfathers, child baby-sitters, or apprentices—that is, household members who could contribute less to the family livelihood—tended babies and children. Caregiving motherhood was less important than advancing the family enterprise, and adoption of kin or nonkin to continue the family line reduced the importance of birth motherhood in early modern and modern Japan.

Interestingly, within one nation or even one community, cultures of rural mothering might diverge. According to a 1991 article by David L. Ransel, two distinct cultures of mothering coexisted side by side in villages in the Volga region of late-nineteenth-century rural Russia, with very different consequences for infant survival. Tatar (Muslim) customs included household and personal cleanliness and breast-feeding on demand for one to three years as well as a peak of births occurring in the winter, and these customs produced far lower infant mortality than Russian customs. For ethnic Russians, despite their custom of breast-feeding, the introduction of solid foods from birth spread germs from foodstuffs and adult bodies to infants, and the peak of births in the summer months coincided with more favorable conditions for the incidence and spread of foodborne and other diseases. Also, Tatar customs seem to have valued motherhood more and allowed women more rest after childbirth, whereas ethnic Russian customs placed greater emphasis on mothers' labor contributions or productivity and their immediate return to agricultural and household labor following childbirth.

People living in highly industrialized societies tend to overlook the fact that many contemporary societies are predominantly agricultural. That is, although industry exists in most countries today, a bare or overwhelming majority of the population may earn a living from farming. In some contemporary societies, expectations of child care are lower because of women's extensive participation in agriculture or handicrafts; in other societies, women are burdened by dual expectations that they will contribute to family livelihood and carry the main burdens of child care and housework.

In late-twentieth-century CHINA, despite regional and ethnic differences in women's economic participation in the north and south, family continuity through birth of a son to carry on the family name remained a cherished goal. In ethnic Chinese households, the senior generation had authority over child rearing, with the birth mother typically caring for the children under her mother-in-law's supervision, or with both women serving as care-giving mothers. For a time, in a rush for economic development, the People's Republic of China developed rural child-care facilities and communal kitchens to aid mothers' domestic and public participation, although these facilities have diminished with the turn to privatized farm and workshop production since the 1980s. Although family reforms have been in place since the 1950s, there is still a tendency for the mother to defer to the authority of coresident in-laws, especially her mother-in-law, in the upbringing of children. Child care also tends to fall on the senior generation for practical reasons, in particular to free mothers to engage in income-earning activities in order to increase family wealth. With a one-child policy in effect to reduce Chinese population growth, mothers, other caregivers, and kin now tend to indulge and to lavish attention on children, collectively nicknamed "Little Emperors." As in China, birth motherhood in INDIA is virtually imperative for family continuity, which is linked to south Asian customs, including religious traditions and the need for a son. Yet emphasis on motherhood as necessary for family continuity may be declining, especially in urban areas, as alternatives to relying on children for support in old age develop and as occupation, status, and wealth rather than maintaining an eternal line of descent become overriding goals for individuals.

Motherhood and Mothering in Industrial Societies

Several changes associated with the rise of industrial societies had a definite impact on the attitudes and practices of motherhood and mothering. First, the low wages, very long working hours, and unhealthy working conditions in early factories had negative effects on poor and working-class mothers' capacity to take care of their children. Second, the separation of home and workplace with the rise of large-scale industries made it more difficult for those engaging in wage work to participate in child rearing and other forms of household labor. Third, besides an impact on mothering, the separation of home and workplace encouraged greater emphasis on female domesticity, especially for the middle class. Middle-class mothers were expected to stay at home rather than engage in wage-earning activities and to devote themselves above all to caring for children and the household. Fourth, middle-class social ideals were often projected onto groups whose economic and cultural conditions did not suit such expectations. Fifth, depressed rural economic conditions or hopes for better employment led peasants to migrate to cities where they entered domestic service, became hawkers or day laborers, or took on other casual, nonindustrial work. In this way, urbanization had a dynamic effect that was partially independent from industrialization (mass production using power-driven machinery). Because urbanization and industrialization tended to occur in urban areas, the examples in this section are mainly drawn from cities. They reveal that despite rising expectations, in the industrial era motherhood and mothering cannot always operate in ways that secure children's survival. The examples illustrate some of the conditions and dynamics shaping motherhood and mothering in early and late industrial societies, but they should not be seen as providing systematic, or even representative, coverage. Similar and divergent examples may be found for other localities, nations, and regions.

For early Russian factory owners, motherhood and the labor of mothering were a low priority. Female factory workers with children therefore made do as best they could. In St. Petersburg in 1912, only one-quarter of working mothers could feed their infants at work, and they breast-fed "in corridors, on stairways, beside the factory buildings" (Glickman, pp. 127–128). Parents working in factories normally could not provide any care for their children. Some busy mothers, however, hired live-in caregivers, usually older women, for their infants. Several families might share a baby-sitter, who provided care in a very small space.

In nineteenth-century France, social stigma and the near impossibility of earning a living led single, especially unwed, mothers to abandon illegitimate children. In the nineteenth century, failure to accommodate motherhood in factories led working-class mothers to place their infants with hired wet nurses. Poor conditions, however, often led to children's deaths. French countermeasures to promote care-giving motherhood included encouraging mothers to breast-feed infants, pregnancy and maternity leaves, and milk depots.

As examples from the United States, France, and Japan reveal, however, the separation of home and workplace and the rise of industrialization also affected middle-class motherhood and mothering. New or altered ideals of womanhood emerged, although regional, class, and ethnic differences led to diversity of ideals and practices. New elements infusing notions of motherhood included expectations of attentive, nurturing, and loving care and the socialization of children from infancy to youth, typically with somewhat reduced emphasis on labor at the household trade, income earning to support the household, or servant or household management. Due to complex interactions of religious or cultural and economic changes, particularly separation of the home and workplace, the measure of womanhood tended to become motherhood or mothering rather than productivity, economic contribution, or industry at the family trade.

The research of Bonnie G. Smith suggests that in northern France, transition to domestic as opposed to productive womanhood took place in the early eighteenth century. In Japan, too, industrious birth motherhood gave way to a more sentimental care-giving motherhood. In the United States, with the decline of multigenerational families and the lessening of fathers' control over land distribution, ideals of motherhood shifted from an emphasis on women as child-bearers (birth motherhood) and anxiety about motherly indulgence to a strong endorsement of women as solicitous care-giving mothers. Tenderness was now permissible not just toward infants but was expected toward older children as well. As workplace was separated from home, the home became defined as women's and children's place. And because children went out to school, the home became above all women's domain. As capitalist competition increased, it became a haven in a heartless world. Society now held that mothers should care for children themselves; it was considered negligent to abandon one's offspring to the care of another, whether servant, grandparent, or other relative.

It can be argued, however, that one or perhaps two more shifts in U.S. motherhood have taken place since the end of the nineteenth century. In her 1975 book, *Women's Proper Place*, Sheila Rothman indicated that in the Progressive era, mothers' responsibilities expanded from the home to the world. The greedy, cruel world of the marketplace and men needed the gentler, nurturing touch of women, thus the mission of care-giving motherhood reached into the public world to reform society and politics. While it remains to be seen whether these ideals were embraced outside the urban middle classes, they tend to confirm the notion of an earlier shift to care-giving motherhood and female domesticity with a modern twist.

Around the third decade of the twentieth century, another change in the ideals of womanhood also had an impact on notions of motherhood and mothering in the United States. With the rise of a companionate ideal of the husband–wife relationship in the 1920s, women were cautioned against lavishing too much attention on their children and told to transfer their affection to their husbands. Too much fuss over children improperly weakened spousal bonds. In addition, rather than trusting their own instincts, women were encouraged to follow medical, psychological, and educational experts. Nevertheless, these changes should not be overstated; the expectation of a strong bond of sentiment between mother and child continued through the twentieth century.

In many late or advanced industrial societies, the construction of women's identities around consumption, leisure, and self-fulfillment rather than marriage, domestic life, or productivity may be undermining motherhood as women's highest goal and mothering as women's highest social task. This shift may of course vary by class, region, religion, ethnicity or race, or other factors. In part, this shift can be seen in falling birthrates. According to Emiko Ochiai's 1997 book, *The Japanese Family System in Transition*, total fertility rates in 1994 were below the 2.1 replacement rate of a married couple: 1.25 in United Kingdom, 1.4 in Germany, 1.5 in Japan, 1.65 in France, and 2.0 in Sweden, and 2.07 in the United States. Other quantitative evidence such as rising ages at first marriage and first birth, falling percentages of women marrying, and increasing female labor force participation rates also suggest a turn away from marriage and motherhood as women's primary or inevitable destiny. Qualitative evidence also suggests a turn away from motherhood as a woman's central reason for existence. Rejection of mothering as confining, unglamorous drudgery or low-status work may replace acceptance of motherhood as a woman's highest calling.

See also: **Family Patterns; Fathering and Fatherhood; Madonna, Secular; Parenting; Surrogacy; Wet-Nursing.**

BIBLIOGRAPHY

Amadiume, Ifi. 1987. *Male Daughter, Female Husbands.* London: Zed Books.

Amadiume, Ifi. 1997. *Reinventing Africa: Matriarchy, Religion, Culture.* London: Zed Books.

Bouvard, Marguerite Guzman. 1994. *Revolutionizing Motherhood: The Mothers of the Plaza De Mayo.* Wilmington, DE: Scholarly Resources.

Brown, Stephanie. 1994. *Missing Voices: The Experience of Motherhood.* Melbourne, Australia: Oxford University Press.

Chodorow, Nancy. 1978. *The Reproduction of Mothering: Psychoanalysis and the Sociology of Gender.* Berkeley: University of California Press.

Coquery-Vidrovitch, Catherine. 1997. *African Women: A Modern History.* Boulder, CO: Westview Press.

Curry, Lynne. 1999. *Modern Mothers in the Heartland: Gender, Health, and Progress in Illinois, 1900–1930.* Columbus: Ohio State University Press.

Degler, Carl. 1980. *At Odds: Women and the Family in America from the Revolution to the Present.* New York: Oxford University Press.

Fernea, Elizabeth Warnock, ed. 1995. *Children in the Muslim Middle East.* Austin: University of Texas Press.

Fox-Genovese, Elizabeth. 1991. *Within the Plantation Household.* Chapel Hill: University of North Carolina Press.

Fuchs, Rachel. 1984. *Abandoned Children: Foundlings and Child Welfare in Nineteenth-Century France.* New York: State University of New York Press.

Glickman, Rose L. 1984. *Russian Factory Women: Workplace and Society, 1880–1914.* Berkeley: University of California Press.

Golden, Janet. 1996. *A Social History of Wet Nursing in America: From Breast to Bottle.* Cambridge, UK: Cambridge University Press.

Hatem, Mervat. 1987. "Toward the Study of the Psychodynamics of Mothering and Gender in Egyptian Families." *International Journal of Middle East Studies* 19, no. 3 (August): 287–306.

Jolivet, Muriel. 1997. *Japan, the Childless Society? The Crisis of Motherhood.* Trans. Anne-Marie Glasheen. New York: Routledge.

Ochiai, Emiko. 1997. *The Japanese Family System in Transition: A Sociological Analysis of Family Change in Postwar Japan.* Trans. the Simul Press. Tokyo: LTCB International Library Foundation.

Oyewumi, Oyeronke. 1997. *The Invention of Women: Making an African Sense of Western Gender Discourse.* Minneapolis: University of Minnesota Press.

Ransel, David L. 1988. *Mothers of Misery: Child Abandonment in Russia.* Princeton, NJ: Princeton University Press.

Ransel, David L. 1991. "Infant-Care Cultures in the Russian Empire." In *Russia's Women: Accommodation, Resistance, Transformation,* ed. Barbara Evans Clements, Barbara Alpern Engel, and Christine D. Worobec. Berkeley: University of California Press.

Rothman, Sheila. 1975. *Women's Proper Place.* New York: Basic.

Ryan, Mary P. 1981. *Cradle of the Middle Class: The Family in Oneida County, New York, 1790–1865.* Cambridge, UK: Cambridge University Press.

Ryan, Mary P. 1983. *Womanhood in America: From Colonial Times to the Present,* 3rd ed. New York: Franklin Watts.

Ryan, Mary P. 1985. *The Empire of the Mother: American Writing about Domesticity, 1830–1960.* New York: Harrington Park Press.

Seymour, Susan Christine. 1999. *Women, Family, and Child Care in India: A World in Transition.* Cambridge, UK: Cambridge University Press.

Sidel, Ruth. 1982. *Women and Child Care in China: A Firsthand Report.* New York: Penguin.

Smith, Bonnie G. 1981. *Ladies of the Leisure Class: The Bourgeoises of Northern France in the Nineteenth Century.* Princeton, NJ: Princeton University Press.

Smith, Robert J., and Ella Lury Wiswell. 1982. *The Women of Suye Mura.* Chicago: University of Chicago Press.

Sussman, George D. 1982. *Selling Mothers' Milk: The Wet-Nursing Business in France, 1715–1914.* Urbana: University of Illinois Press.

Tucker, Judith. 1997. "The Fullness of Affection: Mothering in the Islamic Law of Ottoman Syria and Palestine." In *Women in the Ottoman Empire: Middle Eastern Women in the Early Modern Era,* ed. Madeline C. Zilfi. Leiden, Netherlands: Brill.

Tucker, Judith, and Margaret Meriwether, eds. 1999. *A Social History of Women and Gender in the Middle East.* Boulder, CO: Westview Press.

Ulrich, Laurel Thatcher. 1980. *Good Wives: Image and Reality in the Lives of Women in Northern New England, 1650–1750.* New York: Oxford University Press.

Uno, Kathleen. 1999. *Passages to Modernity: Motherhood, Childhood, and Social Reform in Early Twentieth-Century Japan.* Honolulu: University of Hawai'i Press.

White, Deborah Gray. 1999. *Ar'n't I a Woman? Female Slaves in the Plantation South,* rev. ed. New York: Norton.

KATHLEEN UNO

Movies

Children have always enjoyed good stories and adventures. They are entertained, they learn how to understand and gain insight into the life to which they one day will have to adjust, and in the most serious sense, stories and FAIRY TALES help them to survive. Children have listened to the often very cruel tales of the Brothers Grimm; they have laughed, cried, and shuddered around the campfires; they have read books; and they have held their ears to their RADIO receivers. Today moving images are among their favorite storytellers, and generally, children have had an inquisitive, nonproblematical relationship to film as yet another useful, splendid source of entertainment, knowledge, and insight. However for many adults—parents, pedagogues, and the authorities—this is not the case. We might even go so far as to say that an important approach to understanding the subject "children and the movies" is paved with fear.

There is almost always widespread trepidation about anything new, and such trepidation very much affected film as well. Ever since the birth of film at the end of the nineteenth century there has been widespread concern as to the effects of this emotionally powerful medium on SLEEP and peace of mind, morals, and morality. Children were not the only ones in danger, either. Anybody might be corrupted by witnessing infidelity, murder, and common-or-garden-variety sinfulness displayed on the silver screen! So the agenda of adult discussions on the subject of children and film has often consisted of damage control. Initially this resulted in prohibition and later in censorship, particularly of films containing scenes showing explicit violence and sex. It is worth noting that early discussions of film censorship were not only about shielding children from powerful, violent experiences but very much about the existence of certain matters that were not for adult eyes either. The medium was so powerful, with its rather-too-close resemblance to real life, that it just had to be controlled.

Most countries in Europe introduced film censorship before World War I when film was a phenomenon barely two decades old. In Europe controls were usually administered by the state. Seldom left up to people with any knowledge of film, censorship was delegated to lawyers or people with influential political or religious connections. In more recent times teachers and psychologists have taken over the role of film censor to enable them to decide what is harmful to children. In the United States the film industry chose to submit to self-censorship in order to avoid state or local organs. The MPPDA (the Motion Picture Producers and Distributors of America) was set up in 1922 and its politically experienced leader, former postmaster general Will H. Hays, persuaded the industry to accept a production code. From 1934 onward it was mandatory and its attitude to crime, alcohol, drugs, religion, violence, and sex determined what might, or rather might not, be shown on film. It was a moral straitjacket that was loosened in the 1950s, but with only a few adjustments the Production Code applied until 1968.

People have talked from the beginning of the brutalizing effect of the film medium, a debate repeated in the 1950s when the deleterious effects of cartoon strips and COMIC BOOKS were on the agenda in the United States and Europe, and in the 1980s when it was argued that violent content of videotapes that corrupted youth. But no clear, unequivocal evidence has ever been found of a direct link between violent movies and violent actions in real life. However, a Danish study on the subject concluded that children whose social skills are underdeveloped can become aggressive by watching violence on the screen. The dramatic expansion of the television and video market in the 1990s has rendered censorship practically impossible and so there is now a widespread tendency to replace prohibition with consumer guidelines like those in use in the United States, where a ratings system has been in operation since 1968. Ratings systems typically apply categories such as General Audience or Parental Guidance and impose different age limits, varying from country to country. In general, however, film censorship has evolved from political and moral censorship for adults to exclusively considering suitability for children. Adult censorship is now only found in a small number of countries.

Irrespective of fear and censorship, children have always loved watching films. They have laughed till the tears ran down their cheeks at Charlie Chaplin and Laurel and Hardy, they have wept over Lassie and Bambi, they have shuddered and hidden their faces when the witch appeared in Walt DISNEY's *Snow White and the Seven Dwarfs*, and they have "whooped" and yelled when watching adventures and Westerns. A number of films not produced expressly for children have ended up being cherished by children—as was the case with books by JULES VERNE, James Fenimore Cooper, Captain Marryat, and Edgar Rice Burroughs, originally penned for adults, which ended up in the nursery. Children have always adopted their very own film treasures, for example, *The Adventures of Robin Hood* (1938), *The Crimson Pirate* (1952), *Star Wars* (1977), and *Raiders of the Lost Ark* (1981).

The term *children's films*, that is, films specifically produced for audiences of children, really took shape after World War II. In Britain the production company Rank embarked on the production of children's films and by 1951 this led to the establishment of the Children's Film Foundation. Film as an art form for children was not in focus; what was discussed was what children's films must *not* contain. Films for children were meant to be edifying, pedagogically responsible productions, contributing to their upbringing and education. So they were not to depict war and violence (an attitude which should of course be regarded in the light of the recently concluded world war) and they were not to depict the consumption of alcohol. Marriage was sacrosanct and inviolable, respect had to be paid to the church and monarchy, and the authorities were always good and just, if occasionally strict. Sex was not discussed at all, because it was quite unthinkable.

Children's films from the Children's Film Foundation soon became watered down into cheaply produced films all much of a muchness, an hour in length in order to fit special children's matinees. They introduced the two most enduring genres of children's film: the children's detective story in which hale and hearty youngsters behave like little grown-ups, foiling and catching slightly stupid, absolutely harmless criminals. They have a wonderful time in an anonymous community completely detached from reality, with no divisions or genuine conflicts. The other genre is animal films, in which children cast their affections on hordes of mice, rats, moles, beautiful horses, birds with broken wings, lame deer, and bunnies, dogs, and cats. (Children's detective stories and animal stories are also popular genres in literature.) It is interesting to observe how tenacious these views of children's films remained throughout the second half of the twentieth century, even though a number of children's films did try to break out of these restrictive moral limits, often with little success in terms of reaching their target group. Before the Iron Curtain rusted away, many children's films were made in Eastern Europe and the Soviet Union as an instrument for inculcating the correct ideological stance; but Czechoslovakia in particular managed to rise above time and place and created a powerful tradition of puppet films for children.

The trouble with so-called children's films is that pedagogical correctness and benevolence often weigh more than narrative pleasure and film as an art form. Nobody has ever really managed to decide whether they should be films that children appreciate, films both children and adults appreciate, or films that adults do not necessarily want to see but which they would very much like children to enjoy! The older children become, the more they explore on their own, and adults may think what they like of children's tastes in film and culture (if they ever find out what they are) but these tastes represent independent choices and are one of the ways in which children grow up. Films are quite simply an easy, accessible road to a glimpse behind various closed doors into the world that lies ahead.

As a consequence, the children's films that adults deem politically correct for children do not necessarily seem to be the films in circulation in the children's own, often clandestine, culture. Nevertheless, most good films for children have a number of characteristic features. They have a child in the leading role, and this child has a mission to fulfill. The mission may be tough but the child succeeds, because the message is that a child's actions *do* make a difference. Children's films, such as Albert Lamorisse's French classic *The Red Balloon* (1956) and *Spirit: Stallion of the Cimmaron* (2002) by DreamWorks, share a faith in the triumph of good despite all the odds, and a belief that the world will go on. Young cinemagoers must not be left disillusioned or paralyzed into inaction. For the most part children's films (films targeted specifically to children) are now made in Scandinavian countries and in Canada where there are state subsidies, while commercial cinema operates with the concept of family films (films intended for all age groups), in many countries is usually synonymous with Disney products and their imitators.

See also: **Children's Literature; Media, Childhood and.**

BIBLIOGRAPHY

Balzagette, Cary, and David Buckingham. 1995. *In Front of the Children: Screen Entertainment and Young Audiences.* London: British Film Institute.

Kinder, Marsha. 1991. *Playing with Power in Movies, Television, and Video Games: From Muppet Babies to Teenage Mutant Ninja Turtles.* Berkeley: University of California Press.

Street, Douglas. 1983. *Children's Novels and the Movies.* New York: Ungar.

ULRICH BREUNING

Multiple Births

Throughout history there have been strongly held cultural and religious beliefs about twins. Attitudes to them varied widely from fear, or hostility, to worship and belief in their supernatural powers (e.g., to induce fertility). Misconceptions about the biology of twins have also been rife. In mid-seventeenth-century Europe it was still thought that boy and girl twins could not coexist in the womb because of the *horror incestus,* that two children meant two fathers, and that infertility was inevitable in the female of a boy-girl pair.

Sir Francis Galton (1876) first recognized the potential of twins in research on the effects of heredity and environment on human development. Essential to this research was the new understanding of the two distinct types of twins—monozygotic (MZ) who, arising from the splitting of one fertilized egg, have the same genetic makeup and dizygotic (DZ) twins who share only half of their genes, arising from two separately fertilized ova. (Zygosity was initially, and unreliably, determined by comparing the physical features of twins but DNA analysis later became the preferred method.)

The DZ, but not the MZ, twinning rate varies in different ethnic groups. Since the 1950s all developed countries have seen the same trends. Following a decline between 1950 and the late 1970s, there was a steady increase in DZ twinning after 1980, due largely to the increasing use of infertility treatments such as ovulation stimulating drugs or multiple embryo transfers following IN VITRO FERTILIZATION (IVF). Clomiphene was introduced in the 1960s and injectable gonadotrophins a decade later. The first IVF baby was delivered in 1978 in the United Kingdom, in 1980 in Australia, and in 1981 in the United States. The first IVF twins were born in 1981. There has been a much more rapid rise in the number of higher multiple births with triplet rates increasing three to six fold since the mid 1980s. Triplet rates in some IVF units rose to over 6 percent of pregnancies. At the

beginning of the twenty-first century triplet rates started to decline in a few countries as infertility clinics become more aware of the potential hazards of multiple births. Nevertheless, the twinning rate continued to increase, except in the few countries that adopted a policy of single embryo transfer following IVF. Ovulation induction continued to result in large higher multiple pregnancies with the largest birth by 2003 being of nonoplets (9) and the largest set of surviving children, septuplets (7).

MZ twinning rates are quite different: they were constant worldwide at 3.5 per 1000 births until the 1990s when an unexplained, slight rise was detected. The causes of MZ twinning are unknown but six to twelve times the expected number are found amongst twins and triplets resulting from ovulation inducing forms of treatment for infertility, whether or not these are accompanied by IVF.

By the 2000s, a set of six multiple birth children had reached adulthood in good health and with normal development. However, in general, the degree of prematurity and low birthweight, with all the associated neonatal complications, mortality and long term morbidity, increases with the number of fetuses. Many previously infertile couples face the painful choice of a multifetal pregnancy reduction to twins or continuing a pregnancy which carries a high risk of death or disability for some or all of their children.

See also: **Conception and Birth; Fertility Drugs.**

BIBLIOGRAPHY

Blickstein, Isaac, and Louis Keith. 2001. *Iatrogenic Multiple Pregnancy.* Carnforth, UK: Parthenon Publishing Group.

Bryan, Elizabeth. 2002. "Loss in Higher Multiple Pregnancy and Multifetal Pregnancy Reduction." *Twin Research* 5: 169–174.

Corney, Gerald. 1975. "Mythology and Customs Associated with Twins." In *Human Multiple Reproduction,* ed. Ian MacGillivray, Percy P. S. Nylander, and Gerald Corney. London: WB Saunders.

Galton, Francis. 1876. "The History of Twins as a Criterion of the Relative Powers of Nature and Nurture." *Journal of the Anthropological Institute* 5: 391–406.

Gedda, Luigi. 1961. *Twins in History and Science.* Springfield, IL: Charles Thomas.

ELIZABETH BRYAN

Music Education

In nineteenth-century Europe and North America, school music lessons were mostly designed to foster musical literacy by teaching children to sing at sight using different versions of "sol-fa" (based upon syllables) as an introduction to staff notation. Two key pioneers were Lowell Mason (1792–1872) under whose influence music was introduced into the schools of Boston as an integral subject in the curriculum in 1838, and John Hullah (1812–1884) who conducted a Singing School for Schoolmasters in London for the first time in 1841.

With the development of recording and broadcasting in the early years of the twentieth century, the notion of attentive listening gained a higher profile with the rise of the Music Appreciation movement and the work of Stewart MacPherson (1865–1941) and Frances Elliott Clark (1860–1958). At about the same time the percussion or rhythm band became a regular feature of music in schools, characterized by a rather formal and prescriptive approach. In contrast was the work of Satis Coleman who experimented with creative music for children at the Lincoln School of Teachers College, Columbia University. Simple instruments made by the children themselves were utilized alongside singing, movement, and spontaneous creative improvisation.

The trend towards hands-on, participatory approaches to the teaching of music is exemplified in the work of three key figures: Emile Jaques-Dalcroze (1865–1950), Carl Orff (1895–1982) and Zoltán Kodály (1882–1967). Jaques-Dalcroze devised his system of eurhythmics in Switzerland, and presented his first training course for teachers in 1909. He integrated movement, improvisation, and solfège (the "fixed-doh" system) into music education. Dalcroze's ideas influenced Orff who co-founded a school with Dorothee Günther in Munich in 1924 where music teaching went hand in hand with movement teaching. Musically, students were encouraged to improvise and compose their own music, and to invent a number of unsophisticated musical instruments. The first edition of *Orff-Schulwerk* was published in 1935 and demonstrated Orff's conviction that through speech-rhythms and chants, songs and movements, children were able to discover and demonstrate musical concepts. Meanwhile in Hungary, it was Kodály's aim to build a music culture in schools using national and folk songs. There were three basic elements to his concept of initial musical training: sung folk tunes; movable sol-fa ; and simultaneous clapping and singing, or singing in parts.

In practice, the ideas and methods outlined are adapted, combined, and synthesized by present-day music teachers, whether they are working, for example, within the National Standards for Music Education in the USA (1994), or the National Curriculum in the UK (1992). But the adoption of these ideas should not be regarded as somehow natural or immutable, but rather the result of dialogue, and sometimes conflict, between those who hold widely differing conceptions concerning music and its meaning in children's lives, and how the musical experiences offered to children in schools can reinforce the fundamental aims—the fostering of musical literacy, performance skills, and musical values, along with the cultivation of attentive listening and creative expression—of a general music education.

See also: **Education, Europe; Education, United States.**

BIBLIOGRAPHY

Campbell, Patricia S. 1991. *Lessons from the World: A Cross—Cultural Guide to Music Teaching.* New York: Schirmer.

Coleman, Satis N. 1922. *Creative Music for Children: A Plan of Training based on the Natural Evolution of Music including the Making and Playing of Instruments Dancing-Singing-Poetry.* New York: G. B. Putnam's Sons, The Knickerbocker Press.

Jaques-Dalcroze, Emile. 1967, 1921. *Rhythm Music and Education.* Woking: The Dalcroze Society.

Orff, Carl. 1978. *The Schulwerk.* New York: Schott Music Corp.

Rainbow, Bernard. 1989. *Music in Educational Thought and Practice: A Survey from 800 BC.* Aberystwyth, UK: Boethius Press.

Szönyi, Erzsébet. 1974. *Kodály's Principles in Practice: An Approach to Music Education through the Kodály Method.* Hungary: Corvina Press.

GORDON COX

N

Naming

A name grants a person identity. Yet giving a name to a child is more than just an act of designation or an official registration: names are not superficial phenomena, but are an expression of cultural identity deeply imbedded in sociocultural contexts. Naming is therefore regarded as the social birth of a human being and is frequently carried out in the form of a ritual integration; one example of this is the Christian BAPTISM. In addition to official first names, there are also many informal names, such as nicknames, sobriquets, and pet names.

Identities and a Myriad of Sociocultural References

What is specific to the current culture of naming and trends of the recent past first becomes understandable through a look at historical practices. At the same time, a historical investigation of names can make the past itself accessible, because names reflect important aspects of everyday life, of world views, and of people's social relationships within the family, extended family, and beyond. The practice of naming and the repertoire of names differ in various historical periods and according to cultural and language areas and ethnic and religious affiliation. Even the number of names given to a child is culture-specific, such as the establishment of the middle name during the nineteenth century in the United States. Multiple names are often a sign of social distinction. A concrete name can represent personal memories, general ideas of the past and wishes for the future, social ties or personal preferences, or it can signal conformity or a certain image. To this extent, there is a broad range of orientations that can guide the selection of a name. The following account will concentrate on several relevant criteria for the selection of first names.

Naming results, to a certain extent, in a social placement; with it, parents assume a certain position in their social surroundings for themselves and for their child. Gender-specific differences in naming are manifested at different le-vels, starting with suitability. For example, so-called *theophorous* names—names containing a reference to a divine name—are reserved for men in Judaism and Islam and for women in Christianity.

Naming after Ancestors and Saints

An initial classification of names can be established in terms of whether names are new creations or naming is done in honor of other bearers of the name, which is equally characteristic for the East and the West. The significance of naming in honor of someone else develops in periods and societies in which religious affiliation, ties to family, or both have a high value and cohesiveness. This system of naming in honor of someone else has been superseded by increasing secularization and individualization, which began to have a broader impact over the course of the nineteenth century with regional differentiations. Leitmotifs constitute individuality, the wish for more uncommon names, so that the child might step out from ancestral tradition and from the social surroundings. They also represent the wish—inseparably linked to this—for the so-called "free" choice of names. Naming in honor of someone else, on the other hand, is known as a "bounded" choice of names and has the opposite effect: it is a means of integrating the newborn into the family organization or the religious community. This means that the name has a strongly integrative function. In areas characterized as Catholic or Protestant, a tendency that was dominant throughout the modern era was to name children after ancestors and saints, which represents a form of reverence in addition to other aspects. Yet these two reference systems must not necessarily be regarded as competing or alternative systems. They can also be parallel references, particularly with regard to important saints.

A large number of saints' names came into circulation as the veneration of saints intensified in the High Middle Ages. The various helping and protective functions that were attributed to the saints became more important in everyday life, and the names of saints were disseminated through calendars, pictures in churches, legends, pilgrimages, and the cult of relics. In addition, saints' names came into everyday use in many different ways, such as in designating certain days for the veneration of particular saints. The older form of naming a child after someone in the family or after the ruler was supplemented by the idea of placing the child under the special protection of a certain saint, or patron saint, by giving the child that saint's name. Other factors, such as proximity to a calendar date and local and group-specific traditions, also influenced this choice.

In 1566, several years after the Council of Trent (1545–1563), saints' names were recommended for Catholic naming and then prescribed in the Roman Ritual in 1614. This restriction resulted in a high concentration of a few names and widespread instances of identical names, a process that had already begun in the High Middle Ages and that did not undergo a greater differentiation until the nineteenth century. The name Maria or Mary assumed a special position in Catholic areas, reaching an unrivaled peak in the modern era. The process of linking saints and names was accompanied by the propagation of celebrating the feast days of saints as name days. This included everyone with the same name and was celebrated collectively in some places. In certain regions, the name day was more important than an individual's BIRTHDAY as late as the mid-twentieth century. This was the case in strictly Catholic and Orthodox societies, but also in Finland, where the name day calendar is even updated in keeping with changes in the repertoire of names.

A new component of naming that arose in the wake of the Counter-Reformation was the increased spiritual importance of the office of GODPARENT. The greater role of the godparent was expressed, in part, by naming the child after the godparent. The criteria for choosing godparents reveal information about social relations and forms of organization in a society, depending on which generation they come from, whether or not they are close relatives, whether or not the parents and godparents are social equals, and whether or not there are several godparents for one child. Through godparent patronage, new social relationships, alliances, and networks are created, or existing ones are reinforced; the relationships involved may be reciprocal or one-sided.

In Protestant regions, naming a child after non-biblical saints gradually decreased as a result of the Reformation, whose proponents objected to the exaggerated veneration of saints. Reformed Protestants most frequently followed the maxim of giving only biblical names. Names from the Old Testament—such as Abraham or Isaac, for example—thus came into use again in this context, especially in Puritan England and America, where biblical names constituted over 90 percent of the given names in the seventeenth century. People there additionally attempted to transpose biblical names into their own language in keeping with the original literal meanings.

Prescripts and Regulations

Another distinguishing characteristic of naming, which has already been alluded to, is the standardization of naming. On the one hand, there are cultures in which naming is not regulated either by religion or by the state, and thus it is left up to the parents entirely; on the other hand, there are cultures with normative specifications for naming. Names in the former cultures are naturally less uniform. In the latter cultures standardizations consist of limiting the choices through prescripts determining which names are acceptable at all. The non-acceptance of certain names results from historical religious regulations against blasphemy; contemporary legal restrictions, on the other hand, primarily focus on the well-being of the child and are intended as protection against ridiculous, offensive, or unreasonable names. The extent to which unusual names—or names that stand out from the conventional repertoire of names in a social environment—may be accepted or rejected by the bearers of the name themselves, regarded with pride, hate, or indifference, depends on the personal situation and the social environment. In some restrictive societies of Western Europe, children born out of wedlock were given very specific names that stigmatized them as such. (For example, in the 1830s and 1840s in France, priests often gave the name Philomene—after Saint Philomena, who was associated with virginity—to illegitimate girls, thereby marking their status.)

In conjunction with naming a child after members of the same family, in some regions there were also relatively strict rules for naming within the family, depending on BIRTH ORDER and the sex of the child. For example, the first son, to whom the regulations tended to apply most strictly, had to be named after the paternal grandfather, the first daughter after the paternal grandmother, the second son after the maternal grandfather, the second daughter after the maternal grandmother, and so forth. Conversely, in societies that worshipped ancestors, a practice associated with Confucianism, it was forbidden to name a child after a family member still living. In the Catholic faith a child given the name of a saint was christened on the feast day of that saint. However, a kind of taboo applied to naming a child after a saint whose feast day had already passed in the calendar year. Nevertheless, it could be seen as a kind of obligation to name a child after a recently deceased sibling or relative.

In the context of migration and naturalization, but also in bicultural marriages and relationships, different logics and paradigms of naming can result in legal regulatory difficulties and lead to tensions between personal identities and conformity if the different systems are not compatible. With regards to the conditions for changing first names later in life, the procedures are widely divergent in different countries and cultures. In comparison with many European countries, Anglo-American naming procedures are relatively liberal. A name change can signal a break or a new phase of life, whether it is a self-created nickname or one that is granted as a new official name, for example, when entering a convent. A practice of this kind is also familiar in Japan: there, especially in the early modern era, people changed their names usually between the ages of fifteen and twenty-five to demonstrate transition and taking over property. Finally, names also function as incantations—a magical identification between a name and the bearer of the name can be made in either a positive or a negative sense.

Individualization and Secularization

Just as the concrete practices of naming only gradually changed during the upheaval of the Reformation and Counter-Reformation, naming in the late nineteenth and early twentieth centuries is marked by synchronicities and mixed forms of elements of continuity and transformation rather than radical breaks with earlier notions. Instead of naming children after family members, godparents, and saints, parents began naming their children after figures from novels, opera heroes, actors and actresses, musicians, singers, athletes, friends or acquaintances, and monarchs and other illustrious personalities from public life. At the same time, however, a name of this kind can still be linked with individually defined wishes based on older patterns. The central difference is that the meaning of the individual name is no longer connoted in a collectively recognizable way but is instead highly individualized. The delay in individualization and secularization in naming was due, at least in part, to the fact that the Catholic Church, even in the first decades of the twentieth century, often refused to accept new names for which there was no corresponding saint or made giving these names more difficult.

In other ways as well, the gradual shift from using grandparents, parents, godparents, and saints as naming models requires further examination. Important personal references, such as the names of grandparents, are not entirely dropped but frequently made second or third names. The practice of naming sons after family members occurs more frequently and is upheld longer than with daughters in all social groups and in different European cultural regions. This phenomenon is especially characteristic when the continuity of the male line, often in relation to inheritance, is presumed to have a certain significance. A greater need for continuity through names can also be related to migration and the living situation in the country of immigration: a higher residential concentration of Jewish immigrants in comparison with Italian immigrants might result in a strong concentration of traditional names. Subsequent to wars, there is also a stronger tendency to name children after fallen family members.

Despite the irreversible effects of individualization and secularization, changes in naming practices are not linear processes that are directly parallel to changes in society. In addition, it happens that names and types of names that have been out of fashion for decades are rediscovered.

Name Fashions

Since this break in the nineteenth and early twentieth centuries, which resulted in a massive decrease in exemplary names that had previously been central, tendencies and fashions have alternated with increasing rapidity. Politically motivated names have repeatedly played an important role, especially in nationally charged periods and in conjunction with language purism aspirations. Restrictive prescriptions and registrar interventions are documented for the Nazi era, as well as naming practices marked by fanaticism. Political statements also have been made programmatically in the form of names in keeping with revolutionary actions, as expressions of certain non-conformist attitudes or sympathies. The French Revolution of 1789, for instance, led to a trend in liberal-secularized naming practices in France and in particular, the increased usage of names derived from the ancient Roman tradition; the subsequent boom of the name Jules exemplifies this.

An increase in the repertoire of names may be noted as a more recent tendency at a general level; this phenomenon is due primarily to the use of variants of names and the internationalization of the spectrum of names based on the free and individual choice of names. Whereas 80 to 90 percent of the boys and girls born in the eighteenth century made do with only a few names, 80 percent of the children born in Munich in 1995, for example, were given a name that otherwise occurred at most only four times. At the same time, regional and language-specific characteristics are taken into consideration in annually published statistics of the most popular names, indicating an increasing concentration on certain types and patterns of first names. While this may seem paradoxical in terms of individualization, it documents the presence of a certain spirit of the times behind the individual choice.

The "free" choice of names also leads to the increasing importance of the aesthetic component. For this reason, some speak of "preference names" that have replaced "tradition names": the sound, the pronunciation of the name, or the way it harmonizes with the last name have become more important than the name's origin and meaning. Sounds in common—number of syllables, abundance of vowels, soft consonants—can thus also form name groups.

The social experiences of the parents with their own names or with the bearers of other names also have a more or less conscious effect on the choice of names. The mass media, too, play an important role, specifically as both a reactive and an influencing instance: names chosen for main characters, titles of television series, and feature films intended to reach a broad audience are already in fashion or at least popular. At the same time, however, they can also trigger or strengthen trends on their part. One prominent example that is frequently cited is the film *Home Alone*, which was followed by a significant increase in usage of the name Kevin, the film's main character, in name statistics. Demographic changes must also be taken into account as well: the decrease in the number of children is accompanied by a "staging of childhood" (that is, the orchestrating of childhood as if it were an opera or a play), and this begins with naming. Changes in gender relations have also influenced names, as in English-speaking countries the names given to girls especially have become more androgynous.

BIBLIOGRAPHY

Dupâquier, Jacques, Jean-Pierre Pélissier, and Danièle Rébaudo. 1987. *Le Temps des Jules. Les prénoms en France au XIXe siècle.* Paris: Editions Christian.

Fischer, David Hackett. 1986. "Forenames and the Family in New England: An Exercise in Historical Onomastics." In *Generations and Change: Genealogical Perspectives in Social History*, ed. Robert M. Taylor, Jr., and Ralph J. Crandall. Macon, GA: Mercer.

Hacker, J. David. 1999. "Child Naming, Religion, and the Decline of Marital Fertility in Nineteenth-Century America." *The History of the Family. An International Quarterly* 4: 339–365.

Henry, Louis, ed. 1974. *Noms et prénoms: Aperçu historique sur la dénomination des personnes en divers pays.* Dolhain: Ordina Éditions.

Kaplan, Justin, and Anne Bernays. 1997. *The Language of Names.* New York: Simon and Schuster.

Mitterauer, Michael. 1993. *Ahnen und Heilige. Namengebung in der europäischen Geschichte.* Munich, Germany: C.H. Beck.

Nagata, Mary Louise. 1999. "Why Did You Change Your Name? Name Changing Patterns and the Life Course in Early Modern Japan." *The History of the Family. An International Quarterly* 4: 315–338.

Picard, Jacques. 1990. "Prénoms de naissance et prénoms de baptême. Prénoms usuels. Un aspect de la mentalité religieuse rurale au XIXe siècle." *Annales de Démographie Historique*: 345–356.

Poppel, Franz van, Gerrit Bloothooft, Doreen Gerritzen, et al. 1999. "Naming for Kin and the Development of Modern Family Structures: An Analysis of a Rural Region in the Netherlands in the Nineteenth and Early Twentieth Centuries." *The History of the Family. An International Quarterly* 4: 261–295.

Sangoi, Jean-Claude. 1999. "Forename, Family and Society in Southwest France (Eighteenth–Nineteenth Centuries)." *The History of the Family. An International Quarterly* 4: 239–259.

Smith, Daniel Scott. 1994. "Child Naming Practices, Kinship Ties, and Change in Family Attitudes in Hingham, Massachusetts, 1641 to 1880." *Journal of Social History* 18: 541–566.

Stewart, George R. 1979. *American Given Names: Their Origin and History in the Context of the English Language.* New York: Oxford University Press.

Vroonen, Eugène. 1967. *Les nomes des personnes dans le monde. Anthroponymie universelle comparée.* Brussels: Éditions de la Librairie Encyclopedique.

Watkins, Susan Cotts, and Andrew S. London. 1994. "Personal Names and Cultural Change: A Study of the Naming Patterns of Italians and Jews in the United States in 1910." *Social Science History* 18: 169–209.

MARGARETH LANZINGER
TRANSLATION BY AILEEN DERIEG

Nancy Drew. *See* Carolyn Keene; Series Books.

National Child Labor Committee

In 1902 an Episcopalian minister, the Reverend Edgar Gardner Murphy, founded the Alabama Child Labor Committee. The next year representatives of thirty-two New York City settlement houses formed the New York Child Labor Committee. These groups collaborated on August 15, 1904, to establish the National Child Labor Committee (NCLC), which was incorporated in 1907 with a board that included prominent Progressive reformers such as JANE ADDAMS, Florence Kelley, Edward T. Devine, and Lillian Wald. From that point on, the NCLC led the national child labor reform movement.

Children had always worked in America. In 1790, Rhode Island's Samuel Slater hired nine children ages seven through twelve to work in the nation's first factory. According to the 1870 U.S. Census, about one in every eight children in America worked for wages. In 1900 this ratio was one in six, and the proportion continued to grow through 1910. While children working in agriculture seemed consistent with America's past history, to many Americans youngsters laboring for meager wages in industry seemed brutal and cruel.

From 1908 through 1921, the NCLC sought to mine such sympathies. It paid the photographer LEWIS HINE to take pictures of child laborers that would pull at the nation's heartstrings. At the same time the NCLC organized state-centered campaigns. Alexander McKelway acted as the NCLC's chief investigator for the southern United States, and Owen Lovejoy oversaw the organization's efforts in northern states. The NCLC also called for the establishment of a federal children's bureau that would investigate and report on the circumstances of all American children. President William Howard Taft signed the act establishing the U.S. CHILDREN'S BUREAU on April 9, 1912. In a symbolic gesture, he handed the signature pen to the NCLC's Alexander McKelway. Over the next three decades the NCLC worked closely with the U.S. Children's Bureau to promote child labor reforms at both the state and federal levels.

The effort faced strong opposition from manufacturers and newspaper editors. In addition, many working-class parents saw little advantage to keeping their children in school instead of the workplace. Despite such resistance, in 1916 the NCLC convinced Congress to pass the Keating-Owen Act. This legislation used the federal government's authority over interstate commerce to regulate child labor. Just before the act was to go into effect, however, the U.S. Supreme Court praised the law's intent, but declared its method unconstitutional (HAMMER V. DAGENHART, 1918). The NCLC then switched its strategy to passage of a federal constitutional amendment. In 1924, Congress agreed, but by 1932 only six states had voted for ratification, while twenty-four had rejected the measure.

From 1910 to 1930 passage of various local and state compulsory school attendance laws contributed to a decline in the percentage of wage-earning children, despite the federal amendment's dismal progress. The onset of the GREAT DEPRESSION temporarily reversed this downward trend. Pressured by child welfare advocates and labor unions, Franklin D. Roosevelt's administration included child labor regulations in the 1933 National Industrial Recovery Act (NIRA), which set up the National Recovery Administration (NRA). The NRA was shortlived, however, for the U.S. Supreme Court declared it unconstitutional on May 27, 1935, thereby leaving the United States again without federal restrictions on child labor.

Nevertheless, the NCLC continued to lobby for ratification of the 1924 Child Labor Amendment. Sensing a new attitude in the Supreme Court, advocates included child labor regulations in the 1938 Fair Labor Standards Act. This New Deal legislation prohibited the employment of those under fourteen years of age and placed restrictions on young workers ages fourteen through seventeen. In February 1941, in the case of *United States v. Darby*, the U.S. Supreme Court reversed its earlier stance by upholding the right of Congress to regulate child labor through the interstate commerce clause of the Constitution. The NCLC understood, however, that even with this support the 1938 law did not protect all children. Since the 1930s the group has continued to lobby to prevent the exploitation of children in the workplace in the United States and around the world.

See also: **Child Labor in the West; Work and Poverty.**

BIBLIOGRAPHY

Bremner, Robert H., et al. 1974. *Children and Youth in America: A Documentary History*, vols. II and III. Cambridge, MA: Harvard University Press.

Lindenmeyer, Kriste. 1997. *"A Right to Childhood": The U.S. Children's Bureau and Child Welfare, 1912–1946*. Urbana: University of Illinois Press.

Trattner, Walter I. 1970. *Crusade for Children: A History of the National Child Labor Committee and Child Labor Reform in America*. Chicago: Quadrangle Books.

INTERNET RESOURCE

National Child Labor Committee. 2003. "NCLC Fact Sheet." Available from <www.kapow.org/nclc.htm> (NCLC Papers [1904–1953] are housed in the Library of Congress).

KRISTE LINDENMEYER

Native American Children

The original native American Indians are believed to be Asians who, twenty thousand years ago, hiked across the treeless plain that is now the Bering Strait in search of food on the hoof and eventually moved into the diverse environments of North America. Thus it is customary to divide the Indians of North American not into ethnic groups but rather into culture areas, each of which includes nations that, in response to the regional environment, adopted substantially the same ways of life.

Pre-European Cultures

When the European invaders began arriving in the sixteenth century, farming was the dominant activity on the eastern part of the continent in the culture areas of the northeast (from the Atlantic to the Great Lakes and from lower Canada to Illinois and North Carolina) and the southeast (from the Atlantic to the Mississippi River). Hunting predominated elsewhere, save for some coastal areas where fishing prevailed and parts of the dry Southwest where gathering was more important. Where farming was more intensive, settlement was more sedentary. Yet even in the farming areas, though men aided women in clearing the land, it was the women and children who did the agricultural labor—cultivating, weeding, and harvesting corn, beans, and squash; hunting and picking wild berries, fruits, and nuts—while men (and sometimes younger women) were on the hunt in the spring, early summer, and fall. In the hunting regions, where the game was larger and journeys after it longer, the Indians remained nomadic. These native economies, seemingly primitive, supported a population of five to ten million in what is now the United States and Canada.

The Eastern Woodland Indians. The natives of the culture areas in North America first affected by the European presence, those of the northeast and southeast, are customarily referred to as the Eastern Woodland Indians. They spoke different languages, and their places of residence varied in size from several thousand inhabitants to a few score of souls. Politically, organization ranged from democratic and libertarian to hierarchical and authoritarian. But within all the Eastern Woodland tribes there were clans, each claiming a single ancestor. Most tribes were matrilineal, probably because women carried on the predominant economic activity of farming. And the tribes had similar ways of regarding and rearing children. The importance of the child, unborn and born, was evident. Male missionaries and traders who visited the Indians, though barred from witnessing the delivery of the newborn, gave testimony that prospective mothers enjoyed good health during pregnancy and a painless delivery, after which they quickly reentered normal life.

The newborn child was also immediately prepared for the world. Most Indians immersed children at birth, the water temperature notwithstanding; some circumcised the boys. Other customary rituals included ear piercing, hanging wampum or other ornaments around the baby's neck, and feeding the little one oil or grease. There was a 50 percent child mortality rate due to the rigors of Indian life and the

A young Native American boy and his French father travel down the Missouri River to trade furs. *Fur Traders Descending the Missouri* (c. 1845), George Caleb Bingham. © Geoffrey Clements/CORBIS.

recurrent smallpox EPIDEMICS as a result of contact with Europeans. Children were born at approximately four-year intervals due to protracted breast feeding, prohibitions on sexual relations while nursing, abortions, and even infanticide. All these factors stabilized the size of the population. Families were small by European standards; three or four children appears to have been the average.

It was common to name a child at birth, possibly from a supply of names available to the clan, or in response to an event or the appearance of the child, or after an animate or inanimate object (an eagle, the wind). Boys took on nicknames that captured their exploits (as did men), which probably put pressure on them for further achievements. Huron males apparently changed names as they moved through life stages, to combat illness, and in response to dreams. (Most Huron believed they had two souls, one of which remained with the body unless it was reborn as a child, explaining why some children resembled their dead ancestors.) Finally, the name of a recently deceased person would be passed on to another member of the tribe so the name was not lost. But it was impolite to call a person by his or her own name; instead one used a term that expressed the relationship of the speaker to the person addressed, my sister's son, for example. Even if there was no family affinity, terms such as brother or nephew could still be used.

European observers, hardened to INFANT MORTALITY, were impressed by the fondness shown toward and good care taken of Indian children by their mothers. This quality was nowhere better demonstrated than in the feeding of the infant. Unlike European upper-class parents, Indians did not put their children out to be nursed. If the mother happened to die before the child was weaned the father might fill his mouth with water in which corn had been boiled and pass the liquid on to the infant. Nursing went on for several years. During this time the child stayed close to its mother, usually transported on a cradleboard tied to the mother's back. As the child grew and was allowed to crawl it was carried without a board, again on the back of the mother, who grasped it by one leg and the opposite arm. Weaned at approximately three years, the young Indian who had been so carefully attended was suddenly left to his or her own devices, unconfined and now learning from the example of elders. Still, young children must have remained under the watchful eyes of their parents and, probably, the entire village community.

Children were considered to be specially linked to the spiritual world, and in general were indulged rather than punished. Nothing shocked the Europeans more than the absence of physical punishment as a means to DISCIPLINE Indian children. Sometimes they were chastised by having a little water thrown in their faces, and there were reports of Creek parents occasionally scratching disobedient children and, along with the Chickasaws, allowing young ones to be beaten by someone outside the household. Nevertheless, corporal punishment was very much the exception rather than the rule, although ridicule or fear of the supernatural might be used to produce obedience. Surely the example of parents, especially warrior-fathers, shunning corporal punishment must have contributed to children, especially sons, mimicking the restraint shown by their elders. Indeed, in a milieu which placed a premium on withstanding pain and suffering without flinching, corporal punishment—a blatant manifestation of feeling—had no place. The development of self-restraint and stoicism, initiated in childhood, was closely linked to the cultivation of autonomy, highly prized in adulthood.

The aim of these native American parents was to train male hunter-warriors, who would be required to act individualistically yet always conform to the demands of a communal, conservative, homogeneous society. Scantily clad in winter, boys hardened their bodies as they did their minds; their elders expected of them self-control and absence of "womanly" emotion. Females were instructed as planter-gatherers, who must possess wilderness survival skills as keen as those of the males. Children were expected to adopt the clearly defined gender roles assigned to them. Education of the young was primarily but not exclusively imparted by the example of elders. Religious and moral training came from the parents, seconded by the whole community. A related but different means of instruction was storytelling. This oral literature was entertaining but, more important, conveyed cultural beliefs and practices. Often the leading characters of legend and myth were children or youths, making it clear that the young were targets of these stories.

The test of childhood training would be in adulthood, and the transit from one stage of life to the other was well-defined. For girls there were sometimes rituals surrounding the onset of menstruation. For boys, whose passage through PUBERTY was less biologically evident, there were more elaborate ceremonies: the *huskinaw*, a rigorous physical trial, and the vision quest, a spiritual journey. Both involved isolation as well as sensory deprivation and stimulation; their purpose was to begin life on a new course, though without forfeiting the training of childhood, and to locate through visions the spirits which dominated the young person's life. Sometimes the tribal adults gave the young man a new name, the meaning of which might shame, exalt, or even assign a personality to the recipient.

The endurance of native American customs after European contact varied by region. The Eastern Woodland custom of carrying children in cradleboards, illustrated in this 1940 photograph from Tower Rice Camp, Minnesota, persisted in some areas into the twentieth century. © CORBIS.

And so the line between childhood and adulthood was clearly drawn. Eastern Woodland Indians would draw upon the lessons instilled in the early years to govern the behavior of the later ones. Sex after puberty was considered normal. Marriage partners might be tentatively chosen by parents, and a young man could be expected to consult the parents of his intended. Yet there was no coercion: both young men and young women had a choice when it came to marrying and deciding whether to remain wed.

The Plains and Pueblo Indians. Tribal organization, intertribal relations, and child rearing among the Plains Indians resembled that of the Eastern Woodland Indians. However, most of the Plains tribes, being hunters rather than farmers, were on the move rather than settled. Fathers were frequently absent, leaving mothers with additional chores. Hence, grandparents ordinarily filled the void left by otherwise-occupied parents.

The experience of childhood among the sixteenth-century Pueblo Indians of southwestern North America, whose culture dated back centuries to the by-then-extinct Anasazi, was both similar to and different from that of their distant cousins on the Atlantic coast and the Plains. The Pueblo Indians led lives governed by ritual. The umbilical cord of the newborn was buried inside the house (female) or in a cornfield (male), making clear the sexual division of space and labor. The boy's penis was sprinkled with water, while the girl's vulva was covered with a seed-filled gourd, just as in the natural (adult) world clouds (men) poured their rain on seeds (women), causing them to germinate. On the fourth day the medicine man presented the infant to the rising sun, named it, gave it an ear of corn (representing the Corn Mothers who gave life) and, if it was a male, a flint arrowhead (to create thunder and lightning). A female remained attached to her place of birth, while a male changed houses, living with his mother as a boy and moving at adolescence into a kiva to learn male lore.

Gender was not the only social division among the Pueblo Indians—age also mattered. Children were considered to be indebted to their parents, who had to pay the religious elders for their birth rituals, and there continued a dyadic relationship between givers and receivers, seniors and juniors. None were more senior or more powerful than the kachina, or spirit forces. All adolescents were initiated into the kachina cult, and quickly learned what dire punishment awaited those who did not respect generational reciprocity. With menstruation girls entered womanhood through initiation into clan-based groups, while boys had to kill an enemy before induction into the warrior fellowship through a physical ordeal reminiscent of the Eastern Woodland *huskinaw*.

With the Spanish conquest and the imposition of Christianity in the seventeenth century, Pueblo Indian society was fundamentally altered. The Franciscan priests set about their goal of conversion by upsetting the age relationship, attempting to turn sons from their natural to their spiritual fathers, beginning with BAPTISM. Parents were humiliated by casting adults in the roles of devils in religious dramas, fathers were emasculated by violating the gender division of labor, and children were courted with gifts, as the Franciscans played upon the Indian belief that favors must be reciprocated. Gifts of livestock and lessons in animal husbandry not only yielded baptisms and pious lives; they also undermined the authority of the Indian hunt chiefs. The friars also offered Indian youth the nurturing benefits associated with mothers. Only those Indians who strongly resisted Christianity, among them the Hopi, remained matrilineal societies.

The Nineteenth Century and Beyond

In the mid-nineteenth century the western half of the United States was inhabited by almost a quarter million Indians: Eastern Woodland Indians (including Winnebago, Cherokee, and Chippewa) who had been forced to resettle; Plains Indians (Sioux, Blackfoot, Cheyenne, Crow, Arapaho, Pawnee, Kiowa, Apache, Comanche); Pueblo Indians of the southwest (Hopi, Zuni, Navajo), and the Indians of Califor-

nia and the Pacific Northwest. Advancing European-American settlement, including plans for a transcontinental railroad, and intermittent Indian-white warfare led to the creation of reservations in the late 1860s. Continuing conflict was resolved in the next decades through the United States government's policy of forced assimilation. Indian children were required to attend white schools, often far from home; by 1900 there were twenty-five off-reservation boarding schools, supplemented by reservation boarding schools and day schools, public schools (attended by both Indian and white students), and mission schools. In all cases the Indian child was expected to forsake his or her own culture for the European American.

The Hopi managed to remain remote from European-American culture into the mid-twentieth century. The cradleboard remained, as did long-term nursing on demand. Mainstream medicine was rejected (and infant mortality was high); punishment (when administered, by the maternal uncle) was notably absent while rewards persisted; children grew up always in the presence of others. Girls were taught domestic chores by mothers, and boys, taught by fathers, learned farming; some games remained that were reminiscent of the warrior past. Initiation rites continued as a way of introducing youth to the Hopi world. Children were forced to go to school, but they did not internalize what they were taught, since their elders had conditioned them to believe in basic Hopi values. Thus, the Hopi maintained a strong cultural link with the past.

Usually, however, the contact between native American Indians and European Americans had a much greater impact on the former; a traditional group usually could not survive in the face of a more aggressive, more powerful, and far more intolerant society. The Delawares, for example, an Eastern Woodland tribe, went through a cultural decline from the early sixteenth into the mid-twentieth century, by which time they had lost their original identity, lost their lands east of the Mississippi, and moved into Indian Territory in Oklahoma. There they lived in frame houses, wore European clothes, accepted dependence on the federal government, sent their children to missionary (later government) schools, changed the basis of their kinship system, and became hardly distinguishable from poor rural whites.

The Winnebagos, also an Eastern Woodland tribe, were less dramatically affected. Forced to cede land to the government, they were able to remain in Wisconsin and, although they sent their children to missionary schools, the youngsters did not leave their parents' homes. But by the third decade of the twentieth century babies were being born in hospitals, and many methods of child rearing changed to a less indulgent regime, including even corporal punishment. Brothers and sisters quarreled, in adolescence the sexes mixed, and masculine tasks disappeared (as males were more affected by cultural change than females). English was taught in the home, and the dress, housing, and transportation of the dominant culture was appropriated. In the mid-twentieth century psychoanalyst ERIK ERIKSON visited the Dakota Sioux, a Plains Indian tribe, where he found that children received traditional training at home but faced the demands of European-American society in school. Yet they neither rebelled openly nor showed signs of inner conflict. Rather, students were apathetic or passively resistant, and they viewed the world as dangerous and hostile.

World War II proved disruptive to Native Americans: men joined the armed services and women as well as men took defense jobs. City living was nontraditional, as was some of the work done by rural women in the absence of manpower. But disruption also heightened cultural awareness and even inspired a return to practices long abandoned, such as war chants and prayers for victory, as well as traditional dances. After the war the government began implementing its so-called termination policy: doing away with tribal governments and the trust protection for Indian territories while granting land to individual Indians who would now pay taxes and obey the laws of the states they inhabited. As a corollary to termination, Indians were encouraged to relocate in cities, and by 1958 about one hundred thousand had done so, most without federal assistance.

Relocation was a failed attempt at assimilation; it resulted in continuing ghettoization and poverty. The deplorable living conditions of native Americans described by anthropologist Lewis Merriam in 1928, though they may have been temporarily improved due to rising incomes during World War II, were reconfirmed by reports from California in 1966 and University of Michigan anthropologist Joseph G. Jorgenson in 1971, and again by the census of 1990. Perhaps the most serious problem of all, alcohol, was confronted when the Indian Health Service (IHS) was created in 1954. Though underfunded, IHS has addressed itself to the endemic (and epidemic) matter of fetal alcohol syndrome. Why Indians have been particularly vulnerable to alcohol abuse is unclear, but they died of it at five times the rate of other Americans in the 1990s.

Alcoholism and suicide, poverty and unemployment: these realities more closely describe the life context of Native Americans than of any other group in the United States today. Although the federal government has been paying more attention to the needs of Indian children, as evidenced by such legislation as the Indian Education Act (1972), the Indian Self-Determination and Education Assistance Act (1975), the Indian Health Care Improvement Act (1976), the Tribally Controlled Community College Assistance Act (1978), and the Indian Child Welfare Act (1978)—and there is no denying the impact of this attention—nevertheless the situation for Indian children today is often grim.

See also: **American Indian Schools; Canada.**

BIBLIOGRAPHY

Axtell, James, ed. 1981. *The Indian Peoples of Eastern America. A Documentary History of the Sexes.* New York: Oxford University Press.

Boyer, Bryce L. 1979. *Childhood and Folklore: A Psychoanalytic Study of Apache Personality.* New York: Library of Psychological Anthropology.

California State Advisory Commission on Indian Affairs. 1966. *Indians in Rural and Reservation Areas.* Sacramento.

DeMallie, Raymond J., and Alfonso Ortiz, eds. 1994. *North American Indian Anthropology: Essays on Society and Culture.* Norman: University of Oklahoma Press.

Dennis, Wayne. 1940. *The Hopi Child.* New York: Appleton-Century.

Eggan, Dorothy. 1970. "Institution and Affect in Hopi Cultural Continuity." In *From Child to Adult,* ed. John Middleton. Garden City, NY: Natural History Press.

Erikson, Erik H. 1950. *Childhood and Society.* New York: Norton.

Ferrero, Pat. 1983. *Hopi: Songs of the Fourth World.* San Francisco: Ferrero Films.

Gutierrez, Ramon A. 1991. *When Jesus Came, the Corn Mothers Went Away: Marriage, Sexuality, and Power in New Mexico, 1500–1846.* Stanford: Stanford University Press.

Hilger, M. Inez. 1951. *Chippewa Child Life and Its Cultural Background.* Washington, DC: U.S. Government Printing Office.

Illick, Joseph E. 2002. *American Childhoods.* Philadelphia, University of Pennsylvania Press.

Jorgenson, Joseph G. "Indians and the Metropolis." In *The American Indian in Urban Society,* ed. Jack O. Waddell and O. Michael Watson. Boston, MA: Little, Brown.

Mann, Henrietta. 1997. *Cheyenne-Arapaho Education, 1871–1982.* Niwot: University Press of Colorado.

Mannes, Marc. 1996. "Factors and Events Leading to the Passage of the Indian Child Welfare Act." In *A History of Child Welfare,* ed. Eve P. Smith and Lisa A. Merkel-Holguin. New Brunswick, NJ: Rutgers University Press.

Mead, Margaret. 1932. *The Changing Culture of an Indian Tribe.* New York: Columbia University Press.

Meriam, Lewis, et al. 1928. *The Problem of Indian Administration.* Baltimore, MD: Johns Hopkins University Press.

Newcomb, William W. 1956. *The Culture and Acculturation of the Delaware Indians.* Ann Arbor: University of Michigan Press.

Newcomb, William W. 1974. *North American Indians: An Anthropological Perspective.* Pacific Palasades, CA: Goodyear.

Pettitt, George A. 1946. *Primitive Education in North America.* Berkeley: University of California Press.

Rawls, James J. 1996. *Chief Red Fox Is Dead: A History of Native American Indians since 1945.* New York: Harcourt Brace.

Rountree, Helen C. 1989. *The Powhattan Indians of Virginia: Their Traditional Culture.* Norman: Oklahoma University Press.

Sorkin, Alan L. 1978. *The Urban American Indian.* Lexington, MA: Lexington Books.

Swanton, John R. 1946. *The Indians of the Southeastern United States.* Washington, DC: U.S. Government Printing Office.

Szasz, Margaret. 1974. *Education and the American Indian: The Road to Self-Determination, 1928–1973.* Albuquerque: University of New Mexico Press.

Tooker, Elizabeth. 1964. *An Ethnography of the Huron Indians, 1615–1649.* Washington, DC: U.S. Government Printing Office.

Trigger, Bruce. 1969. *The Huron Farmers of the North.* New York: Holt, Rinehart and Winston.

JOSEPH E. ILLICK

Neill, A. S. (1883–1973)

Alexander Sutherland Neill was born in Scotland on October 17, 1883, the son of a village schoolteacher. He spent his childhood in a modest home with a stern father and many sisters and brothers in an atmosphere of modified but ever-present Calvinism. In his youth he worked as a student-teacher, went to the university and to England where he joined the Progressives in their critique of schooling and education. He published his first books, *A Dominie's Log* (1915), *A Dominie Dismissed* (1917), *A Dominie in Doubt* (1920), and *A Dominie Abroad* (1923), about the everyday experiences of a Scottish teacher who was permissive and loving and therefore constantly got into trouble. For some years he ran the journal of PROGRESSIVE EDUCATION, the *New Era*, together with the theosophist Beatrice Ensor. He stayed for some years in Austria and Germany working with followers of Progressive education and Freudianism.

Upon his return to England in 1924 Neill founded Summerhill, a so-called free boarding school that housed sixty children between the ages of five and sixteen. *Free* referred to the children's freedom to do what they pleased as long as they did not interfere with the freedom of others. Lessons were optional and the everyday life of the school was run according to a long list of rules set by the school assembly, where adults' and children's votes were weighed equally. Neill was the headmaster of the school until his death in 1973. He wrote several books on his experience, including *The Problem Child* (1926), *The Problem Parent* (1932), *The Problem Teacher* (1939), *The Free Child* (1953), *Summerhill: A Radical Approach to Education* (1960), and *Freedom, not License* (1966).

Neill believed that schooling dominated children and caused repression and trauma. He shared the Progressive view regarding the importance of respecting and following the interests of the individual child. Later in his life this understanding was merged with a simplified version of the early Freudian concept of libido: the child was by nature good, had infinite life energy, and should have the opportunity for self-government. The teacher's work was to find out where children's interests lay and help them to live them out. Children would then, because of their nature, move toward good, and a new civilization would be born. The free child was a self-regulating individual—a Reichian term—and not an uncontrolled one. The first priority at Summerhill was to allow emotional release, and the second was the organization of the teaching and learning process and the acquisition of knowledge.

Neill was mainly inspired by Homer Lane, Wilhelm Reich, SIGMUND FREUD, and Jesus Christ, whom he saw as an example of perfect humanity, giving love and not expecting anything in return. Neill's message was more simple, more substantial, and more radical than the majority of Progressive educators. He emphasized his message repeatedly in a number of books written in a conversational style combined with examples from the everyday life of the school, although they lacked any systematic analyses of the ongoing educational processes. His books and the school became very popular after 1960, a success probably as much due to Neill's warmth, enthusiasm, and humor as to the antiauthoritarian ideology of the 1960s that was reflected in the principles of the school. His books have been, in times and places of authoritarian discipline, a constant inspiration for more permissive schooling.

See also: **Child Development, History of the Concept of; Child Psychology; Education, Europe.**

BIBLIOGRAPHY

Hemmings, Ray. 1972. *Fifty Years of Freedom: A Study of the Development of the Ideas of A. S. Neill.* London: Allen and Unwin.

Neill, Alexander Sutherland. 1968 [1960]. *Summerhill.* Middlesex, UK: Penguin.

Neill, Alexander Sutherland. 1975 [1915]. *A Dominie's Log.* New York: Hart.

Placzek, Beverly R., ed. 1981. *Record of a Friendship: The Correspondence between Wilhelm Reich and A. S. Neill, 1937–1957.* New York: Farrar, Straus and Giroux.

Popenoe, Joshua. 1970. *Inside Summerhill.* New York: Hart Publishing.

Selleck, R. J. W. 1972. *English Primary Education and the Progressives, 1914–1939.* Boston: Routledge and Kegan Paul.

ELLEN NØRGAARD

New York Children's Aid Society

The New York Children's Aid Society (CAS) was founded in 1853 by CHARLES LORING BRACE, a Connecticut-born minister who had moved to New York City in 1848. Brace was shocked by the thousands of vagrant children he saw on the city's streets, and by the city's practice of incarcerating them in juvenile and adult prisons. He argued that vagrant children were not criminals and that no institution could care for them as effectively as a family home—an assertion that has become one of the primary principals of modern child welfare.

Soon after its founding, the CAS established a series of industrial schools, which provided academic and job education to children whose ragged clothing or need to work meant they could not attend public schools. In 1854, the Society opened its Newsboys' Lodging House, the nation's first youth shelter. Brace wanted to preserve residents' independence, so he made them pay a nominal fee, which got them not just a bed for the night, but food, a bath, clothes, and a host of other services. By far the most influential and controversial of CAS programs was its Emigration Plan, which, between 1854 and 1929, placed 105,000 poor city children with farm families in all of the lower forty-eight states (except Arizona). Beginning, essentially, as a job placement service, the Emigration Plan became the inspiration for modern foster care.

Brace's work was widely imitated throughout the nineteenth century. Indeed, many other wholly independent organizations (most notably in Boston, Philadelphia, and Canada) even named themselves after the CAS. But as time passed, Brace was subjected to increasingly virulent criticism. In the 1860s the Catholic Church asserted that his main goal, especially through the Emigration Plan, was to convert Catholic children to Protestantism. While it was true that a large percentage of Catholic children sent to the country did end up converting, this was mainly because the American countryside was overwhelmingly Protestant. After Brace's death, in 1890, the CAS banned the placement of Catholic children under the age of fourteen via the Emigration Plan.

Beginning in the 1870s, the CAS was criticized by child welfare advocates who held that Brace was wrong to believe that taking poor children out of their families and neighborhoods was the best way to "save" them. Family preservation, mothers' pensions (which were the direct forerunner of Aid to Families with Dependent Children [AFDC]), and community service programs were held by these critics to be far more helpful and humane.

Other critics charged that there was not enough CAS oversight of the children it placed in rural homes. The CAS responded to such criticisms and new government regulations by placing children ever closer to New York City and increasing screening and supervision of placements. While no longer as influential as it once was, the CAS is still one of the New York City's most respected private FOSTER CARE, ADOPTION, and child welfare agencies. It is now most distinguished for its neighborhood building efforts, such as a block redevelopment program in Harlem, and its eight "Community Schools," public schools through which the society provides family and medical services in addition to a regular public school education.

See also: **Child Saving; Homeless Children and Runaways in the United States; Orphan Trains; Social Welfare; Societies for the Prevention of Cruelty to Children.**

BIBLIOGRAPHY

Brace, Charles Loring. 1973 [1872]. *The Dangerous Classes of New York and Twenty Years Work Among Them.* Silver Spring, MD: National Association of Social Workers.

Holt, Marilyn Irvin. 1992. *The Orphan Trains: Placing Out in America.* Lincoln: University of Nebraska Press.

O'Connor, Stephen. 2001. *Orphan Trains: The Story of Charles Loring Brace and the Children He Saved and Failed.* Boston: Houghton Mifflin.

STEPHEN O'CONNOR

New Zealand

In 1991 the American scholar Mary Gordon observed, in her comprehensive historiographical review published in *Children in Comparative and Historical Perspective,* that much work remained to be done on the history of childhood in AUSTRALIA and New Zealand. Some significant advances have been made since then. Educational and welfare scholars have explored the impact of past social policy on children's lives, while contemporary concerns over child health, abuse, and poverty are fostering research in these areas, particularly in the field of children's rights. Yet there is still no local equivalent to the history of Australian childhood written by Jan Kociumbas. Nor, despite the obvious potential for comparison, are there New Zealand works that parallel such Canadian and U.S. childhood studies as those produced by Neil Sutherland, Elliott West, and Harvey Graff. The challenge for any substantial history of New Zealand childhood is that it should be a worthwhile contribution to the international literature while at the same time providing New Zealand readers—young adults especially—with some youth-centered perspectives on their country's past.

Early History

Childhood experience in New Zealand falls loosely into four distinctive phases. *Firstcomers* covers the period from c. 1200 through the 1700s, during which the first migrants from Hawaiiki (eastern Polynesia) established, and their descendants developed, the communities from which contemporary Maori trace their tribal origins. That *tamariki,* or indigenous children, were loved, instructed, disciplined, and mourned is apparent from traditional proverbs, songs, and prayers. Mobility, adaptability, and intertribal conflict were commonplace. Life expectancy was short; living was a labor-intensive process. There was no prolonged period of dependency.

Newcomers characterizes a second period, from the 1770s through the 1850s, when the arrival of European explorers, adventurers, evangelists, and settlers initiated the experience of cultural encounter for youngsters in both societies. *Tamariki* were exposed to new smells and sounds, commodities and values—and diseases against which they and their kin had no immunity. Where Maori and Pakeha, or non-Maori, lived in close proximity, as in shore-based whaling settlements or mission stations, the children of each culture could grow up with some knowledge of the other's language and customs. From the 1840s, as the patterns that had evolved over centuries changed within the lifetime of a single generation, Maori became a steadily diminishing minority within

Children's Games (c. 1910–1915), Arthur James Northwood. In the nineteenth and early twentieth centuries, some Maori and Pakeha (non-Maori) children grew up in close proximity to each other and could gain some knowledge of each other's customs. However, the rapidly dwindling Maori population made it rare after the 1840s that European immigrants and their children would know anything but the British culture that dominated New Zealand at that time. Northwood Collection, Alexander Turnbull Library, Wellington, N.Z.

their own land. Relatively few of the immigrants' children had meaningful contact with Maori. It would be *tamariki*, not Pakeha youth, who developed a bicultural awareness.

The Colonial Period

Young colonials reflects a period marked by conflict, internal and external, from the 1860s through the 1940s. These were years of prosperity and development, but with periods of disruption, dispossession, and depression. The varying effects of these periods on the colony's children crossed cultural, regional, and class divides. The New Zealand Wars of the 1860s were a conflict of sovereignty, not race; the legislative consequences of confiscation and land alienation were devastating for the tribal communities involved. The wars reflected both Maori resistance to the insatiable immigrant demand for land and the failure of the Crown to uphold guarantees of indigenous sovereignty as agreed in the colony's founding charter, the Treaty of Waitangi, signed between the Crown's representatives and Maori chiefs in 1840. The subsequent unfair confiscation of land from tribes

deemed to have been rebellious, together with the continuing land alienation through the legislative process of a Native Land Court, impoverished the tribal communities involved and severely affected the diet, health, and living conditions of their children.

The well-being of Pakeha youngsters was also affected during the latter half of the nineteenth century. Gold rushes during the 1860s prompted state legislation to provide for neglected children, particularly those whose fathers failed to provide for their maintenance, while a colony-wide recession in the 1880s put additional pressure on many migrant families, especially on those for whom the dream of owning a small farm was largely dependent on child labor. And whereas Maori children were raised within extended *whanau*, or family networks on which they could depend for support, immigrants had to create such connections. At times the bonds proved too fragile and death or desertion led to children becoming dependent on institutional care. The lives of the colonial-born of both societies were also being shaped by a wider constitutional context as colonial politicians fashioned a new Britain of the south, and in so doing gave legislative expression to the dominant cultural values.

State education and health and welfare measures applied to all children, regardless of ethnicity: legalized apartheid has never been part of the New Zealand childhood experience. Yet legislation promoting economic development continued to undermine the communal principles of tribal life and failed to redress impoverishment. Maori children developed a clear understanding of the negative impacts of colonial rule upon their lives; Pakeha youngsters remained largely ignorant of the circumstances, culture, or language of the people whose assistance and cooperation, through food supplies, labor, and initial land sales, for example, had been so fundamental to the colony's establishment. They grew up knowing themselves to be British. The cultural differences of the small enclaves of other European migrants were scarcely acknowledged except when the xenophobia of 1914 through 1918 made ethnicity an issue. Both Maori and Pakeha fought in World War I; the injury and death rates were high and the legacies long term as youth absorbed without question the stories of heroism and sacrifice. There was also no initial shortage of volunteers for World War II.

Recent History

Emergent New Zealanders highlights the issues of identity that characterized much public discussion during the second half of the twentieth century, from the 1950s through 2000. Britain's entry into the Common Market, coupled with high rates of Maori urbanization and Polynesian immigration, challenged Pakeha to acknowledge and reconsider their monoculturalism. Globalization, television, the Internet, and the pervasive influence of American culture have all contributed to changing lifestyles for young New Zealanders, but the greater transformation has been internal. Multicultural immigration policies and the consequences of economic restructuring during the 1980s that diminished the role of the state in favor of market-led competition have contributed to greater social inequality within the country. Children and youth are bearing the brunt of these changes. High levels of youth suicide, sexually transmitted diseases, teenage pregnancy, single parenthood, alcohol and drug abuse, and criminal offending are matters of widespread public concern, as is the increasing awareness of violence against children.

Thousands of New Zealand youth still grow up healthy, happy, and emotionally secure, actively pursuing sporting and cultural interests and planning a future of worthwhile employment and travel overseas. But hundreds do not, and the correlation between poverty, ethnicity, ill health, low educational achievement, and abuse is increasingly obvious. New Zealanders have long cherished the belief that theirs is a great country in which to bring up children. More detailed research into both past and present childhood experience may suggest the need for some modification of that view.

See also: **Comparative History of Childhood.**

BIBLIOGRAPHY

Dalley, Bronwyn. 1998. *Family Matters: Child Welfare in Twentieth-Century New Zealand.* Auckland, NZ: Auckland University Press in association with the Historical Branch, Dept. of Internal Affairs.

Gordon, Mary. 1991. "Australia and New Zealand." In *Children in Historical and Comparative Perspective: An International Handbook and Research Guide,* ed. Joseph M. Hawes and N. Ray Hiner. Westport, CT: Greenwood Press.

Graham, Jeanine. 1992. "My brother and I . . . : Glimpses of Childhood in Our Colonial Past." Hocken Lecture, 1991. Dunedin, NZ: Hocken Library, University of Otago.

Ihimaera, Witi, ed. 1998. *Growing Up Maori.* Auckland, NZ: Tandem Press.

Metge, Joan. 1995. *New Growth from Old: The Whanau in the Modern World.* Wellington, NZ: Victoria University Press.

Simon, Judith, and Linda Tuhiwai Smith. 2001. *A Civilising Mission? Perceptions and Representations of the New Zealand Native Schools System.* Auckland, NZ: Auckland University Press.

Tennant, Margaret. 1994. *Children's Health, the Nation's Wealth: A History of Children's Health Camps.* Wellington, NZ: Bridget Williams Books.

JEANINE GRAHAM

Nursery Schools

The history of nursery schools is intimately related to the history of mass schooling. Provision of nursery schools and other institutions for the education and care of young children (generally under the age of six) came relatively late in the development of school systems. Not until it was accepted that early childhood was a highly significant stage in human development and one during which the contours of the later stages were formed was there much interest in making formal arrangements for the education of the young. Just how young was dependent on the age set for starting school, which varied from country to country, as school systems developed with the coming of industrialization and urbanization. Schools for children under the compulsory age for school attendance were motivated by a combination of a desire for moral regulation, social control, and CHILD SAVING. Demand for the provision of care for young children increased as women, many of whom were mothers, were increasingly drawn into the labor market.

The Early Infant Schools and Kindergartens

In England, the first country in the world to undergo the industrial revolution, large numbers of working-class children below the age set for school attendance and as young as one year old were being sent to school. This was either a school organized for older children or an infant school, the first of which was opened by the utopian socialist reformer Robert Owen (1771–1858) in Scotland in 1816. The infant schools that followed were promoted by infant school societies. They lacked a uniform purpose, curriculum or pedagogy, but preparation for the subjects taught in elementary schools came to predominate. A similar process took place in other industrializing countries, such as France, where the first preschools had been opened by Jean-Frédéric Oberlin (1740–1826). There, schools for young children were called *salles d'asile*, literally, "rooms of the asylum," or refuges for working-class children.

The realization that young children in infant schools needed specialized treatment adapted to their age did not take hold until the ideas and practices of JOHANN HEINRICH PESTALOZZI (1745–1827) attracted the attention of a small number of educational reformers in England. Schools run on Pestalozzian lines attempted to recognize the specific requirements of young children rather than treating them as being no different than older pupils. In 1836, the Pestalozzian Home and Colonial Infant School Society began training teachers for infant schools in its college in London. Not only did this school emphasize the need to educate young children differently but it also introduced the idea that the care and education of children in their early years was a skilled task, which should not be left to anyone prepared to work for the very low wages that were commonly paid to the "motherly" girls who looked after young children. This was made difficult when forms of various CHILD CARE, from wet nurses to dame schools, abounded and teachers received no training.

Further impetus for the idea that the education of young children should be different from that provided for older ones was provided by the international spread of the KINDERGARTEN and the theories of its founder, FRIEDRICH FROEBEL (1782–1852). The first kindergarten in England was opened in 1851 and was followed by the opening of one in the United States in 1856. While the kindergarten was a school, Froebel's educational vision encompassed both home and kindergarten. The school and the home were meant to be complementary in their organization of the play materials and activities by means of which young children from their first year on could become educated. But the conditions of the existing schools that were provided for the laboring poor in England created many obstacles to the adoption of the kindergarten. Among these were large classes, untrained teachers, and the pressure of examinations in the higher grades, which percolated down to the lower ones. Similarly, when the kindergarten entered the public school system in the United States, much that was distinctive was lost due to the bureaucratic nature of the school system and particularly the need to prepare children for the more formal approaches of the elementary schools.

Toward the end of the nineteenth century, the free kindergarten movement in the United States, and similar initiatives in England and other countries, began to stress the role of the kindergarten in the rescue of the children of the urban poor. More social workers than teachers, the women who organized the free kindergartens gradually rejected Froebel's

formal system, with its detailed directions on how to use his apparatus or "gifts" and "occupations," in favor of a wider conception of play combined with domestic tasks. Legitimation for this new approach came from the theories of the psychologist G. STANLEY HALL (1844–1924) and the philosopher JOHN DEWEY (1859–1952).

The Nursery School

In England, Margaret McMillan (1860–1931), a Christian Socialist, went further and substituted sense training and a focus on the health of the young child for the Froebelian emphasis on play and self-activity. Margaret McMillan is regarded as the originator of the nursery school concept, although when state support became available for nursery schools after 1918 the majority of the recognized nursery schools were former free kindergartens. Together with her sister Rachel, Margaret McMillan opened an open-air nursery school in a deprived part of London in 1913. At the same time, in Italy, MARIA MONTESSORI (1870–1952), was working along similar lines to produce her educational method aimed at the rescue of the children of the urban poor through an emphasis on health and sense training by means of her specially devised apparatuses, such as solid insets, sandpaper letters, and blocks that could be made into a long stair. The high rates of INFANT MORTALITY and disease both provided a major stimulus to the advocates of the nursery school.

In the United States, the first nursery schools for children under five were privately financed and often sponsored by and affiliated to universities. They were characterized by their use of CHILD STUDY and psychological theories about children and their families, such as those of SIGMUND FREUD (1856–1958) and later JEAN PIAGET (1896–1980). As such, they formed part of a broader development of the professionalizing field of child welfare. Unlike the ones in the United Kingdom, they catered mainly to upper- and middle-class children whose mothers were not undertaking paid labor. In the 1920s, the cooperative nursery school that involved parents in its running was developed in the United States. This marked a departure from the European model of the nursery school, which previously had been dominant.

The adoption of the nursery school by public education systems throughout most of the twentieth century was constrained by their cost and by the view that the best place for most children below school age was with their mothers in their homes. Exceptions to this were made for the children of the urban poor and in times of national emergency as in the GREAT DEPRESSION and World War II, but provision of nursery schooling trailed behind that of day-care centers and other forms of child-minding that lacked the educational rationale of nursery schools.

In the United States in the 1960s, War on Poverty programs such as Project HEAD START and the Ypsilanti, Michigan, Perry Preschool Project stimulated the growth of nursery schools as a means to combat social inequalities. In recent decades, public and private provision of preschools has increased dramatically in many countries, as the number of women entering the labor market has steadily grown. At the beginning of the twenty-first century the general trend is for the nursery school, which provides a play-based, developmentally appropriate curriculum, to be eclipsed by classes and institutions designed solely to prepare children for school.

A broad pattern may be observed in the history of nursery schools. When they were privately funded they were able to adopt play methods more widely than when they were publicly funded, but there were too few of them to meet the demand. Public funding of nursery schools, on the other hand, while it enabled more children to attend them, has almost always led to their subordination to the demands of the schools for older children.

See also: **Child Development, History of the Concept of.**

BIBLIOGRAPHY

Beatty, Barbara. 1995. *Preschool Education in America: The Culture of Young Children from the Colonial Era to the Present.* New Haven: Yale University Press.

Clark, Linda L. 2000. *The Rise of Professional Women in France: Gender and Public Administration since 1830.* Cambridge, UK: Cambridge University Press.

Deasey, Denison. 1978. *Education under Six.* New York: St. Martin's Press.

Lascarides, V. Celia, and Blythe F. Hinitz. 2000. *History of Early Childhood Education.* New York: Falmer Press.

McMillan, Margaret. 1919. *The Nursery School.* New York: E. P. Dutton.

Read, Katherine H., and June Patterson. 1980. *The Nursery School and Kindergarten: Human Relationships and Learning,* 7th ed. New York: Holt, Rinehart, and Winston.

Spodek, Bernard, and Olivia N. Saracho. 1994. *Right from the Start: Teaching Children Ages Three to Eight.* Boston: Allyn and Bacon.

Steedman, Caroline. 1990. *Childhood, Culture, and Class in Britain: Margaret Mcmillan, 1860–1931.* London: Virago.

Whitbread, Nanette. 1972. *The Evolution of the Nursery-Infant School: A History of Infant and Nursery Education in Britain, 1800–1970.* London: Routledge and Kegan Paul.

INTERNET RESOURCE

European Primary School Association. "A History of Preschool Education in Europe." Available at <www.epsaweb.org/preschool_education.htm>.

KEVIN J. BREHONY

Obstetrics and Midwifery

Obstetrics and midwifery are two distinct but overlapping fields of medical knowledge and practice which focus on the care of the pregnant and parturient (laboring) woman. Obstetrics focuses on the problems and difficulties of pregnancy and labor; midwifery emphasizes the normalcy of pregnancy while acknowledging the vulnerability associated with the reproductive process. Midwifery arose from the social and physical support women traditionally have given to one another, while obstetrics developed gradually as a combination of the medical traditions practiced in ancient Greece and Rome and the rise of modern anatomical research and surgery developed in premodern Europe. Obstetrics had its greatest impact at the end of the eighteenth century as the fundamentals of parturition, including its anatomy, physiology, and pathology, were recognized and as large numbers of male medical practitioners began to deliver babies. Anesthesia and antisepsis advanced nineteenth-century obstetrics, but it was not until the third decade of the twentieth century with the advent of sulfa drugs that infections related to medical intervention during childbirth ceased to be the leading cause of maternal death. In the twenty-first century, obstetrics is increasingly technological in its orientation and is focused on the pathology of pregnancy while midwifery continues to maintain its emphasis on the normalcy of pregnancy and the importance of providing pregnant and parturient women with practical and emotional support.

Antiquity and the Medieval and Early Modern Period

In ancient Greece and Rome, birth was usually an all-female event which affirmed the parturient's status as mother of the patriarchal family, especially when she produced a male child. Laboring women prayed to Asclepias and Artemis for support. Midwives came from a range of socioeconomic backgrounds, and they enjoyed varying amounts of prestige according to their training. In Greece, male and some female healers who were trained in empirically based knowledge derived from Hippocratic medicine enjoyed high social status,

attended births, and sometimes worked together during both normal and problem deliveries. A midwife untrained in Hippocratic medicine relied on a variety of folk nostrums as well as on charms and amulets.

In situations where a baby's abnormal birth position slowed its delivery, the birth attendant turned the infant *in utero* or shook the bed to attempt to reposition the fetus externally. A dead baby who failed to be delivered would be dismembered in the womb with sharp instruments and removed with a "squeezer." A retained placenta was delivered by means of counterweights, which pulled it out by force. Pain relievers and sedatives were employed only for excessive maternal suffering due to birth complications; pain associated with normal labor was seen as productive and as a part of the birthing process.

Soranus, a second-century Greek physician practicing in Rome, published a gynecological treatise in which he discussed obstetrical theory and proposed protocols for normal and abnormal births. He introduced a procedure called *podalic version*, which was a method of delivering a baby that presents in the transverse position by reaching for the leg within the womb and pulling the infant out feet first. Soranus also described the use of a birthing stool and listed the duties and skills of the midwife. Sometimes he advised using a forceps to assist with difficult births.

Historians speculate that the infant and mortality rates in antiquity were probably similar to premodern rates, even though women in classical Greece married before the age of twenty while the average age of marriage for premodern women was twenty-five. Later marriage correlated to a lower overall risk to mother and baby. Puerperal fever caused some maternal deaths, while malaria and tuberculosis constituted special risks, especially due to the lack of modern HYGIENE and efficacious drugs.

During the medieval and Renaissance periods, childbirth was a home-centered social event involving the collaboration of the birthing mother, her female relatives, and a midwife. Birth was a RITE OF PASSAGE for the woman that affirmed her fertility and new status as a mother. In spite of the biblical injunction that "in sorrow thou shalt bring forth children" (Genesis 3:16) midwives administered narcotic or pain-relieving herbs and wine. Catholic mothers also sought solace in praying to St. Margaret, the patron saint of pregnant women, while Protestant women prayed directly to their Lord without the intercession of saints.

To hasten delivery, a midwife massaged the mother's belly and genitalia with oil. Bloodletting at an ankle vein also might be administered. During labor, the pregnant woman moved constantly about the lying-in room, trying to find a comfortable position from which to give birth. Birth stools were common, especially in Germany. For abnormal deliveries, the skilled midwife had several options: she could burst the amniotic sac to induce labor, she could tie cloth to an impacted fetus and pull, or she could reposition the infant internally or externally using manipulation or abdominal massage. In instances of breech presentations, stillbirths, twins, or other problems caused by the mother's pelvic deformities, a surgeon was called in as a last resort. Sometimes he would have to dismember and extract the fetus with crochet hooks and knives to save the life of the mother.

From the late thirteenth to the late eighteenth century, a midwife's social background, occupational status, and skill level varied within and among countries. Her workload, pay, and range of tasks also varied. Popular and learned images of the midwife ranged from ignorant and unskilled to skilled and respectable. The modern notion of the midwife as witch had very little basis in reality. Court records document that midwives were rarely accused of witchcraft. In fact, ecclesiastical and municipal authorities entrusted midwives with a variety of medical and legal responsibilities. With increasing frequency, the midwife was called upon to testify as an expert witness in cases of contested pregnancy, infanticide, virginity, and rape; to mediate domestic squabbles; and to attest to religious conformity, illegitimate birth, or infanticide.

Religious concerns motivated the first official regulation of midwives in 1277 (at the Trier Synod). Midwives were enjoined to learn how to perform an emergency BAPTISM when there was no time to call in a priest. Beginning in the sixteenth century, municipal authorities regulated midwives under the aegis of the emerging male medical hierarchy. A midwife's morals, religiosity, and sometimes her skill were evaluated. In England and the United States, however, midwives received only sporadic regulation.

Studies by Roger Schofield, B. M. Wilmott Dobbie, and Irvine Loudon estimate that maternal mortality rates between 1400 and 1800 were between 1 and 3 percent. Most often, women died in childbirth due to protracted labor caused by a narrow or deformed pelvis, fetal malpresentation, postpartum hemorrhage, or puerperal fevers. The health risk was renewed at each pregnancy. Since a woman averaged five pregnancies, 10 percent of these women died during or soon after childbirth.

During the sixteenth and seventeenth centuries, the systematic study of human anatomy, the recovery of ancient medical knowledge, and a renewed interest among male medical practitioners in human reproduction encouraged the growth of obstetrics and obstetrical innovation. The advent of printing technology facilitated the spread of knowledge. The French surgeon Ambroise Paré (1510–1590) reintroduced podalic version in 1550. Other talented surgeons, as well as a few midwives, published obstetrical texts that included protocols for normal and abnormal labor and deliveries. Indeed, the French paved the way for the English surgeons and surgeon-apothecaries of the next century to become birth attendants for the aristocracy.

In the eighteenth century in England and Scotland, surgeons and physicians refined their methods for recognizing and managing normal and abnormal labor and delivery, both with and without instruments. Accurate illustrations of the gravid uterus were described for the first time. Scottish surgeon William Smellie (1697–1763) made the use of forceps during delivery a viable option; in 1752 he introduced a new and improved instrument that avoided the uterine and vaginal mutilation which an earlier prototype had often caused. In spite of these advances, however, pregnant women remained reluctant to call a surgeon because of his traditional association with death; moreover, husbands and moralists expressed concerns that a male presence during labor could easily compromise a woman's virtue. By the end of the eighteenth century, however, men attended 50 percent of all deliveries in many parts of England. The tendency was similar in France, and it became increasingly true in the United States as well.

The founding of maternity hospitals for poor women contributed to the eventual predominance of obstetrics as a medical specialty. Hospitals provided an endless supply of patients on which males could practice birthing techniques for normal and abnormal deliveries. In addition, famous surgeon *accoucheurs* and physicians set up private lecture courses for an all-male clientele on obstetrics, surgery, and dissection. A "hands-on" learning approach improved the students' skill and confidence.

The rise of obstetrics had a mixed effect on midwifery. Some midwives clung to their traditional ways. Others embraced the new science and sought retraining. National policies also shaped the contours of midwifery practice. While American and British midwives were rarely regulated and essentially were excluded from the hospitals and proprietary schools that employed the new techniques, instruments, and obstetrical knowledge, European midwives were re-educated and regulated under the auspices of local and national authorities. In France, for example, the fear of depopulation induced King Louis XV in 1759 to sponsor Madame du Coudray to educate rural midwives. Utilizing obstetrical mannequins and an illustrated manual, she trained an estimated ten thousand peasant women to deliver babies using advanced life-saving methods.

The Modern Period

Women's search for a painless childbirth experience created a decisive turning point in the history of obstetrics. The discovery of drugs such as ether, morphine, and chloroform between 1792 and 1834, and scopolamine in 1902, made pain manageable. The movement for "twilight sleep," or labor under anesthesia, began in Germany in the early twentieth century and soon spread to England and America. Upper- and middle-class women abandoned their midwives in order to be anesthetized with scopolamine and other drugs during childbirth. The potential danger that accompanied the use of anesthesia required a physician in attendance in a hospital setting. Women's erratic behavior under the anesthesia compelled their attendants to tether them to the hospital bed. Moreover, the mothers' delirious state made them totally unaware of the birth process. In addition, many infants of anesthetized mothers suffered from neonatal depression. By 1900, in the United States and Britain 50 percent of physician-assisted births involved the use of chloroform or ether in a hospital. A 1997 report by British researcher Irvine Loudon found that hospital deliveries rose from 24 percent of all births in 1932 to over 54 percent in 1946. No longer seen as interlopers in an all-female life cycle event, male physicians began to exercise more control over the prenatal and birth processes.

Following the pain management revolution, a newly emerging group of physicians who called themselves *obstetricians* instituted protocols for hospital birth that became routine in the United States and in many other Western countries. Anesthesia, forceps delivery, shaving the pregnant woman's pubic area, administering an enema and refusal of any food or drink for the mother prior to labor, episiotomy, lithotomy position for birth, and administering pitocin or other drugs to induce and control labor all became routine. Fetal monitoring, scanning, and IV infusions for the mother also became standard practice by the end of the twentieth century, as did cesarean section and birth induction, especially in the United States.

Ironically, as the obstetrical revolution gathered momentum between 1900 and 1930, maternal mortality rates increased. These deaths were almost always the result of "childbed" or puerperal fever, an infection of the female genital tract caused by the bacterium *Streptococcus pyogenes*. While the appearance of maternity hospitals in the eighteenth century already had raised the problem of puerperal fever to epidemic proportions, the fever proved fatal in hospitals as well as in many home deliveries, even after the acceptance of the germ theory of disease in the late nineteenth century. Consequently, Loudon reports in his 1997 book that the risk of dying in childbirth in 1863 and 1934 were virtually identical. The high death rate was the result of lax antiseptic practices and poorly trained birth attendants who engaged in unnecessary and dangerous obstetrical interventions, especially forceps deliveries. This fact became evident when national differences were taken into account. In his 1992 published report, Loudon found that in 1935 the rate of obstetrical interference in Holland was 1 percent and in New York 20 percent. When interference occurred, the death rate due to sepsis (infection) was 40 per 10,000 births, while the rate for spontaneous deliveries was 4 per 10,000. Maternal mortality rates did not decrease until the virulence of the streptococcus bacterium decreased and until the introduction of sulfa drugs after 1935. Maternal morality rates continued to fall after World War II with the development of safe blood transfusions, treatments for toxemia, and the introduction of ergometrine, a drug which prevents hemorrhaging after childbirth.

Cesarean Section

The rationale for birth by cesarean section initially was religious. The operation was performed when the mother appeared to be dying in order to ensure that the fetus could be baptized. During the nineteenth century cesarean section gained wider acceptance as antiseptics, anesthesia, aseptic surgery, and new kinds of uterine sutures greatly improved the survival rates of mother and child. The discovery of a purified form of penicillin in 1940 further reduced infection, uterine rupture, and other pathology.

In the United States, successful cesarean section techniques resulted in a steep increase in that form of delivery. Jane Sewell found that in 1970 the U.S. cesarean rate was about 5 percent; by 1988 the rate had reached nearly 25 percent. Judith Pence Rooks found that in 1990, the cesarean birth rate in the United States was about double that of many European countries. Efforts to reduce this rate in America because of maternal health risks have succeeded somewhat. In 1994 the rate fell to 21 percent from a high of 23 percent in 1992. The reduction has been attributed to a reduced number of same-patient cesarean sections after repeated challenges to the statement "once a cesarean section always a cesarean section."

Premature Birth

The invention of the incubator in France in the 1880s constituted a major advance in the field of what is now called neonatology. The first hospital specializing in the care of premature infants opened in Chicago in 1923. Since home birth was still the norm, parents were reluctant to have their child stay in a hospital to undergo experimental treatments. This changed dramatically during the 1960s when major advances in assisted breathing technology, improved nursery equipment, new surgical techniques, innovative INFANT FEEDING methods, and new therapeutic drugs made neonatology a viable subspecialty within PEDIATRICS. Since the 1960s medical advances have increased substantially the survival rates of premature and low-weight-for-gestational-age infants.

Prenatal Care

Routine prenatal care is a relatively recent phenomenon. Its effectiveness in ensuring the health of mother and child varies by country and within the United States by class and ethnicity. In Europe, where all citizens are protected by a national health care system, prenatal care is standard and usually performed by midwives. Women from all races and ethnic backgrounds tend to avail themselves of these services, develop few health problems, and experience premature delivery infrequently. Due to the lack of universal health care in the United States, however, the availability and usage of prenatal clinics vary tremendously. Healthy, educated, middle-class women who have planned pregnancies are more apt to visit their physicians or midwives and to follow their advice. Women who are disadvantaged and lack access to prenatal care and/or are ambivalent about having children tend to have a higher rate of preterm deliveries and other health-related problems. Cultural and social reasons inhibit such women from taking advantage of prenatal services even when they are free and accessible. African-American women deliver low-birth-weight babies at a rate twice as high as white women. Some studies on prenatal care in the United States reinforce the advisability and efficacy of the European model for prenatal care: low-income, high-risk, and/or African-American women who have access to nurse-midwifery care at prenatal clinics as opposed to standard prenatal care from obstetricians have better birth outcomes.

Infant Mortality

INFANT MORTALITY rates reflect the overall welfare and sanitary conditions of the population. In premodern Europe, one out of every four or five children died during their first year of life, and almost one child in two failed to survive to the age of ten. Social class has remained a key factor in determining infant mortality rates; according to experts, this is unlikely to change. In contrast to maternal mortality rates, infant mortality declined throughout the Western world from the early twentieth century until the mid-1930s. This trend suggests that there is no close link between maternal and infant mortality

Midwifery from 1900 to the Present

Between 1900 and 1930, the rise of obstetrics and the medicalization of birthing challenged the identity and autonomy of European midwives. These challenges occurred amid falling birth rates, obstetrician shortages, challenges from public health care workers, and economic crises. Midwives responded in a variety of ways. Swedish midwives acquired the training and right to use forceps, while midwives in other European countries acquired new medical skills to help them compete with physicians. By contrast, during the same peri-

od, American midwives' lack of organization, political power, and economic resources made it extremely difficult for them to defend themselves against the medical profession. Physicians labeled them as incompetent and ignorant in spite of many contemporary studies that contradicted these charges. A few notable exceptions included the continued practice of some immigrant midwives in the North and the founding of the Maternity Center Association in New York (1918) and the Frontier Nursing Service in Kentucky (1925) which trained nurses to become midwives for the poor. In almost all other instances, obstetric nursing practiced by registered nurses in hospitals under the supervision of physicians replaced midwifery until the rise of the alternative birth movement of the 1960s and 1970s.

At the beginning of the twenty-first century, obstetrics and its perception of pregnancy and childbirth as potentially pathological and dangerous continues to dominate Western culture. Midwives who work in hospital settings also have been influenced by this view, although by and large they are trained to view birth as a normal and healthy process. While midwives play a much larger role in the care of pregnant mothers in Europe than in America, the medicalized model of birth has gradually permeated those countries as well.

The midwifery model of pregnancy and childbirth as a normal and healthy process plays a much larger role in Sweden and the Netherlands than the rest of Europe, however. In the latter nation, one out of every three births takes place in the home. The safety and cost-effectiveness of national health care insurance combined with support of a home-birth tradition has allowed the Dutch midwife to enjoy greater autonomy vis-à-vis the medical profession than midwives in almost any country. The Dutch infant mortality rate in 1992 was the tenth-lowest rate in the world, at 6.3 deaths per thousand births, while the United States ranked twenty-second. Swedish midwives stand out as well, since they administer 80 percent of prenatal care and more than 80 percent of family planning services in Sweden. Midwives in Sweden attend all normal births in public hospitals and Swedish women tend to have fewer interventions in hospitals than American women. Midwives in the Netherlands and Sweden owe a great deal of their success to supportive government policies.

American midwives made a comeback in the late twentieth century after their earlier decline. A consumer and feminist revolt against over-medicalized birthing led to a resurgence of interest in self-taught or apprentice-trained midwives for home births, called "lay" or "direct-entry" midwives. Despite gaining legal recognition in some states, direct-entry midwives remain on the medical fringe.

Certified nurse-midwives who also are registered nurses with postgraduate training in midwifery have enjoyed greater acceptance. Middle-class and feminist women who demanded a more natural birth experience in a "safe" but "homey" hospital environment created the alternative birth movement, in which nurse-midwives played an important role. Shortages of physicians in the 1970s also encouraged the federal government to support nurse practitioners and nurse-midwives to staff the newly-funded family planning centers for the poor. At the beginning of the third millennium, certified nurse-midwives enjoyed almost universal legal recognition throughout the United States. Data demonstrate that their expertise results in equal or better outcomes for low-risk pregnancies. Between 1980 and 1995, U.S. policy makers considered nurse-midwives as a potential low-cost solution to lowering the nation's persistently high infant mortality rate, in part linked to the inability to pay for obstetrical care of many poor, high-risk pregnant women.

Obstetrics plays a life-saving and life-affirming role for many women and children who face various kinds of medical complications and emergencies. However, its emphasis on pathology has overshadowed other customs and practices related to pregnancy and childbirth. While a medicalized birth is a rite of passage, it reinforces the rational and scientific values of Western medicine, relying excessively on technology and on the authority of the physician. Critics of technologically dependent and depersonalized obstetrical approaches to pregnancy and childbirth point to the massive amount of data obtained from clinical trials and cross-cultural studies. These data support the view that many aspects of the low-technology, "natural," and health-promoting model implicit in midwifery is not only more cost-effective, but also can offer equal or better outcomes for low-risk mothers and their offspring. Moreover, the midwifery approach to childbirth provides the pregnant woman with a variety of ways to support her own emotional and physical health as well as that of her child.

See also: **Conception and Birth.**

BIBLIOGRAPHY

Demand, Nancy. 1994. *Birth, Death, and Motherhood in Classical Greece.* Baltimore, MD: Johns Hopkins University Press.

Devitt, Neal. 1996. "The Transition from Home to Hospital Birth in the United States, 1930–1960." In *Childbirth: Changing Ideas and Practices in Britain and America 1600 to the Present.* New York: Garland Publishing.

Davis-Floyd, Robbie. 1988. "Birth as an American Rite of Passage." In *Childbirth in America: Anthropological Perspectives,* ed. Karen Michaelson. Beacon Hill, MA: Bergin and Garvey.

DeVries, Raymond. 1996. *Making Midwives Legal: Childbirth, Medicine, and the Law,* 2nd ed. Columbus: Ohio State University Press.

Dobbie, B. M. Willmott. 1982. "An Attempt to Estimate the True Rate of Maternal Mortality, Sixteenth to Eighteenth Centuries." *Medical History* 26: 79–90.

Enkin, M., M. J. N. C. Keirse, and I. Chalmers, eds. 1995. *A Guide to Effective Care in Pregnancy and Childbirth,* 2nd ed. New York: Oxford University Press.

French, Valerie. 1986. "Midwives and Maternity Care in the Roman World." *Helios* 13, no. 2 (special issue): 69–84.

Gélis, Jacques. 1984. *L'arbre et le fruit: La naissance dans l'Occident moderne XVIe–XIXe siècle.* Paris: Fayard.

Green, Monica. 2000. *Women's Healthcare in the Medieval West.* Burlington, VT: Ashgate.

Harley, David. 1990. "Historians as Demonologists: The Myth of the Midwife-Witch." *Social History of Medicine* 3: 1–26.

Jordan, Brigette. 1993. *Birth in Four Cultures: A Crosscultural Investigation of Childbirth in Yucatan, Holland, Sweden, and the United States.* rev. ed. expanded by R. Davis-Floyd. Prospect Heights, IL: Waveland Press.

King, Helen. 1998. *Hippocrates' Woman: Reading the Female Body in Ancient Greece.* London: Routledge.

Leavitt, Judith Walzer. 1986. *Brought to Bed. Childbearing in America, 1750–1950.* New York: Oxford University Press.

Lingo, Alison Klairmont. 1999. "Midwifery." In *Women's Studies Encyclopedia,* 2nd edition, ed. H. Tierney. Westport, CT: Greenwood Press.

Loudon, Irvine. 1992. *Death in Childbirth: An International Study of Maternal Care and Maternal Mortality, 1800–1950.* Oxford: Clarendon Press.

Loudon, Irvine. 1997. "Childbirth." In *Western Medicine,* ed. Irvine Loudon. Oxford: Oxford University Press.

Marland, Hilary, ed. 1993. *The Art of Midwifery: Early Modern Midwives in Europe.* London: Routledge.

Marland, Hilary, and Anne Marie Rafferty, eds. 1997. *Midwives, Society and Childbirth: Debates and Controversies in the Modern Period.* London: Routledge.

Porter, Roy. 1996. "Hospitals and Surgery." In *The Cambridge Illustrated History of Medicine,* ed. Roy Porter. New York: Cambridge University Press.

Rollet, Catherine, and Marie-France Morel. 2000. *Des bébés et des hommes: Traditions et modernité des soins aux tout-petits.* Paris: Albin Michel.

Rooks, Judith Pence. 1997. *Midwifery and Childbirth in America.* Philadelphia: Temple University Press.

Schofield, Roger. 1986. "Did Mothers Really Die? Three Centuries of Maternal Mortality in the 'World We Have Lost'." In *The World We Have Gained,* ed. Lloyd Bonfield, et al. Oxford, UK: Basil Blackwell.

Strong, Jr., Thomas H. 2000. *Expecting Trouble: The Myth of Prenatal Care in America.* New York: New York University Press.

INTERNET RESOURCES

Cochrane Pregnancy and Childbirth Group. 2003. Abstracts of Cochrane Reviews. Available from <www.cochrane.org/cochrane/revabstr/g010index.htm>.

Sewell, Jane Eliot. " Cesarean Section—A Brief History." Brochure for an exhibit at the National Library of Medicine, Bethesda, MD. Available from <www.nlm.nih.gov/exhibition/cesarean/cesarean_1.html>.

ALISON KLAIRMONT LINGO

Oliver Twist

The eponymous child hero of Charles Dickens's *Oliver Twist* became a crucial cultural icon of Victorian childhood. Indeed, Dickens published the novel serially from 1837 to 1839, coinciding with the commencement of Queen Victoria's long reign in 1837. The novel follows the nine-year-old orphaned child Oliver Twist from the provincial workhouse ORPHANAGE where boys are brutally mistreated to the metropolis of London where, under the tutelage of the master criminal Fagin, boys like Oliver are initiated into the criminal underworld. In dramatizing the harshness of the workhouse the novel contributed to an increasing public awareness and growing outrage at the miserable conditions to which children were sometimes subjected in such institutions.

The central dramatic concern of the novel, however, is Oliver's struggle to preserve his spiritual innocence within the criminal context of Fagin's gang. Dickens clearly articulates the Victorian tenet of childhood's innocence, which was synthesized from a variety of earlier ideological strands including Christian theology, the enlightened ideals of JEAN-JACQUES ROUSSEAU, and the Romantic intimations of William Wordsworth. Dickens, in *Oliver Twist* and in his later novels as well, discovered a melodramatic formula for capturing the hearts of the Victorian public by representing a child whose innocence is menaced by an evil world.

Fagin trains the boys to pick pockets, and Oliver is eventually expected to participate in burglary. Yet he desperately objects to such conduct: "Oh! pray have mercy on me, and do not make me steal. For the love of all the bright Angels that rest in Heaven, have mercy upon me!" (p. 154). Dickens suggests that a child like Oliver dreads compromising his innocence for fear of succumbing to utter corruption. In Fagin's world, children are criminally exploited, perhaps even sexually exploited—though Dickens is not explicit about this—by vicious and unscrupulous adults. Dickens was, however, well aware of the irony that it was legal institutions like the workhouse that by their brutality actually drove children like Oliver Twist into the illegal machinations of exploitative criminals.

Oliver is finally redeemed by his own resistance to evil and ends the novel under the kindly adoptive care of bourgeois patrons, but only after it has been recognized that the boy has successfully preserved his embattled innocence. In one scene a respectable doctor and a beneficent young lady observe Oliver asleep and speculate about his possibly criminal history:

"Vice," sighed the surgeon, replacing the curtain, "takes up her abode in many temples; and who can say that a fair outside shall not enshrine her?"

"But at so early an age!" urged Rose.

"My dear young lady," rejoined the surgeon, mournfully shaking his head; "crime, like death, is not confined to the old and withered alone. The youngest and fairest are too often its chosen victims." (p. 197)

In the Victorian ideology of childhood, the child was conceived as naturally innocent but also profoundly susceptible to the forces of moral, criminal, and sexual corruption. Indeed the Victorian cult of the innocence of childhood, in which Dickens was certainly some sort of high priest, was all the more intense inasmuch as innocence was seen as terrifyingly precarious.

Though Oliver survives with his innocence intact to the end of the novel, Dickens in later works would wring even more sentimental effect from the early deaths of children in their utmost innocence, notably Paul Dombey in *Dombey and Son* and Little Nell in *The Old Curiosity Shop*. In the twentieth century *Oliver Twist* would continue to exercise its sentimental spell, translated into new forms including the silent movie of 1922 with the child star Jackie Coogan, the classic film version of 1948 directed by David Lean, and the stage musical *Oliver!* of 1960, which, when made into a film in 1968, won the Oscar for best picture. Both of the novel's central concerns—the institutional mistreatment of children and the criminal exploitation of children—remain matters of tremendous social concern all over the world at the beginning of the twenty-first century. Dickens's *Oliver Twist* played a pioneering part in formulating that concern at the threshold of the Victorian age.

See also: **Child Abuse; Child Labor in the West; Theories of Childhood.**

BIBLIOGRAPHY

Dickens, Charles. 1993. *Oliver Twist*, Norton Critical Edition, ed. Fred Kaplan. New York: Norton.

Donovan, Frank. 1968. *Dickens and Youth*. New York: Dodd, Mead.

Kaplan, Fred. 1988. *Dickens: A Biography*. New York: Morrow.

Wolff, Larry. 1996. "'The Boys Are Pickpockets and the Girl Is a Prostitute': Gender and Juvenile Criminality in Early Victorian England from *Oliver Twist* to *London Labour*." *New Literary History* 27, no. 2.

LARRY WOLFF

Open Air School Movement

The open air school movement was created to prevent the development of tuberculosis in children. It required the establishment of schools that combine medical surveillance with pedagogy adapted to students with pre-tuberculosis. The new institution was established by doctors researching new prophylactic methods, and educators interested in an open air educational experience.

In 1904, Dr. Bernhard Bendix and pedagogue Hermann Neufert founded the first school of this kind: the *Waldeschule* of Charlottenburg, near Berlin, Germany. Classes were conducted in the woods to offer open-air therapy to young city dwellers with pre-tuberculosis. The experiment, conducted by the International Congresses of Hygiene, was immediately attempted throughout Europe and North America: in Belgium in 1904, in Switzerland, England, Italy, and France in 1907, in the United States in 1908, in Hungary in 1910, and in Sweden in 1914. The schools were called "schools of the woods" or "open air schools." Often they were remote from cities, set up in tents, prefabricated barracks, or repurposed structures, and were run during the summer. Some of the more noteworthy experiments were the School in the Sun, in Cergnat, Switzerland and the school of Uffculme near Birmingham, England. The School of the Sun used heliotherapy (1910)—doctor Auguste Rollier sent the children up to the mountains every morning equipped with portable equipment. The school of Uffculme, noted for its architecture, allowed each class to occupy its own independent pavilion (1911).

After World War I the movement became organized. The first International Congress took place in Paris in 1922, at the initiative of The League for Open Air Education created in France in 1906, and of its president, Gaston Lemonier. There were four more congresses: in Belgium in 1931; in Germany in 1936; marked by the involvement of German doctor Karl Triebold; in Italy in 1949; and in Switzerland in 1956. National committees were created. Jean Duperthuis, a close associate of Adolphe Ferrière (1879–1960), the well-known pedagogue and theorist of New Education, created the International Bureau of Open Air Schools to collect information on how these schools worked. Testimonies described an educational experience inspired by New Education, with much physical exercise, regular medical checkups, and a closely monitored diet, but there has been little formal study of the majority of these schools.

According to the ideas of the open air school, the architecture had to provide wide access to the outdoors, with large bay windows and a heating system that would permit working with the windows open. The most remarkable of these schools were in Amsterdam, Holland by architect Jan Duiker (1929–1930), in Suresnes, France by Eugène Beaudoin and Marcel Lods (1931–1935), and Copenhagen, Denmark by Kai Gottlob (1935–1938).

Later, the movement had an influence on the evolution of education, HYGIENE, and architecture. School buildings, for example, adopted the concept of classes open to the outdoors, as in Bale, Switzerland (1938–1939, architect Hermann Baur), Impington, England (1939, Walter Gropius and Maxwell Fry), and in Los Angeles (1935, Richard Neutra). This influence is the major contribution of the open air schools movement, although the introduction of antibiotics, which increasingly provided a cure for tuberculosis, seemed to make them obsolete after World War II.

See also: **Children's Spaces; School Buildings and Architecture.**

BIBLIOGRAPHY

Châtelet, Anne-Marie, D. Lerch, and J.-N. Luc. 2003. *The Open-Air Schools: An Educational and Architectural Experience in the Europe of the Twentieth Century.* Paris: Recherches.

Cruickshank, M. 1977. "The Open-Air School Movement in English Education." *Paedagogica Historica* 17: 62–74.

ANNE-MARIE CHÂTELET

Opie, Iona and Peter

Iona Opie (b. 1923) and Peter Mason Opie (1918–1982) were British collectors, publishers, and archivists of children's folklore. Peter Opie was president of the anthropology section of the British Association in 1962–1963 and of the British Folklore Society in 1963–1964. The husband-and-wife team began their research together in 1944. Their first major work was *The Oxford Dictionary of Nursery Rhymes* (1951; 2nd edition, 1997), a collection of more than five hundred rhymes, songs, nonsense jingles, and lullabies. For each item the known facts about origin, variants, non-English equivalents, and earlier publication are stated. In the introduction, the Opies outline a suggestion for a general categorization of children's rhymes. This volume stands out as one of the standard collections of English-language children's rhymes.

The path-breaking *The Lore and Language of Schoolchildren* (1959) efficiently refuted the idea that the growing impact of mass media and the entertainment industry would inevitably extinguish children's own, genuine traditions. Leaving the parent-guarded nurseries behind, this unexpurgated collection of jokes, riddles, rhymes, rituals, beliefs, and secret spells provides a vivid testimony of multitudinous children's traditions thriving in streets and school yards. The material is grouped into categories and presented together with folkloristic and historical comments, as well as international comparisons.

Unlike many of their predecessors, the Opies collected schoolchildren's lore directly from six- to fourteen-year-olds and not from adults reminiscing about their own childhood traditions. Their method of work foreshadowed a paradigm shift in folklore research in the 1960s that emphasized the study of contemporary folklore and fieldwork among representatives of a culture rather than text analyses of archival material. They conducted large-scale surveys during the 1950s and 1960s, with contributions from 135 state schools throughout England, Scotland, and Wales, and tape-recorded children in playgrounds all over Britain during the 1970s. The mass of information collected provided material for a further three books, all on children's games: *Children's Games in Street and Playground* (1969), *The Singing Game* (1985), and *Children's Games with Things* (1997), the last two of which Iona Opie produced after her husband's death, as well as publishing her own playground observations as *The People in the Playground* (1993). Aside from their work on children's folklore the Opies also dealt with FAIRY TALES, most notably in *The Classic Fairy Tales* (1974). The Opies' inspiring example contributed to the emergence of children's folklore as a thriving field of research within folklore studies.

The Opie Collection of Children's Literature, housed in the Bodleian Library in Oxford, was originated by the Opies as a private research library in 1944. Upon Peter Opie's death in 1982, Iona Opie decided to place the collection, then amounting to twenty thousand titles, in a public institution. The transfer to the Bodleian library was made possible by a national fund-raising campaign (led by Prince Charles) and by Opie's donation of half the collection. The largest single category is made up of twelve thousand bound volumes of children's stories and nursery rhymes. Other substantial categories include primers, alphabets and other instruction books, chapbooks, comics, and children's magazines. Some eight hundred of the titles were published before 1800, including among other rare books a 1706 edition of *The Arabian Nights* and an early printing of *Robinson Crusoe*. The collection is accessible to the public in microfiche form.

See also: **Children's Literature; Theories of Childhood; Theories of Play.**

BIBLIOGRAPHY

Opie, Iona. 1993. *The People in the Playground.* Oxford, UK: Oxford University Press.

Opie, Iona, and Peter Opie. 1959. *The Lore and Language of Schoolchildren.* Oxford, UK: Clarendon Press.

Opie, Iona, and Peter Opie. 1997 [1951]. *The Oxford Dictionary of Nursery Rhymes.* Oxford, UK: Oxford University Press.

ULF PALMENFELT

Organized Recreation and Youth Groups

Efforts to organize children's play have predominantly arisen within the last century. It was not until the early twentieth century that children's use of their free time became an issue for anyone but the child. Throughout much of history, children's PLAY was essentially a time for aimless frivolity, left over after the pressing demands of survival had been met. Sweeping societal changes in the late nineteenth century focused attention on what children were doing in their free time and how they were doing it. This scrutiny led adults to believe that it was important for them to organize children's play and to provide structured opportunities and resources.

From Free Play to Organized Recreation

By the last half of the nineteenth century, industrialization brought about sweeping changes in Europe and the United States. As the industrial labor force organized into craft unions, working conditions improved, levels of pay increased, and hours of work were cut back. Children, who had worked long, hard hours in factories, mines, and big-city sweatshops, were freed of this burden through CHILD LABOR legislation. Increasing numbers of children and youth now had significant periods of unoccupied free time available, and they were lured by the attraction of adults' recreations, including drinking, gambling, and boisterous lawbreaking. The misuse of free time by children came to be viewed as a widespread social problem and the provision and regulation of wholesome play activities became an instrument of social reform. A number of reformers sought to develop agencies and institutions to solve the emerging social problems created by this new era in which children now had too much unsupervised play time. Public demands for increased structured play opportunities and supervision became more frequent and vociferous. The PLAYGROUND MOVEMENT grew out of the public concern, especially in large cities, that children needed a protected, stimulating, and safe place to play. Increasingly, organized recreation programs were promoted by churches, law enforcement agencies, and civic associations in an attempt to help children resist street play and commercialized forms of play such as amusement arcades. By the 1880s and 1890s, church leaders widely encouraged "sanctified amusement and recreation" as alternatives to the undesirable play forms they were witnessing. Settlement houses also provided a variety of organized occasions and facilities for supervised play. Similarly, various ethnic associations organized athletic and gymnastic clubs such as the German Turnverein and Jewish SUMMER CAMPS.

The idea that city governments should organize and provide recreation programs, services, and facilities became widely accepted, and more and more states passed laws authorizing local governments to operate structured recreation programs. In the opening decades of the twentieth century, a number of important nonprofit organizations serving youth were formed. The National Association of Boys' Clubs was founded in 1906, the BOY SCOUTS and the Camp Fire Girls in 1910, and the GIRL SCOUTS in 1912. By the end of the 1920s, these organizations had become widely established in American life and were serving substantial numbers of children and youth. A number of urban school boards initiated structured after-school and VACATION play programs as early as the 1890s, and this trend continued throughout the twentieth century. Education for the "worthy use of leisure" was vigorously supported as an important goal for secondary schools throughout the United States. Between 1910 and 1930, thousands of school systems established extensive programs of extracurricular activities, particularly in SPORTS and hobbies.

Government Plays a Role: The Institutionalization of Organized Recreation

From the end of World War II to the turn of the twenty-first century, recreation programs evolved from a relatively minor area of government and nonprofit agency responsibility to an enormous, complex, profit-seeking enterprise. In the years immediately after World War II there was a dramatic rise in the birth rate, with millions of children and youth flooding the schools and recreation centers. Within a few years, many of these new families moved from the central cities to homes in surrounding suburban areas. In these suburban communities, recreation for growing families became a significant concern. Most suburbs were quick to establish recreation departments to develop organized programs to serve children of all ages. At the same time, the population within the inner cities changed dramatically. An important development of the 1960s was the expanded role given to organized recreation as an important element in President Johnson's War on Poverty. In the mid-1960s, destructive riots erupted in a number of major American cities, and in many cases they stemmed from the overall lack of recreation facilities and programs in inner-city neighborhoods as compared to wealthier sections of the city. In an effort to prevent further rioting, many of the antipoverty programs of the mid- and late 1960s placed their emphasis on serving minority groups in urban slums through organized recreation programs. A new wave of legislation, including the Economic Opportunity Act of 1964, the Housing and Urban Development Act of 1964, and the Model Cities Program of 1967 provided funding for locally directed organized recreation programs to be conducted in depressed urban neighborhoods. Hundreds of millions of dollars were granted each year to local governments to provide recreation services aimed primarily at youth, including sports and social programs, cultural programs, and trips.

In addition, thousands of governmental and nonprofit organizations also expanded their organized programs for children and youth in response to these trends. While youth sports programs have existed in the United States since the beginning of the twentieth century, they played a relatively minor role in organized recreation. In the latter half of the twentieth century, organized sports programs for children and youth surged. Founded in 1939, Little League Baseball, with a televised World Series, has grown to be widely recognized. It was incorporated under a bill signed by President Johnson in 1964, and it is the only youth sports organization with a charter granted by the U.S. Congress. An estimated four million children from preschoolers and up participate in a variety of youth sports each year, organized, structured, and governed by a number of agencies, including municipal park and recreation departments, Little League baseball, Biddy Basketball, American Legion Football, Pop Warner football, U.S. Ice Hockey Association, American Youth Soccer Organization, Boys and Girls Clubs, Girls Incorporated, Boy Scouts of America, YMCAs, and YWCAs.

The Shift to Private and Commercial Sectors: Organized Recreation as Big Business

The organized recreation movement faced a serious threat in the 1970s and 1980s as the mounting cost of government led to tax protests and funding cutbacks in states and cities across the United States. In the mid-1970s a number of older industrial cities in the nation's "rust belt" began to suffer from increased energy costs, welfare and crime problems, and expenses linked to rising infrastructure maintenance costs. Along with some suburban school districts confronted by skyrocketing enrollments and limited tax bases, such communities experienced budget deficits and the need to freeze expenditures. By the end of 1979, statutory provisions had been approved in thirty-six states that either reduced property, income, or sales taxes or put other types of spending limits in place. This resulted in major funding cutbacks for organized recreation services for children and youth.

The demand for organized recreation programs and services for children did not diminish, however, and it was addressed in a dramatically new way. Replacing earlier publicly subsidized recreation programs was a growing sector that provided an entrepreneurial, market-oriented approach to organized recreation. Organized recreation became an industry, and it was made up of a mosaic of thousands of businesses directly or subtly woven into the American economy. It was argued that in order to compete effectively, public recreation agencies had to adopt the philosophy and businesslike methods of successful companies. This meant that at every stage of agency operations—from assessing potential target populations and planning programs to pricing, publicizing, and distributing services—sophisticated methods of analysis and marketing had to be used.

As a second type of response to the era of austerity that began in the 1980s, many organized recreation providers resorted to privatization—subcontracting or developing concession arrangements with private organizations—to carry out functions that they could not themselves fulfill as economically or efficiently. This has become a major thrust in American life as the role of government has been challenged. Numerous public departments have contracted with private businesses to operate swimming pools, golf courses, tennis complexes, marinas, community centers, and other facilities under contractual agreements that govern the standards they must meet and the rates they may impose. Organized recreation has now moved from the public sector to the private, as profit-making businesses now provide structured opportunities for children's play and recreation. Many have decried this shift, arguing that the bottom line is no longer the healthy and safe provision of play, but rather how much profit can be gleaned from providing recreation to youth.

See also: **Indoor Games; Street Games; Theories of Play.**

BIBLIOGRAPHY

Cross, Gary A. 1990. *A Social History of Leisure since 1600.* State College, PA: Venture Publishing.

Hans, James S. 1981. *The Play of the World.* Amherst: University of Massachusetts Press.

Kraus, Richard. 2001. *Recreation and Leisure in Modern Society.* 6th ed. Boston: Jones and Bartlett.

Russell, Ruth V. 2002. *Pastimes: The Context of Contemporary Leisure.* 2nd ed. Champaign, IL: Sagamore Publishing.

Schwartzman, Helen B. 1978. *Transformations: The Anthropology of Children's Play.* New York: Plenum Press.

Sutton-Smith, Brian. 1997. *The Ambiguity of Play.* Cambridge, MA: Harvard University Press.

LYNN A. BARNETT

Orphanages

In the middle of the fourteenth century, religious orders, confraternities, and municipalities established orphanages and FOUNDLING hospitals all over Europe as a response to the plague and to increasing poverty. A Parisian confraternity founded an orphanage, Hôpital du Saint-Esprit-en-Grève, in 1366, and in Italy the Florentine Innocenti opened in 1444. Although most orphanages were established in western and southern Europe, a few were also established in eastern and northern Europe. The Church took care of abandoned and illegitimate infants, and from the fifteenth century on foundling hospitals could be found in many German, Italian, and French cities.

Orphanages in the United States

Few orphanages existed in the United States before the nineteenth century. Religious groups usually founded orphanages as a response to wars and epidemics. In 1734, the Ursuline Sisters, a French Catholic order, turned their school in New Orleans into an orphanage to care for children left by an Indian massacre at Natchez. In 1737, the followers of the German missionary AUGUST HERMANN FRANCKE established the Salzburger orphanage in Ebenezer, Georgia. A year later, the Anglican reverend George Whitefield established an orphanage in Bethesda, Georgia. By the early nineteenth century, about two dozen more had been built in big cities, and from the 1830s on orphanages opened rapidly in most cities in the country.

Industrialization, urbanization, and immigration contributed to the proliferation of child-care institutions. In preindustrial America, orphans were indentured to foster families in exchange for their work. But during the nineteenth century, growing towns with struggling immigrants could not rely on indentured service to solve the problem of orphaned and homeless children. Wage laborers experienced periods of unemployment, and often succumbed to illness and accidents, creating large groups of children with no parents or with parents who were unable to care for them. Religion and ethnicity separated the immigrants from the towns' residents. Catholic immigrants feared the influence of Protestant families over their children. Within the Catholic Church, the Germans resented the Irish and preferred to establish German institutions. Later on, other Catholic immigrants (Italians, Poles, French Canadians) also established orphanages to preserve their culture and language. Nondenominational orphanages usually were built by groups of Protestant churches to serve established nonimmigrant communities.

By the mid-nineteenth century education was emphasized over work, and middle-class women, who dedicated their time to nurturing their children and doing charity work, were actively involved in social issues pertaining to children. They played an important part in the antebellum reform movement, from the 1830s to 1860s. The reformers, responding to growing urban poverty and influenced by the transcendentalists, sought to provide shelter and education in the midst of nature for orphaned, neglected, abused, abandoned, and delinquent children. They believed that separating children from adults in almshouses, placing them in institutions in rural areas, structuring their activities, and educating them would turn them into good citizens. For children who had already experienced a life of vice in the city, the reformers established industrial homes, houses of refuge, and reformatories with an emphasis on work and vocational education. The innocent poor—orphaned, abandoned, and neglected children—were educated in orphanages. Some institutions were defined by gender and others had age restrictions. By 1860 orphanages could be found in almost all states of the union. Only a few new states, and small states without urban centers, did not have any orphanages.

Post–Civil War Orphanages

After the Civil War, states became involved in building orphanages for the war orphans, which later included orphans of the Spanish-American War. As industry expanded rapidly and immigration increased, more children lost one or both parents to accidents, illness, and despair. Jewish orphanages and fraternal orphanages were established, as well as county orphanages financed by local governments. African-American and Indian-American communities built orphanages for their children. Philanthropists outside these communities also established orphanages specifically for racial minorities (black, Chinese, Japanese, Korean, and Indian Americans). A few orphanages accommodated racially mixed populations.

States without public orphanages (New York, California, and Maryland) placed their wards in private institutions and paid for their board. But most private child-care institutions were supported by contributions from individuals, the children's surviving parent or relatives, and their communities, with little or no aid from the state. Boards of trustees, whose members were the respectable and wealthy citizens of the community, ran the orphanages. They usually volunteered their service, considering it a religious and communal obligation. They raised funds, made policies, admitted children, and hired and supervised the superintendent and staff. During the nineteenth century, the superintendents were educators or religious leaders who viewed their work as a vocation. Many stayed in their positions for decades, shaping their institutions' policies, maintaining contacts with their communities, and providing stability and continuity of care.

By the Progressive Era (1890–1920), the superintendents of orphanages were graduates of the evolving discipline of social work, specializing in the new field of CHILD CARE. Orphanages at the end of the nineteenth century were considered the best method of care for dependent children; their popularity increased and single poor parents often regarded them as places they could leave their children temporarily until circumstances improved, or as places where their children could get a good education. Many orphanages became crowded, and some restricted admission to only full and half-orphan children. The majority of children in orphanages in the late nineteenth century had at least one parent living. Those who had both parents living had been placed by the court, by a welfare agency on account of abuse and neglect, or by parents who were unable or unwilling to take care of them. Parents often used the courts to secure admission to institutions by declaring their children delinquent or incorrigible.

Many orphanages did not admit young children. Few orphanages had nurseries. Big cities had foundling hospitals, but single working mothers often used baby farms for their newborns. In baby farms, foster mothers nursed the babies, waited for them to die, or sold them for adoption. The death rates in all infant institutions were staggering, either because the abandoned children arrived at the hospital already starved and sick from exposure to the elements or because CONTAGIOUS DISEASES such as scarlet fever, diphtheria, and whooping cough caused high mortality rates, especially among infants. FOUNDLINGS who survived early childhood and were not adopted were transferred to orphanages. Unlike infant institutions, the mortality rates in orphanages were low, despite epidemics and diseases. Children in orphanages generally enjoyed far better medical care, nutrition, hygiene, and fresh air than were available in the neighborhoods from which they had come.

Late nineteenth-century reformers viewed children as a key for reforming and redeeming the republic. These "child savers" fought against child labor and for compulsory education, playgrounds, and libraries in poor urban neighborhoods. Orphanages played an important role in that reform. By the early twentieth century, many orphanages had playgrounds, libraries, athletic facilities, musical training, recreation, and vocational education. Children were either schooled inside the orphanage or attended neighborhood public schools. Talented students attended high schools and were encouraged to obtain a college education.

Orphanages differed in the kind of population they housed, based on the children's ethnicity, religion, class, and gender, and sometimes on academic ability. But although there was no single model of the Progressive orphanage, they all strove to give their children an edge in life through education.

The Attack on Orphanages

By the late nineteenth century, some reformers began to attack orphanages for being overly regimented and sheltering their children too long. Influenced by social Darwinism, Amos Warner, the prominent social welfare researcher, argued in *American Charities* (1875) that clustering children with similar backgrounds bred pauperism, and that institutionalized children were not prepared adequately for life struggles. He advocated dispersing the children into families. Beginning in 1854, American reformer CHARLES LORING BRACE had been sending dependent children from New York to live with and work in families in the Midwest. These PLACING-OUT operations, carried out by the NEW YORK CHILDREN'S AID SOCIETY and copied in other cities, were later known as the ORPHANS' TRAINS. Children's Aid Societies continued the tradition of indenture and were the precursor to FOSTER CARE. Some children were adopted and some were exploited. Many lost contact with their natural families and were barely supervised by the agency after they were placed. By contrast, orphanages rarely sought to break up families; most encouraged connections with families and kept siblings together. The majority of children returned to their families once circumstances changed. Parents, and especially immigrant parents, preferred orphanages to giving their children to Children's Aid societies.

Progressive-era reformers intensified their criticism of orphanages, blaming them for obliterating individuality. In 1909, at a White House conference called by President Theodore Roosevelt to discuss children's welfare, two hundred social workers declared that the best method of caring for dependent children was at home or in an alternative family. Institutions, they said, should be considered the last resort. For children who needed an alternative home, they suggested placements in screened, unpaid foster homes under the supervision of social workers. The children were expected to attend school and work for their board.

Orphanages responded to the criticisms by striving to create homelike institutions. They broke the large congregate bedrooms into small units, built cottages in which small groups of children lived with a home mother, relaxed the discipline, added more recreation and enrichment programs, and cultivated children's individual talents. Orphanages that could not modernize were closed or consolidated. The remaining institutions attempted to be boarding schools for dependent children.

Post–World War I Orphanages

From the 1920s on, charities started to close their institutions, creating foster care agencies adhering to the social work preference for foster care over institutionalization. Catholic Charities resisted the trend and was slow to change. The 1910s pension laws for widows and their children allowed many single mothers to keep their children at home, and the restrictions on immigration in the early 1920s reduced the number of dependent children. But during the 1930s, orphanages became crowded again. The Depression years depleted the institutions' resources and forced them to place out children in foster families. The 1935 Aid for Dependent Children legislation made it possible for more families to care for children whom they might otherwise have had to place in orphanages. By then, many orphanages had shifted their mission to caring for children with mental, emotional, and physical problems. Social workers preferred to put healthy children in foster families and pay for their board. Disabled children were left in institutions. By the 1950s, most states had taken responsibility for the care of their dependent children, foster care had developed special care for disabled children, and orphanages had become residential treatment centers and temporary shelters until foster families were located.

The anti-institution movement of the 1960s closed most of the remaining orphanages. Federal Aid for Families with Dependent Children legislation (AFDC), which began in the 1960s, aimed at preserving biological families and preventing children from being placed out.

But the number of children in foster care did not diminish, and by the 1980s foster care was in crisis. The system faced a shortage of foster parents, inadequate supervision, high staff turnover, and children who were moved from one placement to another. In some cases there was also abuse, neglect, and death of children in foster homes. In 1994, Congressman Newt Gingrich, suggested a return to orphanages. His remarks reopened a century-old debate. Opponents looked at research done on residential treatments from the 1950s on and pointed to problems that arose when troubled children were concentrated in one place. Supporters emphasized the permanency, family preservation, and educational benefits that the Progressive Era's orphanages had provided. During the 1980s, historians and graduates of orphanages discovered that orphanages were discarded with little research and that the century-old debate was largely based on fiction and movies. The combination of their research and personal accounts cast institutions in a much more positive light than that in which they had previously been depicted. Some states and private philanthropists started building residential academies for preteens and teenagers who were not likely to be adopted or find placements. Others responded to the renewed debate and the continuing crisis in foster care by terminating parental rights in order to release children for adoption, by establishing permanent foster care units, and by enhancing services for families in crisis.

See also: **Abandonment; Baby Farming; Child Saving; Dependent Children; Orphans; White House Conferences on Children.**

BIBLIOGRAPHY

Ashby, Leroy. 1984. *Saving the Waifs: Reformers and Dependent Children, 1890–1917.* Philadelphia: Temple University Press.

Bogen, Hyman. 1992. *The Luckiest Orphans: A History of the Hebrew Orphan Asylum of New York.* Urbana: University of Illinois Press.

Boswell, John. 1990. *Kindness of Strangers: The Abandonment of Children in Western Europe from Late Antiquity to the Renaissance.* New York: Pantheon.

Broder, Sherri. 2002. *Tramps, Unfit Mothers, and Neglected Children: Negotiating the Family in Late Nineteenth-Century Philadelphia.* Phildelphia: University of Pennsylvania Press.

Cmiel, Kenneth. 1995. *A Home of Another Kind: One Chicago Orphanage and the Tangle of Child Welfare.* Chicago: University of Chicago Press.

Crenson, Matthew A. 1998. *The Invisible Orphanage: A Prehistory of the American Welfare System.* Cambridge, MA: Harvard University Press.

Dulberger, Judith A. 1996. *"Mother Donit Fare the Best," Correspondence of a Nineteenth-Century Orphan Asylum.* Syracuse, NY: Syracuse University Press.

Friedman, Reena Sigman. 1994. *These Are Our Children: Jewish Orphanages in the United States 1880–1925.* Hanover, NH: University Press of New England, for Brandeis University Press.

Fuchs, Rachel. 1986. *Abandoned Children, Foundlings, and Child Welfare in Nineteenth-Century France.* Albany: State University of New York Press.

Hacsi, Timothy A. 1997. *Second Home: Orphan Asylums and Poor Families in America.* Cambridge, MA: Harvard University Press.

Holt, Marilyn Irvin. 2001. *Indian Orphanages.* Lawrence: University Press of Kansas.

McKenzie, Richard B. 1996. *The Home: A Memoir of Growing Up in an Orphanage.* New York: Basic Books.

McKenzie, Richard B. 1998. *Rethinking Orphanages for the 21st Century.* Beverly Hills, CA: Sage Publication

Molat, Michel. 1986. *The Poor in the Middle Ages: An Essay in Social History.* Trans. Arthur Goldhammer. New Haven, CT: Yale University Press.

Polster, Gary Edward. 1990. *Inside Looking Out: The Cleveland Jewish Orphan Asylum, 1868–1924.* Kent, OH: Kent State University Press.

Rothman, David J. 1971. *The Discovery of the Asylum: Social Order and Disorder in the New Republic.* Boston: Little, Brown.

Rothman, David J. 1980. *Conscience and Convenience: The Asylum and Its Alternatives in Progressive America.* Boston: Little, Brown.

Zmora, Nurith. 1994. *Orphanages Reconsidered: Child Care Institutions in Progressive Era Baltimore.* Philadelphia: Temple University Press.

NURITH ZMORA

Orphans

In the past, numerous children were orphaned. In societies where people married early and had many children, and a high death rate was common in the adult population, many children lost one of their parents, and some both, before coming of age.

Orphans suffered from a higher death rate than other children did. They often had to live outside of standard households, either because they were placed in a foster family or, as was more often the case, because they were placed as servants or apprentices at an earlier age than was common. Charitable societies first, then towns or nations, organized to improve these children's living conditions and to make it easier for them to become integrated into society.

How Many Orphans Were There?

The number of orphaned children in a society is connected to the political and economic environment (war, famine, epidemic) and to the demographic situation. As the death rate declined from the seventeenth century onwards, as people began to marry later in many Western countries, and as people died at an older age on average, children lost their parents later and the number of underage orphans decreased.

Starting in early modern times, orphans can be precisely numbered. Estimates concerning some French, English, or Spanish villages in the seventeenth and eighteenth centuries indicate that at least one-third of the children lost one of their parents during childhood. In nineteenth-century Milan, one child out of two had lost at least one parent by age twenty. In nineteenth-century China, almost one-third of boys had lost one parent or both by age fifteen. In early modern times, the younger children were, the greater chance they stood of losing their mothers rather than their fathers, because many women died in childbirth. In western Europe, a woman's risks of dying within the sixty days following childbirth declined from 1 percent in the seventeenth century to 0.5 percent in 1900. After age twelve, children's risk of losing their fathers increased due to the higher death rate among the male population. In nineteenth century Venice, at age five, 5.4 percent of children had lost their fathers, 6 percent their mothers, and 1 percent both. At age fifteen, 22 percent had lost their father, 15 percent their mother, and 6 percent both parents.

Weakened Children

All studies indicate a higher death rate among orphans than among other children. In addition to emotional and psychological trauma, the impact on their living conditions was serious. Among the working class, the father's death generally resulted in the household's fall into destitution.

Most of the time, children were worse off if they lost their mothers; this phenomenon was recognized in nineteenth-century Europe, China, and Japan. For example, in Linkoping, Sweden, in the nineteenth century, 60 percent of the children who had lost their mothers before their first birthdays died before age fifteen, as opposed to 30 percent of those who had lost their fathers, and 25 percent of those who still had both parents. The consequences of the mother's death could sometimes be mitigated by the father's prompt remarriage.

The child's age at the time of the parent's death was also a factor: the younger the child was when the father or mother died, the higher the mortality risk. In 1915 Baltimore, the death rate among children who had lost their mothers before their second month of life was 526 out of 1000. In addition, orphans' survival seems to have been linked to their sex because the child's sex influenced the intervention of family or outside help. Girls were more prepared than boys to take over cleaning and cooking and they could take better care of themselves even at a young age. Therefore, more help was usually offered to boys, but the survival of boys and girls depended on familial arrangements. A few surveys also mention the role played by religion. For example, in nineteenth century Venice the death rate among children in general and orphans in particular was twice as low among Jews. This seems to have been connected to various factors, including personal HYGIENE, attitudes towards illness and medicine, and the efficiency of the community's institutions in the event of a parent's death.

Orphans and the Household

When a child's father or mother dies, the household's survival is endangered and several possibilities can be considered: (1) the household may survive, deprived of the deceased parent; (2) the household may be altered by the departure of some of the children or the arrival of a newcomer (aunt, mother-in-law, etc) who is willing to help the surviving parent; (3) the household may be recomposed by the arrival of a stepfather or stepmother, sometimes accompanied by his or her children, if the surviving parent remarries; or (4) the household may be scattered, with the orphans being separated from their surviving parent. From the sixteenth century onward in European societies widowers generally remarried more often and more quickly than widows. Therefore, the recomposed household in which orphans were brought up included a stepmother more often than a stepfather. A few surveys hint that orphans, more often than other children, may have been the victims of sexual abuse especially from their stepfathers or stepmothers, but the sources offer little of substance.

When the father died, the widow could become head of the household, but this role could also be transferred to an orphan, generally a boy in his late teens. In preindustrial Japan, orphan boys could succeed their fathers as head of the household as early as age sixteen, but these orphans had to take on an adult's responsibilities precociously. In countries where this was possible, the orphans sometimes benefited from an early emancipation.

In the event of the father's death, it was sometimes difficult for a widow who did not remarry to keep many of her children with her. Consequently orphans left home precociously more often than other children. GRANDPARENTS seem to have played a very limited part in the accommodation of young orphans, probably because they were so seldom still alive. Orphans were often placed as servants or apprentices. However, family solidarity seems to have resulted in orphans being placed whenever possible as servants or apprentices with relatives.

From Family to Collective Support

During the Middle Ages and well into the seventeenth century, because little material support was available from charitable societies, orphans from modest backgrounds were sometimes doomed to live in destitution. Novelists have dwelt on the portrait of the homeless boy reduced to begging or DELINQUENCY, or the homeless girl forced into prostitution. But institutions were gradually organized to look after them. In many European countries, boards of guardians were set up; these were generally composed of the orphan's relatives and they were responsible for the orphan's education and for the safekeeping of his or her property.

One of the first people appealed to for care of the orphaned child was the godfather or godmother. However, the GODPARENT's role as guardian seemed to decline after the end of the Middle Ages in western Europe, although it probably remained strong in eastern and southern Europe. In France, the revolution instituted the civil BAPTISM, in which the godfather and godmother publicly and solemnly pledged to provide for the child's needs until he or she came of age should the parents die or become unable to look after him or her.

Orphans could also be adopted, a practice already documented in ancient Greece. In early modern times, the godfather and godmother were the first to be appealed to, which is why they had to be chosen from among relatively young people from a good background. In France, famous people such as Montaigne, Corneille, and Voltaire are known to have adopted their orphaned godchildren.

The orphan could also be adopted by a hospital or a charitable society. In Europe, this mainly occurred from the sixteenth century onwards. In western Europe, there is evidence of some orphans who had been entrusted to hospitals being adopted by middle-class people unrelated to them. This seems to have remained in practice until the eighteenth century, notably in Germany. In Venice, the first ORPHANAGE was created in 1811 as part of a campaign meant to reduce begging. Before that, vagrant orphans would be locked up with tramps and people with disabilities in the main hospitals, which were more like detention centers than treatment centers. To be accepted in Venice's orphanage, an orphan had to be seven to twelve years old, legitimate, born and living in Venice, in good health, and fit for work. Because the orphanage had limited accommodation, other orphans, particularly those who were very young, ill, illegitimate, or immigrants, were rejected. Though they could get some help from other charitable societies, which occasionally provided clothes, food, or shelter, they had to rely mainly on their relatives and connections.

In modern Europe illegitimate children had a high risk of being abandoned. For illegitimate orphans the only hope for survival was to be taken in by a hospital or charitable institution. Most orphaned illegitimate children, like thousands of abandoned children, were placed in a caretaker's home and lost contact with their families. Others were confined to workhouses where they had to work to pay for the help they received.

In the nineteenth century, states became more and more active in providing for orphans, particularly by financing and controlling the running of orphanages. The particular case of war orphans must be mentioned—those whose fathers were killed in action or were crippled for life. For example, after World War I France created a special status for war orphans, who were called *Pupilles de la Nation*. Adopted by the state, these orphans benefited from material and moral support that could extend beyond their legal majority.

Fortunately, the living conditions of orphans improved during the twentieth century, at least in developed countries. Because adult mortality among parents of minor children is low, orphans are less numerous and most orphanages have shut down. Surviving parents often receive support from insurance and public funds; the welfare state will attempt to provide education and care if both parents have died and relatives are unable to care for the child; and adoption of orphans by childless couples (which was not allowed by law in the nineteenth century in many countries) has become frequent since the last half of the twentieth century.

See also: **Abandonment; Adoption in the United States; Foundlings; Homeless Children and Runaways in the United States; Stepparents in the United States.**

BIBLIOGRAPHY

Akerman, Sune, Ulf Högberg, and Tobias Andersson. 1996. "Survival of Orphans in 19th Century Sweden." In *Orphans and Foster Children: A Historical and Cross-Cultural Perspective*, ed. Lars-Göran Tedebrand. Umeå, Sweden: Umeå University.

Bideau, Alain, Guy Brunet, and Fabrice Foroni. 2002. "Orphans and Their Family Histories: A Study of the Valserine Valley (France) during the 19th and the 20th Centuries." *The History of the Family: An International Quarterly* 5: 315–325.

Campbell, Cameron, and James Lee. 2002. "When Husbands and Parents Die: Widowhood and Orphanhood in Late Imperial Liaoning, 1789–1909." In *When Dad Died: Individuals and Families Coping with Distress in Past Societies*, ed. Renzo Derosas and Michel Oris. New York: Peter Lang.

Derosas, Renzo. 2002. "Fatherless Families in 19th Century Venice." In *When Dad Died: Individuals and Families Coping with Distress in Past Societies*, ed. Renzo Derosas and Michel Oris. New York: Peter Lang.

Faron, Olivier. 1999. "The Age of War Orphans: Construction and Realities of a Group of State Wards between Education and Assistance (1917–1935)." *The History of the Family: An International Quarterly* 4: 17–29.

Faron, Olivier, and Jacques Renard. 2002. "The Varied Repercussions Caused by the Demise of the Father among Past Populations." In *When Dad Died: Individuals and Families Coping with Distress in Past Societies*, ed. Renzo Derosas and Michel Oris. New York: Peter Lang.

Gager, Kristin E. 1996. *Blood Ties and Fictive Ties: Adoption and Family Life in Early Modern France*. Princeton, NJ: Princeton University Press.

Kurosu, Satomi, and Emiko Ochiai. 1995. "Adoption as a Heirship Strategy under Demographic Constraints." *Journal of Family History* 20: 261–288.

Oris, Michel, and Emiko Ochiai. 2002. "Family Crisis in the Context of Different Family Systems." In *When Dad Died: Individuals and Families Coping with Distress in Past Societies*, ed. Renzo Derosas and Michel Oris. New York: Peter Lang.

Vassberg, David E. 1998. "Orphans and Adoption in Early Modern Castilian Villages." *The History of the Family: An International Quarterly* 3: 441–458.

Wall, Richard. 2002. "Elderly Widows and Widowers and Their Coresidents in Late 19th and Early 20th-Century England and Wales." *The History of the Family: An International Quarterly* 7: 139–156.

GUY BRUNET

Orphan Trains

The term *orphan trains* refers to the mid-nineteenth- and early- twentieth-century method of placing destitute, urban children in the homes of largely rural families. Mid- and late-nineteenth-century reformers were increasingly concerned with the accumulating social ills of an advancing industrial society, including child poverty. Growing numbers of mostly immigrant, poor children filled the streets of nineteenth-century urban America. For instance, in 1849 approximately 3,000 HOMELESS CHILDREN lived and sometimes worked on the sidewalks of New York City. CHARLES LORING BRACE was one of the most well-known of the reformers to respond to the plight of these children. In 1853 Brace established his famed Protestant child welfare organization, the Children's Aid Society (CAS) of New York, that provided an alternative to the almshouses, ORPHANAGES, and jails where destitute and vagrant children were typically housed. Initially, the voluntary CAS developed shelter and lodging centers for urban youth, provided vocational and religious instruction, and looked to place children in family homes within the city. Yet these solutions alone were not alone sufficient and the CAS soon began its experiment with its "Emigration Plan," which later became known as the orphan trains. The trains challenged the conventional practice of institutionalizing dependent children, and their advocates argued that children were best cared for in family settings. Most scholars consider the trains the origin of modern FOSTER CARE.

Children who rode the orphan trains were usually sent in groups out to rural America where local residents greeted them and took them home via an informal auction. The term ORPHAN is actually a misnomer, as less than half of the children who rode the trains were actually orphans and approximately 25 percent had two living parents. Brace believed that country living and training could prevent the development of negative habits and vices characteristic of the evil city. This partially reflected the period's romanticization of rural America and the West. The system deeply resembled earlier indentureship practices, although Brace and the CAS rejected this term. In contrast to indentureship, the CAS or the natural parent remained the guardian of the placed children and children were theoretically able to leave if problems arose. Like indentured children, those who rode the orphan trains were expected to work in their new family homes, which mirrored other informal nineteenth-century fostering arrangements. Many of the boys performed farm labor and many of the girls engaged in domestic work. Yet the new families were also expected to treat the children like "one of their own" and provide love as well as shelter.

Brace enjoyed great fame for his PLACING-OUT system, but he was far from alone in his practice. Agencies such as the Children's Mission to the Children of the Destitute of Boston actually developed a rural placing-out system before the CAS did and many other groups followed in Brace's footsteps, some even as far away as Western Europe. The New York Foundling Hospital, a Catholic organization, was one of the largest American agencies to employ a like system. Catholic agencies were highly critical of the CAS and accused the agency of placing Catholic children in Protestant homes in an effort at conversion. NY Foundling was successful at finding Catholic homes for Catholic children, but its task was more difficult given that fewer Catholic families lived in rural areas.

Along with religion, the racism of the period shaped the fate of children riding the orphan trains. As author Stephen O'Connor argues, the CAS and other orphan train programs generally neglected the African-American community, although the nationally known Colored Orphan Asylum developed a similar program and placed their wards with African-American farmers close to New York. There are instances of the CAS placing African-American children, but these were generally children who could "pass" for white and many of them encountered racism within their host families. A national scandal erupted when NY Foundling placed white Catholic children of European descent with Mexican families in Arizona. The children were forcibly removed from their placements by a group of local Anglo men, the incident almost erupted into violence, and NY Foundling endured highly negative press as a result.

Thus, while the orphan trains enjoyed significant support, they were not without their critics. In addition to sectarian rivalries, others challenged the quality and outcomes of the orphan train placements. The CAS often boasted of astronomically high "success rates" by noting the significant accomplishment of some of its children. Although it is difficult to evaluate the orphan trains as the agencies engaged in little systematic research, historians suggest that many children served through the programs found loving families and went on to distinguished careers. For instance, John Brady, the governor of Alaska, was a CAS ward. Yet historians also recognize that many children were exploited and abused. Nineteenth- and early-twentieth-century critics argued that orphan train programs and the CAS in particular provided little oversight of their placements. CAS agents rarely visited homes after the children were placed, partially due to a lack of funds and logistical complications. Although agents claimed to maintain communication through writing, it was not uncommon for the agencies to lose all contact after initial placement. Critics also argued that the foster families were rarely well screened and agency representatives briefly interviewed the families—if at all—and collected only the most superficial information about them. While CAS and other agencies became more careful about family screening and oversight, this did not appease detractors and by 1900 several midwestern states adopted legislation limiting and regulating the placement of children. In the Progressive Era a new generation of children's advocates suggested that dependent children should remain with their families of origin whenever possible, striking a deep blow to the placing out philosophy. Although the trains continued to run through the first decades of the twentieth century, they served relatively few children in these later years. The last CAS orphan train ran its route in 1929. By then, the orphan trains had served more than 200,000 children. Like the child welfare system of the late twentieth century, the orphan trains leave a mixed legacy and speak to the complexities of assisting children in need.

See also: **Aid to Dependent Children; Apprenticeship; Dependent Children; New York Children's Aid Society; White House Conferences on Children.**

BIBLIOGRAPHY

Holt, Marilyn. 1992. *The Orphan Trains: Placing Out in America.* Lincoln: University of Nebraska Press.

O'Connor, Stephen. 2001. *Orphan Trains: The Story of Charles Loring Brace and the Children He Saved and Failed.* New York: Houghton Mifflin.

Tiffin, Susan. 1982. *In Whose Best Interest?: Child Welfare Reform in the Progressive Era.* Westport, CT: Greenwood Press.

LAURA CURRAN

P

Pacifier

The oral behaviors of infancy, thumb sucking, and the sucking of pacifiers (or *dummies*, as they are called in British Commonwealth countries), have been noted for centuries. It appears that mothers have always been aware that sucking provides comfort, sleep, and pleasure to babies. Sucking rags were described in the sixteenth century. These were later replaced with teething rings and corals, and increasingly with the rubber pacifier after 1900. A number of fifteenth-century Italian paintings depict thumb sucking, and thumb sucking and blanket attachment are the characteristics of the Linus character in the contemporary cartoon *Peanuts*. For most of this time, such oral behaviors have been seen as distinctive of infancy and a source of comfort and pleasure for both the child and parent. But this benign view changed in the late nineteenth century and in the early decades of the twentieth century. Members of the medical profession began to exhibit marked hostility to these infantile habits and in 1926 they influenced the French Chamber of Deputies to carry a motion prohibiting the sale of the *sucette* (pacifier).

This change in attitude was associated with two beliefs: one, that this type of infantile sucking was a threat to the health and development of babies and posed a risk of both infection and damage to the teeth and jaws, and two, that sucking provided the infant with a pleasure that was inherently sexual. These ideas were formed against a background of a medical and societal interest in child behavior and its implications for specifically hereditary degeneration, but also for a possible general societal degeneration manifested by poverty, declining industries, and, in the United Kingdom, poor performance in the Boer War (1899–1902). The analysis of child behavior was in turn influenced by theories of INFANT SEXUALITY and its implications for the moral development of the child and the subsequent adult.

These oral behaviors are unique to infancy and had previously been judged to be normal in that context, but this changed with the new emphasis on potential consequences for the adult whom the child would become. Such common habits could now be defined as abnormal in order to prevent future pathology. Popular belief therefore made a transition from seeing sucking as a comfort and a sign of health to a medical problem, which had to be corrected to produce normal adults.

Thus in the late nineteenth century thumb sucking and associated oral behaviors emerged in the literature of the diseases of children as pathology: a pathology of ugly dental malformation and worrying infant sexual behavior. The issue was first mentioned in 1878 by an American physician, Thomas Chandler, as a cause of mouth and tooth deformities. Other authors subsequently associated such facial deformities with negative moral development. A German pediatrician, S. Lindner, introduced a sexual element, associating it with MASTURBATION. His writings were cited by SIGMUND FREUD, who identified thumb sucking as the classic example of his idea of infant autoeroticism and as a manifestation of infant sexuality. In pediatric texts, masturbation and thumb sucking became grouped together first under injurious habits of infancy and subsequently within functional neurological diseases. A number of aspects were repeatedly emphasized: the dangers for future neurological development; the pleasure a child derived from it, and the laxity shown toward it by parents, nurses, and some physicians. The medical profession was urged to reeducate parents and make them see the habit for the danger physicians believed it posed.

These attitudes persisted in the first third of the twentieth century. Treatment was directed at breaking the habit through destruction of the pacifier and diversion techniques for thumb sucking, including cotton mittens and sleeves pinned or sewed down over the hand. Over the remaining part of the century, however, the attitude gradually changed so that sucking behavior was seen increasingly as a common and harmless activity of infancy and early childhood. Indeed it was often identified as a necessary part of development and the thumb or pacifier a transitional object, a psychoanalytical concept relating to the transition from inner reality to external life. At the same time, residual ambivalent attitudes can still be detected in medical and child-rearing texts. In essence, the representation of such infant behaviors has at any one time reflected the prevailing view of child rearing, child sexuality, and child development.

See also: **Child Development, History of the Concept of; Child Psychology.**

BIBLIOGRAPHY

Gale, Catherine, and Christopher Martyn. 1995. "Dummies and the Health of Hertfordshire Infants, 1911–1930." *Social History of Medicine* 8: 231–255.

Gillis, Jonathan. 1996. "Bad Habits and Pernicious Results: Thumb Sucking and the Discipline of Late-Nineteenth Century Paediatrics." *Medical History* 40: 55–73.

Levin, S. 1971. "Dummies." *South African Medical Journal* 45: 237–240.

JONATHAN GILLIS

Parades

Any nation, city, village, or religious or ethnic group must articulate its sense of community. Since antiquity, processions, pageants, and parades have been one important way of making communal bonds visible, and children have always played a significant though changing role in these celebrations, in which communities say who they are and where they are going.

Ancient and Medieval Celebrations

In his *Laws*, PLATO states that nothing is of more benefit to the state than the mutual acquaintance of its citizens. As manifested by the frieze around the temple of Parthenon, Athens demonstrated its unity in the procession of the great Panathenaen festival. The Greek word for procession, *pompē*, was taken over by the Romans as *pompa*, which can still be found in some form in most European languages, as for example in "pomp and circumstance."

Originally the processions were religious. But their form has survived for centuries, easily metamorphosing from religious processions into royal entries, popular festivals, and, since the beginning of the twentieth century, commercial events such as the American parade.

In ancient as well as modern parades the city very often functions as a theatrical setting. The drama begins with the arrival of the parade into this scene along the major thoroughfares. The protagonist is welcomed by people waving with palm leaves, flags, or similar props. The protagonist is followed by long lines of people and "floats" that make the lavishly decorated streets come alive. Along the streets and at the destination of the parade, children stand praising and chanting.

History shows, however, that communities on a smaller scale are also in need of parading their collective memory or their collective longings. If urban parades often reflect the politics of those in power or the aspirations of those out of power, parades in villages and thinly populated areas either express local conditions or serve to establish a feeling of community among people who do not get together on a daily basis.

Parades are characterized by sociability, participation, and sometimes a temporary abolition of the existing order. But they also often teach moral lessons. Integral to all processions are the moral lessons told by the tableaux displayed on the floats. These lessons may be primarily religious, but they may also be military, political, nostalgic, utopian; efforts are made to give these lessons a spectacular shape. In the early Middle Ages, for example, around 800, a meeting between the Pope and the emperor Karl the Great was celebrated by an entry into Rome, where they were received by a complete and concrete enumeration of all the classes of this society—clerics, political rulers, the military, the people, and lastly the schoolchildren. Medieval carnival celebrations, on the other hand, turned the world upside down and sometimes placed children first in the procession, electing "boy bishops." In the later Middle Ages, the growing importance of the burghers (middle-class citizens) was reflected in the processions.

The early modern age (fifteenth to eighteenth centuries) saw a growing gap between popular culture and elite cultures, but in spite of political efforts to eradicate popular culture, processions continued to be an important part of city life. If the city was torn by religious, political, or economic tensions, this might be reflected in rival parades.

Parades in America

Still, however, processions remained primarily a tool for shaping a sense of community, as seen in the development of the American parade. In small town America the family is at the center of the parade. Everybody takes part in the procession, and if the parade features religious or patriotic symbols this of course makes the children feel the links between family, church, and nation. But these parades may also offer a playful comment on everyday life, as in the New Orleans Parade during Mardi Gras, where African Americans dress up in stupendous feather costumes as American Indians, staging a kind of racial theater. Thus in a parade the child participant not only experiences the reality of metaphors such as "joining your neighbor," "marching together," and "standing side by side" but also learns that social identities and relations may change.

In the rapidly growing cities of nineteenth-century America this ritualized, collective movement took a distinctive form. Inspired by military parades, these celebrations provided a tool for asserting diverse social identities. Holidays such as Fourth of July, Washington's Birthday, and more local anniversaries were celebrated by different nationalities, occupations, and organizations. Whether national, ethnic, occupational, or moral (for example, the temperance movement), each social identity would form a marching unit within the parade. In contrast to most European processions, these parades did not have a plot or a goal such as arriving at a temple or handing over the keys of the city; participants simply wanted to proclaim their social identities to spectators along the streets.

The display of these identities often demonstrated the power of American society to synthesize its various components, but could also demonstrate uncompromising differences. After an 1876 Centennial parade in New York City, the *New York Tribune* noted "incongruous" units were assembled in the parade, including German bands, Irish temperance societies, Spanish, French, and Italian associations, trade unions, and the Ancient Order of Hibernians. In later years, as more and more parades became ethnic rituals rather than broad civic celebrations, the potential for conflict—both among different ethnic groups and with authorities—increased. Carnival and control form the two poles of the history of parades. In modern New York City the Irish are still allowed to parade down Fifth Avenue on Saint Patrick's Day, but for many other ethnic groups it has become increasingly difficult to be allowed to use the prominent parts of the city. It is doubtful whether parades kept under close surveillance by the police have the same appeal to children as those in which the child enjoys the experience of being part of an enlarged, playful family.

Rise of Commercialism in Parades

At the turn of the twentieth century, politicians and merchants saw a common interest in basing parades on the identity of the consumer. The parade would show the commitment of the city to the "democratizing" commercial culture, and children would embody this democracy, which paid no heed to social, ethnic, or religious distinctions. The religious sinner, the nationalist, and the worker were replaced by the consumer, particularly the child consumer.

Since the middle of the nineteenth century, Thanksgiving Day had been celebrated in New York City by so-called ragamuffin parades, probably originating in European carnival traditions. Here, scarcity was the point of departure, with masquerading children begging for money. During the first decades of the twentieth century, however, abundance became the point of departure, with the great department stores arranging spectacular parades. In 1924 Macy's started its gigantic Thanksgiving Day parade, and during the Depression of the 1930s this parade, with its enormous floating balloons of comic figures such as Felix the Cat and the Katzenjammer Kids became immensely popular, attracting an audience of over 1 million along the parade route.

Commercial parades reflected a new attention to children as a special group. Department stores allied themselves with

Thanksgiving parades date back to the nineteenth century. The most well-known, Macy's Thanksgiving parade, was founded in 1924 and continues to be popular at the start of the twenty-first century. © Gail Mooney/CORBIS.

psychologists and other experts in order to capitalize on this attention and to counter the still prevalent belief that "spoiling" children with too many TOYS would make them sinful. Thus when Macy's organized an extensive exposition of toys in 1928, they enlisted the help of child experts such as Sidonie Gruenberg, president of the Child Study Association, who argued that children are beyond good and bad, and that though their instincts must be channeled, they have a right to imaginative PLAY and should not suffer from "repressive penalties imposed by an arbitrary puritanism which suggests every desire and impulse of being Satanic."

The parades turned Gruenberg's suggestions into reality, and department stores profited from the close connection between commercial culture and Santa Claus. But at present the idea of a parade as a free space for imaginative play seems to be counteracted by the reduction of children to spectators being held under close surveillance by armed police.

See also: **Consumer Culture; Theme Parks; Vacations; Zoos.**

BIBLIOGRAPHY

Ladurie, Emmanuel Le Roy. 1979. *Le Carnaval de Romans: De la Chandeleur au mercredi des Cendres 1579–1580.* Paris: Gallimard.

Leach, William. 1993. *Land of Desire: Merchants, Power, and the Rise of a New American Culture.* New York: Vintage.

Lipsitz, George. 1994. *Dangerous Crossroads: Popular Music, Postmodernism, and the Poetics of Space.* New York and London: Verso.

Ryan, Mary. 1989. "The American Parade: Representations of the Nineteenth-Century Social Order." In *The New Cultural History,* ed. Lynn Hunt. Berkeley, Los Angeles, and London: University of California Press.

Tenfelde, Klaus. 1987. "Adventus: Die fürstliche Einholung als städtisches Fest." In *Stadt und Fest: Zu Geschichte und Gegenwart europäischer Festkultur,* ed. Paul Hugger and Walter Burkert. Stuttgart, Germany: Verlag.

MARTIN ZERLANG

Parenting

Anxiety is the hallmark of modern parenthood. Early-twenty-first century parents agonize incessantly about their children's physical health, personality development, psychological well-being, and academic performance. From birth, parenthood is colored by apprehension. Contemporary parents worry about SUDDEN INFANT DEATH SYNDROME, stranger ABDUCTIONS, and physical and sexual abuse, as well as more mundane problems, such as SLEEP disorders and HYPERACTIVITY.

Parental anxiety about children's well-being is not a new development, but parents' concerns have taken dramatically different forms over time. Until the mid-nineteenth century, parents were primarily concerned about their children's health, religious piety, and moral development. In the late nineteenth century, parents became increasingly attentive to their children's emotional and psychological well-being, and during the twentieth century, parental anxieties dwelt on children's personality development, gender identity, and their ability to interact with peers. Today, much more than in the past, guilt-ridden, uncertain parents worry that their children not suffer from boredom, low self-esteem, or excessive school pressures.

Shifting Assumptions about Parenting

In the early twenty-first century, we consider early childhood life's formative stage, and believe that children's experiences during the first two or three years of life mold their personality, lay the foundation for future cognitive and psychological development, and leave a lasting imprint on their EMOTIONAL LIFE. We also assume that children's development proceeds through a series of physiological, psychological, social, and cognitive stages; that even very young children have a capacity to learn; that PLAY serves valuable developmental functions; and that growing up requires children to separate emotionally and psychologically from their parents. These assumptions differ markedly from those held two or three centuries previously. Before the mid-eighteenth century, most adults betrayed surprisingly little interest in the very first years of life and AUTOBIOGRAPHIES revealed little nostalgia for childhood. Also adults were far less age conscious than they have since become, and tended to dismiss children's play as trivial and insignificant.

The basic assumptions that underlie parenting are cultural constructs that arise at particular points in history. Parenting has evolved through a series of successive and overlapping phases, from a seventeenth-century view of children as "adults-in-training" to the early-nineteenth-century emphasis on character formation; the late-nineteenth century notion of SCIENTIFIC CHILD REARING, stressing regularity and systematization; the mid-twentieth-century focus on fulfilling children's emotional and psychological needs; and the late-twentieth-century stress on maximizing children's intellectual and social development.

Childhood in Colonial America

Diversity has always been a hallmark of American parenting. At no time was this more readily apparent than during the colonial era. Parenting took quite different forms among Native Americans, enslaved African Americans, and European colonists of various regions and religious backgrounds.

European observers were shocked by the differences between their child-rearing customs and those of the Indian peoples of the Eastern woodlands. There were certain superficial similarities. Native peoples, like Europeans, surrounded pregnancy with rituals to ensure the newborn's health, and practiced rites following a childbirth that Europeans regarded as perversions of baptism and CIRCUMCISION (such as rubbing an infant in bear's fat and piercing the newborn's tongue, nose, or ears). The differences in child rearing were especially striking. Girls were not expected to spin, weave, or knit, as they were in Europe, and boys were not expected to farm. Nor were children subjected to corporal punishment, since this was believed to produce timidity and submissiveness.

Maturation among Indians was much more enmeshed in religious and communal rituals than among Europeans. For boys, there were ceremonies to mark one's first tooth, killing of one's first large game, and a vision quest, in which boys went alone into the wilderness to find a guardian spirit. Many girls were secluded at the time of first menstruation. Among certain Southeastern tribes, there was a ceremony called *huskinaw* through which boys and girls shed their childish identity and assumed adult status.

English colonists regarded children as "adults-in-training." They recognized that children differed from adults in their mental, moral, and physical capabilities, and drew a distinction between childhood, an intermediate stage they called youth, and adulthood. But they did not rigidly segregate children by age. Size and physical strength were more important than chronological age in defining a young person's roles and responsibilities. Parents wanted children to speak, read, reason, and contribute to their family's economic well-being as soon as possible.

Infancy was regarded as a state of deficiency. Unable to speak or stand, infants lacked two essential attributes of full humanity. Parents discouraged infants from crawling, and placed them in "walking stools," similar to modern walkers. To ensure proper adult posture, young girls wore leather corsets and parents placed rods along the spines of very young children of both sexes. The colonists rarely swaddled their infants, and not surprisingly some youngsters fell into fireplaces or wells.

Colonial America's varied religious cultures exerted a profound influence on child rearing. The New England Puritans encouraged children to exhibit religious piety and to conquer their sinful nature. To encourage children to reflect on their morality, the Puritans spoke frequently about death. They also took children to hangings so that they would contemplate the consequences of sin. To encourage youthful piety, Puritan parents held daily household prayers; read books, such as James Janeway's *Token for Children*, offering examples of early conversion; and expected even young children to attend Sabbath services. One of the Puritans' most important legacies was the notion that parents were responsible not only for their children's physical well-being, but also for their choice of vocation and the state of their soul.

In the Middle Colonies (New York, New Jersey, Pennsylvania, and Delaware), a very different pattern of parenting arose. Quaker households, in particular, were much less authoritarian and patriarchal than the Puritans'. They were also more isolated since fewer families took in other families' children as servants as Puritans did. Instead of emphasizing sinfulness, Quaker parents sought to gently nurture each child's "Light Within," the spark of divinity that they believed was implanted in each child's soul, through "holy conversation." Quaker parents, unlike those in New England, emphasized early independence, providing their children with land at a relatively early age.

In the Chesapeake colonies of Maryland and Virginia, a sharply skewed sex ratio and a high death rate produced patterns of parenting very different from those in the Middle Colonies or New England. Marriages in the seventeenth-century Chesapeake were brief, and orphanhood and step-parenthood were common. Fathers, who could not expect to see their children reach adulthood, granted their children economic independence at an early age. The seventeenth-century Chesapeake included large numbers of teenage indentured servants who were under very strict DISCIPLINE and frequently suffered corporal punishment.

Eighteenth-Century Ferment

During the eighteenth century, the world of childhood underwent dramatic shifts. Fewer first children were named for parents, who also abandoned the custom of NAMING later-born children for recently deceased SIBLINGS. Children also received middle names, suggesting a greater recognition of each child's individuality. Representations of childhood changed. Stiffly posed portraits depicting children as miniature adults gave way to more romantic depictions of childhood, showing young people playing or reading. Meanwhile, such educational toys as globes, jigsaw puzzles, and board games, appeared, as did children's books, with wide margins, large type, and pictures. Animal stories, morality tales, and science books sought to entertain as well as instruct.

Eighteenth-century child-rearing tracts suggest a shift in parental attitudes. Alongside an earlier emphasis on instilling religious piety, there was a growing stress on implanting virtue and a capacity for self-government by teaching "the Government of themselves, their Passions and Appetites." Many manuals embraced JOHN LOCKE's argument that "a Love of Credit, and an Apprehension of Shame and Disgrace" was much more effective in shaping children's behavior than physical beatings. Yet the eighteenth century also saw a growing obsession with MASTURBATION, following the publication in 1710 of *Onania: Or the Heinous Sin of Self Pollution*. As childhood became associated with asexual innocence, behavior that ran counter to this ideal was rigorously repressed.

Contrasting conceptions of childhood coexisted in eighteenth-century America. These included the Lockean notion of the child as a tabula rasa, or blank slate whose character could be shaped for good or bad; a Romantic association of childhood with purity, imagination, and organic wholeness; and an evangelical conception of children as potentially sinful creatures who needed to be sheltered from the evil influences of the outside world and whose willfulness must be broken in infancy. These views of childhood tended to be associated with distinct social groups. The evangelical emphasis on submission to authority and early conversion was most often found among rural Baptist, Methodist, and Presbyterian families. The southern gentry and northern merchants were especially likely to shower children with affection, since day-to-day discipline was in the hands of servants or slaves. Meanwhile, the middling orders, especially upwardly mobile farm, shopkeeping, and artisan families, emphasized self-control and internalized discipline.

The American Revolution accelerated antipatriarchial currents already underway. An emphasis on order and restraint gave way to a Romantic insistence on the importance of personal feeling and affection. Fewer parents expected children to bow or doff their hats in their presence or stand during meals. Instead of addressing parents as "sir" and "madam," children called them "papa" and "mama." By the end of the eighteenth century, furniture specifically designed for children, painted in pastel colors and decorated with pictures of animals or figures from nursery rhymes, began to be widely produced, reflecting the popular notion of childhood as a time of innocence and playfulness.

According to the ideal of "republican motherhood" that flourished in the late eighteenth century, mothers were responsible for implanting the republican virtues of civility and self-restraint in their sons and ensuring that America's republican experiment would not follow the path of the Greek and Roman Republics. To ensure that women could fulfill this responsibility late eighteenth century saw a surge in female academies and a marked increase in female literacy.

By the early nineteenth century, mothers in the rapidly expanding Northeastern middle class increasingly embraced an amalgam of earlier child-rearing ideas. From John Locke, they absorbed the notion that children were highly malleable creatures and that a republican form of government required parents to instill a capacity for self-government in their children. From JEAN-JACQUES ROUSSEAU and the Romantic poets middle-class parents acquired the idea of childhood as a special stage of life, intimately connected with nature and purer and morally superior to adulthood. From the evangelicals, the middle class adopted the idea that the primary task of parenthood was to implant proper moral character in children and to insulate children from the corruptions of the adult world.

Parenting in Nineteenth-Century America

Early-nineteenth-century travelers reported that American children were far more independent and much less rigorously disciplined than their European counterparts. A British visitor, Frederick Marryat, offered a particularly shocking example. After a youngster disobeyed his father's command, the man described his son as "a sturdy republican," while "smiling at the boy's resolute disobedience."

Yet as early as the second quarter of the nineteenth century, a new kind of urban middle-class family, much more emotionally intense than in the past, was emerging. These families were much smaller than their colonial counterparts, as parents rapidly reduced the birth rate from an average seven to ten children in 1800 to five children in 1850 and three in 1900. These families were also more sharply divided along generational lines, as child rearing was increasingly concentrated in the early years of marriage. They were also more mother-centered, as fathers left home to go to work and mothers assumed nearly exclusive responsibility for child rearing. Meanwhile, middle-class children remained within their parents' home longer than in the past. Instead of shifting back and forth between the home and work experiences outside the home, the young remained at home into their late teens or early twenties.

As socialization within the home was prolonged and intensified, child rearing became an increasingly self-conscious activity—a development underscored by a proliferation of advice manuals, mothers' magazines, and maternal societies, where pious mothers discussed methods for properly raising and disciplining children. The advice, which increasingly came from secular authorities rather than ministers, emphasized several themes. One was the crucial significance of the early years. As the Rev. Horace Bushnell wrote in 1843, "Let every Christian father and mother understand, when the child is three years old, that they have done more than half of what they will do for his character." Another key theme was the critical importance of mothering. As Lydia Maria Child put it in 1832, her "every look, every movement, every expression does something toward forming the character of the little heir to immortal life." The goals and methods of child rearing were conceived of in new terms. Mothers were to nurture children—especially sons—who were resourceful and self-directed; they were to do so by internalizing a capacity for inner discipline and self-control not through physical punishment, but through various forms of maternal influence, including maternal example, appeals to a child's conscience, and threats to withdraw love.

Class, Ethnic, and Regional Diversity

At the same time that the northeastern middle class embraced the idea of intensive mothering and a sheltered childhood, very different patterns prevailed among slave, farm, frontier, mining, and urban working-class families. Their children actively contributed to their family's well-being by hunting and fishing, assisting in parents' work activities, tending gardens or livestock, toiling in mines or mills, scavenging or participating in street trades, and caring for younger siblings.

Parenting under SLAVERY was especially difficult. As a result of poor nutrition and heavy labor during pregnancy, half of all slave newborns weighed five-and-a-half pounds or less, or what we would consider dangerously underweight, and fewer than two out of three slave children reached the age of ten. Nearly half of the former slaves interviewed by the Works Progress Administration were raised apart from their father, either because he resided on another plantation, their mother was unmarried or widowed, or their father was a white man. By the time they reached the age of sixteen, fully a third of those interviewed had been sold or transferred to another owner.

Childhood represented a battlefield in which parents and masters competed over who would exercise primary authority over children. One of enslaved children's harshest memories was discovering that their parents were helpless to protect them from abuse. Still, slave parents managed to convey a sense of pride to their children and to educate them about how to maneuver through the complexities of slavery. Through their naming patterns, transmission of craft skills, religious customs, music, and folklore, slave parents gave their children the will and skills necessary to endure slavery and sustained a sense of history, morality, and distinctive identity.

Urban working-class and immigrant families depended for subsistence on a cooperative family economy in which all family members, including children, were expected to contribute to the family's material support. During the nineteenth century, as much as twenty percent of many working-class families' income was earned by children under the age of fifteen. Key decisions—regarding emigration, school attendance, and the timing of entry into the workforce and marriage—were based on family needs rather than individual choices, and working-class and immigrant parents frequently invoked their authority to ensure that children handed over their unopened paychecks.

Rural families also depended heavily on their children. On the western frontier, parents encouraged children to act independently and to assume essential family responsibilities at an early age. Even very young children were expected to perform essential tasks such as cutting hay; herding cattle and sheep; burning brush; gathering eggs; churning butter; and assisting with plowing, planting, and harvesting. In rural areas schooling tended to be sporadic and intermittent.

Turn-of-the-Century Parenting

The late nineteenth and early twentieth century witnessed far-reaching improvements in children's health, as physicians successfully treated digestive problems such as diarrhea, dysentery, and worms; respiratory problems such as consumption, croup, pneumonia, and whooping cough; and such diseases as scarlet fever and infections. The pasteurization of milk was particularly important in reducing child mortality. These medical successes encouraged well-educated parents to embrace the notion that child rearing itself should be more scientific. During the 1880s and 1890s, the CHILD STUDY movement, spearheaded by the psychologist G. STANLEY HALL, collected information from mothers and teachers and promoted greater awareness of the stages of childhood development (including ADOLESCENCE, a term that he popularized) and increased sensitivity to children's fears, insecurities, and anxieties.

The belief that scientific principles had not been properly applied to child rearing produced new kinds of child-rearing manuals, of which the most influential was Dr. Luther Emmett Holt's *The Care and Feeding of Children*, first published in 1894. Holt emphasized rigid scheduling of feeding, bathing, sleeping, and bowel movements and advised mothers to guard vigilantly against germs and undue stimulation of infants. At a time when a well-adjusted adult was viewed as a creature of habit and self-control, he stressed the importance of imposing regular habits on infants. He discouraged mothers from kissing their babies, and told them to ignore their crying and to break such habits as thumb-sucking. Upperclass and upper-middle-class mothers, like Dr. BENJAMIN SPOCK's mother, were much more likely to adopt Holt's ad-

vice than were working-class mothers. The behaviorist psychologist JOHN B. WATSON—who, in the 1920s, told mothers to "never hug and kiss" their children or "let them sit in your lap"—claimed Holt as his inspiration.

During the 1920s and 1930s, the field of CHILD PSYCHOLOGY exerted a growing influence on middle-class parenting. It provided a new language to describe children's emotional problems, such as sibling rivalry, phobias, maladjustment, and inferiority and Oedipus complexes; it also offered new insights into forms of parenting (based on such variables as demandingness or permissiveness), the stages and milestones of children's development, and the characteristics of children at particular ages (such as the "terrible twos," which was identified by ARNOLD GESELL, Frances L. Ilg, and Louise Bates Ames). The growing prosperity of the 1920s made the earlier emphasis on regularity and rigid self-control seem outmoded. A well-adjusted adult was now regarded as a more easygoing figure, capable of enjoying leisure. Rejecting the mechanistic and behaviorist notion that children's behavior could be molded by scientific control, popular dispensers of advice favored a more relaxed approach to child rearing, emphasizing the importance of meeting babies' emotional needs. The title of a 1936 book by pediatrician C. Anderson Aldrich—*Babies Are Human Beings*—summed up the new attitude.

CHILD-GUIDANCE clinics, founded in the late 1910s to treat juvenile DELINQUENCY, attracted an expanding clientele of middle-class parents, concerned about eating and sleeping disorders, nail biting, bed-wetting, phobias, sibling rivalry, and temper tantrums, and by problems involving school failure, running away, disobedience, and rebellious behavior. Yet many parents failed to address children's informational needs regarding SEXUALITY, especially girls' need for information about menstruation, and increasingly favored having schools assume this responsibility. As early as 1922, half of all schools offered some instruction in "social hygiene," an early form of SEX EDUCATION.

The Depression, World War II, and the Baby Boom

The GREAT DEPRESSION imposed severe strains on the nation's parents. It not only threw breadwinners out of jobs and impoverished families, it also forced many families to share living quarters and put off having children. More than 200,000 vagrant children wandered the country. Many fathers were overwhelmed by guilt because they were unable to support their families, and unemployment significantly lowered their status within the family. The father's diminished stature was mirrored by a great increase in the money-saving and -earning roles of mothers.

Wartime upheavals caused by World War II also had a profound impact on parenting. The war produced a sudden upsurge in the marriage and birth rate; spurred an unprecedented tide of family separation and migration; and thrust millions of mothers into the workforce. The war also accelerated a trend toward more affectionate child rearing, as mothers took the position that it was normal and healthy to embrace their children. At the same time, the war temporarily reduced opposition to CHILD LABOR, both paid and volunteer work—such as gathering scrap materials or tending victory gardens—since work might reduce juvenile delinquency, which appeared to be a mounting problem.

World War II produced intense concerns about "faulty" mothering, especially maternal overprotectiveness and its mirror opposite, maternal neglect. Americans were shocked by the number of men, more than 5 million, rejected for military service on the basis of physical or psychological deficiencies. Philip Wylie, author of the 1942 best-seller *A Generation of Vipers*, blamed such problems on the combination of a dominant, overly protective mother and a passive or absent father. There was also a tendency to blame juvenile delinquency, latchkey children, illegitimacy, truancy, and runaways not on unsettled wartime conditions, but on neglectful mothers. An important wartime legacy, based on JOHN BOWLBY's studies of British children separated from their parents during the war, was a heightened stress on the significance of maternal attachment in developing feelings of security and competence in children.

No families were more deeply affected by the war than Japanese Americans. In the spring of 1942, 120,000—two-thirds of them U.S. citizens—were relocated from homes on the West Coast to detention camps located in barren and forbidding parts of Arizona, Arkansas, California, Colorado, Idaho, Utah, and Wyoming. Toilets, showers, and dining facilities were communal, precluding family privacy. The internment camps inverted traditional family roles and loosened parental controls.

Severe problems of family adjustment followed the war. Many returning GIs found it difficult to communicate with children, while many wives and children found the men excessively strict, nervous, or intolerant. Estrangement and problems with alcohol were not infrequent as families tried to readjust after the war. The next decade witnessed a sharp reaction to the psychological stresses of wartime. Americans married at a younger age and had more children than in preceding generations. Responding to the postwar housing shortage, millions moved to new single-family homes in the suburbs. Many war-weary parents, scornful of the child-rearing homilies of their parents and grandparents, embraced the advice of Dr. Benjamin Spock, who rejected the idea of rigid feeding, bathing, and sleeping schedules, and told parents to pick up their babies and enjoy them.

Nevertheless, class and ethnic differences in parenting practices remained widespread. Allison Davis and Robert Havighurst found that middle-class parents began training children in achievement, initiative, personal responsibility, and cleanliness earlier than working-class parents, who placed a higher premium on obedience and relied more on corporal punishment; and that African-American parents had a more relaxed attitude toward INFANT FEEDING and weaning than their white counterparts.

Postwar parenting was characterized by an undercurrent of anxiety, sparked partly by concern over children's physical and mental health. The early 1950s was the last period when large numbers of children were left crippled by POLIO or meningitis. Psychologists such as Theodore Lidz, Irving Bieber, and ERIK ERIKSON linked schizophrenia, homosexuality, and identity diffusion to mothers who displaced their frustrations and needs for independence onto their children. A major concern was that many boys, raised almost exclusively by women, failed to develop an appropriate sex role identity. In retrospect, it seems clear that an underlying source of anxiety lay in the fact that mothers were raising their children with an exclusivity and in an isolation unparalleled in American history.

During the 1960s, there was a growing sense that something had gone wrong in American parenting. Books with titles like *Suburbia's Coddled Kids* criticized permissive child rearing and parents who let their children bully them. Meanwhile, maverick social critics, including Edgar Z. Friedenberg and Paul Goodman, argued that middle-class parents were failing their children by conveying mixed messages, stressing independence and accomplishment but giving their offspring few avenues of achievement or autonomy. At a time when Americans were worrying about gaps of all kinds—such as the so-called missile gap and the "credibility" gap—the generation gap was the most distressing of all. This gap was easily exaggerated and romanticized, and social scientists demonstrated that there was little divergence of ideas between the young and their parents on most moral and social issues, and that the biggest division was among youth themselves, especially between white middle-class and white working-class adolescents. Nevertheless, many families witnessed bitter clashes over dress, language, music, sexual morality, and, especially, politics.

Trends in Parenting since 1970

Since the early 1970s, parental anxieties greatly increased both in scope and intensity. Many parents sought to protect children from every imaginable harm by baby-proofing their homes, using car seats, and requiring bicycle helmets. Meanwhile, as more mothers joined the labor force, parents arranged more structured, supervised activities for their children. Unstructured play and outdoor activities for children three to eleven declined nearly 40 percent between the early 1980s and late 1990s.

A variety of factors contributed to this surge in anxiety. One factor was demographic. At the end of the twentieth century most children had one sibling or none. As parents had fewer children, they invested more emotion in each child, and many lived in fear that their offspring would underperform academically, athletically, or socially. An increase in professional expertise about children, coupled with a proliferation of research and advocacy organizations, media outlets, and government agencies responsible for children's health and safety made parents increasingly aware of threats to children's well-being and of ways to maximize their children's physical, social, and intellectual development. Unlike postwar parents, who wanted to produce normal children who fit in, middle-class parents now wanted to give their child a competitive edge.

Excessive efforts to overload children with activities led experts such as David Elkind to decry a tendency toward "hyper-parenting" as ambitious middle-class parents attempted to provide their children with every possible opportunity by filling up their afterschool time with lessons, enrichment activities, and sports. These experts feared that overscheduling and overprogramming placed excessive pressure on children and deprived them of the opportunity for free play and hanging out.

Shocking news reports intensified parental fears, including the revelation in 1973 of the serial murders of twenty-seven juveniles by Elmer Wayne Henley and Dean Corll, and the poisoning of eight-year-old Timothy O'Bryan by cyanide-laced Halloween candy in 1974. These incidents were followed by highly publicized claims that young people's well-being was rapidly declining. During the mid-1970s there was alarm about an epidemic of teenage pregnancy. This was followed by a panic over stranger abductions of children, triggered by the mysterious disappearance of Etan Patz in New York City in 1979 and the abduction and murder of Adam Walsh in 1981 in Florida. Other panics followed, involving the sexual abuse of children in day care centers; violent YOUTH GANGS and juvenile "superpredators"; youthful substance abuse; and declining student performance on standardized tests.

These panics were highly exaggerated. The teenage pregnancy rate had peaked in 1957 and was declining, not rising. A federal investigation disclosed that few missing children were abducted by strangers; the overwhelming majority were taken by noncustodial parents or were runaways. No cases of multiple caretaker sexual abuse in day-care centers were substantiated. Although youth violence did rise in the late 1980s and early 1990s (in tandem with violence by adults), the rate fell sharply in the mid- and late 1990s until it declined to levels unseen since the mid-1960s. Similarly, rates of drug, alcohol, and tobacco use by juveniles dropped until they were lower than those reported in the 1970s. Finally, the reported decline in student performance on standardized tests reflected an increase in the range of students taking the tests, not deteriorating student achievement.

Nevertheless, these panics produced a nagging, if inaccurate, sense that recent shifts in family life—especially the increasing divorce rate and the growing number of single parent households and working mothers—had disastrous consequences for children's well-being. They also left an imprint on public policy, as many municipalities instituted curfews for juveniles; many schools introduced dress codes, random drug tests for student athletes, and "abstinence-only" sex education programs; and states raised the drinking age, adopted graduated driver's licenses, and made it easier to try juveniles offenders as adults in the court system. Other efforts to restore parental authority and discipline included the establishment of a rating system for CDs and video games; installation of v-chips in TVs to allow parents to restrict children's television viewing; and enactment in some states of laws requiring parental notification when minors sought abortions.

In evaluating recent changes in parenting, there is a tendency to exaggerate evidence of decline and ignore the genuine gains that have occurred. There is no evidence to suggest that most parents are less engaged in childcare than in the past or that adults have become "anti-child." While fewer parents participate in PTAs, many more take an active role in soccer leagues and Little League. While parents are having fewer children, they are investing more time and resources in those they do have. Contemporary parents are much more aware of the children's developmental needs and of the dangers of abuse, and most fathers are more engaged in child rearing than their fathers were.

Rising divorce rates and increasing numbers of working mothers have not had the negative psychological consequences that some have claimed. Research suggests that children suffer more when their parents stay together but have high levels of conflict than when they divorce. Also, working mothers are less likely to be depressed than stay-at-home mothers, and provide valuable role models, especially for their daughters.

There can be no doubt that contemporary parenting is more stressful than it was in the early postwar era. Today's parents are beset by severe time pressures and work-related stress, and fewer have supportive kin or neighbors to help out in a pinch. Their children are growing up in a violent, sex-saturated environment, where the allure of drugs, alcohol, cigarettes, and consumer products is widespread. Many of the vacant lots and other "free" spaces where earlier generations were able to play without adult supervision have disappeared. The result has been a hovering, emotionally intense style of parenting and a more highly organized form of child rearing, which may have made it more difficult for children to forge an independent existence and assert their growing maturity and competence.

See also: **Baby Boom Generation; Child Care; Child-Rearing Advice Literature; Fathering and Fatherhood; Mothering and Motherhood; Same-Sex Parenting; Theories of Childhood.**

BIBLIOGRAPHY

Beekman, Daniel. 1977. *The Mechanical Baby: A Popular History of the Theory and Practice of Child Raising.* Westport, CN: Lawrence Hill.

Davis, Allison, and Robert J. Havighurst. 1946. "Social Class and Color Differences in Childrearing." *American Sociological Review* 11: 698–710.

Elder, Glen H., Jr. 1974. *Children of the Great Depression: Social Change in Life Experience.* Chicago: University of Chicago Press.

Grant, Julia. 1998. *Raising Baby by the Book: The Education of American Mothers.* New Haven, CT: Yale University Press.

Greven, Philip J. 1977. *The Protestant Temperament: Patterns of Child-Rearing, Religious Experience, and the Self in Early America.* New York: Knopf.

Griswold, Robert L. 1993. *Fatherhood in America: A History.* New York: Basic Books.

Hardyment, Christina. 1983. *Dream Babies.* New York: Harper and Row.

Holden, George W. 1997. *Parents and the Dynamics of Child Rearing.* Boulder, CO: Westview Press.

Hulbert, Ann. 2003. *Raising America: Experts, Parents, and a Century of Advice about Children.* New York: Knopf.

Jones, Kathleen W. 1999. *Taming the Troublesome Child: American Families, Child Guidance, and the Limits of Psychiatric Authority.* Cambridge, MA: Harvard University Press.

Ladd-Taylor, Molly, ed. 1986. *Raising a Baby the Government Way: Mothers' Letters to the Children's Bureau, 1915–1932.* New Brunswick, NJ: Rutgers University Press.

Mead, Margaret, and Martha Wolfenstein, eds. 1955. *Childhood in Contemporary Cultures.* Chicago: University of Chicago Press.

Mintz, Steven, and Susan Kellogg. 1988. *Domestic Revolutions: A Social History of American Family Life.* New York: Free Press.

Owens, Timothy J., and Sandra L. Hofferth. 2001. *Children at the Millennium.* New York: Elsevier Science.

Phister, Joel, and Nancy Schnog, eds. 1997. *Inventing the Psychological: Toward a Cultural History of Emotional Life in America.* New Haven, CT: Yale University Press.

Ryan, Mary P. 1983. *Cradle of the Middle Class: The Family in Oneida County, New York, 1790–1865.* Cambridge, UK: Cambridge University Press.

Siegel, Alexander W., and Sheldon H. White. 1982. "The Child Study Movement: Early Growth and Development of the Symbolized Child." In *Advances in Child Development and Behavior,* ed. Hayne W. Reese, 17: 234–85.

Stearns, Peter N. 2002. *Anxious Parents: A History of Modern Childrearing in America.* New York: New York University Press.

Tuttle, William M., Jr. 1993. *"Daddy's Gone To War": The Second World War in the Lives of America's Children.* New York: Oxford University Press.

West, Elliott. 1989. *Growing Up with the Country: Childhood on The Far-Western Frontier.* Albuquerque: University of New Mexico Press.

STEVEN MINTZ

Parents Magazine

Founded in 1926 in New York City, *Parents Magazine* became the key vehicle for transmitting the message of parent education in the twentieth century. This mass-circulation monthly, initially called *Children, The Magazine for Parents,* popularized scientific knowledge on child development to help parents rear their children. Over the course of the twentieth century, it reached into millions of homes.

The magazine reflected and shaped the booming parent education movement of the 1920s. Experts in child health, psychology, and education translated research studies into popular terms and offered practical suggestions. Official cooperation came from four universities and a distinguished board of advisory editors. Extensive advertising promoted such items as ready-made baby food, preparatory schools, and summer camps. The magazine's motto, "on rearing children from crib to college," suggested the middle-class expectations readers held for their children.

The founder and publisher for over fifty years was George J. Hecht, a businessman and social service worker who had earned an economics degree from Cornell, then worked for Creel's Committee on Public Information during World War I. Hecht believed that even educated, middle-class parents needed access to knowledge and assistance in raising their children. He received funding for his venture from the LAURA SPELMAN ROCKEFELLER MEMORIAL Foundation, a chief benefactor of the parent education movement.

Hecht recruited Clara Savage Littledale to serve as editor of the new magazine, a position she held for thirty years until her death in 1956. Littledale was a graduate of Smith College, a journalist, and the mother of two children. To make the latest findings in child development research available to parents, Littledale published articles on such topics as infant care, DISCIPLINE, character building, and SEX EDUCATION. Yet she was wary of parents relying too much on expert advice rather than their own common sense. She balanced research material with pieces based on humor, sentiment, and everyday experience, and included tips that readers sent in. She urged parents to relax and to enjoy their children—a message that presaged by at least a decade BENJAMIN SPOCK's *Baby and Child Care.*

In its attention to expertise and research, *Parents Magazine* reflected the privatized and professional orientation of parent education that took hold in the 1920s. But the reformist impulse shaped the magazine as well. Hecht and Littledale, who had both come of age in the Progressive Era, exhorted parents to look beyond the concerns of their own families and to support legislation on behalf of children and families. The magazine thus linked the private realm of child rearing with larger public concerns.

The popularity of *Parents Magazine* was immediate and enduring. Within a year of its founding, the magazine was selling 100,000 copies a month. Circulation reached 400,000 subscribers at ten years and almost a million by the magazine's twentieth anniversary in 1946. By then, the publishing company had created a series of childcare books and children's magazines. The magazine achieved acclaim as the most popular educational periodical in the world. It has continued to be popular, with over two million subscribers in 2002.

See also: **Child-Rearing Advice Literature; Parenting.**

BIBLIOGRAPHY

Schlossman, Steven L. 1981. "Philanthropy and the Gospel of Child Development." *History of Education Quarterly* 21: 275–299.

Schlossman, Steven. 1986. "Perils of Popularization: The Founding of Parents' Magazine." In *History and Research in Child Development: In Celebration of the Fiftieth Anniversary of the Society*, ed. Alice Boardman Smuts and John W. Hagan. Chicago: Published by the University of Chicago Press for the Society for Research in Child Development.

DIANA SELIG

Parent–Teacher Associations

As long as children have been attending school, parents and teachers have shared in their education. Both have participated in decisions about what would be taught, who would do the teaching, and how it would be done. Their relationship was informal and unstructured in the United States until mothers' clubs and parent–teacher associations began to appear in the 1880s. Gradually, these local organizations became a national movement in American education. Renamed in 1924, the National Congress of Parents and Teachers (NCPT) had convened for the first time as the National Congress of Mothers twenty-seven years before. Because African Americans were not welcome in the NCPT, they formed their own organization in 1926; the two remained separate for forty-four years. What is now known simply as the National PTA has almost 6.5 million members in twenty-six thousand local chapters. Countless others belong to home and school associations and parent–teacher organizations that are not affiliated.

From the beginning parents joined such organizations to meet one another, educate themselves, and perform school and community service. While men were welcome to attend meetings and become members, parent–teacher associations were (and still are) organizations primarily for women. They attracted mostly white, middle-class mothers who wanted to be more involved in their communities. Taking their talents outside the home, they applied them at their children's schools. Through the PTA they expected to exercise influence, if not authority, in education.

Before 1890 most educators held parents at arms length. Because their own lack of training and experience made it easy for them to be treated with disrespect, teachers did not reach out to parents. But at the end of the nineteenth century many began to realize that it was better to have parents for allies than adversaries. The best way to do that, they thought, was through parent–teacher organizations. School administrators gave PTAs a place to meet, attended their meetings, and collaborated with them on projects like fundraising, schoolhouse repairs, and parent education. Mothers responded by joining up. In 1928 membership in the NCPT stood at 1.25 million, and it climbed dramatically over the next thirty years, reaching almost nine million by the early 1950s.

But soon thereafter PTAs began to lose ground. Overcrowded classrooms, teacher strikes, and the civil rights movement changed the way many parents felt about public schools. Having promised time and again that public education would solve personal and social problems, educators now found themselves caught in the grip of rising but unfulfilled expectations. Beginning in the 1970s federal and state legislation guaranteed students with disabilities access to public schools and mandated parental involvement in these children's individual educational plan (IEP), convincing many parents that they did not have to defer to professionals. In a world shaped by developments like these, PTAs began to appear anachronistic—a relic from the past that was part of the problem, not the solution. Parent councils, community school boards, and charter schools seemed to offer parents more power. While parent–teacher organizations continue to play a significant role in American education, they are not as respected or admired as they used to be.

See also: **Education, United States; Parenting; Progressive Education; Urban School Systems, The Rise of.**

BIBLIOGRAPHY

Cutler, William W., III. 2000. *Parents and Schools: The 150-Year Struggle for Control in American Education.* Chicago: University of Chicago Press.

Woyshner, Christine A. 1999. "'To Reach the Rising Generation through the Raising Generation': The Origins of the National Parent–Teacher Association." Ph.D. diss., Harvard University.

WILLIAM W. CUTLER III

Parochial Schools

Parochial schools belong to the complex expectations about the education of children in a pluralistic American society. In the United States the line between parental and state authority over education has long been at issue, and Americans have tenaciously clung to the conviction that schooling has a profound influence upon democracy and national unity.

Parochial Education through the Nineteenth Century

Catholics followed the same patchwork approach to education that Protestants adopted in colonial and early-nineteenth-century America. The large majority of boys and girls learned the fundamentals and religion in parish schools supported by parishioners' donations, clergy's services, and parents' small fees. Academies taught by nuns or laywomen offered the "refinements" to daughters of wealthier Catholics in cities. The first opened in New Orleans in 1727. Men's colleges for boys as young as eight and as old as twenty-four were operated by clerics; with Georgetown as the early model, the fourteen established by 1830 often combined prep school, college, and seminary under one roof.

The flood of Catholic immigrants from Ireland and Germany gave new immediacy and shape to parochial education in the 1840s. Catholics scrambled to provide ethnic parishes with schools and to find sister-teachers who spoke the parents' language and could instruct in lessons of the old world and new. Urban middle and upper classes began to set their children apart by expanding Catholic school opportunities; fifty-six new Catholic secondary schools for girls opened in the decade of the 1840s. At this same time, Protestant American reformers were placing new emphasis on education as the means to transmit democratic values. Following the lead of HORACE MANN of Massachusetts, other educators began to develop free tax-funded schools, usually Protestant-controlled and undergirded by readings from the Protestants' King James Bible. Parish and public schools went up within the same few blocks while bricks and mortar drained scarce dollars. Education became a lightning rod for midcentury ethnic and religious tensions once matters of faith were wrapped up in matters of money.

Nativists like the Know Nothing party exploited Protestant fears that a foreign, authoritarian pope would control Catholic schools to the detriment of democracy. Catholics countered that their taxes went to public schools where hostile teachers used the Protestant rather than Catholic Bible and could not transmit parents' language or cultural heritage. This was not what they expected from the freedoms America promised. New York City's Bishop John Hughes ignited the "school wars" in 1840 when he rallied Catholics to petition for tax support of parochial schools. For over a decade, similar efforts disrupted many northern and midwestern communities. Catholics failed to win a share of tax revenues but persevered on their separate course, with some parents and dioceses more willing or able to support parochial education. Boston and the New England region lagged behind New York, where nearly 20 percent of all children attending school were in parochial schools; in Detroit, Catholic schools accounted for nearly 40 percent of total enrollment. A proliferation of parish schools took form according to local circumstances, quality of sister-teachers, and parents' preferences; Irish nuns for Irish children, German nuns for Germans. Catholic publishers printed textbooks for religious education and conscientious nuns insisted upon additional books and lessons equal to the best of the public schools.

When the American bishops met in 1884 for the Third Plenary Council, parochial education was a cornerstone of their discussion and underscored their disagreement. "Americanists" wanted schools planted within the American culture. "Pluralists" argued for ethnic schools and opposed any form of public control. Debate raged for the next fifteen years. The disparate array of parish schools, Catholic boys' prep schools, and convent boarding schools continued to defy any bishop's ambition for an orderly system despite Protestants' belief that Catholic schools followed papal dictates.

When Catholic immigrants from central and southern Europe surged into America's industrial centers between the 1890s and 1920s, the model of ethnic parish schools was in place. Polish pupils of diverse ages crowded parish elementary schools taught by newly developed congregations of Polish-American nuns using textbooks written for them in Polish. Second- and third-generation immigrants distanced themselves in new middle-class parishes boasting high schools; their children studied Greek, Latin, and chemistry with college-educated nuns and priests.

Twentieth Century

Ambitions for an American melting pot and "100 percent Americanism" promoted renewed attacks on parochial schools after World War I. In several states ballot proposals aimed to require public school attendance. The 1925 Supreme Court ruling PIERCE V. SOCIETY OF SISTERS affirmed parents' right to select nonpublic schools. Catholics, meanwhile, embraced external accreditation standards to validate their schools. By the mid-1960s, 12 percent of all elementary-age children attended parochial schools.

Throughout the remainder of the twentieth century, parochial education adapted to new realities inside and outside the Catholic church. Upward mobility, a shrinking pool of teachers from religious congregations, and changing attitudes about public schools led some schools to close and others to open or expand. The historical controversy about the place of nonpublic, church-related schooling in a democratic America continues. Parochial schools remain also, justifiably regarded as the single most impressive accomplishment of America's Catholic immigrants.

See also: **Catholicism; Education, United States; Private and Independent Schools; Sunday School.**

BIBLIOGRAPHY

Dolan, Jay P. 1985. *The American Catholic Experience: A History from Colonial Times to the Present.* Garden City, NJ: Doubleday, 1985.

Ravitch, Diane. 1974. *The Great School Wars: New York City, 1805–1973.* New York: Basic Books.

Sanders, James. 1977. *The Education of an Urban Minority.* New York: Oxford University Press.

Shananbruch, Charles. 1981. *Chicago's Catholics: The Evolution of an American Identity.* Notre Dame, IN: University of Notre Dame Press.

Vinyard, JoEllen McNergney. 1998. *For Faith and Fortune: The Education of Catholic Immigrants in Detroit, 1805–1925.* Urbana: University of Illinois Press.

Walch, Timothy. 1996. *Parish School: American Catholic Parochial Education from Colonial Times to the Present.* New York: Crossroad.

JoEllen McNergney Vinyard

Pediatrics

The care of children is as old as our species, but the discipline of pediatrics emerged barely a century ago. In this progression, the history the field of pediatrics follows the general pattern of the history of medicine: the timeless traditions of informal health care in the home; the roots of modern medicine in ancient Greece, Rome, and the Arab world; the gradual emergence of science in the 1600s; the provision of health care by medical professionals working in ever-larger institutions during the 1800s; and the recent faith that technically sophisticated medicine will cure disease and improve health. What distinguishes pediatrics from other branches of medicine is the notion that children are our future, and consequently that their health and well-being are a matter of broad social concern. Since antiquity, political and medical leaders have argued that healthy children are necessary to the well-being of the state. Each nation-state's response to such arguments has affected both the health of children and how societies have organized pediatric health services.

Ancient and Medieval Medical Writings

Although many observers in ancient and medieval eras may have viewed children as merely small adults, most medical writers focused on the special health concerns of children. The first few years of life, for example, were thought to require special care, especially during times when teeth were emerging. Hippocrates (c. 460–377 B.C.E.) wrote a small treatise, "On Dentition," on the subject of teeth, and noted how children differ from adults in various ways in his "Aphorisms." Spring and full summer are the best seasons for children, Hippocrates suggested, while late summer and early fall are the healthiest seasons for adults. Soranus of Ephesus (2nd century C.E.) completed a more detailed work on children's diseases, which included explanations on how to feed, bathe, and swaddle an infant. Rhazes (c. 865–932), who studied and taught in Baghdad, was one of the first medical scholars to write an entire treatise on children.

Home and Foundling Asylums

These scholarly efforts had little affect on the vast majority of children. Most health care was delivered by family members in the home. When a child became more ill than the family could handle, they may have turned to local untrained specialists, usually religious leaders or women in the community with reputations for expertise in medical matters. There were no special medical services or providers for children. In 787 Archbishop Datheus opened one of the first

TABLE 1

Discovery dates of selected bacteria, antibiotics, vaccines

Bacteria

1882	tuberculosis	Robert Koch
1883	cholera	Robert Koch
1884	pneumonia	Albert Fraenkel
1894	plague	Alexandre Yersin, Shibanuro Kitasato
1905	syphilis	Fritz Schaudinn

Antibiotics

1910	salvarsan	Paul Ehrlich
1929	penicillin	Alexander Fleming
1935	sulfa drugs	Gerhard Domagk

Vaccines

1923	diphtheria toxoid	A. T. Glenny, Barbara Hopkins, Gaston Ramon
1955	polio vaccine	Jonas Salk, Albert Sabin
1962	measles vaccine	John Franklin Enders

SOURCE: Courtesy of author.

foundling asylums at Milan. Over the next thousand years, religious leaders opened many more places of refuge for abandoned or orphaned babies. Such institutions provided little or no medical treatment, however, and most infants and children died soon after being taken in.

Renaissance Medical Writings

With the invention of movable type in the 1400s, medical works became more accessible to scholars, at least to those who read Latin. The first medical book to be printed was a pediatrics treatise by the Italian Paolo Bagellardo (c. 1425–1495). It was based on Greek and Arab works, though it included some of his own experience, such as medicines that could be used to soothe a crying baby. In 1545 Thomas Phaer wrote the first English-language work on pediatrics. The *Boke of Children* included a long section on dentition: teething caused swelling of gums and jaw, crying, fever, cramps, palsies, etc. He advocated washing the child in camomile and applying oil of roses, fresh butter with barley flour or honey, or frankincense and licorice mixed in a fine powder. In their content and reliance on centuries-old Greek, Roman, and Arab sources, Bagellardo's and Phaer's books were typical of pediatric medical works prior to 1600.

Rise of Empiricism

In the 1600s, scholars eschewed traditional theories and supernatural accounts, and began to value their own observations of the natural world. The so-called scientific revolution was heralded by the empiricism of Francis Bacon (1561–1626) in his *Advancement of Learning* (1605). By the late 1600s the concept of a scientific *fact*, as distinct from theory, emerged as the basis for creating reliable knowledge about the natural world. In medicine, this meant more realistic studies of anatomy and physiology, including William Harvey's (1578–1657) experimental demonstration of the

TABLE 2

Selected pediatric institutions

Outpatient facilities
1761	Lying-in Hospital of Stockholm, Sweden
1769	Dispensary for the Infant Poor, London
1787	Dispensary for Children, Vienna

Hospitals
1802	Hospital des Enfants Malades, Paris
1852	Hospital for Sick Children in Great Ormond Street, London
1855	Children's Hospital of Philadelphia, Pennsylvania

Professional associations
1880	American Medical Association, Section on Pediatrics
1883	Gesellschaft der Naturforscher und Aerzte, Pediatric Section, Germany
1885	Russian Pediatric Society
1888	American Pediatric Society

Pediatric journals
1834	*Analekten uber kinderkrankheiten*, Germany
1841	*Clinique des hopitaux des enfants*, France
1883	*Archivio di patologia infantile*, Italy
1895	*Pediatrics*, United States

Professorships
1845	T. T. Berg, Karolin Medico-Chirurgical Institute
1860	Abraham Jacobi, New York Medical College, United States
1888	Thomas Rotch, Harvard Medical College, United States

SOURCE: Courtesy of author.

circulation of blood through the body. In clinical medicine, classification and description of disease became central topics for medical scholars. Thomas Sydenham (1624–1689), for example, developed a sophisticated system for categorizing diseases, and his description of the movement disorder that accompanies rheumatic fever (Sydenham's chorea) is a model of clinical observation. To treat such fevers, Sydenham subscribed to the medical therapeutics espoused since ancient times: he would drain seven ounces of blood, then purge with senna, black-cherry water, and laudanum.

Heroic Therapeutics

While the seventeenth-century clinical observations of Sydenham and others would still be familiar today, the blood-letting and purging regimens now appear barbaric. However, such therapeutics fit squarely with contemporary concepts of health and disease; they were rational responses to widely accepted theories of disease causation. Medical scholars and the general public agreed that the balance of various body humors (e.g., blood, bile, phlegm) was the key to maintaining health. Specific diseases were thought to occur when the humors were out of balance. If the blood ran high during fevers, then cutting open a vein or applying leeches was a logical response. With generally high mortality rates, most people were resigned to the frequent deaths of children and young adults. Physicians gained notoriety not for their ability to cure but for how accurately they predicted outcomes and how heroically they tried to rebalance the humors through bleeding and purging. When a patient survived such interventions, the therapy was deemed successful

and the physician could take credit for his therapy; when the patient died, then the intervention was said to have occurred too late or to have been applied too gently. God's will was often invoked. Pre-nineteenth-century therapeutics was dramatic, and when someone died no one could argue that the doctor had not tried to intervene.

Vaccination

The most famous therapeutic intervention of the 1700s was a conceptual anomaly. Inoculation against smallpox had been practiced in India and parts of the Arab world for centuries, but it never fit the model of disease and cure implied by the balance of body humors. Lady Mary Wortley Montagu (1689–1762) brought the practice to the West when she had her son inoculated with material from a smallpox victim in Constantinople in 1718. She championed the idea of inoculation before physicians and royalty as a way to lessen the burden of smallpox: nearly every child contracted signs and symptoms of the disease and many were permanently scarred by the skin lesions. Some estimated that as many as 30 percent of all children died from smallpox. In the 1790s, Edward Jenner (1749–1823) noted that young women who milked cows and became infected with cowpox did not get smallpox. Since the consequences of contracting cowpox were less severe than those of inoculation with smallpox, vaccination with cowpox became common practice. Indeed, it was made compulsory in Bavaria in 1807 and in Denmark in 1810.

Rise of Hospitals

Modern therapeutics owes less to Jenner and Montague than to the hospitals of Paris, which became the center of medical research in the late 1700s. With large numbers of patients confined to institutions, French scholars such as Pierre-Charles-Alexandre Louis (1787–1872) were able to follow the natural course of specific diseases. Louis used clinical statistics to correlate the signs and symptoms of specific diseases with particular abnormalities found inside the body. He relied on the work of Xavier Bichat (1771–1802) and others who had previously matched clinical symptoms with pathological findings on autopsy. For example, a yellowish discoloration of the skin and eyes predicted an abnormal liver; microscopic analysis of liver tissues revealed disrupted cells and scarring. By routinely applying new technologies such as the stethoscope, the microscope, and statistical reasoning to hospitalized patients, French scholars created the basis for modern clinical medicine. Perhaps most importantly, they noted that medical interventions of the past two millennia—bleeding and purging—did not seem to improve survival.

Germ Theory

When French medicine overturned centuries of faith in body humors as the cause of disease, physicians were left to pursue many different strategies to explain disease and heal their patients. Medical sects such as homeopathy, osteopathy, and hydrotherapy (water cure) flourished through the late 1800s, offering stiff competition to practitioners of "regular" medicine. Germ theory was just one of many plausible explanations for disease causation until the work of Robert Koch (1843–1910) and Louis Pasteur (1822–1895). In dozens of now-famous experiments, they demonstrated that specific germs (bacteria) caused specific diseases. Although Koch, Pasteur, and their many colleagues worked differently, in general the process was the same: the microbiologist obtained fluids from animals or people with a particular disease, isolated bacteria present in such body fluids, created techniques for growing the bacteria, then injected these bacteria into healthy subjects to recreate the signs and symptoms of the disease. Germ theory not only provided a way of understanding the etiology and patterns of many infectious diseases, but it also suggested therapies such as antibiotics and vaccines. The history of pediatric science in the twentieth century reads like a list of victories over specific infections (see Table 1), whether through the discovery of penicillin by Sir Alexander Fleming (1881–1955) or the disappearance of POLIO in the Western Hemisphere with the vaccines introduced by Jonas Salk (1914–1995) and Albert Sabin (1906–1993).

Emergence of the Field of Pediatrics

Although there had been pockets of scholarly focus on children for centuries, the field of pediatrics did not take shape until the mid-1800s. In part, the emergence of pediatrics as a medical specialty was merely one example of a broader trend in institutional medicine. Before 1800, physicians in most parts of the world claimed broad expertise for various diseases, populations, and therapeutic techniques. Surgery and DENTISTRY were considered the only legitimate areas of specialization; doctors who claimed to be experts in specific fields were likely to be viewed as quacks. As medical knowledge expanded in the 1800s, many medical scholars found intellectual justification for focusing on particular areas of the body such as the brain (psychiatry, neurology) or on particular surgical techniques (orthopedics, ophthalmology). Even if they continued a general medical practice, groups of physicians gathered around shared interests at medical meetings, created specialty journals, and began to control medical school curricula and clinical teaching. In the mid-1800s, pediatrics was closely associated with obstetrics, but by the early 1900s, pediatrics had its own hospitals, journals, professional associations, and medical school professorships (see Table 2).

The Economics of Specialization

Given the intellectual plausibility of medical specialization, many physicians were also motivated by the economic advantages. Before 1900, medicine was not necessarily a lucrative profession. Indeed, in many parts of the world, only those physicians who tended to rich families found economic or social security in the practice of medicine. With the growth of concentrated populations in cities, a medical practice devoted exclusively to a medical specialty became economically viable. Specialization was one strategy for competing for the limited number of families who could afford to pay for medical care. A young physician could distinguish himself from his peers by affiliating with the specialty practice of a hospital, clinic, or medical school. In pediatrics, formal training programs have existed for more than a hundred years in Europe and North America. To certify pediatricians, each nation has developed its own criteria for training after graduation from medical school; most also require successful completion of a standardized written or oral examination. The American Board of Pediatrics, for example, was founded in 1933 to certify pediatricians in the United States.

Changing Emotional Reasons Underwriting Pediatrics

For physicians in the 1800s, the emergence of pediatrics may have seemed to be a logical response to economic pressures and to evidence from developmental biology and clinical medicine that distinguished children's bodies from those of adults. However, pediatrics emerged as a specialty in the context of a broader appreciation for the emotional value of children: no longer a mere economic asset of the father, each child was considered to be a priceless human being who deserved some protection by society. Although this new view of children emerged at different times in different places, by 1900 most nations had instituted laws providing education to children, protecting them against physical abuse from their fathers, and outlawing excessive or dangerous labor before a certain age. To some degree, the field of pediatrics owes its genesis to the new view of children as special and distinct from adults, along with a growing belief that children's deaths could and should be prevented.

Pediatric Specialists or General Medical Care

Specialization in pediatrics has deepened our scientific understanding of children and improved the training of physicians and nurses. The practice of pediatrics by specialists, however, has had little direct impact on most families. It is only in the last two hundred years or so that the average family might have access to a trained medical professional such as a physician, let alone a specialist. In many parts of the world medical care is still difficult to find, and pediatric specialty care an unusual luxury. Indeed, the specific configuration of the field of pediatrics in each nation depends more on social, political, and economic factors than on the intellectual content of pediatric medicine. In most nations children receive medical care from physicians or nurse practitioners with training in general medicine. Physicians with specialty training in pediatrics are consulted when a child or adolescent has a medical issue that goes beyond the expertise of the general practitioner. Even in industrialized nations, rural families and those living in poverty remain less likely to see a pediatric specialist.

Pediatrics in the United States

The United States is unique in that pediatrics has become a primary care specialty. In 1910 there were approximately one hundred physicians who confined their practice to pediatrics; by 1935 there were several thousand. The American Academy of Pediatrics' membership in 2000 was more than fifty thousand pediatricians, which means one pediatrician for every fifteen hundred children. This allows most children to visit a physician with specialty training in pediatrics for routine check-ups and mild illnesses. Other children are cared for by family medicine practitioners and pediatric nurse practitioners, but nearly all children in the United States have access to pediatric subspecialists. These are physicians who obtain two to three years of additional training after general pediatrics to gain expertise in areas such as pediatric cardiology, neonatology, and pediatric gastroenterology. Pediatric subspecialists may be found in academic centers in many other nations, but few families outside the United States would expect to be routinely referred to such practitioners.

Women and Pediatrics

Women have long had an important role in the field of pediatrics, especially in the United States. Many without medical training, such as Julia Lathrop (1858–1932), the first director of the U.S. CHILDREN'S BUREAU, held leadership positions in government and philanthropic organizations designed to improve the health and well-being of children. Within the field of medicine, women physicians accounted for 20 percent of practitioners in some U.S. cities in the early 1900s. They directed hospitals, medical schools, and city health departments. Because many women felt a special obligation to provide medical care to women and children, they often specialized in obstetrics and pediatrics; many took academic positions and some gained national prominence in pediatrics. Following the reforms in medical education in the early 1900s, the number of women physicians fell to approximately 5 percent of all doctors. As their numbers have increased since 1970, however, women have again moved toward pediatrics as a field of specialization. In the year 2000 approximately half of all pediatricians in the United States were women, and they represent about two-thirds of pediatricians-in-training.

Social Implications of Child Health

The science of pediatrics has rarely been divorced from the social implications of child health. Since antiquity, scholars and political leaders have assumed that healthy children were essential to the well-being of the state. Medical authorities have generally agreed, and they have consistently viewed the proper upbringing and education of children as within the province of medicine. Persian medical scholar Avicenna (980–1037) wrote that all the study and work of physicians should focus on forming and molding the character of the child. Medical writers over the centuries have echoed his remarks, and in the twenty-first century pediatricians frequently use their status as the experts in child health to suggest the most effective ways of raising and educating children. On the other hand, the importance of child health has also led philosophers and political writers to enter medical matters. Thus the Greek scholar Plutarch (c. 46–120) wrote *The Education of Children* to teach ruling-class families how to properly mold their children such that the future strength of the state might be secured. Among his many medical suggestions, he implored mothers to breast-feed because it makes a "bond of good feeling." Political leaders through the centuries have continued to approach the health of children as a social issue, whether through the extremes of EUGENICS programs aimed to secure the racial health of the state or through the emptiness of campaign slogans designed to emphasize a politician's commitment to the future.

Infant Mortality and the Fate of Nation-States

The history of the INFANT MORTALITY rate is a good example of how the field of pediatrics combines science and social policy. As early as 1761, British physician William Buchan (1729–1805) noted that one half of the human race dies in infancy, with ominous consequences for the health of the state. In the 1800s, improvement in health statistics led to increased attention to the death rate of infants throughout Europe. Such deaths were seen not as mere medical failings but as indictments of the economic, political, and moral well-being of the nation. Theophile Roussel (1816–1903), the French physician and politician, was perhaps the most vocal of national leaders. He is credited with the *loi Roussel*, a set of laws that protected infants sent out to nurse (1874), protected abused and abandoned children (1889), and organized medical charity (1893).

Throughout Europe in the late 1800s, governments instituted programs to protect pregnant women (e.g., paid maternity leave) because they believed that healthy infants were crucial to the future economic and political well-being of the state. In 1892 Paris physician Pierre Budin (1846–1907) started the first infant consultations, when mothers would bring their well babies to be weighed and examined. Such well-child care was duplicated throughout Europe and the United States in hopes that advice and clean milk might prevent infant deaths. Such preventive health visits remain central to the practice of pediatrics, even as the infant mortality rate has dropped from three hundred deaths out of every one thousand births to less than ten per thousand in many parts of the world. The result—the regular check-up—is a huge change in the experience of children and parents alike in the more affluent groups and regions.

Emerging and Persisting Child Health Problems

Viewed as a medical discipline, pediatrics has shifted in response to each generation's understanding of which diseases seemed most important among children. While Hippocrates focused on climate and special vulnerable periods for children, later scholars wrote about the most common infectious diseases, from smallpox in the 1700s to infantile diarrhea in the late 1800s. The dramatic decrease in infectious diseases in developed nations over the last century has led pediatricians to focus on rare chronic illnesses and behavioral and developmental conditions. The mapping of the human genome promises new ways to eliminate disabilities and prevent chronic illness in the twenty-first century.

Some of this success has been shared by all the children in the world—the eradication of smallpox in 1970 is the crowning achievement of a public health system applying a specific therapy to a specific disease. Millions of children in Africa and Asia continue to die from measles, tuberculosis, and infant diarrhea, however, demonstrating that antibiotics, vaccines, and modern hospitals only go so far. Even as the incidence of AIDS decreases in the West, more and more African and Asian babies are born infected with HIV in the early twenty-first century. In these nations, pediatricians and public health officers continue to focus on nutrition, sanitation, and maternal education as the most effective ways to reduce mortality from common infectious diseases.

Pediatrics and Social Activism

Abraham Jacobi (1830–1919) is generally considered to be the "father" of modern pediatrics. A German physician who was once arrested for participating in the revolution of 1848, Jacobi moved to New York, where he built a career of scientific discovery, clinical practice, and tireless advocacy on behalf of children. He argued that the health and well-being of children required appropriately trained medical practitioners as well as social and economic investment in their lives and neighborhoods. His words have been remembered by pediatricians, scholars, and political leaders for over a hundred years, and perhaps best embody the science and social activism that characterizes the field of pediatrics: "It is not enough, however, to work at the individual bedside in the hospital. In the near or dim future, the pediatrician is to sit in and control school boards, health departments, and legislatures. He is the legitimate advisor to the judge and the jury, and a seat for the physician in the councils of the republic is what the people have a right to demand" (quoted in Burke).

See also: **Children's Hospitals; Contagious Diseases; Epidemics; Obstetrics and Midwifery.**

BIBLIOGRAPHY

Abt, Arthur, and Fielding Garrison. 1965. *Abt-Garrison History of Pediatrics.* Philadelphia: Saunders.

Ackerknecht, Erwin. 1982. *A Short History of Medicine.* Baltimore, MD: Johns Hopkins University Press.

Brosco, Jeffrey P. 1999. "The Early History of the Infant Mortality Rate in America: A Reflection Upon the Past and a Prophecy of the Future." *Pediatrics* 103: 478–485.

Burke, E. C. 1998. "Abraham Jacobi, MD: The Man and His Legacy." *Pediatrics* 101: 309–312.

Charney, Evan. 1994. "The Field of Pediatrics." In *Principles and Practice of Pediatrics,* 2nd ed., ed. Frank A. Oski et al. Philadelphia: Lippincott.

Cone, Thomas E. 1979. *History of American Pediatrics.* Boston: Little, Brown.

Dwork, Deborah. 1987. *War Is Good for Babies and Other Young Children: A History of the Infant and Child Welfare Movement in England, 1898–1918.* London: Tavistock.

Halpern, Sydney. 1988. *American Pediatrics: The Social Dynamics of Professionalism, 1880–1980.* Berkeley and Los Angeles: University of California Press.

Kevles, Daniel. 1985. *In the Name of Eugenics: Genetics and the Uses of Human Heredity.* Berkeley and Los Angeles: University of California Press.

Klaus, Alisa. 1993. *Every Child a Lion: The Origins of Maternal and Infant Health Policy in the United States and France, 1890–1920.* Ithaca, NY: Cornell University Press.

McKeown, Thomas. 1979. *The Role of Medicine: Dream, Mirage, or Nemesis?* Princeton, NJ: Princeton University Press.

Meckel, Richard. 1990. *Save the Babies: American Public Health Reform and the Prevention of Infant Mortality.* Baltimore, MD: Johns Hopkins University Press.

Pearson, Howard A. 1994. "The History of Pediatrics in the United States." In *Principles and Practice of Pediatrics,* 2nd ed., ed. Frank A. Oski et al. Philadelphia: Lippincott.

Preston, Samuel H., and Michael R. Haines. 1991. *Fatal Years: Child Mortality in Late Nineteenth-Century America.* Princeton, NJ: Princeton University Press.

Stern, Alexandra Minna, and Howard Markel, eds. 2002. *Formative Years: Children's Health in the United States, 1880–2000.* Ann Arbor: University of Michigan Press.

Still, George. 1931. *The History of Paediatrics: The Progress of the Study of Diseases of Children up to the End of the XVIIIth Century.* London: H. Milford Oxford University Press.

Viner, Russell. 1997. *Healthy Children for a New World: Abraham Jacobi and the Making of American Pediatrics.* Cambridge, MA: University of Cambridge.

Zelizer, Vivian. 1985. *Pricing the Priceless Child: The Changing Social Value of Children.* New York: Basic Books.

JEFFREY P. BROSCO

Pedophilia

The word *pedophilia* originates from the Greek words *paidos,* meaning child, and *philia,* meaning love. A pedophile is characterized by sexual attraction to and maybe love for children. The first scientist to use the concept was the German sexologist and physician Richard Krafft-Ebing. In his monograph *Psychopatia Sexualis,* published in 1886, he defined pedophilia as a psychosexual perversion, open to cure. This was in sharp contrast to the prevailing religious and moral judgment on sexual relations between adults and children. To Krafft-Ebing, pedophilia could be caused by senility or other mental deficiencies. Around 1906, his British counterpart Havelock Ellis presented pedophilia as an extreme version of normal masculine sexuality. Currently, pedophilia is understood as a divergence of personality, caused by psychological damage in early childhood. This concept was rarely used in English before the 1950s.

It is generally believed that pedophiles vary as much as any other group of human beings. The majority consists of men, who seek contact with children, mainly boys, in early puberty. Some wish to stimulate the child, some seek mutual

The Snake Charmer (c. 1870), Jean-Léon Gérôme. By displacing the scene onto a foreign landscape, nineteenth-century European artists could hint at an erotic view of children that would be unacceptable using Western subjects. © Sterling and Francine Clark Art Institute, Williamstown, Massachusetts.

stimulation, and others want to have intercourse with the child. A minority, who get most of the press coverage, are fascinated by sadistic elements in their relation to children, as was the case among a group of pedophiles in Holland and Belgium who were discovered during the 1990s in a widely publicized case.

Until relatively recently, pedophiles had fairly easy access to children, who were left largely unattended by parents. During the last two decades of the twentieth century, growing attention to the phenomenon has made it more difficult for pedophiles to act out their sexual urges. This is why easy access to CHILD PORNOGRAPHY and chat rooms on the Internet play such a prominent role in stimulating the fantasies of pedophiles and, probably, alleviating the desire for more aggressive behavior.

The first British and American surveys of sexual CHILD ABUSE date from the 1920s. More substantial surveys were conducted from the 1950s on, with the Kinsey Reports taking the lead. A comparative study of Anglo-American surveys covering the years 1940 though 1990 showed no noticeable change in the prevalence of abuse of girls younger than

fourteen. Between 10 and 12 percent are thought to have been sexually abused. There are no comparable figures for boys. The surveys of the 1990s produced highly contradictory data, which vary depending on differences in study populations and design. The number of college students who claim to have been sexually abused as children varies from 15 to 30 percent. Of these, only five or six percent mention that they have experienced intercourse during childhood. Scandinavian surveys show a similar picture. Official crime statistics indicate a much lower incidence of child sexual abuse, which suggests a large number of unreported instances, especially for severe crimes in family settings. To what degree the sexual abuse is caused by pedophiles—in the figure of the "dirty old man"—and not by relatives or other persons known to the child is impossible to discern from the existing statistical sources. But all research suggests that the most severe sexual abuses of children are related to incestuous relations within the family.

The Cultural History of Pedophilia

Despite the lack of statistics, other sources indicate that sexual relations between adults and children have always existed. Attitudes toward this have changed over the course of history, and these relations have been condemned since late antiquity. Despite this we can find examples of prominent figures, including Saint Augustine (354–430), Muhammad (570–632), and Gandhi (1869–1948), who publicly enjoyed the company of young children and may have had sexual relations with them.

In the strictly hierarchical society of classical Greece, sexual relations between an adult man and a boy were seen as contributing to the boy's education. In late antiquity this view was questioned by, among others, the poet Ovid and the philosopher Plutarch. They argued that such a relationship was not fulfilling for the adult, since the boy, due to his inferior social status, was not allowed to express his own desire. This devaluated the joy of his adult partner and so men were better served by having sexual relations with women.

With the rise of Christianity, approved sexuality came to be located within heterosexual marriage, with procreation as its sole purpose. This was reflected in medieval legislation that established minimum marriage ages and prohibitions against INCEST and homosexual relations. With the EN-LIGHTENMENT and the French Revolution in the eighteenth century, morality was no longer the responsibility solely of the Church. The gatekeeper of public and private morals was to be the state, and nineteenth-century penal legislation built upon this base, adding sections on sexual offenses.

The penal code did not prevent adults from having sexual relations with children. The most severe sexual abuse can be detected in legal sources, from rape to sexually related child murder. Between 1830 and 1890, two-thirds of all documented sexual offenses in London had children as victims. Nineteenth-century institutional and educational sources show a less dramatic picture, with some ambiguity about the line between physical and sexual abuse of children by teachers or priests.

Discourse on the sexual abuse of children was renewed in France and England around 1850 as a result of the rise of the middle-class family, with its romantic concept of the child, as well as the establishment of the new scientific professions of psychiatry and forensic medicine. Two French physicians, Adolphe Toulmouche and Ambrose Tardieu, undertook the first forensic medical studies of child victims of sexual abuse.

But it was not until the publication of a series of articles entitled "The Maiden Tribute of Modern Babylon" in the British newspaper the *Pall Mall Gazette* in 1885 that sexual abuse of children became a topic for public discussion. The articles, written by the journalist W. T. Stead, dealt with CHILD PROSTITUTION. They had an enormous effect on a public that cultivated the image of the innocent girl-child as encountered in *Alice in Wonderland* and in the many contemporary photos and paintings of naked children. About a quarter of a million people marched in the streets of London demanding a higher AGE OF CONSENT for sexual acts. This

In 1996, a mass protest was held in Brussels, Belgium, in response to the perceived mishandling by the police of the Marc Dutroux case. Dutroux had abducted, sexually abused, and killed several young girls in the 1990s; his crimes went undetected for years, even though informants had warned the police of his activities a number of times. © BISSON BERNARD/CORBIS SYGMA.

demand was echoed all over the Western world, and at the outbreak of World War I the age of consent had been raised in most countries from ten or twelve to fifteen, sixteen, or eighteen.

The people responsible for bringing sexual child abuse to the public's attention were not physicians. Despite the occurrence of sexually transmitted VENEREAL DISEASES among children, both at ORPHANAGES and in families, physicians tended to profess belief in the so-called innocent explanation: that the children had caught the diseases after sharing sheets, sponges, or towels. The physicians were motivated not only by fear of losing customers if they interfered in the domain of the family. The epidemiology of venereal diseases was not completely known. Furthermore, it was not yet possible in their society to speak about children and SEXUALITY within the context of the innocent child. To the nineteenth-century child savers, the subject could not be mentioned without evoking the image of the masturbating boy and the precocious working-class girl.

In this situation, the subject was left to the women's movement, the philanthropic societies, and individual child savers. Due to their work, a new image—that of the sexually innocent child who was easy prey for sexually depraved adult men—was introduced into the culture.

Even though children were considered sexually innocent, however, they were not always trusted in court. The skepticism facing the child witness was great, and it was supported by new scientific studies of child witnesses and by a Freudian understanding of children's sexuality. This new knowledge could also be used to acquit the child of bad intentions, since it framed childhood sexuality as by its very nature innocent.

The moral panic about sexual child abuse at the end of the nineteenth century was followed by a series of media panics during the twentieth century. With a foundation in sexology, forensic medicine, and EUGENICS, the image of the sexual psychopath dominated the discourse of the 1930s through 1950s. This interpretation was gradually replaced by psychoanalysis, the sexual revolution, and an understanding of and belief in resocializing sexual criminals. In the late 1960s the picture changed again with the development of the women's movement and movements concerned with the rights of various groups. This period climaxed with the first accusations against preschool teachers. Among the first cases was the McMartin Preschool in California. The case opened in 1983. Seventeen years later all the accused were acquitted.

During the 1970s through 1990s, revelations of the existence of child pornography as well as pedophile chat groups on the Internet, in addition to a series of sensational child murders in the United States and Europe, resulted in a new moral panic, which led to an insistence on stronger punishments for child sexual abuse and a demand for national registers of sexual offenders. The first world conference on sexual child abuse, held in Stockholm in the summer of 1996, supported these. In the United States, thirty-five states implemented the so-called MEGAN'S LAWS during the years 1994 through 1996. These laws contain a community notification provision. Forty-nine states have introduced state registers. In the early twenty-first century a reaction to what came to be seen as a witch-hunt against pedophiles became visible. It produced a growing awareness of the legal rights of the accused.

The Serial Pedophile of the 1990s

At the dawn of the twenty-first century, pedophilia as well as sexual child abuse are no longer private matters, as they were a century before. They are public matters that keep a collection of professionals, from physicians, psychiatrics, and psychologists to lawyers busy. They also sell well in the media. Whereas sexual abuse within the family has been known and publicly condemned for generations, the twentieth century has seen a growing awareness of sexual child abuse in public settings, from preschools to the Catholic Church. Public awareness has shifted its focus from the adult to the child, and concern is not only for girls but, since the 1930s, has grown to include boys as well.

The growing discussion of pedophilia and the sexual abuse of children has been seen as characteristic of the cultural and mental changes of the twentieth century. Researchers seem to agree that the increased number of cases has not, by itself, been the driving force behind the discussion. Here the agreement stops, and a variety of different explanations are to be found in the existing literature. They range from pointing out the responsibility of the scientific professions as well as the media to explaining the public debate about pedophilia as an element in disciplining heterosexual normality. The question of continuity and change has also been introduced. When 250,000 people marched in the streets of Brussels, Belgium, in the summer of 1996, was this a repetition of the London march of 1885 against the white slave trade and a demand for a higher age of consent? Or was it the harbinger of a radical new phase, since the child in contemporary society could be considered the last remaining, irrevocable, unexchangeable primary reflection of adult dreams of a long-lost world of purity and stability. The strong reactions to sexual child abuse are in reality an exhibition of adult insecurity at being confronted with a late-modern, reflexive society, where human relations are constantly changing. A final statement in this debate over the rationality of the pedophilia discourse comes from the American literary critic James Kincaid. He has advocated the provocative thesis that the contemporary concept of the child, which praises innocence and asexuality, inevitably produces its own erotic counterpart. In our longing for children, the erotic desires are banned and projected onto the pedophile. In other words, the focus on pedophilia fulfils an existential need.

The above-mentioned studies focus on the discourse on pedophilia and sexual abuse of children. Analysis of legal practices has revealed gendered, racial, and social biases as well as concealment, ambivalences, and distortions when the many words had to be turned into action. Knowledge of the reality of sexual child abuse has been based on studies of court records. They reveal that girls historically have been thought to be the most vulnerable group, especially girls from lower social strata and of non-white descent. They also reveal that the sexual abuse of children often continued unpunished for many years because, on the one hand, children were not trusted as witnesses in such cases, and, on the other, mothers were often blamed for not having been watchful enough. Studies of court materials have also revealed how difficult it can be to untangle the accusation of child abuse—especially sexual child abuse—from social and racial prejudices of the juridical system.

See also: **Child Saving; Lolita.**

BIBLIOGRAPHY

Fass, Paula S. 1997. *Kidnapped: Child Abduction in America.* New York: Oxford University Press.

Feldman, W., et al. 1991. "Is Childhood Sexual Abuse Really Increasing in Prevalence?" *Pediatrics* 88: 29–33.

Freedman, E. B. 1987. "'Uncontrolled Desires.' The Response to the Sexual Psychopath 1920–1960." *Journal of American History* (June): 83–106.

Jackson, Louise A. 2000. *Child Sexual Abuse in Victorian England.* New York: Routledge.

Jenks, Chris. 1994. "Child Abuse in the Postmodern Context: An Issue of Social Identity." *Childhood* 2: 111–121.

Jenkins, Phillip. 1998. *Moral Panic: Changing Concepts of the Child Molester in Modern America.* New Haven, CT: Yale University Press.

Kincaid, James R. 1998. *Erotic Innocence: The Culture of Child Molesting.* Durham, NC: Duke University Press.

NING DE CONINCK-SMITH

Perpetua, Saint

Among the few preserved texts from antiquity written by women, the visions recorded by the Roman *matrona*, or formally married woman of elevated social status, Vibia Perpetua while awaiting execution for lèse-majesté (harming the ruler) are among the most widely studied. This is not surprising, for Perpetua's visions form part of a larger account that details her execution in the then-customary manner: she was savaged by a wild cow as part of an elaborate public spectacle (a form or gladiatorial games known as *ad bestias*) staged on March 7, 203 C.E., in her hometown of Carthage, in North Africa, for the birthday of the emperor's son Geta.

Perpetua's crime had been adherence to Christianity, at the time outlawed as a dangerous superstition that, among other crimes, denied the emperor's divine character. Her death made her, in Christian eyes, a martyr. Perpetua is one of the earliest female martyrs known, and she was a remarkable woman. Then around twenty years old, Perpetua was the nursing mother of a newborn. She was accompanied, even in death, by her slave Felicitas, herself highly pregnant. Both Perpetua's visions as well as the account of the two women's death highlight their maternal status. Perpetua speaks of her aching breasts and is tormented over her son's fate, and Felicitas' pregnancy causes her great concern.

Public executions of women in the context of gladiatorial games were very rare in antiquity, those of high-status women were even rarer, and pregnancy was virtually an excluding factor. Later accounts document that "martyrdoms" of pregnant women had became illegal, and Perpetua's story emphasizes the authorities' attempts to prevent her execution; the judge asked Perpetua repeatedly to have pity on her child and recant. Indeed, the framing narrative highlights the audience's reaction to Perpetua's leaking breasts and Felicitas' pregnancy—compassion, pity, and outrage directed against the authorities. In fact, the mere presence of a *matrona* in the arena was a shocking sight: the reversal of all norms that defined and maintained society. Perpetua's own account, as well as the framing narrative, leave no doubt that

this was the point of the exercise. By admitting her Christianity, Perpetua explicitly defied her father and his powerful tutelage (called *patria potestas*) and hence his role as *paterfamilias*, of an elite household, the cornerstones of Roman society. Her insistence on being executed, against the will of the authorities, meant abandoning her son to almost certain death, since he would be without her milk—so unthinkable an act that a miracle had to occur to prevent it (in the framing narrative, the child no longer required milk).

Perpetua's husband is never mentioned (Felicitas' companion is, but there was no formal marriage for slaves). Further, the manner of Perpetua's death, nearly naked and in public, classified her as a prostitute, the antithesis of a *matrona*. For the early Christian audience of this text, all these factors symbolized the destruction of the Roman Empire and its power in favor of the apocalyptically desired "heavenly kingdom." But even this audience could take only so much disruption: The narrator reestablishes (and elevates) Perpetua's status as married mother by calling the deceased *matrona Christi*, and elevates Felicitas by freeing her posthumously. This authorial act is significant: both women, as martyrs and mothers, became exemplars of the highest order for subsequent generations of Christians until the early fifth century. By then Christianity had become the official religion of the Roman Empire, and in the hands of Bishop Augustine, who wrote several sermons celebrating both women, the highborn Perpetua loses her motherhood to become a chaste virgin. Her slave Felicitas is now married and gives birth before her public death. Thus in Augustine's reinterpretation both women are still martyrs but no longer explicitly martyr-mothers—far less threatening to the social fabric their religion now upheld.

See also: **Ancient Greece and Rome; Christian Thought, Early.**

BIBLIOGRAPHY

Coleman, Katherine. 1990. "Fatal Charades: Roman Executions Staged As Mythological Enactments." *Journal of Roman Studies* 80: 44–73.

Elm, Susanna. 1994. *Virgins of God: The Making of Asceticism in Late Antiquity.* New York: Oxford University Press.

Salisbury, Joyce E. 1997. *Perpetua's Passion: The Death and Memory of a Young Roman Woman.* New York: Routledge.

SUSANNA ELM

Pestalozzi, Johann Heinrich (1746–1827)

Johann Heinrich Pestalozzi was a writer, political and social reformer, and educator. Born and educated in Zurich, Switzerland, in 1765 he ended his university studies abruptly due to his active engagement in the radical republican youth movement aiming towards the restoration of republican values and morals. Influenced by the ancient Roman ideal of the citizen as "landed man" and inspired by JEAN-JACQUES ROUSSEAU's *Julie ou la Nouvelle Héloïse* (1761) and the fifth book of *Émile* (1762), Pestalozzi apprenticed himself to a farmer (1767–1768). In 1769 Pestalozzi married Anna Schulthess, of a wealthy burgher family. Overhasty purchase of a large tract of land in Birr in the Swiss canton of Aargau (under the control of Bern), debts on his Neuhof estate, and the agricultural crisis in Europe in 1771–1772 led Pestalozzi into great financial difficulties. He attempted to avert financial disaster by employing children of the poor in a proto-industrial enterprise at Neuhof, promising parents education of their children. However, he had overestimated the children's productivity and was soon forced to raise funds through public appeals to charity. But the monies collected were not sufficient, and the institution closed in 1780. Nevertheless, Pestalozzi's public reflections on the meaning and purpose of education of the poor led to his career as a commentator on politics, education, and economics. His novel *Lienhard und Gertrud*, published in 1781, enjoyed great literary success; three further volumes had a lesser reception.

It was during this phase of his work that Pestalozzi first used the term *childhood*. Although Pestalozzi revised his understanding of childhood many times, his idea of childhood as a period of transformation remained constant throughout his long life. In *Lienhard und Gertrud*, the predominant idea is a sensualistic view of childhood as the life phase when the young child is shaped by external conditions.

Pestalozzi's efforts and experiences at proto-industry forced him to revise his agrarian-oriented republicanism. After 1782 he came into contact with the Berliner ENLIGHTENMENT, which led him to political reflections upon natural law and the theories of the social contract. For Pestalozzi, who remained under the influence of republican ideals, the life of the family, which would be a largely independent economic unit, would allow for family socialization and thus the instilling of virtues. Here Pestalozzi equates childhood with the human being in a natural state but in contrast to Rousseau, the connotation is a negative one: in a passage in the fourth volume of *Lienhard und Gertrud* (1787) entitled "the philosophy of my book," Pestalozzi wrote, "By nature, and when people grow up left to their own devices, they are lethargic, ignorant, careless, thoughtless, foolish, gullible, timorous, greedy without bounds, . . . crooked, sly, insidious, distrustful, violent, foolhardy, vindictive, and prone to acts of atrocity" (p. 330). It therefore follows that stringent socialization to the constraints of societal life through work and the workplace must precede religious moral training.

The development of the human race and the development of the individual were seen to take a parallel course. Pestalozzi thus interpreted childhood as an unspoiled, natural state, in which—following Rousseau—needs and faculties, or powers, are in perfect equilibrium. However, Pesta-

lozzi did not believe that this natural state could be maintained, for in the life of an individual it existed only at the moment of birth. Through life's experiences, the needs of young persons growing up were greater than their ability to satisfy them. It was thus unavoidable that the person became "depraved." In an ideal political system, education could bring the person to recreate the self, to develop into a "moral" being. Pestalozzi maintained that "the circumstances make the man," but in an extension based on Christianity, he found that human beings had within themselves the power to influence those circumstances according to their own will and to create ideal contexts. This faculty, or "self-power," was seen as highly individual and independent of natural and societal determinants. Human beings achieved morality (in a religious sense) dependent upon two conditions: politics and education. Pestalozzi made it his own principle to follow the noble principle of Jesus Christ: to first make the inner person pure in order to make the outside pure. This religiously inspired theory of education was based on the principle of the family, to which the school should also acquiesce.

Philipp Albert Stapfer, Minister of Arts and Sciences of the Helvetic Republic, believed that Pestalozzi would be the ideal person to help him enact various school reforms. His hope was based on a belief that Pestalozzi had developed a completely unique method of teaching children to read. Paradoxically, Pestalozzi became a national educator just at the time when he had lost faith in the restoration of the republic, and he was given responsibility for a modern school system just as he had wanted to subordinate schooling to education within the family.

From this time in his life onwards, Pestalozzi was to head a number of educational institutions. His efforts at education theory centered upon the development of a comprehensive method of elementary education that would promote the natural acquisition of basic learning in all disciplines and, at the same time, go hand in hand with the unfolding of the child's moral-religious as well as physical propensities. A first draft of his main principles of education was presented in 1801 in his book *Wie Gertrud ihre Kinder lehrt* (How Gertrude teaches her children). The underlying concept was that human nature is made up of mechanically structured innate predispositions and self-powers, whereby the innate teleological structured predispositions are too weak to develop on their own. According to this view, Pestalozzi equated childhood with the need for (Pestalozzi's) object lesson books, the only lesson books that succeeded in drawing out and evolving children's God-given inherent propensities.

After 1802, Pestalozzi began to develop a more organic perspective of mankind. He did not follow the contemporary discussion of the Romantic period in Germany, which in 1800—inspired by Rousseau—equated childhood with a state of holiness and propagated the historical-philosophical progression of Paradise, The Fall, and Redemption. Pestalozzi saw in the child a natural innocence, but even the holy in the child could not develop without the necessity of education. In this apolitical view, it is the mother who takes on the central role in the process of societal regeneration; in her religious mission, she becomes first of all the natural "intermediary between the child and the world" before she deflects the child's love of herself towards God. It is this sacred educational function that allows the child to maintain itself as an independent and religious person in the face of a corrupted world.

For Pestalozzi, children have divine predispositions, which must be fostered. Pestalozzi believed that he himself had discovered the correct method of education. He made frequent references to his own very difficult biography full of privation in his writings. In this connection Pestalozzi saw himself as an educational Jesus Christ.

Following great personal difficulties and the death of Pestalozzi's wife in 1815, his third institute at Yverdon slowly fell apart, and in 1825, Pestalozzi returned to Neuhof in Birr at the age of 79. He died two years later, largely forgotten by the world. It was only through the efforts of teachers, who were becoming organized in the nineteenth century, and through a need in Switzerland (torn religiously and politically) for a guiding, unifying figure that the tireless reformer came to be remembered and honored. It was as an educator that Pestalozzi became the most important national figure in Switzerland, providing sense and a purpose to the whole nation. However, his books were little read, and his pedagogical concepts of the "method" were not put into practice.

See also: **Basedow, Johann Bernhard; Child Development, History of the Concept of; Education, Europe; Salzmann, Christian Gotthilf**

BIBLIOGRAPHY

Pestalozzi, Johann Heinrich. 1927–1996. *Complete Works, Critical Edition*, ed. Artur Buchenau et al. Zurich, Switzerland: Orell Füessli Verlag.

Pestalozzi, Johann Heinrich. 1946–1996. *Complete Letters, Critical Edition*, ed. Emanuel Dejung. Zurich, Switzerland: Orell Füessli Verlag.

DANIEL TRÖHLER

Peter Pan and J. M. Barrie

The children's drama *Peter Pan*, by J. M. (James Matthew) Barrie, first presented on the London stage in 1904 and then in the form of a novel in 1911, created a literary character who has potently played upon children's imaginations through the entire twentieth century and into the early twenty-first century. Barrie offered to the adult public a particular vision of childhood from the Edwardian threshold of the twentieth century: Peter Pan, the child hero who never grows up and therefore must remain radically elusive and inassimilable to the adult world.

The story tells of Peter's visit to the nursery of the Darling children—Wendy, Michael, and John—and his seductive invitation to them to escape from home and parents by flying to the magical island of the Neverland, where a colony of lost boys pursue boyish adventures involving fairies and pirates. In particular they do battle against Peter Pan's archenemy, the pirate Captain Hook, whom Peter heroically vanquishes before returning the Darling children to their home in London so that they may eventually grow up. The part of Peter Pan onstage has been traditionally assigned to an adult actress impersonating a young boy.

If the nineteenth century fostered a Victorian cult of childhood's innocence, preserved according to rigorous forms of domestic propriety, the drama of *Peter Pan* in 1904 represented a literal escape from Victorian childhood as the Darling children flew right out the window. It was reenacted every year at Christmas time. Though the character of Peter evolved from Victorian fairy stories, and he was always accompanied by the fairy Tinker Bell, the drama reached the stage in an age of early modernism, and its vision of children's minds is in many ways curiously modern. The novel of 1911 presents Mrs. Darling, the children's mother, sorting through their minds like chests of drawers while they sleep: "When you wake up in the morning, the naughtiness and evil passions with which you went to bed have been folded up small and placed at the bottom of your mind; and on the top, beautifully aired, are spread out your prettier thoughts, ready for you to put on." Barrie goes so far as to suggest that one might try to make a "map" of a child's mind, a "rather confusing" map, on which one might find the Neverland (pp. 5–7). Such whimsy was not altogether remote from the contemporary spirit of SIGMUND FREUD, who was also making maps of the mind, who also recognized that the mind had folded elements at the bottom, and who, especially, discerned "evil passions" or amoral impulses in children. Barrie was whimsical but not necessarily sentimental about children. The aptness of his insight was confirmed by the returning troops of children who came to the play every Christmas season to watch the Darling children cheerfully abandon home and parents.

Indeed, with the recurrence of the Christmas theater seasons, new generations of children attended the drama while the children of past seasons did what all children (except Peter Pan) do: grow up. The sentiment of the drama and the novel were peculiarly pitched at adults: reminding them that the insides of their children's minds would always be alien, and at the same time that their children would inevitably grow up and cease to be children. Rather than carrying on the Victorian cult of childhood, *Peter Pan* played to a new breed of ambivalent nostalgia for childhood. At the conclusion of the story, Wendy is an adult and Peter Pan returns to carry off her child to the Neverland. "And thus it will go on," comments Barrie, with his concluding flourish, "so long as children are gay and innocent and heartless" (p. 192). The joint attribution of innocence and heartlessness gave *Peter Pan* its own peculiar post-Victorian twist before a public of ever-aging, and always renewed, generations of children.

After Barrie's death in 1937, the rights to Peter Pan passed, by the author's beneficent bequest, to the children's hospital of Great Ormond Street in London, further enhancing the already mythological quality of the story. There was a silent film of 1924, still in Barrie's lifetime. Walt Disney put his own animated American mark on the legend with the movie *Peter Pan* in 1953, and a Peter Pan ride for children, aloft, remains part of the experience of Disney World in the twenty-first century. Broadway weighed in with *Peter Pan* in 1954, starring Mary Martin, singing and flying, as the boy who never grew up. Steven Spielberg, the cinematic master of American fantasy, created his own version of the story in 1991, with a slight shift in emphasis, under the title *Hook*. In the meantime, scholarship and biography also made important contributions to interpreting *Peter Pan*. The biographer Andrew Birkin's *J. M. Barrie and the Lost Boys*, published in 1979, explored Barrie's close personal relationship with the five little boys of the Llewellyn Davies family and suggested the possibility of pedophile fantasy as one of the ingredients that went into the making of the children's classic. In 1984 the literary critic Jacqueline Rose published *The Case of Peter Pan, or, The Impossibility of Children's Fiction*, arguing that the work's cultural sway came from its bundling of the sexual and political contradictions inherent in the adult enterprise of representing children.

A crucial aspect of the history of childhood ever since the Renaissance has been an increasing cultural attention to the fundamental differences between children and adults. The literary legend of Peter Pan, still potent a century after its creation, finds its sentimental force in the aching consciousness of that difference. When Peter returns for Wendy, years later, she confesses what he is too childishly self-absorbed to recognize: "I am old, Peter. I am ever so much more than twenty. I grew up long ago." When he offers to teach her to fly again, with a sprinkling of fairy dust, she replies, "O Peter, don't waste the fairy dust on me" (p. 189). Invoking the Victorian theatrical nonsense of fairy dust, Barrie conjured with remarkable modernity the abyss that separates adults from children.

See also: **Children's Literature; Theories of Childhood.**

BIBLIOGRAPHY

Barrie, J. M. 1987. *Peter Pan*, Signet Classic Edition. Afterword by Alison Lurie. New York: New American Library.

Birkin, Andrew. 1979. *J. M. Barrie and the Lost Boys: The Love Story that Gave Birth to Peter Pan*. New York: C. N. Potter.

Green, Roger Lancelyn. 1954. *Fifty Years of Peter Pan*. London: P. Davies.

Rose, Jacqueline. 1984. *The Case of Peter Pan, or, The Impossibility of Children's Fiction*. London: Macmillan.

Larry Wolff

Pets

The association of childhood with pet-keeping is easy to see in contemporary culture. Children's intimacy with pets is a stock image of life in suburban America, a theme deployed throughout the world by global capitalism, intensifying the message of childhood as timeless, happy, and safe, fixed both within nature and in a protective, snapshot moment. It is a kinship acknowledged in calendars, stories, stuffed animals, commercials, and mail-order catalogues.

How did this relationship come about? Tess Cosslett suggests in "Child's Place in Nature" that for nineteenth-century people, the link between children and animals was clear and unmediated. When a child encounters an object in nature, French philosopher and historian Hippolyte Taine argued, "animal or tree, she immediately meets it as a person and wants to know its thoughts and words; that is what she cares about; by a spontaneous induction she imagines it like herself, like us; she humanizes it" (quoted in Cosslett, p. 481). Cosslett shows how these views found expression in CHILDREN'S LITERATURE. In the story "Inferior Animals" by Margaret Gatty, author of *Parables from Nature* and other books about nature for children, for example, we are directed to "see the little child as she babbles to her cat on the rug, and would fain be friends" (p. 482). Children were like "primitive peoples," Taine explained. In Old Norse poetry and in the folk tales of medieval Wales, for example, "animals have also the gift of speech."

Children are feminized by the pronouns employed by Taine and Gatty, closer to nature than to men. Gatty mourned the "necessary unlearning" of our childhood instinct for intercommunication with the animals, a theme which the stories in the *Jungle Book* by RUDYARD KIPLING also address. Mowgli's trajectory from wild child—half animal, half human ("I am two Mowglis," he sings)—to adult is, Cosslett explains, "part of growing up and leaving the childhood space of play and ambivalence between human and animal natures" (p. 487). Children feel an affinity for nature, one that adults, males, and modern people, have lost. In children's literature, in the fantasy interactions of child and beast, that infantile closeness is recaptured. "Perhaps the child can reclaim as fiction what the adult has to lose as primitive superstition," Cosslett suggests, explaining this nineteenth-century point of view (p. 481). "Only children, or child-like men . . . have any chance of breaking through the charm which holds nature thus as it were frozen around us, like a petrified magic city," German romantic writer Novalis explained (quoted by Cosslett, p. 483).

Research by cognitive scientists into how children perceive the relationship between themselves and other animals belies the "natural" connection assumed by these nineteenth-century thinkers. Gregg Solomon and Deborah Zaitchik show in a 2000 essay, "Les enfants et la pensée animale" (Children and animal thought), that children intuitively recognize themselves as humans to be "ontologically unique," essentially different from other animals: "Consequently, they are reluctant about attributing such essentially human characteristics as the ability to pretend or imagine to other animals" (p. 166). Their research shows how tenacious is the idea of difference—of the separateness of species, of the alienation of human and beast—among young children. Indeed, they show how hard it is to unlearn intuitive ideas about the radical difference between humans and other animals, and how culturally specific that process of unlearning is. A study cited by Solomon and Zaitchik compared two groups of children living in the same Midwestern town. One group was made up of the children of fundamentalist Christians, the other excluded them. The young children of both groups were essentialist in their thinking about species, that is, they believed people were—in essential, defining ways—completely different. Adolescents and adults differed, however. The nonfundamentalists had overcome that so-called bias, while fundamentalists remained locked into the beliefs of their childhood. At the very least, Solomon and Zaitchik conclude, these studies suggest the critical role cultures may play in modifying early notions of the human–animal divide.

The work of anthroplogist Rita Astuti on the Vezo of Madagascar is instructive along these lines. In "Les gens ressemblent-ils aux poulet?" (Do people resemble chickens?), Astuti describes Vezo children torturing animals. As a form of PLAY, they tear the legs off crabs, stab the eyes and wounds of captured sea turtles, and hunt and gratuitously hurt birds, butterflies, grasshoppers, lizards, frogs, and all manner of creatures. Only adults treat animals with respect. Vezo behavior changes when individuals are old enough to understand the restrictions of taboo, which recognizes the moral kinship between humans and certain privileged animals. Thus it is adults who have created an imagined connection between childhood and animal life.

Children and pets are often paired in popular culture, but not because of any natural or indisputable affinity on the part of children for animals. It may be cultural habit alone that prompts Nicholas Orme in *Medieval Children* to state that "children bonded with animals, too, as they do today, because of animals' comparable size, their different activities, and the apparent friendliness of many of them" (p. 68). Much of the evidence of bonding, however, is slight. We read in Orme of a girl "knocked in the water by a pig" she was feeding, and another drowned while washing the skull of a bird she may have been tending. In addition, a few "household animals" are named in fifteenth-century schoolbooks. The fact that these were named suggests an emotion-

Miss Anna Ward with Her Dog (1787), Joshua Reynolds. In the eighteenth and nineteenth centuries, the pairing of children and animals signified the instinctual affinity of children for nature, an affinity that overcivilized adults had long lost. © Kimbell Art Museum/CORBIS.

al connection. These include a hen, a cock, and, possibly, a dog named Whitefoot. Some royal children hunted with hawks and hounds, "animals cared for by others," Orme notes, "but which the child could fancy to be its own." Steven Ozment notes a few incidents like these in *Ancestors: The Loving Family in Old Europe*, including children playing with tame birds and pretending to be horses and goats (pp. 71–72).

More typical of human–animal relationships in the Middle Ages is cruelty to animals on the part of children. Thomas More mentions that boys loved to play cock-stele. The cock-stele, Orme explains, "was a stick to throw at a cockerel in the cruel sport of burying the bird in the ground and aiming sticks and arrows at its head"(p. 179). Boys, and possibly girls, too, Orme suggests, organized cock-fights on Shrove Tuesday, a day "particularly important in the children's calendar[,] . . . a public holiday and one when children had their own activity: cock-fighting" (p. 185). Another favorite pastime was raiding birds' nests—breaking eggs and killing baby birds—an activity which along with cock-fighting helped to galvanize the European animal-protection movements of the eighteenth and nineteenth centuries.

The relationship between children and animals, although often romanticized, is not always a loving one. William Hogarth's print *The First Stage of Cruelty* (1751) shows the abuse of animals as the first step down a road of crime, ending in robbery and murder. The British Museum.

Keith Thomas in *Man and the Natural World* and Erica Fudge in *Perceiving Animals* have shown the importance of Puritan and humanist thought in recasting European's relationship to animals—from one of simple dominance to stewardship and even kinship. It makes sense, then, that the pairing of children and pets enters the historical record during the Dutch Golden Age of the sixteenth and seventeenth centuries. The United Provinces was a stronghold of both humanist and Calvinist cultures, and a haven for the English Puritans. In Dutch paintings of the time we find dogs and cats within the home, playing with children, participants in and witnesses to family life. We can interpret the place of pets within Dutch culture as part of the transformation in European attitudes toward animals, but, more particularly, as we shall see below, as an expression of beliefs about family life.

What does this evidence tell us? Historian Simon Schama in *The Embarrassment of Riches* shows us that in paintings of Dutch domesticity, "we are not merely glimpsing snapshots from the family album, but scenes from the interior of the Dutch mental world" (p. 495). In Jacob Gerritszoon Cuyp's *Portrait of a Child*, for instance, a "chubby-cheeked" little girl is shown holding the leash of an even smaller dog, perhaps a puppy, as Schama argues, and holding an outsized pretzel.

The dog is at once the child's pet and an emblem of her status as a Christian child, educable, trainable, tied by "leading bands" to the values of her home. In another example, the girl in Jacob Ochtervelt's *Family Portrait* (1663), is training her small spaniel to sit up on his back paws, begging in a familiar way for a cookie or treat. Her father sits behind them, facing us, with his hand on a page of his Bible, while her mother stands, pointing a finger at the dog. These paintings evince a "tradition in which the instruction of children is reinforced by the visual analogue of training dogs in obedience," a tradition within which kittens or cats, in contrast, signal opposite qualities, and "function as symbols of fecklessness or unteachability" (p. 547).

Pets seem to amplify the message that children are meant to broadcast in Dutch life. They form part of a system of signs that tells viewers that a home is ordered, as in Pieter de Hooch interiors, or disordered, as in Jan Steen's *The Dissolute Household* (1668), where the prettified dog (it seems to be wearing a bow) scrounges for food on platters dropped on the floor as the children steal from their drunken mother. Whether, or to what extent, children and pets were bound together in social life is hard to tell. That they have linked meanings within the cultural universe of the Dutch is less in doubt.

We find a similar figurative quality assigned to pets in the nineteenth-century practice of pet-keeping. Pet-care books, which begin to be published in the 1850s for a middle-class audience, speak to the sanctity of the home and the role of dogs in guarding that domain both from strangers and from the pressures of modern life. Dogs, especially, come to form part of the emotional furniture of the bourgeois home, as Pierre Auguste Renoir implied in his portrait of *Madame Georges Charpentier et ses enfants* (1878). There, one Charpentier child sits on the shaggy Newfoundland while another is perched on the sofa, the dog as much a component and defining feature of the home as the children themselves.

What is surprising about nineteenth-century pet-keeping practice is the extent to which it is defined as an adult activity. Harriet Ritvo's work on the development of dog breeds shows how grounded in adult needs for status dog breeding institutions were. And although children figure in dog-care books, it is only at a remove, metaphorically, as in the stories of BEATRIX POTTER. Far from being directed to children or children's needs, much of the literature on pet-keeping describes pets as replacement children, or imitation children, or better children. According to Kathleen Kete's *The Beast in the Boudoir*, dogs lived "in an eternal childhood, a minority without end" (p. 82).

Like children, pets demanded attention, training, food, and sometimes clothing. But in return, it was promised, they were faithful to the grave. Pets took the "place of dead or departed children, of daughters who have been seduced, of spouses who have been ungrateful" (Kete, pp. 35–36). They were buried in pet cemeteries with tombstones, as if marking human loss, then replaced. They found a place within an adult culture marked by the loneliness of modern life. The importance of pets as replacement children continues in contemporary America. For example, suburban towns might have both a pet bakery and an upscale shop for canine and feline toys and clothes, often directly across the street from an equally upscale clothing store for children. For some women a new puppy seems to herald the end of reproduction. The last "child" is canine, a substitution for what the family cannot afford, an outlet for nurturing not yet exhausted.

A custody case reported by Adam Liptak in the *New York Times* on July 12, 2002 ("Man Loses a Best Friend"), describes some of the issues involved in treating pets like children. A divorcing couple in Pennsylvania had agreed that the wife would have custody of their dog, Barney, and the husband would have visiting rights. The law refused to recognize the arrangement made between the couple, however. A state appeals court ruled that although the former husband "appears to treat Barney, a dog, as a child," legally he had the status of "a table or a lamp." The status of animals—pets included—is of increasing concern to the practice of law in the United States, where a growing number of law schools offer courses in the subject, and the animal rights movement in general has called into question the boundaries between human and animal.

Research in psychology helps explain why we might treat animals like children. As Kete reported in *The Beast in the Boudoir*, talking to pets is shown to lower blood pressure. People's "voice tones and facial expressions," in speaking to pets are the same as those used by "lovers or by mothers with small children"(p. 37). It is for this reason that pets are being used in therapy, especially as tools in the treatment of older people. Psychologically, they *are* replacement people—a transference made more easily by the physical resemblance of pets to children. Both are cuddly and cute, at least in the views of their handlers.

The anthropocentric culture of European America is becoming increasingly anthropomorphic. A tension exists, however, between the blended imagery of pets and children today and the wide range of children's behavior, both toward animals and people. Earlier pet-keeping cultures were bolder. The feral children of eighteenth- and nineteenth-century Europe—Peter the Wild Boy and Victor the Wild Boy of Aveyron, for example—anti-pets, as it were, allowed for discussion of the "brutish" nature of humans, though ideas about the natural goodness of children and nature also prevailed. Even among the child-happy Dutch, it was the trainability of children, not their innocence, that canines depicted. The animal protection movement in nineteenth-century Britain and France recognized that children, like adults, were prone to abuse animals. The movement was clear about the dangers this behavior posed to society. "The child is father to the man" was an often-repeated slogan of reformers. William Hogarth's print *The Four Stages of Cruelty* (1750–1751) illustrated this point in the mid-eighteenth century, showing the juvenile abuser of dogs and the later robber and murderer.

A 2003 article on dog fighting by Shane DuBow makes a point similar to the animal protectionist arguments of an earlier age, though it is an echo now rarely heard: the inner-city children who grow up training pit bulls to rip each other apart will, in their turn, become violent. "You're going to see a spike in violence" as these children grow up, one police sergeant is quoted as saying. The menace of violence implied in the pairing of child and pit bull is as important, however, as the image of peace and prosperity marketed by the puppies in the clothing catalogues. It is this menace that pet-keeping culture today seeks to efface. Perhaps it hides from us the gap between an ideal conception of the child and the more prosaic and versatile range of human behavior.

Children and pets are twinned in European-American culture as two moons might be, the one occasionally obscuring the other—the child, the pet—each reflecting, and together amplifying, the power of adult needs. The history of that association says little about the actual relationships between children and animals but suggests a continuity across European cultures in the power of childhood to speak to ideas of nature and for animals, real and imagined, to stand in for the human.

See also: **Theories of Childhood; Zoos.**

BIBLIOGRAPHY

Astuti, Rita. 2000. "Les gens ressemblent-ils aux poulets? Penser la frontiere homme-animal a Madagascar," trans. Christine Langlois. *Terrain 34: Les animaux pensent-ils?* March: 89–106.

Candland, Douglas Keith. 1993. *Feral Children and Clever Animals: Reflections on Human Nature.* Oxford, UK: Oxford University Press.

Carpenter, Humphrey. 1989. "Excessively Impertinent Bunnies: The Subversive Element in Beatrix Potter," in *Children and Their Books: A Celebration of the Work of Iona and Peter Opie*, ed. Gillian Avery and Julia Briggs. Oxford: Clarendon Press.

Cosslett, Tess. 2001. "Child's Place in Nature: Talking Animals in Victorian Children's Fiction." *Nineteenth-Century Contexts* 23, no. 4: 475–495.

DuBow, Shane. 2003. "Dog Bites Dog." *New York Times Magazine*, September 29: 50–51.

Fudge, Erica. 1999. "Calling Creatures by Their True Names: Bacon, the New Science, and the Beast in Man." In *At the Borders of the Human: Beasts, Bodies, and Natural Philosophy in the Early Modern Period*, ed. Erica Fudge, Ruth Gilbert, and Susan Wiseman. New York: St. Martin's Press.

Fudge, Erica. 2000. *Perceiving Animals: Humans and Beasts in Early Modern English Culture.* New York: St. Martin's Press.

Kete, Kathleen. 1994. *The Beast in the Boudoir: Pet-Keeping in Nineteenth-Century Paris.* Berkeley and Los Angeles: University of California Press.

Newton, Michael. 1999. "Bodies without Souls: The Case of Peter the Wild Boy." In *At the Borders of the Human: Beasts, Bodies, and*

Natural Philosophy in the Early Modern Period, ed. Erica Fudge, Ruth Gilbert, and Susan Wiseman. New York: St. Martin's Press.

Orme, Nicholas. 2001. *Medieval Children*. New Haven, CT: Yale University Press.

Ozment, Steven. 2002. *Ancestors: The Loving Family in Old Europe*. Cambridge, MA: Harvard University Press.

Ritvo, Harriet. 1987. "Prize Pets." In *The Animal Estate: The English and Other Creatures in the Victorian Age*, ed. Harriet Ritvo. Cambridge, MA: Harvard University Press.

Schama, Simon. 1987. *The Embarrassment of Riches: An Interpretation of Dutch Culture in the Golden Age*. New York: Knopf.

Solomon, Gregg, and Deborah Zaitchik. 2000. "Les enfants et la pensee animale," trans. Christine Langlois. *Terrain 34: Les animaux pensent-ils?* March: 73–88.

Thomas, Keith. 1983. *Man and the Natural World: A History of the Modern Sensibility*. New York: Pantheon Books.

Waldau, Paul. 2001. "Will the Heavens Fall? De-radicalizing the Precedent-Breaking Decision." *Animal Law* 7: 75–117.

KATHLEEN KETE

Photographs of Children

From the moment portrait photography become technically feasible in the 1840s, children have figured among the most popular and compelling of camera subjects. U.S. households spent $9.1 billion on photography in 1999, and in 1995, 40 percent had a professional portrait photo taken. Yet by the turn of the twenty-first century, photographs of children had also become caught up in issues of child SEXUALITY and child sexual abuse. In Europe and the United States in the second half of the nineteenth century, photography played a crucial role in reflecting, producing, and disseminating a Romantic ideal of children as innocent, vulnerable, emotionally priceless beings in need of special nurturance and protection from adult forms of work and social interchange. The contentiousness that surrounds photographic representations of children in the twenty-first century is symptomatic of the breakdown of this long-held Romantic ideal and the emergence of a post-Romantic child whose qualities and status remain radically in doubt.

Portraits

Popular commercial culture embraced portrait photography as a powerful new instrument in the formation and extension of the bourgeois liberal subject, that sovereign individual born of ENLIGHTENMENT values who is possessed of a psychologically complex sense of self and is entitled to certain inalienable human rights. For the first time in human history, a popular, affordable, and accessible medium of heretofore unimaginable verisimilitude recorded the visual presence of children neither rich nor famous enough to command the painter's attention. The children depicted in the early daguerreotypes (1839–1850s) make their appearance predominantly as members of a nuclear, middle-class family. Often they pose with one or both parents, but frequently they appear singly or in sibling groups, their likenesses preserved in one-of-a-kind images placed in ornate, hand-held cases. These early photographs often possess a solemn aspect due to the long exposure times required and to the social formality of the occasion. The making of postmortem photographs of deceased infants and children was a common ritual aspect of mourning and loss throughout the nineteenth century.

While child and family portraiture remained a mainstay of commercial photography, the advent of George Eastman's Kodak Company in the 1880s transformed the popular culture of photographic imagery. By adapting a number of advances in photographic technology (e.g., flexible roll film, more light-sensitive emulsions, simpler and smaller cameras, assembly-line photo processing) and by implementing an ambitious marketing strategy, the Kodak company convinced a U.S. and European middle class to take up photography as an essential attribute of family life. The amateur snapshot became as familiar and ritualistic as the BIRTHDAYS, holidays, graduations, weddings, reunions, and VACATION travels it served to commemorate. No childhood now goes undocumented. While the aesthetic and/or commercial value of this plenitude of self-generated familial imagery may be negligible, it constitutes a vast, collective visual unconscious informing our deepest understandings of self in relation to family history and the social order.

Fine Art Photography

While the family snapshot has served conventionally to construct and affirm a narrative of family well-being, the history of photography includes a distinguished tradition of artist-photographers from Julia Margaret Cameron (1815–1879) and LEWIS CARROLL (1832–1898) to Gertrude Kasebier (1852–1934) and SALLY MANN (b. 1951) for whom children have served as powerful iconographic figures. In these images the empirical fact of the subject's historical presence in front of the camera becomes enmeshed with literary references and aesthetic programs inherited from painting and printmaking. So, for example, the young members of Cameron's extended upper-class Victorian household embodied ideals of angelic transcendence from Renaissance painting while Carroll's images of his prepubescent friends represented his personal efforts to forge relationships based on play and fantasy that evaded conventional strictures segregating children from adults.

Throughout the nineteenth century and into the first decades of the twentieth, child nudity as portrayed in art photographs signaled a complex amalgam of associations composed of prelapsarian sexual innocence, family sentiment, nostalgia, and spiritual rejuvenation. This limited and socially acceptable range of meanings was secured by a fine-arts tradition inherited from the Renaissance in which nude forms, both male and female, constituted the outward, physi-

Self-Portrait with Hydroglider (1904), Jacques-Henri Lartigue. Lartigue's pride in a particularly favored toy is evident in this turn of the twentieth century photograph. The ease of using cameras has allowed children to be photographers as well as the subjects of photographs, giving viewers an image of childhood from the child's point of view. Photograph J. H. Lartigue. © Ministère de la Culture-France/AAJHL.

cal embodiment of abstract, philosophical, and aesthetic ideals. By the latter half of the twentieth century, however, the production and circulation of images of naked children by artist-photographers such as Robert Mapplethorpe (1946–1989), Jock Sturges (b. 1947), and Sally Mann had become the focus of public controversy, state and federal legislation, and legal prosecution. In these post-Freudian proceedings, allegations of CHILD PORNOGRAPHY and child sexual abuse are countered by free-speech arguments often accompanied by sophisticated postmodern theories of representation that insist upon the fictive, unstable, and ideological nature of photographic realism.

Social Documentary

Beginning with the novels of Charles Dickens and Lord Shaftesbury's speeches in the 1830s and 1840s, the child has figured prominently in the rhetoric and politics of social reform as unconscionable victim of social injustice and symbolic hope of a better future. In the 1870s, Dr. Thomas John Barnardo (1845–1905) commissioned a series of "before and after" albumen prints to illustrate the success of his CHILD-SAVING evangelical missionary activities in London. Photographs have been deployed ever since to solicit political and financial support from a reform-minded public. In the United States, Jacob Riis (1849–1914), a journalist and early advocate of slum clearance, used camera images of the New York tenement districts in order to illustrate and dramatize for a middle-class audience the systemic social problems arising from industrial capitalism's exploitation of immigrant wage labor. While children figure poignantly as innocent victims of slum conditions in many of these images, it is only with the five thousand photographs taken by LEWIS HINE (1874–1940) for the NATIONAL CHILD LABOR COMMITTEE between 1907 and 1918 that the image of the working-class child takes center stage as the object of Progressive reform.

Documentary photography as a consciously articulated, professional genre, came into being in the 1930s in response to the social and economic upheavals of the GREAT DEPRESSION. Dorothea Lange (1895–1965) and Walker Evans

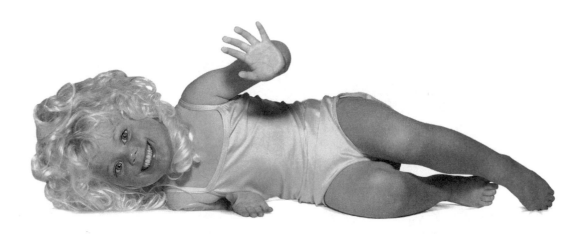

Dutch-born artist Inez van Lamsweerde has used computer manipulation of digital photographs—giving her girl models the tight grins of adult males—to represent the blurring of the lines between childhood and adulthood (*Final Fantasy, Ursula* [1993]). © Inez van Lamsweerde and Vinoodh Matadin.

(1903–1975) are only the best known of a talented group of photographers who worked under the auspices of the New Deal to record the plight of rural America in order to justify the federal programs aimed at providing assistance. A subsequent generation of photojournalists, spawned by a burgeoning picture press, included W. Eugene Smith (1918–1978), Roy DeCarava (b. 1919), and HELEN LEVITT (b. 1913). Almost invariably, they depicted children as immensely appealing beings whose unguarded happiness or unwarranted sufferings stood in dramatic contrast to the harsh and knowing circumstances of adult life. This liberal-humanist viewpoint became a foil for a subsequent generation of photographers, including Robert Frank (b. 1924), Diane Arbus (1923–1971), Ralph Eugene Meatyard (1925–1972), and Emmet Gowin (b. 1941), who tended to portray children as more directly implicated in the more awkward, confusing, conflicted, unsavory, materialistic, erotic, or emotionally disturbing aspects of American social life. It remained for such photographers as Mary Ellen Mark (b. 1941), Larry Clark (b. 1943), Chris Killip (b. 1946), Sebastião Salgado (b. 1944), Nan Goldin (b. 1953), and Lauren Greenfield (b. 1966) to create difficult bodies of work portraying runaway, refugee, alienated, precocious, and delinquent youths as symptomatic of a social landscape

in which the Romantic child figures only negatively as a lost possibility or grand illusion.

Beginning in the 1970s, photography came to be understood by an increasing number of artists as a medium that could be manipulated, re-contextualized, and thereby turned back against itself in order to highlight the complexity and instability of representation. Photographs of children that play with and against realist conventions have proven particularly useful to such postmodern artists as Jeff Wall (b. 1946), Christian Boltanski (b. 1944), Nancy Burson (b. 1948), and Carrie Mae Weems (b. 1953) in disrupting prevailing assumptions concerning photographic transparency and documentary truth.

Related Topics

Commericial photography. Photographs of children have figured ubiquitously as catalysts for consumer desire since the coming of age of advertising and photo-reproduction technologies in the 1920s. In keeping with advertising photography's unrivaled capacity to imbue constructions of fantasy with the immediacy of "the real," icons of romantic innocence, familial bliss, and physical perfection saturate popular culture as the promise of happiness attendant upon the consumption of goods and services—everything from automobile tires to health insurance. No matter how sophisticated and critical viewers, including very young ones, have become about the discrepancies between magazine fictions and lived experience, these images greatly influence common understandings and expectations as to who children are and how they fit into the adult world. Likewise, advertising imagery, in its ongoing search for new and more effective ways to solicit the viewer's attention, continues to make use of long-standing collective confusion, ambivalence, and repression regarding the erotic appeal of the child body.

Fetal imagery. Photographs of the human fetus (in conjunction with sonograms and related medical imaging technology) have had a powerful influence on conceptions of childhood by conferring personhood upon ever more immature stages of embryonic development. Lennart Nilsson's (b. 1922) color photographs, first published in *Life* magazine (April 30, 1965), vividly portrayed the fetus as a cosmic "star child" floating free from the mother's body, thereby providing a powerful ideological construct for the anti-abortion movement in which virtually all prenatal existence is redefined and reimagined as "the life of the unborn child."

Child as photographer. Children, by definition, lack the power to define themselves and their world. Yet photography, given its mechanical ease and its independence from language, holds out the promise of transparency and immediacy in communicating a child's vision or point of view. In the history of photography, the work of Jacques-Henri Lartigue (1894–1986) has long been celebrated as an aristocratic boy's-eye-view of the French belle epoque. In the United States, WENDY EWALD (b. 1951) has worked with Southern rural working-class young people, encouraging them to use photography as a tool of personal expression and cultural empowerment.

Family history. Photography's ability to arrest and preserve the temporal moment even as it signals its irremediable passage has always operated with a particular, sentimental force with regard to the portrayal of childhood, understood as a transitory, future-oriented state of innocence and dependence that must give way to worldly knowledge and adult responsibilities. Photographs of childhood offer a formidable epistemological challenge and can often serve as catalysts for the exploration of the intersections between individual life stories and more collective and distanced forms of social history.

See also: **Images of Childhood.**

Alice Liddell as the Beggar Maid (c. 1859), Lewis Carroll. Girlhood was a source of inspiration for Lewis Carroll, as it was for a number of Victorian artists. Whether or not Carroll was aware of the sexual overtones in his portraits of his young friends—immediately apparent to twenty-first-century viewers—has been a subject of intense debate among scholars. © Bettman/CORBIS.

BIBLIOGRAPHY

Brown, Marilyn R., ed. 2001. *Picturing Children: Constructions of Childhood between Rousseau and Freud.* London: Ashgate.

Dimock, George. 2002. *Priceless Children: American Photographs 1890–1925: Child Labor and the Pictorialist Ideal.* Seattle: University of Washington Press.

Ewald, Wendy, and Alexandra Lightfoot. 2001. *I Wanna Take Me a Picture: Teaching Photography and Writing to Children.* Boston: Beacon Press.

Hacking, Ian. 1991. "The Making and Molding of Child Abuse." *Critical Inquiry* 17 (winter): 253–288.

Higonnet, Anne. 1998. *Pictures of Innocence: The History and Crisis of Ideal Childhood.* New York: Thames and Hudson.

Hirsch, Marianne. 1997. *Family Frames: Photography, Narrative, and Postmemory.* Cambridge, MA.: Harvard University Press.

Hirsch, Marianne, ed. 1999. *The Familial Gaze.* Hanover, NH: University Press of New England.

Holland, Patricia. 1992. *What Is a Child? Popular Images of Childhood.* London: Virago.

Kincaid, James R. 1992. *Child Loving: The Erotic Child and Victorian Culture.* London: Routledge.

Kuhn, Annette. 1995. *Family Secrets: Acts of Memory and Imagination.* London: Verso.

Mann, Sally. 1992. *Immediate Family.* New York: Aperture.

Marks, Laura U. 1990. "Minor Infractions: Child Pornography and the Legislation of Morality." *AfterImage* 18, no. 4 (November): 12–14.

Mavor, Carol. 1995. *Pleasures Taken: Performances of Sexuality and Loss in Victorian Photographs.* Durham, NC: Duke University Press.

McCauley, Elizabeth Anne. 1980. *Likenesses: Portrait Photography in Europe, 1850–1870.* Albuquerque, NM: University of New Mexico Press.

Spence, Jo, and Patricia Holland, eds. 1991. *Family Snaps: The Meanings of Domestic Photography.* London: Virago.

Stange, Maren. 1989. *Symbols of Ideal Life: Social Documentary Photography in America, 1890–1950.* New York: Cambridge University Press.

Stanley, Lawrence. 1989. "The Child Porn Myth." *Cardozo Arts and Entertainment Law Journal* 7, no. 2: 295–358.

Stanley, Lawrence. 1991. "Art and Perversion: Censoring Images of Nude Children." *Art Journal* 50, no. 4 (winter): 20–28.

Stott, William. 1973. *Documentary Expression and Thirties America.* New York: Oxford University Press.

GEORGE DIMOCK

Physical Education

Physical education (sometimes referred to as GYMNASTICS or physical training) has a long tradition. National interests, cultural values, and much more have affected the attention it has received. In the *Republic* PLATO set forth two branches of education: *music* (that over which the Muses preside) for the mind; *gymnastics* for the body. Balanced development of the two—as well as harmonious development of the body—was the desired goal. Physical education has also retained strong connections with classical ideas regarding HYGIENE and preventative medicine. Since the late 1800s, efforts have been made to incorporate knowledge from physiology, psychology, and other disciplines into its practice.

In the eighteenth century a remarkable number of treatises were written in which exercise appropriate to children's age and sex was declared an essential part of their education. JOHN LOCKE's *Some Thoughts Concerning Education* (1693), which opens with the dictum *mens sana en corpore sano*, was frequently cited. Physician Jean Charles Desessertz's *Traité de l'Éducation Corporelle des Enfants en Bas Âge* (1760), who some suggest influenced JEAN-JACQUES ROUSSEAU, would have boys engage in activities like running, jumping, shuffleboard, swimming, and fencing. Desessertz and the Comtesse de Genlis (*Leçons d'Une Gouvernante à ses Éleves*, 1791) were among many who declared that girls should receive much more exercise than their education typically provided. JO-HANN BASEDOW's Philanthropium (1774) set aside three hours a day for recreation. JOHANN CHRISTOPH FRIEDRICH GUTSMUTHS (called by some the grandfather of modern physical education) had a major impact on developments in the nineteenth century.

During the 1800s formalized programs of calisthenics and gymnastics, each with its particular motives and style, developed in various European countries. The usual form of exercise in the state-aided schools of England was gymnastics/calisthenics. Games-playing (with its presumed poten-

tial for developing character) dominated at public schools like Harrow and Rugby and the grammar schools that sought to emulate them. In 1826, the same year that gymnastics (Turnen) was introduced at the Round Hill School, the *American Journal of Education* included an article titled "Physical Education" that declared: "The time we hope is near, when there will be no literary institution unprovided with proper means of healthful exercise and innocent recreation." Antebellum health reformers repeatedly urged parents and teachers to attend to the laws of growth, health, and exercise. The *Boston Medical and Surgical Journal* and numerous educational publications did likewise. Catharine Beecher's popular *Physiology and Calisthenics for Schools and Families* (1856) included chapters on the circulatory and other systems of the body and described (with illustrations) schoolroom exercises for girls and boys.

During the last decades of the nineteenth century "physical training" was dominated by biomedical interests. Nine of the first ten presidents of the American Association for the Advancement of Physical Education (1885) were physicians. In his opening remarks at the 1889 Boston Conference on Physical Training U.S. Commissioner of Education William T. Harris referred to the importance of exercise and commented on its benefits. The conference was devoted mostly to discussing the several gymnastic systems (such as the German, Swedish, and American systems) then in vogue; sport was barely mentioned.

In the twentieth century games, SPORTS, and dance increasingly replaced formal gymnastic/calisthenic systems as the focus of the curriculum. Young people found games more appealing, and INTERSCHOLASTIC ATHLETICS (for boys) were gaining prominence. Most important from a pedagogical standpoint, proponents of PROGRESSIVE EDUCATION were emphasizing the importance of PLAY and games in psychosocial as well as physical development. *The Pedagogical Seminary*, which G. STANLEY HALL initiated in 1893, published many articles like LUTHER GULICK's "Psychological, Pedagogical, and Religious Aspects of Group Games." As did numerous other leaders of the emerging field of physical education, Gulick made important contributions to the YMCA, the Playground Association of America (1906), and other organizations that worked with children. In 1903 he established the New York City Public School Athletic League, which served as a model for similar organizations across the country. The focus of these was *educational athletics*, that is, sports for large numbers of boys and girls organized around developmental principles, not highly competitive athletics for the few.

Although they may seem similar, physical education and interscholastic/intercollegiate athletics differ in their goals and other significant ways. (The distinction was set down by Plato more than two thousand years ago.) Articles published in the *American Physical Education Review* (later called the *Re-*

search Quarterly for Exercise and Sport) in the early 1900s reflect the nature of concerns that have been repeated since then. By 1920, education *through* the physical was rapidly replacing education *of* the physical as the dominant ideology in physical education. Through the contributions of individuals like Dr. Thomas Denison Wood, physical education retained connections with health education, which emerged as a separate field following World War I. Thomas Storey, the nation's first State Director of Physical Education (New York in 1916), was among many who believed that the goals of school hygiene and physical education (which put textbook information into practice) were identical as the object of both was health. Similar views were expanded upon in *School Program in Physical Education* (1922), prepared for the N.E.A.'s Commission on the Revision of Elementary Education. *Physical Education in the Elementary School* (1951), published by the California State Department of Education, is an example of other extensive works that have provided teachers with information and described hundreds of games, rhythmic, and other activities adjusted for grades one through eight.

In the late 1800s research focused upon posture and studying physical growth by means of anthropometric measures. During the 1920s attention was directed to measuring physical efficiency (such as strength and coordination). *Motor Performance During Adolescence* (1940), published by the Society for Research in Child Development, launched important work in motor development. Following the enactment in 1975 of PL–142, physical educators produced important studies involving children with disabilities. After the 1970s the volume of research relevant to physical activity, children, and youth expanded enormously across several disciplines. Studies of children's anxiety in sport that appear in publications like the *Journal of Sport Psychology* may reflect growing tendencies for some youngsters to participate in highly organized competitive programs.

During the 1960s the daily high school physical education requirements that most states had enacted declined, in part due to the initiation of more elective subjects, which required flexible scheduling. The Presidents Council on Physical Fitness and Sports, created in 1955, reported in 1976 that fewer than forty percent of public school students participated in daily lessons. The Centers for Disease Control and Prevention's "Guidelines for School and Community Programs" (1997) point out that in spite of extensive evidence from PEDIATRICS, epidemiology, physiology, and other fields confirming its importance, large numbers of children and adolescents do not engage in regular physical activity. Other countries are reporting similar findings. The inactivity brought about by the attraction of TELEVISION and other electronic media is one reason for the decline. In addition, the attraction of high performance sports, in which relatively few children and youth participate, has drawn attention away (unintentionally) from the broad-based curricular and after-school intramural programs that physical educators once insisted form the basis of the schools' offerings.

See also: **Baseball; Basketball; Organized Recreation and Youth Groups; Playground Movement; Title IX and Girls' Sports.**

BIBLIOGRAPHY

Dauer, Victor P., and Robert P. Pangrazi. 1983. *Physical Education for Elementary School Children.* Minneapolis: Burges Publishing Company.

Gerber, Ellen W. 1971. *Innovators and Institutions in Physical Education.* Philadelphia: Lea and Febiger.

Hackensmith, Charles W. 1966. *History of Physical Education.* New York: Harper and Row.

Haley, Bruce 1978. *The Healthy Body and Victorian Culture.* Cambridge, MA: Harvard University Press.

Massengale, John D. and Richard A. Swanson, ed. 1997. *The History of Exercise and Sport Science.* Champaign, IL: Human Kinetics.

National Center for Chronic Disease Prevention and Health Promotion, Centers for Disease Control and Prevention. 1997. "Guidelines for School and Community Programs to Promote Lifelong Physical Activity Among Young People." *Journal of School Health* 67: 202–219.

Van Dalen, Deobold, and Bruce L. Bennett. 1971. *A World History of Physical Education, Cultural, Philosophical, Comparative.* Englewood Cliffs, NJ: Prentice-Hall.

INTERNET RESOURCE

American Alliance for Health, Physical Education and Dance. Available from <www.aahperd.org>.

ROBERTA PARK

Piaget, Jean (1896–1980)

Born on August 9, 1896, in Neuchâtel, Switzerland, Jean Piaget grew up among passionate intellectuals in a basically Protestant environment. At a very early age, he became interested in issues connected with natural science, philosophy, logic, metaphysics, and theology. After studying science and being awarded his doctorate in zoology in 1919 with a thesis on molluscs, he moved to psychology with the hope of developing new ways to study empirically the old philosophical question "What is knowledge?" To achieve this, he started exploring the world of childhood. He studied in Zurich and at ALFRED BINET's laboratory in Paris. In 1921, he was called to direct research at the Jean-Jacques Rousseau Institute at the University of Geneva by Edouard Claparède and his former teacher Pierre Bovet. He was a professor of philosophy at the University of Neuchâtel from 1925 to 1929 before becoming a professor of the history of scientific thought at the University of Geneva, where he remained until his death in 1980.

Piaget played an important part in the thinking of the active school movements, and became involved in the foundation of the International Bureau of Education, of which he was the first director. His research inquiries during that period (1920–1936) bear on logic in the child's thought and moral judgment, and on the originality of child development in a non-adult-centered perspective. From 1936 onward, he began collaborating with other researchers, notably Bärbel Inhelder and Alina Szeminska, who contributed to the enrichment of his critical interview method and to the gathering of a very rich collection of empirical data on children's cognitive development in the main areas of thinking. Piaget developed a theoretical model characterized by its focus on the child's own activity in a search for equilibrium and by an attempt to formalize the structures underlying the cognitive functioning of observed children at given ages. He described four main developmental stages: sensori-motor, preoperationals, concrete operations, and formal operations.

From 1952 to 1963, Piaget also taught psychology, including the psychology of childhood, at the Sorbonne in Paris. During that time, his research moved to encompass a wider understanding of knowledge development. In 1955 he founded the International Center for Genetic Epistemology, an interdisciplinary meeting point where he could discuss, with specialists from all over the world, his main preoccupation: "How is knowledge possible?" He compared ideas and facts, the philosophy of science and the observation of children, working out the fundamental principles of genetic epistemology. He pursued his empirical research on the genesis of knowledge with collaborators who inventively multiplied the tasks to be presented to children, and he offered a general constructivist theory explaining the order in which, according to his observations, phenomena are understood. According to Piaget, the first stage of development is *objectal*; that is, the young child concentrates on the supposed properties of objects and does not distinguish him- or herself from these objects. The next stage is *interobjectal* (the child is able to connect self, objects, and phenomena) and at the final stage, the child is able to think hypothetically and to go beyond the present appearance of objects, actions, and phenomena.

Jean Piaget was wary of any attempt to imprison the child's autonomous thinking with ready-made answers that would call on memory and docility rather than on intelligence and critical reflection. Piaget illustrated how knowledge is possible because learners actively strive for mastery and understanding. He offered evidence for a constructivist understanding of intelligence, that is, a view of cognitive development as not merely the fruit of biological maturation, or of simple cumulative self-experience, or of the direct interiorization of cultural transmissions, but an interplay of all of these different factors. Piaget's findings have become the basis for much research in teaching, cognitive psychology, remedial education, and socialization and have penetrated so deep into almost all higher education programs in education and psychology that they have become accepted as simply common sense for many.

See also: **Child Development, History of the Concept of; Child Psychology.**

BIBLIOGRAPHY

Piaget, Jean. 1952. *The Child's Conception of Number.* Trans. C. Gattegno and F. M. Hodgson. London: Routledge and Paul.

Piaget, Jean, et al. 1965. *The Moral Judgment of the Child.* Trans. Marjorie Gabain. New York: Free Press.

Piaget, Jean. 1971. *Biology and Knowledge: An Essay on the Relations Between Organic Regulations and Cognitive Processes.* Trans. Beatrix Walsh. Chicago: University of Chicago Press.

Piaget, Jean, and Bärbel Inhelder. 1969. *The Psychology of the Child.* Trans. Helen Weaver. New York: Basic Books.

INTERNET RESOURCE

The Jean Piaget Archives. Available from <www.unige.ch/piaget>.

ANNE-NELLY PERRET-CLERMONT
MARIE-JEANNE LIENGME BESSIRE

Pierce v. Society of Sisters

In *Pierce v. Society of Sisters*, the U.S. Supreme Court declared unconstitutional a 1922 Oregon law that compelled children aged eight to sixteen to attend not just a school, but the *public* schools. The Oregon compulsory public education law was sponsored by the Ku Klux Klan, Federated Patriotic Societies, the Masons, and smaller groups that appealed to white supremacist, anti-Catholic, anti-Semitic, and nativist beliefs. Drawing on popular anxieties, the reformers argued that private schools allowed un-American elements to persist, and that compelling attendance to public schools was the only way to assimilate these diverse masses to white American Protestant culture. This method was not unique to Oregon, but had emerged from the ideals of the COMMON SCHOOL movement of the mid-nineteenth century. The reform movement was able to win in Oregon partly because it gained support from the educational establishment of the state, including the *Oregon Teacher's Monthly* and a large proportion of public school teachers. In addition, Governor Walter Pierce had won his office through the support of the Ku Klux Klan, and he actively supported the law.

The bill helped align civil libertarians, Lutherans, Catholics, Adventists, Jews, and African Americans first against passage, and then against the constitutionality of the law. It seems likely that the KKK and their allies pushed the reform in Oregon because they held an overwhelming native white majority in the state, but there were also initiatives in other states awaiting the outcome of the court battle. The operators of two private schools, the Society of the Sisters of the Holy Name of Jesus and Mary and the Hill Military Academy, filed complaints, gained an injunction against the law from a lower court, and won in the U.S. Supreme Court in 1925. The decision rested on two basic principles of American law. First, the state cannot seize private property, or grant monopolies that will destroy livelihoods, unless it can show that a compelling public interest requires the action. Therefore, the state does not possess the power to put all the private schools out of business. Second, juvenile law must balance the will of the majority and parental authority.

Pierce is significant because it helped limit the power of the state to socialize children at a moment when this power was advancing. Writing for a unanimous court, Justice James C. McReynolds penned what has become an often-quoted phrase, "The child is not the mere creature of the state." It should be noted that *Pierce* was not decided on the basis of the rights of the child, but the rights of property owners and parents. It supported previous rulings such as *Meyer v. Nebraska* that had granted the state considerable power to exercise its interest to "foster a homogeneous people with American ideals." This assimilationist justification for public schooling still has standing in educational policy, but it has been challenged periodically since the 1940s.

See also: **Children's Rights; Education, United States; Law, Children and the; Parochial Schools.**

BIBLIOGRAPHY

Arons, Stephen. 1976. "The Separation of School and State: Pierce Reconsidered." *Harvard Educational Review* 46: 76–104.

Tyack, David, Thomas James, and Aaron Benavot. 1987. *Law and the Shaping of Public Education, 1785–1954.* Madison: University of Wisconsin Press.

PATRICK J. RYAN

Piggy Bank

Objects in which to collect coins have been found in Greek and Roman excavations. They were simple containers of clay or wood, usually pots and jars with slots, shaped by hand or turned on the wheel. To gain access to the contents of the bank, the owner would either have had to break it or slide the coins carefully out through the slot with the aid of a knife. The shapes of these banks changed little before the eighteenth century, when glazed earthenware (delftware) was introduced.

Piggy banks date from about the seventeenth century, when they were made of pottery. There is some debate about why the pig became a symbol of thrift. It is possible that it derives from *pygg*, the orange clay used to make pots in the Middle Ages. The name *pig* was probably retained after the clay stopped being used. Pigs were also considered to be symbols of good luck in many parts of the world.

In Germany and the Netherlands, piggy banks are given as good luck gifts and New Year presents. In the 1800s, England's Staffordshire potters made money boxes to meet the public's preference for rural scenes, castles, and flower-covered cottages. They were crude and simple but when decorated with glazes they became attractive ornaments, which were often displayed rather than used, although small ones were given to children to use.

American money boxes followed European patterns until the mid-nineteenth century, when they were made extensively of metal. Between 1870 and 1900, hundreds of cast-iron mechanical banks, often representing a topical, patriotic, or amusing scene, were made. Banks shaped like buildings were made to represent real banks. In Britain, pillar box savings banks were introduced in the late nineteenth century, and post office savings books, which could be locked, were issued. It was usual to give a child a savings bank as a birth or christening present. Thrift and the cultivation of wise savings habits were actively encouraged, while any inclination towards frivolous spending was discouraged. In the nineteenth century, working-class children who earned money helped to support their families with their earnings. Children who were better off received pocket money from visiting relatives, which was often supplemented by money paid for running errands and helping with household chores. In the pre-welfare state era before World War II (1939–1945) a firm control over one's finances was vital if one wished to acquire possessions and property of one's own; sometimes even one's survival depended on good financial housekeeping. Banks and building societies gave away money boxes to encourage saving. (This custom endured into the late twentieth century; the most famous of these building society money boxes were the National Westminster Bank's pigs of the 1980s.)

A variety of money boxes in different shapes and materials were available. New technology coupled with gradual improvements in lifestyle and increasing interest in child rearing prompted manufacturers to design more interesting shapes and colors, intended for children. Printed tin plate was often used for their manufacture in the 1920s and 1930s, and plastics were used to produce cheap money boxes after 1945. Many children had some pocket money. Attractive novelties were also made, which could be used as toys or as containers for sweets and cookies. These would often also be used as advertising tools for various companies. Brightly colored miniature vending banks rewarded children with a small treat when they put their money in and also encouraged saving.

Despite all these innovations, temptations, and computerized banking, the piggy bank remains the shape that children associate with special treats and with saving all over the world.

See also: **Allowances.**

BIBLIOGRAPHY

King, Constance Eileen. 1983. *Money Boxes: Antique Pocket Guide.* Guildford, UK: Lutterworth Press.

Moore, Andy, and Susan Moore. 1984. *The Penny Bank Book: Collecting Still Banks.* Philadephia: Schiffer.

HALINA PASIERBSKA

Placing Out

In 1607 the British Virginia Company commenced its colonization of the North American coastline with a settlement at Jamestown. Unfortunately, few of the early gentleman adventurers were personally amenable to the colossal physical challenges involved in creating settlements in the wilderness. With some urgency the authorities in London looked for sources of cheap labor, and many convicted felons were reprieved and despatched to Virginia. However, the demand for labor was insatiable and the available prison population proved insufficient. Sir Thomas Smythe, director of the Virginia Company, considered the possibilities of rounding up London "vagrants," that is, abandoned, illegitimate, and runaway children and teenagers—poor, idle, and normally male—and "placing them out" in the Americas as indentured servants.

In the seventeenth and eighteenth centuries, placing out children in the American colonies where labor was needed was popularly associated with either the criminal justice system or common kidnapping. The first hundred "vagrants" were despatched from the London area to Virginia in 1618, their passage arranged by the city fathers. The Privy Council legalized the dispatch of "vagrant and recalcitrant" children to Virginia on January 31, 1620. Two further groups were sent by 1623. The requirements of the colonial labor market were met, partly from the recruiting activities of religious enthusiasts and philanthropists, but mainly by the organized efforts of emigration agents, known as *spirits* in popular parlance. The term had pejorative overtones; the dark underside of normal indentured servant recruitment was kidnapping. It was easier to snatch young people than it was to suborn adults, and some children living near major ports were simply kidnapped for indentured service in the Americas.

Child migration (in English parlance) or placing out (the American usage) had a long and checkered history, almost always surrounded by controversy and scandal. It was, actually, never a single policy pursued continuously; rather it was a complex tangle of competing private schemes, government initiatives, charismatic personalities, muddled priorities, and confused agendas. It was critically affected by the economic, political, and social pressures of particular times. Placing out young people as servants or apprentices was common in Elizabethan and Jacobean England. Service was the norm for plebeian youth until they came of age or married. During the American War of Independence and the long Napoleonic wars, the British army and navy absorbed tens of thousands of teenagers and young men who would previously have found indentured service in the North American colonies.

After the wars, amid great social distress in Britain, two small philanthropic efforts were made to place children abroad. In the years 1830 through 1841, the Children's Friend Society sent some boys to the Cape Colony in South Africa and to Toronto in CANADA; and in the 1850s, Lord Shaftesbury supported the St. Pancras Board of Guardians sending a small number of teenagers to the British West Indies. In the 1850s, placing out at-risk children from the grim slums of east-coast American cities such as New York, Boston, and Baltimore was begun by the Reverend CHARLES LORING BRACE. The children were despatched in groups by rail on what were called ORPHAN TRAINS, to be fostered by families in the farming states of the Midwest. In the years 1854 to 1932, over 100,000 were placed out in this program.

Placing Out Peaks

Child migration to Canada peaked from the 1870s until the start of World War I and was triggered by desperate economic conditions over the previous few years: the social havoc caused by the 1866 cholera epidemic; the bad harvest of 1867; and widespread unemployment during a cyclic downturn in the economy. It was during this period that Annie Macpherson, Thomas Barnardo, and William Booth (the founder of the Salvation Army) commenced their work among the poorest and most destitute in the East End of London. To them, and to many other religious workers, emigration, including the forced migration of abandoned children, seemed the one certain way for the desperately poor to better themselves. Some eighty thousand children were sent to Canada during those years.

Child migration to the Australian states came toward the end of a long experience with the policy elsewhere. In the early twentieth century, new migration enthusiasts got involved, stressing that children should be trained in colonial orphanages before they were placed with colonial farmers. The dominating figure in this phase was Kingsley Fairbridge, who was offered land south of Perth by the Western Australian government in 1911 to pioneer his farm-school initiative. After an epic struggle Fairbridge and his supporters established their venture securely, and other farm schools followed in New South Wales and Victoria.

With the outbreak of World War I, migration from the British Isles was suspended, and when it recommenced in 1920, the numbers of children sent were never on the same scale. By 1920, powerful interest groups in Canada opposed the entry of unaccompanied juveniles and throughout the following decade child migration to Canada diminished. The Great Depression finally ended the program. As Canada barred the entry of unaccompanied juveniles, the voluntary societies focused their attention increasingly on AUSTRALIA, where, in the buoyant 1920s, governments favored their entry. Barnardo sent 872 children to New South Wales in the 1920s; Fairbridge continued his work and 918 children arrived in Western Australia during this period.

After World War II, nearly five hundred child migrants were brought to Australia, most of them under Catholic auspices and most sent to Western Australia. Thereafter, Fairbridge and Barnardo and many other groups brought in some children, but numbers remained small. Overall, about thirty-five hundred children came to Australia, around half of them to Catholic institutions. In 1950, Maltese child migrants were placed in orphanages in Western Australia. During the next decade some 280 boys arrived under this scheme. However, by this stage the enduring phenomenon in social engineering was becoming anachronistic. Times had changed; the social conditions and attitudes that had led to children being sent abroad were disappearing. Grinding poverty was being reduced and the social services of the welfare state were being extended, and it became the norm to care for children closer to home.

See also: **Apprenticeship; Foster Care; Orphans; Work and Poverty.**

BIBLIOGRAPHY

Corbett, Gail H. 2002. *Nation Builders: Barnardo Children in Canada.* Toronto: Dundum Press.

Holt, Marilyn. 1992. *The Orphan Trains: Placing Out in America.* Lincoln: University of Nebraska Press.

Sherington, Geoffrey, and Chris Jeffrey. 1998. *Fairbridge: Empire and Child Migration.* Nedlands: University of Western Australia Press.

BARRY M. COLDREY

Plato (427–348 B.C.E.)

Plato was born into an aristocratic Greek family in the fifth century B.C.E. Like all youngsters of his status, he initially intended to go into politics. In his twenties, he came into the circle of Socrates, who was to be the lasting influence on his thought. After the execution of Socrates on accusations of the corruption of youth, Plato abandoned direct involvement in politics and turned to writing and education. All his works are in the form of dialogues, in most of which the main speaker is Socrates (469–399 B.C.E.). In 385 B.C.E. he founded the Academy in Athens, the first known institution of research and higher learning in the Greek world, which he headed until the end of his life. Plato deals with childhood in the context of education. He discusses early education mainly in the *Republic*, written about 385 B.C.E., and in the *Laws*, his last work, on which he was still at work at the end of his life.

The State as an Educational Entity

Plato saw the state primarily as an educational entity. In the *Republic* he discusses the principles of a state that is based on knowledge and reason, personified in the philosopher, and not on mere opinion or desire for power. This state is a strict meritocracy, where the citizen body is divided into the functions (commonly but erroneously called "classes") of producers, auxiliaries (in charge of internal and external security), and philosophers, the last two jointly referred to as "guardians." This book is not so much a blueprint for a future state as a standard by which all states are to be measured. The *Republic* is concerned with the education of the guardians, but in the *Laws*, where Plato draws up an actual system of laws for a state conforming as much as possible to that standard, the same education is provided to all citizens, according to their abilities.

Plato devotes much attention to the education of the child as a future citizen. As such, he believes that the child belongs to the state and its education is the responsibility of the state (*Republic*, bk. 2, 376.). Education must be compulsory for all. State funds should pay for gymnasiums and for instructors, officials, and superintendents in charge of education, both cultural and physical (*Laws*, bk. 7, 764, 804, 813).

Plato is not concerned with training children for a trade but rather with giving them an education in virtue, which is to produce "a keen desire to become a perfect citizen who knows how to rule and be ruled" in turn (*Laws*, bk. 1, 643). Reason is man's true nature, but it has to be nurtured from childhood by irrational means. Education is thus the correct channeling of pains and pleasures (*Laws*, bk. 2, 653), aiming at establishing "a nature in which goodness of character has been well and truly established" so as to breed a familiarity with reason (*Republic*, bk. 3, 398, 401).

Prenatal and infant care. Plato recommends that the care of the soul and body of the child begin even before birth, with walks prescribed for the pregnant woman. The first five years of life see more growth than the next twenty, necessitating frequent and appropriately graduated exercise. Children should be kept well wrapped up for the first two years of life, but they should be taken to the country or on visits. They should be carried until they are old enough to stand on their own feet, which should happen by the age of three, to prevent subjecting their young limbs to too much pressure. The main importance of movement, however, lies in its influence on the early development of a well-balanced soul (*Laws*, bk. 7, 758–759), and the cultivation of the body is mainly for the soul's sake (*Republic*, bk. 3, 411).

Storytelling and literature. Storytelling is the main tool for the formation of character in Plato's view, and begins at an earlier age than physical training. Stories should provide models for children to imitate, and as ideas taken in at an early age become indelibly fixed, the creation of fables and legends for children, true or fictional, is to be strictly supervised. Mothers and nurses are not to scare young children with stories of lamentations, monsters, and the horrors of hell, to avoid making cowards of them. That some such stories are enjoyed as good poetry is all the more reason for keeping them away from children (or even grown men) who should be trained to be free and unafraid of death (*Republic*, bk. 2, 377–383).

Play. Plato believes that a child's character will be formed while he or she plays. One should resort to DISCIPLINE, but not such as to humiliate the child. There should be neither a single-minded pursuit of pleasure nor an absolute avoidance of pain—not for children and not for expectant mothers (*Laws*, bk. 7, 792). Luxury makes a child bad-tempered and irritable; unduly savage repression drives children into subserviency and puts them at odds with the world. Children and adults should not imitate base characters when playing or acting, for fear of forming a habit that will become second nature (*Republic*, bk. 3, 395).

Teachers must provide children with miniature tools of the different trades, so that they can use the children's games to channel their pleasures and desires toward the activities they will engage in when they are adults (*Laws*, bk. 1, 643). Children are to be brought together for games. The sexes are to be separated at the age of six, but girls too should attend lessons in riding, archery, and all other subjects, like boys. Similarly, both boys and girls should engage in dancing (for developing grace) and wrestling (for developing strength and endurance). Plato attached much importance to children's games: "No one in the state has really grasped that children's games affect legislation so crucially as to determine whether the laws that are passed will survive or not." Change, he maintained, except in something evil, is extremely dangerous, even in such a seemingly inconsequential matter as children's games (*Laws*, bk. 7, 795–797).

Physical education. "Physical training may take two or three years, during which nothing else can be done; for weariness and sleep are unfavorable to study. At the same time, these exercises will provide not the least important test of character" (*Republic*, bk. 7, 537). Children who are sturdy enough should go to war as spectators, if one can contrive that they shall do so in safety, so that they can learn, by watching, what they will have to do themselves when they grow up (*Republic*, bk. 5, 466; bk. 7, 537). Girls should be trained in the same way and learn horseback riding, athletics, and fighting in armor, if only to ensure that if it ever proves necessary the women will be able to defend the children and the rest of the population left behind (*Laws*, bk. 7, 804–805, 813).

Reading and writing, music, arithmetic. In Plato's educational system, a child, beginning at the age of ten, will spend three years on reading, writing, and the poets, and another three learning the lyre, and will study elementary mathematics up to the age of seventeen or eighteen, all with as little compulsion as possible, in order to learn "enough to fight a war and run a house and administer a state" (*Republic*, bk. 7, 535–541). Neither child nor father are to be allowed to extend or curtail that period, either out of enthusiasm or distaste. Children must work on their letters until they are able

to read and write, but any whose natural abilities have not developed sufficiently by the end of the prescribed time to make them into quick or polished performers should not be pressed (*Laws*, bk. 7, 810). The child's lessons should take the form of PLAY, and this will also show what they are naturally fit for. Enforced exercise does no harm to the body, but enforced learning will not stay in the mind (*Laws*, bk. 7, 536).

Family Control

In the *Republic* Plato abolishes the family for the guardians, to avoid nepotism and amassing of private wealth (*Republic*, bk. 5, 464). Wives and children are to be held in common by all, and no parent is to know his own child nor any child his parents—"provided it can be done" (*Republic*, bk. 5, 457). In the *Laws* Plato allows family raising for all citizens, with restrictions on child rearing and inheritance (*Laws*, bk. 5, sec. 729). Each family is to have only one heir, to avoid subdivision of the agrarian lots into small parcels. In cases where there is more than one child, the head of the family should marry off the females and the males he must present for adoption to those citizens who have no children of their own—"priority given to personal preferences as far as possible." If too many children are being born, measures should be taken to check the increase in population; and in the opposite case, a high birth-rate can be encouraged and stimulated (*Laws*, bk. 5, 740).

Plato stands at the fountainhead of Western philosophy. He established its themes and posed its problems. Plato's views on education have greatly influenced educational thought to this day and have become the basis of many educational policies. Such diverse thinkers as Montaigne, JEAN-JACQUES ROUSSEAU, JOHN DEWEY, John Stuart Mill, Nietzsche, and many others owe much to Plato's direct influence. His view of philosophy as an educational activity and of education as the development of reason, the responsibility of which lies squarely with the state, is still a living educational challenge.

See also: **Ancient Greece and Rome; Aristotle.**

BIBLIOGRAPHY

Marrou, Henri-Irénée. 1956. *A History of Education in Antiquity.* Trans. George Lamb. New York: Sheed and Ward.

Plato. 1941 [385 B.C.E.]. *The Republic of Plato.* Trans. Francis Macdonald Cornford. New York: Oxford University Press.

Plato. 1970 [348 B.C.E.]. *The Laws.* Trans. Trevor J. Saunders. Harmondsworth, UK: Penguin.

Scolnicov, Samuel. 1988. *Plato's Metaphysics of Education.* London: Routledge.

SAMUEL SCOLNICOV

Play

When considering the history of children's play, the very notion of when conceptions of childhood began must be con-

Pieter Brueghel the Elder depicts over ninety different games in *Children's Games* (1560), many of which would still be familiar to children in the twenty-first century, including hide-and-seek, leapfrog, and piggyback rides. © Francis G. Mayer/CORBIS.

sidered. Historian PHILIPPE ARIÈS, in his *Centuries of Childhood* (1962), contended that the idea of childhood did not exist in medieval society. Ariès also argued, however, that there was no clear separation of the world of adults and children prior to and during this period. He did not deny that children played among themselves or with adults. In fact, this entry examines play based on historical and contemporary studies from the fourteenth century through the late twentieth century. Although far from exhaustive, this work covers several distinct periods and highlights common themes in children's play over time.

Play in Medieval London

The best source on children's play in the fourteenth and fifteenth centuries is Barbara Hanawalt's 1993 book *Growing Up in Medieval London*. Hanawalt maintained that during this period children played ball and tag, ran races, rolled hoops, and engaged in role playing in imaginary parades, Masses, and marriages. Support for Hanawalt's claims came from court and coroner's records of injuries and deaths. For example, one young boy fell to his death when he climbed from a window to retrieve a ball from a gutter. In another case, a seven-year-old boy was climbing and jumping from timbers of wood with two other boys when a timber fell on him and broke his right leg. In her book, Hanawalt dramatizes the

story of eight-year-old Richard Le Mazon. Richard was on his way back to school after his midday meal when he joined his friends to play a popular but risky game—hanging by the hands from a beam that protruded out from the side of London Bridge. The boys competed to see who could swing out the farthest on the beam. Feeling brave, Richard swung far but, having forgotten to remove his school satchel from his back, he lost his grip due to the extra weight and fell to his death in the river.

Richard's death prevented him from participating in the boy-bishop celebration. This celebration was of special importance in the Middle Ages because it was reserved for children and coincided with St. Nicholas Day. St. Nicholas was considered the patron saint of children, and his feast day (December 6) marked the beginning of the Christmas season. The best or most favored scholar from each school would be elected to impersonate the bishop. The rest of the boys formed his clergy. The boys ousted the real bishop and took over for him, presiding over services and preaching the sermon. As Hanawalt notes: "It was one of those medieval, world-turned-topsy-turvy events. The boys, whose life seemed all discipline, were given a taste of power to discipline" (p. 79). The boy bishop and his clergy traveled in style, wearing ceremonial capes, rings, and crosses, and they

Children playing hopscotch at school, England, c. 1990s. Iona and Peter Opie chronicled the playground games and lore of mid-twentieth-century children in exhaustive detail. The Opies' studies showed that children possessed remarkably enduring traditions of games, stories, and expressions all their own. Jennie Woodcock; Reflections Photolibrary/CORBIS.

stopped at parish homes to receive offerings, meals, and gifts.

Hanawalt's work challenges notions that there was no clear conception of childhood at the time. It also shows that even though most children entered the world of adults and work at an early age, this did not mean there was no time for play. The study also, by its omission of specific references to the play of or special celebrations for girls, suggests that girls had far less autonomy and opportunities for play than boys. Girls were less likely to be educated, and their work inside and outside the home was probably more closely supervised.

Play in Eighteenth- and Nineteenth-Century America

Reports on the lives of slave children in the pre–Civil War South provide us some idea of how children played at that time, even in very oppressive conditions. Based on a belief that slaves would be more productive workers if they were not brought to the fields until early adolescence, slave children (especially boys) lived rather autonomous lives on the plantation. Lester Alston (1992) and David Wiggins (1985) captured these children's lives in their respective analyses of narratives collected from former slaves as part of the

1936–1938 Federal Writers' Project. According to these accounts, older slave women who were too frail to continue to work in the fields cared for the very young children. At the age of two or three, however, children joined a group of older youth who cared for them while they performed daily chores such as hauling water, fetching wood, tending gardens, and feeding livestock.

There was, however, more to these children's lives than chores and caretaking. They had some freedom to explore the physical world and to play. Older children especially had a good deal of autonomy. Most boys (and some girls) who had more stringent caretaking responsibilities made good use of their time by hunting and fishing during the day with peers and with their fathers at night. Not only were hunting and fishing enjoyable, but those activities also generated feelings of self-worth in the children because of their contributions to the family table.

Slave children engaged in both traditional and improvised play and games. As did the children of medieval London, slave children enjoyed dramatic role-playing. These children especially liked to emulate social events like church services, funerals, and auctions. One former slave recounted the game of auction, where one child would become the auctioneer and conduct a simulated slave sale. The fact that slave children knew early on that they themselves could be sold and separated from their families displays the power of such play for dealing with fears and anxieties. In another game, "Hiding the Switch," several children would look for a switch hidden by another child. The one who found the switch ran after the others attempting to hit (and some cases actually hitting) them. The relation of this game to the often brutal treatment of adult slaves should be obvious.

Slave children played a number of organized games, such as jump rope and various chasing games. They did not typically play elimination games like dodge ball or tag, however; if they did, they altered the rules. In a 1985 book, American historian David Wiggins links this finding to real fears among these children that members of their families (and eventually they themselves) could be sold or hired out at any time.

Historical studies have also been conducted of children's play with TOYS (especially DOLLS) from the mid-1850s until the turn of the century. According to a 1992 article by Miriam Forman-Brunell, doll play before the Civil War was rare; it often was linked to domestic training, such as teaching girls to sew. In the decades after the Civil War, however, adults encouraged middle- and upper-class girls "to imbue their numerous dolls with affect, to indulge in fantasy, and to display their elaborately dressed dolls at ritual occasions such as tea parties and while visiting" (Forman-Brunell, p. 108). Although girls adopted this attitude to some degree, they did not simply internalize adult values. To the contrary, girls often used their dolls for purposes other than practicing the skills of mothering. Contemporary autobiographical reports describe girls rebelling against holding sedate tea parties by sliding their dolls down banisters atop tea trays and turning tea parties into fights among their dolls. In addition, girls often physically punished their dolls for bad behavior.

Such behavior was seen by adults as the expression of repressed anger. In fact, adults encouraged a form of play that now might be considered horrific or at least in bad taste: the enactment of doll funerals. According to Forman-Brunell, doll funerals were more common than doll weddings among middle-class girls in the 1870s and 1880s. She notes that mourning clothes were packed in the trunks of French lady dolls, and that fathers constructed tiny coffins for their daughters' dolls. Such play was not seen as morbid; rather, it was viewed as helping to develop the comforting skills that often were needed at a time when many relatives and friends died young. The similarity of this type of play to the auctions of slave children is striking.

Girls often went further than enacting imaginary funerals, however; some created harrowing scenes of ritualized executions and gruesome fatal accidents. Again we see that the adult model for play was appropriated and embellished, not simply internalized.

David Nasaw's Children of the City, published in 1985, portrays the work and play of immigrant children in large cities from the late 1890s until about 1920. Nasaw's historical study (relying on records compiled by child reformers, oral histories, and autobiographies) shows that even poor children became active consumers in the booming economy of the period. Immigrant children engaged in many types of work (selling newspapers, candy, and personal items; making deliveries; scavenging; and caretaking) that contributed to the family's economic well-being. Despite this hard work, however, there was still time for play and for the development of a robust peer culture. Boys played ball, tag, and other games after school while they awaited the delivery of newspapers they would hustle for sale throughout the city. Children also took time out from scavenging in the dumps to forge make-believe battles and to play king-of-the-hill. Also children (mainly boys) held back from their parents small sums of their earnings to buy candy and watch movies, shown initially in nickelodeons and later in the first movie houses. Girls had less autonomy to play, since most of them assisted their mothers in the home with housework and the care of younger siblings. However, they were also given small allowances to purchase consumer items.

Play in Contemporary Times

Studies of children's play in the twentieth century moved from reliance on historical and indirect sources to direct observations and ethnographies of play from a variety of disciplinary perspectives. Much useful information was gleaned from anthropological and sociological studies of children's play and peer cultures. The most well-known observational studies are IONA AND PETER OPIE's The Lore and Language of Schoolchildren (1959) and Children's Games in Street and Playground (1969). These works included exhaustive details, in the tradition of descriptive folklore. Later work moved from detailed descriptions to a focus on children's actual engagement in play from a cross-cultural perspective. Much of this work was reviewed and evaluated in Helen Schwartzman's 1978 groundbreaking book Transformations: The Anthropology of Children's Play.

More recently, research on children's play has been tied theoretically and empirically to the notion of children's peer culture. In his 1997 book The Sociology of Childhood William Corsaro defines peer culture as "a stable set of activities or routines, artifacts, values, and concerns that children produce and share in interaction with peers" (1997, p. 95). Play is at the heart of peer culture.

Recent technological advances have enabled researchers to acquire audiovisual recordings of the fantasy play of three- to five-year-old children for intensive microanalysis. In preschools, spontaneous fantasy often develops around sandboxes or tables and in building and construction areas. The expectations children bring into these areas are not well defined. They know they will play with certain objects (toy animals, blocks, cars, and so on), but they seldom enter the areas with specific plans of action. The play emerges in the process of verbal negotiation; shared knowledge of the adult world, although referred to occasionally, is not relied upon continually to structure the activity.

In spontaneous fantasy, children use a number of identifiable communicative strategies which include: paralinguistic cues such as voice, intonation, and pitch; repetition; descriptions of actions; semantic linking of turns at talk; and gestures and movement of objects to structure the play as it unfolds. The play involves underlying themes important in children's lives and present in FAIRY TALES and children's films: danger and rescue, lost and found, and death and rebirth. The children do not simply produce copies of fairy tales or films, however, but they embellish existing stories and create new ones through highly creative improvisation. In fact, three- to five-year-old children are more skilled at creating, sharing, and enjoying fantasy play than are most older children and adults.

Children continue to enjoy and engage in dramatic role play. Children frequently display power, discipline, and authority in these games, as they gain a sense of control compared to their everyday lives when they are continually in a subordinate position to adults. Comparative studies of role play across cultures and social class groups show that children project to their future lives as adults; in the process, they adopt orientations that contribute to social perpetuation of class, race, and gender inequalities.

Children also produce spontaneous games with rules in order to identify and avoid monsters or threatening agents. Such play is attractive to children because it creates tension and fear, but it allows them always to be in control and to escape to safety. In fact, in such play, threatening agents are taunted and mocked as children gain control of real ambiguities and underlying fears in their lives.

In these various types of play, much has been made of the gender separation that begins when children are around six years of age and reaches its peak in the early years of elementary school. Such separation surely does occur; it is likely a reflection of differences in play preferences by gender and the organizational structure of the social institutions (especially schools) where children spend a great deal of their time. Some scholars have gone so far as to argue that there is a separate peer culture for boys and girls leading to clear gender differences in personality and social interactive styles. Others, however, relying on comparative studies of children of various races and classes, as well as analysis of children's actual play, have found that the gender relations, personality, and interactive style are much more complex. In most cases, gender separation is not nearly as complete as was often depicted in the past.

Finally, it is clear that children's play has been affected by what has been termed the "institutionalization of childhood": children's lives are increasingly scheduled and structured with less time available for spontaneous play. Also, with fewer siblings, children's increased time spent playing alone with the computer or video games suggests that advanced technology and the media more generally discourage collective play and dilute the creativity of children's peer cultures. Studies are needed to examine these trends more closely to estimate their effects and the possible consequences on the nature of children's play.

See also: **Indoor Games; Playground Movement; Street Games; Theories of Play.**

BIBLIOGRAPHY

Alston, Lester. 1992. "Children as Chattel." In *Small Worlds*, ed. Elliott West and Paula Petrik. Lawrence: University Press of Kansas.

Ariès, Philippe. 1962. *Centuries of Childhood*. Trans. Robert Baldick. New York: Knopf.

Corsaro, William A. 1993. "Interpretive Reproduction in Children's Role Play." *Childhood* 1: 4–74.

Corsaro, William A. 1997. *The Sociology of Childhood*. Thousand Oaks, CA: Pine Forge Press.

Evaldsson, Ann-Carita. 1993. *Play, Disputes, and Social Order: Everyday Life in Two Swedish After-School Centers*. Linköping, Sweden: Linköping University.

Forman-Brunell, Miriam. 1992. "Sugar and Spice: The Politics of Doll Play in Nineteenth-Century America." In *Small Worlds*, ed. Elliot West and Paula Petrik. Lawrence: University Press of Kansas.

Gilligan, Carol. 1982. *In a Different Voice: Psychological Theory and Women's Development*. Cambridge, MA: Harvard University Press.

Goldman, L. R. 1998. *Child's Play: Myth, Mimesis, and Make-Believe*. New York: Oxford University Press.

Goodwin, Marjorie H. 1998. "Games of Stance: Conflict and Footing in Hopscotch." In *Kids Talk: Strategic Language Use in Later Childhood*, ed. Susan Hoyle and Carolyn T. Adger. New York: Oxford University Press.

Hanawalt, Barbara. 1993. *Growing Up in Medieval London*. New York: Oxford University Press.

Nasaw, David. 1985. *Children of the City*. New York: Anchor Books.

Opie, Iona, and Peter Opie. 1959. *The Lore and Language of Schoolchildren*. New York: Oxford University Press.

Opie, Iona, and Peter Opie. 1969. *Children's Games in Street and Playground*. Oxford, UK: Clarendon Press.

Qvortrup, Jens. 1991. "Childhood as a Social Phenomenon: An Introduction to a Series of National Reports." *Eurosocial Report No. 36*. Vienna, Austria: European Centre for Social Welfare Policy and Research.

Sawyer, C. Keith. 1997. *Pretend Play as Improvisation: Conversation in the Preschool Classroom*. Mahwah, NJ: Lawrence Erlbaum Associates.

Schwartzman, Helen. 1978. *Transformations: The Anthropology of Children's Play*. New York: Plenum.

Seiter, Ellen. 1993. *Sold Separately: Parents and Children in Consumer Culture*. New Brunswick, NJ: Rutgers University Press.

Sutton-Smith, Brian. 1976. *The Dialectics of Play*. Schorndoff, Germany: Verlag Hoffman.

Thorne, Barrie 1993. *Gender Play: Girls and Boys in School.* New Brunswick, NJ: Rutgers University Press.

Wiggins, David. 1985. "The Play of Slave Children in the Plantation Communities of the Old South." In *Growing Up in America: Children in Historical Perspective*, ed. N. Ray Hiner and Joseph M. Hawes. Urbana: University of Illinois Press.

WILLIAM A. CORSARO

Playground Movement

In the summer of 1885 the Massachusetts Emergency and Hygiene Association (MEHA) placed a pile of sand in the yard of the Parmenter Street Chapel, a mission in Boston's North End. The pile was called a sand garden, and its purpose was to provide a supervised PLAY area for the immigrant children in the immediate vicinity. At first, an average of fifteen children came three mornings a week. They dug in the sand, made sand pies, sang songs, and had parades. The supervisors took the opportunity to instill desirable moral conduct during play.

The sand yard became such a popular magnet for the neighborhood kids that the following summer MEHA opened three more sand gardens. In 1887 the program expanded to eleven locations—one in a school yard. The Boston School Board gave MEHA permission to use vacant school yards during the summer as supervised play areas for very young children. MEHA changed the sand garden name to *playground* and began transferring the responsibility for operations to the school board and park commission. School yards and park playgrounds expanded their programs to include activities for older children.

The playground idea spread to other cities through the public media and communications between settlement house workers. In 1887 the New York State Legislature authorized the purchase of property in lower New York City (immigrant ghetto areas) for small parks. In 1888 Philadelphia formed the Small Parks Association to develop playgrounds, and in 1892 the Boston Park Commission made plans for playgrounds in the midst of dense populations citywide. JANE ADDAMS, of Chicago's Hull-House, designed a model playground in 1894 to advance a higher social morality among the participants in her settlement house activities.

In 1900, fourteen U.S. cities were sponsoring playgrounds. By 1906, the year the Playground Association of America (PAA) was formed in Washington, D.C., a movement was evident, with twenty-five cities having playground operations. By 1910, there were fifty-five cities with playground programs. Also by 1910, 113 colleges and universities were offering classes in "The Normal Course in Play," a recreation leadership curriculum developed by the PAA in 1909. These classes identified the personnel and types of programs needed to operate playgrounds effectively.

The playground idea became a movement because it was an effective instrument to attract children into a fun environment so as to teach them lessons in manners, morals, and sportsmanship. Playgrounds also were designed to be safe havens in which children could temporarily escape, through play, the dire circumstances of their urban environments. Throughout the 1920s and 1930s playgrounds, supervised and guided by rules and regulations, continued to be the responsibility of public school boards and parks and recreation departments.

Play was an effective means for facilitating learning. Many municipalities and reform-oriented agencies began using organized play as the nucleus for other youth sport and service programs aimed at developing character and fitness. The Public School Athletic League, Police Athletic League, and the youth services of the Young Men's Christian Association were such programs.

World War II devastated many urban areas in Western Europe and children in these areas began creating their own play space in bombed out areas in their neighborhoods, using whatever materials and equipment could be found. These pocket play areas sparked in the United States the idea of adventure playgrounds where children could use their imagination in creating their own play environments. The playground leader's role changed from supervisor to enabler, encouraging children to act on their own ideas of play.

Today, playgrounds are a multibillion dollar business, and design, construction, and operations are too diverse for any general description to be meaningful. The National Program for Playground Safety offers up-to-date information on all aspects of contemporary playgrounds.

See also: **Children's Spaces; Progressive Education; Sandbox; Social Settlements; Theories of Play.**

BIBLIOGRAPHY

Dickason, Jerry G. 1983. "The Origin of the Playground: The Role of the Boston Women's Clubs, 1885–1890." *Leisure Sciences* 6: 83–98.

Rainwater, Clarence E. 1922. *The Play Movement in the United States.* Chicago: University of Chicago Press.

Riess, Steven A. 1996. *City Games: The Evolution of American Urban Society and the Rise of Sports.* Urbana and Chicago: University of Illinois Press.

Sessoms, H. Douglas. 1993. *Eight Decades of Leadership Development.* Arlington, VA: National Recreation and Park Association.

INTERNET RESOURCE

National Program for Playground Safety. 2003. <www.uni.edu/playground>.

JERRY G. DICKASON

Police, Children and the

The police have often played ambiguous roles in the lives of children, acting both as agents of crime control and as unofficial providers of social welfare services. On the one hand, police have treated children and youths as potential criminals, seeking to regulate their behavior by intimidating them, arresting them, detaining them, referring them to courts, and sometimes using force on them. On the other hand, police have also treated children and youths as vulnerable urchins in need of protection. Police officers throughout the years have found lost children, safeguarded them from traffic, referred them to social agencies, and organized recreation for them.

Before the Police

Children and youths have always misbehaved and committed crimes, but in the early modern world, juvenile conduct was governed by families or by others acting in their stead rather than external agencies. In France, Italy, and other European countries between the sixteenth and eighteenth centuries, youths themselves sometimes regulated the behavior of others by parading publicly at night, mocking, harassing, and occasionally assaulting people who had violated moral or social norms. More commonly, parents or other adult authorities managed youthful misconduct. At the colleges and academies of seventeenth- and eighteenth-century France, teachers did their best to manage student duels and mutinies against school authority. Most often in urban Europe, a system of APPRENTICESHIP governed youth. Masters fed, housed, and taught trades to their sons and other young men, and in return these youths accepted their masters' moral authority for as long as they remained in that household. And in both England and the American colonies, authorities depended directly on families to correct wrongdoing. In seventeenth-century Massachusetts, magistrates regularly returned young offenders to their families for court-mandated whippings or punishments.

In the eighteenth century, these familial and household controls began to break down. Migration brought increased poverty to the cities of Europe and America, while the apprenticeship system deteriorated as an increasingly commercial and manufacturing-oriented economy made older trades less viable. Commentators noted a rising number of poor and vagrant children and youths visible in the streets of urban centers such as London and Philadelphia, and worried that they were turning to petty theft to survive. By the early nineteenth century, traditional mechanisms of control no longer seemed adequate to restrain a rising tide of crime and disorder in European and American cities. In response, public agencies—both state authorities and private philanthropies—assumed responsibility for regulating misconduct. States created penitentiaries for adult criminals, but nineteenth-century reformers assumed a special responsibility for wayward young offenders and thus established separate Houses of Refuge for youths, first in New York in 1825 and subsequently in Boston in 1826 and in Philadelphia in 1828. The creation of the modern police in American cities in the mid-nineteenth century represents part of a larger process of building a criminal justice system.

The Nineteenth Century

Police departments are innovations of the nineteenth and twentieth centuries. London's Metropolitan Police, considered the first modern police department, was founded in 1829. Boston established the first police force in the United States in 1838. New York followed suit in 1845 and Chicago in 1855. According to historian Wilbur R. Miller, modern police organizations were defined by their efforts to prevent crime rather than to detect it after the fact, to establish a centralized administration, to conduct full-time day and night patrols, and to wear visible symbols of authority such as badges and uniforms.

In the nineteenth-century United States, police forces were primarily urban institutions, oriented more toward service than toward crime control. Police officers—all male, and usually working-class whites drawn from the same first- and second-generation immigrant neighborhoods that they policed—performed their jobs mainly by walking beats. Our most detailed understanding of what patrolmen actually did comes from the 1895 diary of one Boston officer, Stillman Wakeman. Rather than devoting his time to enforcing the law or making arrests, Wakeman more regularly mediated neighborhood disputes. In particular, he dealt with youth when local home owners and storekeepers complained to him about boys breaking windows, setting fires, and committing petty thefts. Wakeman gauged his response according to the circumstances. Sometimes he made boys cease misbehaving; at others he forced them to apologize to their victims; only in the most extreme cases did he arrest the boys and bring them to court.

When police interacted with younger children, they mainly provided social services. Policemen aided children hurt in accidents involving wagons, trains, and public transportation by investigating what caused the incidents and ensuring that injured children received medical aid. Police also recovered lost children. In large and impersonal late-nineteenth-century cities, families could easily lose track of young children whom they allowed to play unsupervised and often turned to the police for help. Every year, urban police departments recovered and returned home hundreds of children, generally under age ten.

Police monitored older children in ways that combined social service and law enforcement functions. Beginning in 1883, for example, the Detroit police assigned men to serve as truant officers to enforce Michigan's compulsory education law. The stated purpose for this work was to prevent boys lacking "proper control" from drifting into crime. Likewise, urban police supervised boys working in street trades. In the 1890s, police officials in Pittsburgh expressed concern that street employment—particularly work as messengers—forced boys to frequent pool halls and brothels, and exposed them to gambling, drinking, and vice. Similarly, police officials worried that girls engaged in street trades (such as selling newspapers) had taken the first step toward prostitution. In short, police sought to exercise control over street arabs because they regarded them as both potential victims of degradation and as potential perpetrators of crime.

Police often enforced the law in an extralegal, discretionary manner, with adolescents as well as with adults. Nineteenth-century police used violence as a means of control, even against youth. Making arrests required that police subdue suspects and transport them to the station, so officers sometimes preferred to simplify matters and punish offenders themselves. In particular, police used violence to reprimand youth, believing that it deterred teenagers from future crime. As late as the 1920s, Chicago policemen boasted that they routinely corrected young offenders by physically abusing them and letting them go.

At the turn of the century, urban police also acquired a reputation for arresting youth arbitrarily. In an 1884 study of Chicago law enforcement, future Illinois governor John Peter Altgeld reported that police detained hundreds of boys each year for sleeping in public, mainly to deter future mischief. Even so, children constituted a small portion of total arrests. In 1890s Detroit, for example, David Wolcott (2003) reports that boys and girls under age seventeen represented less than one in ten total arrests. Like urban populations as a whole, youths arrested were typically the children of working-class and immigrant parents. They were arrested for a mix of minor property crimes and offenses defined by their status as juveniles (such as truancy or curfew violations). When police did arrest children and youth, however, they sought to protect them by keeping them out of courts or jails, instead turning them over to their parents or social service agencies far more often than they did adults.

The Twentieth Century

In the twentieth century, police underwent a long-term process of professionalization that reshaped their interactions with children and youth. In the 1910s, police administrators such as Richard Sylvester in Washington, DC, and August Vollmer in Berkeley, California, began to encourage greater centralization, more officer training, greater specialization, recruitment of better-educated officers, and a new orientation toward legal norms. More generally, they sought to shift the function of urban police away from providing social services (such as finding lost children) in favor of more efficient crime control.

The creation of JUVENILE COURTS—first in Chicago in 1899 and subsequently in most major cities by 1910—changed the legal and institutional context in which police dealt with children. Early advocates of juvenile courts such as Chicago activists Julia Lathrop and Timothy Hurley based their arguments in part on criticism of urban police. They maintained that police and courts detained children in jails together with adults, tried them before unsympathetic magistrates, and unnecessarily exposed them to danger and corruption. Juvenile courts were designed to remove children from the criminal justice system and instead offer individualized treatment, either via probation or in reform schools. One purpose of juvenile courts was to reduce the influence that police exercised over youth.

In fact, the new juvenile courts did not fully remove the police from the emerging JUVENILE JUSTICE system. Police remained the primary source of complaints, arrests, and referrals to juvenile courts. Most big-city police departments designated specialized juvenile bureaus to investigate complaints about children and to work closely with juvenile courts. These officers determined which cases required hearings and which cases police could decide on their own. Essentially, they screened juvenile court caseloads (usually with the court officials' approval). In the early twentieth century, police juvenile bureaus resolved a majority of complaints without court hearings. Additionally, police exercised authority over youth by deciding whether to detain young offenders following arrests but prior to court hearings. Even in jurisdictions such as Los Angeles, where juvenile courts were legally in charge of detention decisions, police juvenile bureaus made recommendations that were almost always implemented.

Police departments also developed innovations aimed at addressing the distinctive needs of female juvenile offenders. Departments hired female officers whose primary duty was to safeguard girls from the perceived threat of urban vice. The first policewoman was appointed in Portland, Oregon, in 1905, but the 1910 appointment of social worker Alice Stebbins Wells to the Los Angeles Police Department began a national movement for women police. Wells and policewomen like her, hired at the insistence of women's civic organizations, sought to appropriate police authority to expose immorality, to regulate commercial amusements, and to rescue girls whom they viewed as sexually vulnerable. Most big-city police departments hired policewomen by 1920, but until the 1970s usually defined their roles merely as supervising teenage girls and young children, thus marginalizing women within policing.

In the 1920s and 1930s, however, a number of departments did seek to professionalize the traditional connection between social services and crime control by establishing new "crime prevention" programs for youth. Berkeley's Vollmer proposed that authorities should intervene aggressively into the lives of "predelinquent" youth. Police, Vollmer argued in 1919, should not only enforce laws, but also act as social workers in order to prevent children from becoming delinquents and criminals. By monitoring everyday behavior, police could identify troubled youth and refer them to treatment agencies. To implement these ideas, Vollmer established a "coordinating council" of police, court officials, educators, and social workers to share information about at-risk youth and to determine the most efficient means of intervention. These plans achieved their fullest implementation in Los Angeles in the 1930s, where the police established large-scale recreation and mentoring programs and participated in a county-wide coordinating council. Similarly, the New York Police Department established its well-known Police Athletic League in 1932 to organize SPORTS and activities. These crime prevention programs were directed mainly at boys, seeking to establish masculine bonds between police and youth.

In the 1930s, police also emphasized fighting crime among youth. In light of highly publicized crime sprees by well-known bandits and strong rhetoric from law enforcement officials such as FBI director J. Edgar Hoover, public concerns over serious crime surged in the Depression-era United States. In response, police priorities de-emphasized providing social services in favor of arresting and punishing offenders, even if they were juveniles. In addition, as African Americans migrated to northern industrial cities and Hispanics migrated to the urban West, police increasingly blamed these groups for crime and delinquency, and increasingly targeted them for arrest. In 1930s Los Angeles, police shifted from arresting juveniles mainly for minor property crimes and status offenses to arresting them for felonies. In addition, they disproportionately arrested African Americans and Hispanics, rounding up groups of young men or pulling over youths in automobiles on the suspicion that the vehicle had been stolen.

In the decades following World War II, the social service and crime control functions of policing youth coexisted in an uneasy balance. Police departments maintained separate juvenile divisions and continued to offer character-building programs, mainly for boys. Filtering young offenders out of juvenile courts and referring them to social service agencies had become a standard duty for police within the juvenile justice system. Participant–observer studies such as those of Donald Black and Albert Reiss and of Robert Lundman found that, in the postwar decades, complaints about mischief and petty theft remained the main cause of police interaction with youth, much as they had in the 1890s. At the same time, juvenile crimes began to be perceived as more like those of adults. In the postwar decades, both boys and girls increasingly participated in gangs, took DRUGS, and committed violent offenses. Although police continued to incorporate social service functions into their work with children, the demands of crime control more and more determined the nature of police interactions with youth in the latter half of the twentieth century.

See also: **Delinquency; Guns; Law, Children and the; School Shootings and School Violence; Street Arabs and Street Urchins; Teen Drinking; Youth Gangs.**

BIBLIOGRAPHY

Appier, Janis. 1998. *Policing Women: The Sexual Politics of Law Enforcement and the LAPD.* Philadelphia: Temple University Press.

Ariès, Philippe. 1962. *Centuries of Childhood: A Social History of Family Life.* New York: Knopf.

Black, Donald J., and Albert J. Reiss, Jr. 1970. "Police Control of Juveniles." *American Sociological Review* 35: 63–77.

Escobar, Edward J. 1999. *Race, Police, and the Making of a Political Identity: Mexican Americans and the Los Angeles Police Department, 1900–1945.* Berkeley: University of California Press.

Haller, Mark H. 1976. "Historical Roots of Police Behavior: Chicago, 1890–1925." *Law and Society Review* 10: 303–323.

Kelling, George L. 1987. "Juveniles and the Police: The End of the Nightstick." In *From Children to Citizens, Volume II: The Role of the Juvenile Court,* ed. Francis X. Hartmann. New York: Springer-Verlag.

Liss, Julia, and Steven Schlossman. 1984. "The Contours of Crime Prevention in August Vollmer's Berkeley." *Research in Law, Deviance, and Social Control* 16: 79–107.

Lundman, Robert J., Richard E. Sykes, and John P. Clark. 1979. "Police Control of Juveniles: A Replication." *Journal of Research in Crime and Delinquency* 18: 74–91.

Mennel, Robert M. 1973. *Thorns and Thistles: Juvenile Delinquents in the United States, 1825–1940.* Hanover, NH: University Press of New England.

Miller, Wilbur R. 1999 [1973]. *Cops and Bobbies: Police Authority in New York and London, 1830–1870.* Columbus: Ohio State University Press.

Monkkonen, Eric H. 1981. *Police in Urban America, 1850–1920.* New York: Cambridge University Press.

Von Hoffman, Alexander. 1992. "An Officer of the Neighborhood: A Boston Patrolman on the Beat in 1895." *Journal of Social History* 26: 309–330.

Walker, Samuel. 1977. *A Critical History of Police Reform.* Lexington, MA: D. C. Heath.

Wolcott, David. 2001. "'The Cop Will Get You': The Police and Discretionary Juvenile Justice, 1890–1940." *Journal of Social History* 35: 349–371.

Wolcott, David. 2003. "Juvenile Justice before Juvenile Court: Cops, Courts, and Kids in Turn-of-the-Century Detroit." *Social Science History* 27: 111–138.

DAVID WOLCOTT

Polio

Poliomyelitis, or infantile paralysis, is a virus disease affecting the central nervous system. The infection passes from person to person by the fecal-oral route. Throughout most of human history the polio virus was ubiquitous and infected almost all children as soon as they were weaned from breast milk to a mixed diet, but infection caused symptoms in only a small minority. Infants exposed to the polio virus when they were first weaned retained some residual maternal immunity, or else the virus was less virulent before the early twentieth century when the disease began occurring in EPIDEMICS of paralytic poliomyelitis. For either or both of these reasons, the infection usually passed unnoticed since it caused neither symptoms nor signs.

Early History

Poliomyelitis occurs when the virus invades the nervous system and attacks nerves that activate muscle movement, but in many cases infection with the polio virus causes no signs or symptoms at all. The symptoms include fever, headache, and muscle pains, rapidly followed by the onset of localized muscle paralysis, which is permanent. Depending on which nerves are attacked—that is, which muscles are paralyzed—the outcome varies from mild weakness of part of an arm or leg to death if nerves in the brain stem that control muscles required for breathing and swallowing are paralyzed. Until about the 1920s polio was a disease of infants and young children, but older children, adolescents, and adults occasionally got it too. When a limb was paralyzed in childhood, the muscles wasted away and the limb did not continue to develop at the same rate as that on the unaffected side, leading to a shriveled arm or leg or some worse deformity, depending upon the severity of the disease.

We know that poliomyelitis has existed for thousands of years. A stone carving from Egypt, dated about 1500 B.C.E., shows a youth with the deformed shrunken leg that is characteristic of polio and has virtually no other possible cause. The old name for the disease, infantile paralysis, recalls the time when it was primarily a disease of infants and very young children and its outcome was paralysis of the affected muscles. Both the little crippled boy who could not follow the Pied Piper of Hamelin and Tiny Tim in Charles Dickens' classic *A Christmas Carol*, were probably victims of infantile paralysis. Because of its fecal-oral transmission route and because of ecological factors such as the prevalence of flies to carry fecal contamination to food in summer, poliomyelitis was always predominantly a summertime disease.

Polio Epidemics

When standards of domestic HYGIENE and environmental sanitation began to improve in the rich nations of Europe and North America after the sanitary reforms of the late nineteenth and early twentieth centuries, infants often escaped infection and the disease began to have a greater impact on older children, adolescents, and young adults, and began to occur in epidemics. Repeated epidemics affecting significant numbers of children, adolescents, and young adults became commonplace in North America, Europe, and Australia early in the twentieth century.

These epidemics had dramatic effects on family life and society at a time when INFANT MORTALITY and family size were declining. The life and health of every child seemed more precious to most people than perhaps it had in the days when it was an accepted fact of life that a great many newborn infants did not survive. And it was almost as bad for parents to see their children struck down by a disease that left them crippled as to see them die. Parents sometimes took extraordinary precautions to protect their children. Polio was known to be due to an infectious pathogen but until the 1950s it was not known how this pathogen was transmitted. In the large epidemics of the 1930s and 1940s, schools, cinemas, public swimming pools, and sports arenas were closed,

perhaps reinforcing a mood of mass anxiety bordering on hysteria that the size and true impact of these epidemics did not justify. The epidemics were in fact numerically small in comparison to the great epidemics of cholera, typhus, and smallpox of the nineteenth century.

The Medical Response

The medical response was more rational. Special hospital facilities were developed to deal with the care of children and young adults with paralyzed respiratory muscles. Modern intensive-care nursing and specialized intensive care units evolved from the early treatment of severe epidemic poliomyelitis, which was still often called infantile paralysis. Cecil Drinker (1887–1956), an American physiologist, invented a respirator commonly known as an iron lung, in which children with paralyzed respiratory muscles were nursed, often for many months or even years, and their breathing was maintained by means of a pistonlike device that kept air pressure below atmospheric level, expanding the chest as air was sucked into the lungs. The machines, the intensive nursing care that was required with them, the prolonged aftercare with skilled physiotherapy, and appliances to assist paralyzed people to get about, were costly. When Franklin Delano Roosevelt was struck down with severe polio in 1921, the disease and its expensive treatment and aftercare acquired a high public profile. The charitable foundation March of Dimes, founded in 1935, was born in a wave of massive public sympathy for the young victims of infantile paralysis. Unlike other charitable foundations of that time, the March of Dimes relied on innumerable small donations rather than a few large ones, and in this way it was able to raise enough money not only to pay for many of the expensive treatment facilities but also to invest in research.

Research focused partly on improved treatment and rehabilitation methods, but it was much more important to find a way to prevent the disease. This required discovery of the causative organism, epidemiological studies to elucidate the way polio was spread, and development of ways to prevent the spread and immunize infants and children. All these advances were among the achievements of medical science in the first half of the twentieth century. The virus responsible for the infection was discovered in 1908 by the Austrian microbiologist Karl Landsteiner (1868–1943) and the discovery was confirmed in 1910 by Simon Flexner (1863–1946) at the Rockefeller Institute in New York. These discoveries, in the early years of virology, were based on inference as much as on direct observation.

Development of a vaccine to protect against infection could not begin until ways to cultivate the virus artificially were developed. Before this happened, several therapeutic innovations emerged, sometimes with unhappy consequences. Vaccine trials in 1935, using convalescent human serum, may actually have enhanced the risk of paralytic polio and may also have transmitted other virus diseases such as hepatitis. Sister Elizabeth Kenny, an Australian nurse, advocated movement and massage of affected limbs, in contrast to the then-orthodox procedures of immobilization for prolonged periods. Her ideas were theoretically sound but in practice sometimes did more harm than good.

The first important breakthrough on the way to developing polio vaccines was the work by John Enders (1897–1985) and colleagues, who successfully grew the polio virus in tissue cultures in 1949. Jonas Salk (1914–1995) used tissue cultures of polio virus to produce the first successful vaccine that could provide immunological protection against poliomyelitis. The Salk vaccine was tested in the early 1950s and licensed for general use in 1955. The Salk vaccine had to be given by injection and was sensitive to temperature extremes. Albert Sabin (1906–1993) developed a vaccine that used live attenuated polio virus, which could be orally administered as a drop of vaccine on the tongue (or on a sugar lump) and was better able to withstand tropical temperatures; the Sabin vaccine came into general use around 1960 and superceded the Salk vaccine, despite the small (and mostly theoretical) risk that the live virus vaccine might mutate under some circumstances into a more virulent strain that could cause paralytic poliomyelitis.

The use of polio vaccines has virtually eliminated poliomyelitis from much of the world. The disease was declared eradicated from the western hemisphere in 1994. It remains a risk in low-income countries in Africa and Asia and among small groups of people such as members of certain religious sects who for reasons connected with their faith refuse to accept vaccination against poliomyelitis and other diseases.

See also: **Contagious Diseases; Vaccination.**

BIBLIOGRAPHY

Paul, J. R. 1971. *A History of Poliomyelitis.* New Haven: Yale University Press.

Robbins, F. C. 1999. "The History of Polio Vaccine Development." In *Vaccines,* 3rd edition, ed. S. A. Plotkin and W. A. Orenstein. Philadelphia: Saunders.

Zuber, P. L. F. 2002. "Poliomyelitis." In *Encyclopedia of Public Health,* ed. L. Breslow, B. D. Goldstein, L. W. Green, et al., pp. 932–933. New York: Macmillan.

JOHN M. LAST

Posture

The modern history of children's posture involves an important episode of intense concern, followed by an equally interesting relaxation. Around 1900 American parents were told to devote a great deal of attention to the posture training of their children, but roughly fifty years later the campaign was receding dramatically. Posture history in other societies remains to be traced, but the beginnings of modern posture standards in Western Europe emerged in the seventeenth and eighteenth centuries, as part of the growing concern about precise MANNERS and body discipline in the middle and upper classes. Children, and particularly boys, were urged to hold themselves erect. While most boys did not serve in the military, growing attention to formal military training may have played a role in the wider posture concern.

Books about manners dealing with children's posture spread to North America by the 1760s and 1770s. Middle-class Americans such as John Adams began to write about their concern for proper carriage of the body, so that social relationships would not be troubled by slouching or twitching. These new posture standards became a regular part of child-rearing advice through the nineteenth century, as a means to help children grow up to be respectable. Proper posture began to denote self-discipline. Doctors supported the movement, arguing that good posture was essential for proper health. At the same time, there is no indication that many people worried greatly about posture training, except perhaps in urging children to sit up straight at the dinner table. Rigid furniture and stiff clothing for formal occasions, including corseting of young women, helped maintain posture without too much effort.

This situation changed at the end of the nineteenth century, as a flurry of posture advice emerged. Doctors stepped up their campaign, arguing that a number of modern conditions, including cramped school desks, were leading to widespread physical deformity. More important still was the emergence of posture testing and training in the schools, backed by a growing body of physical education instructors. An American Posture League was formed early in the twentieth century, staffed mainly by the physical education group. Posture kits allowed teachers to evaluate children's posture. A number of school districts set up active posture programs, involving thousands of children. Children identified with bad posture were sent to a variety of remedial lessons, and in severe cases physical devices were imposed to straighten the body. More informally, habits such as walking with a book on the head gained in popularity as a means of acquiring attractive posture. The posture movement spread to American colleges in the 1920s, particularly for women. Schools like Vassar actively tested the posture of all entrants, often photographing them, and mandatory courses included posture training.

Several factors propelled this striking new concern. First, clothing and furniture became looser and more relaxed, and the posture programs were deliberately set in this context, seeking more generally to compensate for the growing indulgence of modern life. Second, the professional self-interest of doctors and physical education instructors supported what was a sincere but obviously advantageous interest in convincing parents and children that most young people suffered from posture defects. Third, the posture program served as an expression of anxiety about a number of more general features of modern society, including compulsory schooling and the lures of consumerism. Posture standards were now imposed quite widely, and not just for the respectable middle classes, though elite colleges developed a special concern. The democratization of standards was juxtaposed with concerns about immigrants and the need to use school programs to help bring their children into line.

By the 1940s the posture movement was past its peak. National associations disappeared. School programs were dropped or diluted. By the 1960s, doctors began to attack the old posture anxieties as false and misleading; few children had posture problems, according to the new wisdom, and those that did could be helped through medical treatments. Posture interests did not fade entirely, however. Interview manuals of college students still included reminders about good posture, and conservatives continued to lament the slouching of modern young people as part of their claims that character standards were deteriorating. In general, however, presenting oneself in a relaxed, informal mode replaced stiff posture as the expression of choice for American young people.

See also: **Child-Rearing Advice Literature.**

BIBLIOGRAPHY

Kasson, John F. 1990. *Rudeness and Civility: Manners in Nineteenth-Century Urban America.* New York: Hill and Wang.

Roodenburg, Herman. 1997. "How to Sit, Stand or Walk: Toward a Historical Anthropology of Dutch Paintings." In *Looking at Seventeenth-Century Dutch Art: Realism Reconsidered,* ed. Wayne Franits. New York: Cambridge University Press.

Yosifon, Davis, and Peter N. Stearns. 1996. "The Rise and Fall of American Posture." *American Historical Review* 103: 317–344.

PETER N. STEARNS

Potter, Beatrix (1866–1943)

Helen Beatrix Potter was born in South Kensington, London, on July 28, 1866. She was the first child of Rupert Potter, a barrister, and Helen Leech Potter. To avoid confusion with her mother, young Helen Beatrix was called Beatrix, or often, just B. Beatrix's parents were quite wealthy and absorbed themselves in the social life of London, while Beatrix lived a quiet life at home under the guardianship of a governess. Beatrix was left to find her own amusement. She spent her time tending to her many PETS, while also studying and drawing them.

During summers, Beatrix traveled with her parents to their country home. The plants and animals fascinated her, and she found it difficult to return to London after the freedom offered by the countryside. Influenced by the preservationist views of family friend Hardwicke Rawnsley, Beatrix's love for the beauty of nature and its animals continued to grow deeper. In her mid-teens Beatrix began keeping a journal. She wrote it in a simple code that remained undeciphered for over eighty years. As the years passed, her journal increasingly revealed that Beatrix was emerging from her cloistered, lonely childhood. She never neglected her animals and her paintings, however. Rawnsley continued to encourage her drawing, and Beatrix made a series of greeting cards and began work on a book. He encouraged her to publish. After failing to find a publisher, Potter privately published 250 copies in 1901. Only after these copies sold did Frederick Warne publish *The Tale of Peter Rabbit* in 1902.

Over the next decade, Beatrix wrote and illustrated more than twenty books for children, including such favorites as *The Tale of Benjamin Bunny* (1904), *The Tale of Jemima Puddle-Duck* (1908), and *The Tale of Mr. Tod* (1912). Many of her stories take place in the actual country locations where Beatrix spent time during her childhood. Several qualities of Beatrix Potter's books set her apart from other children's authors and illustrators. Her integration of story and illustration remains unmatched in CHILDREN'S LITERATURE. Her recognition of the beauty of animals, and her ability to convey it truthfully set her illustrations apart from the grotesque, caricature-like images typical of most animal stories for young children during the Victorian era. Potter was acutely aware of the fact that it was unnecessary to make her animal characters humorous or exaggerated in order to tell her story. Her books also reveal her love of the countryside and her appreciation of its natural beauty. They are marked by an absence of sentimentality and reflect the realities of nature with subtly ironic humor. Lastly, Beatrix Potter's books were innovative in their unique size. They were small enough for a child to hold and were easily transportable. Unlike the typically large and elaborate children's books of the period, Potter's were clearly for children, rather than for parents to read to children. Also, each book cost only a shilling, and thus children from all backgrounds could enjoy the world of Beatrix Potter.

In 1913 Beatrix Potter married William Heelis, a solicitor. With her marriage began the next stage of her life. Her creative period came to an end, aside from the publication of miscellaneous sketches and notes that lacked the charm and poetry of her earlier works. Beatrix and William Heelis lived a simple yet happy and comfortable life. She spent much of her time hill-farming and acting as president of the Herdwick Sheepbreeders' Association. Beatrix also focused her efforts toward acquiring as much Lake District property as possible for the National Trust. Beatrix Potter died on December 22, 1943, at the age of seventy-seven. To this day her works are widely read, and she is remembered as one of the most beloved children's authors and artists of all time.

See also: **Victorian Art.**

BIBLIOGRAPHY

Battrick, Elizabeth. 1987. *The Real World of Beatrix Potter*. London: The National Trust.

The Beatrix Potter Papers at Hill Top: A Catalogue of the Manuscripts, Miscellaneous Drawings and Papers at Hill Top, Sawrey. 1987. London: The National Trust.

Crouch, Marcus. 1960. *Beatrix Potter*. London: Bodley Head.

Grinstein, Alexander. 1995. *The Remarkable Beatrix Potter*. Madison, CT: International Universities Press.

Hobbs, Anne Stevenson. 1989. *Beatrix Potter's Art*. London: Frederick Warne.

Hobbs, Anne Stevenson, and Joyce Irene Whalley. 1985. *Beatrix Potter, the Victoria and Albert Collection: The Leslie Linder Bequest of Beatrix Potter Material, Watercolours, Drawings, Manuscripts, Books, Photographs and Memorabilia*. London: The Victoria and Albert Museum and Frederick Warne.

Jay, Eileen, Mary Noble, and Anne Stevenson Hobbs. 1992. *A Victorian Naturalist: Beatrix Potter's Drawings from the Armitt Collection*. London: Frederick Warne; New York: Penguin.

Lane, Margaret. 1946. *The Tale of Beatrix Potter: A Biography*. London: Frederick Warne.

Linder, Leslie. 1966. *The Journal of Beatrix Potter, 1881–1897*. London: Frederick Warne.

Linder, Leslie. 1971. *A History of the Writings of Beatrix Potter*. London: Frederick Warne.

Linder, Leslie. 1972. *The Art of Beatrix Potter*. London: Frederick Warne.

MacDonald, Ruth K. 1986. *Beatrix Potter*. Boston: Twayne.

Potter, Beatrix. 1989. *Beatrix Potter's Letters*. London: Frederick Warne.

Potter, Beatrix. 1992. *Letters to Children from Beatrix Potter*. London: Frederick Warne.

Taylor, Judy. 1986. *Beatrix Potter: Artist, Storyteller, and Countrywoman*. New York: Frederick Warne.

Taylor, Judy, et al. 1987. *Beatrix Potter, 1866–1943: The Artist and Her World*. London: Frederick Warne.

VICTORIA SEARS

Pram

The pram, a baby carriage for infants and toddlers, is mainly a Western and urban phenomenon that developed in the 1800s. Before 1800 babies were seldom carried outside of the home. When transporting babies was necessary, they were swaddled in clothing or, among the upper classes, carried by nannies. Between 1650 and 1800, a few examples of children's carts, copies of the adult equipage or cart, are known to have existed in the aristocracy. The famous English architect William Kent presumably designed an abundantly decorated baby carriage for the children of the Third Duke of Devonshire in 1733.

The first prams normally were made of wicker—not unlike a cradle mounted on (often three) wheels. The child sat in the carriage, but in the mid-1800s prams were altered so that they could be pushed and not pulled and the child could lie down to sleep. From the 1860s through the 1870s use of the pram was widespread in bourgeois families across Europe and Northern America, as prams and promenade carriages became status symbols. In the 1920s the pram became common in all social groups. Single mothers were given prams by charitable organizations or social institutions.

The production of early prams involved the collaboration of a wicker worker, a smith, and an upholsterer or saddler, but soon pram production was overtaken by carriage builders who specialized in the manufacture of complicated wheels. Later, prams were produced in particular factories. In the 1880s multiple folding prams were introduced in the United States, Germany, Denmark, and Holland. Manufacturers in England and Germany made a number of improvements to the pram, including suspension, brakes, massive rubber tires, and, after World War II, plastic handles, fiberglass exteriors, and power steering.

The general design of prams has varied greatly over the years, running the gamut from the horse-drawn carriage to automobiles. From 1870 to 1920 prams had exceptionally high wheels, but in the 1920s and even more so in the 1930s the body of the pram was made deeper and the wheels smaller, which made the pram more steady and secure. At the same time the design was streamlined and made more functional. After World War II, the pram, inspired by American and English automobile fashion, again was made higher. The stroller or push chair dates from the 1920s, but it did not become widespread until the 1950s and 1960s due to increased mobility.

The use of prams reflects broad cultural changes concerning HYGIENE, urbanization, social development, and changing views of childhood, parenthood, and gender. With the introduction of pavement in urban and suburban areas in the mid-1800s, the pram became a practical means of transportation. Yet transportation was not the only purpose for prams, for in the 1880s light and fresh air were considered important in the nursing and care of young children, and doctors recommended that all parents use prams. The general economic welfare after World War II made prams more available to middle-class families, and the pram and stroller industry grew. The pram provided women—both mothers and nannies—with greater mobility. They were liberated from home and enjoyed a wider radius of action.

In the 1970s, discussion arose about child care and physical proximity, specifically whether young children are better off sleeping in a pram or being carried. Most children continue to be carried by their mothers, older sisters, or other persons in the family or community, and baby slings are common in Europe and in the United States. In Western countries a wide range of prams and strollers for special use have appeared in recent years as a result of the changing needs of parents. For example, baby joggers designed for both men and women enable them to simultaneously care for their child and maintain their health. The baby carriage industry is now concerned with accessories—beds, swings, buggies, doll's prams, high chairs, and other FURNITURE— corresponding with the twenty-first century's conception of childhood and the various materialistic possibilities in a very differentiated world.

See also: **Children's Spaces.**

BIBLIOGRAPHY

Dick, Diana. 1987. *Yesterday's Babies, a History of Babycare.* London: The Bodley Head.

Gathorne-Hardy, Jonathan. 1972. *The Rise and Fall of the British Nanny.* London: Hodder and Stoughton.

LENE FLORIS

Premature Birth. *See* Obstetrics and Midwifery.

Private and Independent Schools

There are private schools in most countries of the world, although many of them are religious schools. Most have curricula that parallel those of state-controlled schools, and are under some form of government regulation, although their private status allows them greater flexibility in programs and personnel. Unlike most public schools, the parents of private-school students must pay for their schooling, a fact that makes them less accessible to low-income families. Families tend to choose private schools based on their belief that their children will obtain a better education or be educated in a better or safer environment than in public schools, or because the private school has a more sympathetic educational philosophy.

In colonial America, there was much blurring between private and public education, with many variations. In general, however, most schooling was designed to provide students with a minimum of essential skills, often under AP-PRENTICESHIP arrangements. Secondary education was uncommon, although some towns had Latin GRAMMAR SCHOOLS. From the Revolution to the Civil War, the country saw a rise in the presence of academies that provided secondary education, often associated with the religious fervor of the Great Awakening. The curriculum varied, with both classical and more modern and practical curricula available. There was originally little age grading, and there were few schools for girls. Initially, all were day schools without boarding facilities; if students were not staying with their own families, they boarded with families in the town. Schools such as Phillips Academy in Andover and Phillips Exeter Academy (founded in 1778 and 1781, respectively) did not build dormitories until the late 1820s. However,

once students began to live within the school, the schools began to plan activities for every moment, partly as they had assumed the role of *in loco parentis*, and partly to keep their charges from any potential harm.

Private schools for girls had a separate history. Since education beyond the rudiments was seen as unnecessary for most girls, it was varied and sporadic during the colonial era and the early Republic. Much of what was available took the form of finishing schools, which emphasized social graces as much as learning. Three pioneering women, Catharine Beecher, Mary Lyon, and Emma Willard, provided curricula that differed greatly from this pattern during the 1820s and 1830s. The schools they founded were boarding schools that emphasized science, mathematics, history, and literature. The older conception of education designed to provide "feminine" virtues did not disappear, however, and was important in the founding of new schools for girls in the mid-nineteenth century. However, as WOMEN'S COLLEGES increased in numbers and more colleges became coeducational, the curriculum of even these schools became primarily academic.

Day schools have an extremely varied history, particularly among primary schools, which are generally smaller and less costly to operate than secondary schools and therefore can be established more simply. In colonial times and the early Republic these schools often provided basic education, with the idea that the family and the church would provide the rest. Later, more private schools emphasized secondary education, as tax-supported public schools offered primary education for large segments of the society. One special type, the country day school, emerged for many of the same reasons that boarding schools were placed in rural settings: avoidance of the perceived physical and spiritual hazards of the city. These schools had curricula much like the boarding schools, but the students returned to their families each evening. Although the day schools followed the main trends in American education, their private status allowed them to follow a wide range of philosophies: the Waldorf schools, for example, emphasized the arts and manual skills as paths to the development of the child, while Ethical Culture schools favored an experimental approach to education.

However, as was true for most schools, one of the key influences from the late nineteenth century to the middle of the twentieth century was the Progressive school movement, which broadened the programs of the school to reflect the needs of a citizen in a complex society and included concern for vocations, health, and family life. The emotional development of the child was considered to be very important. Private day schools today include a bewildering variety of orientations and purposes, from community schools to Montessori schools to nongraded schools, among many others. One consequence, of course, is that families who can afford it have a great variety of choices in the education of their children.

The history of private schools is entwined with current research controversies about the effects and social consequences of schooling. These controversies concern the effectiveness of schools on the learning of students, the social effects of private education (and the consequences for the social perspectives of their students), and the role of private schools in the formation and continuance of social and economic elites. First, because private schools charge tuition, they tend to limit their enrollments to students whose parents can afford them. This fact leads to schools that emphasize high achievement on standardized tests of vocabulary, reading, and mathematics as a measure of their value. However, international comparisons suggest that private schools' academic results are due more to family expectations and encouragement than to the special educational power of the schools.

A second concern is the overall effect of schools whose students come chiefly from the more affluent segments of society. The concern is that schooling where students from a narrow strata of society interact will lead to a similarly narrow range of social and economic options. Beginning with E. Digby Baltzell and C. Wright Mills, a series of writers have contended that elite boarding schools provide an environment that prepares students not only for college but for the vicissitudes of corporate and political life. Based on the fact that disproportionate numbers of CEOs and high government officials attended these schools, they argue that one of their key purposes is "preparing for power." Concentrated in the northeastern part of the United States, such schools offer rigorous academic programs, often using college-level texts. The days and nights are carefully scheduled, with an emphasis on SPORTS, mandatory study hours, and a wide range of extracurricular activities, particularly music. High culture is emphasized in campus art collections and guest speakers. Classes are usually small and emphasize discussion and writing. The schools claim that they develop "character," which is reflected in class discussions and school codes of conduct. Almost all activities are done in groups in the presence of others with great efforts to treat all students the same.

However, many researchers have noted the psychological costs of these "total environments" to the students' need for privacy and uncontrolled self-expression. Analyses of the student cultures in these schools further suggests high levels of competitiveness. Despite the stressful aspects of student life, these schools are unusually successful in placing their students in prestigious colleges. More importantly, these schools have been seen as models for other schools by some researchers, who note a community and culture of learning that values academic achievement, sets goals for students, and provides personal attention. Arthur Powell believes their practices provide lessons that other schools may use to good effect with average students. Other researchers have argued that these schools are successful because of their academic

content, and the fact that some wealthy families send their children to the school is secondary.

Comparisons with European schools are difficult because of the wide variety of educational systems. However, British educational history is roughly analogous to that of the United States, with most private schools being boarding or day schools, along with a large number of church-related schools and a historically "elite" set of schools. In recent years, both countries have witnessed a proliferation of private day schools. The British elite boarding schools have been described as being "total" environments with strong student cultures. These schools are also seen as providing the basis for elitist values among their students, who later implement these values in positions of power.

See also: **Girls' Schools; Latin School; Parochial Schools; Public Schools: Britain; Progressive Education.**

BIBLIOGRAPHY

Baird, Leonard L. 1977. *The Elite Schools: A Profile of Prestigious Independent Schools.* Lexington, MA: Lexington Books.

Baltzell, E. Digby. 1971 [1957]. *Philadelphia Gentlemen: The Making of a National Upper Class.* Chicago: Quadrangle Books.

Cookson, Peter W., and Caroline H. Persell. 1985. *Preparing for Power: America's Elite Boarding Schools.* New York: Basic Books.

Cremin, Lawrence A. 1977. *Traditions of American Education.* New York: Basic Books.

Krausharr, Otto. 1972. *American Nonpublic Schools: Patterns of Diversity.* Baltimore: Johns Hopkins University Press.

Powell, Arthur G. 1996. *Lessons from Privilege: The American Prep School Tradition.* Cambridge, MA: Harvard University Press.

Walford, Geoffrey, ed. 1991. *Private Schooling: Tradition, Change, and Diversity.* London: Chapman Publishing.

LEONARD L. BAIRD

Progressive Education

Progressive education was a far-flung array of ideas and practices designed to enliven teaching and learning. As with other amorphous constructs, the meaning of Progressivism varied from person to person, place to place, and era to era. At its most diffuse, the word was synonymous with "new" or "good" education. Even so, there were several core ideas in this heterogeneous and influential movement that took shape in the late nineteenth century, spread rapidly and widely in the early twentieth century, and receded by the 1950s.

Progressive versus Traditional Education

Nearly all Progressives knew what they opposed and thus identified themselves by what they were not. Traditional education was the enemy. Students were required to memorize endless facts and formulas from a dreary academic curriculum remote from their own youthful interests. Most teachers defined good pedagogy as drill and practice; their job was to hear recitations, not lead discussions. Classroom life was austere. Teachers established unilaterally the rules and regulations, and they punished misconduct harshly. Administrators deferred to school boards often enmeshed in factionalism and political patronage.

In contrast to that unflattering sketch of traditional education, Progressives juxtaposed their vision of a more pleasant and practical education. They often said that education should be "child centered" rather than grounded on the authority of a ponderous textbook or a stern teacher. Children were not willful, obstreperous creatures that had to be tamed; they were by nature curious and creative, with a wide range of worthwhile interests. A broader curriculum and a humane pedagogy would honor those interests.

Education of the "whole child" steadily expanded the scope of the school curriculum during the first half of the twentieth century. For the very young, opportunities multiplied for music, art, drama, and recreation. For the early adolescent, there were JUNIOR HIGH SCHOOLS for the unique needs of that stage of life. For older teens, the HIGH SCHOOL offered more "tracks," or programs of study such as vocational, commercial, academic, and general. At all levels of schooling there was growth in extracurricular activities as clubs and teams proliferated. Another area of rapid expansion was health care and social services for the physical and emotional needs of the whole child.

Instructional methods and materials also changed. Progressives envisioned teachers as facilitators who should encourage student participation and activity through discussions and group projects. Learning could be fun: games, field trips, and films blurred the lines between work and PLAY. Teachers should be kind and patient, not strict and aloof. The good classroom would be a democratic community where rules were fair, everyone had a say, and all felt comfortable and successful. As a result, fewer students would fail or drop out, an important consideration in light of soaring school enrollments throughout the first two thirds of the twentieth century. The enlarged and diverse student body would get more from education and like it better, the Progressives believed.

Aside from burgeoning enrollments, why did those ideas and practices take hold in the very late nineteenth and early twentieth centuries? Progressive educators addressed three of the most important developments in American life. First, a broader curriculum could match the shifting needs of employers in an age when the demand for semiskilled and clerical labor surged. With more students in new vocational and commercial tracks, the fit between graduates' preparation and the needs of the labor market improved. Second, the massive and unprecedented immigration from Europe filled urban schools with students who seemed to need nonacademic training more than Shakespeare or trigonometry in order to become loyal, virtuous, and productive citizens. Third, Progressive education drew strength from more expansive notions of the scope of governmental intervention, which included fostering the well-being of children. Heightened concern for the vulnerabilities of youth spurred successful crusades for CHILD LABOR laws, JUVENILE COURTS, public playgrounds, mothers' pensions, and other methods to rescue youth from the perils of life in a rapidly changing society. The Progressives' advocacy of a kinder and broader schooling matched the spirit and scale of child-saving interventions elsewhere in America.

Most Progressives also saw themselves as scientific. In the 1880s and 1890s they deplored the haphazard management of many urban schools. Elected officials often based decisions on partisan considerations; many policies were either wasteful or corrupt. Progressives urged the appointment of well-trained managers to oversee the rapidly expanding schools. Expertise, rationality, standardization, and predictability were the traits valued in a good administrator. Not every school system by the early twentieth century was a sleek bureaucracy, but that was the ideal within the profession, notwithstanding the preference of many for local control and freedom from state regulations.

A similar quest for certainty marked the Progressives' support of INTELLIGENCE TESTING. Measuring the innate mental abilities of youngsters seemed a rigorous and fair way to assign students to particular courses and tracks. Grouping children by ability seemed more democratic to the Progressives than holding all children to the same standards. Within a decade of the first large-scale use of IQ tests in World War I, school districts throughout the nation used them. Not every Progressive championed IQ tests, to be sure, but even the skeptics favored "child study," detailed and continuous scrutiny of the social, emotional, and intellectual growth of the young.

Controversies and Influence

Not everyone admired and adopted Progressive practices. The changes were greatest in elementary schools, in PRIVATE SCHOOLS, and in wealthier communities. In those enclaves the Progressive notions of the care and training of the young matched parents' views of how to rear their children. Elsewhere the impact was modest, with educators taking bits and pieces in addition to, not in place of, their old routines. Progressive education could easily exhaust teachers who took its tenets seriously. For instance, the constraints of teaching 150 students in a high school without plentiful supplemental materials made it hard to be a facilitator of projects suited to the individual needs and interests of each student.

The ultimate purpose of the broader curriculum, gentler pedagogy, and scientific outlook was a point of dispute among Progressives. One prominent faction boldly called for the "reconstruction" of American society to empower the disenfranchised, strengthen government, and regulate corporations. On the political left, the reconstructionists embraced the New Deal reforms of the 1930s, and some leaders even admired socialist and communist regimes. In contrast, a larger faction rallied under the banners of "efficiency" and "adjustment." The goal of education was to equip youth to fit, not challenge, society as it was. A useful education prepared a graduate to earn a living, vote intelligently, shop wisely, and in other ways conform to the demands of adult life. What both factions shared was the conviction that schooling mattered enormously and that educators held the future of the race in their hands.

In addition to internal schisms, Progressives encountered stinging criticisms of their ideas. Whenever their praise of the goodness of children sounded too rapturous, they were mocked as sentimental and soft, willing to coddle rather than discipline the young. If their political preferences drifted too far to the left, they were condemned as subversive and anti-American. Should their innovations require higher tax rates, frugal voters might spurn Progressive education as superfluous "fads and frills." Above all, critics doubted if Progressive schools were academically rigorous. Students who enjoyed school and felt good about themselves might never learn chemistry and calculus, many parents feared. Those anxieties intensified as college enrollment became, after World War II, not just a wish but an expectation for middle-class youth. Progressivism might be appropriate in elementary schools, but there were enduring doubts that it would prepare a talented teenager for admission to and success in a first-rate college.

The most influential theorist of Progressivism, the philosopher JOHN DEWEY, regretted the anti-intellectual misinterpretations of his ideas. He never doubted the importance of a challenging academic curriculum. Dewey envisioned Progressive pedagogy as a means to, not an avoidance of, intellectual exertion. The curiosity of children and the flexibility of teachers should enhance, not diminish, the life of the mind. But Dewey's prose was frequently so convoluted that his admirers misconstrued his ideas. The most egregious misrepresentations downplayed the wit and will of average-ability students. Pseudo-Progressives claimed that most students either could not, would not, or need not undertake serious academic work.

In the late 1940s, the most prominent educational reform, called "Life Adjustment," displayed the dangers of misreading Dewey. The Adjusters believed that the majority of high school graduates acquired neither the know-how nor the social skills they would later use far more than French or algebra. What every teenager needed, they argued, were lessons in practical matters such as FRIENDSHIPS, hobbies, and family life. Instead of urging more students to attend college or acquire vocational skills, the adjusters envisioned a curriculum full of practical pointers on how to get along with others.

As a formal movement, Life Adjustment disappeared by the mid-1950s. Articulate critics lampooned it as pretentious, pernicious, and vapid. In their opinion, it was ridiculous and dangerous to give the mundane aspects of life a place, let alone center stage, in a school's curriculum. Furthermore, most parents were unwilling to let teachers and students disengage from academic work for the purpose of discussing social and personal concerns. Those topics belonged at the family dinner table, not in the classroom.

The underlying ideas of Progressivism outlived the Life Adjustment debacle. Many parents and teachers remained loyal to its vision of more practical and pleasant education. School curricular and extracurricular offerings, as well as social services, continued to expand in the 1960s and 1970s. Groups previously ill-served, especially racial minorities and SPECIAL EDUCATION students, had more opportunities. Teaching methods never reverted to the old rigidities of the nineteenth century. Administrators were still wedded to the norm of dispassionate expertise. Whenever the central ideas of the Progressives were put forth cautiously and presented without overselling, the odds of success were good.

See also: **Child Saving; Education, United States; Vocational Education, Industrial Education, and Trade Schools.**

BIBLIOGRAPHY

Cremin, Lawrence A. 1988. *American Education: The Metropolitan Experience, 1876–1980.* New York: Harper and Row.

Cuban, Larry. 1993. *How Teachers Taught: Constancy and Change in American Classrooms, 1880–1990.* New York: Teachers College Press.

Dewey, John. 1916. *Democracy and Education.* New York: Free Press.

Fass, Paula S. 1989. *Outside In: Minorities and the Transformation of American Education.* New York: Oxford University Press.

Jervis, Kathe, and Carol Montag, eds. 1991. *Progressive Education for the 1990s: Transforming Practice.* New York: Teachers College Press.

Kliebard, Herbert M. 1995. *The Struggle for the American Curriculum, 1893–1958.* New York: Routledge.

Ravitch, Diane. 2000. *Left Back: A Century of Failed School Reforms.* New York: Simon and Schuster.

Reese, William J. 2001. "The Origins of Progressive Education." *History of Education Quarterly* 41: 1–24.

Tyack, David, and Elisabeth Hansot. 1982. *Managers of Virtue: Public School Leadership in America, 1820–1980.* New York: Basic Books.

Zilversmit, Arthur. 1993. *Changing Schools: Progressive Education, Theory, and Practice, 1930–1960.* Chicago: University of Chicago Press.

ROBERT L. HAMPEL

Proms

The high school prom is an iconic event in contemporary American society, often heralded as one of the most important coming-of-age rites for adolescents today. Part of school institutions, repositories for the formation of youth cultures, and shaped by an expanding commodity culture, the meaning of the American prom is ever changing.

The expansion of schooling in the early twentieth century, stemming from rapid urbanization and industrialization, played a key role in the American prom's development. Prior to the late nineteenth century only the wealthy attended school beyond elementary levels. With a steady increase of student enrollment, public schools emerged as major socializing agents in U.S. society. School dances, clubs, and student government increasingly became a part of young Americans' lives as the role of school changed. As a growing number of young people began attending college in the 1920s, the university emerged as a meaningful site for leisure and learning. By the 1920s the traditional academic concerns of the university lost ground as youth-centered social activities such as the college junior prom captured the attentions of a changing young America.

High school proms did not gain in popularity until the 1930s. Their popularity stems largely from the changes in how youth had been defined culturally as a distinct age group. Though scholars had treated youth as a cohort having distinctive habits and traits since the mid-nineteenth century, by the 1930s the idea of the adolescent was firmly entrenched in both popular cultural lore and scholarly work. At the threshold of adulthood, adolescence signified a tumultuous stage in the life course, one characterized by uncertainty and angst. Consequently, adolescents were thought to need moral and social guidance. Well-structured, adult-supervised social activities served as perfect opportunities to socialize youth to the practices and values of a middle-class adult world.

By the 1940s the leisure lives of adolescents were tied less to family and were increasingly bound to a rapidly expanding commodity culture. The emergence of a teen leisure market led to a mounting concern among (middle-class) adults about youth SEXUALITY, DELINQUENCY, and complacency. The earlier concern for adolescents' moral development, combined with the fact that young people's lives were increasingly consumed by activities outside of the home, gave rise to more concerted efforts to manage and often overtly regulate youth activities and spaces. By the mid-twentieth century high school proms, along with teen canteens and sock hops, were a mainstay of middle-class American cultural life.

The prom's popularity receded in the 1960s and early 1970s as a growing number of American youth participated in the antiwar, civil rights, and free speech movements. Many youth refused to attend the prom as an act of symbolic resistance to middle-class Anglo conformity, adult authority, and the status quo. With shifts in the political culture of the 1980s and early 1990s, combined with concerted efforts by marketers to carve out and expand youth markets, proms once again gained in popularity and were radically transformed by the pull of consumerism such that limousines, expensive dresses, and luxury hotels became important to the experience of the prom for many American youth. Yet proms of today, like those of the past, serve as events where youth struggle to create and reshape American history. In 1981 a gay high school student sued his Rhode Island high school to attend the prom with another gay student. In 1994 the students of an Alabama school organized an alternative protest prom after the principal canceled the prom in an effort to forestall interracial dating among the school's student body. In 1995 high schoolers in California attended the first gay prom.

See also: **Adolescence and Youth; High School; Youth Culture.**

BIBLIOGRAPHY

Best, Amy L. 2000. *Prom Night: Youth, Schools and Popular Culture.* New York: Routledge.

Fass, Paula. 1977. *The Damned and the Beautiful: American Youth in the 1920s.* New York: Oxford University Press.

Graebner, William. 1990. *Coming of Age in Buffalo: Youth and Authority in the Post War Era.* Philadelphia: Temple University Press.

Kett, Joseph F. 1977. *Rites of Passage: Adolescence in America, 1790 to the Present.* New York: Basic Books.

Palladino, Grace. 1996. *Teenagers: An American History.* New York: Basic Books.

AMY L. BEST

Property. *See* Inheritance and Property.

Protestant Reformation

The Protestant Reformation began in Germany in 1517, following Martin Luther's attempt to provoke discussion about reforming the Catholic Church. It rapidly blossomed into an international struggle, resulting in the permanent destruction of Catholic unity in Europe and the creation of many new Christian denominations and sects. By the early 1520s, once it was clear that the break with the Catholic Church was permanent, the reformers faced the challenge of creating stable new churches that could endure the religious conflict of the sixteenth century.

Children were a critical component in the response to this challenge. The reformers were anxious to ensure that the children of their churches would be properly and completely nurtured and educated in the newly defined Christian faith. Protestant reformers saw the family as the fundamental unit for fostering both religious belief and social stability;

therefore, they directed more attention to children and families than had the late-medieval Catholic Church. As envisioned by the reformers, the ideal family was a patriarchy in which fathers held ultimate responsibility and authority, but within which mothers were also held accountable for the nurture and education of their offspring. The reformers viewed children as tainted with original sin, like all human beings, yet educable and in need of careful oversight to protect them from the temptations and vices of the world. They insisted on the duty of both fathers and mothers to teach their children Christian beliefs and practices and to discipline them with love and restraint, always with the support of the church community. Another significant contribution was the insistence on the importance of basic education and the attempt to spread literacy so that reformed Christians would be able to read the Bible for themselves.

Protestant Children and Church Ritual

Most reformers, including Martin Luther (1483–1546) in Germany and John Calvin (1509–1564) in Geneva, kept the rite of infant BAPTISM as a sacrament in their churches. The more "radical" or Anabaptist reformers, such as Menno Simons (1496–1561) in the Netherlands and northern Germany, rejected infant baptism and asserted that a person had to proclaim his or her faith and *choose* to be baptized as an adolescent or adult. While Luther and Calvin maintained the practice of infant baptism, they each altered the Catholic interpretation of what occurred during the sacrament, indicating a changed understanding of the nature of children. Medieval Catholics believed that the sacrament of baptism washed away the original sin that weighed upon the soul of a newborn child. In contrast, the Protestant reformers emphasized the burden that original sin placed on all human beings, including baptized children. There was no exact Protestant consensus on the effects of baptism, but generally they held that it was not an act of purification that automatically protected the child from future harm, but rather a sign of God's grace and covenant with the child, the parents, and the wider church community. The baptismal ceremony also marked the commitment of parents and community to raise the child in the Christian faith. Children were considered to be particularly susceptible to the distractions and vices of the world, and adolescents even more so. For this reason they required careful supervision and loving discipline to help them learn piety and Christian responsibility.

Another change that occurred with the Protestant Reformation was the delay of CONFIRMATION until adolescence. While confirmation was no longer understood to be a sacrament, Protestant churches still marked a child's profession of faith and official entrance into the church with some ceremony. In medieval Catholicism, children received confirmation sometime between the moment of baptism and age seven. The reformers held that such an act required that the child have achieved some level of spiritual maturity, which they generally believed coincided approximately with physical maturity. In delaying confirmation until ADOLESCENCE (in the most extreme cases until the age of eighteen), the reformers were pushing back the age of discretion, thereby extending the time during which children were not held fully responsible for their actions.

Education

Both the delay of confirmation, in the case of Luther and Calvin, and the delay of baptism, in the case of the Anabaptists, made the proper education of children imperative. A main premise of the Protestant Reformation was that individual Christians could communicate directly with God through prayer and study of the Scripture. The reformers sought to foster this relationship by providing catechisms and establishing schools to teach both boys and girls to read. Luther and Calvin each, in their efforts to aid in the training of children, produced catechisms that could be used by parents and ministers to teach children and adults in need of religious instruction. Such catechisms were written in the form of questions and responses about the basic tenets of the Christian faith. They were printed in the vernacular (for example, German or English, rather than Latin), in simple language, and could be expeditiously published and distributed across a region with the aid of the printing press, which had been in use in Europe since the 1450s.

Both boys and girls were expected to learn such catechisms at home, at church, and even at school. Girls' schools and coeducational schools were both established during the sixteenth and seventeenth centuries, but schools for boys appeared more rapidly. Girls were more often expected to receive their education at home, focusing on the catechism in order to learn pious behavior. Scholars continue to debate the effectiveness of these efforts at education and indoctrination in different parts of Europe. It is generally agreed that, while the reformers' efforts at education did not succeed as perfectly or completely as they hoped, literacy rates across sixteenth- and seventeenth-century Europe improved more quickly in Protestant areas than in Catholic areas. Ultimately, the schools created during the Reformation became a part of the standard European educational systems.

Discipline and Obligation

Luther, Calvin, and Simons all insisted upon the obligation of children to respect, obey, and assist their parents. Parents had a corresponding duty to love, nurture, and discipline their children, both for the protection of the children and in the interest of creating a stable community. It is noteworthy that this obligation extended to illegitimate children as well. While Catholic authorities were more willing to expend resources on caring for abandoned children in the interest of protecting the honor of unwed mothers, Protestant officials went to great lengths to ensure that parents took responsibility for raising their children born out of wedlock.

"Godly" parents were expected to nurture their children physically and spiritually; this included a strict but compassionate discipline. Corporal punishment, including beating, was acceptable in moderation in order to help children learn to resist the many vices that the world pressed upon them. But extreme abuse, neglect, and overindulgence were all seen as threats to children. To combat these various extremes, the reformers emphasized the notion that nurturing their children according to Protestant teachings was one way that Christian parents served God. Calvin wrote, "Unless men regard their children as the gift of God, they are careless and reluctant in providing for their support" (quoted in Pitkin, p. 171). In the case of Anabaptists, children depended upon their parents not for Christian instruction that built upon their baptism, but rather for the education in the Christian faith that would one day enable them to choose to be baptized. While the issue of infant baptism was a significant division between Anabaptists and other Protestants, in practice they took similar steps to raise their children as both faithful Christians and responsible citizens. Simons advised Anabaptist parents regarding their children, "If they transgress, reprove them sharply. If they are childish, bear them patiently. If they are of teachable age, instruct them in a Christian fashion. Dedicate them to the Lord from youth" (quoted in Miller, p. 208).

The Protestant Influence

Reformers' thoughts on child care were made popular by numerous books on child rearing. Church and state authorities attempted to reinforce these ideas through such instruments as the consistories, or morals courts, established in Reformed ("Calvinist") communities. But despite these efforts, it is important to remember that the reformers' views were not consistently put into practice by all Protestant parents. Indeed, it is likely that few parents—fathers or mothers—lived up to the reformers' mandate to instruct their children fully in Protestant theology and beliefs. While reformers sometimes criticized parents for disciplining their children too harshly, a more frequent complaint was that parents were indulging their children, and thus neglecting their spiritual and moral welfare. Another area of dispute involved selecting GODPARENTS for a newborn child. Calvin and the Genevan reformers insisted that parents should choose godparents only from among the Reformed community, so that they might serve as spiritual mentors for children. But, maintaining earlier traditions, some parents insisted upon inviting relatives from Catholic towns to be godparents. Finally, the belief that baptism cleansed a child of original sin and was a prerequisite for salvation persisted among some Protestants, despite the reformers' teachings to the contrary. Practices such as "reviving" dead infants in order to baptize them continued throughout the early modern period.

Nonetheless, the Protestant Reformation had significant and lasting effects on the treatment of and attitudes toward children in early modern Europe. Where the reformers clashed with parents regarding their children, it was because both parents and church officials had strong opinions about

the best way to raise a child to become a responsible citizen, a faithful Christian, and a dutiful son or daughter. The Protestant reformers began efforts at widespread education that would come to the forefront once again during the ENLIGHTENMENT of the eighteenth century. They emphasized the notion that childhood was a period of nurture, discipline, and learning. And they reiterated frequently the mutual obligation that parents and children had toward one another.

See also: **Catholicism; Islam; Judaism.**

BIBLIOGRAPHY

Ben-Amos, Ilana Krausman. 1994. *Adolescence and Youth in Early Modern England.* New Haven, CT: Yale University Press.

DeMolen, Richard L. 1975. "Childhood and the Sacraments in the Sixteenth Century." *Archiv für Reformationsgeschichte/Archive for Reformation History* 66: 49–70.

Fletcher, Anthony. 1994. "Prescription and Practice: Protestantism and the Upbringing of Children, 1560–1700." In *The Church and Childhood,* ed. Diana Wood. Cambridge, MA: Blackwell.

Harrington, Joel. 1998. "Bad Parents, the State, and the Early Modern Civilizing Process." *German History* 16:16–28.

Luke, Carmen. 1989. *Pedagogy, Printing, and Protestantism: The Discourse on Childhood.* Albany: State University of New York Press.

Marshall, Sherrin. 1991. "Childhood in Early Modern Europe." In *Children in Historical and Comparative Perspective: An International Handbook and Research Guide,* ed. Joseph M. Hawes and N. Ray Hiner. Westport, CT: Greenwood Press.

Miller, Keith Graber. 2001. "Complex Innocence, Obligatory Nurturance, and Parental Vigilance: 'The Child' in the Work of Menno Simons." In *The Child in Christian Thought,* ed. Marcia J. Bunge. Grand Rapids, MI: W. B. Eerdmans.

Ozment, Steven. 1983. *When Fathers Ruled: Family Life in Reformation Europe.* Cambridge, MA: Harvard University Press.

Pitkin, Barbara. 2001. "'The Heritage of the Lord': Children in the Theology of John Calvin." In *The Child in Christian Thought,* ed. Marcia J. Bunge. Grand Rapids, MI: W. B. Eerdmans.

Pollock, Linda. 2001. "Parent–Child Relations." In *Family Life in Early Modern Times, 1500–1789,* ed. Marzio Barbagli and David I. Kertzer. New Haven, CT: Yale University Press.

Strauss, Gerald. 1978. *Luther's House of Learning: Indoctrination of the Young in Reformation Germany.* Baltimore, MD: Johns Hopkins University Press.

Tudor, Philippa. 1984. "Religious Instruction for Children and Adolescents in the Early English Reformation." *Journal of Ecclesiastical History* 35: 391–413.

Watt, Jeffrey R. 2001. "The Impact of the Reformation and Counter-Reformation." *In Family Life in Early Modern Times, 1500–1789,* ed. Marzio Barbagli and David I. Kertzer. New Haven, CT: Yale University Press.

Wiesner, Merry E. 1993. *Women and Gender in Early Modern Europe,* 2nd ed. New York: Cambridge University Press.

KAREN E. SPIERLING

Puberty

Puberty is the experience of sexual maturation for girls and boys; it encompasses certain hormonal, physical, and physio-

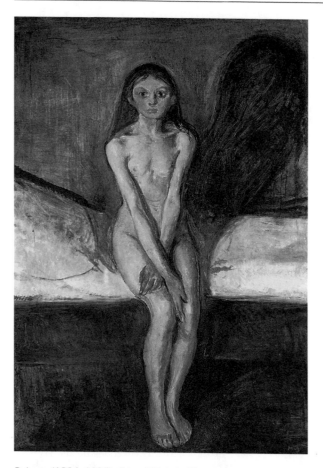

Puberty (1894–1895), Edvard Munch. The ambiguous expression on the face of Munch's young model leaves it unclear whether she welcomes or dreads the changes that await her. © 2003 The Munch Museum/The Munch-Ellington Group/Artists Rights Society (ARS), New York. The Art Archive/Nasjonal Galleriet Oslo/Album/Joseph Martin.

logical changes that manifest themselves in the lives of young people in all times and places. During puberty, boys and girls experience a rise in hormone levels and undergo an increase in height, known as the *growth spurt.* The secondary sex characteristics appear and boys and girls develop the potential for reproduction. Within these broad parameters, however, the way the biological process of puberty has been experienced by young people has varied considerably across cultures and historical time periods. One of the most notable changes in the experience of puberty in industrialized countries has been the decline in the average age of MENARCHE, or first menstruation, due to improvements in health care and nutrition. Along with changes in the biological process itself, puberty has been conceptualized differently in different times and places. Such varying views of and expectations for puberty have significantly influenced the ways young people have experienced the process of sexual maturation.

In the West, meanings and experiences of puberty have taken shape in relationship to meanings and experiences of

the stage of life known as ADOLESCENCE AND YOUTH. Ancient and medieval views of puberty recognized it as a period of heightened sexual interest, which was associated both with personal vitality and social benefit and, particularly under the rising influence of Christianity, with immorality and social danger. In the turbulent social climate of sixteenth and seventeenth-century England, Puritan moral theologians concerned with the threat posed to the social order by disgruntled urban apprentices decisively linked the sensuality of male youth with sin, temptation, and disruptive behavior and called upon the family, the school, and the church to act as disciplining agents. Colonial New Englanders, in contrast, were more confident about the hold their orderly, hierarchical, and patriarchal society had over youth, and so displayed much less anxiety about puberty, at least during the first generations of settlement. Beginning at the end of the seventeenth century, a confluence of demographic and economic changes, most notably population growth, geographical mobility, and commercial development, began to undermine the stability of many New England families and towns. Some, but not all, of the adult controls over the lives of youth were loosened. The result was a rising conflict in age relations and a new attention by religious authorities to the potentially perilous manifestations of youthful SEXUALITY.

By the middle of the eighteenth century, however, the emphasis on authoritatively controlling youth during their period of sexual maturation was supplemented by ENLIGHTENMENT views that sanctioned some degree of social and sexual independence, for boys in particular. Ideally, boys would learn to control their powerful passions from within and emerge from their youth as autonomous individuals. Not invested with the same capacity for self-determination, girls were increasingly regarded as pure and passionless, and any expression of female sexual desire was deemed deviant. At the same time, a Romantic sensibility came to associate the volatility of puberty less with danger and destruction than with vigor, creativity, and the awakening of love and compassion. The seminal text here was JEAN-JACQUES ROUSSEAU's *Émile* (1762), which posited that the difficulties puberty seemed to pose were more the artifact of society than nature and were best managed by an educational regimen that allowed for the gradual development of the body, mind, and heart.

During the nineteenth century, scientific theories dominated discussions about puberty, establishing it as the primary determinant of sexual difference, as well as a marker of race and class hierarchy. Physicians and evolutionary theorists maintained that male and female development were largely similar during childhood. The biological changes that occurred with the maturation of the reproductive organs established the ineradicable differences between male and female bodies, minds, behaviors, and social roles and responsibilities. Maintaining such differences among men and women of the white middle class was thought to be essential to preserve social order and ensure the ongoing progress of Western civilization. With the exception of anxieties about the physically and morally depleting effects of MASTURBATION, male puberty was not discussed by scientific authorities with any great specificity. According to the developmental theory of this period, nature intended the growth of the white middle-class male to proceed along a gradual, steady course and endowed such "civilized" boys with the capability of managing the benignly vitalizing physical changes wrought by the onset of puberty. The "civilized" girl, in contrast, was described in medical and evolutionary discourse as being rendered completely vulnerable and passive in the face of the much more volatile, complex, and consequential changes her body experienced during the process of sexual maturation. Female puberty indicated not the onset of sexual desire, but the future capacity for maternity. Any expenditure by the girl of physical, mental, or emotional energy was thought to further compromise an already taxing process, thereby threatening her health, her mental stability, and her ability to fulfill her essential function as reproducer of the "civilized" white race later in her life. While not all doctors regarded female puberty as inherently dangerous, many prominent physicians advanced such a notion as the primary justification for limiting girls' activities during their youth, most especially their access to institutions of higher education, to which women aspired by the second half of the nineteenth century.

Nineteenth-century scientific discourse, under the influence of an evolutionary schema applied to social science, also attended to the timing of puberty as evidence for the existence of natural gender, racial, and class hierarchies. It was widely noted that the white middle-class girl grew more rapidly and reached puberty earlier than her "civilized" brother. Once her body stopped growing, the explanation went, her intellectual and moral development ceased as well, thereby determining her inferior status in relation to the more slowly, but ultimately more fully, maturing boy. Likewise, girls and boys who lived in or were descended from peoples living in tropical regions of the world or who were members of the working class were thought to complete the process of pubertal growth sooner than their "civilized" counterparts (due to the effects of warm climates and a greater tendency to sexual licentiousness), and so were biologically incapable of advancing to the highest stages of evolutionary development. Even so, while all girls and nonwhite and lower-class boys were deemed naturally precocious, and hence developmentally inferior to "civilized" boys, the *sexual* precocity of the "civilized" girl was restricted, since it was her purity that served as the hallmark of her racial and class superiority. Advice to white middle-class parents abounded about protecting their girls from a whole range of dangerous activities that could excite the sexual passions, including masturbation, reading novels, eating meat or sweets, and, of course, engaging in any sort of physical encounter with men. At the end of the century, campaigns to end the white slave trade and

raise the AGE OF CONSENT emerged in further defense of female purity. The sexual precocity of nonwhite and working-class girls was more likely to be expected, though no more tolerated, and the late nineteenth century also saw the foundation of numerous organizations and institutions intending to reform and/or punish the transgressive sexual behaviors of female youth.

In 1904 the pioneering developmental psychologist G. STANLEY HALL published his seminal text *Adolescence*, which reaffirmed puberty as the originator of sexual differentiation, while also significantly modifying some of the gendered assumptions about the process of sexual maturation. Undermining earlier claims as to the steadiness of male growth, Hall maintained that the biological changes that occurred at puberty universally gave rise to "storm and stress" in the developing adolescent, rendering boys and girls alike somatically vulnerable, emotionally volatile, and socially awkward. Conversely, he enthused about the pubertal awakening of sexual desire in girls as well as boys. However, Hall sanctioned female desire only in so far as it was productive of male pleasure and reserved most of his zealous characterization of the sex instinct for the role it played in furthering the noble purpose of racial regeneration. Moreover, despite his recognition of certain shared qualities of the pubertal experience, Hall depicted the girl as growing into her biological and emotional self at puberty, with the sensibilities and functions then established determining her personality and role for the rest of her life. For his part, the boy's capacity for autonomy and rationality would ultimately enable him to outgrow the physical and psychological vulnerabilities wrought by puberty, so that he could assume his rightful position of leadership in the ongoing quest for social progress.

In the twentieth century, puberty was reinterpreted through the lenses of several new approaches to the study of human development. Psychoanalytic theory pushed the initial experience of sexual desire and the onset of sexual difference back from puberty to infancy and the Oedipal complex of early childhood, respectively. While SIGMUND FREUD deemed the prepubertal stages of psychosexual development to be the most consequential for the health of the personality, he also retained earlier notions of the diminished sexual and psychological capacity of girls. His daughter, psychoanalyst ANNA FREUD, reasserted the significance of puberty, arguing that the emergence of the genital drive gave rise to significant psychological conflicts during adolescence. Challenging the biological determinism that had characterized much of the theorizing about puberty and adolescence, cultural anthropologist MARGARET MEAD's widely read *Coming of Age in Samoa* (1928) made use of cross-cultural comparison to assert that the difficulties of adolescence were not the result of biological puberty, but of the complex demands placed on youth by modern civilization. Mead also emphasized that the process of sexual maturation did not limit the development of the Western girl in any way. Beginning in the 1920s, the rise of the science of endocrinology provided a new biological framework for conceptualizing puberty. However, in seeking to understand the role of the hormones in shaping pubertal development, researchers increasingly attended to the interaction between biological and social factors in shaping the psychology and behavior of the adolescent, as well as the causes and manifestations of sexual difference. In addition to scientific authority, puberty in the twentieth century was also mediated by the ascendancy of the CONSUMER CULTURE. For girls, especially, the buying of sanitary products, bras, and other beauty items encouraging conformity to dominant cultural standards of femininity have shaped, without ever fully determining, the meaning and experience of the process of sexual maturation.

See also: **Adolescent Medicine; Age and Development; Boyhood; Child Development, History of the Concept of; Girlhood.**

BIBLIOGRAPHY

Brumberg, Joan Jacobs. 1997. *The Body Project: An Intimate History of American Girls.* New York: Random House.

Freud, Anna. 1969. "Adolescence as a Developmental Disturbance." In *Adolescence*, ed. G. Caplan and S. Lebovici. New York: Basic Books.

Freud, Sigmund. 1954. *Collected Works*, Standard Edition. London: Hogarth Press.

Hall, G. Stanley. 1904. *Adolescence: Its Psychology and Its Relations to Physiology, Anthropology, Sociology, Sex, Crime, Religion and Education*, 2 vols. New York: Appleton.

Mead, Margaret. 1928. *Coming of Age in Samoa: A Psychological Study of Primitive Youth for Western Civilization.* New York: William Morrow and Company.

Prescott, Heather Munro. 1998. *A Doctor of Their Own: The History of Adolescent Medicine.* Cambridge, MA: Harvard University Press.

Rotundo, E. Anthony. 1993. *American Manhood: Transformations in Masculinity from the Revolution to the Modern Era.* New York: Basic Books.

Rousseau, Jean-Jacques. 1979 [1762]. *Émile or On Education.* Trans. Alan Bloom. New York: Basic Books.

Russett, Cynthia Eagle. 1989. *Sexual Science: The Victorian Construction of Womanhood.* Cambridge, MA: Harvard University Press.

Tanner, J. M. 1981. *A History of the Study of Human Growth.* New York: Cambridge University Press.

CRISTA DELUZIO

Public Schools: Britain

The British public school can be characterized by institutional independence, an emphasis on the ideal of a "liberal" curriculum, and a fee-paying student body that frequently boards at the school. Although there are no formal criteria governing an institution's status as a public school in Britain, a general qualification is representation in the Headmasters' Conference, the coalition founded in 1869 under the stewardship of Edward Thring of Uppingham. However, the increasing membership of this organization, which rose from an initial thirty-seven schools to stabilize around two hundred by 1937, masks the predominance of a much smaller group of prestigious institutions that make up the core of the public school system. This elite group is defined either as the "Great Nine" (Winchester [founded in 1382], Eton [1440], St. Paul's [1509], Shrewsbury [1552], Westminster [originally conceived in 1179 and refounded in 1560], Merchant Taylors' [1561], Rugby [1567], Harrow [1572], and Charterhouse [1611]) or the wider coterie of around sixty schools that acknowledged each other's comparable status through regular SPORTS meetings. Although the earliest of the public schools were originally intended to provide clerical training for the poor, the increasing demands for fees meant that the schools quickly became the sole preserve of the wealthy and attendance became a rite of passage for the elite of British society. Although boarding is not unknown in continental Europe, in their social prestige, organizational culture, and emphasis on the development of gentlemanly qualities, the public schools are unique to Great Britain.

The coalescence of long-established institutions, endowed GRAMMAR SCHOOLS, and a significant number of new Victorian schools into a uniform system with a common ethos was a product of the later nineteenth century. The eighteenth and early nineteenth century had seen public schools accused of brutality, inefficiency, and corruption, both financial and moral. A series of high profile student rebellions, particularly during the period of the French Revolutionary, had further tarnished the reputation of the established schools. However, under the influence of Thomas Arnold, headmaster of Rugby from 1828 to 1842, the public schools were recast as agents of moral and spiritual development and their role as the cultivators of Christian gentlemen was affirmed. Although schools guarded their individual traditions and idiosyncrasies, those institutional features set in place by Arnold and his imitators: pupil prefectures, the house system, organized games, the cult of the amateur, and a renewed sense of importance vested in the study of the classics, had become typical by the end of the nineteenth century.

Children's life at public school was shaped by the schools' preoccupation with the formation of their "character." Although Arnold had emphasized the achievement of manliness through waging an unending war against sin, from the later Victorian period this evangelical conception had given way to an emphasis on the secular virtues of determination, self-control, and a sense of duty. For the pupils this translated into a cult of athleticism and the celebration of games as the mainspring of those qualities of fair play, unselfishness, and *esprit de corps* deemed the foundation of gentlemanly conduct. In the classroom, study was similarly geared toward the cultivation of moral and behavioral attributes fitting for the social elite rather than scholarship for its own sake. Much of the pressure exerted on the late Victorian public school to expand its curriculum beyond the dominant core of the classics was based on a subjects' perceived capacity to aid the process of character formation. Stern discipline, reinforced by the generous use of corporal punishment, the devolving of disciplinary power onto prefects, and the practice of fagging, whereby younger pupils were required to perform services for older boys, were justified in these terms: that they taught boys those habits of obedience, self-command, and authority necessary for a future role in public life and the administration of empire.

For some, these conventions resulted in unhappy experiences in which floggings and bullying exacerbated the already harsh conditions of the schools. Although to criticize one's school was considered dishonorable and "bad form," accounts of the hardships engendered by the public school regime are not hard to find. In the early 1800s, in an Eton governed by the formidable Dr. Keate, famed for flogging eighty pupils in one session, the poet Shelley was a victim of ferocious bullying, partly occasioned by his refusal to submit to the fagging system. Twenty years later, the English novelist Anthony Trollope might reasonably have expected to escape the severity of prefect discipline at Winchester after his elder brother Tom was elected his "tutor." Instead, as his autobiography recalls, he was daily thrashed with a stick. Nevertheless, for others, the Old School was an object of almost fanatical loyalty. The interpretation of World War I as an extended cricket match, fought for the sake of school as much as country, was common in the letters and diaries of the trenches, and the glorification of the public schools in popular literature for boys bolstered the image of the school as an object of devotion.

Prevailing conceptions of gender were entrenched in the public school and boys were urged to interpret effeminacy as the antithesis of the public school ideal and a menace to national life. Similarly, the developing provision for girls in institutions such as the North London Collegiate School and Cheltenham Ladies' College, despite reproducing elements of the curricula and organizational culture of the boys' schools, attempted to mediate the cultivation of character with traditional feminine ideals: boys were to be made manly and girls were to be womanly. The spread of coeducation from the early twentieth century was resisted on these grounds, though by this time the public schools faced other diverse challenges. From an egalitarian assault on elitism to accusations of fostering national decline through an anti-industrial ethos, the public school was not without its critics in the twentieth century. However, the institutions proved largely able to navigate change while retaining their independence and many of those characteristics that have distinguished public schools from those of the state sector. The path from the public school to the higher echelons of political and professional life remained well trodden in twentieth-century Britain.

See also: **Coeducation and Same-Sex Schooling; Education, Europe; Private and Independent Schools.**

BIBLIOGRAPHY

Bamford, Thomas William. 1967. *Rise of the Public Schools: A Study of Boys' Public Boarding Schools in England and Wales from 1837 to the Present Day.* London: Nelson.

Fraser, George MacDonald, ed. 1977. *The World of the Public School.* London: Weidenfeld and Nicholson.

Gathorne-Hardy, Jonathan. 1977. *The Public School Phenomenon, 597–1977.* London: Hodder and Stoughton.

Mangan, James A. 1981. *Athleticism in the Victorian and Edwardian Public School: the Emergence and Consolidation of an Educational Ideology.* Cambridge, UK: Cambridge University Press.

McCrone, Kathleen E. 1988. *Sport and the Physical Emancipation of English Women, 1870–1914.* London: Routledge.

Parker, Peter. 1987. *The Old Lie: The Great War and the Public-School Ethos.* London: Constable.

Simon, Brian, and Ian Bradley, eds. 1975. *The Victorian Public School: Studies in the Development of an Educational Institution.* Dublin: Gill and Macmillan.

Stanley, Arthur P. 1844. *The Life and Correspondence of Thomas Arnold.* London: B. Fellowes.

NATHAN ROBERTS

R

Radio

In the 1930s and 1940s, when radio still was regarded as a new medium, special children's programs were broadcast in order to attract young listeners. As such programs became popular, production increased. Children and teenagers took pleasure in listening to programs specifically aimed at children as well as other programs. By this time, American children aged nine to twelve listened to radio approximately two to three hours a day, especially during the evening. Girls preferred romantic and historical dramatizations and boys listened more to popular and novelty programs, but one study came to the conclusion that the differences mattered less than the similarities. With some variations, comedy and mystery radio plays were preferred above others by both boys and girls of all ages. Thus children enjoyed a variety of programs, including those produced for adults.

As with other electronic media, radio was met with worries from the adult world. In Sweden, as in other countries, it was a common anxiety that too much listening could make children passive and less eager to play. In the 1940s, Swedish teachers expressed worries about being regarded as mere "loudspeakers" by children accustomed to passively listening to radio. However, compared with reactions to other electronic media, radio seems to have incited relatively few "moral panic" attacks. Partly this can be explained by radio's supposed usefulness in education (discussed below).

In the 1950s, when TELEVISION was introduced, researchers in Britain came to the conclusion that television reduced radio listening more than it reduced any other activity. In spite of this, one in three children said that if they had to do without radio they would miss it quite a lot. The study also noticed that children who had been watching television for several years listened a little more often to the radio. This was described as a revival in line with reports of adults' media behavior. While radio plays could not compete with television plays, other types of programs held listeners' interest, including panel games, discussions, music, and sports commentaries.

Other studies have arrived at the similar conclusion that, with increasing age, children spent more time with radio than with television. TEENAGERS in particular have been found to be regular radio listeners. Researchers have attributed this to the socialization effects of radio, although explanations of what those effects are have varied over time. In the 1970s socialization to political virtues was considered to be an important factor, while in the 1980s, radio was seen as a source for identity formation in a peer group. This change can be related to the shift of content in programs addressed to teenagers. In the 1980s and 1990s teenagers listened more to music than to anything else on radio.

Radio in Education

From the start, in both Europe and America radio was greeted with hopes for its pedagogical value. Radio had the power to bring the world to the classroom, and programs could be presented as textbooks of the air.

In America, commercial and educational stations received licenses starting in the 1920s to produce classroom broadcasting, and eventually national networks also provided educational programs. Even though most programs were in line with traditional school subjects, some attempted to connect this content with progressive ideas about education and democracy. Radio allowed children and teachers to engage in the production of programs, preparing talks on, for example, automobiles, farming, and science. Together with the fact that parents supplied schools with radio receivers, this reflected a certain degree of local engagement in the implementation of radio in schools. However, this is not a perspective that has been emphasized in research. On the contrary, the organization of radio in education in America has been described as top down implementation. One example of this was the fact that superintendents, not teachers, were supposed to answer questionnaires, indicating that teachers were not included in the implementation process.

In July 1937, Amelia Earhart's niece and nephew eagerly follow reports of the search for their missing aunt and her plane. Other children too were exposed to a world far beyond their own homes through the medium of radio. © Bettman/CORBIS.

In contrast to America, broadcast systems in Europe were organized as nationwide networks that could be used for the inculcation of national values and virtues. Issues regarding educational as well as social and cultural policy were included in the broadcast organizations—in other words, they became part of welfare policy. In this context, children became a special interest.

In Scandinavian countries and Britain, special departments for educational programs were organized in the late 1920s or early 1930s. In general these programs were in line with the overall curriculum. However, a study on the use of radio in classrooms in Sweden reveals that there were contrasts between the content of ordinary schoolbooks and the content of radio programs. Radio programs emphasized contemporary progressive ideas on education and progressive political notions that were not represented in schoolbooks at that time. Citizenship, a new subject, was also given a particularly radical formulation in the school programs. This

meant that children who listened to educational programs on the radio, discussed the programs, and did assignments on them, encountered views of society that differed from prevailing traditional middle-class representations. Reoccurring subjects included the everyday lives of the working or lower-middle classes as well as the need for health reform and an expanded welfare system.

In Sweden, educational broadcasts addressed children not only as future citizens but also as active contemporary citizens. Children were included in the actual broadcasts, where they were displayed, with references to famous scientific explorers like Sven Hedin, as competent explorers of their own society. Further, these children were enlisted to represent various parts of society in accordance with notions of society proposed by progressive policymakers. Each pupil was supposed to have his or her own program sheet where each program was presented in texts and pictures. The notion was that the material should help children to create "listening pictures" (*hörbilder*) when listening to programs. This practice was implemented out of a strong belief that a will to change the way people thought had to start with strategies that changed the way they talked.

In contrast to America, and in spite of the centralized organization, in Sweden teachers were included in the implementation of radio in education. They participated continually in surveys where they reported their own and the pupils' responses to programs. Active teachers were invited to annual conferences about the use of radio in classrooms. It was argued by teachers and by the organizers of school broadcasts that elementary schoolteachers were more competent than academics and experts in communicating with pupils and therefore were invited to produce programs.

In Britain, educational radio programs were regarded as an important way to influence individual children and adolescents when they had problems or needed guidance in societal matters. Radio was also used to inculcate new notions of citizenship.

Further Research

Studies of children's radio programs, particularly educational programs, offers an area of research that brings new perspectives to social, cultural, and political history. Such research also expands investigations of children's increased visibility and status as a special group in society, for instance as reflected in the UN CONVENTION ON THE RIGHTS OF THE CHILD (1989). Children's programs provide material for inquiries into children's place in society as well as representations of childhood from a historical perspective, particularly during the period from 1920 to 1960, when radio was regarded as the major electronic medium in society. It is also a field well attuned to further developments of theoretical and methodological issues. In addition to actual programs, manuscripts, program sheets, and other documents concerning children's broadcasts, a number of studies measure children's reading and comprehension skills in relation to radio. Such materials could be used to investigate the systems of knowledge and meaning that have affected the child in different decades of the twentieth century.

See also: **Media, Children and the.**

BIBLIOGRAPHY

Christenson, Peter G., and Peter DeBenedittis. 1986. "'Eavesdropping' on the FM Band: Children's Use of Radio." *Journal of Communication* 36, no. 2: 27–38.

Cuban, Larry. 1986. *Teachers and Machines. The Classroom Use of Technology since 1920.* New York and London: Teachers College Press.

Lindgren, Anne-Li. 1999. "'Att ha barn med är en god sak': Barn, medier och medborgarskap under 1930-talet" ("Including children is a good thing": Children, media and citizenship in the 1930s). *Linköping Studies in Arts and Science* 205.

Paik, Haejung. 2000. "The History of Children's Use of Electronic Media. In *Handbook of Children and the Media*, ed. Dorothy G. Singer and Jerome L. Singer. Thousand Oaks, CA, London, and New Delhi: Sage.

Palmer, Richard. 1947. *School Broadcasting in Britain.* London: BBC.

ANNE-LI LINDGREN

Recovered Memory

Recovered memory, often called repressed memory, emerged as a significant concept in mental health therapy in the early 1980s. The theory postulates that a variety of complaints in adulthood, ranging from eating disorders to marital problems, stem from childhood sexual abuse by a family member, usually of a daughter by her father. This experience is so traumatic that the child represses the memory and from then on has no conscious awareness that the abuse occurred. But at a subconscious level, the repressed memory continues to fester, producing symptoms that disrupt the victim's adult life. Therapeutic treatment consists of memory enhancement techniques to unblock the memories, allowing the patient to confront the source of her problems (an estimated 90 percent of these cases are female) and by doing so, "heal."

The roots of recovered memory theory can be traced to attitudes toward the middle-class family in parts of the feminist movement. Social worker Florence Rush was especially influential, arguing that INCEST was far more common than generally believed and was permitted because it prepared the female to accept a subordinate role in society. The theory provided an explanation for the gap between textbook estimates of incest (one to two for every million women in the United States) and its supposed common occurrence. The theory's most influential advocates include psychiatrists Judith Herman and Lenore Terr and law professor Catherine MacKinnon. But the single most influential book was written by lay people: *The Courage to Heal* by Ellen Bass and Laura Davis, originally published in 1988, which provides checklists of symptoms suggesting past abuse. It has sold close to a million copies.

Both the theory and the therapy are controversial. The theory assumes that memory functions like a camcorder, keeping repressed memories intact in a special part of the brain. But memory experts have demonstrated that memory does not function in this way: forgetting is extensive and memories are continually reconstructed into what memory expert Elizabeth Loftus has called "creative blendings of fact and fiction." There is no scientific evidence that memories of traumas are processed and/or stored differently from other memories. The theory assumes that certain symptom profiles—especially eating disorders—are signposts of child sexual abuse. However, according to American Psychiatric Association guidelines, "no specific unique symptom profile has been identified that necessarily correlated with abuse experiences."

The techniques therapists use to recover memories are equally controversial. The most common are hypnosis, guided imagery (the therapist helps the patient visualize scenes of childhood abuse), dreamwork, participation in "survivor groups," massage therapy to uncover "body memories" of abuse in infancy, and injections of sodium Amytal as a truth serum. There is no scientific evidence for the existence of "body memories." As for hypnosis, in a report issued in 1984, the American Medical Association's Council on Scientific Affairs stated that contrary to what the public believes, recollections obtained during hypnosis are "generally less reliable than nonhypnotic recall." According to the Council, hypnosis increases suggestibility, promoting vivid pseudomemories. Memory researcher Martin Orne has noted that sodium Amytal is even more problematic than hypnosis in producing false memories. Researchers like Loftus, who has performed experiments in which she implanted "memories" in college students, including memories of traumatic events (such as being lost as a child in a shopping mall) believe therapists, wrongly convinced their patients' problems derive from childhood sexual abuse, implant false memories in their patients.

Recovered memory therapy has wreaked a great deal of damage on patients and their families. Therapists have encouraged patients to confront the perpetrator, typically the father, and sever all ties with their parents (the mother is often viewed as an accomplice), even to sue them in civil or criminal court. It is estimated that roughly 15 percent of patients who recover false memories of sexual abuse eventually go on to recover memories of being forced to participate in Satanic cults in which they engaged in ritual murders and cannibalism. Many of these patients have been wrongly diagnosed as suffering from multiple personality disorders, which supposedly had enabled them to compartmentalize their terrible experiences, and some have been hospitalized for long periods.

Since 1995 a number of factors have led to a waning of recovered memory therapy. The False Memory Syndrome Foundation, established in 1992 by and for accused families, assembled leading U.S. and Canadian memory researchers on its board and widely disseminated their findings. But the most important factor has been malpractice suits against therapists brought by ex-patients, some of which have resulted in multimillion-dollar judgments. As a result, insurance companies have become unwilling to insure therapists practicing recovered memory therapy.

See also: **Child Abuse; Mental Illness.**

BIBLIOGRAPHY

Bass, Ellen, and Laura Davis. 1988. *The Courage to Heal: A Guide for Women Survivors of Child Sexual Abuse.* New York: Harper and Row.

Herman, Judith L. 1992. *Trauma and Recovery.* New York: Basic Books.

Isaac, Rael Jean. 2000. "Down Pseudo-Memory Lane." *Priorities for Health* 12, no. 4: 17–22, 60–61.

Loftus, Elizabeth, and Katherine Ketcham. 1991. *The Myth of Repressed Memory.* New York: St. Martin's Press.

Ofshe, Richard, and Ethan Watters. 1994. *Making Monsters: False Memories, Psychotherapy, and Sexual Hysteria.* New York: Scribner.

Prendergast, Mark. 1995. *Victims of Memory: Incest Accusations and Shattered Lives.* Hinesburg, VT: Upper Access.

Terr, Lenore. 1994. *Unchained Memories: True Stories of Traumatic Memories, Lost and Found.* New York: Basic Books.

RAEL JEAN ISAAC

Religious Revivals

Since the pioneering work of William J. McLoughlin, historians have tended to isolate four periods when revivals—or mass religious meetings for prayer, preaching, song, and conversion—were especially prominent features of American cultural history. The first, the so-called Great Awakening of 1735 to 1745, featured what Jonathan Edwards called "surprising conversions" across New England and the Middle Colonies. Among the most surprising of these conversions were many among children and youth. Child converts were accorded special status because supporters of the revivals saw in them evidence of the miraculous character of the events, while detractors used the prominence of children in the revivals to dismiss them as irrational "enthusiasm." Later observers, noting how both the ritual performances of children and the reports on the revivals by elders followed some definable patterns, have emphasized a wide range of potential social and political causes for them. Most explanations imply that the presence of children as public converts signified the appearance of a more malleable conception of the self and life-course in America, at least in contrast to typical Calvinist understandings. That this malleable self was still under severe social strictures, as Philip Greven has pointed out, goes without saying. As converts, however, children asserted themselves as agents in history. They did so under the cover of a transcendent God, and within the boundaries of an ecclesiastical ritual, but their assertion of agency gained attention not least because it was consistent with the need for both producers and consumers in emerging market economies.

The link between markets, revivals, and children and youth is solidified when historians turn to the second period of revivals, which dominated the first half of the nineteenth-century and culminated in a series of "businessmen's revivals" across the Northeast in 1857 to 1858. Some historians have identified a "Great Revival" in the South from 1800 to 1805, through which Baptists and Methodists gained their enduring foothold in the region, and their predominance in the African-American community. Southern revivals featured charismatic lay leadership over educated clergy, thus providing spiritual (and economic) leadership opportunities to enterprising young men (and, on occasion, young women). At such meetings, which quickly spread North and

West, flashing especially at Cane Ridge in Kentucky, intergenerational events held in the open air were free from the constraints of local social hierarchies, and provided for what anthropologists have called experiences of ecstatic *communitas*, and what has since been called entertainment. The young were quick to capitalize on the spiritual, as well as the social, opportunities, further "democratizing" Christianity in the process, and opening up a social space for the agency of young women, who sometimes joined young boys as child preachers. By the time a series of revivals swept across upstate New York in the 1830s, the most famous evangelist of the day, Charles Grandison Finney, had developed the technique of calling both young men and women to come before him to the "anxious bench" to consider their salvation. Finney also, in company with his wife, Elizabeth, furthered the revivalist emphasis on the malleable self, arguing that revivals were not only the result of a miracle, but also "the right use of the constituted means," or what has come to be called marketing. Such an emphasis on technique led theologians such as Horace Bushnell, who advocated for less dramatic Christian nurture for children, such as the SUNDAY SCHOOL, to dub revivalism a form of CHILD ABUSE. Nevertheless, entrepreneurial revivalism led directly to new evangelical bible schools and colleges, such as Oberlin, which quickly filled the market niche abandoned by "rationalist" schools like Harvard and Yale. Evangelical schools then provided seedbeds for youthful activism in causes of social reform, notably abolitionism, although white Baptists and Methodists for obvious reasons preferred to promote temperance in the South. By the time of the businessmen's revivals of 1857 and 1858, young men were especially prominent, although female leaders like Phoebe Palmer also began to assert themselves. Such a public presence of young male converts as a cohort in an urban venue fostered a distinct "boy culture," according to John Corrigan, which both coincided with and promoted the growth of the earliest YOUTH MINISTRIES in the United States.

A third series of revivals marked the years from 1890 to 1925, now largely in urban areas, and drawing extensively on the existence of cadres of young men devoted to the YMCA's "muscular Christianity." The leading evangelists—Dwight L. Moody, Billy Sunday, and Aimee Semple McPherson—developed Finney's rationalized techniques by holding separate meetings in large tents or "tabernacles" for young men and women, featuring swing-tinged "gospel" music. Such meetings sanctioned both an emerging popular culture for youth and a separate-spheres ideology defined along age-lines. This segregation of youth coincided well with G. STANLEY HALL's popular identification of ADOLESCENCE as a particular stage of life marked by such attributes as piety and turbulence. Both attributes were amply in evidence in the tabernacle meetings, where sexual energy was sublimated into passionate prayer and turbulence given vent in dramatic conversions and upbeat music. Now, though, the converts were expected to follow conventions of behavior that ac-

corded with carefully cultivated civic values, rather than the spontaneous *communitas* of frontier revivals. The public presence of youthful converts, once the sign of a malleable self, was now becoming a defined market niche. At the same time, some of the social reforms sought by revivalists for the good of youth, namely Prohibition, came to fruition. This "success" ironically led to scorn among cultural elites such as H. L. Mencken and Sinclair Lewis and scrutiny of the links between adolescence and conversion in the emerging social scientific disciplines. In reaction to such reductionism, the anti-intellectual elements in revivalism, always significant in particular communities, came further to the fore as revivalists became allied with the fundamentalist movement, and began to feel like a besieged minority.

A fourth period of revivals can be traced to the founding of Youth for Christ during World War II, led by Billy Graham, with fruition in the so-called new Christian right, represented by leaders such as James Dobson, and in movements like the "Promise Keepers." Such movements owe much to the links between Christian conversion, commerce, and cultural change, now also associated with nationalist politics. At the same time, however, contemporary revivalism no longer promotes a malleable life course. Now, revivalists seek to contain children and youth, rendering them subject to various state, church, and family projects (such as HOMESCHOOLING), all marketed through the most current technologies.

See also: **Protestant Reformation.**

BIBLIOGRAPHY

Blumhofer, Edith L. and Randall Balmer, ed. 1993. *Modern Christian Revivals.* Urbana: University of Illinois Press.

Carpenter, Joel A. 1997. *Revive Us Again: The Reawakening of American Fundamentalism.* New York: Oxford University Press.

Corrigan, John. 2002. *Business of the Heart: Religion and Emotion in the Nineteenth Century.* Berkeley: University of California Press.

Greven, Philip. 1977. *The Protestant Temperament: Patterns of Child-Rearing, Religious Experience, and the Self in Early America.* New York: Knopf.

Hardesty, Nancy. 1999. *Women Called to Witness: Evangelical Feminism in the Nineteenth-Century.* 2nd ed. Knoxville: University of Tennessee Press.

Long, Kathryn Teresa. 1998. *The Revival of 1857–58: Interpreting an American Religious Awakening.* New York: Oxford University Press.

McLoughlin, William G. 1978. *Revivals, Awakenings, and Reform.* Chicago: University of Chicago Press.

Putney, Clifford. 2001. *Muscular Christianity: Manhood and Sports in Protestant America, 1880–1920.* Cambridge: Harvard University Press.

Thomas, George M. 1989. *Revivalism and Cultural Change: Christianity, Nation Building, and the Market in the Nineteenth-Century United States.* Chicago: University of Chicago Press.

JON PAHL

Renaissance. *See* Medieval and Renaissance Europe.

Retardation

Mental retardation is a construct with many interpretations. In some periods of history, mental retardation has been referred to as a disease. In other periods it has been thought of as a disability. Often mental retardation has been represented as social deviance. Most modern professionals in the United States adopt the definition published in 1992 by the American Association for Mental Retardation (AAMR). This definition describes mental retardation as neither a disease nor a disability but a functional state with limitations in both intelligence and adaptive skills. People classified as mentally retarded obtain an Intelligence Quotient (IQ) below seventy when tested with an appropriate standardized instrument. They demonstrate difficulties with adaptive skills, and their problems develop before the age of eighteen. The prevalence of mental retardation has been estimated to be under 3 percent of the general population. The majority of individuals with mental retardation need minimal supports and their disability may go undetected in tolerant environments. Some people require more extensive support, including assistance from family members and professionals. The causes of mental retardation are about evenly divided between organic and nonorganic problems. Organic causes are attributed to prenatal difficulties such as metabolic and genetic disorders, perinatal distress including prematurity and birth injury, and childhood diseases and traumas. Nonorganic causes are associated with environmental deprivation. In many cases the etiology is unknown. Treatment usually requires a multidisciplinary approach to provide a variety of supports that people with mental retardation need in order to function adequately in their homes, schools, places of work, and communities.

Although the AAMR definition is widely accepted in the twenty-first century, traditional interpretations of deviance, disability, and disease lie deeply imbedded in Western culture. These interpretations, usually disparaging, have influenced the ways societies have thought about and responded to people with mental retardation. Their roots lie in philosophical debates, religious beliefs, scientific discoveries, and social developments of the past. The historical record reveals the various meanings associated with mental retardation and its analogous conditions, including idiocy, foolishness, feeblemindedness, and mental deficiency. A review of this history depicts the many ways that mental retardation has been and continues to be defined.

The origins of the construct of mental retardation appear in the writings of Greek and Roman philosophers reflecting on the nature of the intellect. Both PLATO and ARISTOTLE associated human value with the ability to reason. They differentiated mankind from other living beings by the quality of the intellect. People who lacked the capacity to reason were considered barely human and therefore socially inferior. Writings attributed to Hippocrates in the late fifth century B.C.E. adopted a physiological explanation. This work localized the intellect in the brain and explained the intellect's function with humoral theories. In the most intelligent individuals properties of heat and moisture balanced. Those who lacked intelligence were thought to possess an excess of moisture and a deficit of warmth. Variations in the speed of the elements also affected the intellect. In their medical treatises, the Hippocratic writers defined healthy states and illness, and introduced the concept of the mean which would serve as a basis in the future identification of people with mental retardation. The Galenists, writing in Rome in the late second century, adopted the Hippocratic theories of the intellect, systematized them, and elaborated on the humoral interpretation. Galen's understanding of the nature of the intellect was adopted by many scientists and philosophers well into the eighteenth century.

The laws of ancient Rome contributed to Western legal systems the concept of clemency for criminals who acted without intention. Linking incompetence with infancy, Romans established the law that punishment for crimes depended on the understanding and intent of the criminal. The principle is central in Western legal systems, although in the United States the problem of competence and mental retardation in criminal cases remains a contentious issue at the beginning of the twenty-first century. Another legal precedent with economic and political implications appeared in medieval England: in the thirteenth century the English king claimed the property of people who were then called idiots who were unable to manage their personal affairs. The intention was to provide guardianship for people thought to be idiots while also enriching the coffers of the king. The law differentiated idiocy from madness and instituted rudimentary assessments to determine competence. In the early modern period English and American colonial laws provided guardianship and welfare relief for people with mental retardation who were without family support. Tests of competence were developed to assess the eligibility of welfare beneficiaries and people convicted of capital crimes. Those tests, and the laws in general, extended assistance to some needy people while they also reinforced images of dependency, incompetence, and infantilism.

In the ancient world most people attributed the mysteries they witnessed to pagan gods, and in medieval Europe they ascribed them to the supernatural powers of witches, devils, and magic. Yet Western views were gradually transformed by the infusion of beliefs and practices of the monotheistic religions JUDAISM, Christianity, and ISLAM. All three religions contributed to the modern social ethic as it concerns mental retardation. This ethic was essentially optimistic, for it recognized intrinsic value in humans created in the image of God. It established principles of justice and affirmed charity on behalf of disadvantaged people. In Christian societies, idiocy, as it was known, provided evidence of God's creativity and a manifestation of the diversity of his universe. Furthermore, idiocy could be construed by Christians as a condition of blessed simplicity and innocence. Despite such magnanimity, however, religious belief also served to reinforce images of idiots as childish, dependent individuals, worthy recipients of beneficence, yet helpless and hopelessly afflicted. Indeed, both Catholics and Protestants banned people thought to be idiots from the sacraments, thereby denying salvation. Such contradictory portrayals of mental retardation have persisted throughout the years and are still evident in the twenty-first century.

The work of the English anatomist Thomas Willis (1621–1675) represented the first modern scientific account of idiocy. Willis adopted the view that idiocy constituted a structural defect in the brain that might be inborn or caused by serious illness or injury. He theorized that the condition could be related to the smallness of the brain, and he distinguished between two types of idiots, one more capable than the other. Willis was probably the first to define idiocy as a disease, to speculate on its causes, and to suggest treatments. Like most physicians of his time, however, Willis believed that in most cases idiocy was permanent and incurable.

Physicians continued to explore the functions of the brain throughout the 1800s. Franz Joseph Gall (1758–1828), for example, concluded that the development of specific regions of the brain accounted for variations of intellect. Influenced by Gall's ideas, other physicians developed the system of phrenology, which associated intelligence with the structure of the head. By the 1870s, phrenology was no longer practiced, although for many years it was commonly believed that brain size was related to the intellect. Other theories drew parallels between intelligence and morality. In his 1866 book *Mongols,* John Langdon Down concluded that congenital idiocy represented atavism, a degeneracy of the race. Soon after the publication in 1859 of Charles Darwin's *On the Origin of Species,* Francis Galton (1822–1911) proposed methods to improve society by selectively breeding the human species. He named this system EUGENICS, a method of social control with profound implications for humanity in the twentieth century. Frustrated with attempts to prove the correlation between intelligence and the structure of the head, ALFRED BINET (1857–1911) set about to develop an alternative system to measure the intellect. With his student Theodore Simon (1873–1961), Binet produced in 1905 the first test of intelligence to identify children with learning difficulties.

Other scientists in nineteenth century Europe were interested in classification systems in order to differentiate idiocy from madness and to define levels of idiocy based on capability. Their purpose, in part, was to separate those people who were considered more suitable for treatment from those considered incurable. The French physician Édouard Séguin (1812–1880) went further than others and developed his own system of classification which included four types of idiocy. Unlike his colleagues, Séguin adopted more optimistic views of people considered least capable. He protested conditions at the Bicêtre, Paris's notorious mental institution, and introduced treatment programs for idiots who were considered unable to profit from instruction. In 1848 he emigrated to the United States, where he continued his work establishing educational programs based on a physiological method.

Séguin's optimistic approach did not last, however, and by the middle of the nineteenth century idiocy acquired once again the meaning of permanent and incurable disability. In the United States schools originally intended for educating children with mental retardation were gradually converted to custodial facilities with the admission of more seriously disabled people and failures in rehabilitation. By the 1920s the eugenics movement had aroused the public's fear of people with mental retardation, who were denounced as morally degenerate. Institutional settings grew in power and size in order to accommodate the growing numbers of individuals with mental retardation who were rejected by society. Although most people continued to be cared for by family members at home with minimal public support, the social abandonment of thousands of people in large public institutions into the 1970s signified an era of pervasive dehumanization and hopelessness.

In response to the failure of public programs in the United States, parents whose children were mentally retarded organized in the mid-1900s to advocate on their behalf. Encouraged by the civil rights movement of the 1960s, parents and their professional allies sought educational opportunities, medical treatment, community living situations, and basic human rights. The concept of normalization coincided with the deinstitutionalization movement in the 1970s to promote services for people with mental retardation in local communities. At the same time, achievements in medicine produced methods for the amelioration and prevention of physiological problems. Responsive politicians and a favorable economy provided the impetus for legislation that established programs and provided services. In addition, successful challenges in courts of law contributed to expanded policies and programs on behalf of people with mental retardation. In particular, all children, including those who previously had been excluded from schools due to their disability, were granted the right to be educated at public expense. Early in the twenty-first century most children with mental retardation are educated in public schools with their peers, although many with severe disabilities are still consigned to segregated settings. Remaining issues for people with mental retardation include meaningful participation in all aspects of community living, social integration, equal opportunities in school and work, justice in the courts of law, and self-determination.

See also: **Birth Defects; Education, Europe; Education, United States; Intelligence Testing; Special Education.**

BIBLIOGRAPHY

American Association on Mental Retardation. 2002. *Mental Retardation: Definition, Classification, and Systems of Supports*, 10th ed. Washington, DC: AAMR.

Blatt, Burton, and Fred Kaplan. 1974. *Christmas in Purgatory: A Photographic Essay on Mental Retardation.* Syracuse, NY: Human Policy Press.

Bogdan, Robert, and Steven J. Taylor. 1994. *The Social Meaning of Mental Retardation: Two Life Stories.* New York: Teachers College Press.

Dykens, Elisabeth M., Robert M. Hodapp, and Brenda M. Finucane. 2000. *Genetics and Mental Retardation Syndromes: A New Look at Behavior and Interventions.* Baltimore, MD: Paul H. Brookes.

Ferguson, Philip W. 1994. *Abandoned to Their Fate: Social Policy and Practice Toward Severely Retarded People in America 1820–1920.* Philadelphia: Temple University Press.

Finger, Stanley. 1994. *Origins of Neuroscience: A History of Explorations of Brain Function.* New York: Oxford University Press.

Hankinson, R. J. 1991. "Greek Medical Models of the Mind." In *Psychology*, ed. Stephen Everson. Cambridge, UK: Cambridge University Press.

Robinson, Daniel N. 1995. *An Intellectual History of Psychology*, 4th ed. Madison: University of Wisconsin Press.

Scheerenberger, R. C. 1983. *A History of Mental Retardation.* Baltimore, MD: Paul H. Brookes.

Stainton, Tim. 2001. "Reason and Value: The Thought of Plato and Aristotle and the Construction of Intellectual Disability." *Mental Retardation* 39: 452–460.

Trent, James W., Jr. 1994. *Inventing the Feeble Mind: A History of Mental Retardation in the United States.* Berkeley: University of California Press.

Wright, David, and Anne Digby, eds. 1996. *From Idiocy to Mental Deficiency: Historical Perspectives on People with Learning Disabilities.* London: Routledge.

Zigler, Edward, and Robert M. Hodapp. 1986. *Understanding Mental Retardation.* Cambridge, UK: Cambridge University Press.

PARNEL WICKHAM

Rites of Passage

Rites of passage are found in all societies in all periods, but they differ not only from culture to culture but over time within a particular culture. They change as societies change and, while they are often perceived as traditional, they are by no means timeless. Rites of passage are at least as common in modern as in premodern societies. In the case of Western cultures, they have increased over time. Rites of passage are highly scripted dramatic performances initiated on the occasion of a change in the life of an individual that affects relationships within a group or between groups. These are as

much directed to changing perceptions as changing behavior. The rite itself has a tripartite structure, which begins with the separation of the main actor from his or her former status. This is usually accomplished by a change of clothing, locale, or behavior. Then follows a liminal moment when the individual is thought to be in a transitional state. The rite is completed when the central actor is reintegrated into society in his or her new role or identity. The most obvious contemporary example of a rite of passage is the big white wedding in which the female is separated from unmarried women as a group by her dress and deportment, then is cloistered as "bride" for a period of time before being reintegrated into society as a married woman. The white wedding is a highly dramatic performance which alters the relationship not only of the bride to the groom, but of the couple to their peers, family, and community.

While rites of passage may appear to be the product of tradition and seem to represent consensus about the way things ought to be done in a particular society, they are in fact ways of coping with the ambiguities, uncertainties, and conflicts inherent in any social order. When life flows smoothly and there are no contradictions, there is no need for these cultural interventions. But in all societies there are certain moments in the life of the individual and the group which seem to require something more, something that will mediate the apparent contradictions and restore a sense of order. Rituals allow this to happen smoothly and unthinkingly. "Ritual inevitably carries a basic message of order, continuity, and predictability. New events are connected to preceding ones, incorporated into a stream of precedents so that they are recognized as growing out of tradition and experience. By stating enduring and underlying patterns, ritual connects past, present, and future, abrogating history and time," writes Barbara Myerhoff (p. 306). Rites of passage do not so much change things as give meaning to changes that are occurring.

In the Western world rites of passage have changed dramatically since the onset of modernity in the eighteenth century. Premodern rites were collective and communal performances, coping with ambiguities and tensions in the preindustrial social order. At that time lives were perceived spatially rather than temporally. Society understood itself as a static hierarchy—as a great chain of being—in which people moved up and down rather than forward and backward through time. In preindustrial society senior did not necessarily mean older. In that world very young men and women could attain very high rank.

Premodern Western rites of passage were not keyed to age as such. Instead, they marked changes in status within a larger community. The first and almost universal rite of passage was BAPTISM, symbolic of membership in the Christian community. It usually happened within a few days of birth, but in some denominations was postponed until a much later point in life. BIRTHDAYS as such were rarely celebrated before the nineteenth century. For some young people the ceremonies associated with entry into a religious calling constituted their ultimate rite of passage. The rites of apprentices, journeymen, and masters were equally dramatic performances. Village youth groups also had their rites of passage, but the most elaborate ceremony was the wedding, which in both town and country marked the biggest single change of status. Only those who could sustain a household were allowed to marry in this manner. The very public performance of wedding, which involved the entire community and not just the families involved, acknowledged the change in public status and power involved. It was less about personal than collective transformation.

By contrast, modern rites of passage are more personal and familial. They are less concerned with adjustments in the order of society than with the changing age identities of individuals. Rites of passage have become much more age-specific as numerical age itself becomes more important in assigning status. But because age is as much a cultural construct as a natural fact, some events, like MENARCHE and PUBERTY, which one might expect to draw considerable ritual attention, do not necessarily do so. On the other hand, birth dates, which do not indicate any great change, are now the occasion of sometimes elaborate ceremonies. In this secular era, it is birth, not baptism, which is life's first rite of passage.

Transitions from infancy to BOYHOOD were marked by BREECHING in the early modern period, and in the nineteenth century such ceremonies as FIRST COMMUNION, CONFIRMATION, and BAR MITZVAH came to be the standard passages to adolescence. In the twentieth century the transition from adolescence to young adulthood was marked for men by elaborate graduation and enlistment ceremonies, while elite women had their debutante balls and various coming-out parties. Today, these ceremonies are overshadowed by such landmarks as getting a driver's license and having one's first legal drink, but ADOLESCENCE AND YOUTH remain a time of intense ritualization; and so too does young adulthood, that long drawn-out affair marked variously by graduation from university, the first "real" job, leaving home, getting married, getting a mortgage, and having children. Never has the life course been so full of ritualized events that have become modern rites of passage, almost all of which are celebrated within the confines of family and friends.

The development of modern rites of passage in the modern world has followed a certain pattern. Elaborate ceremonies appeared first among the upper classes and were later appropriated by lower classes and various ethnic groups. It is worth noting that they multiplied first among males and spread later to women. In the Jewish religion the modern bar mitzvah for boys developed long before it was felt necessary to have a similar ceremony (bat mitzvah) for girls. The reasons for this class and gender pattern have to do with the greater degree of uncertainty and ambiguity experienced initially by males in modern capitalist society. Elite men were the first to be expected to forge their own way as individuals, while elite women's lives as daughters and wives were more predictable and continuous, at least until marriage, when their one great rite of passage, the white wedding, dealt with the uncertainties generated by that event.

Today's rites of passage are less exclusive, though class, ethnic, and gender variation is very evident. Every group now has its own version of the standard rites of passage. African-American families make much of their young people's graduations. Latino female coming-of-age parties rival the old debutante balls in expense and significance. Bat mitzvahs have attained a parity with bar mitzvahs, and the white wedding is now universal in Western societies, exported worldwide as the modern way to be married in Japan, Mexico, and many parts of Africa. Today gay and lesbian people also have their own rites of passage, including commitment ceremonies. But, while there are more and more varied rites of passage today than ever before, they are less inclusive of the community and more family oriented.

Western society has become extraordinarily child-centered, and virtually every stage of childhood is given ritual treatment. The reason for this lies in the increasingly uncertain and conflicted nature of growing up in modern society. In this era of the "hurried child," when there is such pressure on children to meet certain norms, rites of passage are one of the ways adults try to reassure themselves that there are still "enduring and underlying patterns" and that childhood itself has not yet been lost. Rites assure us that our children have a proper childhood and that we are good parents and grandparents after all. In today's highly ritualized family life, to miss a birthday or graduation is regarded as neglect or worse. One could even go so far as to say that the modern family is a group of people sharing a set of rituals. Everywhere we turn, especially where there is tension and unpredictability, there are rites of passage. This is not to say that ritual always works as intended. It can also be its own source of tension and controversy. This is one reason why rites of passage are always mutating. They are one of the most prominent but also one of the most protean features of modern life, deserving much more attention by historians and other cultural observers.

See also: **Life Course and Transitions to Adulthood.**

BIBLIOGRAPHY

Chudacoff, Howard. 1981. *How Old Are You? Age Consciousness in American Culture.* Princeton, NJ: Princeton University Press.

Davis-Floyd, Robbie E. 1992. *Birth as an American Rite of Passage.* Berkeley and Los Angeles: University of California Press.

Gillis, John. 1996. *A World of Their Own Making: Myth, Ritual, and the Quest for Family Values.* New York: Basic Books.

Lowe, Donald. 1982. *History of Bourgeois Perception.* Chicago: University of Chicago Press.

Myerhoff, Barbara. 1986. "Rites and Signs of Ripening: The Intertwining of Ritual, Time, and Growing Older." In *Age and An-*

In the 1950s Elvis Presley's music and " suggestive " dancing was the subject of considerable controversy. Critics saw him as a dangerous influence on American teenagers, particularly if those teenagers were white, Northern, and middle class. © Bettman/CORBIS.

thropological Theory, ed. David Kertzer and Jennie Keith. Ithaca, NY: Cornell University Press.

Pleck, Elizabeth. 2000. *Celebrating the Family: Ethnicity, Consumer Culture, and Family Rituals.* Cambridge, MA: Harvard University Press.

Sheehy, Gail. 1995. *New Passages: Your Life Across Time.* New York: Random House.

JOHN R. GILLIS

Rock and Roll

Beginning around 1955, rock and roll, a music of outlandish performers, amplified guitars, and aggressive lyrics, replaced jazz and pop standards in commercial prominence. It is often discussed as the charged collision of two racially separate genres: African-American rhythm and blues (R&B) and white country music. Yet it is more accurately viewed as a different hybrid. These outsider musical styles, and the often working-class, Southern, and/or black performers who championed them, were embraced by TEENAGERS who were often middle class, Northern, and white and who had

emerged in the affluence of that decade as an economic force to be reckoned with. As controversy raged about Elvis Presley's gyrating hips and the "leerics" of hit songs, a music industry veteran argued that the music had only become controversial because "the [white] pop kids started buying the R&B disks and playing them at home" (Martin and Segrave, p. 17).

Youth Culture

The union of YOUTH CULTURE and popular music has periodically sent shockwaves through American society ever since: variants include hippies, teenyboppers, punks, metalheads, rappers, and ravers. As the U.S. model of consumerism has spread worldwide, phenomena akin to rock and roll have cropped up time and again—from subcultures like the English mods and skinheads and the French *yeh yeh*s to the emergent sounds of Jamaican reggae, South African *mbaqanga*, Balkan turbofolk, and Algerian *rai*. Music, and the styles of clothing, language, and behavior so closely linked to it, has provided adolescents with the essential basis for a common sense of identity.

Yet rock and roll has evolved with every decade, and so have the youth phenomena associated with it. The teenagers of the 1950s were categorized as juvenile delinquents (the boys) or insipid sock hoppers screaming for manufactured idols on the television show *American Bandstand* (the girls); either way, a decadent, selfish breed compared to the generation that had withstood the Depression and fought World War II. Sociologists, and the media that followed their lead, looked at rock and rollers as deviants or as innocents manipulated by mass culture. In retrospect, however, rock had a radicalizing effect on these children, listening to brand-new transistor radios in their bedrooms and learning to identify with musicians from society's most marginal groups—the heavily pompadoured Little Richard, for instance, who sang in a falsetto taken from the Southern drag-queen club circuit.

By the 1960s, the subterranean energies that had fueled rock and roll's rise were bubbling over. The children of the BABY BOOM, that demographic bulge lasting from 1946 to 1964, were hitting their teenage years. Rock and roll, formerly a genre devoted to fun and loudness, had now become rock, a more serious Anglo-American art form with cultivated links to politicized folk music and the hippie generation's notion of youth as a self-consciously oppositional counterculture. New heroes like Bob Dylan, the Beatles, and the Rolling Stones, essentially akin to the boomers in background, inspired them to pick up electric guitars, grow their hair long, and experiment with sex and DRUGS. Woodstock, a three-day antiwar festival that drew hundreds of thousands to upstate New York in 1969, epitomized how sixties rock offered a mass cultural vision of authenticity and community.

Yet soon after, as the Stones played a different festival in Altamont, California, a young black attendee was murdered by Hell's Angels bikers who had foolishly been hired to protect the stage. Rock had lost its innocence, and as the music's popularity grew in the 1970s and 1980s it became a far more standardized industry. Young female teenyboppers were encouraged by TEEN MAGAZINES and AM radio to consume airbrushed pinups like Donny Osmond and the Bay City Rollers. Boys read *Rolling Stone*, listened to FM radio, and learned about arena rock, the cartoonishly heavy metal sounds of bands like Led Zeppelin and Black Sabbath. The music's cross-racial alliances faded as black and Latin disco and funk separated from white singer-songwriter earnestness. MTV, a cable network relying on music videos for its programming, appeared in 1981, linking rock to television around the clock. The youth market was bigger than ever. Stars like Michael Jackson, Madonna, Prince, and Bruce Springsteen enjoyed global popularity. It was now possible to find kids in virtually every location on earth obsessed with the same musical icons.

Divisions

As rock aged, however, cracks unsurprisingly started to appear in its dominance over youth culture. Punk, a movement from within rock that began in the mid-1970s, gradually became the music's oppositional wing, inspiring an audience that still looked to rock to behave as the antithesis of manufactured pop music. From the Sex Pistols in 1977 to Nirvana in 1991, often called "the year punk broke," a generation of college students used punk much as an early generation had used folk music, positioning themselves outside a corrupted mainstream. Alternative rock, a commercial variant of punk that briefly held sway in the 1990s, was epitomized by the Lollapalooza festivals, a post–baby boomer Woodstock of sorts. Then it splintered, a victim of its own anticorporate mainstream contradictions.

But rock was now simply one established genre among many competing for the younger demographic. Rappers replaced rock stars as icons of youth rebellion: although Eminem was white, most of the other major performers were African American, including Public Enemy, N.W.A, Notorious B.I.G., and Tupac Shakur. Country music, including Garth Brooks, Shania Twain, and the Dixie Chicks, courted suburban youth with a slicked-up twang. A new breed of boy bands like N'Sync and the Backstreet Boys, revived the teenybopper for the MTV era. Dance beats appealed to a subculture of ravers, whose consumption of the party drug Ecstasy terrified parents who had grown up experimenting with marijuana to the sounds of rock. Nerds more inspired by their computers and video games than by the radio downloaded songs on MP3, much to the chagrin of the music industry, which saw album sales plummet at the turn of the century.

Globally, local music inspired by rock and its affiliated sounds but taking a particularly homegrown slant, has steadily rolled back the dominance of American music. Rappers

can be found in Wales, Senegal, and South Korea; an alternative rock scene exists in Singapore; Japanese reggae bands have created a vibrant scene out of the Jamaican sounds of dancehall. The story gets steadily more complicated, but certain basic patterns never change: emotional affiliation across lines of identity; the tension between the pop marketplace and subcultures driven by a notion of personal authenticity; and the endless ability of new cohorts of young people to cobble together new blends of sound and style.

See also: **Adolescence and Youth; Media, Childhood and the.**

BIBLIOGRAPHY

De Curtis, Anthony, and James Henke, with Holly George-Warren, eds. 1992. *The Rolling Stone Illustrated History of Rock & Roll: The Definitive History of the Most Important Artists and Their Music.* New York: Random House.

Frith, Simon. 1982. *Sound Effects: Youth, Leisure, and the Politics of Rock'n'Roll.* New York: Random House.

Frith, Simon, Will Straw, and John Street, eds. 2001. *The Cambridge Companion to Rock and Pop.* New York: Cambridge University Press.

Hebdige, Dick. 1979 *Subculture: The Meaning of Style.* London: Methuen.

Martin, Linda, and Kerry Segrave. 1988. *Anti-Rock: The Opposition to Rock'N'Roll.* Hamden, CN: Archon Books.

Mitchell, Tony, ed. 2002. *Global Noise: Rap and Hip-Hop Outside the U.S.A.* Middleton, CT: Wesleyan University Press.

ERIC WEISBARD

Rousseau, Jean-Jacques (1712–1778)

Jean-Jacques Rousseau was born in Geneva, Switzerland, and grew up motherless. He received no systematic education; instead his father provided him with various kinds of lectures. Sent to an engraver to learn a profession, Rousseau ran away in 1728 to Turin and later France. In France he pursued his self-education, supported by a noblewoman. Rousseau was a man of many professions and many failures. He acquired his first public recognition as a musicologist and composer. In his *Discours sur les sciences et les arts* (Discourse on the sciences and the arts [1750/1751]) he criticized the conviction of the ENLIGHTENMENT that knowledge and science would bring progress to mankind. In 1755 he published his *Discours sur l'origine et les fondements de l'inégalité parmi les hommes* (Discourse on the origin and the foundations of inequality among men). Because of his wayward opinions, difficult character, and a supposed persecution complex, Rousseau more and more came into conflict with other intellectuals, among them his friend Denis Diderot, his lifelong enemy Voltaire, his later defender David Hume, and even French musicians. In 1761 Rousseau's novel *Julie, ou la Nouvelle Héloïse* (Julie, or the New Heloise) was a best-seller in Paris and made him popular all over Europe. A year later *Du contrat social* (The Social Contract) was published, and a year later *Émile, ou Traité de l'éducation* (Émile, or A Treatise on Education) appeared. Both works were banned and burned in public, both in Catholic France and in Calvinist Geneva. To make things worse, Voltaire accused Rousseau of severe neglect of his wife and children in the pamphlet *Sentiments de citoyen* (Sentiments of a citizen [1764]). Rousseau wrote several apologies, including *Lettres écrites de la montagne* (Letters written from the mountain [1764]). Condemnation of Rousseau's publications, especially of *Émile*, forced him to flee to Switzerland in 1762 and to England in 1766, where Hume gave him shelter. Rousseau returned to France the following year under a false name—Jean-Joseph Renou. In the last years of his life he wrote his *Les Confessions* and two other autobiographical works: *Rousseau juge de Jean-Jacques. Dialogues* (Rousseau, judge of Jean-Jacques. Dialogues [1775]) and *Les Rêveries du promeneur solitaire* (The reveries of a solitary walker [1776]). He died July 2, 1778 in Erenonville, France.

Ideas

Today Rousseau is considered one of the pivotal figures in the history of education and of childhood. More specifically, he is credited with the discovery of the distinctive character of the unique viewpoint of the child; the modern practice of educating in accordance with nature; the recognition of the child as a valuable person; and the cult of emotion—that is, that emotion is central in life and for learning—and the importance of the child's internal motivation. This image of the romantic Rousseau led to the conviction that Rousseau is one of the founding fathers of anti-authoritarian education. This interpretation is supported by the first three books of *Émile*. Here, indeed, the child grows up as an isolated individual with an uncorrupted nature and without any intervention by the educator. The educator safeguards the child from social influences (negative education), for nature is good and perfect, whereas society can only bear evil. Rousseau describes the developmental stages of the child's inner nature and the way the child learns from the external nature (natural education, or education "by things").

However, this picture is incomplete and presents a rather superficial comprehension of Rousseau's work. The central problem of Rousseau is that man is not only an individual, but that he is also condemned to live in society. Man's original and benevolent nature (natural state) is an intellectual experiment, a theoretical construction, not a reality. Central to Rousseau's philosophy is how man can cope with the break between nature and society, between individuality and sociality, between humankind and citizenship, and remain happy. Émile has to learn to function in society. This is the theme of the two last books of *Émile*, which deal mainly with the problem of Émile's relationship with another character, Sophie. Through negative education, the educator earns the confidence of the child; this trust is used to urge the child toward the goal of virtuousness.

In accordance with this social education are Rousseau's proposals for the organization of public education in Corsica and Poland. According to Rousseau, the gap between individual and public education is bridged by moral education: the education of virtue. The key feature of this education is self-limitation: if man wants to approach the (imaginary) happiness of the natural order, then he has to limit his desires (*vouloir*) to his power and ability (*pouvoir*). However, virtuousness is always threatened by the social condition of man. It is not surprising that Rousseau planned to write another novel in which the fate of Sophie and Émile would be described as a continuous and vain battle for virtuousness. The struggle for virtue is also the main theme of Rousseau's other educational novel—*Julie, ou la Nouvelle Héloïse*. Contrary to *Émile*, the protagonist here is a girl and the educational setting is the family.

Influence

The impact of Rousseau on educational theory cannot be underestimated. Rousseau romanticized the idea of childhood. Indeed, according to Rousseau, the main educational question should not be how to bring the child as fast as possible to adulthood, but rather how to do justice to the specificity of childhood. The characteristics of childhood, according to Rousseau, are the features of "natural man." Just like man in the original condition, the child is not yet corrupted by society. As such, childhood is linked with the promise of a perfect world and the possibility to make mankind better. Rousseau therefore argued that the child be kept away from society as long as possible, so that the child can develop according to his or her own needs and in accordance with nature.

This image of the child as inherently good has inspired a number of romantic educational theories. For example, FRIEDRICH FROEBEL's founding of the KINDERGARTEN system is a practical translation of Rousseau's idea of education. Kindergarten is an isolated and safe place where children, as young as possible, can develop without being disturbed by adults. In this natural condition the educator is only stimulating the child by things, which in turn stimulate the child's innate possibilities. Rousseau inspired also the English romantic poet William Wordsworth and the American transcendentalist Ralph Waldo Emerson. The Russian novelist Leo Tolstoy, who refers explicitly to Rousseau in his educational writings, established a school (Yasnaya Polyana School) for peasant children on his estate between 1859 and 1862.

At the end of the nineteenth century and the beginning of the twentieth century, Rousseau's idea of childhood was revisited through many educational experiments labeled as *éducation nouvelle* in France and *reformpedagogik* in Germany. The Swedish social reformer ELLEN KEY, whose *Barnets århundrade* (1900; CENTURY OF THE CHILD, 1909) is about the natural rights of the child, forever linked Rousseau with the art of education. In the second half of the twentieth century the anti-authoritarian movement and its pedagogy claimed to be the real inheritors of the ideas of Rousseau by stressing the idea of the original goodness of the child, as exemplified by A. S. NEILL's *Summerhill: A Radical Approach to Child Rearing* (1960).

This reception, however, is mostly one-sided and historically problematic. In the first place, contrary to the romantics (e.g., Froebel, Wordsworth), Rousseau was very much opposed to imagination as a key feature of childhood and education. According to Rousseau, imagination is a social dynamic that causes unhappiness and as such is not an element of the natural state of man and childhood. In the second place, there are a number of individuals who have put forth educational theories—including the German philosophers Immanuel Kant and JOHANN FRIEDRICH HERBART and the Swiss educational reformer JOHANN HEINRICH PESTALOZZI—that do not cultivate a romantic image of the child even though these individuals claim to be inheritors of Rousseau's ideas. Instead of cultivating the idea of the original goodness of the child, they are inspired by Rousseau's insight that children have to become adults and have to function in a society, and that the educator has to make use of the child's naïveté to impose moral principles and social skills.

Currently in educational historiography, Rousseau is recognized for exploring and rejecting several educational ideas. What is more, there is a growing awareness that in Rousseau's philosophy several contradictory traditions of educational thought come together. Given that Rousseau used the ideas of PLATO, Quintilian, FRANÇOIS DE SALIGNAC DE LA MOTHE-FÉNELON, JOHN LOCKE, and many others, his own contradictions are understandable.

See also: **Education, Europe; Theories of Childhood; Tolstoy's Childhood in Russia.**

BIBLIOGRAPHY

Cassirer, Ernst. 1954. *The Question of Jean-Jacques Rousseau.* Trans. and ed. Peter Gay. New York: Columbia University.

L'Aminot, Tanguy. 1992. *Images de Jean-Jacques Rousseau de 1912 à 1978.* Oxford: Voltaire Foundation.

Rousseau, Jean-Jacques. 1969. *Oeuvres complêtes.* Paris: Gallimard.

Rousseau, Jean-Jacques. 1979 [1762]. *Emile: or, On Education.* Trans. Allan Bloom. New York: Basic Books.

Starobinski, Jean. 1988. *Jean-Jacques Rousseau: Transparency and Obstruction.* Trans. Robert J. Morrissey. Chicago: University of Chicago Press.

van Crombrugge, Hans. 1995. "Rousseau on Family and Education." *Paedagogica Historica* 31: 445–480.

HANS VAN CROMBRUGGE

Rowling, J. K. *See* Harry Potter and J. K. Rowling.

Runaways. *See* Homeless Children and Runaways in the United States.

Russia. *See* Tolstoy's Childhood in Russia.